# Life Histories of
# North American Wood Warblers

# Life Histories of
# North American Wood Warblers

by

Arthur Cleveland Bent

*in two parts*

Part 1

Dover Publications, Inc.

New York

Published in the United Kingdom by Constable and Company, Limited, 10 Orange Street, London W. C. 2.

This Dover edition, first published in 1963, is an unabridged and unaltered republication of the work first published in 1953 by the United States Government Printing Office, as Smithsonian Institution United States National Museum *Bulletin 203*.

*Standard Book Number: 486-21153-3*

Manufactured in the United States of America

Dover Publications, Inc.
180 Varick Street
New York 14, N. Y.

## ADVERTISEMENT

The scientific publications of the National Museum include two series, known, respectively, as *Proceedings* and *Bulletins*.

The *Proceedings* series, begun in 1878, is intended primarily as a medium for the publication of original papers, based on the collections of the National Museum, that set forth newly acquired facts in biology, anthropology, and geology, with descriptions of new forms and revisions of limited groups. Copies of each paper, in pamphlet form, are distributed as published to libraries and scientific organizations and to specialists and others interested in the different subjects. The dates at which these separate papers are published are recorded in the table of contents of each of the volumes.

The series of *Bulletins*, the first of which was issued in 1875, contains separate publications comprising monographs of large zoological groups and other general systematic treatises (occasionally in several volumes), faunal works, reports of expeditions, catalogs of type specimens, special collections, and other material of similar nature. The majority of the volumes are octavo in size, but a quarto size has been adopted in a few instances in which the larger page was regarded as indispensable. In the *Bulletin* series appear volumes under the heading *Contributions from the United States National Herbarium*, in octavo form, published by the National Museum since 1902, which contain papers relating to the botanical collections of the Museum.

The present work forms No. 203 of the *Bulletin* series.

REMINGTON KELLOGG,
*Director, United States National Museum.*

# CONTENTS

# INTRODUCTION

This is the nineteenth in a series of bulletins of the United States National Museum on the life histories of North American birds. Previous numbers have been issued as follows:

107. Life Histories of North American Diving Birds, August 1, 1919.
113. Life Histories of North American Gulls and Terns, August 27, 1921.
121. Life Histories of North American Petrels and Pelicans and Their Allies, October 19, 1922.
126. Life Histories of North American Wild Fowl (part), May 25, 1923.
130. Life Histories of North American Wild Fowl (part), June 27, 1925.
135. Life Histories of North American Marsh Birds, March 11, 1927.
142. Life Histories of North American Shore Birds (pt. 1), December 31, 1927.
146. Life Histories of North American Shore Birds (pt. 2), March 24, 1929.
162. Life Histories of North American Gallinaceous Birds, May 25, 1932.
167. Life Histories of North American Birds of Prey (pt. 1), May 3, 1937.
170. Life Histories of North American Birds of Prey (pt. 2), August 8, 1938.
174. Life Histories of North American Woodpeckers, May 23, 1939.
176. Life Histories of North American Cuckoos, Goatsuckers, Hummingbirds, and Their Allies, July 20, 1940.
179. Life Histories of North American Flycatchers, Larks, Swallows, and Their Allies, May 8, 1942.
191. Life Histories of North American Jays, Crows, and Titmice, January 27, 1947.
195. Life Histories of North American Nuthatches, Wrens, Thrashers, and Their Allies, July 7, 1948.
196. Life Histories of North American Thrushes, Kinglets, and Their Allies, June 28, 1949.
197. Life Histories of North American Wagtails, Shrikes, Vireos, and Their Allies, June 21, 1950.

The paragraphs on distribution for the Colima and Kirtland's warblers were supplied by Dr. Josselyn Van Tyne with his contributions on these species.

All other data on distribution and migration were contributed by the Fish and Wildlife Service under the supervision of Frederick C. Lincoln.

The same general plan has been followed as explained in previous bulletins, and the same sources of information have been used. It does not seem necessary to explain the plan again here. The nomenclature of the Check-List of North American Birds (1931), with its supplements, of the American Ornithologists' Union, has been followed. Forms not recognized in this list have not been included.

Many who have contributed material for previous Bulletins have continued to cooperate. Receipts of material from several hundred contributors has been acknowledged in previous Bulletins. In addition to these, our thanks are due to the following new contributors: G. A. Ammann, O. L. Austin, Jr., F. S. Barkalow, Jr., Ralph Beebe, H. E. Bennett, A. J. Berger, Virgilio Biaggi, Jr., C. H. Blake, Don Bleitz, B. J. Blincoe, L. C. Brecher, Jeanne Broley, Maurice Broun, J. H. Buckalew, I. W. Burr, N. K. Carpenter, May T. Cooke, H. L. Crockett, Grace Crowe, Ruby Curry, J. V. Dennis, E. von S. Dingle, M. S. Dunlap, J. J. Elliott, A. H. Fast, Edith K. Frey, J. E. Galley, J. H. Gerard, Lydia Getell, H. B. Goldstein, Alan Gordon, L. I. Grinnell, Horace Groskin, F. G. Gross, G. W. Gullion, E. M. Hall, R. H. Hansman, Katharine C. Harding, H. H. Harrison, J. W. Hopkins, N. L. Huff, Verna R. Johnston, Malcolm Jollie, R. S. Judd, M. B. Land, Louise de K. Lawrence, R. E. Lawrence, G. H. Lowery, J. M. Markle, C. R. Mason, D. L. McKinley, R. J. Middleton, Lyle Miller, A. H. Morgan, R. H. Myers, W. H. Nicholson, F. H. Orcutt, H. L. Orians, R. A. O'Reilly, A. A. Outram, G. H. Parks, K. C. Parkes, M. M. Peet, J. L. Peters, F. A. Pitelka, Mariana Roach, James Rooney, Jr., O. M. Root, G. B. Saunders, James Sawders, Mary C. Shaub, Dorothy E. Snyder, Doris Heustis Speirs, E. A. Stoner, P. B. Street, H. R. Sweet, E. W. Teale, A. B. Williams, G. G. Williams, R. B. Williams, Mrs. T. E. Winford, and A. M. Woodbury.

As the demand for these Bulletins is much greater than the supply, the names of those who have not contributed to the work during recent years will be dropped from the author's mailing list.

Dr. Winsor M. Tyler has again read and indexed for this volume a large part of the current literature on North American birds and has contributed four complete life histories. Dr. Alfred O. Gross has written stories on the yellowthroats (*Geothlypis trichas*) and has contributed three other complete life histories. Edward von S. Dingle, Alexander Sprunt, Jr., and Dr. Josselyn Van Tyne have contributed two complete life histories each.

William George F. Harris has increased his valuable contribution to the work by producing the entire paragraphs on eggs, including descriptions of the eggs in their exact colors, assembling and averaging the measurements, and collecting and arranging the egg dates, as they appear under Distribution; the preparation of this last item alone required the handling of over 5,600 records.

Clarence F. Smith has furnished references to food habits of all the species of wood warblers. Aretas A. Saunders has contributed full and accurate descriptions of the songs and call notes of all the species with which he is familiar, based on his extensive musical records. Dr. Alexander F. Skutch has sent us full accounts of all the North American wood warblers that migrate through or spend the winter in Central America, with dates of arrival and departure. James Lee Peters has furnished descriptions of molts and plumages of several species and has copied several original descriptions of subspecies from publications that were not available to the author.

Eggs were measured for this volume by American Museum of Natural History (C. K. Nichols), California Academy of Sciences (R. T. Orr), Colorado Museum of Natural History (F. G. Brandenburg), C. E. Doe, W. E. Griffee, W. C. Hanna, E. N. Harrison, H. L. Heaton, A. D. Henderson, Museum of Comparative Zoology (W. G. F. Harris), and Museum of Vertebrate Zoology (M. Jollie).

The manuscript for this Bulletin was written in 1945; only important information could be added. If the reader fails to find in these pages anything that he knows about the birds, he can only blame himself for failing to send the information to—

THE AUTHOR.

# LIFE HISTORIES OF
# NORTH AMERICAN WOOD WARBLERS

---

## Order PASSERIFORMES: Family PARULIDAE

---

By ARTHUR CLEVELAND BENT
*Taunton, Mass.*

---

### GENERAL REMARKS ON THE FAMILY PARULIDAE

#### CONTRIBUTED BY WINSOR MARRETT TYLER

The family of wood warblers, Parulidae, is the second largest family
of North American birds, surpassed only in number of species by the
family Fringillidae. The wood warblers occur only in the Western
Hemisphere; they are distinct from the Old World warblers, Sylviidae,
although the two families play a similar rôle in nature's economy.

The wood warblers are largely nocturnal migrants, whose long
journeys in the dark of night over sea and lake and along the coast
expose them to many perils, one being the lighthouses they strike
with frequently fatal results. Their notes are seldom heard from the
night sky during their spring migration, but on many a calm, quiet
night in August and September, as they fly overhead, their sharp,
sibilant, staccato notes punctuate the rhythmic beat of the tree-crickets
singing in the shrubbery and stand out clearly among the soft, whistled
calls of the migrating thrushes.

The length of migration varies greatly; the pine warbler withdraws in winter only a short distance from the southern limit of its
breeding range, whereas the most northerly breeding blackpolls migrate from Alaska to the Tropics. In spring many species migrate at
nearly the same time, apparently advancing northward in intermittent waves of great numbers during favorable nights. Flocks made
up of sometimes a dozen species together flash about in their bright
plumage during the week or two at the height of the migration and
furnish days of great excitement to ornithologists. Their return in
late summer and autumn is more leisurely and regular; in loose flocks
they drift slowly by for several weeks, their southward passage evident even in daytime. The flocking begins early, soon after nesting is
over, and to the north is apparent early in July, if closely watched for,
even before the leaves begin to wither. The mixed fall flocks, with
adults in winter plumage and young birds in duller colors, present
many fascinating problems in identification as the birds move quietly
along.

[AUTHOR'S NOTES: When I asked Dr. Tyler to contribute these remarks we discussed Professor Cooke's (1904) theory of trans-Gulf migration, which has been generally accepted until recently, when it was challenged by George C. Williams (1945). This paper started a discussion in which George H. Lowery, Jr. (1945), has taken a prominent part, and of which we have not yet heard the last. Routes of migration from South America to the United States are evidently well established through the West Indies and the Bahamas to the southeastern States; across the Caribbean to Jamaica, Cuba, and Florida; through Central America and directly across the Gulf from Yucután to the Gulf States; through eastern Mexico and Texas; and through western Mexico to the southwestern States. Professor Cooke was probably correct in assuming that the majority of wood warblers breeding in eastern North America migrate directly across the Caribbean or the Gulf. Some species may confine themselves to only one of the routes named, but we need more data to say just which species uses what route.]

The literature contains descriptions of several warblers not recognized as established species by the A.O.U. Check-List (1931). Some, described and illustrated by older writers such as Wilson and Audubon, cannot be identified; others are presumably hybrids; and one, *Sylvia autumnalis* Wilson, the autumn warbler, is clearly the blackpoll in fall plumage. The first category includes *Dendroica carbonata* (Audubon), the carbonated warbler, of which the Check-List says "the published plates may have been based to some extent on memory"; *D. montana* (Wilson), the blue mountain warbler, which is "known only from the plates of Audubon and Wilson"; and *Wilsonia* (?) *microcephala* (Ridgway), the small-headed flycatcher, of which it says: "Known only from the works of Wilson and Audubon whose specimens came from New Jersey and Kentucky respectively. There is some question whether they represent the same species."

In the second category is *Vermivora cincinnatiensis* (Langdon), the Cincinnati warbler, described in 1880. "The unique type is regarded as a hybrid between *Vermivora pinus* (Linnaeus) and *Oporornis formosa* (Wilson)." Recently, in a letter dated August 3, 1948, Dr. George M. Sutton reports to Mr. Bent the discovery of a second Cincinnati warbler, taken in Michigan on May 28, 1948. He says: "Its bill and feet are large for *Vermivora* and its under tail coverts proportionately too long for that genus. It has only a faint suggestion of wing-barring and the merest shadow of a pattern on the outer rectrices. One of its most interesting and beautiful characters is the gray tipping of the feathers at the rear of the crown, as in *O. formosus*. The effect is very unusual, for the gray-tipped feathers are yellow. It is, in short, obviously a cross between *Vermivora* and *Oporornis*."

The status of *Vermivora leucobronchialis* and *V. lawrencii* and the relationship between them puzzled ornithologists for upward of two generations. William Brewster (1876) described the former as a new species, and since that time, as Walter Faxon (1911) writes, "almost every conceivable hypothesis has been advanced by one writer or another to fix its true status in our bird-fauna." In addition to being considered a valid species, it has been regarded as a hybrid (Brewster, 1881), as a dichromatic phase, that is, a leucochroic phase of *V. pinus* (Ridgway, 1887), as a mutant (Scott, 1905), and finally as a phase, "ancestral in character" (atavistic) of the goldenwing (C. W. Townsend, 1908).

Lawrence's warbler is a very rare bird. The first specimen was described in 1874 (Herold Herrick, 1874), and since that time the bird was taken or seen infrequently, chiefly in regions where the breeding ranges of *V. chrysoptera* and *V. pinus* overlap. Consensus of opinion in the main regarded it as a hybrid between *V. chrysoptera* and *V. pinus*, as it combined characters of both the supposed parents. John Treadwell Nichols (1908) some years ago brought new light to the problem. He says:

> In any discussion of the status of Lawrence's and Brewster's Warblers it is well to bear in mind the facts, including the much greater abundance of Brewster's, are in accord with Mendel's Law of Heredity, supposing both forms to be hybrids between *Helminthophila pinus* and *H. chrysoptera*. * * * All the first generation hybrids will be Brewster's Warbler in plumage. In the next generation there will be pure Golden-winged Warblers, pure Blue-winged Warblers, pure Brewster's Warblers, and pure Lawrence's Warblers; also mixed birds of the first three forms, but none of the last form, which, being recessive, comes to light only when pure. The original hybrids then (which will be all Brewster's in plumage) must be fertile with one another or with the parent species for any Lawrence's to occur; and if they are perfectly fertile Lawrence's must still remain a small minority. After the first generation the proportion of plumages of birds with mixed parentage should be: 9 Brewster's, 3 *chrysoptera*, 3 *pinus*, 1 Lawrence's.

This explanation removed the stumbling block, long believed to be insurmountable, that a black-throated bird, mating with a yellow-throated bird, could produce progeny having a white throat. Under Mendel's Law the dominant color (white) of *chrysoptera* would appear by the suppression of the recessive black throat.

Fortunately, Walter Faxon (1913) not long afterward found a female blue-winged warbler mated with a goldenwing and was successful in following the resulting brood of young birds until they had acquired their first winter plumage when, fulfilling Mendel's Law, they were all in "the garb of *Helminthophila leucobronchialis*," thus establishing beyond a doubt the hybrid nature of the bird. At the end of his paper, Walter Faxon (1913) relates a bit of interesting ancient history regarding these three species of *Vermivora*. He says:

In my paper published in 1911, after stating the different hypotheses proposed in order to explain the relations existing among the Golden-winged, Blue-winged, Brewster's, and Lawrence's Warblers I added, half in jest, that the only hypothesis left for a new-comer in the field was this: that the Golden-winged and the Blue-winged Warblers themselves were merely two forms of one species. Curiously enough, not long after this I found that this very opinion had been expressed, and in a most unexpected quarter: in a letter dated Edinburgh, Sept. 15, 1835, Audubon wrote to Bachman that he suspected the golden-winged warbler and the blue-winged warbler were one species! That Audubon at that early date, ignorant (as he was assumed to be) of the existence of Brewster's and Lawrence's warblers, and but superficially acquainted with the golden-wing, should suspect that two birds so diverse as the blue-wing and the golden-wing were one species seemed incomprehensible, and in the light of what we now know about these birds, his surmise seemed to presuppose an almost superhuman faculty of prevision.

As a possible explanation of Audubon's letter I have only this to offer: in the winter of 1876–77 Dr. Spencer Trotter discovered in the collection of the Academy of Natural Sciences of Philadelphia a specimen of Brewster's warbler without a label, the third specimen known up to that time; on the bottom of the stand was written in the autograph of John Cassin, "J. C., 20 October, 1862," and also a badly blurred legend "Not [note?] from Bell." An appeal to J. G. Bell elicited the response that he remembered shooting a peculiar warbler in Rockland Co., N. Y., about the year 1832—a warbler something like a golden-wing, but lacking, although in high plumage, the black throat of that species; a great many years afterward, he sold this specimen in Philadelphia but knew nothing of its ultimate fate. Dr. Trotter justly inferred that the Philadelphia Academy specimen was in all probability the very bird shot by Bell.

Now as Audubon was intimately associated with Bell, is it not possible that he had examined this example of Brewster's warbler? In that case, seeing that this bird's characters were in part those of the blue-wing, in part those of the golden-wing, he may have inferred the interbreeding of these two birds, and so (rather unwarrantably, it is true) their identity. If this be not the explanation of the passage in Audubon's letter to Bachman I have no other to suggest.

When Audubon came to publish his account of the Golden-winged Warbler in 1839 (Ornithological Biography, 1839, 5, p. 154) he said not a word about its connection with the Blue-winged Warbler.

Recently Karl W. Haller (1940) described "a new wood warbler from West Virginia" from two specimens, male and female, which he collected on May 30 and June 1, 1939, respectively, at points 18 miles apart, and proposed for it the new name *Dendroica potomac*, Sutton's warbler. These birds resemble the yellow-throated warbler in plumage but lack streaks on the sides. They also suggest the parula warbler in having a faint yellowish wash on the back and, in the male, "an almost imperceptible hint of raw sienna" on the upper breast. The male sang a song much like the parula's, but doubled by repetition.

Two more Sutton's warblers have been carefully observed in the field: one at the point where the type was collected on May 21, 1942, by Maurice Brooks and Bayard H. Christy (1942); the second about 18 miles to the westward on June 21, 1944, by George H. Breiding and

Lawrence E. Hicks (1945). Another aberrant warbler has been described by Stanley G. Jewett (1944), who examined four specimens which show a curious intermingling of the plumage characters of the hermit and Townsend warblers.

[AUTHOR'S NOTE: Since the above was written, Kenneth C. Parkes (1951) has published a study of the genetics of the golden-winged–blue-winged warbler complex, to which the reader is referred.]

### MNIOTILTA VARIA (Linnaeus)

### BLACK-AND-WHITE WARBLER

### HABITS

### CONTRIBUTED BY WINSOR MARRETT TYLER

### PLATES 1–3

The black-and-white warbler is one of the earliest spring warblers to reach its breeding-ground in the Transition Zone. Most of the other members of this family arrive in or pass through the region in mid-May or somewhat later, according to the season, when the oaks are in bloom and the opening flowers attract swarms of insects.

The black-and-white warbler, however, owing to its peculiar habit of feeding on the trunks and the large limbs of the trees, does not have to wait for the bounty supplied by the oaks but finds its special feeding-ground well stocked with food long before the oaks blossom or their leaves unfold. It comes with the yellow palm warbler late in April, when many of the trees are nearly bare, and not long after the pine warbler.

*Mniotilta* is a neat little bird, dressed in modest colors, at this season singing its simple but sprightly song as it scrambles over the bark—the black-and-white creeper, Alexander Wilson calls it.

Milton B. Trautman (1940), speaking of the spring migration at Buckeye Lake, Ohio, shows that the male birds are preponderant in the earliest flights. He says: "The first spring arrivals, chiefly males, were noted between April 16 and 30, and between May 1 and 5, 2 to 15 birds, mostly males, could be daily noted. The peak of migration usually lasted from May 6 to May 18, and then from 3 to 42 individuals, consisting of a few old males and the remainder females and young males, were daily observed. On May 18 or shortly thereafter a decided lessening in numbers occurred, and by May 23 all except an occasional straggler had left."

*Courtship.*—Forbush (1929) gives this hint of courtship, which resembles the activities of most warblers at this season: "When the females arrive there is much agitation, and often a long-continued intermittent pursuit, with much song and fluttering of black and white plumage, and much interference from rival males before the happy pair are united and begin nesting."

*Nesting.*—The black-and-white warbler usually builds its nest on the ground, tucking it away against a shrub or tree, or even under the shelter of an overhanging stone or bank. The nest is generally concealed among an accumulation of dead leaves which, arching over it, hides it from above. It is made, according to A. C. Bent (MS.), "of dry leaves, coarse grass, strips of inner bark, pine needles and rootlets, and is lined with finer grasses and rootlets and horsehair." I have seen a nest made chiefly of pine needles on a base of dry leaves.

Henry Mousley (1916), writing of Hatley, Quebec, mentions moss as a component part of the nest, and says of three nests that they were all "heavily lined with long black and white horse hairs," a peculiarity of coloration mentioned in one of Mr. Bent's nests. Thomas D. Burleigh (1927b) speaks of a nest in Pennsylvania "built of dead leaves and rhododendron berry stems, lined with fine black rootlets and a few white hairs." H. H. Brimley (1941) describes an exceptional nest. He says: "There was no particular departure from normal in its construction except for the fact that it was lined with a mixture of fine rootlets and very fine copper wire, such as is used in telephone cables. Fragments of such cable, discarded by repair men, were found nearby where a telephone line ran through the woods."

Cordelia J. Stanwood (1910c) speaks of a nest "built in a depression full of leaves, behind a flat rock. * * * The cavity was shaped on a slant, the upper wall forming a partial roof. * * * It looked not unlike a small-sized nest of an Oven-bird. On the inside, the length was 2½ inches, width 1½ inches, depth 2 inches. On the outside, length 3½ inches, width 2½ inches, depth 2½ inches. Thickness of wall at the top of nest, 1 inch; at the bottom, ½ inch." Henry Mousley (1916) gives the average dimensions of three nests as "outside diameter 3¾, inside 1¾ inches; outside depth 2¼, inside 1½ inches."

F. A. E. Starr (MS.) writes to A. C. Bent from Toronto, Ontario, that all the nests he has found have been in broken-off stumps in low woods. "The cavity in the top of the stump," he says, "is filled with old leaves, and the nest proper is made chiefly of strips of bark with grass and fiber." Guy H. Briggs (1900) reports a nest "in a decayed hemlock stump, fifteen inches from the ground." In such cases, of course, while the nest is well above the ground level, it rests on a firm foundation.

Audubon (1841) says: "In Louisiana, its nest is usually placed in some small hole in a tree," but he quotes a letter to him from Dr.

T. M. Brewer on the subject, thus: "This bird, which you speak of as breeding in the hollows of trees, with us always builds its nest on the ground. I say always, because I never knew it to lay anywhere else. I have by me a nest brought to me by Mr. Appleton from Batternits, New York, which was found in the drain of the house in which he resided."

Minot (1877) speaks of two nests found near Boston, Mass., well above the ground. He says: "The first was in a pine grove, in the cavity of a tree rent by lightning, and about five feet from the ground, and the other on the top of a low birch stump, which stood in a grove of white oaks."

Gordon Boit Wellman (1905) states: "Toward the last of the incubation time one of the birds was constantly on the nest. I found the male sitting usually at about dusk, but I think the female sat on the eggs over night."

*Eggs.*—[AUTHOR'S NOTE: The black-and-white warbler usually lays 4 or 5 eggs to a set, normally 5, seldom fewer or more. These are ovate to short ovate and slightly glossy. The ground color is white or creamy white. Some are finely sprinkled over the entire surface with "cinnamon-brown," "Mars brown," and "dark purplish drab"; others are boldly spotted and blotched with "russet" and "Vandyke brown," with underlying spots of "brownish drab," "light brownish drab," and "light vinaceous-drab." Speckled eggs are commoner than the more boldly blotched type. The markings are usually concentrated at the large end, and on some of the heavily spotted eggs there is a solid wreath of different shades of russet and drab. The measurements of 50 eggs average 17.2 by 13.3 millimeters; the eggs showing the four extremes measure 18.8 by 13.7, 17.9 by 14.7, 15.7 by 12.7, and 16.3 by 12.2 millimeters (Harris).]

*Young.*—Cordelia J. Stanwood (MS.) speaks of the nestlings a few days from the egg as "very dark gray, much like young juncos and Nashville warblers." But when they leave the nest they are clearly recognizable as young black-and-white warblers, although they are slightly tinged with brownish. By mid-July, here in New England, they assume their first winter plumage, and, as both sexes of the young birds have whitish cheeks, they resemble very closely their female parent.

Unlike the young of some of the other warblers which remain near the ground for many days, the young black-and-white warblers shortly ascend to the branches of trees where they are fed by the old birds.

I find no definite record of the length of the incubation period, but in a nest I watched in 1914 it was close to 10 days. Burns (1921) gives the period of nestling life as 8 to 12 days.

*Plumages.*—[AUTHOR'S NOTE: Dr. Dwight (1900) calls the natal down mouse gray, and describes the juvenal plumage as follows: "Above, wood-brown streaked with dull olive-brown, the upper tail coverts dusky; median crown and superciliary stripe dingy white. Wings and tail dull black, edged chiefly with ashy gray, the tertiaries (except the proximal which is entirely black) broadly edged with white, buff tinged on the middle one. Two buffy white wing bands at tips of greater and median wing coverts. The outer two rectrices with terminal white blotches of variable extent on the inner webs. Below, dull white, washed on the throat and sides with wood-brown, obscurely streaked on throat, breast, sides and crissum with dull grayish black."

A postjuvenal molt begins early in July, involving everything but the flight feathers; this produces in the young male a first winter plumage which is similar to the juvenal, but whiter and more definitely streaked. "Above, striped in black and white, the upper tail coverts black broadly edged with white; median crown and superciliary stripe pure white. The wing bands white. Below, pure white streaked with bluish black on sides of breast, flanks and crissum, the black veiled by overlapping white edgings; the chin, throat, breast and abdomen unmarked. Postocular stripe black; the white feathers of the sides of the head tipped with black."

The first nuptial plumage is acquired by a partial prenuptial molt in late winter, which involves a large part of the body plumage, but not the wings or the tail. "The black streaks of the chin and throat are acquired, veiled with white, and the loral, subocular and auricular regions become jet-black. The brown primary coverts distinguish young birds and the chin is less often solidly black than in adults."

The adult winter plumage is acquired by a complete postnuptial molt, beginning early in July. It differs from the first winter dress "in having the chin and throat heavily streaked with irregular chains of black spots veiled with white edgings, the wings and tail blacker and the edgings a brighter gray. * * * The female has corresponding plumages and moults, the first prenuptial moult often very limited or suppressed. In juvenal dress the wings and tail are usually browner with duller edgings and the streaking below obscure. In first winter plumage the streakings are dull and obscure everywhere, a brown wash conspicuous on the flanks and sides of the throat. The first nuptial plumage is gained chiefly by wear through which the brown tints are largely lost, the general color becoming whiter and the streaks more distinct. The adult winter plumage is rather less brown than the female first winter, the streaking less obscure and the wings and tail darker. The adult nuptial plumage, acquired partly by moult, is indistinguishable with certainty from the first nuptial."]

*Food.*—McAtee (1926) summarizes the food of the species thus:

In its excursions over the trunks and larger limbs of trees the Black and White Creeper is certainly not looking for vegetable food, and only a trace of such matter has been found in the stomachs examined. The food is chiefly insects but considerable numbers of spiders and daddy-long-legs also are eaten. Beetles, caterpillars, and ants are the larger classes of insect food, but moths, flies, bugs, and a few hymenoptera also are eaten. Among forest enemies that have been found in stomachs of this species are round-headed wood borers, leaf beetles, flea beetles, weevils, bark beetles, leaf hoppers, and jumping plant lice. The hackberry caterpillar, the hackberry psyllid, an oak leaf beetle *Xanthonia 10-notata*, and the willow flea beetle, are forms specifically identified. Observers have reported this warbler to feed also upon ordinary plant lice, and upon larvae of the gypsy moth.

Forbush (1929) adds the following observation: "The food of this bird consists mostly of the enemies of trees, such as plant-lice, scale-lice, caterpillars, both hairy and hairless, among them such destructive enemies of orchard, shade and forest trees as the canker-worm and the gipsy, brown-tail, tent and forest tent caterpillars. Wood-boring and bark-boring insects, click beetles, curculios and many other winged insects are taken. Sometimes when the quick-moving insects escape its sharp bill, it pursues them on the wing but most of its attention is devoted to those on the trees."

H. H. Tuttle (1919), speaking of the male parent feeding the young birds, says: "The fare which he provided was composed entirely of small green caterpillars, cut up into half-lengths."

*Behavior.*—The black-and-white warbler seems set apart from others of the group, perhaps because of its marked propensity for clambering over the trunks of trees and their larger branches. Although, like other warblers, it seems at home among the smaller twigs, it spends a large part of its time on upright surfaces over which it moves easily and quickly, upward, downward, and spirally, with great agility and sureness of footing, constantly changing direction, and not using the tail for support. As it scrambles over the bark, it switches from side to side as if at each hop it placed one foot and then the other in advance, and even on slim branches it hops in the same way, the tail alternately appearing first on one side of the branch and then on the other; it reminds us of a little schoolgirl swishing her skirt from side to side as she walks down the street. The bird is alert and watchful, and if it starts an insect from the bark, or sees one flying near, it may pursue it and catch it in the air.

H. H. Tuttle (1919) describes an extreme example of behavior simulating a wounded bird. He says: "She struck the leaves with a slight thud and turned over on her side, while the toes of one upstretched leg clutched at the air and her tail spread slowly into a pointed fan. * * * Deceived for a moment then, I turned a step in her direction. She lay quite still except for a quivering wing. I reached out toward her with a small stick and touched her side; she screamed pitifully; I stretched out my hand to pick her up, but with a last effort she righted herself, and by kicking desperately with one leg, succeeded in pushing forward a few inches."

We associate this warbler with dry, rocky hillsides where the ground is strewn with dead leaves, but the bird may breed also in the dry portions of shady, wooded swamps.

*Voice.*—The black-and-white is one of the high-voiced singers. Its song is made up of a series of squeaky couplets given with a back-and-forth rhythm, a seesawing effect, like the ovenbird's song played on a fine, delicate instrument. It may be suggested by pronouncing the syllables *we see* rapidly four or five times in a whispered voice. In the distance the song has a sibilant quality; when heard near at hand a high, clear whistle may be detected in the notes. The final note in the song is the accented *see*.

Albert R. Brand (1938), in his mechanically recorded songs of warblers, placed the black-and-white's song as the fourth highest in pitch in his last of 16 species, the blackpoll, blue-winged, and the Blackburnian being higher. He gives the approximate mean (vibrations per second of the black and white as 6,900 and of the blackpool as 8,900.

Aretas A. Saunders (MS.) says: "The pitch of the songs varies, according to my records, from B''' to E'''', a range of three and a half tones more than an octave. A single song, however, does not vary more than three and a half tones."

A second song, not heard, I think, until the bird has been on its breeding ground for some time, is rather more pleasing, less monotonous, than the first. It is longer, somewhat faster, more lively, and is modulated in pitch. Francis H. Allen (MS.) speaks of it thus: "Later in the season a more elaborate song is very commonly heard. I have been accustomed to syllabify it as *weesy, weesy, weesy, weesy, woosy, woosy, weesy, weesy*. The notes indicated by *woosy* really differ from the others only by being pitched lower."

Occasionally we hear aberrant songs which prove puzzling until we can see the singer. Allen remarks that he has heard several such songs, and I remember hearing one in which the lower note of each couplet was reduplicated, thereby strongly suggested one of the songs of the Blackburnian warbler. Sometimes *Mniotilta* sings during flight. I once heard a song from a bird flying within a few feet of me—at this range a sound of piercing sharpness.

Of the minor notes Andrew Allison (1907) says: "I know of no other warbler except the Chat that can produce so great a variety of sounds; and since nearly all of the notes resemble those of other warblers, this is a most confusing bird to deal with during the busy season of 'waves'."

The call note often has a buzzing quality, and often runs into a long chatter (also characteristic of the young bird), but it may be given so sharply enunciated that it suggests the *chip* of the blackpoll. Allen (MS.) writes it *chi*, "like pebbles struck together," and Cordelia J. Stanwood (1910) renders it *sptz*, saying "the sound resembled the noise made by a drop of syrup sputtering on a hot stove."

*Field marks.*—The blackpoll, in its spring plumage, and the black-and-white warbler resemble each other in coloration, but the latter bird may be readily distinguished by its white stripe down the center of the crown and the white line over the eye. The contrast in the behavior of the two birds separates them at a glance.

*Enemies.*—Like other birds which build on the ground, the black-and-white is subject, during the nesting season, to attacks by snakes and predatory mammals. A. D. DuBois (MS.) cites a case in which maggots destroyed a nestful of young birds.

Harold S. Peters (1936) reports that a fly, *Ornithoica confluens* Say, and a louse, *Myrsidea incerta* (Kellogg), have been found in the plumage of the black-and-white warbler.

Herbert Friedmann (1929) says: "This aberrant warbler is a rather uncommon victim of the Cowbird, only a couple dozen definite instances having come to my notice. * * * The largest number of Cowbirds' eggs found in a single nest of this Warbler is five, together with three eggs of the owner." George W. Byers (1950) reports a nest of this warbler, in Michigan, that held two eggs of the warbler and eight of the cowbird, on which the warbler was incubating. His photograph of the eggs suggests that they were probably laid by four different cowbirds.

*Fall.*—Several of the warblers show a tendency to stray from their breeding grounds soon after their young are able to care for themselves, perhaps even before the postnuptial molt is completed and long before the birds gather into the mixed autumn flocks. Among these early wandering birds the black-and-white warbler is a very conspicuous species, perhaps because it is one of our commoner birds or, more probably, because of its habit of feeding in plain sight on the trunks and low branches of dead or dying trees and shrubs instead of hiding, like other warblers, high up in the foliage. It may be that the warblers we see at some distance from their breeding grounds thus early in the season have already begun their migration toward the south: they often appear to be migrating.

Behind the house in Lexington, Mass., where I lived for years, there was a little hill, sparsely covered with locust trees, to the southward from my dooryard. This hill was a favorite resort for warblers in late summer. No warbler bred within a mile of the spot, except the summer yellowbird, to use the old name, yet soon after the first of July the black-and-white warblers began to assemble there. Not infrequently I have seen a single bird come to the hill, flying in from the north across Lexington Common, and join others there. The small company might remain for an hour or more, frequently singing (evidently adult males) as the birds fed in the locust trees.

Later in the season, as August advances, migration appears more evident. The birds now gather in larger numbers, sometimes as many as eight or ten; they pause in the locust trees for a shorter time before flying off; they are no longer in song; and the majority of the birds have white cheeks, most of them presumably young birds. Although they are almost silent as they climb about feeding, if you stand quietly in the midst of a company of four or five, now and then you may hear a faint note, and at once the note comes from all sides, each bird apparently reporting its whereabouts—a sound which calls to mind the south-bound migrants as they roam through the quiet autumn woods. Other warblers, unquestionably migrants, visit this hillside in August, notably the Tennessee, an early arrival who has already traveled a long way.

The fall migration of the black-and-white is long-drawn-out. The bird does not depend, like many of the warblers, on finding food among the foliage, so it may linger long after the trees are bare of leaves, sometimes, here in New England, well into October. I saw a bird in eastern Massachusetts on October 23, 1940, a very late date.

*Winter.*—Dr. Alexander F. Skutch (MS.) sent to A. C. Bent the following comprehensive account of the bird on its winter quarters: "None of our warblers is more catholic in its choice of a winter home than the black-and-white. Upon its departure from its nesting range, it spreads over a vast area from the Gulf States south to Ecuador and Venezuela, from the Pacific coast of Mexico and Central America eastward through the Antilles. And in the mountainous regions of its winter range it does not, like so many members of the family, restrict itself to a particular altitudinal zone, but on the contrary scatters from sea level high up into the mountains. As a result of this wide dispersion, latitudinal and altitudinal, it appears to be nowhere abundant in Central America during the winter months, yet it has been recorded from more widely scattered localities than most other winter visitants. On the southern coast of Jamaica, in December 1930, I found a greater concentration of individuals than I have ever seen in Central America during midwinter.

"Wintering throughout the length of Central America, from near sea level up to 9,000 feet and rarely higher, the black-and-white warbler is somewhat more abundant in that portion of its altitudinal range comprised between 2,000 or 3,000 and 7,000 or 8,000 feet above sea level. It is found in the heavy forest, in the more open types of woodland, among the shade trees of the coffee plantations, and even amid low second-growth with scattered trees. It creeps along the branches in exactly the same fashion in its winter as in its summer home. Solitary in its disposition, two of the kind are almost never seen together. The only time I have heard this warbler sing in Central America was also one of the very few occasions when I found two together. Early on the bright morning of September 1, 1933, when the warblers were arriving from the north, I heard the black-and-white's weak little song repeated several times among the trees at the edge of an oak wood, at an altitude of 8,500 feet in the Guatemalan highlands. Looking into the tree tops, I saw two of these birds together. Apparently they were singing in rivalry, as red-faced warblers, Kaup's redstarts, yellow warblers, and other members of the family solitary during the winter months will sing in the face of another of their kind, at seasons when they are usually silent. Often such songs lead to a pursuit or even a fight; but I have never seen black-and-white warblers actually engaged in a conflict in their winter home.

"Although intolerant of their own kind, the black-and-white warblers are not entirely hermits; for often a single one will attach itself to a mixed flock of small birds. In the Guatemalan highlands, during the winter months, such flocks are composed chiefly of Townsend's warblers; and each flock, in addition to numbers of the truly gregarious birds, will contain single representatives of various species of more solitary disposition, among them often a lone black-and-white, so different in appearance and habits from any of its associates.

"This warbler arrives and departs early. It has been recorded during the first week of August in Guatemala, and by the latter part of the month in Costa Rica and Panamá. In Costa Rica, it appears not to linger beyond the middle or more rarely the end of March; while for northern Central America my latest date is April 22.

"Early dates of fall arrival in Central America are: Guatemala—passim (Griscom), August 3; Sierre de Tecpán, August 23, 1933; Santa María de Jesús, August 6, 1934; Huehuetenango, August 14, 1934. Honduras—Tela, August 19, 1930. Costa Rica—San José (Cherrie), August 20; Carrillo (Carriker), September 1; San Isidro de Coronado, September 8, 1935; Basin of El General, September 19, 1936; Vara Blanca, September 5, 1937; Murcia, September 11, 1941. Panamá—Canal Zone (Arbib and Loetscher), August 24, 1933, and

August 29, 1934. Ecuador— Pastaza Valley, below Baños, October 17, 1939.

"Late dates of spring departure from Central America are: Costa Rica— Basin of El General, February 23, 1936, March 10, 1939, March 26, 1940, March 3, 1942, March 18, 1943; Vara Blanca, March 13, 1938; Guayabo (Carriker), March 30; Juan Viñas (Carriker), March 21. Honduras—Tela, April 22, 1930. Guatemala—Motagua Valley, near Los Amates, April 17, 1932; Sierra de Tecpán, February 20, 1933."

The bird has a wide winter range, as shown above. Dr. Thomas Barbour (1943) speaks of it thus in Cuba: "Common in woods and thickets. A few arrive in August, and by September they are very abundant, especially in the overgrown jungles about the Ciénaga."

Edward S. Dingle (MS.) has sent to A. C. Bent a remarkable winter record of a black-and-white warbler seen on Middleburg plantation, Huger, S. C., on January 13, 1944.

### DISTRIBUTION

*Range.*—Canada to northern South America.

*Breeding range.*—The black-and-white warbler breeds **north** to southwestern Mackenzie, rarely (Simpson and Providence; has been collected at Norman); northern Alberta (Chipewyan and McMurray); central Saskatchewan (Flotten Lake, probably Grand Rapids, and Cumberland House); southern Manitoba (Duck Mountain, Lake St. Martin, Winnipeg, and Indian Bay); central Ontario (Kenora, Pagwachuan River mouth, and Lake Abitibi; has occurred at Piscapecassy Creek on James Bay, and at Moose Factory); southern Quebec (Lake Tamiskaming, Blue Sea Lake, Quebec, Mingan, and Mascanin; has occurred at Sandwich Bay, Labrador); and central Newfoundland (Deer Lake, Nicholsville, Lewisport, and Fogo Island). **East to** Newfoundland (Fogo Island and White Bear River); Nova Scotia (Halifax and Yarmouth); the Atlantic coast to northern New Jersey (Elizabeth and Morristown); eastern Pennsylvania (Berwyn); Maryland (Baltimore and Cambridge); eastern Virginia (Ashland and Lawrenceville); North Carolina (Raleigh and Charlotte); South Carolina (Columbia and Aiken); and central Georgia (Augusta and Milledgeville). **South** to central Georgia (Milledgeville); south central Alabama (Autaugaville); north-central Mississippi (Starkville and Legion Lake); northern Louisiana (Monroe; rarely to southern Louisiana, Bayou Sora); and northeastern and south-central Texas (Marshall, Dallas, Classen, Kerrville, and Junction). **West to** central Texas (Junction and Palo Dura Canyon); central Kansas (Clearwater); central-northern Nebraska (Valentine); possibly eastern Montana (Glasgow); central Alberta (Camrose, Glenevis, and Lesser

Slave Lake); to southwestern Mackenzie (Simpson). There is a single record of its occurrence in June at Gautay, Baja California, 25 miles south of the international border.

*Winter range.*—In winter the black-and-white warbler is found **north** to southern Texas (Cameron County, occasionally Cove, and Texarkana); central Mississippi, occasionally (Clinton); accidental in winter at Nashville, Tenn.; southern Alabama (Fairfield); southern Georgia (Lumber City, occasionally Milledgeville, and Athens); and rarely to central-eastern South Carolina (Edisto Island and Charleston). **East** to the coast of South Carolina, occasionally (Charleston); Georgia (Blackbeard Island); Florida (St. Augustine, New Smyrna, and Miami); the Bahamas (Abaco, Watling, and Great Abaco Islands); Dominican Republic (Samana); Puerto Rico; Virgin Islands and the Lesser Antilles to Dominica; and eastern Venezuela (Paria Peninsula). **South** to northern Venezuela (Paria Peninsula, Rancho Grande, and Mérida); west-central Colombia (Bogotá); and central Ecuador (Pastazo Valley). **West** to central and western Ecuador (Pastazo Valley and Quito); western Colombia (Pueblo Rico); western Panamá (Dvala); El Salvador (Mount Cacaguatique); western Guatemala (Mazatenango); Guerrero (Acapulco and Coyuca); Colima (Manzanillo); northwestern Pueblo (Metlatayuca); western Nuevo León (Monterey); and southern Texas (Cameron County). It also occurs casually in the Cape region of Baja California and in southern California (Dehesa and Carpenteria). There are also several records in migration from California and from western Sinaloa.

*Migration.*—Late dates of spring departure from the winter home are: Venezuela—Yacua, Paria Peninsula, March 20. Colombia—Santa Marta region, March 12. Panamá—Gatún, March 26. Costa Rica—El General, April 9. Honduras—Tola, April 22. Guatemala—Quiriguá, April 17. Veracruz—El Conejo, May 15. Puerto Rico—Algonobo, April 27. Haiti—Île à Vache, May 6. Cuba—Habana, May 25. Bahamas—Abaco, May 6. Florida—Orlando, May 21. Georgia—Cumberland, May 26. Louisiana—Avery Island, April 27.

Early dates of spring arrival are: South Carolina—Clemson College, March 20. North Carolina—Weaverville, March 3. Virginia—Lawrenceville, March 23. District of Columbia—Washington, March 30. New York—Corning, April 18. Massachusetts—Stockbridge, April 16. Vermont—St. Johnsbury, April 19. Maine—Lewiston, April 27. Quebec—Montreal, April 26. Nova Scotia—Wolfville, April 29. Mississippi—Deer Island, March 4. Louisiana—Schriever, March 8. Arkansas—March 12. Tennessee—Nashville, March

20. Illinois—Chicago, April 17. Michigan—Ann Arbor, April 6. Ohio—Toledo, April 7. Ontario—Guelph, April 22. Missouri—Marionville, April 3. Iowa—Grinnell, April 16. Wisconsin—Milwaukee, April 20. Minnesota—Lanesboro, April 23. Kansas—Independence, April 1. Omaha—April 21. North Dakota—April 28. Manitoba—Winnipeg, April 28. Alberta—Edmonton, May 6; McMurray, May 15. Mackenzie—Simpson, May 22.

Late dates of fall departure are: Alberta—Athabaska Landing, September 11. Manitoba—Aweme, September 22. North Dakota—Argusville, October 2. Minnesota—Minneapolis, October 10. Iowa—Davenport, October 1. Missouri—Columbia, October 24. Wisconsin—Madison, October 7. Illinois—Port Byron, October 15. Ontario—Hamilton, October 3. Michigan—Detroit, October 15. Ohio—Youngstown, October 15. Kentucky—Danville, October 14. Tennessee—Athens, October 17. Arkansas—Winslow, October 17. Louisiana—New Orleans, October 25. Mississippi—Gulfport, November 19. Quebec—Quebec, September 18. New Brunswick—St. John, September 19. Nova Scotia—Yarmouth, September 23. Maine—Portland, October 17. New Hampshire—Ossipee, October 18. Massachusetts—Cambridge, October 15. New York—New York, October 6. Pennsylvania—Atglen, October 29. District of Columbia—Washington, October 18. Virginia—Charlottesville, October 18. North Carolina—Raleigh, October 29. South Carolina—Charleston, November 15. Georgia—Savannah, October 29.

Early dates of fall arrival are: South Carolina—Charleston, July 19. Florida—Pensacola, July 12. Cuba—Artemisa, Pinar del Río, August 1. Dominican Republic—Ciudad Trujillo, September 27. Puerto Rico—Mayagüez, October 9. Louisiana—New Orleans, July 21. Mississippi—Bay St. Louis, July 4. Michoacán—Tancitaro, August 7. Guatemala—Huehuetenango, August 14. Honduras—Cantarranas, August 7. Costa Rica—San José, August 20. Panamá—Tapia, Canal Zone, August 24. Colombia—Bonda, Santa Marta region, August 21. Ecuador—Pastaza Valley, October 17. Venezuela—Estado Carabobo Las Trincheras, October 9.

*Banding.*—A single banding recovery is of considerable interest: A black-and-white banded at Manchester, N. H., on August 31, 1944, was found on March 17, 1945, at Friendship P. O., Westmoreland, Jamaica.

*Casual records.*—This warbler is casual in migration or winters in Bermuda, having been recorded in six different years from October to May.

At Tingwall, Shetland Islands, north of Scotland one was picked up on November 28, 1936. This is almost as far north as the northernmost record of occurrence in North America and later than it is normally found in the United States.

A specimen was collected near Pullman, Wash., on August 15, 1948, the first record for the State.

*Egg dates.*—Massachusetts: 31 records, May 18 to June 14; 17 records, May 25 to June 3, indicating the height of the season.

New Jersey: 7 records, May 18 to June 8.

Tennessee: 3 records, May 1 to 17.

North Carolina: 6 records, April 20 to 28.

West Virginia: 7 records, May 6 to 29 (Harris).

PROTONOTARIA CITREA (Boddaert)

## PROTHONOTARY WARBLER

PLATES 4–6

HABITS

I do not like the above name for the golden swamp warbler. The scientific name *Protonotaria*, and evidently the common name, were apparently both derived from the Latin *protonotarius*, meaning first notary or scribe. I sympathize with Bagg and Eliot (1937), who exclaimed:

What a name to saddle on the Golden Swamp-bird! Wrongly compounded in the first place, wrongly spelled, wrongly pronounced! We understand that Protonotarius is the title of papal officials whose robes are bright yellow, but why say "First Notary" in mixed Greek and Latin, instead of Primonotarius? Proto is Greek for first, as in prototype. Why and when did it come to be misspelled Protho? Both Wilson and Audubon wrote Protonotary Warbler, a name seemingly first given to the bird by Louisiana Creoles. Both etymology and sense call for stress on the third syllable, yet one most often hears the stress laid on the second. Here, certainly, is a bothersome name fit only to be eschewed!

The scientific name cannot be changed under the rules of nomenclature, but a change in the common name would seem desirable. However, the name does not make the bird or detract from its charm and beauty. It will still continue to thrill with delight the wanderer in its swampy haunts.

The center of abundance of the prothonotary warbler as a breeding bird in this country is in the valleys of the Mississippi River and its tributaries, notably the Ohio, the Wabash, and the Illinois Rivers. Its summer range extends eastward into Indiana and Ohio, northward into southern Ontario, Wisconsin, Michigan, and Minnesota, and westward into Iowa, Nebraska, Kansas, Oklahoma, and eastern Texas—wherever it can find suitable breeding grounds.

It also breeds in the Atlantic Coast States from Virginia to Florida. It is essentially a bird of the damp and swampy river bottoms and low-lying woods, which are flooded at times and in which woodland pools have been left by the receding water. Perhaps this warbler abounds more than anywhere else in the valley of the lower Wabash, where William Brewster (1878) found it to be—

one of the most abundant and characteristic species. Along the shores of the rivers and creeks generally, wherever the black willow (*Salix niger*) grew, a few pairs were sure to be found. Among the button-bushes (*Cephalanthus occidentalis*) that fringed the margin of the peculiar long narrow ponds scattered at frequent intervals over the heavily timbered bottoms of the Wabash and White Rivers, they also occurred more or less numerously. Potoka Creek, a winding, sluggish stream, thickly fringed with willows, was also a favorite resort; but the grand rendezvous of the species seemed to be about the shores of certain secluded ponds lying in what is known as the Little Cypress Swamp. Here they congregated in astonishing numbers, and early in May were breeding almost in colonies. In the region above indicated two things were found to be essential to their presence, namely, an abundance of willows and the immediate proximity of water. * * * So marked was this preference, that the song of the male heard from the woods indicated to us as surely the proximity of some river, pond, or flooded swamp, as did the croaking of frogs or the peep of the Hylas.

Dr. Chapman (1907) writes of this bird in its haunts:

The charm of its haunts and the beauty of its plumage combine to render the Prothonotary Warbler among the most attractive members of the family. I clearly recall my own first meeting with it in the Suwanee River region of Florida. Quietly paddling my canoe along one of the many enchanting, and, I was then quite willing to believe, enchanted streams which flowed through the forests into the main river, this glowing bit of bird-life gleamed like a torch in the night. No neck-straining examination with opera-glass pointed to the treetops, was required to determine his identity, as, flitting from bush to bush along the river's bank, his golden plumes were displayed as though for my special benefit.

Dr. Lawrence H. Walkinshaw (1938) says that the golden swamp warbler "nests rather abundantly along southwestern-Michigan rivers. * * * Winding streams, bordered densely with oak, maple, ash, and elm, shallow ponds with groups of protrudnig willows and flooded, heavily shaded bottom-lands are favorite nesting habitats for the Prothonotary Warbler (*Protonotaria citrea*). Such habitats occur along the banks of the Kalamazoo River and its tributary the Battle Creek River in Calhoun County, Michigan."

*Territory.*—The males arrive on the breeding grounds a few days or a week before the females come and immediately try to establish their territories, select the nesting sites, and even build nests. Dr. Walkinshaw (1941) writes:

The Prothonotary Warbler is a very strongly territorial species. When a male takes possession of a certain area he continually drives off all opponents if he is able. At certain areas in Michigan I have watched these birds battle intermittently for two or three days, usually for the same bird house, one male finally taking possession. In addition I have observed them to drive off House Wrens (*Troglodytes aedon*), Black-capped Chickadees (*Penthestes atricapillus*) and Yellow Warblers (*Dendroica aestiva*). * * * The male Prothonotary Warbler selects the territory, selecting the nesting site before he becomes mated for the first nest, but thereafter both birds inspect the new nest sites.

On observations made near Knoxville, Tenn., Henry Meyer and Ruth Reed Nevius (1943) found that—

three males established territories. Male I arrived April 14. By the next day he was singing on an area 550 feet long and for the most part not more than 200 feet wide. It included three kinds of habitats: (a) a grassy terrace on which several nesting boxes were located, (b) river banks densely covered with small trees and bushes, and (c) a small open orchard which constituted the connecting link between the terrace and the river bank. Male II arrived on April 18 and occupied a narrow territory along a brook confined by wooded slopes and which contained two lotus ponds. The area was about 400 feet long and 100 feet wide. A nesting box was on a stake above one of the ponds. Male III appeared May 5 in the terraced area being claimed by Male I. During the day, the 2 males sang energetically and flew often only a few inches apart. Male I maintained his territory and Male III disappeared.

There were a number of nesting boxes on the area that the males investigated, carrying nesting material into some of them while they were waiting for the females to arrive. The mate of the first male came on April 20, and—

on this day this pair communicated by their full call-note. Twice the male was seen pursuing the female rapidly in a small semi-circle and pausing, called a soft, full note which was later heard only when the two sexes were together.

The mate of Male II came April 22, four days after the latter's arrival.

Combat with other species found within the territories of these birds was observed. Combat with the Bluebird was most frequent but one or more indications of opposition was noticed with the Flicker, Downy Woodpecker, Acadian Flycatcher, Tufted Titmouse, Robin, and Cardinal.

The males sing persistently and energetically from the time that they arrive on their territories, hoping to attract their mates, but they are not always successful, especially in regions where the species is rare or not very common, and their nest-building brings no occupant. Edward von S. Dingle writes to me that, at Summerton, S. C., a male prothonotary warbler built a nest in a low stub, but no female was ever seen. He sang frequently and remained in the vicinity for several weeks. And Frederic H. Kennard, in far-away Massachusetts, mentions in his notes that he saw one and watched it for several days, June 16–20, 1890. "He sang loudly and clearly and sweetly, and seemed to like a particular place by the side of the river, for when I returned later in the day, he was still there, on the other side of the river." On June 19, he watched him for half an hour. He was always in the same locality.  On a later search, no nest or no mate could be found.

*Courtship.*—Brewster (1878a) gives the following full account of this performance:

Mating began almost immediately after the arrival of the females, and the "old, old story" was told in many a willow thicket by the little golden-breasted lovers.  The scene enacted upon such occasions was not strikingly different from that usual among the smaller birds; retiring and somewhat indifferent coyness on the part of the female; violent protestations and demonstrations from the male, who swelled his plumage, spread his wings and tail, and fairly danced around the object of his affections.  Sometimes at this juncture another male appeared, and then a fierce conflict was sure to ensue.  The combatants would struggle together most furiously until the weaker was forced to give way and take to flight.  On several occasions I have seen two males, after fighting among the branches for a long time, clinch and come fluttering together to the water beneath, where for several minutes the contest continued upon the surface until both were fairly drenched.  The males rarely meet in the mating season without fighting, even though no female may be near.  Sometimes one of them turns tail at the outset; and the other at once giving chase, the pursuer and pursued, separated by a few inches only, go darting through the woods, winding, doubling, now careering away up among the tree-tops, now down over the water, sweeping close to the surface until the eye becomes weary with following their mad flight.  During all this time the female usually busies herself with feeding, apparently entirely unconcerned as to the issue.  Upon the return of the conqueror her indifference, real or assumed, vanishes, he receives a warm welcome, and matters are soon arranged between them.

*Nesting.*—The prothonotary warbler and Lucy's warbler are the only two American warblers that habitually build their nests in cavities, usually well concealed.  The normal, and probably the original, primitive, nestling sites are in natural cavities in trees and most nests are still to be found in such situations today.  The prothonotary is not at all particular as to the species of trees, nests having been found in many kinds of trees, although perhaps a slight preference is shown for dead willow stumps.  Nor is it particular as to the size or condition of the cavity, or its location, though quite often choosing one over water or near it.  The height above the ground or water varies from 3 feet or less to as much as 32 feet but there are more nests below 5 feet than there are above 10, the height of the majority being between 5 and 10 feet.  The size and shape of the cavity are of little concern; if the cavity is too deep, the industrious little birds fill it with nesting material up to within a few inches of the top; sometimes a very shallow cavity is used, so that the bird can be plainly seen from a distance as it sits on the nest.  The old deserted holes of woodpeckers or chickadees are favorite nesting sites; the entrances to these have often been enlarged by other agencies, or are badly weathered.  In very rotten stumps, the warblers have been known to excavate partially or to enlarge a cavity.

The nests built by the males in early spring, referred to above, are probably rarely used as brood nests and might be classed as dummy nests. The family nest is built almost entirely by the female, with encouragement and a little help from her mate, who accompanies her to and from the nest and in the search for material; much of the soft, green moss used extensively in the nest is often obtainable from fallen logs and stumps in the vicinity.

Brewster (1878a) mentions a nest taken from a deep cavity that "when removed presents the appearance of a compact mass of moss five or six inches in height by three or four in diameter. When the cavity is shallow, it is often only scantily lined with moss and a few fine roots. The deeper nests are of course the more elaborate ones. One of the finest specimens before me is composed of moss, dry leaves, and cypress twigs. The cavity for the eggs is a neatly rounded, cup-shaped hollow, two inches in diameter by one and a half in depth, smoothly lined with fine roots and a few wing-feathers of some small bird."

In Dr. Walkinshaw's (1938) Michigan nests, "moss constituted the bulk of the nesting material in nearly all cases, completely filling the nest space whether it was large or small. On top of this the nest proper was shaped and a rough lining of coarse grape-bark, dead leaves, black rootlets procured from the river-banks, and poison-ivy tendrils was added. Above this a lining of much finer rootlets, leaf-stems, and very fine grasses was used."

In addition to the materials listed above Meyer and Nevius (1943) mention hackberry leaves, hairs, pine needles, horsehair, and cedar bark in their Tennessee nests. They say that from 6 to 10 days were required for nest construction, and that from 3 to 5 days more elapsed before the first eggs were laid. Their four nests were all in bird-boxes; one was in an orchard over plowed ground, one over a lotus pond in a wooded ravine, and two were over lily pools near buildings.

Dr. Walkinshaw (1938) publishes a map showing the location of 21 nesting boxes along the winding banks of the Battle Creek River, in Calhoun County, Mich., and writes: "Of the 28 nests found during 1937, 19 were in bird-houses over running water, 6 were in stubs over water (2 of which were over running water), and the other 3 were in natural holes back from the river bank. Of 44 nests found from 1930 through 1937, excluding the 21 in bird-houses, six were over running water in old woodpecker holes, one in a bridge-support in a slight depression, and nine in natural holes over standing water. Seven were in old woodpecker holes from two to a hundred and sixty feet back from the river-bank."

Many and varied are the odd nesting sites occupied by prothonotary warblers. Dr. Thomas S. Roberts (1936) writes:

The vagaries of this bird in choosing artificial nesting-places are shown by the positions of the following nests. On the La Crosse railroad bridge: in a cigar-box nailed on the engine-house on top of the draw; on one of the piers; in a metal ventilator-cap four inches in diameter, that had fallen and lodged just at the point where the draw banged against the pier, and close under the tracks; in a shallow cavity in a piece of slab-wood nailed to a trestle-support close under the road-bed of the railroad; these all far out in the middle of the Mississippi River. Still others are: in a Bluebird box on a low post by a switching-house and busy railroad platform; in a cleft in a pile in the river; in a tin cup in a barn, to reach which the birds entered through a broken pane of glass; in a pasteboard box on a shelf in a little summer-house; in an upright glass fruit jar in a house-boat; and other similar situations. In most cases the birds had to carry the nesting-material long distances, especially to the places on the bridge.

John W. Moyer (1933) relates an interesting story that was told to him by people living in a farm house along the Kankakee River. A pair of these warblers built their nests and raised their broods for three consecutive seasons in the pocket of an old hunting-coat, hung in a garage; each year the man cleaned out the nest and used the coat in the fall, and the next spring the birds used it again. M. G. Vaiden tells me of a similar case.

Nests have been found in buildings, on beams and other supports. Louis W. Campbell (1930) reports two on shelves in sheds, one in a small paper sack partly filled with staples and another in a coffee can similarly filled. Nests in cans in various situations have been found a number of times, and others have been reported in a tin pail hung under a porch, in a mail box, in a box on a moving ferry boat, in a Chinese lantern on a pavilion, and in an old hornets' nest.

Dr. Walkinshaw writes to me: "At Reelfoot Lake, Tenn., during July, 1940, I found 8 nests of the prothonotary warbler, all built a few feet above the water in small natural holes in cypress knees. Evidently these are regular late-summer nesting sites." The knees were farther under water earlier in the season. Most of his 76 Michigan nests were over water, or less than 100 feet from it; but 10 were 300 or more feet away from it and 2 were over 400 feet away. M. G. Vaiden tells me of a pair that nested in the tool box of a log-loading machine that was in daily operation, hauling logs.

*Eggs.*—From 3 to 8 eggs have been found in nests of the prothonotary warbler, from 4 to 6 seem to be the commonest numbers, 7 is a fairly common number, and at least 3 sets of 8 have been reported; in the J. P. Norris series of 70 sets are 34 sets of 6, 15 sets of 7, and 2 sets of 8.

The eggs vary in shape from ovate to short ovate, and they are more or less glossy. The eggs are undoubtedly the most striking of the warblers' eggs, with their rich creamy, or rose-tinted cream, ground color, boldly and liberally spotted and blotched with "burnt umber," "bay," "chestnut brown," and "auburn," intermingled with spots and undertones of "light Payne's gray," "Rood's lavender," "violet-gray," and "purplish gray." There is quite a variation in the amount of markings, which are generally more or less evenly scattered over the entire egg; some are sparingly spotted and blotched, while others are so profusely marked as almost to obscure the ground color (Harris).

J. P. Norris (1890b), in his description of his 70 sets, describes 2 eggs in each of 2 sets as "unmarked, save for four or five indistinct specks of cinnamon." These were in sets of 6 eggs each. Pure white, unmarked eggs were once taken by R. M. Barnes (1889). Dr. Walkinshaw (1938) gives the measurements of 78 eggs as averaging 18.47 by 14.55 millimeters; the eggs showing the four extremes measured 20 by 15, 19 by 16, and 17 by 13 millimeters.

*Incubation.*—The eggs are laid, usually one each day, very early in the morning; Dr. Walkinshaw (1941) says between 5:00 and 7:00 a. m. in Michigan; Meyer and Nevius (1943), in Tennessee, saw the female enter the nest to lay as early as 5:00 a. m. on May 2, and as early as 4:44 on May 23, remaining in the nest from 28 to 36 minutes on different occasions. The period of incubation is recorded as 12, 13½, and 14 days by different observers; about 13 seems to be the average, according to Dr. Walkinshaw (MS.), probably depending on conditions and the method of reckoning. Incubation seems to be performed entirely by the female, but the male feeds her to some extent while she is on the nest. Incubation starts the day before the last egg is laid.

*Young.*—Meyer and Nevius (1943) write:

The adults shared feeding duties, and both removed fecal sacks. During the first three days the female steadily brooded the young. One female, observed from 4:55 to 8:10 a. m., when the young were one day old, spent a total of 70 minutes off and 155 minutes on the nest. Trips from the nest lasted an average of 8.6 minutes, while periods on the nest averaged 19.4 minutes. * * * At one nest when the young were eight days old, activities were noted during the eight and one half hours from 8:30 a. m. to 5:30 p. m. The young were fed an average of 16 times an hour. * * * The adults were seen carrying spiders and insects, small green caterpillars frequently being used. Mr. H. P. Ijams saw a male offer a 10-day old nestling a mayfly. An incubator-hatched bird accepted egg-yolk, ants, ant larvae, crickets, earthworms, and spiders.

They say of the development of the young: "The young on the day of hatching had orange-red skin. The mouth lining was red. Down was distributed over the frontal and occipital areas of the capital tract, spinal tract, femoral, altar, and humeral tracts. Feather sheaths of the alar tracts penetrated the skin the first day after hatching. On the second day after hatching the eye-slits began to open. Feather sheaths of the humeral, femoral, and crural tracts emerged on the third day; those on the dorsal and ventral tracts emerged on the fourth day, and those of the capital and caudal tracts on the fifth day. On the fifth day the sheaths began breaking." During the next five days the young developed rapidly and became more and more active, and on the tenth day began to leave the nest.

Young observed by Dr. Walkinshaw (1914) at Reelfoot Lake "averaged 11 days of age when leaving the nest in 1939, while 21 young in Michigan during 1939 and 1940 remained in the nest for a period of 10¾ days." Of the comparative nesting success in the two localities, he says:

In Michigan from 1930 through 1940, 121 nests of the Prothonotary Warbler were observed. Only 28, or 23.14 per cent, were successful. Out of 413 eggs, 159 (38.47 per cent) hatched and 100 young were fledged (.87 per total nest; 3.78 per successful nest). The fledgling success was 25.66 per cent of eggs laid. More failures in Michigan resulted in more nestings by individual birds.

In Tennessee during 1939, 30 nests were observed until terminated or successful; 19 were successful (63.33 per cent) while out of 139 eggs, 78 hatched and all the young lived to leave the nest or 56.11 per cent fledging success of eggs laid; 2.6 young were fledged per total nest; 4.1 per successful nest.

He also notes that in Michigan the species is typically single-brooded if the first nesting is successful, but that in Tennessee it is typically double-brooded.

*Plumages.*—According to Dr. Dwight (1900) the natal down, located as indicated above, is brownish mouse-gray. Ridgway (1902) gives rather the best description of the juvenal plumage as follows: "Pileum, hindneck, back, and scapulars dull olive-greenish; wing-coverts, tertials, rump, and upper tail-coverts slate-gray, tinged with olive, the middle and greater wing-coverts narrowly tipped with light olive-greenish, producing two very indistinct bands; secondaries, primaries, and rectrices as in adults; sides of head pale yellowish olive; chin, throat, and chest dull light grayish olive, darkest on chest rest of under parts dull white, passing on sides and flanks into olive-grayish."

In very young birds, according to Dr. Dwight, there is a variable amount of brownish wash on the back, which fades out to gray. And Dr. Chapman (1907) says that the white on the inner webs of the tail feathers is more restricted than in adults and more or less mottled with blackish. This first plumage is followed in June and July by a partial postjuvenal molt involving all the contour plumage and the wing coverts but not the rest of the wings or the tail. The young bird now becomes a golden swamp warbler, the young being nearly like the adults, the females being considerably duller in color than the males and having less white in the tail.

The crown and hind neck in both sexes, both old and young, are washed with dusky or olive in the fall. Spring plumages are produced by very slight wear without molt. There is one complete, annual molt in late summer.

*Food.*—Very little seems to have been recorded on the food of the prothonotary warbler. It is evidently highly insectivorous, obtaining most of its food from the trunks and branches of trees and shrubs and from fallen logs. Brewster (1878) says: "This Warbler usually seeks its food low down among thickets, moss-grown logs, or floating débris, and always about water. Sometimes it ascends tree-trunks for a little way like the Black-and-White Creeper, winding about with the same peculiar motion."

Dr. Roberts (1936) lists "ants, and other insects and their larvae," as its food. Some of the food of the young is mentioned above, most of which is doubtless included in the food of the adults. Spiders, beetles, mayflies, and other insects should be included, as well as many caterpillars and the larvae of water insects. Audubon (1841) says: "It often perches upon the rank grasses and water plants, in quest of minute molluscous animals which creep upon them, and which, together with small land snails, I have found in its stomach."

*Behavior.*—Brewster (1878a) observes:

When seen among the upper branches, where it often goes to plume its feathers and sing in the warm sunshine, it almost invariably sits nearly motionless. Its flight is much like that of the Water-Thrush (either species), and is remarkably swift, firm, and decided. When crossing a broad stream it is slightly undulating, though always direct. * * *

In general activity and restlessness few birds equal the species under consideration. Not a nook or corner of his domain but is repeatedly visited through the day. Now he sings a few times from the top of some tall willow that leans out over the stream, sitting motionless among the yellowish foliage, fully aware, perhaps, of the protection afforded by its harmonizing tints. The next moment he descends to the cool shades beneath, where dark, coffee-colored water, the overflow of the pond or river, stretches back among the trees. Here he loves to hop about on floating drift-wood, wet by the lapping of pulsating wavelets; now following up some long, inclining, half-submerged log, peeping into every crevice and occasionally dragging forth from its concealment a spider or small beetle, turning alternately his bright yellow breast and olive back towards the light; now jetting his beautiful tail or quivering his wings tremulously, he darts off into some thicket in response to a call from his mate; or, flying to a neighboring tree-trunk, clings for a moment against the mossy bole to pipe his little strain or look up the exact whereabouts of some suspected insect prize.

*Voice.*—The same gifted writer and careful observer (Brewster, 1878) gives the following good account of the distinctive song of this warbler:

The usual song of the Prothonotary Warbler sounds at a distance like the call of the Solitary Sandpiper, with a syllable or two added,—a simple *peet, tweet, tweet, tweet,* given on the same key throughout. Often when the notes came from the farther shore of a river or pond we were completely deceived. On more than one occasion, when a good opportunity for comparison was offered by the actual presence of both birds at the same time, we found that at the distance of several hundred yards their notes were absolutely undistinguishable; nearer at hand, however, the resemblance is lost, and a ringing, penetrating quality becomes apparent in the Warbler's song. It now sounds like *peet, tsweet, tsweet, tsweet,* or sometimes *tweet, tr-sweet, tr-sweet, tr-sweet.* When the bird sings within a few yards the sound is almost startling in its intensity, and the listener feels inclined to stop his ears. The male is a fitful singer, and is quite as apt to be heard in the hot noontide or on cloudy days, when other birds are silent, as during the cool morning and evening hours. The ordinary note of alarm or distress is a sharp one, so nearly like that of the Large-billed Water Thrush (*Siurus motacilla*) that the slight difference can only be detected by a critical ear. When the sexes meet a soft *tchip* of recognition common to nearly all the Warblers is used. In addition to the song above described the male has a different and far sweeter one, which is reserved for select occasions,—an outpouring of the bird's most tender feelings, intended for the ears of his mate alone, like the rare evening warble of the Oven-Bird (*Siurus auricapillus*). It is apparently uttered only while on the wing.

Although so low and feeble as to be inaudible many rods away, it is very sweet, resembling somewhat the song of the Canary, given in an undertone, with trills or "water-notes" interspersed. The flight during its delivery is very different from that at all other times. The bird progresses slowly, with a trembling, fluttering motion, its head raised and tail expanded. This song was heard most frequently after incubation had begun.

Dr. Roberts (1936) refers to this flight song, as delivered "after the manner of the Maryland Yellow-throat, * * * consisting first of the usual rapid monotone of five or six notes and ending with a pleasing, varied warble, full and strong in some of its notes and far sweeter than the usual utterance."

Dr. Walkinshaw (1938) says of the usual song: "Uttered at the rate of five or six times per minute, the song lasts slightly over one second. It is given all day long from the time of arrival until the young have left the nest and has been heard as late as the 16th of August (1931). The frequency is much greater during the early nesting season and during the earlier hours. During midday on warmer days the number of times per hour seems much less. Later, from four until near sundown, it again increases. During late nesting, when the young are about to leave the nest, the rate again decreases, but it is heard several days after the young leave the nest." Aretas A. Saunders tells me that the songs are pitched at C′′′′ or B′′′, and the call note, *tseek*, at A′′′.

*Field marks.*—The golden swamp warbler could hardly be mistaken for anything else. The rich, brilliant yellow of the head and breast, sometimes almost orange on the head, only slightly paler in the female, the absence of wing bars, and the large amount of white in the tail will distinguish it.

*Enemies.*—Dr. Walkinshaw (1941) says that the house wren is a serious competitor with the prothonotary warbler in Michigan, contending with it for nesting sites in the bird-boxes.

The cowbird is a persistent enemy of this warbler in spite of its hole-nesting habits; perhaps if the warbler nested in deeper holes it might find some relief from this pest. Among 70 sets of eggs of this warbler in the J. P. Norris collection, 18 contain cowbirds' eggs. Dr. Friedmann (1929) found no less than 36 records of such parasitism in the literature, and says: "As many as four eggs of the Cowbird have been found in a single nest together with four of the Warbler's. There are several cases on record of doubled-storied nests of this bird, with a Cowbird's egg buried in the lower story. Such cases are, however, not common, and usually the Warbler seems to make no attempt to get rid of the strange eggs." E. M. S. Dale wrote to me of a nest, found near Toronto in 1933, that contained seven eggs of the cowbird and none at all of the warbler!

Snakes sometimes destroy the eggs or young.

*Fall.*—Dr. Walkinshaw (1938) says that "the majority of the Prothonotaries leave our rivers [Michigan] by the second or third of July. One may canoe some years a good many miles during the latter part of July or the early part of August without finding a single Prothonotary, whereas in other years many groups can be found. The majority evidently are early migrants. Very few remain until late August or early September, the latest date being September 9, 1934, at Battle Creek."

The 1931 A. O. U. Check-List states that this warbler apparently crosses the Gulf of Mexico in migration "and is not found in Mexico north of Campeche," but probably some migration is along the coast of Texas and Mexico, as suggested by George G. Williams (1945).

Dr. Chapman (1907) says: "The route of the Prothonotary Warbler in its fall migration is interesting; the breeding birds of the Middle Atlantic States apparently pass southwest to northwestern Florida and then take a seven-hundred-mile flight directly across the Gulf of Mexico to southern Yucatan, instead of crossing to Cuba and thence to Tucatan."

Alexander F. Skutch writes to me: "Unrecorded from Guatemala, the prothonotary warbler is a rare bird of passage and very rare winter resident in the more southerly portions of Central America. When Carriker published his list of Costa Rican birds in 1910, he had a few records from the highlands—apparently of migrating birds—and from the Pacific lowlands, but none from Caribbean lowlands. But on March 4, 1934, I found it not uncommon at Puerto Limón, where I saw one among the royal palms in Vargas Park, and several among the shrubbery about the outlying cottages, all within a hundred yards of the Caribbean Sea. It has been recorded a number of times from the Canal Zone, but it is not common there. It is almost always seen in the vicinity of water."

*Winter.*—Apparently the main winter range is in Colombia and perhaps Venezuela. Referring to Magdalena, Colombia, P. J. Darlington, Jr. (1931), writes: "The Prothonotary Warbler swarms during the winter in the mangroves at Sevillano and in the fresh swamps at Cienaga. It was seen also in bushes on the sea beach at Donjaca September 15, and along the Rio Frio River in the edge of the foothills, where it was especially common in February. The birds usually occur near water, but numbers were noted again and again in yellow-flowering, acacia-like trees on the border of stump land and dry forest, far from water."

## DISTRIBUTION

*Range.*—Eastern United States to northwestern South America.

*Breeding range.*—The prothonotary warbler breeds **north** to southeastern Minnesota (Cambridge, Lake Pekin, and La Crescent); central Wisconsin (New London and Shiocton); southern Michigan (Hesperia, Lansing, and Ann Arbor); northern Ohio (Toledo and Cleveland); extreme southern Ontario (Rondeau); western New York (Buffalo and Oak Orchard); northern West Virginia (Parkersburg); central Maryland (Seneca and Bowie); and southern Delaware (Gumboro). **East** to southern Delaware (Gumboro); eastern Virginia (Dyke, near Alexandria, and Dismal Swamp); and the Atlantic coast to central Florida (Lake Gentry and Padgett Creek). **South** to central Florida (Padgett Creek and possibly Puntarossa); the Gulf coast to southeastern Texas (Cove, Houston, and Bloomington). **West** to central Texas (Bloomington, Fort Worth, and Gainesville); central Oklahoma (Norman and Oklahoma City); eastern Kansas (Emporia and Manhattan); northwestern Iowa (Lake Okoboji); and southeastern Minnesota (Rochester, Red Wing, and Cambridge).

The prothonotary warbler has been recorded as casual or accidental **west** to southeastern Nebraska (Powell and Lincoln); southeastern South Dakota (Yankton and Sioux Falls); and central Minnesota (Brainerd). **North** to southern Ontario (London and Hamilton); central New York (Ithaca); Massachusetts (Northampton, Amherst, and Concord); New Hampshire (Concord); and Maine (Matinicus Island and Calais).

*Winter range.*—The winter home of the prothonotary warbler is in Central America and northwestern South America where it has been found **north** to northwestern Costa Rica (Bolson); Nicaragua (Escondido River). **East** to northwestern Venezuela (Mérida and Encon-

trados) ; and western Colombia (San José de Cucuta and Villavieja).
South to southwestern Colombia (Villavieja); and northwestern
Ecuador (Esmeraldas). West to northwestern Ecuador (Esmeraldas) ; western Colombia (Antioquia) ; western Panamá (Paracote
and David) ; and Costa Rica (Puntarenas and Bolson). It has been
reported to occur in winter in Campeche and on Cozumel Island,
Mexico, and casually or accidentally in Cuba (Habana), Jamaica,
and St. Croix, Virgin Islands.

*Migration.*—The probable route of the prothonotary warbler between its summer and winter homes is across the Gulf of Mexico,
from the Yucatan peninsula where it occurs in both spring and fall
migration. The casual or accidental occurrences of this warbler in
Cuba (Habana); Jamaica; and St. Croix, Virgin Islands, are in
migration.

Late dates of spring departure are: Colombia—Villavieja, February
5. Panamá; Canal Zone—Barro Colorado, March 10. Nicaragua—
Edén, March 23. Quintana Roo—Cozumel, April 6. Cuba—Habana,
April 4.

Early dates of spring arrival are: Yucatán—Mérida, March 28.
Jamaica—Black River, February 28. Cuba—Habana, March 31.
Florida—Pensacola, March 18. Alabama—Booth, April 4. Geor-
gia—Fitzgerald, March 21. South Carolina—Yemassee, March 27.
North Carolina—Greenville, April 6. Virginia—Suffolk, April 10.
Mississippi—Gulfport, March 18. Louisiana—Morgan City, March
10. Texas—Cove, March 28. Arkansas—Huttig, March 31. Mis-
souri—St. Louis, April 17. Kentucky—Bowling Green, April 5.
Illinois—Murphysboro, April 17. Ohio—Berlin Center, April 18.
Michigan—Grand Rapids, May 3. Iowa—Iowa City, April 26. Wis-
consin—Madison, May 2. Minnesota—Red Wing, May 7. Oklahoma—Tulsa, April 2. Kansas—Manhattan, April 26. Nebraska—
Blue Springs, April 30.

Late dates of fall departure are: Nebraska—Watson, September 1.
Oklahoma—Oklahoma City, September 14. Texas—Kemah, September 11. Wisconsin—Racine, September 22. Iowa—Sioux City, August 31. Michigan—Three Rivers, September 13. Ohio—Columbus,
October 5. Illinois—Oak Park, October 17. Kentucky—Lexington,
October 6. Tennessee—Elizabethton, October 19. Louisiana—Monroe, October 8. Mississippi—Deer Island, September 27. North
Carolina—Raleigh, August 26. South Carolina—Charleston, September 17. Georgia—Atlanta, October 8. Yucatán—Chichén-Itzá, October 18.

Early dates of fall arrival are: Florida—Fort Myers, August 8.
Yucatán—Chichén-Itzá, October 7. Honduras—Tela, September 8.

Nicaragua—Río Escondido, September 2.    Costa Rica—Bonilla, August 28.    Panamá—Obaldia, September 15.    Colombia—Gaira, September 11.

*Banding records.*—Banding provides a hint as to the life-span of the prothonotary warbler.    One banded as an immature on June 16, 1940, in Convis township, Calhoun County, Mich., was color banded when it returned to the same place in 1942.    Subsequently it was identified by the colored band on May 14, 1944, and May 10, 1945.

*Casual records.*—The prothonotary warbler was reported at Nassau, Bahamas, on August 29, 1898.    It has been twice reported at Bermuda: one shot from a flock in the fall of 1874, and another specimen collected in November 1903.    A single bird was observed at Mammoth Hot Springs, Yellowstone Park, Wyo., on September 10, 1931.    There are two records for Arizona.    On May 1, 1884, a specimen was taken near Tucson at an altitude of 2,300 feet, the highest record of the species in the United States.    Another specimen was taken September 8, 1924, at Cave Creek, 4 miles northeast of Paradise in the Chiricahua Mountains.

*Egg dates.*    Florida: 8 records, April 18 to May 9; 5 records, April 28 to 30.

Illinois: 79 records, May 6 to June 21; 46 records, May 20 to June 4, indicating the height of the season.

Iowa: 56 records, May 15 to June 26; 36 records, May 27 to June 6 (Harris).

## LYMNOTHLYPIS SWAINSONII (Audubon)

### SWAINSON'S WARBLER

#### CONTRIBUTED BY EDWARD VON SIEBOLD DINGLE

#### PLATES 7–9

#### HABITS

"The history of our knowledge of Swainson's Warbler," write Brooks and Legg (1942), "is a curious one, falling into definite periods."    This bird was discovered in the spring of 1832 by the Rev. John Bachman "near the banks of the Edisto River, South Carolina." His discovery of the bird is described as follows: "I was first attracted by the novelty of its notes, four or five in number, repeated at intervals of five or six minutes apart.    These notes were loud, clear, and more like a whistle than a song.    They resembled the sounds of some extraordinary ventriloquist in such a degree, that I supposed the bird much farther from me than it really was; for after some trouble caused by these fictitious notes, I perceived it near to me and soon shot it" (Audubon, 1841).    Dr. Bachman took five specimens; then, up to the spring of 1884, Swainson's warbler remained almost a lost species, for according to Brewster (1885a) there is no record of more than eight or nine birds being collected. Wayne, through collections and field work near Charleston, opened a productive 25-year period in the history of *swainsonii*, in which many valuable contributions were made by various observers. From 1910 to 1930 the name *swainsonii* was practically absent from the pages of current ornithological literature.

Brewster (1885a) has given us the best description of the bird's haunts in the low country:

> The particular kind of swamp to which he is most partial is known in local parlance as a "pine-land gall." It is usually a depression in the otherwise level surface, down which winds a brook, in places flowing swiftly between well-defined banks, in others divided into several sluggish channels or spreading about in stagnant pools, margined by a dense growth of cane, and covered with lily leaves or other aquatic vegetation. Its course through the open pine-lands is sharply marked by a belt of hardwood trees nourished to grand proportions by the rich soil and abundant moisture. Beneath, crumbling logs cumber the ground, while an under-growth of dogwood (*Cornus florida*), sassafras, viburnum, etc., is interlaced and made well-nigh impenetrable by a net-work of grapevines and greenbriar. These belts—river bottoms they are in miniature—rarely exceed a few rods in width; they may extend miles in a nearly straight line.

The writer has had a long acquaintance with Swainson's warbler in the low country of Carolina. Except during September (fall migration) the birds were almost never seen out of sight of substantial growths of cane, even when the nests were built in bushes, low trees, or vines. This has been the experience of practically all observers and, as Brooks and Legg (1942) remark, "an idée fixe among ornithologists" existed; the familiar description of habitat by Brewster (1885a) became a dictum: "Briefly, four things seem indispensible to his existence, viz., water, tangled thickets, patches of cane, and a rank growth of semi-aquatic plants."

Hence, the ornithological world received a surprise to learn that *swainsonii* was a summer resident and breeder in different localities of high altitude in the Appalachian Chain. Although several observers have found the bird nesting beyond the limits of the Coastal Plain, even in Piedmont territory, as La Prade (1922) did at 1,050 foot above sea level, it was F. A. Williams (1935) who first detected it in a truly mountainous terrain. During two successive summers he found birds near Tryon, N. C., "in open woods."

Loomis (1887) was quite prophetic when, in recording a Swainson's warbler from Chester, S. C., "in the heart of the Piedmont Region, one hundred and fifty miles from the coast," he wrote: "It awakens the mind to the possibility of an Up-Country habitat, yet awaiting discovery, where the true centre of abundance will finally be located."

The efforts of Brooks and Legg (1942) have shown Swainson's warbler to be a locally common summer resident in south-central West Virginia up to an elevation of 2,000 feet above sea level; no positive evidence of breeding has been found, but it undoubtedly does breed. In Tennessee, Wetmore (1939) has found the bird in mountainous country at 3,000 feet.

The question naturally arises, Did Swainson's warbler always inhabit higher altitudes, or is this a recent extension of range and partial change of habitat? The answer will probably never be found; but study of changing conditions in its low country habitat for the past several decades may throw light on this interesting problem. Within the writer's experience the canebrake areas have long been exposed to forest fires, timber cutting, overgrazing, drainage, and the construction of a hydroelectric project, as a result of which thousands of acres of timbered swampland are now under water.

*Spring.*—The birds that winter in Jamaica enter the United States through Florida, but it is probable that those from Yucatán make a direct flight across the Gulf to the delta of the Mississippi. The earliest recorded spring arrival in the United States was on March 22, 1890, on the lower Suwanee River. The same year the species was taken at the Tortugas, March 25 to April 5 (Chapman, 1907). The earliest arrival near New Orleans, was March 30, 1905 (Kopman, 1915). Meanley (MS.) records it from central Georgia on March 31, 1944. Swainson's warbler reaches the vicinity of Charleston, S. C., during the first week of April, the earliest being the fifth of that month.

*Nesting.*—Nests are built in bushes, canes, masses of vines, and briers; 10 feet seems to be the maximum height from the ground, while some nests have been found as low as 2 feet. The average elevation would be around 3 feet. As many nests are built over dry ground as over water. The nest is quite bulky and loosely constructed; a typical one in situ looks like a bunch of leaves lodged in a bush or cane, as the stems point upward. The outer walls of the nest are composed of various leaves such as oak, gum, maple, tupelo, and cane; the inner walls are usually of cane, while the lining is of pine needles, black fiber of moss (*Tillandsia*), cypress leaves, rootlets, or grass stems. Sometimes horsehair is also present.

[AUTHOR'S NOTE: A few more notes on the nesting of Swainson's warbler may well be added to the above general statements. Brewster's (1885b) nests, taken by Wayne in the low country of South Carolina, are evidently typical for that region. All four of these nests were in canes. Wayne (1886) says that the nests "are generally built in canes," but he has also found them "in small bushes, and in one instance in a climbing vine, by the side of a large public road." Brewster (1885b) gives the measurements of two of his nests; the smallest of the four measures—

externally 3.50 in diameter by 3.00 in depth; internally 1.50 in diameter by 1.50 in depth; the greatest thickness of the rim or outer wall being 1.00. * * *

The nest June 27 is very much larger, in fact quite the largest specimen that I have seen, measuring externally 5.00 in diameter by 6.00 in depth; internally 1.50 in diameter by 1.25 in depth; with the rim in places 1.75 thick. It is shaped like an inverted cone, the apex extending down nearly to the point of junction of the numerous fascicled stems which surround and support its sides. Its total bulk fully equals the average nest of our Crow Blackbird, while it is not nearly as finished a specimen of bird architecture. Indeed it would be difficult to imagine anything ruder than its outer walls,—composed of mud-soaked leaves of the sweet gum, water oak, holly, and cane, thrown together into a loose mass, bristling with rough stems, and wholly devoid of symmetry or regularity of outline. The interior, however, lined with pine needles, moss fibre, black rootlets, and a little horse-hair, is not less smooth and rounded than in the other specimens.

Troup D. Perry (1887), with his friend George Noble, found no less than 24 nests near Savannah, Ga., in 1887; some of these were in gall or myrtle bushes and one was in a saw palmetto 2½ feet high. S. A. Grimes has sent us a photograph of a nest on the broad leaf of a saw palmetto (pl. 7). Albert J. Kirn (1918) says of the nesting sites of Swainson's warbler in Oklahoma: "A well shaded clump of trees in the woods, such a place as would suggest itself for a Wood Thrush, yet not exactly so, with considerable 'buck brush' undergrowth, but no grass or weeds is selected for a nesting site. In the top of this 'buck brush' usually about two feet high the nest is built; about half of the nests found were close to the river bank—the Little Caney River. All but two were built in the brushy undergrowth. These two were fastened to briers and slender brush and were higher up, 3.5 and 4 feet."

F. M. Jones wrote to Brooks and Legg (1942) of a nest found in southwestern Virginia: "This nest was in a very dense growth of rhododendron bushes close to a stream of water where the sunlight never penetrated. It was 5 ft. 6 in. up, built in the forks of a slender beech limb which grew across the top of a rhododendron bush (*R. maximum*) and partly supported by the top of the rhododendron. * * * The outside of the nest measured 7 in. wide by 5 in. deep and the inside 2 in. wide by 1¹³⁄₁₆ in. deep."

It is evident, from the above and other similar accounts that, at higher elevations northward and westward, Swainson's warbler nests in bushes and vines where there are no canes to be found.]

*Eggs.*—Swainson's warbler usually lays three eggs; sets of four are rare and of five very rare. Although there are records of nests containing two incubated eggs or two young birds, these probably represent incomplete sets or cases where an egg or a nestling has been destroyed.

Eggs are quite globular, the two ends sometimes scarcely distinguishable; the shell is thick and has a distinct polish; the ground color is white with a bluish tinge; however, a set of three eggs in the writer's collection had a faint greenish tinge, while several observers describe sets of pale pink or buffy white.

Rarely, spotted eggs are found. Wayne (1910) says: "Spotted eggs are, however, very rare and I have found only four or five nests containing them." The only spotted egg the writer has found is in the set referred to above; of these, two are immaculate, while the third is "faintly though distinctly speckled around the larger end with reddish brown" (Dingle, 1926).

Brewster (1885b) describes a set collected by the late Arthur T. Wayne: "One is perfectly plain; another * * * has two or three minute specks which may be genuine shell markings; while the third is unmistakably spotted and blotched with pale lilac. Over most of the surface these markings are fine, faint, and sparsely distributed, but about the larger end they become coarser, thicker, and deeper colored, forming a well-defined ring or wreath."

Burleigh (1923) writes: "Unlike all the descriptions I had read, and the few eggs I had seen, these were light pink in ground color and dotted distinctly over the entire surface with light brown spots, this almost forming a wreath at the larger end of one egg." These eggs were found near Augusta, Ga., and the parent was secured.

Wayne (1910) was of the opinion that two broods are raised in a season.

[AUTHOR'S NOTE: The measurements of 50 eggs average 19.5 by 15.0 millimeters; the eggs showing the four extremes measure 21.6 by 14.2, 20.8 by 16.0, 18.0 by 14.1, and 19.5 by 13.5 millimeters (Harris).]

*Plumages.*—[AUTHOR'S NOTE: Ridgway (1902) describes the juvenal plumage of Swainson's warbler as follows: "Head, neck, back, rump, upper tail-coverts, chest, sides, and flanks plain brown (varying from broccoli to bister); rest of under parts whitish or dull pale yellowish, more or less clouded with brown; middle and greater wing-coverts indistinctly tipped with cinnamon-brown; otherwise like adults, but no trace of lighter superciliary nor darker postocular stripes." Specimens that I have seen in this plumage are more nearly "cinnamon-brown" than the colors named above on the back and wing coverts, and the latter show very little evidence of cinnamon tips.]

The postjuvenal molt, which evidently includes only the contour plumage and the wing coverts, occurs early in the summer; I have seen young birds beginning to acquire the first winter plumage as early as June 12, and others that had nearly completed the molt on July 20; these birds were not yet fully grown. Wayne (1910) writes: "I have taken young birds which were as large as the adults and which were acquiring their autumnal plumage as early as June 2, but it must be borne in mind that the season in which these young were taken (1906) was exceptionally advanced."

Brewster (1885a) describes the young bird in its fall plumage as follows: "Entire upper parts rich olive strongly tinged with reddish-brown, the crown scarcely deeper-colored than the back, the wings a trifle redder; loral stripe blackish; superciliary stripe tinged with yellow; under parts strongly yellowish, otherwise like the adult." The nuptial plumage is apparently assumed by wear and fading, the reddish-brown and yellowish colors becoming much duller. There are no specimens available of either young or adult birds that indicate a prenuptial molt.

The postnuptial molt seems to occur mainly in August, but perhaps earlier, and is evidently complete; I have seen birds in full, fresh autumn plumage as early as August 28. This fresh plumage is similar to the spring plumage, but the crown and back are nearly uniform brown, the crown is darker than in spring, the back is browner than in spring, and the breast and flanks are more or less clouded with grayish.

*Food.*—Howell (1924) says that "four stomachs of this bird from Alabama contained remains of caterpillars, spiders, and Hymenoptera (ants, bees, etc.)."

Brewster (1885a) considered the principal food to be small coleopterous insects, "as well as some small green worms that are found on water plants, such as the pond lily (*Nymphaea odorata*) and the Nelumbium (*Cyamus flavicomus*).

*Behavior.*—Swainson's warbler is an unsuspicious bird and can be easily observed in its haunts where the vegetation is not too dense and tangled and the tree canopy overhead partially open. The neutral color of the bird is often apt to conceal him in the shadowy undergrowth. Singing males usually remain on the same perch during their periods of song, apparently disinclined to move. He often sings from the ground during insect hunting; Meanley (MS.) says: "It was so wrapped up in its song as to be absolutely unconcerned; it sang at my very feet with its head thrown back, its beak pointing perpendicularly toward the sky, pouring forth its resounding melody in the best of warbler fashion."

The female is a close sitter, and the observer has usually to touch her before she leaves the nest. Grimes (1930) writes: "This bird would not leave her eggs until *pushed* off, and when I held my hand over the nest she straddled my fingers in trying to get back onto it. * * * When I did drive her away from the nest she fluttered along on the ground in the manner of a crippled bird, her actions manifestly intended to induce me to follow. This bird certainly was not badly frightened, for within a few minutes she was back on her nest, accepting deerflies from my fingers and swallowing them with apparent relish."

Brewster (1885a) gives an admirable portrayal:

His gait is distinctly a walk, his motions gliding and graceful. Upon alighting in the branches, after being flushed from the ground, he assumes a statuesque attitude, like that of a startled Thrush. While singing he takes an easier posture, but rarely moves on his perch. If desirous of changing his position he flies from branch to branch instead of hopping through the twigs in the manner of most Warblers. Under the influence of excitement or jealousy he sometimes jets his tail, droops his wings, and raises the feathers of the crown in a loose crest, but the tail is never jerked like that of a *Geothlypis*, or wagged like that of a *Siurus*. On the contrary, his movements are all deliberate and composed, his disposition sedentary and phlegmatic.

*Voice.*—The bird student who hears the song of Swainson's warbler as he sings in his wooded retreat is fortunate, for it is one of the outstanding warbler songs and, once heard, leaves a lasting impression upon the listener. At a distance it bears much resemblance to the songs of the hoooded warbler and the Louisiana waterthrush. Close up, however, the appealing quality, lacking in the other two, impresses the listener strongly. The song has, in the majority of individuals, a highly ventriloquial effect, but the writer has listened to birds whose notes did not in the slightest degree possess this quality.

The song varies in length and number of notes but can be separated into two distinct parts; the first few notes are uttered rather slowly, the last ones more rapidly and on a descending scale. The second part closely follows the first, with no apparent separation. Brooks and Legg (1942) write: "It might be translated as *whee, whee, whee, whip-poor-will*, the first two (or three) introductory notes on an even pitch, the last *whee* a half-tone lower, and the slurred phrase with *will* separated into two syllables, and accented on the *whip* and on the *wi*-part of the *will*. The last phrase sounded at times remarkably like one of the songs of the White-eyed Vireo."

When the singer begins his performance, the bill is pointed directly up, and he seems entirely unconscious of anything but his own musical efforts. "During his intervals of silence," says N. C. Brown (1878), "he remains motionless, with plumage ruffled, as if completely lost in musical reverie." Brewster (1885a) adds:

It is very loud, very rich, very beautiful, while it has an indescribably tender quality that thrills the senses after the sound has ceased. * * * Although a rarely fervent and ecstatic songster, our litle friend is also a fitful and uncertain one. You may wait for hours near his retreat, even in early morning, or late afternoon, without hearing a note. But when the inspiration comes he floods the woods with music, one song often following another so quickly that there is scarce a pause for breath between. In this manner I have known him to sing for fully twenty minutes, although ordinarily the entire performance occupies less than half that time. Such outbursts may occur at almost any hour, even at noontide, and I have heard them in the gloomiest weather, when the woods were shrouded in mist and rain.

Several times the writer has seen males when the inspiration had not quite come to them; the bird would throw back its head but utter only one or two opening notes of his song.

The call note is a chip, which Brewster calls "a soft *tchip* indistinguishable from that of *Parula americana.*" But Murray (1935) writes that it is "more throaty and full-bodied than that of most Warblers." Brooks and Legg (1942) describe it as "clear, penetrating chirps, having (to our ears) much the same quality as do the chirps of the Mourning Warbler. They are not quite so loud, but have a more ringing quality than those of the Hooded Warbler."

*Field marks.*—[AUTHOR'S NOTE: Swainson's warbler is a plainly colored bird, with no conspicuous field marks. It is brownish olive above and whitish below, with no white in either wings or tail; there is a whitish line over the eye and a dusky streak through it; but the bill is long and sharply pointed.]

## DISTRIBUTION

*Range.*—Southeastern United States to southern Mexico.

*Breeding range.*—Until about 1935 Swainson's warbler was considered to be confined in summer to the southern canebrakes and coastal marshes. It is now known to breed **north** to extreme southern Illinois, probably (seen in breeding season to Olive Branch, Duquoin, and Mount Carmel); southeastern Kentucky (Big Black Mountain); central to northern West Virginia (Charleston, Mount Lookout, Sutton, and Buzzard Rocks, Monongalia County); and southeastern Maryland (Pocomoke River Swamp). **East** to eastern Maryland (Pocomoke River Swamp); eastern Virginia (Warwick County and Dismal Swamp); eastern North Carolina (New Bern, Lake Ellis, and Red Springs); eastern South Carolina (Summerton, Charleston, and (Yemassee); eastern Georgia (Savannah and Okefinokee Swamp); and northeastern Florida (Jacksonville). **South** to northern Florida (Jacksonville, Oldtown, Whitfield, and Pensacola) and southern Louisiana (Mandeville, New Orleans, and Baton Rouge). **West** to eastern Louisiana (Baton Rouge, Bayou Sara, and Jena); central Arkansas (Camden and Conway); extreme northeastern Oklahoma (Copan); and central Missouri (Concordia).

Within this large breeding area are two almost discontinuous breeding ranges: the coastal and swamp range long considered the only home of the species; and the more recently discovered mountain home along the slopes of the Allegheny Mountains from northern West Virginia nearly to the Georgia line where it has been found to an altitude of nearly 3,000 feet.

*Winter range.*—The winter home of the Swainson's warbler is very imperfectly known from a dozen or more specimens, most of which are from Jamaica where it has been listed as a rare winter resident. There are records also from the Swan Islands (March 1); Santa Lucia, Quintana Roo; Pacaytain, Campeche; and the city of Veracruz. Two specimens have been taken near Habana, Cuba; one on September 25, the other in April; and one near Guantánamo on January 18, 1914.

*Migration.*—Dates of spring departure are: Jamaica, April 8. Cuba—Habana, April 14.

Early dates of spring arrival are: Florida—St. Petersburg, March 25. Alabama—Autaugaville, April 3. Georgia—Savannah, March 25. South Carolina, April 1. Louisiana—New Orleans, March 30. Mississippi—Biloxi, March 31. Tennessee—Memphis, April 20. Texas—Point Bolivar, April 17.

Late dates of fall departure are: Texas—Kemah, September 27. Tennessee—Sulphur Springs, September 9. Mississippi—Gulfport, October 6. South Carolina—Charleston, October 10. Georgia—Savannah, October 18. Alabama—Greensboro, September 6. Florida—Pensacola, October 2; Sombrero Key (4 struck lighthouse November 10).

Dates of fall arrival are: Tamaulipas—Matamoros, August 29. Jamaica, October 1.

*Casual records.*—A specimen was recorded near Corsicana, Tex., on August 24, 1880; another was collected at Kearney, Nebr., on April 9, 1905; and one near Holly, Prowers County, Colo., on May 12, 1913.

*Egg dates.*—Florida: 3 records, May 7. Georgia: 35 records, May 4 to July 13; 19 records, May 29 to June 17, indicating the height of the season. South Carolina: 28 records, May 2 to June 30; 14 records, May 12 to June 12 (Harris).

## HELMITHEROS VERMIVOROS (Gmelin)

### WORM-EATING WARBLER

PLATE 10

HABITS

The breeding range of the worm-eating warbler covers much of the central portion of the United States east of the prairie regions. Its center of abundance seems to be in the vicinity of Pennsylvania, but it breeds less abundantly northward to southern Iowa, New York, and New England and southward to Missouri and to northern Alabama and Georgia, as well as in much of the intervening wooded region, where it is essentially a woodland bird.

The distribution, migration, and habits of this warbler were but poorly understood by the early writers on American birds, and neither Wilson nor Audubon ever saw its nest; the latter's description of the nest, probably from hearsay, is entirely wrong. Frank L. Burns writes to me: "Bartram neglected to list this species, although he had furnished the type to Edwards 35 years earlier, and from the information furnished by the youthful Bartram it doubtless received its name, which is a misnomer perpetuated by Gmelin in his *Motacilla vermivora.*" Mr. Burns says further on in his notes: "I searched for 10 seasons before I found my first nest, and oddly enough it was through the parent bird carrying a 'worm' to its young; nevertheless I have since thought that a more fitting name for the species would have been hillside or laurel warbler."

Hillside warbler would not be a bad name for this bird, which shows a decided preference for wooded hillsides covered with medium-sized deciduous trees and an undergrowth of saplings and small shrubbery. Often a running stream with numerous swampy places, overgrown with brier tangles and alders, bounds the base of the hill as an additional attraction. It is seldom seen outside of its favorite woods and returns year after year to the same chosen haunts.

W. E. Clyde Todd (1940) says that in western Pennsylvania "wooded slopes are its chosen abodes, the shadier and cooler the better. * * * Deep ravines, down which trickle little streams, and the slopes of which support good stands of deciduous trees, with plenty of shrubbery and bushes for cover, are favorite resorts." In Ritchie County, W. Va., William Brewster (1875) found it "most partial to the retired thickets in the woods along water courses, and seldom or never found in the high open groves."

*Spring.*—The northward movement of the worm-eating warbler evidently begins in March, as the earliest arrivals from the Bahamas, the West Indies, and Cuba reach southern Florida during the first week in April. From its main winter resorts in Central America the flight seems to be partially across the Gulf of Mexico. Professor Cooke (1904) says in part: "The time of arrival on the coasts of Louisiana and Texas is about the same as in southern Florida. * * * Houston is the southernmost point in Texas from which it has been recorded to date, and Alta Mira is the northernmost point of record in Mexico. Since the species is apparently not common west of Louisana or north of Vera Cruz, it is probable that the principal line of migration is from Yucatan and the coast immediately west of Yucatan directly north to the northern coast of the Gulf of Mexico." According to Williams (1945) the species is common on the coast of Texas in spring, and it probably migrates along the coast. Thence the migration pro-

ceeds northward through the Mississippi Valley and through the
Atlantic Coast States east of the Alleghenies, the warblers reaching
the more northern breeding grounds by the middle of May, where
nesting activities begin as soon as mates have been selected.

*Nesting.*—Evidently Thomas H. Jackson, of West Chester, Pa., was
the first to report the discovery of the nest of the worm-eating warbler;
he published an account of it in the American Naturalist for December
1869, from which Baird, Brewer, and Ridgway (1874) quote as follows: "On the 6th of June, 1869, I found a nest of this species containing five eggs. It was placed in a hollow on the ground, much
like the nests of the Oven-Bird (*Seiurus aurocapillus*), and was well
hidden from sight by the dry leaves that lay thickly around. The
nest was composed externally of dead leaves, mostly those of the
beech, while the interior was prettily lined with the fine, thread-like
stalks of the hair-moss (*Polytrichium*). * * * So close did the
female sit that I captured her without difficulty by placing my hat
over the nest."

This nest was quite characteristic of the species. Mr. Burns writes
to me: "The nest, well hidden under a drift of dead forest leaves, never
varied in composition in over a hundred examples examined by me, in
partly skeletonized leaves and the characteristic reddish-brown lining
of the flower stem of the hair moss." Every one of 50 nests found
by Mr. Jackson was lined with these flower stems, and out of 34
nests reported by Dr. Samuel S. Dickey (1934) only one failed to
contain this material, being lined with "black and gray horsehair."
Samuel B. Ladd (1887) says that "sometimes fine grass and horse-hair
are used as part of the lining." Dr. Chapman (1907) writes: "Nests
taken by J. N. Clark at Saybrook, Connecticut (C. W. C.) are composed of decayed leaves and lined with stems of maple seeds." And
there are probably a few other exceptions to the rule.

Most observers agree that the worm-eating warbler prefers to nest
on hillsides, either sloping or steep, but a number of nests have been
found on the sides of deep, shady ravines, or on steep banks. Mr.
Ladd (1887), however, states: "I have observed that these birds are
not confined necessarily to hill-sides, as was heretofore supposed, as
I have taken three sets on level ground and in rather open places,
with little shade. The experience of Mr. Thomas H. Jackson of this
place, who has taken ten nests this year, corroborates this fact."

The nests are generally well concealed under a canopy of dead
leaves, drifted by the wind and lodged against a maple, beech, dogwood, or ash sapling, or under hydrangea, laurel, or rhododendron
bushes, or under some bunch of weeds or other obstruction. They
are sometimes concealed under the roots of a tree or in a cavity in a
bank where they are protected somewhat by fallen leaves.

*Eggs.*—The number of eggs laid by the worm-eating warbler varies from 3 to 6, but the set usually consists of 4 or 5. The eggs are ovate or short ovate, sometimes rather pointed, and only slightly glossy. The white ground color is speckled and spotted with shades of "russet," "vinaceous russet," and "auburn," intermingled with "light brownish drab" and "light vinaceous-drab." The markings, usually more thickly grouped at the large end, vary considerably, some eggs being boldly marked, while others are almost immaculate, or have just a few pale freckles of "light brownish drab" and "fawn." The measurements of 50 eggs average 17.4 by 13.6 millimeters; the eggs showing the four extremes measure 20.8 by 14.5, and 15.5 by 12.7 millimeters (Harris).

*Incubation.*—Frank L. Burns (1905) writes:

Incubation does not always commence immediately after completion of set, particularly if the season be young. It is probable that the second night witnesses the beginning of that period and, as far as my experience goes, I believe it is performed by the female alone. The male feeds her when covering newly hatched young.

The home-coming of a brooding bird, after a brief airing and feeding, is heralded several hundred yards distant by frequent *chips* and short flights from branch to branch near the ground, in leisurely fashion and circuitous route, until at length, arriving above the nest, she runs down a sapling and is silent. The bird is a close sitter and if approached from the open front will often allow a few minutes' silent inspection, eye to eye, at arm's length, sometimes not vacating until touched, then she runs off in a sinuous trail, not always feigning lameness before the young are out. When disturbed with young in the nest she will flutter off with open wings and tail, and, failing to lead one off, will return with her mate, who is seldom far off at this period, circling about the nest or intruder, and, if the young are well feathered, she will dash at them, forcing them from the nest and to shelter. Once this brave little bird dashed at me and ran up to my knee, scratching with her sharp little claws at every step. On the return the birds always make the vicinity ring with their protests— a quickly repeated *chip*. The period of incubation in one instance was thirteen days.

*Young.*—Mr. Burns continues:

Young fear man soon after their eyes are open, and a menacing finger will cause them to scamper out and away, repeated replacing in the nest proving of no avail after they became panic-stricken. At three days of age they made no outcry but opened their mouths for food, which consisted of a species of white moth, or "miller," and soft white grubs, supplied by either of the parent birds. At that period they were naked except a fluff on head and wing quills, just showing feathers at tips. In the presence of an intruder and absence of the parents, they will sit motionless if not threatened, and, but for the blinking, beady eyes, one might mistake them when well fledged, at very close range, for dead leaves. The head stripes became visible under the nestling down on the seventh day, and they left the nest ten days after leaving the shell, in the one case I have kept record of. The parents keep the young together for several days at least, just how long is impossible to say. One brood is all that is reared in a season, I think.

*Plumages.*—Dr. Dwight (1900) calls the natal down "brownish mouse-gray," and describes the juvenal plumage as follows: "Whole body plumage and the wing coverts cinnamon, palest on the abdomen. Wings and tail olive-brown edged with olive-green. Two indistinct lateral crown stripes brownish mouse-gray. A transocular streak dusky." Ridgway's (1902) description is somewhat different: "Head, neck, and under parts buff, the pileum with two broad, but strongly contrasted, lateral stripes of wood brown or isabella color; a post-ocular streak of the same color; back, scapulars, rump, and upper tail-coverts wood brown or isabella color; wing-coverts light buffy olive, the middle and greater broadly but not sharply tipped with cinnamon-buff; remiges and rectrices grayish olive-green, as in adults." Young birds seem to vary considerably in the color of the upper parts.

A partial postjuvenal molt occurring in late June or early July involves all the contour plumage and the wing coverts but not the rest of the wings or the tail. The young bird in its first winter plumage is practically indistinguishable from the adult at that season, except for the juvenal wings, in which the tertials are lightly tipped with rusty brown.

There is apparently no spring molt, but a complete postnuptial molt occurs in July. Spring birds are slightly paler, grayer and less buffy than in the fall. The sexes are practically alike in all plumages.

*Food.*—As I have said, the name worm-eating warbler seems to be somewhat of a misnomer for this bird. Edward H. Forbush (1929) writes: "I find no records of any consumption of earthworms by this species, which although a typical ground warbler spends some of its time hunting among the branches of trees, where it finds span-worms. It also hunts on the ground in damp places frequented by army-worms. Nevertheless these are not worms but caterpillars. Probably, however, in its perambulations and peregrinations upon the surface of the earth the bird now and then does pick up a small earthworm, for earthworms form a staple food for many birds when the ground is moist."

Arthur H. Howell (1924) says: "Little is known of the food of this species, but it seems doubtful whether it lives up to its name of 'worm-eater.' Two stomachs of this bird from Alabama contained remains of weevils, beetles, bugs, caterpillars, and Hymenoptera." Howell (1932) further reports: "The stomachs of three individuals taken in Florida in April contained small grasshoppers, caterpillars, sawfly larvae, beetles, and spiders. One dragon-fly, one bumblebee, and one 'walking stick' were also included in the contents." Professor Aughey (1878) included the worm-eating warbler among the birds seen catching locusts in Nebraska.

*Behavior.*—Brewster (1875) gives the best account of the activities of the worm-eating warbler as follows:

They keep much on the ground, where they *walk* about rather slowly, searching for their food among the dried leaves.  In general appearance they are quite unique, and I rarely failed to identify one with an instant's glance, so very peculiar are all their attitudes and motions.  The tail is habitually carried at an elevation considerably above the line of the back, which gives them a smart, jaunty air, and if the dorsal aspect be exposed, in a clear light, the peculiar marking of the crown is quite conspicuous.  Seen as they usually are, however, dimly flitting ahead through the gloom and shadow of the thickets, the impression received is that of a dark little bird which vanishes unaccountably before your very eyes, leaving you quite uncertain where to look for it next; indeed, I hardly know a more difficult bird to procure, for the slightest noise sends it darting off through the woods at once.  Occasionally you will come upon one winding around the trunk of some small tree exactly in the manner of *Mniotilta varia,* moving out along the branches with nimble motion, peering alternately under the bark on either side, and anon returning to the main stem, perhaps in the next instant to hop back to the ground again.  On such occasions they rarely ascend to the height of more than eight or ten feet.  The males are very quarrelsome, chasing one another through the woods with loud, sharp chirpings, careering with almost inconceivable velocity up among the tops of the highest oaks, or darting among the thickets with interminable doublings until the pursuer, growing tired of the chase, alights on some low twig or old mossy log, and in token of his victory, utters a warble so feeble that you must be very near to catch it at all, a sound like that produced by striking two pebbles very quickly and gently together, or the song of *Spizella socialis* heard at a distance, and altogether a very indifferent performance.

*Voice.*—Aretas A. Saunders has contributed the following study of the song of this warbler:

The song of the worm-eating warbler is a simple trill, varying from 1⅖ to 2⅕ seconds in length.  It is usually all on the same pitch, but a few songs rise or fall a half tone, and one record I have rises a full tone and then drops a half tone at the end.  The quality is not musical, but rather closely resembles some forms of the chipping sparrow's song.  The pitch varies from G sharp ′′′ to F sharp ′′′′, one tone less than an octave.

The majority of songs are a continuous trill, that is, the notes are too fast to be separated and counted by ear.  I have three examples that are broken into short, very rapid notes.  Two of these were of 18 notes and one was of 28.  Most of the songs vary in loudness, becoming loudest in the middle, or beginning loud and fading away toward the end.  One record becomes louder toward the end and ends abruptly.

Francis H. Allen describes in his notes a song "remarkably like that of the chipping sparrow, but more rapid than is usual with that species, I think, and perhaps shorter, though not so short as the chippy's early-morning song.  The bill quivers with the song, but does not close between the *chips.*  The bird sang constantly as it flitted about, usually 10 or 20 feet from the ground, seeming to prefer dead branches and twigs."

Almost everyone emphasizes the resemblance of the song to that of the chipping sparrow. Burns (1905) says: "I can distinguish no difference between the notes of this species and the Chipping Sparrow; the first may be a trifle weaker perhaps." But, in some notes recently sent to me, he writes: "The song has often been described as easily mistaken for that of either the chipping sparrow or slate-colored junco, but by no means by an expert. The notes of the worm-eater have a buzzing or bubbling quality not easily described, but are quite distinct from the flat notes of the species named above." And Eugene P. Bicknell (1884) writes: "The songs of no other three birds known to me are more alike than those of the Worm-eating Warbler, the Chipping Sparrow, and the Slate-colored Snowbird." He is in agreement with Saunders and Burns that this bird sings from the time of its arrival until the last of June or early July, but he also says: "On July 10, 1881, several of these birds were silently inhabiting a small tract of woodland, their first season of song having passed; here, on August 14, and again on the 21st, they were found in fine plumage and in full song." Evidently there is a cessation of singing during the molting period.

Burns (1905) says of the song: "The series of notes may be uttered while perched, or creeping about the lower branches of the trees, sapling tops, bushes or fallen brush, or while on the ground. With slightly drooping tail and wings, puffing out of body plumage, throwing its head back until the beak is perpendicular, it trills with swelling throat an unvarying *Che-e-e-e-e-e*, which does not sound half so monotonous in the woods as does the Chippy's lay in the open."

Dr. Chapman (1907) adds: "Mr. W. DeW. Miller of Plainfield, New Jersey, tells me that he has on two occasions heard a flight song from this species. It is described by him as much more varied and musical than the ordinary song, though lacking in strength. It was given as the bird flew through the woods at an even level, not rising above the tree-tops, as does the Oven-bird and other flight singers."

*Field marks.*—When seen walking around on the ground the worm-eating warbler might be mistaken for an ovenbird, but the conspicuous black stripes on the head of the former are quite distinctive, very different from the head markings of the latter. Moreover, the ovenbird is distinctly spotted on the breast, whereas the warbler has a plain, unmarked breast and no conspicuous wing bars. Except for the bold stripes on the head it is just a plain olive and buffy warbler in all plumages.

*Enemies.*—Says Burns (1905): "This Warbler's enemies are woodmice, red squirrels and hunting dogs; the latter will sometimes push up and overturn the nest; an occasional weasel or blacksnake may destroy a few young. The percentage of loss while in the nest cannot be high."

Friedmann (1929) regards the worm-eating warbler as a "rather uncommonly imposed upon species" by the eastern cowbird. "Twenty-one definite records, and as many more indefinite ones have come to my notice."

*Winter.*—Dr. Alexander F. Skutch contributes the following: "Widely distributed as a winter resident in Central America, the worm-eating warbler appears to be everywhere very rare. It occurs from Guatemala to Panamá on both coasts, and upward in the mountains to at least 5,000 feet. On February 26, 1935, I found one in the forest on Barro Colorado Island, Canal Zone, which appears to represent a slight southward extension of the known range. I have recorded this rare visitant from every part of Central America below 6,000 feet in which I have made an extended sojourn during the months of the northern winter, yet only one or two in each locality, except on the Finca Mocá on the Pacific slope of Guatemala at 3,000 feet above sea-level, where in one day—January 21, 1935—I saw three. The worm-eating warbler is found in the Tropics beneath dense thickets or in the undergrowth of the forest, usually near the ground; but at times one will rise to the lower branches of the trees to investigate curled dead leaves caught up among them. It is solitary rather than social in its habits.

"The records of the occurrence of this warbler in Central America are too few to indicate clearly the dates of its arrival and departure. I found one at Tela, Honduras, on August 19, 1930; but the next early record is for October 14, at the same locality. Griscom quotes a record by Dearborn for the occurrence of this warbler at Patulul, Guatemala, on April 2; but except for this, the latest record I have seen is from El General, Costa Rica, March 11, 1939."

## DISTRIBUTION

*Range.*—Eastern United States to Panamá.

*Breeding range.*—The worm-eating warbler breeds **north** to northeastern Kansas (Lawrence); possibly central southern Nebraska (Red Cloud); probably south-central Iowa (Des Moines); probably southern Wisconsin (Wyalusing, Madison, and Milwaukee); northeastern Illinois (Hinsdale); southern Indiana (Terre Haute, Bloomington, and Indianapolis); central Ohio (Columbus, East Liverpool, and possibly Cleveland); southern New York (Penn Yan and Albany), and southern Connecticut (New Haven and Saybrook). It has been found in summer north to London, Ontario; Northampton, Ipswich, and North Eastham, Massachusetts. **East** to Connecticut (Saybrook); Long Island (Newtown); northern New Jersey (Elizabeth and Morristown); eastern Pennsylvania (Norristown and Philadelphia); northern Delaware (Wilmington); central Maryland (Baltimore; rarely east of Chesapeake Bay); eastern Virginia (Cobham and Dismal Swamp); central North Carolina (Chapel Hill and Statesville); northwestern South Carolina (Caesars Head, Mount Pinnacle, and Sassafras Mountain); and northern Georgia (Brasstown Bald and Atlanta). **South** to northern Georgia (Atlanta); central Tennessee (Nashville and Wildersville); northern Arkansas (Newport and Winslow); and, occasionally, extreme northern Texas (Bowie County and Gainesville). **West** to northern Texas (Gainesville); northeastern Oklahoma (Jay); and eastern Kansas (Lawrence). It has been recorded in summer, but with no evidence of breeding, at Red Cloud, Nebr., and at London and Vineland Station, Ontario.

*Winter range.*—In winter the worm-eating warbler is found **north** to southern Tamaulipas (Altamira); northern Florida, casually (Blue Springs and Amelia Island), and the Bahamas (Abaco, Nassau, and Great Inago). **East** to the Bahamas (Great Inago); Jamaica and central Panamá (Río Chepo). **South** to Panamá (Río Chepo, Barro Colorado, and Chiriquí). **West** to western Panamá (Chiriquí); Costa Rica (Escasú and Volcán Tonorio); El Salvador (Mount Cacaguatique); Guatemala (Dueñas, Patulul, and Naranjo); southern Chiapas (Huehuetan); western Veracruz (Jalapa); Hidalgo (Pachuca); and southern Tamaulipas (Altamira).

*Migration.*—Late dates of spring departure are: Panamá—Darién March 16. Costa Rica—El General, March 19. El Salvador—Barra de Santiago, April 8. Guatemala—Patulul, April 2. Yucatán—Mérida, April 9. Cuba—Habana, May 1. Bahamas—Abaco, April 29. Florida—Seven Oaks, May 14. Georgia—Cumberland, May 7. Alabama—Barachias, May 1. Mississippi—Biloxi, April 27. Louisiana—Avery Island, April 23.

Early dates of spring arrival are: Florida—Pensacola, March 26. Georgia—Savannah, April 4. South Carolina—Mount Pleasant, April 7. North Carolina—Bat Cave, April 16. Virginia—Richmond, April 19. West Virginia—Morgantown, April 4. District of Columbia—Washington, April 21. Pennsylvania—Beaver, April 29. New York—Jones Beach, April 20. Louisiana—Grand Isle, April 3. Mississippi—Bay St. Louis, April 5. Tennessee—Chattanooga, April 15. Kentucky—Bowling Green, April 3. Indiana—Brookville, April 17. Ohio—Columbus, April 18. Texas—Brownsville, March 29. Missouri—St. Louis, April 15. Iowa—Keokuk, April 21.

Late dates of fall departure are: Missouri—St. Louis, September 20. Ohio—Austinburg, September 23. Kentucky—Middlesboro, September 27. Tennessee—Athens, October 5. Mississippi—Biloxi,

October 11. Louisiana—Monroe, September 30. New York—Balston, September 23. Pennsylvania—Atglen, October 10. District of Columbia—Washington, September 13. West Virginia—Bluefield, September 19. Virginia—Salem, October 24. North Carolina—Andrews, October 11; Raleigh, November 3. South Carolina—Charleston, October 11. Georgia—Atlanta, October 10. Florida—Fernandina, October 3.

*Casual records.*—A specimen was collected in Bermuda on October 4, 1899. An individual was present at Wood Pond near Jackson, Somerset County, Maine, September 1 to 12, 1935; and one was reported seen at Mayagüez, Puerto Rico, on October 15, 1943, following a small hurricane.

*Egg dates.*—Connecticut: 7 records, May 27 to June 29.

New Jersey: 4 records, May 21 to 30.

Pennsylvania: 75 records, May 15 to June 30: 45 records, May 24 to June 5, indicating the height of the season (Harris).

## VERMIVORA CHRYSOPTERA (Linnaeus)

## GOLDEN-WINGED WARBLER

PLATES 10, 11

CONTRIBUTED BY WINSOR MARRETT TYLER

### HABITS

The golden-winged warbler is one of the daintiest among this group of gay-colored little birds. Its plumage is immaculate white below and delicate pearl-gray on the upper parts, the crown and wings sparkle with golden yellow, and on the throat and cheeks is a broad splash of jet black.

It is only within comparatively recent years that we have become well acquainted with the goldenwing: the older ornithologists, Wilson, Audubon, and Nuttall, knew it only as a rather uncommon migrant, drifting through from the south, and they had no idea where it bred. At a much later date J. A. Allen (1870) says of it: "This beautiful warbler has been taken, so far as I can learn, but few times in the western part of the State; it seems to be more common in the eastern, where it breeds." He cites the first record of the finding of a nest in the State in 1869. There is, however, an earlier record of its nesting. Dr. Brewer (1874) states: "Dr. Samuel Cabot was the first naturalist to meet with the nest and eggs of this bird. This was in May, 1837, in Greenbrier County, Va."

William Brewster (1906), speaking of the bird in 1874, when he first found it in eastern Massachusetts, says: "If the species inhabited any part of the Cambridge Region before the year just mentioned, it was overlooked by several keen and diligent collectors, among whom may be mentioned Mr. H. W. Henshaw and Mr. Ruthven Deane." Since that time the bird has increased in numbers here until at present it is common in suitable localities.

*Spring.*—The goldenwing appears in eastern Massachusetts about the middle of May, or sometimes a little earlier, at the time when many of the resident warblers are arriving on their breeding-grounds. At this season the bright green leaves are beginning to open in the thickets and trees on the borders of woodlands where the goldenwing finds its food; and under the trees in the wooded swamps where the bird will build its nest, fresh new growth—skunkcabbage, ferns, and a host of spring plants—is pushing through the dead leaves, spreading a green carpet on the forest floor. But even thus early in the year, when the trees are nearly bare, it is not easy to see as it feeds high up in the trees, far out near the tips of the branches. Indeed, but for its queer little song, we should rarely suspect that it had come back to its summer home.

*Nesting.*—The golden-winged warbler builds its nest on the ground, generally raised somewhat by a substratum of dead leaves. The nest is supported by stalks of herbs—often goldenrod or meadow rue— or by fern fronds, or it may be hidden deep in a clump of grass, or it may lean against the base of a small shrub or tree with grass all about it. The leaves above the nest develop as the season advances and soon completely conceal it, and the plants, by their growth, may raise the nest a little above the ground. The cup of the nest is made chiefly of long strands of dry grass and narrow strips of grapevine bark, with a few hairs in the lining. This fine, flexible material is pressed down on the inside by the weight of the incubating bird and the nestlings, becoming smooth and firm like a mat, whereas on the outside wall the long grass blades and fibrous vegetable shreds are left free and, protruding loosely in all directions for some distance from the cup, produce a disorderly, unkempt appearance, like a little loose handful of fine hay.

Edward H. Forbush (1929) quotes an account of the goldenwing by Horace O. Green who has had an extensive experience with the species and who gives the following interesting details of the construction of the nest:

The nest of the Golden-wing usually has a bottom layer of coarse dead leaves on which is placed a ring of large dry leaves, arranged with the points of the leaves downward, so that the leaf stems stick up noticeably around the edges of the nest proper, which is built within and upon this circular mass of leaves, and is made of rather wide strips of coarse grass or rushes, and usually has considerable grape vine bark interwoven in it. The nest lining is coarse and rough, sometimes the eggs being laid on the rough grape vine bark, and in some nests other coarse fibers are used. A very characteristic feature of the nest lining is fine shreds of light reddish-brown vegetable fiber, which at first glance might easily be mistaken for dry needles from the pitch pine—but careful examination shows it to be the inner layers of the bark from the grape vines. The nest is very bulky for the size of the bird and is rather loosely put together by crossing the materials diagonally, so that it slightly resembles a rather coarse basket-work. I never saw a nest of this species which had a soft lining, such as many other warblers use—the eggs are apparently always deposited on rough material.

The general color of the nest is very dark, especially just after a rain, when the materials of which it is composed look almost black—this being one thing which helps to distinguish these nests from those of the Maryland Yellow-throat, which generally builds a much lighter colored nest, lined with fine grass, and sometimes with horse hair. Another small point of difference which is noticeable on close examination is that the lining in the Yellow-throat's nest is usually of a much finer and lighter colored material, and appears to be woven in horizontally, or at least to show some traces of such a design, especially around the upper edge—while the Golden-wing closely adheres to the diagonal criss-cross pattern with the loose ends of the nesting materials sticking up at an angle above the rim of the nest cavity.

Mr. Green describes the surroundings of the nest thus:

For their summer home these birds prefer the border of deciduous woods, where tall trees give plenty of shade, to an adjacent clearing with a growth of briers, bushes and grass, and the nest is usually placed just outside the line of the forest proper, but within the shade of the trees. A meadow wholly surrounded by woods is frequently selected. The ideal place to search for a nest of the species is in one of those woodland meadows, which has a clear brook flowing through it, with briers, tussocks of grass and a fresh growth of goldenrod scattered around in profusion, with birch trees and wild grape vines growing near the edges where the meadow meets higher ground and all this bordered by tall oak, chestnut and maple trees which furnish an abundance of shade to the vegetation of the meadow itself.

J. Warren Jacobs (1904) describes the nest much as above and adds: "The opening is not straight down, but slightly tilted, the jaggy leaf-stems and bark sometimes reaching two or three inches above the rim of the nest proper. As incubation advances, the rough rim on the lower edge of the nest becomes broken down, and by the time the young birds are ready to leave, this part of their home is worn smooth by the attendant parents."

He gives the measurements of 17 nests as follows: "Outside 3.6 to 5.0 inches in diameter, and 3.0 to 5.0 inches in depth; and on the inside, from 1.7 to 2.5 inches in diameter by 1.3 to 2.5 inches deep." These measurements agree very closely with the records of several other observers. Jacobs continues: "Seemingly before the birds have had time to complete their nest, the female begins the deposition of the eggs. Generally, where I had opportunity to watch the nests daily, or at intervals between the beginning and completion of the set, the eggs were laid on consecutive days, but in two or three instances it was noticed that the laying missed a day."

*Eggs.*—The set for the golden-winged warbler may consist of anywhere from 4 to 7 eggs; 5 is perhaps the commonest number, but 4
is a common number, and the larger numbers are increasingly rare.
The eggs are ovate or short ovate, and have only a slight luster.
They are white or creamy white, with a wide variety of markings in
"auburn," "argus brown," "Mars brown," "hazel," "Hay's brown,"
"liver brown," and "burnt umber," with underlying speckles or spots
of "light brownish drab" and "light vinaceous drab." There is, also,
much variation in the amount of markings, some being very sparingly
speckled and others are quite heavily marked, with some of the
spots assuming the proportions of blotches. Occasionally small hair-
line scrawls, or scattered spots, of brown so dark as to appear almost
black, are found. The markings are usually denser toward the large
end. The measurements of 50 eggs average 16.7 by 13.0 millimeters;
the eggs showing the four extremes measure 18.6 by 13.0, 16.8 by 13.7,
15.5 12.5, and 15.9 by 12.3 millimeters (Harris).

*Young.*—Jacobs (1904) states that the incubation period is 10 days
and that the young birds are able to leave the nest 10 days after
hatching. In a nest which Maunsell S. Crosby (1912) watched closely,
the eggs hatched on June 1 and the young flew on June 10.

The fledglings are delicate little birds, brownish olive on the back,
washed with yellow below, and have two widely separated yellow
wing bars. They have astonishingly long legs and soon become very
active, fluttering about in the shrubbery and clinging to the branches.
Walter Faxon (1911) in speaking of them gives this lively picture
which could well be applied to them soon after leaving the nest: "In appearance and habit they were grotesque little fellows, clinging with
their disproportionately long legs to the low herbage, like peeping
Hylas in the springtime clinging to the grasses and weeds above the
surface of the water. The little thread-like natal plumes still waving
from the tips of their crown feathers enhanced the oddity of their
appearance." Mr. Faxon, to be exact, is speaking here of some young
birds of mixed parentage, but his words apply equally well to the
behavior and appearance of the young of *chrysoptera* which he and
I watched year after year together. Both parents are very attentive
to their young brood, bringing to them food which they find both
on low plant growth and high in the overshadowing branches.

The fledglings call to their parents with a very characteristic note,
a little quavering, high, fine chirp which I find written in my journal
*crrr* and *tzzz*. It suggests somewhat a note of young chipping sparrows, but is less sharp and crisp. In form it also resembles the call of
the young cowbird, but again it is gentler and weaker in tone. Mr.
Faxon (1911) refers to it as the "cricket note." The young birds ac-

quire their first winter plumage about a month after they leave the nest, and hence to the eye are indistinguishable from their parents, but as they still continue to use the call of their babyhood, they may be recognized as immature birds even when they are feeding high up in the trees.

*Plumages.*—[AUTHOR's NOTE: I can find no description of the natal down. Dr. Dwight (1900) describes the juvenal plumage, in which the sexes are practically alike, as "above, grayish or brownish olive-green. Wings and tail slate-black edged chiefly with bluish plumbeous gray, the coverts and tertiaries with olive-green. Below, pale olive-yellow, the throat dusky. Transocular streak dusky. * * *

"First winter plumage acquired by a partial postjuvenal moult, beginning early in July, which involves the body plumage and wing coverts, but not the rest of the wings nor the tail, young and old becoming practically indistinguishable." He describes the young male in this plumage as—

above, plumbeous gray veiled with olive-green edgings; the crown bright lemon-yellow veiled posteriorly only. Below, grayish white, with yellow edgings here and there, the chin, jugulum, lores and auriculars jet-black veiled slightly with pale buff. Broad submalar stripes joining at angle of the chin, and superciliary lines white. Outer half of median and greater coverts bright lemon yellow forming an almost continuous wing patch, lesser coverts plumbeous gray, edged with olive-green.

First nuptial plumage acquired by wear, through which the buff edgings of the black areas, the olive edgings of the back and the yellow edgings below are almost completely lost, the plumage becoming clear gray, white, yellow and black.

Of the female, he says: "In first winter and other plumages olive-gray, dusky on the lores and auriculars, replaces the black areas of the male, and olive-yellow marks the crown. Above, the plumage is greenish; the submalar stripes are grayish." Subsequent plumages are acquired by a complete postnuptial molt in late June and July and by wear in early spring.]

*Food.*—Little exact information has been gathered regarding the food of the goldenwing. The insects it feeds on are mainly so small that it is generally impossible to identify them. Jacobs (1904) states. "Once I saw a female carry a small brownish butterfly to her young; and several times I have discovered the birds taking small smooth green worms—such as strip the leaves of their green coat, leaving the ribbed skeleton—to their nestlings. The legs of a spider protruded from a bird's bill as she approached her nest."

The little pale green larva which Jacobs mentions impresses us as the chief article of food, as we watch the birds. It is ½ to ¾ inch long and appears to have a smooth, hairless skin. These larvae are obtained, I believe, chiefly in the large trees.

In the following note A. L. Nelson (1933) furnishes an interesting detail of the bird's diet:

The following observation on the food habits of a Golden-winged Warbler (*Vermivora chrysoptera*), made in the vicinity of Port Tobacco (Charles Co.), Maryland on May 6, 1933, seems worthy of mention, inasmuch as little specific information on the dietary habits of this species has been recorded. About 1:30 we observed a single individual of this species actively feeding in a low shrubbery growth of pawpaw (*Asimina triloba*), which was in full bloom at this date. Closer observation revealed that the bird was probing about inside the flowers, and apparently was getting some kind of larvae. Examination of the flowers revealed that they were infested with a small, brown-headed lepidopterous larva. Dissection of a large number of flowers indicated that the infestation was high, the majority of flowers having one larva, although in many cases two were present. Several infested flowers were collected for the purpose of rearing the insects to the adult stage under laboratory conditions. The cycle was completed without difficulty, the adults emerging within twelve days. These were examined by Dr. Carl Heinrich of the U. S. National Museum and found to be *Talponia plummeriana* Busck, a small brightly colored Tortricid, the only known food plant of which is the pawpaw.

*Behavior.*—A favorite locality for the golden-winged warbler to spend the summer in eastern Massachusetts may be the border of a wooded swamp where tall elm and maple trees shade a dense undergrowth of ferns and other moisture-loving plants, a swamp which runs out toward drier ground where abounds a growth of gray birches or a tangle of raspberry canes, wild grapevines, and goldenrod. Such a spot furnishes countless situations for hiding the nest in the thick vegetation growing in the half-wet half-dry ground, and also a source of food near at hand in the high branches of the trees. Much the same conditions exist along the course of a brook winding through second growth, or near orchards or old neglected weedy pastures.

Sometimes, as William Brewster (1906) points out, the bird may frequent "dry hillsides covered with a young sprout growth of oak, hickory or maple."

In a more southern latitude the habitat may be quite different. Maurice Brooks (1940), speaking of the bird in the central Allegheny Mountain region, says: "Shunning the swamps which it frequents in other portions of its range, it is highly characteristic of the 'chestnut sprout' association, where the males choose dead chestnuts for perches from which to sing. It is also fairly common in the pitch and scrub pine regions on the hills just back of the Ohio river, but becomes less common toward the eastern portion of the territory with which this paper deals. It ascends to at least 4,000 feet in Giles Co., Va."

We can watch the little golden-winged warblers best, and often at very short range, when they are feeding their fledglings recently from the nest. The little birds sit quietly in the shrubbery near the ground, waiting for their parents. We can find them easily, for they frequently utter their characteristic "cricket note," and we can approach them closely, for they scarcely heed us. The parents, too, when they are feeding the young birds, pay little attention to us and come fearlessly to them even when we stand near. At such times they work in a seeming panic of hurry, flying about in the low growth searching for food, or visiting the smallest branches high up in the trees, where they cling to the terminal twigs, hanging like chickadees as they probe among the curled up leaves (insect nests) for food hidden there, then back to the waiting young, seemingly in continuous motion and without the slightest pause in their nervous activity. At this season when the parents are busy with the young birds, about the third week in June in eastern Massachusetts, they are so occupied in searching for food that the male rarely sings.

In two particulars—their tameness, or indifference to our presence, and the almost complete cessation of singing thus early in the season— the goldenwing differs from the other common birds which breed in much the same regions, the chestnut-sided warbler, redstart, northern yellowthroat, ovenbird, and veery.

Jacobs (1904) speaks of the anxiety of the parent birds if the nest is disturbed when the nestlings are nearly ready to fly. He says: "If the hand is placed near the nest at this period of their growth, they will scramble out and flutter away, all giving vent to their chipping note, which brings down upon the intruder the wrath of both old birds, who fly close to his face, snapping their beaks and chipping loudly; then down upon the ground they fall and feign the broken wing act as long as one of the young continues to chirp."

*Voice.*—The song of the golden-winged warbler is an inconspicuous little buzzing sound which one might pass by unnoticed, or hearing it for the first time, might ascribe it to a mechanical sound made by some insect, not suspecting it to be the song of a bird. Only after we have become thoroughly familiar with the song do we grasp its definite character, so that we can pick it out even when we hear it in the distance among a medley of other voices. In this particular it resembles the songs of Henslow's and the grasshopper sparrows, which are scarcely audible, and pass unregarded until well known.

The male goldenwing sings generally from a high perch, often from a branch bare of leaves; hence, once we find him, we can see him plainly. When he sings he throws his head back so far that his bill points almost to the zenith, and sings with it widely open, as if he were pouring out a great volume of sound. The bird sings freely from his arrival in spring until mid-June, about a month, often devoting himself to long periods of singing from the same perch.

Later in the season, after the young have hatched, he sings only fitfully.

The song most often heard is composed of four notes, the first prolonged, and followed, after an almost imperceptible pause, by three shorter notes on a lower pitch. All four notes are delivered in a leisurely manner, drawling in tempo, and might be written *zeee, zer-zer-zer*. The first note takes up about half the time of the song. The quality of the voice is buzzing, and when heard near at hand, slightly rasping, with a lisping suggestion throughout. The song carries well; curiously it seems little louder when heard at close range, but from a distance it sounds smoother and, losing much of the buzzing quality, suggests a long drawn out *thth, th-th-th*, like a whispering wind. Occasionally there may be four short notes, and sometimes only two following the long initial note.

Like some of the other warblers, notably the black-and-white, chestnut-sided, and black-throated green, the goldenwing sings two distinct songs. In the second form the buzzing tone is nearly or wholly absent. It begins with about half a dozen short notes given in a quick series on the same pitch, and ends with one long note on a higher key, *th-th-th-th-th-th-theee*.

I have heard two males singing antiphonally, the responses repeated with perfect regularity for several minutes.

Of the minor notes the commonest is a short, slightly roughened *dz*. When much excited both adults use a chattering *tchu-tchu-tchu*, suggesting in manner of delivery the song of the short-billed marsh wren, although it is higher pitched and not so loud.

Francis H. Allen (MS.) mentions two other songs, only slightly different from the above. One goes something like "*tick tick chick chick chick chick shree.* The *shree* is a beady note resembling one of the cedar waxwing's familiar notes." Another song he writes as "*see-see-see-see-see-see-see-see-see-dz'-dsee.*"

*Field marks.*—The golden-winged warbler is easy to recognize; it is the only warbler that combines a blue-gray back and yellow in the wing. In the two other common warblers with a black throat, the black-throated blue and the black-throated green, the black runs down the sides a little way so that the white of the breast comes up in a peak in the middle of the breast, whereas in the goldenwing the line of division between the black and white runs straight across. From directly below, the goldenwing appears wholly black and white, and from this angle is marked like a chickadee, but a glance at its long, needle-sharp bill proclaims it a warbler of the genus *Vermivora*.

*Enemies.*—Prowling mammals, the enemies of ground-nesting birds, and predatory hawks are a danger to the bird. In its relation to the cowbird, Friedmann (1929) reports the bird as "a very uncommon victim." He says: "I have only six definite records, but the species is listed as a molothrine victim by Bendire and by Short. As many as four eggs of the Cowbird have been found in a single nest of this Warbler."

*Fall* and *winter.*—We lose sight of the goldenwing early in the season. Silent amid the dense foliage of July and August, the bird is rarely seen. During the years between 1907 and 1920, when I kept a daily record of birds seen, I met it only four times in August and only twice in September, the latest September 12.

Dr. Alexander F. Skutch sends to A. C. Bent the following account of the bird in its winter quarters: "I am familiar with the golden-winged warbler in its winter home only in Costa Rica. In this country it winters on the Caribbean slope from the lowlands up to about 6,000 feet above sea-level, and on the Pacific slope at least in the region between 2,000 and 4,000 feet. While it appears to be nowhere abundant, I found it most numerous at Vara Blanca, on the northern slope of the Cordillera Central at an elevation of about 5,500 feet. Here on one day—November 2, 1937—I saw three individuals, the greatest number I have ever recorded. This is a region of dense vegetation, subject to much cloudiness and long-continued, often violent rainstorms—one of the wettest districts of all Central America. Most of the published records are from this generally wet side of the country. Yet the bird winters sparingly in the Basin of El General on the Pacific slope, which during the first 3 months of the year may be nearly rainless. While in the Tropics, it appears never to associate with others of its own kind, but at times may roam about with mixed flocks of other small birds. It may forage among low, fairly dense, second-growth thickets, or among the tangled vegetation at the forest's edge, or at times in the forest itself, or in groves of tall trees, high above the ground. It investigates the curled dead leaves caught up among the branches, and devours such small creatures as it finds lurking in their folds. I have not heard it sing while in its winter home.

"In Costa Rica, it appears to arrive late and to depart early, not having been recorded before September 15, nor later than April 9. Early dates of fall arrival are: Costa Rica—San José (Cherrie), September 15 and October 2; La Hondura (Carriker), September 21; Basin of El General, October 18, 1936; Vara Blanca, October 5, 1937.

"Late dates of spring departure are: Costa Rica—Basin of El General, April 8, 1936, April 7, 1937, March 30, 1939, and April 9, 1943; Vara Blanca, April 9, 1938; Guápiles (Carriker), March 30."

DISTRIBUTION

*Range.*—Eastern United States to northwestern South America.

*Breeding range.*—The golden-winged warbler breeds **north** to central Minnesota (Detroit Lakes, Onamia, and Cambridge); central Wisconsin (St. Croix Falls, New London, and Shiocton); northern peninsula of Michigan (McMillan and Mackinac Island); southern Michigan (Kalamazoo, Locke, and Detroit); southern Ontario (London and Port Rowan, has occurred north to Collingwood and Bowmanville); central New York (Medina, Rochester, and Waterford); central Vermont (Rutland), and northern Massachusetts (Winchendon, Newton, and Lynn). It has been found in summer and may possibly breed in southern New Hampshire (Concord and Durham); and southwestern Maine (Emery Mills and Sandford). **East** to eastern Massachusetts (Lynn, Boston, and Rehoboth); southern Connecticut (New Haven and Bridgeport); northern New Jersey (Morristown); central Pennsylvania (near State College); and south through the mountains to western North Carolina (Weaverville, Waynesville, and Highlands); northwestern South Carolina (Caesars Head and Highlow Gap); and northern Georgia (Young Harris, Margret, and Oglethorpe Mountain). **South** to northern Georgia (Oglethorpe Mountain and Rising Faun); central Tennessee (Maryland); northern Ohio (Steuben, Port Clinton, and Wauseon); northern Indiana (Waterloo); and northern Illinois (Riverside). **West** to northern Illinois (Riverside); central and western Wisconsin (Baraboo Bluffs and Durand); and central Minnesota (Minneapolis, Elk River, and Detroit Lakes). It has been noted in summer, or in migration, west to St. Louis, Mo.; Lake Quivira and Lawrence, Kans.; and Omaha, Nebr.

*Winter range.*—In winter the golden-winged warbler is found **north** to central Guatemala (Cobán); and northern Honduras (Lancetilla); casually or in migration to the Yucatán Peninsula (Campeche and Mérida). **East** to Honduras (Lancetilla); eastern Nicaragua (Escondido River); Costa Rica (Guápiles and Guayabo); central Panamá (Lion Hill, Canal Zone); and central Colombia (Santa Marta region, Bogotá, and Villavicencio); rare or accidental in western Venezuela (Mérida). **South** to central Colombia (Villavicencio and El Eden). **West** to northwestern Colombia (El Eden, Medellín, and Antioquia); western Panamá (Chiriquí); Costa Rica (El General and Nicoya); and central Guatemala (Cobán).

*Migration.*—Late dates of spring departure are: Colombia—Fusagasugá, March 24. Panamá—Volcán de Chiriquí, April 16. Costa Rica—Vara Blanca, April 9. Florida—Pensacola, April 22. Alabama—Hollins, May 7. Georgia—Athens, May 13. South Carolina—Clemson College, May 3. North Carolina—Raleigh, May 7.

District of Columbia—Washington, May 20. Mississippi—Gulfport, April 18. Missouri—St. Louis, May 25.

Early dates of spring arrival are: Florida—Pensacola, April 5. Alabama—Barachias, April 22. Georgia—Milledgeville, April 12. South Carolina—Clemson College, April 21. North Carolina—Asheville, April 23. Virginia—Lynchburg, April 19. West Virginia—Bluefield, April 19. District of Columbia—Washington, April 24. Pennsylvania—Beaver, April 24. New York—Rochester, April 29. Massachusetts—Belmont, April 28. Louisiana—Grand Isle, April 6. Mississippi—Gulfport, April 10. Tennessee—Memphis, April 12. Illinois—Olney, April 17. Indiana—Sedan, April 27. Michigan—Plymouth, April 30. Ohio—Youngstown, April 27. Ontario—London, April 30. Missouri—St. Louis, April 18. Iowa—Keokuk, April 27. Wisconsin—Sheboygan, April 30. Minnesota—Minneapolis, April 30. The golden-winged warbler ranges west to central Iowa in migration, and in the lower Mississippi Valley is much less abundant in spring than in fall.

Late dates of fall departure are: Minnesota—Minneapolis, September 30. Wisconsin—Madison, October 11. Ontario—Point Pelee, September 2. Ohio—Ellsworth Station, September 23. Michigan—Ann Arbor, October 6. Indiana—Lyons, September 27. Illinois—Chicago, October 7. Missouri—La Grange, September 30. Kentucky—Versailles, September 25. Tennessee—Athens, September 29. Louisiana—New Orleans, September 25. Mississippi—Gulfport, October 8. Massachusetts—Danvers, September 7. New York—Brooklyn, October 2. Pennsylvania—Jeffersonville, October 2. District of Columbia—Washington, September 14. West Virginia—French Creek, September 15. North Carolina—Piney Creek, October 3. South Carolina—Chester, September 22. Georgia—Atlanta, October 9. Alabama—Greensboro, October 4.

Early dates of fall arrival are: Mississippi—Bay St. Louis, July 23. District of Columbia—Washington, August 8. Virginia—Naruna, August 23. North Carolina—Highlands, August 15. South Carolina—Charleston, August 20. Georgia—Athens, August 14. Alabama—Greensboro, August 11. Florida—Pensacola, August 14. Costa Rica—San José, September 15. Colombia—Bonda, September 6.

*Casual record.*—One reported seen at Fort Thorn, N. Mex., in April 1854 by Dr. Joseph Henry. Since no specimen was taken this remains on the hypothetical list for the State.

*Egg dates.*—Massachusetts: 14 records, May 27 to June 24; 9 records, May 30 to June 7, indicating the height of the season.

Michigan: 33 records, May 13 to June 10; 18 records, May 17 to 30.

New York: 6 records, June 3 to 24.

New Jersey: 7 records, May 25 to June 5 (Harris).

## VERMIVORA PINUS (Linnaeus)

## BLUE-WINGED WARBLER

PLATES 12, 13

HABITS

Bagg and Eliot (1937) write: "According to Wilson, this species was discovered by William Bartram, who gave it the descriptive name *Parus aureus alis caeruleis* (Blue-winged Golden Tit), and sent a specimen to 'Mr. Edwards' by whom it was drawn and etched. Edwards suspected its identity with the Pine Creeper of Catesby: hence its present inappropriate name, *pinus.*" As there are other warblers whose wings are more distinctly blue, those of this warbler being only bluish gray, the old familiar name, blue-winged yellow warbler, which stood for many years, seems more appropriate and more truly descriptive.

The blue-winged warbler is a bird of the so-called Carolinian Life Zone, with a rather restricted breeding range in the Central States and not quite reaching our northern borders. Its center of abundance in the breeding season seems to be in southern Ohio, Indiana, Illinois, northern Kentucky, northern Missouri, and southern Iowa. Its range extends northeastward to New Jersey, southeastern New York, and southern Connecticut. It is fairly common in the latter State, and I know of one small colony in eastern Rhode Island within a mile or two of the Massachusetts line. North of these points in New England it occurs only as a straggler or casual breeder. In southern New England I have found it in rather open situations, in neglected pastures where there is low shrubbery, brier patches, and bushy thickets around the edges; or in similar growth along the borders of woods, usually on dry uplands; and sometimes in the rank growth of tall grasses and weeds near the borders of swamps or streams.

Frank L. Burns wrote to Dr. Chapman (1907) of its haunts in Pennsylvania: "This species is here an inhabitant of the rather open swampy thickets, upland clearings, neglected pastures and fence rows, where the grass and weeds have not been choked out by a too thick growth of briers, bushes, saplings and vines." Dr. Lawrence H. Wilkinshaw tells me that, in southern Michigan, "this species loves deep swampy woods, where the golden-winged warbler and cerulean warbler are found." This is quite different from the haunts in which we find it in the east, though Dr. Chapman (1907) says: "It is not, as a rule, a deep woods warbler, though I have found it nesting in heavy forest, but prefers rather, bordering second growths, with weedy openings, from which it may follow lines or patches of trees to haunts some distance from the woods."

*Spring.*—From its winter home in Central America the blue-winged warbler seems to migrate from Yucatán straight across the Gulf of Mexico to the Gulf States and along the eastern coast of Texas to Louisiana.   It is apparently very rare anywhere in Florida or the Keys, and along the Atlantic coast, where it is comparatively rare, it is found at low elevations.   It migrates northward mainly west of the Alleghenies, seeming to avoid the mountains; the main body of the species seems to travel through the Mississippi Valley to the centers of abundance in the central States.   Perhaps the birds that settle in southern New York and New England travel up the Ohio River, drift-ing through Pennsylvania and New Jersey to their destination.   According to Milton B. Trautman (1940) this warbler seems to be a rare or uncommon spring migrant in central Ohio, and "in some migrations only 2 individuals were noted" at Buckeye Lake; this adds support to the theory that the birds follow the river along the southern border of the State.

*Nesting.*—Although Wilson (1831) gave a very good description of the nest of the blue-winged yellow warbler, very little was known of its nesting in southern New England prior to about 1880, when nests were found in southern Connecticut, where it is now known to be a fairly common breeder.   I found two nests near West Haven, Conn., on June 3, 1910; both were close to the ground but not quite on it; one was in a clump of blackberry vines, weeds, and grasses, in a swampy corner of a scrubby lot; the other was in a bunch of grass and rank weeds on some sprout land among some mixed bushes.   Again, on June 1, 1934, I photographed (pl. 12) a nest near Hadlyme, Conn., on the edge of an open, neglected field and close to the border of some young woods. It was built among and attached to the upright stems of a clump of tall goldenrod.   These were all typical of the nests described below.

Massachusetts nests are very rare; Forbush (1929) gives but two nesting records for this State, and only one for Rhode Island, though I am confident that its breeds regularly in the latter State.   Horace W. Wright (1000b) gives a very full account of a nest found near Sudbury, Mass., in some mixed woods, placed between the exposed roots of a decayed stump and partially concealed by a growth of ferns.

T. E. McMullen has sent me the data for several Pennsylvania nests, three in old fields, one under a cherry sprout, one under a small bush, and one 6 inches up in a tussock of goldenrod; another was under a birch sprout along the edge of an old woods road.

The nest of the blue-winged warbler is unique and quite distinctive, often shaped like an inverted cone, usually very narrow and very deep and supported by a firm cup of strong, dead leaves. I cannot improve on the excellent description given to Dr. Chapman (1907) by Frank L. Burns as follows:

Outwardly composed of the broad blades of a coarse grass, the dead leaves of the maple, beech, chestnut, cherry and oak trees; the leaf points curving upward and inward forming a deep cuplike nest in which the bird's head and tail seem almost to meet over her back. Occasionally grass stems, coarse strips or wild grapevine bark, shreds of corn fodder, and fragments of beech and wild cherry bark appear in the make-up. Lined most frequently with wild grapevine bark laid across, instead of bent around in a circle, shredded finest on top, to which is added an occasional long black horse-hair or split grass stem, with now and then a final lining of split grass stems in place of fine bark. The shape varies in accordance to situation, outwardly a short cornucopia, a round basket, and once a wall-pocket affair, would best describe the shapes I have noticed.

*Eggs.*—From 4 to 7 eggs may be found in the nest of the blue-winged warbler; 5 seems to be the commonest number, and sets of 6 are not very rare. The eggs are ovate, with a tendency to short ovate, and they have only a slight gloss. The white ground color is finely speckled or sparingly spotted with "chestnut brown," "mummy brown," and "sayal brown," with under markings in shades of "drab-gray." Some sets have three or four eggs that are almost immaculate, with one egg sparingly spotted; other sets occasionally are prominently spotted with "drab-gray," "light Quaker drab," and "dark vinaceous-drab," or, less often, with spots of dark "mummy brown." Usually the majority of the markings are confined to the large end. The measurements of 50 eggs average 15.7 by 12.5 millimeters; the eggs showing the four extremes measure 16.8 by 13.0 and 14.2 by 11.6 millimeters (Harris).

*Young.*—An egg is laid each day until the set is complete, and incubation generally begins when the last egg is laid. The period of incubation is 10 or 11 days, and the young remain in the nest from 8 to 10 days. Mr. Burns gave Dr. Chapman (1907) the following full account of the nest life:

The task of incubation falls on the female alone. It appears that an airing is taken in the early morning or a little before midday, and again in the early evening, though perhaps not regularly every day. I have not seen the male about the nest with food at this period. The female will allow a close approach, looking into one's eyes with that hunted look so common in wild animals, and often flushing without a protesting note. The period of incubation in the one instance was exactly ten days.

On June 13, at 6.30 p. m., five young just hatched were blind, naked and prostrate from chin to sternum. The shells were disposed of immediately, in what manner I am unable to state; the female was reluctant to vacate.

On June 15, at 2.45 p. m., the young were able to raise their heads slightly and a fluffy bit of down had appeared about the head, also a dark stripe along the back bone. The female appeared, accompanied by the male, and fed the young with small green larvae—such as may be found on the under-side of oak and chestnut leaves—and then shielded the callow young from the hot rays of the sun.

On June 16, at 6.30 p. m., when the young were three days old, a downy puff appeared between the shoulders, wing quills being dark. The strongest bird had the eyes partly open and the mouth wide open for food.

On June 18, at 7 p. m., the heads and bodies were no longer flesh-colored but were well enough covered to appear dark. The eyes were open. At a *cluck* from me their mouths flew open. Both parents fed them with green-colored larvae. When the male rested a moment on a brier above the nest, the female flew down and drove him away, fed the young, re-appearing with excrement in her beak, which was carried in an opposite direction from the regular approach via maple bough and poplar sapling. The male fed the young from a mouthful of very minute larvae or eggs, which were gathered from the silken nests in the unfolding leaves of a nearby poplar; after this (7.30 p. m.) the female covered the young for the night.

On June 20, at from 6.50 to 7.35 p. m., the young had been seven days in the nest. They were well feathered and of a yellowish-green cast, the short tails being tipped with yellow. The parents were more suspicious. The female came to the maple bough with something in her beak and flew down to the briers and back again several times before she dropped to the edge of the nest and fed her young. The male appeared immediately but swallowed a green grub himself upon discovery of me twenty-five feet away. The female came again in five minutes with a brownish object in her bill, but appeared more timid and refused to drop to the nest until the male set her an example of courage.

On June 21, at 6.12 p. m., the young were fully fledged in green plumage above and dirty yellow beneath. They showed fear of me for the first time, eyeing me in the same manner as the parent bird when on the nest. They were evidently ready to vacate at a moment's notice or hasty movement on my part. The parents appeared, scolding rapidly. The female fed the young as soon as I retired to my old stand under a bush, with a rather large green grub (6.20 p. m.) and flew out to the top of a blackberry bush, followed immediately by the topmost fledgling. It could do little more than run. The adults flew to within a yard of my head, making a great outcry, and in the midst of the excitement the remainder of the young vacated the nest with feeble *chips*. The male gave his attention to them, while the female followed me as I beat a hasty retreat to enable them to collect their little family before dark. Eight days had elapsed since incubation was completed, and it is not at all unusual for the young of this species to leave the nest while so tiny and ragged.

*Plumages.*—Dr. Dwight (1900) calls the natal down "mouse-gray," and describes the juvenal plumage, in which the sexes are alike, as, "entire body plumage olive yellow darkest on the back and throat. Wings and tail slate-gray largely edged with plumbeous gray, the tertiaries and coverts with olive-yellow; the greater and median coverts tipped with white, yellow tinged. Rectrices largely white. Lores dusky."

A partial postjuvenal molt begins early in July, involving the contour plumage and the wing coverts, but not the rest of the wings or the tail. This molt produces the first winter plumage in which the sexes are very much alike, the female being duller in color, especially the streak through the eye, and having less yellow on the crown. Dr. Dwight (1900) describes the first winter male as "above, bright olive-green, lemon-yellow on the crown veiled by greenish tips. Below, bright lemon-yellow, the crissum white or merely tinged with yellow. Transocular streak black. Wing coverts plumbeous gray, edged with olive-green, the greater and median tipped with white, yellow tinged, forming two broad wing-bands."

The birds are now practically adult in plumage. The first and subsequent nuptial plumages are acquired by wear, which produces little change beyond removal of the greenish tips. Subsequent winter plumages are acquired by a complete postnuptial molt each July.

The interesting hybrids between this and the golden-winged warbler are discussed on pages 3 and 4. Kumlien and Hollister (1903) mention a probable mating of this with the Nashville warbler.

*Food.*—Nothing seems to have been published on the food of the blue-winged warbler beyond that mentioned above as food given to the young, which is doubtless eaten by the adults as well. It is apparently wholly insectivorous, seeking its food near the ground in the weed patches and underbrush where it lives and among the lower branches of the trees in its haunts. Probably any small insects that it can find in such places, as well as their larvae and eggs, including many small caterpillars, are eaten. Small grasshoppers and spiders are probably included. Prof. Aughey (1878) observed it catching small locusts in Nebraska. It is evidently a harmless and a very useful bird in destroying insects that are injurious to foliage.

*Behavior.*—Dr. Chapman (1907) writes: "It is rather deliberate in movements for a Warbler, and is less of a flutterer than the average member of the genus *Dendroica*. Some of its motions suggest those of the tree-inhabiting Vireos, while at times, as the bird hangs downward from some cocoon it is investigating, one is reminded of a Chickadee." And he quotes Burns as follows:

Perched inconspicuously near the top and well out on the branchlets of a tree or sapling, preferably facing an opening, if in a thicket; it is in itself so minute an object as to be passed unseen by many, more especially as it is much less active than most of our Warblers. With body feathers puffed out to a delightful plumpness, except for the backward sweep of the head while in the act of singing, it remains motionless for quite a while. When it moves it is with a combination of nervous haste and deliberation, and its song may be heard from quite another part of the landscape with no apparent reason for the change. While it has its favorite song perches, it is quite a wanderer and not infrequently sings beyond possible hearing of its brooding mate, but oftener within fifty to two hundred feet of the nest.

*Voice.*—Aretas A. Saunders contributes the following study of the songs of this warbler: "The territory song of the blue-winged warbler consists of two long, buzz-like notes, the second usually lower in pitch than the first and rougher in sound, *bzzzzzzz–brrrrrrrr.* The pitch interval between the two notes varies from one tone to four and a half tones, but the smaller intervals, one tone and one and a half tones, are much commoner. The second note is lower in pitch than the first in about 75 percent of my records, and higher in most of the others. In a few songs the second buzz is a double note, and one may hear both lower and higher notes from a medium distance, only the lower from a greater distance, and only the higher when very near the bird.

"The pitch is not high as compared to other warblers, ranging from C ′ ′ ′ to D ′ ′ ′ ′, one tone more than an octave. The territory song commonly begins on some note from A ′ ′ ′ to C ′ ′ ′ ′. It varies in time from 1⅕ to 1⅘ seconds, the first note being either equal to or shorter than the second. The second note is often twice as long as the first. In some songs the second note is broken into two notes, and in one record it is in four short notes, so that the song is essentially like that of the golden-winged warbler.

"After the birds have been on the breeding grounds for a week or two, singing of the nesting song begins. This song has the same buzz-like quality as the other, but it is exceedingly variable, considerably longer, and hardly ever twice alike. The song often begins with a series of short notes, like *tsit tsit tsit*, or contains such notes somewhere in the middle. There are usually long buzzes that change pitch by slurring upward or downward. On one occasion, I found a bird that sang a territory song and four different nesting songs. Often the nesting song is sung in flight. By June this song is heard about as frequently as the territory song, and in late summer, after the molt, it is the one most commonly heard.

"The song of this bird is heard from its arrival in spring until early July, when it ceases for a time. It is usually revived in late July or early August, and from then on may be heard fairly frequently until the birds depart about the last of August."

In his notes sent to Dr. Chapman, Burns describes the song as, "a drowsy, locust-like, *swe-e-e-e ze-e-e-e-e*, the first apparently inhaled and the last exhaled. * * * Another song heard on the first day of arrival, on one occasion, uttered by several males in company, possibly transients here, and may be the mating song, suggests the Chickadee's *che-de-de-e*, *che-dee-e*, and *che-de-de-dee*, uttered repeatedly in one form or other in excitement, and while running out on the branchlets. The call and alarm note is a rather weak *chip*." Dr. Chapman (1912) records a longer song, heard later in the season as "*wēē-chǐ-chǐ-chǐ-chǐ, chūr, chēē-chŭr*."

Francis H. Allen tells me that the final note, *ze-e-e-e-e*, as rendered by Burns, "is really a very rapid series of *pips*, as if the bird had lips like ours and vibrated them by forcing the air through them—in other words, giving a sort of avian Bronx cheer, but high in pitch."

The individual *pip* notes are clear, but the effect of the rapid succession is somewhat buzzy."

The songs of the hybrid forms may be like the song of either parent form, more often like that of the goldenwing, or a mixture of the two.

The flight song, as heard by Frank A. Pitelka, is recorded as follows:

*tsee-*

*zweé-*                                          *zweé*

*tzip-*                          *tzip-*

*zee-zee-zee-zee-zee-zee-*                 *zee-zee-zee-zee-zee-zee-*

The song of the blue-winged warbler is one of the high-frequency songs; Albert R. Brand (1938) gives the approximate mean as 7,675, the highest note about 8,050 and the lowest note about 7,125 vibrations per second; this compares with an approximate mean for the blackpoll warbler of 8,900 vibrations per second, the highest frequency of any of the wood warblers, and an average for all passerine birds of about 4,000 vibrations per second.

*Field marks.*—A small warbler with a greenish olive back, yellow forehead and under parts, with a black line through the eye and two white wing bars, is a blue-winged warbler. The female is merely more dull in coloration than the male, and the young even duller. The hybrids between this and the golden-winged warbler are more puzzling, but in a general way they can be recognized; a nearly typical blue-winged warbler with a black throat is probably a Lawrence's warbler; and a golden-winged warbler without a black throat or cheek and with a variable amount of white and yellow on the under parts and in the wing-bars, is probably a Brewster's warbler. But there is an immense amount of individual variation between the two species, due to frequent crossing.

*Fall.*—Most of the blue-winged warblers move southward during August and September, though a few may linger in the southern part of the breeding range into October. Professor Cooke (1904) says: "Most of the individuals of the species migrate across the Gulf of Mexico, apparently avoiding Florida on the east and Texas and Vera Cruz on the west, as there is no record of the occurrence of this warbler in fall in Texas, and but one in Florida—that of a bird taken at Key West August 30, 1887." But this remains to be proved.

Alexander F. Skutch writes to me: "This is another very rare migrant in Central America. It has been recorded only a few times in Guatemala and apparently not at all in Costa Rica. I have seen it only once, on the Finca Mocá, Guatemala, on October 30, 1934."

Very little seems to be known about its winter distribution and still less about its winter habits.

DISTRIBUTION

*Range.*—Eastern United States to Panamá.

*Breeding range.*—The blue-winged warbler breeds **north** to southeastern Minnesota (Lanesboro); southern Wisconsin (Mazomanie, Prairie du Sac, and Glarus); northeastern Illinois (Rockford, Deerfield, and La Grange); southern Michigan (possibly Hastings, and Ann Arbor); northern Ohio (Toledo, Lakeside, Cleveland, and Austinburg); southern Pennsylvania (Carlisle); southern New York (Ossining and Whaley Lake); and Massachusetts (Springfield and Sudbury). **East** to eastern Massachusetts (Sudbury and Lexington); Connecticut (Westfield and Saybrook); Long Island (Mastic and Oyster Bay); New Jersey (Demarest, Morristown, and Elizabeth); southeastern Pennsylvania (Tinicum and Berwyn); probably occasionally in northern Maryland (Cecil County and Sabillasville); eastern and central Ohio (Canfield and Columbus); east-central Kentucky (Berea); central Tennessee (Nashville and Fall Creek); and central northern Georgia (Young Harris). **South** to northern Georgia (Young Harris, Margret, and Atlanta); northeastern Alabama (Long Island); central Tennessee (Wildersville); and northwestern Arkansas (Pettigrew and Winslow). **West** to northwestern Arkansas (Winslow and Fayetteville); west-central Iowa (Warrensburg); eastern Iowa (Lacey, Grinnell, Winthrop, and McGregor); and southeastern Minnesota (Lanesboro). The blue-winged warbler has occurred in summer west to eastern Kansas (Emporia and Leavenworth); central-southern and eastern Nebraska (Red Cloud, Plattsmouth, and Omaha); western Iowa (Sioux City); and north to Minnesota (Minneapolis); southern Ontario (Point Pelee, Strathroy, and West Lake); central New York (Penn Yan and Auburn); and southern New Hampshire (Manchester).

*Winter range.*—The principal winter home of the blue-winged warbler seems to be in Guatemala, though it has been recorded in winter from the Valley of Mexico; Puebla (Metlatoyuca); Veracruz (Tres Zapotes); to eastern Nicaragua (Río Escondido and Greytown). There is one winter record each from Costa Rica (Bonilla), Panamá (Port Antonio), and Colombia (Santa Marta Region).

On January 6, 1900, a dead blue-winged warbler (apparently dead from starvation) was picked up in Bronx Park, New York. It had only recently died and in all probability was the bird seen on December 10, in the same region.

*Migration.*—Late dates of spring departure are: Colombia—Santa Marta Region, March 21. Veracruz—Jalapa, April 7. Florida—Pensacola, April 25. Alabama—Guntersville, May 2. District of

Columbia—Washington, May 30.   Louisiana—Monroe, April 27.
Texas—San Antonio, May 12.

Early dates of spring arrival are: Florida—Pensacola, April 4.
Alabama—Shelby, April 4.   Georgia—Atlanta, March 26.   North
Carolina—Arden, April 18.   District of Columbia—Washington,
April 23.   West Virginia—Wheeling, April 23.   Pennsylvania—
Germantown, April 25.   New York—Yonkers, April 26.   Massachu-
setts—Lexington, May 6.   Mississippi—Bay St. Louis, March 13.
Louisiana—New Orleans, March 23.   Arkansas—Winslow, April 2.
Tennessee—Nashville, April 7.   Kentucky—Eubank, April 10.   Illi-
nois—Springfield, April 29.   Ohio—Columbus, April 22.   Michigan—
Ann Arbor, May 1.   Missouri—St. Louis, April 17.   Iowa—Grinnell,
April 28.   Wisconsin—Reedsburg, April 30.   Minnesota—Lanesboro,
May 7.   Texas—Cove, March 27.   Kansas—Onaga, April 26.

Late dates of fall departure are: Minnesota—Lanesboro, September
1.   Wisconsin—Elkhorn, September 19.   Iowa—Giard, September 20.
Missouri—Monteer, September 17.   Arkansas—Winslow, September
18.   Louisiana—Monroe, October 7.   Michigan—Jackson, September
13.   Ohio—Oberlin, September 27.   Indiana—Bloomington, Septem-
ber 28.   Illinois—Chicago, September 29.   Kentucky—Bowling Green,
October 5.   Tennessee—Memphis, September 11.   Mississippi—Deer
Island, October 13.   Massachusetts—Belmont, September 6.   New
York—New York City, September 25.   Pennsylvania—Jeffersonville,
September 19.   District of Columbia, Washington, September 14.
West Virginia—French Creek, September 28.   North Carolina—
Reidsville, September 26.   South Carolina—Huger, September 10.
Georgia—Tifton, September 27.   Florida—St. Marks, October 9.

Early dates of fall arrival are: District of Columbia—Washington,
August 13.   Georgia—Columbus, July 28.   Alabama—Leighton, August 8.   Florida—Key West, August 30.   Mississippi—Gulfport, August 23.   Texas—Cove, July 29.   Tamaulipas—Matamoros, August
25.   Costa Rica—Bonilla, September 8.

*Banding.*—Few blue-winged warblers have been banded and recovered.   A bird banded at Elmhurst, Long Island, on August 17,
1935, flew into a screened porch at Westbury, Long Island, on May
7, 1937.   The two places are about 15 miles apart.

*Egg dates.*—Connecticut: 30 records, May 25 to June 24; 20 records,
May 29 to June 6, indicating the height of the season.

New Jersey: 40 records, May 16 to June 19; 29 records, May 22 to
30.

Pennsylvania: 27 records, May 28 to July 7; 14 records, May 28 to
June 3 (Harris).

VERMIVORA BACHMANII (Audubon)

## BACHMAN'S WARBLER

CONTRIBUTED BY EDWARD VON SIEBOLD DINGLE

### HABITS

Bachman's warbler was discovered by Dr. John Bachman a few miles from Charleston, S. C., in July, 1833. According to Audubon (1841), who described and named in honor of his "amiable friend" the only two specimens taken, several other birds were seen soon after in the same locality.

More than half a century passed before the bird again appeared in America, this time in Louisiana. Charles S. Galbraith (1888), while securing specimens of warblers at Lake Pontchartrain for the millinery trade in the spring of 1886, took a single bird; in the two succeeding years he collected a number of additional specimens, 6 in 1887 and 31 in 1888. These birds were evidently migrating, for the 31 were all taken between March 2 and 20, and none could be found after the end of March. Chapman (1907) comments on Galbraith's first specimen: "This specimen, now in the American Museum of Natural History, is prepared for a hat piece. The feet are missing, the wings are stiffly distended, the head bent backward in typical bonnet pose, and, had it not been for an interest in ornithology which led Galbraith to take his unknown birds to Mr. Lawrence for identification, this *rara avis* might have become an unappreciated victim on Fashion's altar."

Since then the records have multiplied; but *bachmanii* has always been an extremely local species, even in migrations, and breeds in primeval swamps in small colonies, which are few and far between. At the present writing, the bird is one of the very rarest of North American warblers. It has been an unattained ideal to the writer; yet, having heard much about its habits from the late Arthur T. Wayne and having visited with him the former breeding grounds, he has some consolation for not having met it in life.

Wayne (1901) took a specimen of this species on May 15, 1901, near Mount Pleasant, which was the first record for South Carolina since Dr. Bachman collected the type, and says: "I am positive that I have heard this song nearly every summer in the same localities where the male was found, but I always keep out of such places after April 10 on account of the myriads of ticks and red bugs which infest them. Then, too, such places are simply impenetrable on account of the dense blackberry vines, matted with grape vines, fallen logs piled one upon another, and a dense growth of low bushes."

*Spring.*—From its winter home in Cuba Bachman's warbler enters the United States through Florida, and according to Howell (1932) the earliest date of arrival in that state is February 27. It has also been recorded from Louisiana on the same date (Chapman, 1907). The majority of individuals, however, cross to the United States mainland early in March; apparently the birds that summer in Alabama, Missouri, Arkansas, and Kentucky reach their breeding grounds by skirting the Gulf coast and continuing up the Mississippi Valley. They reach the vicinity of Charleston, S. C., in March and nesting begins at once, for Wayne (1907) found a nest on March 27 containing one egg and another on April 3 with five well-incubated eggs. He calls attention to the fact that Bachman's warbler therefore breeds earlier than the resident pine and yellow-throated warblers.

*Nesting.*—Dr. Bachman did not discover the breeding grounds of this warbler, and it was more than 60 years before the first nests and eggs became known to science; Widmann (1897) found the bird breeding in the St. Francis River country of Missouri and Arkansas on May 13, 1897. The nesting area extended "over two acres of blackberry brambles among a medley of half-decayed and lately-felled treetops, lying in pools of water, everything dripping wet with dew in the forenoon, and steaming under a broiling sun in the afternoon." The first nest, which he describes as being 2 feet from the ground, "was made of leaves and grass blades, lined with a peculiar black rootlet; it was tied very slightly to a vertical blackberry vine of fresh growth and rested lightly on another, which crossed the former at a nearly right angle. From above it was entirely hidden by branchlets of latest growth, and the hand could not have been inserted without at first cutting several vines, overlying it in different directions."

Ridgway (1897) describes this nest as, "a somewhat compressed compact mass composed externally of dried weed- and grass-stalks and dead leaves, many of the latter partially skeletonized; internally composed of rather fine weed- and grass-stalks, lined with black fibres, apparently dead threads of the black pendant lichens (*Ramalina*, species ?) which hang in beard-like tufts from button-bushes (*Cephalanthus*) and other shrubs growing in wetter portions of the western bottomlands. The height of the nest is about 3½ inches; its greatest breadth is about 4 inches, its width in the opposite direction being about 3 inches. The cavity is about 1½ inches deep and 1½×2 inches wide."

In 1906, Wayne (1907) found six nests of Bachman's warbler near Charleston, S. C., from two of which the young had flown. "The swamp in which this warbler breeds is heavily timbered and subjected to overflow from rains and reservoirs. The trees are chiefly of a deciduous character, such as the cypress, black gum, sweet gum, tupelo, hickory, dogwood, and red oak. In the higher parts of the swamp short-leaf pines, water oaks, live oaks, and magnolias abound. The undergrowth is chiefly cane, aquatic bushes, and swamp palmetto, while patches of blackberry brambles and thorny vines are met with at almost every step." The first two nests, found on April 17, are described as follows:

The first nest was placed upon a dead palmetto leaf, being supported by a small aquatic bush, and was completely hidden by a living palmetto leaf which overhung the nest, like an umbrella. It was in a dense swamp, two feet above the ground, and contained four pure white eggs, almost ready to be hatched.

The second nest, which was within one hundred yards of the first one, was built in a bunch of canes (*Arundinaria tecta*), and supported by a palmetto leaf. This nest was three feet above the ground, in a compartively dry situation, and contained four pure white eggs in an advanced stage of incubation. * * *

The two nests are similar, being constructed of fine grass, cane leaves, and other leaves, the latter skeletonized. The second nest, taken April 17, is 6½ inches high, 6 inches wide, 2 inches wide at rim, and 2 inches deep. It is composed almost entirely of dead cane leaves, a little Spanish moss (*Tillandsia usneoides*), and a few skeletonized leaves. * * *

The female is a very close sitter; indeed so close that I found it necessary to touch her before she would leave the nest. This habit was the same in both females.

The other nests were in low bushes, vines, or canes.

During that same year Embody (1907) discovered Bachman's warbler breeding in Logan County, Ky., and later Holt (1920) found it nesting in Autauga County, Ala. The localities in which these birds were breeding and the locations of the nests were not very different from those described above by Wayne.

*Eggs.*—The egg of Bachman's warbler is ovate and pure white, and usually glossy. The only spotted egg on record is one of a set described by Holt (1920) as follows: "The nest contained four eggs, three of them pure, glossy white, the other with a dozen minute dots of light brown, mostly about the large end; all were tinted faint salmon pink by the yolks." Three to five eggs constitute a set; three seem the usual number, with four a close second, while five are unusual.

[AUTHOR'S NOTE: The measurements of 42 eggs average 15.8 by 12.4 millimeters; the eggs showing the four extremes measure 16.6 by 12.9, 16.5 by 13.0, 14.9 by 12.2, and 15.8 by 11.6 millimeters.]

*Plumages.*—[AUTHOR'S NOTE: Two young birds, just able to fly from the nest and taken by Wayne on May 13, are thus described by Brewster (1905):

The male which is now before me may be described as follows:—Top and sides of head and fore part of back faded hair brown with a trace of ashy on the middle of crown; remainder of upper parts dull olive green; wings and tail (which are fully grown) as in the first winter plumage excepting that the greater and middle wing-coverts are rather more broadly tipped with light brown, forming two well-marked wing-bars; chin and throat brownish white tinged with yellow; sides of jugulum smoke gray, its center yellowish; sides of breast gamboge yellow shading into olive on the flanks; middle of breast, with most of abdomen, yellowish white; under tail-coverts ashy white. All the feathers on the under parts which are strongly yellow or olive, and those on the upper parts which are decidedly ashy or greenish, appear to belong to the autumnal plumage or, as it is now called, the first winter plumage, but all the other feathers on the head and body are evidently those of the first plumage. * * *

I have not seen the young female Bachman's Warbler above referred to, but Mr. Wayne writes me that "it differs from the male only in these respects: The yellow on the sides of the breast is very much paler and more restricted and the back is not greenish, but brownish. The white on the tail-feathers is merely indicated on the margins of the inner webs of the tail-feathers."

It would appear from the above that there is a sexual difference even in the juvenal plumage, and that the postjuvenal molt begins before the middle of May. This molt evidently involves all the contour plumage and the wing coverts but not the rest of the wings or the tail. The young male in first winter plumage is similar to the adult male at that season, but the crown is entirely gray, or with very little black; the feathers of the black patch on the throat, which is more restricted, are tipped with yellowish or buffy. There are no specimens available that indicate a prenuptial molt, which is probably very limited. Young males in the first nuptial plumage may be recognized by the worn and faded wings and tail.

The complete postnuptial molt of adults apparently occurs in July or earlier; I have seen no molting birds, but a large series of August birds are all in completely fresh winter plumage. In this plumage the male resembles the spring male, but the black of the crown is widely tipped with gray and the black of the breast is narrowly tipped with yellowish; these tips largely wear away before spring, although Wayne (1910) says that his "breeding males all show the olive yellow edging on the black feathers." Similar molts and changes take place in the female, but she has no black in the crown and much less or none at all on the breast; her colors are duller and she has less white in the tail, as well as olive-green, instead of yellow, lesser wing coverts.

For a full description of individual variations in plumage, the reader is referred to Mr. Brewster's (1891) excellent paper.]

*Food.*—Very little information is to be found concerning the food of this warbler, but insects undoubtedly constitute its diet. Howell (1924) says: "Five stomachs of this species from Alabama contained remains of caterpillars and a few fragments of Hymenoptera, probably ants."

*Behavior.*—Wayne (1907), in writing of this bird on its breeding grounds, says: "Bachman's Warbler is a high-ranging bird, like the Yellow-throated Warbler, and generally sings from the top of a sweet gum or cypress. It appears to have regular singing stations during the breeding season, and upon leaving a tree it flies a long distance before alighting. On this account it is impossible to follow the bird through the dark forest, and it can only be detected by its song. I have occasionally seen the males in low gall-berry bushes within six or eight inches of the ground, but their usual resorts are among the topmost branches of the tallest forest trees."

Brewster (1891) had similar experience with migrating birds in Florida:

Nearly or quite all that has been hitherto written about this Warbler would lead one to infer that its favorite haunts are dense thickets, undergrowth, or low trees, and that it seldom ventures to any considerable height above the ground. Our experience, however, was directly contrary to this. * * * The bird, moreover, not only frequented the tops of the tallest trees, but at all times of the day and under every condition of weather kept at a greater average height than any other Warbler excepting *Dendroica dominica*. In its marked preference for cypresses it also resembled the species just named, but unlike it was never seen in pines. * * *

At the time of our visit the Suwanee bottoms were alive with small birds many of which were doubtless migrants. They banded together in mixed flocks often of large size and motley composition. * * * Such a gathering was nearly certain to contain from one or two to five or six Bachman's Warblers.

These with the Parulas were most likely to be feeding in the upper branches of some gigantic cypress, at least one hundred feet above the earth, where they looked scarcely larger than bumble bees. * * *

The habits and movements of Bachman's Warbler are in some respects peculiar and characteristic. It does not flit from twig to twig nor launch out after flying insects in the manner of most Warblers, and many of its motions are quite as deliberate as those of a Vireo. Alighting near the end of a branch it creeps or sidles outward along a twig, and bending forward until the head points nearly straight down, inserts the bill among the terminal leaflets with a peculiar, slow, listless motion, keeping it there a second or two, and repeating the leisurely thrust many times in succession without changing its foothold. The action is like that of several other members of the genus—notably *H. pinus* and *H. chrysoptera*—under similar conditions, and suggests the sucking in of liquid food, perhaps honey or dew. Not infrequently a bird would hang back downwards beneath a twig and feed from the under sides of the leaves in the manner of a Titmouse, * * *

Many of the hackberry trees along the banks of this stream contained compact bunches nearly as large as a child's head—of dead leaves blackened by exposure to wind and weather. These bunches probably sheltered insects or their larvae, for they attracted several species of birds, especially the Bachman's Warblers which would work at them minutes at a time with loud rustling, sometimes burrowing in nearly out of sight and sending the loosened leaves floating down to the ground. Upon exhausting the supply of food or becoming tired of the spot—whether one of the leaf bunches or the extremity of a cypress branch—the bird almost invariably started on a long flight, often going hundreds of yards through the woods or crossing the river, instead of merely passing to the next branch or tree as almost any other Warbler would have done under similar circumstances. This habit seemed to us characteristic of the species.

Atkins wrote from Key West (Scott, 1890):

Bachman's Warbler in its habits is very much like the Parula Warbler (*Compsothlypis americana*). The resemblance is more noticeable when feeding and in search of food. The birds will then penetrate a thick bunch of leaves and go through, over and all around in the most thorough manner in their exploration after insects that appeal to their taste. They are very active, and constantly in motion. They are also quarrelsome, and resent the intrusion of other species. Frequently I have noticed them fighting away the White-eyed Vireo, and where two or more Bachman's Warblers are observed together, one is pretty sure to see them chasing and fighting among themselves. When disturbed or alarmed they are at once alert; a sharp alarm note, something like that of a Yellow-throated Warbler (*D. dominica*) is uttered, but more forcible and clear cut in its delivery. This is accompanied with a few jerks of the tail, and the bird is off to a neighboring tree. They are found alike in the trees, low bushes, and shrubbery, sometimes on or quite near the ground, and seem to prefer the heavy and more thickly grown woods to trees or bushes more in the open. Young birds are quite tame, but the adults as a rule were very shy and difficult to approach after having been once disturbed.

*Voice.*—The song of Bachman's warbler is of a wiry or insectlike character, and has been widely compared by many observers to the music of the worm-eating and parula warblers and the chipping sparrow. It also resembles, according to Aretas A. Saunders (MS.), one of the songs of the blue-winged warbler. Brewster (1891) says:

The song is unlike that of any other species of *Helminthophila* with which I am acquainted and most resembles the song of the Parula Warbler. It is of the same length and of nearly the same quality or tone, but less guttural and without the upward run at the end, all of its six or eight notes being given in the same key and with equal emphasis. Despite these differences it would be possible to mistake the performance, especially at a distance, for that of a Parula singing listlessly. The voice, although neither loud nor musical, is penetrating and seems to carry as far as most Warblers'. Besides the song the only note which we certainly identified was a low hissing *zee-e-eep*, very like that of the Black-and-white Creeper.

Widmann (1897), observing a singing male for 8 hours, says that "the bird kept singing nearly all the time at the rate of ten times a minute with the regularity of clockwork, and its sharp, rattling notes reminded me strongly of an alarm-clock. In this regard it recalls one of the performances of Parula, whose rattle is of the same length and quality, except that it has a certain rise at the end, by which it is easily distinguished."

Wayne (1910) heard one singing exactly like a prothonotary warbler, this song lasting for more than 20 minutes. And Howell (1924) mentions two Bachman's warblers, observed in Alabama, that "had the habit of singing on the wing, the song being delivered just before the bird alighted on a perch after a short flight."

*Field marks.*—[AUTHOR'S NOTE: Under certain circumstances Bachman's warbler might be mistaken for a black-throated green warbler, but, fortunately, the two species do not frequent similar habitats at the same seasons. Mr. Brewster (1891) calls attention to the difficulty of distinguishing it from the parula warbler, when the two are seen against the sky in a lofty treetop; at such times—

the chestnut throat-markings of the Parula showed quite as dark and distinct as the black cravat of the Bachman's Warbler.

The latter bird, however, was the larger or rather plumper-looking of the two, and if the upper side of the wings could be seen the absence of the white bars which are so conspicuous on the wings of the Parula Warbler was quickly noticed. * * * Of course it is only the male Bachman's Warbler which can be confounded with the Parula, for the female—setting aside occasional individuals which have black on the throat—is most like the Orange-crowned Warbler. * * * Both sexes of Bachman's Warbler habitually carry the feathers of the crown a little raised, giving the head a fluffy appearance.]

*Fall.*—[AUTHOR'S NOTE: Wayne (1925) says: "The Bachman's Warbler has left South Carolina before the advent of August; the latest date I have is a young male taken by me on July 16, 1919." But he records a specimen which struck the lighthouse on Tybee Island, Ga., on September 23, 1924; he thought that this bird might have come from somewhere in the Mississippi Valley region, where the species breeds much later than in South Carolina. Atkins sent the following notes to W. E. D. Scott (1890):

Key West, Florida, 1889. First arrival from north, July 17, one adult male and one young female. Next observed July 23, three birds. Not seen again until July 31, though I was watching for them almost continually; three birds again on this date. August 4, found them more common perhaps a dozen birds in all were seen. From this time till August 25 inclusive, I found them regularly in small numbers. On August 8, 11, and 25 they were most abundant, particularly so on the first-named date, when as many as twenty-five or thirty birds were seen. After the 11th there was a decline in the numbers until the 25th, when they were again almost as numerous as on the 8th, but none were observed after the 25th.

Bachman's warbler is said to spend the winter in western Cuba and the Isle of Pines, migrating through Florida and the Keys.]

### DISTRIBUTION

*Range.*—Southeastern United States and Cuba.

*Breeding range.*—Although Bachman's warbler was described more than a hundred years ago its range is still very imperfectly known. After its discovery near Charleston, S. C., in 1833, the bird remained unknown until rediscovered in 1886 near Lake Pontchartrain, La.

The first nest was found in 1897 in southeastern Missouri, nearly the northwestern border of the range as now known.   It was not until 1901 that the species was again found near Charleston and in 1905 the first young birds were collected in the same swamp where the type specimen was collected.

Bachman's warbler breeds, locally **north** to northwestern Arkansas (possibly Winslow, Big Creek, and Bertig); southeastern Missouri (Grandin, Senath, and has occurred in Shannon County); central Kentucky (Russellville and Mammoth Cave); possibly occasionally in southern Indiana, since a pair was seen throughout the breeding season at Indianapolis; north-central Alabama (Irondale); and southern South Carolina (Charleston).   **East** to the coastal swamps of South Carolina (Charleston), and Georgia (Savannah).   **South** to Georgia (Savannah and possibly the Okefenokee Swamp); southern Alabama (Tensas River); and southern Louisiana (West Baton Rouge Parish).   **West** to southeastern Louisiana (West Baton Rouge Parish) and northwestern Arkansas (Winslow, possibly).   In addition, specimens have been recorded at Fayetteville, Ark.; Versailles, Ky.; Aylett, Va.; and Raleigh, N. C.

*Winter range.*—The only known wintering place for the Bachman's warbler is the island of Cuba.   It has occurred in the Bahamas in fall migration.   Color is given to the theory that this species may occasionally spend the winter in the deep swamps of Georgia and Florida, by the collection of a specimen in Okefenokee Swamp on December 30, 1928, and the occurrence of several in December of 1932.   A specimen was collected at Melbourne, Fla., on January 27, 1898.

*Migration.*—That Bachman's warbler migrates through the Florida Keys is indicated by the large number seen at Key West in fall migration and by the many that have struck the light at Sombrero Key. On March 3, 1889, 21 birds of this species struck the light and five more were killed on April 3.

Early dates of spring arrival are: Florida—Lukens, February 27. Georgia—Atlanta, April 18.   Alabama—Woodbine, March 20.   Mississippi—Deer Island, March 21.   Louisiana—Mandeville, February 27.

In spring the latest date at Dry Tortugas Island, Fla., is April 9 and the earliest fall arrival at Key West, Fla., July 17.

Fall departure dates are: Georgia—Savannah, September 24. Florida—Key West, September 5.

*Egg dates.*—Missouri: 4 records, May 13 to 17.

South Carolina: 19 records, March 27 to June 17; 10 records, March 27 to April 4.

## TENNESSEE WARBLER

PLATE 14

HABITS

Alexander Wilson (1832) discovered this warbler on the banks of the Cumberland River in Tennessee and gave it the common name it has borne ever since, although it seems inappropriate to name a bird for a State so far from its main breeding range in Canada. Only two specimens were ever obtained by him, and he regarded it as a very rare species, possibly a mere wanderer from some other clime, hence the name *peregrina*. Audubon never saw more than three individuals, migrants in Louisiana and at Key West. And Nuttall, it seems, never saw it at all. Its apparent rarity in those early days was, perhaps, due to the fact that it is inconspicuously colored and might easily be overlooked or mistaken for a small plainly colored vireo or for the more common Nashville warbler; its fluctuation in numbers from year to year in different places may also have suggested its apparent rarity. Here in Massachusetts, we have found it very common in certain years and very scarce in others.

*Spring.*—Professor Cooke (1904) says: "In spring migration the Tennessee warbler is rarely found east of the Alleghenies, nor is it so common in the Mississippi Valley as during the fall migration." And he makes the rather surprising statement that "the Biological Survey has received no notes from the South Atlantic States on the spring migration of the Tennessee warbler, nor from Alabama, Mississippi, or Louisiana, though two birds were seen in April in Cuba and some were taken on the island of Grand Cayman, and the species has been noted several times in spring at Pensacola, Fla." Yet he gives April 26, 1885, as the date of its arrival at Rising Fawn, Ga. And H. H. Kopman (1905) writes:

In a small lot of warblers sent Andrew Allison, in the spring of 1902, from the lighthouse on Chandeleur Island, off the southeast coast of Louisiana, was a Tennessee Warbler that had struck the lighthouse April 10. While I had some dubious records of the occurrence of the Tennessee Warbler at New Orleans in the early part of April, it was not until 1903 that I saw the species, in spring, and then in some numbers, singing, and loitering to a degree that surprised me, for the first of these transients appeared April 26, and the last was noted May 9. They were restricted almost to one spot, a thicket of willows beside a pond in the suburbs of New Orleans. I observed others the latter part of April, 1905.

This warbler seems to be a rare spring migrant through Florida; A. H. Howell (1932) gives seven records, from Key West to Pensacola, in March and April.   The few records available seem to indicate that the main migration route is along the eastern coasts of Central America (Dr. Skutch tells me that he sees it both spring and fall in Costa Rica), Mexico, and Texas to the Mississippi Valley, whence it spreads out to reach its wide breeding range.   Some birds may reach Florida via Cuba, and we have some evidence that it migrates across the Gulf of Mexico.   It is common on the coast of Texas in spring.

Gerald Thayer wrote to Dr. Chapman (1907) that about Monadnock, N. H., the Tennessee warbler is "very rare, and seemingly irregular.   It haunts blossoming apple trees, big elms, and roadside copses of mixed deciduous second growth."

At Buckeye Lake, Ohio, according to Milton B. Trautman (1940), "the daily and seasonal numbers of no warbler species fluctuated as greatly as did those of the Tennessee Warbler.   During some spring migrations it was decidedly uncommon, and never more than 5 individuals were recorded in a day nor more than 35 for the spring.   During other years as many as 250 individuals (May 16, 1929) were observed in a day, and more than 800 were noted during the migration. * * *   The birds in spring chiefly inhabited the upper half of the taller trees of both upland and lowland wooded areas and also the upper parts of rows or groups of tall trees along the lake shore, streams, and about farmhouses."

It must have been a very common migrant in Minnesota at one time, for Dr. Roberts (1936) writes:

Formerly, when all Warblers were more abundant than now, the little Tennessee flooded the tree-tops for a week or ten days in such numbers as to equal, if not excel, all other species put together, excepting only the Myrtle.   Insignificant in size and inconspicuous in garb, it made up for these shortcomings by numbers and incessant vocal effort, indifferent performer though it is.   It is still one of the commonest species.   It keeps well up among the topmost branches and moves restlessly about in search of food, singing meanwhile with little apparent effort and announcing its passage from one tree-top to another by a succession of sharp little *yeap-yeaps* that are almost as characteristic to the trained ear as the song itself.

A. D. Henderson, of Belvedere, Alberta, tells me that the Tennessee warbler is probably the most numerous of the warblers which spend the summer in the territory around Belvedere and in the Fort Assiniboine District.   It breeds mainly in poplar woods, but I have also found nests in dry muskeg."

*Nesting.*—Prior to the beginning of the present century very little authentic information on the nesting habits of the Tennessee warbler was available.   Professor Cooke (1904) records two sets of eggs taken by one of the parties of the Biological Survey in 1901 at Fort Smith, Mackenzie, of which he says: "These eggs are among the first absolutely authentic specimens known to science."   And Dr. Chapman

(1907) remarked: "The Tennessee Warbler awaits a biographer." Since then, we have learned much about it, mainly through the writings of B. S. Bowdish and P. B. Philipp, who found it breeding abundantly in New Brunswick. In their first paper (1916) they describe the summer haunts and the nesting habits of this warbler as follows:

The region in question is particularly well adapted to the nesting requirements of the Tennessee Warbler, as we noted them during the above period. Extensive lumbering has removed the greater part of the large growth spruce and balsam timber, which forms the great bulk of the forests of this region, leaving areas of small trees, which, in the older clearings, have grown thickly, and to an average height of ten feet. These are interspersed with areas of more or less open, large timber, and others where the second growth has reached little more than the proportions of somewhat scattered shrubbery. The essentially level surface is frequently scored by slight depressions which form the beds of tiny streams, bordered on either side by boggy ground, dotted with grass tussocks, bushes and small trees, and overspread with a luxuriant growth of moss. Such areas are most numerous in cleared tracts, but not infrequent in the edges and the more open portions of the woods. These are the summer home-sites of the Tennessee Warbler. * * *

At the time of our visit to the breeding country, in the middle of June, nest building was completed and full sets of eggs had been laid. Altogether, ten nests were located, all built on the ground in substantially the same general sort of situation, and all but two were found by flushing the bird. The nest is built in the moss, usually in a wet place at the foot of a small bush, and in most cases in woods, somewhat back from the more open part of the clearings. A hollow is dug in the moss, usually beneath an overhanging bunch of grass. The nest is in nearly every case entirely concealed and it is impossible to see it from any view-point without displacing the overhanging grass. Consequently unless the bird is flushed it would be all but impossible to find it. The outer foundation of the nest is of dry grass forming quite a substantial structure. Several nests had whisps of grass stems extending from the front rim, as noted in description of the first nest below. It is lined, usually, with fine dry grass, to which in some instances the quill-like hairs of the porcupine, or white moose hairs, are added, and more rarely still, fine hair-like roots which were not identified. * * *

This species seems to be somewhat gregarious. In 1914, in one small clearing, five males were heard singing at the same time. In 1915, in the same clearing, three males were heard singing at once, and two nests were found. In almost every clearing of suitable size at least two pairs of birds were found, the nests being sometimes located rather close together. * * *

On the second day of our sojourn, June 19, we visited one of the typical nesting places of this warbler, a boggy cleared swale, with scattering, small second growth, and soon flushed a female from a nest containing six fresh, or practically fresh, eggs. This nest, typical of the majority of those found in both construction and situation, was placed in the side of a small tussock, bedded in moss and completely overhung by the dead grass of the previous year's growth. The nest was composed entirely of fine, nearly white, dead grass stems. From the front rim protruded outward and downward, a wisp of dead grass tips, lying over the lower grasses in the tussock, and shingled over by the overhanging grass, establishing a continuity of the side of the tussock, thus cunningly adding to the perfect concealment. A tiny tree and one or two bush shoots grew from the tussock, close to the nest and this feature was typical of the greater number of the nests found.

They give the measurements of four nests; the outside diameter varied from 3 to 4 inches, the inside diameter from 1⅛ to 2 inches, the outside depth from 2 to 3¼, and the inside depth from 1⅛ to 1½ inches. What nests I have seen, in collections, all appeared much flatter than the above measurements indicate, but they were probably flattened in transit. All that I have seen seemed to consist entirely of very light, straw-colored grass rather lightly arranged. Some observers mention moss in the composition of the nest, but the nests are evidently made in the moss and not of it.

Dr. Paul Harrington mentions in his contributed notes four nests that he found near Sudbury, Ontario: "The nests were all similarly situated in a clump or mound of sphagnum, well arched so that to obtain a full view of the nest it was necessary to part the sphagnum, in shaded areas on the borders of black spruce bogs. These, and others I have examined, have always been constructed entirely of fine straw-colored grasses, whereas in those of the Nashville warbler a few hairs or gold-threads were generally incorporated in the structure."

Philipp and Bowdish (1919) record in a later paper the finding of a number of additional nests in New Brunswick, and say: "The experience of the past two years has demonstrated that while the boggy ground nesting, previously described, is the really typical and by far the most common form, not a few of these birds nest on higher and dryer ground. One such nest, found June 24, 1918, was well up on a steep hillside, in rather open woods, on fairly dry ground, utterly devoid of moss and grass cover. It was built among a thick growth of dwarf dogwood, and under a tiny, crooked stemmed maple sapling, very well concealed, and was rather more substantially built than the average nest of this species."

The nesting history of the Tennessee warbler would not be complete without mentioning two authentic records made in 1901. J. Parker Norris, Jr. (1902), reported receipt of a set of four eggs, collected by Major Allan Brooks on June 15, 1901, at Carpenter Mountain, Cariboo, British Columbia. This is apparently the first authentic set of eggs ever taken, as those mentioned above by Professor Cooke were taken a few days later. In this far western locality, the birds "generally frequented the clumps of aspen trees and Norway pines, where the ground was covered with a thick growth of dry pine grass." Major Brooks found several other nests in the same locality, and says in his notes: "The nests were always on the ground, sometimes at the foot of a small service berry bush or twig. They were all arched over by the dry pine grass of the preceding year, this year's growth having just well commenced."

The Fort Smith nests, referred to by Professor Cooke, were recorded by Edward A. Preble (1908) as follows:

Nests containing eggs were found by Alfred E. Preble on June 20 and 27, the eggs, five in number, being fresh in each instance. The first nest was embedded in the moss at the foot of a clump of dead willows near the edge of a dense spruce forest. It was rather slightly built of dead grass with a lining of the same material, and was protected from above by the overhanging bases of the willows, and by the strips of bark which had fallen from them, so that the nest could be seen only from the side. The second nest was more bulky, was composed outwardly of shreds of bark, coarse grass, and *Equisetum* stems, and was lined with fine grass. It was placed on the ground beneath a small fallen tree, in a clearing which had been swept by fire a year or two previously.

W. J. Brown, of Westmount, Quebec, tells me that he and L. M. Terrill in an hour found 16 nests of this warbler in a corner of a sphagnum bog, and, "there must have been about 100 pairs nesting in this ideal spot at the time."

*Eggs.*—The Tennessee warbler lays large sets of eggs, from four to seven, with sets of six common. Philipp and Bowdish (1919) state, "it appears that more full layings of six eggs are to be found than of five."

The eggs are ovate to short ovate and have only a slight luster. The ground color is white or creamy white, and the markings, in the form of speckles and small spots, are in shades of "chestnut" and "auburn," sometimes intermingled with "light vinaceous-drab." On some the markings are well scattered over the entire surface while on others they are concentrated at the large end, often forming a loose wreath. Only occasionally do the spots assume the proportions of blotches. The measurements of 50 eggs average 16.1 by 12.4 millimeters; the eggs showing the four extremes measure 17.8 by 12.7, 16.8 by 13.1, 14.8 by 12.3, and 15.8 by 11.4 millimeters (Harris).

*Young.*—Nothing seems to have been recorded on the period of incubation, which is performed by the female alone. Nor do we know anything about the care of the young or their development.

*Plumages.*—Dr. Dwight (1900) says that the young Tennessee warbler in juvenal plumage, in which the sexes are alike, is similar to the young Nashville warbler in similar plumage but lacks the brownish cast and has a faint transocular stripe. He describes it as "above dull grayish olive-green, the rump brighter. Wings and tail clove-brown, the primaries whitish edged, the secondaries, tertiaries and wing coverts greenish edged with two yellowish white wing bands. Below grayish buff rapidly fading when older to a greenish gray; abdomen and crissum pale straw-yellow. Trace of ducky transocular streak."

The incomplete postjuvenal molt, involving the contour plumage and the wing coverts, but not the rest of the wings or the tail, begins about the middle of July. This produces the first winter plumage, in which the young male is "above, bright olive-green, gray tinged on the pileum. Below, olive-yellow darker on the flanks, the abdomen and crissum white. Superciliary line and orbital ring buff. Transocular streak dull black." The young female "differs from the male in having the lower parts more washed with olive-green." Young and old birds are now practically indistinguishable.

Dickey and van Rossem (1938) say that the prenuptial molt "begins in late February and is not finished before about the middle of March. The molt involves most of the anterior body plumage, but progresses so slowly that this species never has the ragged 'pin-feathered' appearance so often seen in *Dendroica aestiva* at the spring molt." Dr. Dwight noticed the beginning of this molt as early as January 14. He says it "involves chiefly the head, chin and throat. The ashy gray cap is acquired, the chin, throat, and superciliary line become white, the throat is tinged with cream-buff and the transocular streak black. The yellow tints of the feathers retained below are lost by wear." In the female, this molt is less extensive than in the male, and "the crown never becomes, even in later plumages, as gray as that of the male, but always has a brown or greenish tinge."

Subsequent molts consist of a complete postnuptial in July and a partial prenuptial molt in late winter and early spring as in the young bird.

*Food.*—Bowdish and Philipp (1916) sent four stomachs of birds collected in June to the U. S. Biological Survey for analysis. One of these was empty. Of the other three, one contained 8 small caterpillars (Tortricidae), 35 percent; dipterous fragments, 23 percent; a small spider, 2 percent; and scalelike fragments (perhaps of some catkin), 40 percent. Another held a camponotid ant, 16 percent; at least 78 small caterpillars (Tortricidae), 75 percent; a snail (*Vitrea hammoides*), 4 percent; and unidentified vegetable fragments, 5 percent. The other contained 3 lampyrids (near *Podabrus*), 8 percent; a small coleopterous (?) larva, 3 percent; about 15 small caterpillars (as above), 25 percent; a neuropterous insect (apparently a caddis fly), 50 percent; 2 small spiders, 14 percent; and a trace of unidentified vegetable matter.

Several observers have complained that Tennessee warblers do considerable damage to grapes, and this is undoubtedly true. W. L. McAtee (1904), while investigating the damage done by this and the Cape May warbler, found that—

in the arbor under observation, which was a small one, scarcely a grape and not a cluster was missed. The damage, however, was inconsiderable as the birds did not commence to use their appropriated share of the crop until the owner had taken all he desired. * * * Both species were constantly busy catching insects on the vines, and on a walnut and some appletrees near by. Frequently, however, they dashed into the vines and thrust their bills quickly into a grape. Sometimes they withdrew them quickly; again they poked around in the interior of the grape a little, and always after these attacks, they lifted their heads as in drinking. This action suggested a reason for piercing the grapes, that I am satisfied is the true one, that is, the obtaining of liquid refreshment.

A supply of available drinking water for the birds, might help to protect the grapes. And, as the warblers feed on insects that seriously damage the grapevines, the good work they do may compensate for the grapes that they damage. The stomach of one Tennessee warbler examined by Mr. McAtee contained a *Typhlocyba comes*, an especial pest of the grape, a destructive jassid or leafhopper, 6 caterpillars which were doing all in their power to eat up the leaves remaining on the vines, 2 spiders, a bug (*Corizus*), a weevil, and one parasitic hymenopteron (the only insect that was not harmful).

S. A. Forbes (1883) found that a stomach taken from an orchard infested by canker-worms contained about 80 percent of these destructive larvae and about 20 per cent beetles. Professor Aughey (1878) observed these warblers catching young locusts in Nebraska. Clarence F. Smith adds, in some notes sent to me, that "in the fall, during migration time, Tennessee warblers often glean their food from dense patches of such weeds as sunflower, goldenrod, and ragweed," and that "sumac, poison ivy, and other berries are sometimes eaten in small quantity."

F. H. King (1883) has considerable to say about the damage done to Delaware and Catawba grapes in Wisconsin; as soon as they are wounded, they are attacked by ants, bees, and flies and soon destroyed. But he thinks the service rendered more than compensates for the harm done. He refers to the feeding habits of the Tennessee warbler as follows:

It is very dexterous in its movements, and obtains the greater part of its food upon and among the terminal foliage of trees. Titmouse-like, it often swings pendant from a leaf while it secures an insect which it has discovered. Small insects of various kinds, not especially attractive to larger birds, are destroyed by this species in large numbers; and its slender, acute bill serves it much better in picking up these forms than a heavier, more clumsy one could. * * * Of thirty-three specimens examined, two had eaten two very small hymenoptera (probably parasitic); seven, thirteen caterpillars; three, fifteen diptera; six, thirteen beetles; three, forty-two plant-lice, among which were two specimens of the corn plant-louse *Aphis maidis* (?); three, thirty-five small heteroptera, .09 of an inch long; and one, eleven insect eggs.

Alexander F. Skutch has sent me the following interesting notes on the feeding habits of the Tennessee warbler in Central America: "I was surprised to find last month [March] that these warblers were visiting my feeding shelf on the guava tree in the yard. About the only food I ever serve to the birds on this table is bananas and occasionally plantains; and my chief guests are tanagers of about half a dozen brilliant kinds, a few finches, honeycreepers, and wintering Baltimore orioles. But the Tennessee warblers soon formed the habit of visiting the table and sharing the food with the bigger resident birds.

Some seemed to linger in the vicinity much of the day, making frequent visits to the board and each time eating liberal portions of banana or the somewhat harder ripe plantain. They were intolerant of each other, and one individual would not let a second alight on the board until it had finished its own meal, although there was plenty of room and plenty of food for all. I have noticed also that the Tennessee warblers chase each other as they forage among the trees in wintering flocks. I cannot recall ever having seen any other wood warbler eat banana.

"Last November 14 a Tennessee warbler behaved most surprisingly. The grass in the yard had grown very long, and I had it cut with a machette. Late in the afternoon, after the usual rain, a lone Tennessee warbler flew down on the fallen grass and began to hop over it, catching small insects.

"It also entered the uncut grass, about a foot high, and disappeared momentarily amidst it. Twice driven up by passing people, each time it promptly returned to the grass. Its third visit to the cut grass was longest. While I stood quietly watching, it hopped deliberately about, much in the manner of a house wren, and gathered an abundant harvest from the fallen herbage. Once it found a caterpillar about an inch long, which it carefully bruised in its mandibles before swallowing it. The warbler was amazingly bold, and hopped over the grass within a yard of my feet, and allowed me to follow closely as it moved away. Early the following morning, and again at the close of the day, the warbler foraged over the lawn in the same fashion. In the evening, it continued to creep slowly over the mown grass and after all other birds had disappeared into their roosts, and the light was becoming too dim to see it clearly."

*Behavior.*—Much of the behavior of the Tennessee warbler has been mentioned above, and there is little more to be said. It is a very close sitter on its nest, when incubating, and has been caught there by throwing a hat or a net over it; but, when flushed, it is rather shy about returning to it, usually making its demonstrations of protest by flitting about at a safe distance and nervously uttering a sharp *chip*.

The Prebles (1908) witnessed a rather remarkable flight behavior at Fort Resolution, Mackenzie:

During the forenoon of June 25, an extremely windy day, we observed a remarkable movement of these warblers. They came from the northward, flying over the point of land on which the fort is built in loose flocks of from 10 to 20 individuals. After passing the point, they either struck out directly across the bay or skirted the shore, in either case having to face a strong southeast wind. Some paused a few moments among the low bushes on the point, but the slightest alarm started them off. The flight lasted over two hours, and, during this time, upward of 300 birds were seen from our camp. Two specimens, a male and a female, were collected. The ovaries of the female contained eggs only slightly developed.

*Voice.*—Aretas A. Saunders contributes the following: "The song of the Tennessee warbler is a rapid series of short, loud, unmusical notes. It has been compared to the song of the chipping sparrow, but it varies more in pitch, time, and loudness, and is distinctly in two or three parts. To my ear it is much more like the chippering of a chimney swift.

"In 35 records of this song, the number of notes varies from 9 to 25, the average being 17. Only one song has a true trill in it, that is, notes so rapid that they cannot be counted. Each song is of either two or three parts, each part composed of a series of notes on the same pitch and in uniform rhythm. The parts differ from each other in pitch, time, or loudness. In a number of songs, one of the parts is a repetition of 2-note phrases. Loudness generally increases to the end of the song, but sometimes the reverse is true. Some songs rise in pitch to the end and others fall; my records are about evenly divided in this matter. A typical three part song would be something like

*tit it it it it it it pita pita pita pita pita chit chit    chit    chit chit.*

"Pitch varies from G''' to E'''', or four and a half tones. Single songs vary from half a tone to three and a half tones, averaging one and a half. The length of songs varies from 1⅘ to 3⅕ seconds. An individual bird may sing a dozen different variations of the song in a short time. On the other hand, I have heard three birds in one tree singing alternately, the songs of all three being exactly alike so far as my ear could determine."

Francis H. Allen gives me his impression of the song as follows: "The song bears some resemblance to that of the Nashville warbler, but is easily distinguished. I have written it

*wi-chip wi-chip wi-chip wi-chip, wi-chip wi-chip chip chip chip chip chip chip chip.*

The higher notes in the middle sometimes appear to be monosyllables, and they are sometimes omitted. The series of *chips* at the end are very emphatic, and the last one is perhaps accented somewhat. All the notes are staccato."

Various other renderings of the song have appeared in print, but they all give the same impression of a variable, loud, striking song which, once learned, can be easily recognized. The bird is a very persistent singer rivaling the red-eyed vireo in this respect. Bowdish and Philipp (1916) write: "As a basis for estimating the frequency of song repetition, counts were kept on three singing birds for a period of 5 minutes each, with a result of 32, 36, and 22 songs, respectively, within the period. In one instance, a bird was observed to sing while on the wing, repeating the song twice in the course of a short flight." Albert R. Brand (1938) found the pitch of the Tennessee warbler's song to be well above the average, the approximate mean count being 6,600 vibrations per second, the highest note about 9,150 and the lowest 4,025; this compares with an approximate mean of 8,900 vibrations per second for the black-poll warbler, and about 4,000 for the average passerine song.

*Field marks.*—The Tennessee warbler has no prominent wing-bars and no very conspicuous field marks. It might be mistaken for one of the small vireos, but its bill is much more slender and acute. The male has a gray crown, a light line over the eye, and a dusky line through it; the upper parts are bright olive-green and the under parts grayish white. The female has a greener crown and more yellowish under parts. For more details, see the descriptions of plumages.

*Fall.*—The fall migration starts early in August, but is quite prolonged, many birds lingering in the northern States until early in October and in the southern States all through that month. During some seasons and at certain places the Tennessee warbler is exceedingly abundant, sometimes far outnumbering any other species, but it is very variable in its abundance.

Mr. Trautman (1940) says that at Buckeye Lake, Ohio, "during some years not more than 20 individuals could be recorded in a day in the southward migration, nor more than a 100 in the season. In other years the bird rivaled the Myrtle Warbler in numbers, and as many as 1,000 individuals could be seen in a day and several thousands during a migration. * * * Throughout the southward migration the species did not confine itself to the upper sections of the taller trees as in spring, but was found in almost equal numbers in smaller trees and brushy thickets, in bushes and saplings along fence rows, and in weedy fields."

Professor Cooke (1904) says of the fall migration route: "The principal line of migration is from the Mississippi Valley across the Gulf of Mexico to Mexico and Central America. The eastern part of this route probably extends from the southern end of the Alleghenies across northwestern Florida to the coast of Yucatan and Honduras." A. H. Howell (1932), however, gives several records for central and southern Florida, and says: "In autumn, Weston reports a large migration on October 26 and 27, 1925, when 31 birds were killed at the lighthouse near Pensacola on the two nights, and large numbers seen on the morning of October 26 in vacant lots in the city."

Dickey and van Rossem (1938) say of the migration in El Salvador:

During the fall migration of 1925, Tennessee warblers arrived in the vicinity of Divisadero on October 13. No advance guard, that is, individuals arriving ahead of the main flights, was observed in this case. On the above-mentioned date they were suddenly found to be present in numbers, and from then on were common in every lowland or foothill locality visited. In point of relative abundance this was by far the most common warbler (resident or migratory) throughout the coastal plain and in the foothills, but it was greatly outnumbered by *Dendroica virens* above 3,000 feet.

The manner of occurrence was usually as small flocks of six or eight or even twenty or more birds. These combined with several other species to make up larger flocks which worked ceaselessly through the crown foliage of low, semi-open woodland. However, many were found even in the tall, dense swamp forests along the coast and also in the oak woods on Mt. Cacaguatique.

*Winter.*—Dr. A. F. Skutch has contributed the following account: "The Tennessee warbler winters in Central America in vast numbers. Coming later than many other members of the family, the first individuals appear in mid-September; but the species is not abundant or widely distributed until October. During the year I passed on the Sierra de Tecpán in west-central Guatemala a single Tennessee warbler appeared in the garden of the house, at 8,500 feet, on November 7 and despite frosty nights lingered into December. On November 19, 1935, I saw one on the Volcán Irazú in Costa Rica at 9,200 feet—the highest point at which I have a record of the species. At the other extreme I found a few of these adaptable birds among the low trees on the arid coast of El Salvador in February and among the royal palms at Puerto Limón, on the humid coast of Costa Rica, in March. But Tennessee warblers are most abundant as winter residents at intermediate altitudes, chiefly between 2,000 and 6,000 feet above sea-level. From 3,000 to 5,000 feet they often seem to be the most abundant of all birds during the period of their sojourn. They travel in straggling flocks and form the nucleus of many of the mixed companies of small, arboreal birds. At times 'myriads' is the only term that seems apt to describe their multitudes.

"I think 'coffee warbler' would be a name far more appropriate than Tennessee warbler for this plainly attired little bird; it was merely a matter of chance that Alexander Wilson happened to discover the species in Tennessee rather than at some other point on its long route from Canada to Central America; but the warblers themselves manifest a distinct partiality to the coffee plantations. The open groves formed by the shade trees, whose crowns rarely touch each other, yet are never far apart, seem to afford just the degree of woodland density that they prefer. It matters not whether these trees are Grevilleas from Australia with finely divided foliage, or Ingas with large, coarse, compound leaves, or remnants of the original forest—a mixture of many kinds of trees with many types of foliage: from Guatemala to Costa Rica the Tennessee warblers swarm in the coffee plantations during the months of the northern winter and are often the most numerous birds of any species among the shade trees. Possibly they may at certain times and places be as multitudinous in the high forest as in the plantations. Although I have never found them so, the negative evidence must not be allowed to weigh too heavily, for such small, inconspicuous birds, devoid of bold recognition marks, are not easy to recognize among the tops of trees over a hundred feet high.

"Tennessee warblers are fond of flowers, especially the clustered heads of small florets of the Compositae and Mimosaceae, and of the introduced Grevillea that sometimes shades the coffee plantations. They probe the crowded flower clusters, perhaps seeking small insects lurking there rather than nectar. The white, clustered stamens of the Inga—the most generally used shade tree of the coffee plantations—are especially attractive to them. Local movements within their winter range appear to be controlled by the seasonal abundance of flowers. So, in the valley of the Río Buena Vista in southern Costa Rica, at an altitude of about 3,000 feet, I found Tennessee warblers very abundant during December and January. Here they flocked not only in the forest and among the shade trees of the little coffee groves, but also in great numbers through the second-growth thickets that filled so much of the valley, where at this season there was a profusion of bushy composites with yellow or white flower-heads, and of acacia-like shrubs (*Calliandra portoricensis*) with long, clustered, white stamens. But during February, the third dry month, the thickets became parched and flowered far more sparingly. Now the Tennessee warblers rapidly declined in numbers, and before the end of the month disappeared from the valley. During the following year, which in its early quarter was far wetter, a number remained through March, and a few well into April.

"Tennessee warblers pluck the tiny, white protein corpuscles from the brown, velvety bases of the long petioles of the great-leafed Cecropia trees, taking advantage of these dainty and apparently nutritious tid-bits when the usual Azteca ants fail to colonize the hollow stems; for only on trees free of ants does this ant-food accumulate in abundance.

"While the Tennessee warbler departs during February from some districts where it is common in midwinter, it remains until April in regions where the dry season is not severe. After the middle of April it is only rarely seen in Central America; and there appears to be no record of its occurrence in May."

### DISTRIBUTION

*Range.*—Canada to northern South America.

*Breeding range.*—The Tennessee warbler breeds **north** to southwestern Yukon (Burwash Landing and the Dezadiash River); southern Mackenzie (Mackenzie River below Fort Wrigley, lower

Grandin River, and Pike's Portage); northeastern Manitoba (Churchill and York Factory); central Quebec (Fort George, Lake Mistassini, and Mingan); and possibly southern Labrador (Hawkes Bay). East to southeastern Labrador (Hawkes Bay); central Newfoundland (Lamond and Gaff Topsail). South to central Newfoundland (Gaff Topsail); Nova Scotia (Wolfville); southern New Brunswick (Grand Manan); northern and central western Maine (Mount Katahdin, Livermore, and Lake Umbagog); north-central New Hampshire (Mount Washington); south-central Vermont (Rutland); possibly northwestern Massachusetts (Hancock); southern New York (Slide Mountain); southern Ontario (Ottawa, North Bay, and Biscotasing; probably occasionally farther south); west-central Michigan (Duck Lane); probably northern Wisconsin (Plum Lake); northern Minnesota (Tower, Cass Lake, and Warren); southwestern Manitoba (Margaret and Aweme); central Saskatchewan (Emma Lake; has been found in the breeding season at Indian Head, Old Wives Creek, and Maple Creek); southern Alberta (Flagstaff, Red Deer, and Banff); and south-central British Columbia (150 Mile House and Kimquit). West to western British Columbia (Kimquit, Hazelton, Telegraph Creek, and Atlin); and southwestern Yukon (Dezadiash River and Burwash Landing).

*Winter range.*—In winter the Tennessee warbler is found **north** to central Guatemala (Volcán de Santa María, Cobán, and Gualán). **East** to eastern Guatemala (Gualán); northeastern El Salvador (Mount Cacaguatique); eastern Nicaragua (Río Escondido); eastern Costa Rica (Puerto Limón); eastern Panamá (Barro Colorado and Permé); northern Colombia (Santa Marta region); and northern Venezuela (Caracas). **South** to northern Venezuela (Caracas and Mérida); and northwestern Colombia (Concordia). **West** to western Colombia (Concordia and Antioquia); Panamá (Paracaté); Costa Rica (El General and Liberia); El Salvador (Puerto de Triunfo); and Guatemala (Tecpán and Volcán de Santa María). It has also been found to the first of January (possibly delayed migration) at Knoxville (1936) and at Nashville (1935), Tenn.; and one wintered (1934-35) in Cameron County, Tex.

*Migration.*—Late dates of departure from the winter home are: Colombia—Miraflores, April 19. Costa Rica—San Isidro del General, April 30. El Salvador—San Salvador, April 25. Guatemala—Livingston, April 8. Chiapas—Tixtla Gutiérrez, May 8. Tamaulipas—Gómez Farías, April 27.

Early dates of spring arrival are: Cuba—Habana, April 8. Florida—Sandy Key, April 13. Georgia—Athens, April 13. District of Columbia—Washington, May 2. West Virginia—French Creek, April 20. Pennsylvania—McKeesport, April 27. New York— Corning, May 3. Massachusetts—Northampton, May 8. Maine—Waterville, May 11. New Brunswick—Petitcodiac, May 19. Quebec—Quebec, May 19. Louisiana—Avery Island, April 6. Arkansas—Winslow, April 8. Tennessee—Memphis, April 9. Kentucky—Bowling Green, April 19. Indiana—Bloomington, April 12. Ohio—Columbus, April 25. Michigan—Ann Arbor, April 21. Ontario—Ottawa, May 12. Missouri—Columbia, April 22. Iowa—Sigourney, April 25. Wisconsin—St. Croix Falls, April 25. Minnesota—Clarissa, April 30. Kansas—Winfield, April 19. Nebraska—Red Cloud, April 18. South Dakota—Vermillion, May 1. North Dakota—Fargo, May 1. Manitoba—Margaret, May 3. Colorado—Estes Park, May 14. Wyoming—Torrington, May 12. Montana—Great Falls, May 9. Alberta—Belvedere, May 1. British Columbia—Carpenter Mountain, Cariboo, May 15; Atlin, May 26.

Late dates of spring departure of transients are: Cuba—Habana, May 5. Florida—Fort Myers, May 15. Alabama—Melville, May 3. Georgia—Athens, May 7. North Carolina—Chapel Hill, May 3. Virginia—Falls Church, June 3. District of Columbia—Washington, June 3. Pennsylvania—Warren, May 30. New York—Rochester, June 6. Massachusetts—Beverly, June 3. Vermont—Wells River, June 5. Louisiana—Shreveport, May 15. Mississippi—Oxford, May 15. Arkansas—Delight, May 20. Tennessee—Nashville, May 21. Illinois—Lake Forest, June 3. Ohio—Toledo, June 5. Michigan—Houghton, June 7. Ontario—Toronto, June 7. Missouri—Columbia, May 31. Iowa—Sioux City, June 6. Wisconsin—Racine, June 4. Minnesota—St. Paul, June 1. Kansas—Lawrence, May 24. Nebraska—Omaha, May 28. South Dakota—Faulkton, June 5.

Late dates of fall departure are: British Columbia—Atlin, July 26; 16-mile Lake, Cariboo, August 28. Alberta—Glenevis, September 13. Montana—Fortine, September 11. Wyoming—Laramie, October 5. Saskatchewan—Wiseton, September 29. Manitoba—Aweme, October 3. North Dakota—Fargo, October 8. South Dakota—Arlington, October 8. Nebraska—Lincoln, October 14. Kansas—Lawrence, October 22. Oklahoma—Fort Sill, October 19. Minnesota—Hutchinson, October 11. Wisconsin—Madison, October 19. Iowa—National, October 17. Missouri—St. Louis, October 19. Michigan—Ann Arbor, October 30. Ontario—Port Dover, October 10. Ohio—Columbus, October 31. Illinois—Evanston, October 28. Tennessee—Nashville, October 23. Arkansas—Jonesboro, October 19. Louisiana—New Orleans, November 8. Mississippi—Gulfport, November 12. Quebec—Montreal, September 28. Vermont—Wells River, September 29. Massachusetts—Harvard, October 1. New York—Rhinebeck, October 14. Pennsylvania—Beaver, October 26. District of Columbia—Washington, October 22. North Carolina—Mount Mitchell, October 1.

Georgia—Dalton, October 30, Alabama—Birmingham, October 25. Florida—Pensacola, November 4. Cuba—Habana, November 10.

Early dates of fall arrival are: Wyoming—Laramie, August 28. South Dakota—Lennox, August 30. Kansas—Topeka, August 29. Wisconsin—Delavan, August 19. Illinois—Glen Ellyn, August 17. Missouri—Monteer, August 20. Ohio—Toledo, August 19. Tennessee—Knoxville, September 15. Arkansas—Hot Springs, September 19. Louisiana—Monroe, September 14. Mississippi—Gulfport, September 5. Vermont—Woodstock, August 22. Massachusetts—Lexington, August 11. Pennsylvania—Jeffersonville, August 27. District of Columbia—Washington, August 31. Virginia—Salem, August 23. North Carolina—Blowing Rock, September 1. Georgia—Atlanta, September 9. Alabama—Leighton, September 17. Florida—Fort Myers, September 20. Cuba—Habana, October 13. Guatemala—Huehuetenango, September 11. Nicaragua—Río Escondido, October 24. Costa Rica—San José, September 17. Panamá—New Culebra, October 24. Colombia—Santa Marta Region, October 14.

*Casual records.*—In 1898 an adult male of this species was found dead at Narssag, Greenland. In Bermuda one was seen on March 2, 1914, and it remained about six weeks.

*Egg dates.*—Alberta: 6 records, June 1 to 16.

New Brunswick: 82 records, June 10 to July 10; 46 records, June 17 to 26, indicating the height of the season.

Quebec: 30 records, June 8 to 29; 21 records, June 17 to 27.

## VERMIVORA CELATA CELATA (Say)

## EASTERN ORANGE-CROWNED WARBLER

### HABITS

The type race of the orange-crowned warbler makes its summer home in northwestern Canada and Alaska, from northern Manitoba to the Kowak River, migrating in the fall southeastward through the United States to its winter range in the southern Atlantic States and Gulf States, from South Carolina and Florida to Louisiana. It was discovered and named by Say (1823) early in May at Engineer Cantonment, on the Missouri River, while on its northward migration.

The main migration route is through the Mississippi Valley, northwestward in the spring and southeastward in the fall. It is very rare in spring in the northern Atlantic States, though there are a few records for even Rhode Island and Massachusetts, but there are many fall records for this region, some of them remarkably late. It seems to be rare at either season in Ohio; Milton B. Trautman (1940) gives only 10 records for Buckeye Lake, 5 in spring and 5 in fall. "Eight were noted in lowlands, within 10 feet of the ground, in dense tangles of blackberry bushes, rosebushes, or grapevines. The remaining 2, both fall birds, were in rather well-drained, brushy, and weedy fields."

Dr. E. W. Nelson (1887) says of its status in Alaska:

Throughout the wooded region of Northern Alaska, from the British boundary line west to the shores of Bering Sea, and from the Alaskan range of mountains north within the Arctic Circle as far as the tree-limit, this species is a rather common summer resident. It is known along the shores of Bering Sea and Kotzebue Sound mainly as an autumn migrant, as it straggles to the southward at the end of the breeding season. Wherever bushes occur along the northern coast of the Territory it is found at this season, and at Saint Michaels it was a common bird each summer from the last of July up to about the middle of August, after which it became rare and soon disappeared. I have never noted it on the sea-coast during the spring migration.

The Prebles (1908) found it well distributed and probably breeding throughout the Athabaska–Mackenzie region. MacFarlane (1908) found it breeding as far north as the Anderson River. Kennicott, according to Baird, Brewer, and Ridgway (1874), found it nesting about Great Slave Lake. And Ernest Thompson Seton (1891) reported it as a common summer resident and breeding near Carberry, Manitoba.

*Nesting.*—Herbert Brandt (1943) found two nests of the eastern orange-crowned warbler along the Yukon River in Alaska, about 20 miles up from the sea, on July 1, 1924. His first nest contained five eggs, advanced in incubation. The nest was near the bank of the river, "in a bush 18 inches from the ground. The nest was loosely made of coarse grass held together with bark strips, silvery plant down, and a few feathers, one of which was a mottled feather of the Northern Varied Thrush. Twenty feet away was another nest of the same species, which held three young just hatched and two pipped eggs.    *   *   *   The measurements of the two nests cited are: height, 2.25 to 3.00; outside diameter, 3.5; inside diameter, 1.75; and depth of cup, 1.50 to 1.75 inches."

MacFarlane's (1908) nests, found on the Anderson River, "held from four to six eggs each, and they were made of hay or grasses lined with deer hair, feathers and finer grasses, and were usually placed in a shallow cavity on the ground in the shade of a clump of dwarf willow or Labrador tea."

Baird, Brewer, and Ridgway (1874) write:

The nests of this species, seen by Mr. Kennicott, were uniformly on the ground, generally among clumps of low bushes, often in the side of a bank, and usually hidden by the dry leaves among which they were placed. He met with these nests in the middle of June in the vicinity of Great Slave Lake. They were large for the size of the bird, having an external diameter of four inches, and a height of two and a half, and appearing as if made of two or three distinct fabrics, one within the other, of nearly the same materials. The external portions of these nests were composed almost entirely of long, coarse strips of bark loosely interwoven with a few dry grasses and stems of plants. Within it is a more elaborately interwoven structure of finer dry grasses and mosses. These are softly and warmly lined with hair and fur of small animals.

E. A. Preble (1908) reported a nest found near Fort Resolution that "was placed among thick grass on a sloping bank, and was composed outwardly of grass and *Equisetum* stems, with a layer of finer grass and with an inner lining of hair."

Several nests have been reported from points farther south as being of this warbler, but these are probably all referable to the Rocky Mountain subspecies *Vermivora celata orestera.*

*Eggs.*—The orange-crowned warbler lays from 4 to 6 eggs to a set, probably most often 5. Dr. Brandt (1943) describes his Alaska eggs as follows: "The egg is short ovate in outline, the surface moderately glossy, and the shell delicate. The ground color is white and is prominent because the markings obscure but one-fifth of its area. These spots are very small, and are peppered over the broad end in an ill-defined wreath, while over the smaller two-thirds the egg is almost immaculate. In color the markings range from hydrangea red to ocher red; and underlying these are a few weak spots of deep dull lavender." Probably a series of the eggs would show all the variations shown in eggs of the other races. The measurements of 50 eggs, including those of the Rocky Mountain race, average 16.2 by 12.7 millimeters; the eggs showing the four extremes measure 18.3 by 13.2, 17.0 by 14.2, and 14.7 by 12.2 millimeters (Harris).

*Plumages.*—Dr. Dwight (1900) describes the juvenal plumage as "above, brownish olive-green. Wings and tail olive-brown, broadly edged with bright olive-green, the median and greater coverts tipped with buff. Below, greenish buff paler and yellower on abdomen and crissum. Lores and auriculars grayish buff."

The first winter plumage is acquired by a postjuvenal molt that involves the contour plumage and the wing coverts but not the rest of the wings or the tail. The sexes are alike in the juvenal plumage and much alike in all plumages, except that the female is always duller; in her first winter plumage the orange crown is lacking, and it is more or less suppressed and sometimes wholly lacking in subsequent plumages. Dr. Dwight (1900) describes the young male in first winter plumage as "above, bright olive-green, mostly concealed on the pileum and nape with pale mouse-gray edgings that blend into the green. The crown brownish orange concealed by greenish feather tips. Wing coverts broadly edged with dull olive-green, sometimes the greater coverts with faint whitish tips. Below, pale olive-yellow, grayish on the chin and sides of neck with very indistinct olive-gray streaking.

A dusky anteorbital spot. Lores, orbital ring and indistinct superciliary stripe mouse-gray."

The first nuptial plumage is acquired by a partial prenuptial molt, "which involves chiefly the anterior part of the head and the chin. A richer, half concealed, orange crown patch is acquired; the lores and adjacent parts become grayer, the anteorbital spot darker. Wear makes birds greener above and slightly yellower below. Young and old become practically indistinguishable."

Subsequent molts consist of a complete postnuptial molt in summer and a partial prenuptial molt in early spring, as described above. The adult winter plumage "differs chiefly from first winter dress in possessing a larger, more distinct crown patch," in the male, and more or less of it in the female. "The color below is uniform and paler."

*Food.*—Nothing seems to be known about the summer food of the orange-crowned warbler, but it probably does not differ greatly from that of the lutescent warbler, whose food has been more thoroughly studied. In winter, it probably eats a fair proportion of berries and other fruits, especially when it spends the winter somewhat farther north than insects are to be found in abundance. It has also been known to come to a feeding station and eat suet, peanut butter, and doughnuts. In summer, it is probably almost wholly insectivorous. I can find no evidence that it does any damage to grapes or other cultivated fruits on its fall migration.

*Voice.*—Ernest Thompson Seton (1891) says of an orange-crowned warbler that he shot in Manitoba on May 12, 1883: "It was flitting about with great activity among the poplar catkins, and, from time to time, uttering a loud song like '*chip-e chip-e chip-e chip-e chip-e.*' On May 14 I shot another Orange-crowned Warbler. Its song is much like that of the Chipping Sparrow, but more musical and in a higher key. The bird is extremely restless and lively, moving about continually among the topmost twigs of the trees and uttering its little ditty about once in every half minute."

Dr. Lynds Jones wrote to Dr. Chapman (1907): "The song is full and strong, not very high pitched, and ends abruptly on a rising scale. My note book renders it *chee chee chee chw' chw'.* The first three syllables rapidly uttered, the last two more slowly. One heard late in the season sang more nearly like Mr. Thompson's description: *chip-e, chip-e, chip-e, chip-e, chip-e,* but with the first vowel changed to *e,* thus eliminating what would appear to be a marked similarity to the song of Chippy. Even in this song the ending is retained."

Francis H. Allen tells me that this warbler "has a *chip* note suggesting that of the tree sparrow but sharper."

*Field marks.*—The orange-crowned warbler is a plain bird, with practically no white markings in wings or tail, clad in dusky olive-green, paler below, the underparts sometimes obscurely streaked with olive-gray. The brownish orange crown patch is usually not conspicuous, except in worn summer plumage, and lacking in young birds and some females.

*Fall.*—Orange-crowned warblers begin to leave northern Alaska in August. Dr. Nelson (1887) says that it is rare about St. Michael after the middle of the month, his latest date being August 24. The birds obtained at that season were mainly young of the year. "In fall this species frequents the vicinity of dwellings and native villages, where it searches the crevices of the fences and log houses for insects."

The southeastward migration through central Canada and the United States seems to be leisurely and quite prolonged, mainly in September and early October, but often continuing into November. In Massachusetts, there are numerous late fall records and some winter records. Horace W. Wright (1917) has published an extensive paper on this subject and has collected the following Massachusetts records: "Mr. Brewster's eleven records lie within the period of autumn from September 23 to November 28. There are three for September, namely, the 23rd and the 30th twice; none for October; and eight for November, namely, 7th, 9th, 10th, 17th, 20th–21st, 23rd–24th, 25th, and 28th. On two occasions two birds were present, November 9 and 28. My own records run later. The earliest is November 5, and the latest is January 23. They are November 5, 18, 20, 22, 28, 29, January 10, 19, 23." As Mr. Wright's records cover a period of 8 years ending with January 1916, they indicate that the orange-crowned warbler is not such a rare straggler in Massachusetts as is generally supposed, and may be looked for almost any year in late fall, or even winter. Mr. Forbush (1929) says of its occurrence there:

This warbler may be found almost anywhere in New England during the fall migration wherever there are trees and shrubbery. In my experience the bird has been either in the trees or in the tops of rather tall shrubs and never very high, but like other members of the genus, though it nests on the ground it is said to spend considerable time in the upper parts of trees. It seems fond of the edges of woodlands near water, but it also frequents open woods, orchards, fruit gardens and shade trees, where amid the foliage it is very seldom noticed by the ordinary observer. When approached it divides its attention between the observer and its insect prey, which it hunts assiduously in the manner of others of the genus. This warbler may be seen rarely in small companies, but more often singly or in company with a small group of warblers of other species.

Dr. Winsor M. Tyler contributes the following: "The orange-crowned warbler is a rare bird in New England, but we may look for it with some hope of success in the very late autumn, through November and even into December, during the soft, calm days of Indian Summer. As we walk along over the dead leaves, wet from last night's frost, watching for the bird in the shrubs by the roadside and in neglected pastures, almost the only sound is the ticking of the falling leaves as they hit against the branches; and mistiness is all about us. Several seasons may pass before we hear its sharp *chip*, which stands out clearly from the gentle voice of the late-lingering myrtle warblers, and see it flitting all alone among the twigs, or on the ground—a lonely, dark, obscure little bird, darker and more deliberate than the kinglets. It is strange that a *Vermivora* should linger here with winter so near at hand, but indeed there is evidence which leads us to believe that a few of these warblers may attempt to spend the winter in the southern part of this region, and should any one of them withstand the cold season, it may furnish, when it moves northwards towards its breeding ground, one of the exceedingly rare instances of the occurrence of the bird on the northern Atlantic coast in spring."

*Winter.*—The principal winter home of the orange-crowned warbler seems to be in the southern Atlantic and Gulf States. Of its occurrence in coastal South Carolina, Arthur T. Wayne (1910) writes:

My earliest date for its arrival is October 30, 1897, but it is never abundant until the middle of November, remaining until the second week in April. It is capable of enduring intense cold. I have seen numbers of these highly interesting birds near Charleston when the thermometer ranged as low as 8° above zero and it is always more active and hence oftener seen when the weather is cold and cloudy.

The Orange-crowned Warbler inhabits thickets of lavender and myrtle bushes as well as oak scrub, and its center of abundance is on the coast islands, the greater part of which is veritable jungle, in which it particularly delights. Its only note while it sojourns here is a *chip* or *cheep* which very closely resembles the note of the Field Sparrow in winter.

Dr. Chapman (1907) says: "During the winter I have found the Orange-crowned Warbler a not uncommon inhabitant of the live-oaks in middle Florida where its sharp *chip* soon becomes recognizable. In Mississippi, at this season, Allison (MS.) says that 'its favorite haunts are usually wooded yards or parks, where the evergreen live oak and magnolia can be found; I have seen it most commonly among the small trees on the border of rich mixed woods, above an undergrowth of switch cane. Coniferous trees it seems not to care for, though I have seen it in the cypress swamps.'"

### DISTRIBUTION

*Range.*—From Alaska and northern Canada to Guatemala.

*Breeding range.*—The orange-crowned warbler breeds **north** to northcentral Alaska (Kobuk River and Fort Yukon; a specimen has been collected near Point Barrow); northern and western Mackenzie (Fort McPherson, Fort Anderson, Lake Hardisty, and Hill Island Lake); northern Saskatchewan (near Sand Point, Lake Athabaska);

northeastern Manitoba (Churchill and York Factory) ; and casually to northwestern Quebec (Richmond Gulf). **East** to eastern and southern Manitoba (York Factory, Winnipeg, and Aweme) ; southwestern Saskatchewan (East End and the Cypress Hills) ; southeastern Alberta (Medicine Hat) ; western Montana (Great Falls, Belt, and Bozeman) ; northwestern and southeastern Wyoming (Yellowstone Park and Laramie) ; central Colorado (Denver, Colorado Springs, Wet Mountains, and Fort Garland) ; central New Mexico (Taos Mountains and Willis) ; and southwestern Texas (Guadalupe Mountains). **South** to southwestern Texas (Guadalupe Mountains) ; south-central New Mexico (Capitan Mountains) ; southeastern and northwestern Arizona (Tucson, Santa Catalina Mountains, and north rim of the Grand Canyon) ; southern Nevada (St. Thomas) ; and southern California (Panamint Mountains, San Bernardino Mountains, San Jacinto Mountains, Coronado Beach, and San Clemente Island). **West** to the Pacific coast of California (San Clemente and Santa Rosa Islands, Santa Barbara, San Francisco, and Eureka) ; Oregon (Coos Bay and Tillamook) ; Washington (Cape Disappointment, Stevens Prairie, and Neah Bay) ; British Columbia (Nootka Sound and the Queen Charlotte Islands) ; and Alaska (Sitka, Yakutat, Nushegak, Igiak Bay, St. Michael, and the Kobuk River).

The orange-crowned warbler has been recorded in migration in southern Quebec as far east as Metamek and may occasionally breed. There is a single breeding record for Minnesota at Cambridge.

*Winter range.*—The orange-crowned warbler winters **north** to northwestern Washington (Seattle) ; central California (Marysville, Bigtrees, Atwater, and Victorville) ; southern Nevada (near Searchlight) ; central and southeastern Arizona (Fort Verde, Phoenix, and Tucson) ; southern Texas (El Paso, Fort Clark, and Boerne) ; Louisiana (Monroe) ; rarely Tennessee (Memphis) ; central Georgia (Macon and Augusta) ; and southern South Carolina (Charleston). It has also occurred occasionally in winter as far north as Madison, Wis.; Ann Arbor, Mich.; Canandaigua, N. Y.; and Boston, Mass. **East** to South Carolina (Charleston) ; Georgia (Savannah) ; and Florida (Jacksonville, Coconut Grove, and Royal Palm Hammock). **South** to southern Florida (Royal Palm Hammock) ; the Gulf coast of Florida (Ozona, Wakulla Beach, and Pensacola) ; Mississippi (Biloxi) ; Louisiana (New Orleans) ; Texas (Rockport, Corpus Christi, and Brownsville) ; Tamaulipas (Altamira) ; Veracruz (Orizaba) ; and Guatemala (Chimuy and Tecpán). **West** to western Guatemala (Tecpán and Nenton) ; Guerrero (Chilpancingo and Coyuca) ; Colima (Manzillo) ; Jalisco (Mazatlán) ; Baja California (Cape San Lucas and Santa Margarita Island) ; the Pacific coast of California (San Clemente and Santa Cruz Islands, Santa Barbara,

San Francisco, and Eureka) ; western Oregon (Eugene) ; and northwestern Washington (Tacoma and Seattle).

The above ranges apply to the species as a whole, of which four subspecies or geographic races are recognized: the eastern orange-crowned warbler (*V. c. celata*) breeds from northern Alaska, northern Mackenzie and northern Manitoba south to central Alaska, northern Alberta, and Saskatchewan to southern Manitoba; the Rocky Mountain orange-crowned warbler (*V. c. orestera*) breeds from northern British Columbia, central Alberta, and southwestern Saskatchewan southward east of the Cascades and Sierra Nevadas; the lutescent orange-crowned warbler (*V. c. lutescens*) breeds in the Pacific coast region from Cook Inlet, Alaska, south to southern California and eastward in California to the west slope of the Sierra Nevadas; the dusky orange-crowned warbler (*V. c. sordida*) is resident on the southern coastal islands of California and locally on the adjacent mainland.

*Migration.*—The orange-crowned warbler is of rare occurrence in the northeastern United States where it is reported more often in fall than in spring.

Early dates of spring arrival are: Pennsylvania—Harrisburg, April 21.   New York—Rochester, April 27.   Tennessee—Memphis, April 5.   Kentucky—Bowling Green, April 23.   Ohio—Oberlin, April 14.   Michigan—Ann Arbor, April 26.   Ontario—Queensborough, April 26.   Missouri—Columbia, April 20.   Iowa—Sioux City, April 24.   Wisconsin—Madison, April 19.   Minnesota—Red Wing, April 19.   Kansas—Lake Quivira, April 18.   Nebraska—Fairbury, April 16.   South Dakota—Arlington, April 22.   North Dakota—Fargo, April 22.   Manitoba—Winnipeg, April 25.   Saskatchewan—East End, May 2.   Mackenzie—Simpson, May 21.   New Mexico—Carlisle, April 28.   Colorado—Colorado Springs, April 27.   Wyoming—Laramie, April 21.   Montana—Fortine, April 28.   Alberta—Glenevis, April 28.   Oregon—Portland, March 26.   Washington—Bellingham, March 2.   British Columbia—Courtney, March 24.   Yukon—Carcross, April 26.   Alaska—Ketchikan, April 26; Tanana Crossing, May 18.

Late dates of spring departure of migrants are: Florida—Pensacola, April 20.   Georgia—Atlanta, April 29.   South Carolina—Aiken, May 3.   North Carolina—Hendersonville, May 9.   West Virginia—Wheeling, May 12.   New York—Canandaigua, May 27.   Louisiana—New Orleans, April 3.   Mississippi—Biloxi, April 21.   Tennessee—Knoxville, April 25.   Ohio—Austinburg, May 30.   Ontario—Ottawa, May 28.   Missouri—St. Louis, May 8.   Iowa—Des Moines, June 6.   Wisconsin—Racine, May 24.   Michigan—Sault Ste. Marie, June 3.   Minnesota—Rochester, May 28.   Texas—Lytle, May 19.   Oklahoma—Copan, May 2.   Kansas—Onaga, May 22.   Nebraska—Neligh, May

13. South Dakota—Faulkton, June 1. North Dakota—Fargo, June 6.

Late dates of fall departure are: Alaska—Craig, September 24. British Columbia—Atlin, September 9; Okanagan Landing, October 23. Washington—Semiahmoo, October 8. Oregon—Prospect, October 8. Alberta—Glenevis, October 5. Montana—Fort Keogh, September 22. Wyoming—Laramie, October 25. Utah—St. George, October 12. New Mexico—Gallinas Mountains, October 9. Saskatchewan—East End, September 16. Manitoba—Aweme, October 14. North Dakota—Fargo, October 19. South Dakota—Aberdeen, October 14. Nebraska—Hastings, October 8. Kansas—Wichita, November 2. Oklahoma—Norman, October 19. Minnesota—Minneapolis, October 20. Wisconsin—Milwaukee, October 26. Iowa—Giard, October 19. Ontario—Kingston, October 6. Michigan—Ann Arbor, November 1. Ohio—Toledo, October 27. Illinois—La Grange, October 28. Tennessee—Dover, October 26. Massachusetts—Lynn, November 30. New York—Rochester, October 9. Pennsylvania—Harrisburg, November 19 (bird was banded).

Early dates of fall arrival are: North Dakota—Ryder, August 18. South Dakota—Faulkton, August 23. Nebraska—Hastings, September 16. Texas—Lytle, August 29. Minnesota—Lanesboro, August 3. Wisconsin—New London, August 24. Iowa—National, August 28. Michigan—Blaney, August 19. Illinois—Chicago, August 28. Ontario—Ottawa, September 7. Ohio—Columbus, September 9. Tennessee—Clarksville, October 16. Arkansas—Hot Springs, September 11. Louisiana—New Iberia, November 19. Mississippi—Saucier, October 12. Massachusetts—Concord, October 2. Pennsylvania—Erie, September 15. West Virginia—Bethany, October 20. Georgia—Athens, October 12. South Carolina—Frogmore, September 20. Florida—Key West, October 5.

*Banding.*—Two returns of banded orange-crowned warblers seem worth recording. One banded at Mellette, S. Dak., on September 21, 1939, was found, probably dead, on December 13, 1940 at Webster, Wis. Another banded at Eagle Rock, Calif., on April 3, 1940, was found dead, on June 21, 1940 at Wards Cove, Alaska.

*Casual record.*—An immature orange-crowned warbler was collected October 14, 1906, at Lichtenfels, Greenland.

*Egg dates.*—Alaska: 10 records, June 8 to July 2.

California: 71 records, April 3 to June 24; 36 records, April 20 to May 12, indicating the height of the season.

Washington: 17 records, April 25 to June 25; 9 records, May 13 to 24.

## ROCKY MOUNTAIN ORANGE-CROWNED WARBLER

### HABITS

Although recognized and described by Dr. Harry C. Oberholser (1905) over 45 years ago, this well-marked subspecies was not accepted by the Committee for addition to the A. O. U. Check-List until comparatively recently.

It is described as "similar to *Vermivora celata celata*, but larger and much more yellowish, both above and below." Dr. Oberholser (1905) adds the following remarks: "This new form has usually been included with *V. celata celata*, but breeding specimens recently obtained, principally from New Mexico and British Columbia, indicate its much closer relationship, in all respects except size, with the west coast forms. From *Vermivora celata lutescens* it may, however, readily be distinguished by its duller, less yellowish color, both above and below, and by its much greater size."

He gives its geographical range as: "Mountains of New Mexico, Arizona, and southeastern California to British Columbia; in migration to Minnesota and Pennsylvania, south to Texas, and Mexico to Lower California, Michoacan, Guerrero, and Puebla."

*Nesting.*—Stanley G. Jewett (1934) reports a nest within the range of this race, of which he writes:

On June 18, 1934, a nest of this species was found at 6,000 feet altitude on Hart Mountain, Lake County, Oregon. The location was a rather dense mixed grove of aspen, alder, willow, and yellow pine. The female was on the nest, which was placed on the ground well under a small leaning willow stump, about five inches in diameter, that had been cut off about a foot above the ground, leaving the stump leaning at an angle of about 45 degrees. Weeds had grown over the stump forming a loose canopy of vegetation which protected the nest and sitting bird from being easily seen. The nest was composed of coarse dry strips of willow bark, lined with porcupine hairs. It measured, inside, 50 mm. in width and 33 mm. in depth.

A nest and four eggs of this species, probably *orestera*, is in the Thayer collection in Cambridge; it was collected at Banff, Alberta, on June 9, 1902. The nest was said to be "in root of a shrub, a few inches above the ground". It is compactly made of the finest larch twigs, yellow birch bark, fine shreds of coarse weed stems, other fine plant fibers and fine grasses, fine strips of inner bark, and a little plant down; it is lined with finer pieces of the same materials and some black and white hairs. The outside diameter is about 3 inches, and the height about 2 inches; inside, it measures about 1¾ inches in diameter and 1¼ inches in depth. A set of three eggs in my collection was taken May 14, 1909, near Glacier National Park, Mont.; the nest was on the ground, concealed by grass on a hillside. The measurements of the eggs of this race, which are indistinguishable from those of other races of the species, are included in those of the type race.

### VERMIVORA CELATA LUTESCENS (Ridgway)

### LUTESCENT ORANGE-CROWNED WARBLER

#### HABITS

This brightly colored race of the orange-crowned warbler group is widely distributed during the breeding season along the Pacific coast regions from southern Alaska to southern California and migrates in the fall southward to Baja California, western Mexico, and Guatemala. It differs from typical *celata* in being more brightly olive-green above and distinctly yellow below; in strong light it seems to be a yellow rather than an olive bird.

Dr. Walter K. Fisher sent the following sketch of it in its California haunts to Dr. Chapman (1907) :

Chaparral hillsides and brushy open woods are the favorite haunts of the Lutescent Warbler. Its nest is built on or near the ground, usually in a bramble tangle or under a rooty bank, and the bird itself hunts near the ground, flitting here and there through the miniature jungle of wild lilacs, baccharis and hazel bushes. Its dull greenish color harmonizes with the dusty summer foliage of our California chaparral, and with the fallen leaves and tangle of stems that constitute its normal background. It impresses one chiefly by its lack of any distinctive markings, and the young of the year, particularly, approach that tint which has been facetiously called "museum color."

Ordinarily the crown-patch is invisible as the little fellow fidgets among the undergrowth, but at a distance of 3 feet Mr. W. L. Finley was able to distinguish it when the bird ruffled its feathers in alarm.

In May, 1911, while I was waiting in Seattle, Wash., to take ship to the Aleutian Islands with R. H. Beck and Dr. Alexander Wetmore, we were shown by Samuel F. Rathbun the haunts of the lutescent orange-crowned warbler around Seattle. He says that it is one of the more common warblers of the region and is widely distributed. It favors small deciduous growths in more or less open situations, with or without accompanying evergreens. "It is also partial to the edges of old clearings fringed with a deciduous growth." He says that it is an early migrant, arriving early in April or sometimes in the latter part of March, and departing in September.

On Mount Rainier, according to Taylor and Shaw (1927), it was—

fairly common in the Hudsonian Zone (4,500 feet to 6,500 feet) ; occurs also, but more rarely, in the Canadian Zone between 3,500 and 4,500 feet. * * * The lutescent warbler was commonly found in the mountain ash, huckleberry, azalea, and willow brush, principally in the open meadow country of the subalpine parks. Warm and sunny south-facing slopes were favorite places of resort, especially

after a period of cold or fog. Occasionally the bird was found in patches of
Sitka valerian; at other times in the lower branches of alpine firs. His summer
foraging seems for the most part to be done within 10 feet of the ground, though
in the fall, when migrating, he apparently takes to the tree tops.

*Nesting.*—On May 7, 1911, Samuel F. Rathbun took us over to
Mercer Island in Lake Washington. At that time, this interesting
island was heavily forested in some places with a virgin growth of
tall firs, in which we saw the sooty grouse and heard it hooting, later
finding its nest in an open clearing. While walking through another
open space among some scattered groups of small fir trees, Mr. Beck
flushed a lutescent warbler from her nest in a hummock covered with
the tangled fronds of dead brakes (*Pteridium aquilinum*). The nest
was so well concealed in the mass of dead ferns that we had difficulty in
finding it. It was made of dead grasses and leaves, deeply imbedded
in the moss of the hummock, and was lined with finer grasses and
hairs. It held four fresh eggs. Three days later, Dr. Wetmore took
a set of five fresh eggs at Redmond. This nest was located beside a
woodland path at the edge of a swamp; it was well hidden on the
ground, under a stick that was leaning against a log. It was made of
similar materials and was lined with white horsehair.

Mr. Rathbun mentions three nests (MS.), found in that same vicinity; one was well hidden under some fallen dead brakes; and the other
two were beautifully concealed in the centers of small huckleberry
bushes.

William L. Finley (1904b) records six Oregon nests. The first
"was tucked up under some dry ferns in the bank of a little hollow
where a tree had been uprooted. * * * The second nest was on a
hillside under a fir tree, placed on the ground in a tangle of grass and
briar." Another was "in a sloping bank just beside a woodland path.
A fourth nest was tucked under the overhanging grasses and leaves in
an old railroad cut." He found two nests in bushes above ground.
He saw a female carrying "food into the thick foliage of an arrow-
wood bush. A cluster of twigs often sprouts out near the upper end
of the branch and here, in the fall, the leaves collect in a thick bunch.
In one of these bunches, 3 feet from the ground, the warbler had tun-
neled out the dry leaves and snugly fitted in her nest making a dark
and well-protected home." He found another nest 2 feet up in a
bush, within a few yards of the ocean beach.

Henry W. Carriger, of Sonoma, Calif., (1899) mentions two more
elevated nests of the lutescent warbler. He writes:

On May 31, 1897, I found a nest of the Lutescent Warbler placed three feet
from the ground in a bunch of vines. * * * On May 3, 1899, * * * I
flushed a bird from a nest in an oak tree, and was surprised to see it was a
Lutescent Warbler. The nest was six feet from the ground and three feet from

the trunk of the tree. A horizontal limb branched out from the tree and a small branch stuck up from it for about eight inches, and over this was a great quantity of Spanish moss (*Ramalina retiformis*), which fell over the horizontal limb. The nest is quite bulky, composed of leaves, grass and bark strips, lined with hair and fine grass, and was partially supported by both limbs and the moss, which is all about it and which forms quite a cover for the eggs.

*Eggs.*—The lutescent warbler lays from 3 to 6 eggs to a set, probably most often 4. These are ovate or short ovate and are practically lusterless. The white or creamy white ground color is speckled, spotted or occasionally blotched with shades of reddish brown, such as "russet," "Mars brown," "chestnut," and "auburn," intermingled with underlying shades of "light brownish drab." The markings are usually concentrated at the large end, but some eggs are speckled more or less evenly over the entire surface. Small scrawls of blackish brown may be found on some of the more heavily marked types. The measurements of 50 eggs average 16.2 by 12.6 millimeters: the eggs showing the four extremes measure 17.7 by 12.8, 16.8 by 13.5, 14.7 by 12.2, and 15.9 by 11.1 millimeters (Harris).

*Young.*—We seem to have no information on incubation or on the care and development of the young.

*Plumages.*—The molts and plumages are evidently similar to those of the orange-crowned warbler, though the lutescent is, of course, decidedly more yellow in all plumages.

*Food.*—Prof. Beal (1907) examined the contents of the stomachs of 65 California specimens of this species.

Less than 9 percent of the food is vegetable matter, and is made up of 3 percent of fruit and rather more than 5 percent of various substances, such as leaf galls, seeds, and rubbish. Fruit was found in only a few stomachs, but the percentage in each was considerable; figs were the only variety identified. [Of the 91 percent animal matter,] Hemiptera are the largest item and amount to over 25 percent, mostly leaf-bugs, leaf-hoppers, plant-lice, and scales. Plant-lice were found in only one stomach and scales in 5, of which 3 contained the black olive species. Beetles amount to about 19 percent of the food, and with the exception of a few Coccinellidae are of harmful families, among which are a number of weevils. * * * Caterpillars are eaten rather irregularly, though they aggregate 24 percent for the year. Stomachs collected in several months contained none, while in others they amounted to more than half of the food. * * * Hymenoptera amount nearly to 15 percent, and are mostly small wasps, though some ants are eaten.

Other items were flies, less than 1 percent, and spiders, 7 percent. W. L. McAtee (1912) says that this is one of only two wood warblers known to prey upon codling moths. "The lutescent warbler shows a strong liking for the pupae, two taken in California in May having eaten 10 and 18 pupae, respectively."

*Behavior.*—Mrs. Wheelock (1904) writes thus of its feeding activities: "All day long he flits about through the oak trees, leaning away over the tips of the boughs to investigate a spray of leaves, or stretching up his pretty head to reach a blossom just above him; now clinging head downward underneath a spray, or hovering under the yellow tassels as a bee hovers beneath a flower."

*Voice.*—Samuel F. Rathbun (MS.) gives me his impression of the song of the lutescent warbler as follows: "Its song is a succession of trilling notes on a slightly rising then falling key, the latter more lightly given and faster.   There is an apparent ease in this song that is suggestive of airiness, and, although simple in construction, it is pleasing to hear and further bears the stamp of distinctiveness."

*Fall.*—The fall migration is southward to southern California, western Mexico, and Guatemala.   The movement is apparently leisurely and quite prolonged, for the earliest birds begin leaving western Washington in August and September, and Theed Pearse gives me two October dates for Vancouver Island, with his latest date November 1.   Taylor and Shaw (1927) write of the fall movement on Mount Rainier as follows:

The post-nuptial scatter movement was in full swing by the middle of August. At this time the lutescent warbler was often found in the same flocks with Shufeldt juncos, western golden-crowned kinglets, or chestnut-backed chickadees. It is not unlikely that there is some good reason for this flocking, aside from the companionship involved.   The warblers and the juncos, kinglets, or chickadees probably do not compete for food as would one warbler with another of the same species.   The individual warbler, attached to a flock of kinglets, let us say, may be the more surely guided to available food.   Then, too, differences in alertness of the two or more species concerned may afford greater protection to each than would be the case if they remained separate.

Robert Ridgway (1877) met with these warblers in large numbers in Nevada:

In the fall, the thickets and lower shrubbery along the streams, particularly those of the lower cañons, would fairly swarm with them during the early portion of the mornings, as they busily sought their food, in company with various insectivorous birds, especially the Black-capped Green Warbler (*Myiodioctes pusillus*) and Swainson's Vireo (*Vireosylvia swainsoni*).   At such times they uttered frequently their sharp note of chip.   The brightly-colored specimens representing *H. lutescens* were prevalent in the western depression of the Basin, but were not observed eastward of the upper portion of the Valley of the Humboldt, nor at any locality during the summer; and wherever found, were associated with individuals of the other form, which is the only one found breeding on the mountains.   It is therefore inferred that all these individuals were migrants from the northern Pacific Coast region and the Sierra Nevada, while those of *H. celata* proper were from the higher portions of the more eastern mountains, or from farther northward in the Rocky Mountain ranges, full-fledged young birds being numerous in the high aspen woods of the Wahsatch Mountains in July and August.

VERMIVORA CELATA SORDIDA (Townsend)

## DUSKY ORANGE-CROWNED WARBLER

PLATE 15

HABITS

The subspecific characters of this warbler, as given by the original describer, C. H. Townsend (1890), are: "Adult male: Entire plumage decidedly darker than *H. celata lutescens.* Feet and bill larger; wings slightly shorter. There is an appearance of grayness about the upper plumage, owing to a leaden tinge on ends of feathers. Throat and under parts slightly streaked."

The principal breeding range of the dusky warbler is on the Santa Barbara Islands off the coast of southern California, but it has also been known to breed in San Diego and probably breeds farther south in Baja California, and on the Todos Santos Islands, off that coast.

The dusky orange-crowned warbler was discovered by Dr. Townsend on San Clemente Island January 25, 1889, but it does not seem to be so common there as on some of the other islands. According to A. Brazier Howell (1917) it has been reported from all of the channel islands except San Nicholas, which is too barren for it; and its occurrence on Santa Barbara Island is doubtful, as this precipitous island is not suited for it. It is probably commonest on Santa Catalina Island, "in the darker canyons and on the wooded hillsides."

J. Stuart Rowley writes to me: "I found that the weekend nearest the 15th of April was the ideal time to hunt nests of this warblers on Catalina Island, and after much hiking about this island I finally located a little ravine, only about a mile or so out of the own of Avalon, where these warblers nested abundantly, due to the little trickle of surface water in the bottom of the ravine. Since most of the ravines here are dry, this one was 'made to order' and I enjoyed the chance to find many nests in the short time allotted to me. Around the middle of April this little ravine fairly trilled with the songs of many males, who were constantly pursuing trespassing individuals out of their nesting territories, only to return and continue their melodic songs."

*Nesting.*—Of its nesting habits, J. Stuart Rowley continues: "I have found dusky warblers nesting in every conceivable sort of place, ranging from those placed on the ground in the grass to those placed 15 feet up in toyon trees. The usual nesting site here seems to be in a small toyon bush, rather well concealed, but not over 2 to 3 feet from the ground; the nests are made of fibres and grasses and, although nicely cupped and lined, are rather bulky affairs externally for a warbler to build." Howell (1917) writes:

The usual nesting site of the Lutescent Warbler is on the ground, but I have never heard of *sordida* building in such a situation. On the smaller barren islands, such as the Coronados and Todos Santos (where it is common), they build in a bush or tangle of vines, a foot or so above the ground, and the nest is always mainly constructed of gray moss, where this is to be had, lined with a little fine grass. On the larger islands, where there are good-sized trees, the site chosen may be a thicket of vines several feet above the bed of a stream, a small shrub, say four feet up, or perhaps an oak as much as fifteen feet above the ground. In such case the nest is quite substantially made of leaves, twigs, bark, rootlets, and often a little sheep wool. Three or four eggs constitute a set, and at least two broods of young are raised each year.

A most unusual nesting site for a dusky warbler is described by Clinton G. Abbott (1926). It was—

a decorative fern basket inside a small lath house adjoining the home of Mrs. A. P. Johnson, Jr., at 2470 C Street, San Diego. * * * Her house is in one of the older residential sections of the city, known as Golden Hill. The homes here are large and surrounded by more or less extensive grounds, but the whole aspect is distinctly urban, with streets everywhere paved. Broadway, with double trolley tracks, is only one block away. The lath house, sixteen by twenty-four feet in size, was filled with a luxuriant growth of cultivated plants. A rectangular path within was marked at its corners by four wire fern baskets suspended about four feet from the ground. In one of these were the remains of the two previous years' nests, and in the basket diagonally opposite was the inhabited nest, which contained three eggs. Although the eggs were manifestly not fresh, there was no bird about and they seemed cool to my touch. I waited about for fully ten minutes and was beginning to fear that disaster had overtaken the home, when I heard a low, scolding note overhead. Then down from between the slats hopped the dainty little warbler, and, with no concern whatsoever, she took her place upon the eggs, although I was standing in full view close by. [The nest was] cosily placed in the moss at the base of the ferns.

We soon discovered that not only was the bird practically fearless in the ordinary sense, but that she would even allow us to touch her without leaving her nest. She would permit us to raise her from her eggs with no greater protest than a pecking at the intruding finger. If she was not sitting sufficiently broadside for a good photograph, it was possible to arrange her the way we wanted her! Sometimes, if our familiarity was beyond her patience, she would merely hop among the foliage behind the nest, wait there for a few minutes, and then nestle back on her eggs.

*Eggs.*—Three eggs seem to constitute the average set for the dusky warbler, with occasionally only two or as many as four. Mr. Rowley tells me that, out of at least two dozen nests examined, he found only two sets of four; one nest had only one newly hatched young, and two or three nests held two well-incubated eggs. The eggs are apparently indistinguishable from those of the mainland races. The measurements of 27 eggs average 17.0 by 13.2 millimeters; the eggs showing the four extremes measure 18.5 by 13.5, 17.6 by 14.0, and 16.0 by 12.7 millimeters.

*Winter.*—Many of the dusky warblers, perhaps most of them, desert the islands in the fall when they become dry and uninviting, for the winter spreading widely on the mainland as far north as the San Francisco Bay region and inland to Merced County. Dr. Joseph Grinnell (1898) says: "This subspecies appears in the vicinity of Pasadena in the oak regions and along the arroyos in large numbers during August, and even by the middle of July. Remains in diminishing numbers through the winter; the latest specimen noted in the spring was secured by me, Feb. 29 ('96)."

### VERMIVORA RUFICAPILLA RUFICAPILLA (Wilson)

### EASTERN NASHVILLE WARBLER

#### PLATES 16, 17

#### HABITS

Alexander Wilson discovered this species near Nashville, Tenn., and gave it the name Nashville warbler. Baird, Brewer, and Ridgway (1874) say of its early history: "For a long while our older naturalists regarded it as a very rare species, and knew nothing as to its habits or distribution. Wilson, who first met with it in 1811, never found more than three specimens, which he procured near Nashville, Tenn. Audubon only met with three or four, and these he obtained in Louisiana and Kentucky. These and a few others in Titian Peale's collection, supposed to have been obtained in Pennsylvania, were all he ever saw. Mr. Nuttall at first regarded it as very rare, and as a Southern species."

This is not strange when we stop to consider that this bird is more or less irregular in its occurrence, apparently fluctuating in numbers in different localities and perhaps choosing different routes of migration. Its record here in eastern Massachusetts illustrates this point. Thomas Nuttall never saw the bird while he lived in Cambridge, from 1825 to 1834. Dr. Samuel Cabot, who lived there from 1832 to 1836, told William Brewster (1906) that he was sure that it did not occur regularly in eastern Massachusetts at that time. According to Brewster:

Soon afterwards a few birds began to appear every season. They increased in numbers, gradually but steadily, until they had become so common that in 1842 he obtained ten specimens in the course of a single morning.

In 1868, and for some fifteen years later, I found Nashville Warblers breeding rather numerously in Waltham, Lexington, Arlington and Belmont, usually in dry and somewhat barren tracts sparsely covered with gray birches, oaks or red cedars, or with scattered pitch pines. A few birds continue to occupy certain of these stations, but in all of the towns just mentioned the Nashville Warbler is less common and decidedly less generally distributed in summer now than it was twenty-five or thirty years ago.

Forbush (1929) found it "more common in eastern Massachusetts in the latter quarter of the last century than it is today." And my own experience has been similar; prior to 1900 we used to consider the Nashville Warbler a common bird on migrations and even found it breeding in Bristol County in 1892; but we have seen very little of it since the turn of the century.

*Spring.*—From its winter home in Mexico and Central America, the eastern Nashville warbler seems to migrate mainly northeastward through Texas to the lower Mississippi Valley and then west of the Alleghenies to New England and northward up the central valleys. Some individuals apparently fly straight across the Gulf of Mexico, but it is very rare in Louisiana, for which Dr. Oberholser (1938) gives only three records. It seems to be very rare, or entirely unknown, in any of the southeastern States, east of Louisiana and south of Virginia, except in some of the mountains.

According to Dr. Chapman's (1907) tables, about 18 days elapse between the average date of the first arrival of the species in Missouri and that of its first appearance in Minnesota, and it seems to require exactly the same time to migrate from West Virginia to New Brunswick.

Dr. Dayton Stoner (1932) says of its migration through the Oneida Lake region, N. Y.:

The Nashville warbler here seems to prefer coppices along the edges of woodland such as young aspen and maple and elm thickets and other small growth that springs up in cut-over and burned-over areas. In such situations I have found it singing persistently in late May and the first few days in June. This warbler and the chestnut-sided are often found together. However, it does not confine its activities to thickets, for it not infrequently visits woodlands of tall elm, maple, beech and other deciduous trees, as well as mixed forest and the vegetation in door-yards. The flowering currant is in full bloom at the time this bird reaches the height of its abundance and I have seen it visiting such shrubbery during the first part of May.

In Massachusetts in May, according to Forbush (1929), "among its favorite haunts are the bushy edges of woodlands, whether along roads, railroads or streams, or about ponds, lakes, marshes, swamps or open fields. It may often be found among willows, alders, birches or poplars. Old neglected fields and pastures, with scattered growths of birches and bushes, are favorite feeding grounds, but the bird also visits orchards, gardens and shade trees, even in city parks. It may be found on dry lands where scattered pitch pines grow, and on moist lands with rank shrubbery."

W. E. Clyde Todd (1940) says of the migration in western Pennsylvania: "The Nashville Warbler appears during the flood tide of the warbler migration in both spring and fall and is sometimes inordinately abundant. * * *

Almost every spring there is a day or two of decided movement, when the species is very common and on occasion exceedingly abundant. On May 3, 1901, I witnessed a remarkable flight at Beaver. That morning the woods everywhere were full of Nashville warblers, to the exclusion of almost all other kinds. I counted a dozen in one tree. They kept mostly in the treetops and were singing very little."

These warblers are also sometimes abundant in Ohio, for Milton B. Trautman (1940) noted as many as 80 individuals on May 15, 1932, at Buckeye Lake.

*Nesting.*—The nesting haunts of the eastern Nashville warbler are quite varied, and habitats similar to some of those frequented on the spring migration seem to be suitable for breeding grounds. But the nest is always placed on the ground and generally is well hidden. Gerald Thayer wrote to Dr. Chapman (1907):

Birch Warbler would be a good name for this bird as it appears in the Monadnock region where it breeds abundantly. For here it is nowhere so common as in abandoned fields and mountain pastures half smothered by small gray birches. From the airy upper story of these low and often dense birch copses the Nashvilles sing; and among the club-mosses and ferns, and the hardhacks and other scrubby brushes at their bases and around their borders, the Nashvilles build their nests. But such is merely their most characteristic home. * * * Dark spruce woods they do not favor, nor big, mixed virgin timber; but even in these places, one is likely to find them wherever there is a little "oasis" of sunlight and smaller deciduous growth. They are fairly common among the scanty spruces, mountain ashes, and white birches of the rocky ridge of Mt. Monadnock, almost to the top—3,169 feet.

F. H. Kennard records in his notes two nests found near Lancaster, N. H. One was among some dead weeds on a mossy hummock in a pasture; the other was in a swamp, at the base of and under a clump of alders beside a path. Miss Cordelia J. Stanwood (1910), of Ellsworth, Maine, writes:

When a growth of evergreens—pine, fir, spruce and hemlock—is cut, it is succeeded by a growth of hard wood—gray, white and yellow birches, maple, poplar, beech, cherry and larch—and vice versa. As the woodland is cut in strips, there are always these growths in juxtaposition. Though the nest of the Nashville is always placed among the gray birches, the inevitable strip of evergreen woodland is near at hand, and a swale not far away.

The nest of the Nashville is sometimes placed in comparatively low ground (that is, compared with its immediate surroundings), in soft green moss under an apology for a shrub, again in the side of a knoll covered with bird wheat (hair-cap) moss, or at other times in an open space in the woodlands under a stump, or tent-like mass of grass, or a clump of gray birch saplings. Around the top is usually woven a rim of coarse, soft, green moss; sometimes dried boulder fern or bracken is added. The side coming against the stump or overhanging moss lacks this foundation. The nest is lined with fine hay, if it abounds in the neighborhood, or pine needles if they are nearer at hand. Sometimes both are used. The red fruit stems of bird wheat moss and rabbit's hair are often employed. One or two birds have preferred some black, hair-like vegetable fibre for lining matter, one bird, horse hair.

Ora W. Knight (1908) mentions a Maine nest that "was situated on the ground on an open wooded hillside at the foot of and between two small spruce trees, and was well imbedded in the moss. It measures in depth outside one and three-fourths inches, and inside one inch, the diameter outside was three and a quarter. * * * Nest building begins soon after the birds have arrived, and presumably the female does most of the work, while the male perches in a near by sapling and sings. * * * It takes from seven to nine days to build the nest, and on its completion an egg is laid each day until the set is completed. The eggs are usually laid between six and ten in the morning."

A nest found by Henry Mousley (1918) near Hatley, Quebec, "was located at the foot of a spirea bush on a little mound, well sunk into the surrounding hair-cap moss (*Polytrichum commune*) and dwarf cornel or bunchberry (*Cornus canadensis*) of which the mound was carpeted. It was entirely hidden from sight and would never have been found had I not flushed the female from her set of five eggs."

The only local nest of which we have any record was found by Owen Durfee (MS.) in Rehoboth, Mass., on June 2, 1892. It was only partially concealed among some very low bushes, grass, and other herbage near the foot of a small hill in neglected pasture land; the hill had a scattered growth of oak and beech saplings and had been tramped over by cattle.

Frank A. Pitelka (1940a) found the Nashville warbler breeding in northeastern Illinois in "oak-maple-hickory climax woodland with semi-dense undergrowth, * * * with the stream cutting it and a semi-swampy, sedge-grass area with willow thickets and scattered elms and ashes." In northern Michigan, he found it "in spruce and cedar bogs and in sandy woods of aspen, birch, and Norway pine."

Richard C. Harlow tells me that most of the nests he has found in New Brunswick, about 10, are very frail, but are lined with moose hair. He has found 7 nests in the mountains of Pennsylvania, where the normal lining is deer hair.

*Eggs.*—The first set of eggs for the Nashville warbler seems to be always either 4 or 5; reported sets of 3 are probably incomplete or late sets. The eggs are ovate or short ovate and are only slightly lustrous. They are white or creamy white, speckled with shades of reddish brown, such as "chestnut" and "auburn," mixed with "light brownish drab." On some eggs the markings are fairly evenly scattered over the entire surface, but usually they are concentrated and form a wreath at the large end. Occasionally eggs are more boldly marked with spots and small blotches or short scrawls; others are nearly immaculate. The measurements of 50 eggs average 15.7 by 12.1 millimeters; the eggs showing the four extremes measure 17.2 by 12.7, 16.4 by 13.0, 14.5 by 11.6, and 15.2 by 11.5 millimeters (Harris).

*Young.*—The period of incubation is said to be from 11 to 12 days, and probably the female does most of it, though Mr. Knight (1908) says: "One bird relieves the other on the nest and at times when the eggs are very near the hatching point I have seen the male bring insects to its mate on the nest. Possibly he may feed the female at earlier stages of incubation but I have not seen him do so. Both birds feed the young, giving them at first soft grubs and caterpillars, later on small beetles, flies and similar insects. * * * The young leave about the eleventh day after hatching."

For a further study of the nesting behavior of the Nashville warbler, the reader is referred, to an excellent paper on the subject by Louise de Kiriline Lawrence (1948).

*Plumages.*—Dr. Dwight (1900) calls the natal down "sepia-brown," and describes the juvenal plumage of the Nashville warbler as follows:

"Pileum hair-brown, back darker, olive tinged, and rump olive-green. Below, pale yellowish wood-brown, straw-yellow on abdomen and crissum. Wings and tail olive-brown broadly edged with bright olive-green, the median and greater coverts tipped with pale buff-yellow forming two wing bands. Lores and auriculars mouse-gray, the orbital ring pale buff."

The sexes are alike in juvenal plumage. A postjuvenal molt occurs in July and August that involves the contour plumage and the wing coverts but not the rest of the wings or the tail. This produces a first winter plumage in which young birds become practically indistinguishable from adults in many cases, but the chestnut crown patch is generally smaller and more veiled in the younger male and is often lacking in the young female.

Dr. Dwight (1900) says that the first nuptial plumage is "acquired by a partial prenuptial moult which involves chiefly the crown, sides of head and throat, but not the rest of the body plumage nor the wings and tail. The head becomes plumbeous gray, the edgings only half concealing the rich chestnut of the crown. The orbital ring is white and conspicuous. Wear is marked, bringing the gray of the nape into contrast with the greenish back, later exposing the chestnut of the crown."

A complete postnuptial molt in July and August produces the fully adult plumage. In fresh fall plumage the head is browner than in spring, the back is grayer, the crown patch is more veiled with gray tips, and the breast is tinged with brownish. The females are paler than the males, with less chestnut in the crown. Adults probably have a partial prenuptial molt similar to that of young birds.

*Food.*—Very little has been published on the food of the Nashville warbler. Knight (1908) says that "the food of the adults consists of beetles, larvae of various insects and the eggs of various insects. In fact they eat almost anything which they can glean in the insect line from the shrubbery and ground."

Forbush (1929) says: "As the bird ranges from the ground to the tree-tops it takes most of the insects that any warbler will eat, among them flies, young grasshoppers and locusts, leaf-hoppers and many plant-lice, caterpillars both hairless and hairy, among them the gipsy, brown-tail and tent caterpillar, most of which are taken when young and small; also small wood-boring beetles are eaten, and other small insects of many species. The bird appears to be almost wholly insectivorous."

*Behavior.*—The eastern Nashville warbler is an active, sprightly, restless member of an active family, ranging in its foraging mainly in the lower story of the open woodlands and more often in the low trees and shrubbery around the borders of the forest. When thus engaged it is not particularly shy and often seems quite unconscious of the presence of an observer. On migrations it seems to be sociably inclined and may be seen associated with the mixed flocks of warblers that are drifting through the tree tops. At these seasons it often visits our orchards and the shrubbery in our gardens, giving us a glimpse of green and gold among the blossoms and opening leaves.

J. W. Preston (1891) describes an interesting manner of foraging:

"One will fly to the foot of a fir tree or other conifer and begin an upward search, hopping energetically from branch to branch until the very highest point is reached, when the bird drops lightly down to the foot of another tree, much as does the Brown Creeper. When an insect is discovered the bird secures it by a sudden bound, and, should the object be not easily dislodged, *Helminthophila* sustains himself on flapping wings until his purpose is accomplished, which often requires several moments."

*Voice.*—Gerald Thayer gave Dr. Chapman (1907) a very good description of the songs and calls as follows:

The Nashville has at least two main perch-songs, and a flight-song, all subject to a good deal of variation. It belongs decidedly among the full-voiced Warblers. * * * Its commoner perch-song consists of a string of six or eight or more, lively, rapid notes, suddenly congested into a pleasant, rolling twitter, lower in key than the first part of the song, and about half as long. In the other perch-song, the notes of what correspond to the rolling twitter are separate and richer, and the second part of the song is longer and more noticeable than the first, whose notes are few and slurred, while the whole is more languidly delivered.

The differences are hard to describe intelligibly; but in reality they are pronounced and constant. The flight-song, a fairly common performance in late summer, is sung from the height of five to forty feet above the (usually low) tree-tops. It is like the commoner perch-songs, but more hurried, and slightly elaborated, often with a few *chippings* added, at both ends. Among the Nashville's calls a very small, dry *chip*, and a more metallic, louder *chip*, somewhat Water-Thrush-like, are noteworthy. It also *chippers* like a young Warbler or a Black-throated Green.

Miss Stanwood (1910a) writes:

One common song sounds like *'tsin, 'tsin, 'tsee*, another *sweeten, sweeten, 'tsee*, a third, *sillup, sillup, sillup, 'tsee-e-e-e-e*. At other times the bird sings but part of the song as *sweeten, sweet;* or *sweeten, 'tsee;* or *sweeta, sweeta, 'tsee;* or recombines them differently as *sweeten, sweeten, sweeten, 'tsee-e-e-e-e*. * * *

The song is loud, constant, and heard all over the locality, coming principally from the gray birches, but also from the maples, poplars, and evergreens. The bird sings from the tree-tops, but likewise from the middle branches, and I have seen it singing on the ground and just a few inches above it. My last record of its song in 1908 was made the 17th day of July, the first, May the 14th. Between these dates it sang well-nigh incessantly.

Knight (1908) says that, while the female is building the nest, "the male bird perches in a nearby sapling and sings leisurely *'pea-cie-pea-cie-hit-i-hit-i-hit.'*" Wilson (1832) thought that the "notes very much resembled the breaking of small dry twigs, or the striking of small pebbles of different sizes smartly against each other for six or seven times, and loud enough to be heard at the distance of thirty or forty yards." Rev. J. H. Langille (1884) writes: "The song of the Nashville Warbler is a composition, the first half of which is as nearly as possible like the thin but penetrating notes of the Black-and-white Creeping Warbler, while the last half is like the twitter of the Chipping Sparrow." He writes it in syllables as *"ke-tsee-ke-tsee-ke-tsee-chipe-ee-chip-ee-chip-ee-chip."*

The song has been said to resemble that of the chestnut-sided warbler, but the two are really quite distinct; the song of the latter does not end in a trill or in chipperings. It does, however, more closely resemble the song of the Tennessee warbler. Dr. Roberts (1936) heard the two singing at the same time and noted this difference: "The Nashville's song is an utterance of rather greater volume than that of the Tennessee and differs, also, in the fact that it has a short, rapidly weakening trill or slide, following a rather long and deliberate prelude of four or five notes; while the Tennessee has a brief prelude with a long finishing trill, increasing in loudness and intensity to an abrupt ending."

Aretas A. Saunders contributes the following study of the song: "The territory song of the Nashville warbler is in two parts, the first a series of 2-note phrases, and the second a series of rapid notes, commonly lower in pitch and just twice as fast as the notes of the first part; *pa tipa tipa tipa tipa titititititit*. In 26 of my 29 records the second part of the song is lower than the first. In the other three it is higher. "The pitch of songs varies from G ′′′ to F sharp ′′′′, or five and a half tones. Single songs rarely vary more than one and a half or two tones. They are from 1⅔ to 2 seconds in length. The quality is rather musical, and some individuals have almost as sweet a tone as the yellow warbler. In my experience field students often confuse the songs of these two species.

"The nesting song may be heard commonly on the breeding grounds. I have several records from the Adirondacks. This song is in three or four parts, each part of three or four notes, and a little lower in pitch than the preceeding part. Two-note phrases are not commonly heard in the nesting song."

Francis H. Allen's rendering of the song is not very different from the first one of Mr. Saunders', though he noted some variation, and mentions in his notes an aberrant song, which "doubled the common song, which in this case had a first part consisting of only a single phrase, thus; *chip-ee*–(trill) *chip-ee*–(trill)."

*Field marks.*—The gray head, white eye ring, olive-green back, bright yellow under parts, and the absence of wing bars, with no white in the tail, are the distinguishing marks of the eastern Nashville warbler. The Connecticut warbler has a white eye ring but it has a gray throat, whereas the Nashville is bright yellow from chin to abdomen. The chestnut crown patch is not very conspicuous in the male and is less so, or entirely lacking, in the female; the female is duller yellow below and browner above than the male.

*Enemies.*—Like other ground-nesting birds, this warbler has the usual four-footed enemies to contend with, but its nest is quite well hidden. Perhaps its worst bird enemy is the cowbird, although Friedmann (1934) listed it as an uncommon victim of this parasite and had only six records of it, the nests containing from one to two eggs of the cowbird.

*Fall.*—As soon as the molting season is over and the young birds are freshly clad in their winter dress the migration begins in Massachusetts. This takes place in August, and the last stragglers may be seen passing through in early October.

In Ohio, according to Mr. Trautman (1940), the first migrants are seen about the first of September, the peak of the migration coming during the latter half of that month when from 10 to 100 could be found in a day, and after the 10th of October only an occasional bird remains. He writes: "As with many other transient warblers the southward migration of the Nashville Warbler covered a greater period of time than did the spring movement, which usually lasted less than 30 days, whereas the fall movement generally extended more than 45 days. * * * In spring the species frequented the upper half of large trees and was more numerous in tall trees of woodlands than it was in smaller groups or rows of tall trees. In fall the species tended to inhabit the middle section of large trees, and it also resorted to the taller bushes and saplings, especially the larger hawthorn trees."

The fall migration route is apparently a reversal of the spring route southwestward into Mexico and Central America where it spends the winter.

*Winter.*—The Nashville warbler is evidently very common in winter in certain parts of Mexico, for Dr. C. William Beebe (1905) says: "At times there were twenty and thirty in sight at once near our camp in the Colima lowlands." These may have been the western race.

### DISTRIBUTION

*Range.*—Southern Canada to Guatemala.

*Breeding range.*—The eastern Nashville and the western Nashville (formerly the Calaveras) warblers breed **north** to southern British Columbia (Tahsis Canal and Beaver Creek, Vancouver Island; Pemberton, Lillooet, and Revelstoke); northern Idaho (Clark Fork); northwestern Montana (Fortine); east-central Saskatchewan (Cumberland House); southern Manitoba (Duck Mountain, Lake St. Martin, and Hillside Beach); central Ontario (Casummit Lake, Lake Nipigon, and Lake Abitibi); and southern Quebec (Lake Baskatong, Quebec, Kamouraska, Mingan, and Natashquan River). **East** to southeastern Quebec (Natashquan River and the Magdalen Islands); and Nova Scotia (Baddeck, Halifax, and Barrington). **South** to Nova Scotia (Barrington); Maine (Ellsworth and Bath); northeastern Massachusetts (Haverhill and Beverly); southern Connecticut (Norwich); northern New Jersey (Moe and Beaufort Mountain); northeastern Pennsylvania (Dingman's Ferry, Mount Riga, and Highland Falls); northern West Virginia (Stony River Dam, Canaan Mountain, and Cranesville Swamp); northeastern Ohio (Pymatuming Lake); southern Michigan (Ann Arbor); northeastern Illinois (Deerfield); southern Wisconsin (Lake Koshkonong); central Minnesota (Onamia and Detroit Lakes); reported to breed in northeastern Nebraska but no specific records; northwestern South Dakota (Cave Hills); northern Idaho (Falcon); northwestern Oregon (Powder River Mountains, probably); probably western Nevada (Lake Tahoe); and south-central California (Greenhorn Mountains). **West** to central and western California (Greenhorn Mountains, Paicines, and Yreka); western Oregon (Pinehurst, Gold Hill, Depoe Bay, and Portland); western Washington (Mount Adams, Tacoma, and Blaine); and southwestern British Columbia (Friendly Cove and Tahsis Canal).

There are several records of the occurrence of this species in spring migration in southern Saskatchewan (Regina, East End, and Maple Creek); and in fall at Lake Kimawan, Alberta, west of Lesser Slave Lake. These records imply the existence of a breeding range north of any yet discovered.

*Winter range.*—The Nashville warbler and races are found in winter **north** to central Durango (Chacala); western Nuevo León (Monterrey) and southern Texas (Somerset and Matagorda County). **East** to southern Texas (Matagorda County, Rio Hondo, and Brownsville); eastern Puebla (Metlatoyuca); western Veracruz (Jalapa); Chiapas (Chicharras); and central Guatemala (Barillos, Panajachel, and San Lucas). **South** to Guatemala. **West** to western Guatemala (San Lucas and Sacapulas); Oaxaca (Tehuantepec); Guerrero (Acapulco); Colima (Manzanillo); and Durango (Durango and Chacla).

The Nashville warbler has been recorded as wintering occasionally in southern Florida, but in view of the extreme rarity of the species in southeastern United States it seems best to consider the record hypothetical until specimens are collected.

Like other species that winter regularly in the Tropics, the Nashville warbler can resist low temperatures as long as food is available. Evidence of this is seen in the daily presence of one in a garden in New York City from December 16, 1918, to January 9, 1919 (perhaps longer). Another was noted almost daily from January 1 to March 1, 1938, at a feeding table in Arlington, Va. The latter bird was caught and brought to the U. S. Biological Survey for confirmation of the identification, and was banded. On January 31, 1890, a specimen was picked up in Swampscott, Massachusetts, that had apparently been killed by a shrike about two weeks before.

The ranges as outlined apply to the entire species which includes two geographic races; the eastern Nashville warbler (*V. r. ruficapilla*) breeds from eastern Saskatchewan and Nebraska eastward; and the western Nashville warbler (*V. r. ridgwayi*) breeds west of the Rocky Mountains.

*Migration.*—Some early dates of spring arrival are: West Virginia—French Creek, April 23. District of Columbia—Washington, April 20. Pennsylvania—Beaver, April 25. New York—Canandaigua, April 25. Massachusetts—Taunton, April 24. Vermont—Rutland, April 27. Maine—Presque Isle, May 2. Quebec—Kamouraska, May 2. New Brunswick—Scotch Lake, May 8. Mississippi—Rosedale, April 26. Tennessee—Memphis, April 16. Kentucky—Bardstown, April 28. Indiana—Indianapolis, April 24. Ohio—Oberlin, April 19. Michigan—Ann Arbor, April 25. Ontario—Toronto, April 29. Texas—San Antonio, March 27. Arkansas—Delight, April 14. Missouri—St. Louis, April 21. Iowa—Davenport, April 26. Illinois—Chicago, April 25. Wisconsin—Madison, April 25. Minnesota—Red Wing, April 29. Manitoba—Winnipeg, May 2. Arizona—Tucson, April 6. Montana—Missoula, April 25. Idaho—Coeur d'Alene, April 29. California—Buena Park, March 3. Oregon—Prospect,

April 20. Washington—Tacoma, April 23. British Columbia—
Okanagan Landing, April 21.
Late dates of spring departure are: West Virginia—Wheeling, May
24. District of Columbia—Washington, May 20. Pennsylvania—
Jeffersonville, May 20. Mississippi—Rosedale, May 6. Tennessee—
Nashville, May 19. Kentucky—Bowling Green, May 19. Indiana—
Richmond, June 1. Texas—Ingram, May 10. Arkansas—Monticello,
May 9. Missouri—Columbia, May 28. Iowa—Grinnell, June 2.
Illinois—Rockford, May 30. Kansas—Lake Quivira, May 21. Ne-
braska—Red Cloud, May 24. South Dakota—June 1. Arizona—
Otero Canyon, Baboquivari Mountains, April 29. California—Cabe-
zon, May 7.

Late dates of fall departure are: British Columbia—Okanagan
Landing, September 13. Washington—Port Chehalis, October 11.
California—Los Angeles, October 8. Idaho—Bayview, September
12. Montana—Bozeman, September 12. Arizona—Fort Verde, Sep-
tember 28. Manitoba—Shoal Lake, September 26. North Dakota—
Fargo, October 15. South Dakota—Mellette, October 4. Nebraska—
Blue Springs, October 1. Kansas—Lawrence, October 8. Minne-
sota—St. Paul, October 25. Wisconsin—Racine, October 6; Madison,
November 1. Iowa—Marshalltown, October 14. Missouri—Colum-
bia, October 19. Arkansas—Winslow, October 14. Texas—Cove, No-
vember 15. Ontario—Ottawa, October 7. Michigan—Sault Ste.
Marie, October 7. Illinois—Springfield, October 2. Ohio—Toledo,
October 29. Kentucky—Lexington, October 16. Tennessee—Mem-
phis, October 3. Mississippi—Deer Island, October 16. Quebec—
Hatley, October 18. Maine—Portland, October 13. New Hampshire,
Center Ossipee, October 23. Massachusetts—Danvers, October 12.
New York—New York, October 17. Pennsylvania—Philadelphia,
October 17. District of Columbia—Washington, October 14. West
Virginia—Bluefield, October 19.

Early dates of fall arrival are: California—Los Angeles, August 9.
Arizona—Patagonia, August 8. North Dakota—Rice Lake, August
18. South Dakota—Yankton, August 2. Kansas—Lake Quivira,
August 31. Iowa—Iowa City, August 18. Missouri—Montier, August 8. Arkansas—Winslow, September 8. Texas—Rockport, September 1. Illinois—Glen Ellyn, August 16. Indiana—Bloomington,
August 26. Ohio—Cleveland, August 2. Kentucky—Versailles, August 13. Tennessee—Marysville, September 1. Massachusetts—
Martha's Vineyard, August 17. New York—Rhinebeck, August 13.
Pennsylvania—Pittsburgh, August 28. District of Columbia—Washington, September 5. West Virginia—French Creek, September 7.

The Nashville warbler is a rare species in the lower Mississippi Valley; there are only three records for Louisiana; and it is almost unknown in the Atlantic States south of the Chesapeake Bay.

*Casual records.*—Four specimens have been collected in Greenland: One at Godthaab, about 1835; two at Fiskenaes, October 10, 1823, and August 31, 1840; and one marked "West Greenland," between 1890 and 1899. The three latter were all immature birds. A specimen was collected in Bermuda on September 16, 1907.

*Egg dates.*—Maine: 27 records, May 8 to August 7; 15 records, May 27 to June 14, indicating the height of the season.

Minnesota: 11 records, May 7 to June 15.

Quebec: 32 records, May 28 to July 4; 18 records, June 19 to 29.

California: 23 records, May 17 to July 30; 12 records, May 21 to June 5 (Harris).

## VERMIVORA RUFICAPILLA RIDGWAYI van Rossem

### WESTERN NASHVILLE WARBLER

#### HABITS

This western form of our well-known eastern Nashville warbler, often called the Calaveras warbler, was discovered by Robert Ridgway in the East Humboldt Mountains, Nev., on September 6, 1868, and given the subspecific name *gutturalis*. He (1902) describes it as similar to the eastern bird, "but olive-green of rump and upper tail-coverts brighter, more yellowish, yellow of under parts brighter, lower abdomen more extensively whitish, and greater wing-coverts lighter, more yellowish olive-green." He gives as its range: "Western United States, breeding on high mountains, from the Sierra Nevada (Calaveras Co., California) to British Columbia (Vernon, Nelson, Okanogan district, etc.), eastward to eastern Oregon (Fort Klamath), northern Idaho (Fort Sherman), etc.; southward during migration to extremity of Lower California, and over western and northern Mexico, and southeastward to Texas (San Antonio; Tom Green County; Concho County)." The 1931 A. O. U. Check-List says that this form winters "in Mexico south to Puebla, Oaxaca, Guerrero, Jalisco, and Colima."

Dr. Walter K. Fisher wrote to Dr. Chapman (1907): "The Calaveras Warbler is a characteristic denizen of the chaparral and is found on both slopes of the Sierra Nevadas about as far south as Mt. Whitney. It frequents the belts of the yellow, sugar, and Jeffrey pines, and ranges up into the red fir zone. During the height of the nesting season one may see them flitting about among thickets of manzanita, wild cherry, huckleberry, oak and buck brush, almost always in song; and while the female is assiduously hunting among the dense cover of bushes, the male is often singing in a pine or fir, far above mundane cares. * * * I have observed this Warbler at lower altitudes on the west slope among small black oaks, in company with Hermit Warblers."

Dr. Wilfred H. Osgood (1896) first saw it in the Sierras at 3,500 feet elevation, but more commonly at 3,700 feet. "At 5,000 feet we found them most common, and from 7,000 to 9,000 feet they gradually disappeared, apparently going as high up as the black oak, in which trees they were generally seen, skipping about in search of insects."

Grinnell and Storer (1924) say: "The Calaveras Warbler is common during the summer months in the black oaks and maples along each side of the Yosemite Valley and in similar situations elsewere on the western flank of the Sierra Nevada. Among all the warblers to be seen in the Yosemite Valley during the summer months the present species is the only one which does not forage and nest in the same niche. The Calaveras seeks its food and does its singing well up in trees, but places its nest immediately upon the ground."

C. W. and J. H. Bowles (1906) write of its haunts in Washington:

Like the hermit warbler, a bird of the higher altitudes in the mountains of California, the Calaveras warbler, on reaching the cooler climate of the northwest, is to be found as a rule only on the driest prairies. Here the birds frequent the scattered clumps of young oaks and fir trees that have reached a height of some three or four feet, and which border the large tracts of dense fir timber. It is a noteworthy fact that, while these birds are not often to be found more than a hundred yards outside of the forests, they are seldom or never seen inside of the dividing line where the heavy timber meets the prairie. Also they do not encroach upon the hillside territory of the lutescent warbler, which bird in turn does not appear on the prairies but confines itself to the brush-covered uplands.

*Nesting.*—Dr. Osgood (1896) found three nests of the western Nashville, or Calaveras, warbler near Fyffe in the Sierras; two of these were concealed under dead leaves, one of which was partially concealed by a little sprig of cedar at the foot of a cedar stump, and the other was under a little tuft of "mountain misery"; the third was in a thick patch of "mountain misery" and was "well embedded among the roots of this little shrub, and shaded by its thick leaves."

In the Yosemite Valley, Grinnell and Storer (1924) found a nest in what must be an unusual situation:

The location was only about 75 feet from the much traveled south road on the Valley floor and at the base of the talus pile of huge boulders. The nest was in the face of one of the larger of these boulders, partly in a diagonal fissure. It was on the north side of the rock and so never received any direct rays of sunlight. The whole face of the boulder was covered densely with yellow-green moss which in places was overlaid by olive-gray lichens. The nest was 43 inches from the base of the rock and about 60 inches from the top. Another nest was found in a hollow of the ground at the base of an azalea bush, near an old road along the hillside. The creek itself was about 50 feet distant. This nest was 3 inches across the outside and about 2 inches high, the cavity being 1¼ inches deep. Strips of bark of the incense cedar, plant fibers, and horsehair comprised the building material.

The Bowles brothers (1906) say that the nests are very much like those of the eastern Nashville warbler, as taken by them in Massachusetts. In Washington, "the site chosen is usually at the base of a very young oak, or fir, tho on one occasion we found one built under some blackberry vines at the base of a large fir stub. The nests are sunk well into the ground or moss, and are so well concealed as to defy discovery unless one flushes the bird."

*Eggs.*—The eggs of the western Nashville warbler are practically indistinguishable from those of the eastern form. The measurements of 40 eggs average 15.3 by 12.2 millimeters; the eggs showing the four extremes measure **16.6** by **13.2, 14.3** by 11.9, and 16.0 by **11.5** millimeters (Harris).

We have no information on the incubation of the eggs or care of the young. The changes in plumage parallel those of the eastern bird. Very little seems to be known about the exact food of the Calaveras warbler, and its voice seems to be the same as that of the Nashville, but the following accounts of its habits seem worth quoting. Grinnell and Storer (1924) write:

> The forage range of this warbler lies chiefly in trees other than conifers. Such trees as the black oak and big-leafed maple renew their foliage every spring and the Calaveras Warblers find excellent forage in the insects and larvae which feed upon this tender new leafage during the spring and summer months. Less often these birds may be found in golden oaks and occasionally in Douglas spruces. They usually forage 25 to 40 feet above the ground, keeping within the stratum of new foliage, but they have been seen as low as 10 feet and as high as 70 feet above the earth. When within the foliage their yellow and green coloration makes it difficult to locate them, especially as the birds do not move about as rapidly as some of the other warblers. At times a Calaveras Warbler will poise on rapidly beating wings to capture some insect otherwise out of reach.

Dr. J. C. Merrill (1888) calls them "restless, shy, and very difficult to shoot, and says further, "When alarmed, as they very easily are, the males move rapidly through the trees, often flying a hundred yards or more at once, and were it not that their constant song indicates their movements, it would be impossible to follow them. I have frequently followed one for half an hour or more before I could even catch a glimpse of it, and my pursuit of any particular one was more often unsuccessful than the reverse. * * * I have never found a land bird more wary and difficult to shoot. But as soon as the young leave the nest this extreme shyness disappears, and the parents are readily approached and observed as they busily search for food for their young family."

Dr. William T. Shaw, who collected a specimen of this warbler in northwestern Washington, says in his notes: "This warbler, a singing male, was noticeably a percher upon high, isolated cedar poles when singing, having three or four favorite ones in his territory, which was a hillside grown to a height of about 15 feet with second-growth deciduous trees, following fire. He sang from a height of from 30 to 40 feet up near the top of these old widely-scattered, fire-blasted, weather-bleached trees, clearly out in the open and isolated from green sheltering foliage beneath him, in such a location as one is accustomed to seeing lazuli buntings perch when they sing." Dr. Shaw thought the first part of the song suggested that of Macgillivray's warbler, and the latter notes reminded him of "those heard among the inspirational notes in the song of the lazuli bunting."

The Bowles brothers (1906) say that, in the spring, the males have at times a very pleasing habit while singing, "that of hovering thru the air for a distance of fifteen or twenty yards. The manner of flying at these times is very slow and closely resembles that of one of the marsh wrens, but the beak is turned upwards and the feathers on the swelling throat separate until it seems almost certain that the bird will sing himself into some serious bodily mishap."

VERMIVORA VIRGINIAE (Baird)

VIRGINIA'S WARBLER

PLATE 18

HABITS

This warbler was discovered by Dr. W. W. Anderson, at Fort Burgwyn, New Mexico, and was described by Baird, in a footnote in The Birds of North America, by Baird, Cassin, and Lawrence (1860). The footnote occurs under the explanation of plates in the second volume. The warbler was named for Mrs. Virginia Anderson, wife of the discoverer.

Its range during the breeding season covers portions of Nevada, Utah, Colorado, Arizona, and New Mexico, mainly in the mountain regions, and it retires to Mexico for the winter. It seems to be more abundant in Colorado than elsewhere, breeding from the foothills, where it is a characteristic bird and perhaps the most abundant of the wood warblers, up to 7,500 to 8,000 feet in the mountains. On the spring migration, it is abundant along the valley streams, among the cottonwoods and willows, or sometimes among the pines; but in the summer it is found among the low scrub oak brush on the hillsides.

Bailey and Niedrach (1938) write attractively of Virginia's warbler in its Colorado haunts:

In the broken prairie where the yellow pines have taken their stand upon the crest of the tableland, and in the rocky canyons clothed with the scraggly scrub oaks slipping down to narrow grass-grown creek-bottoms, Virginia's Warbler chooses its nesting grounds.

Plants seem to burst into life during the early weeks in May. * * * The flowers of the scrub oaks tinge the hillsides with a greenish-yellow bloom; the green of bursting leaves and grasses soon blends with the nodding blossoms of the pasque-flower; the beautiful pink plume sways on the hillside, and yellow blossoms of the Oregon grape thrust forth among the holly-like leaves, making one think of flowering Christmas wreaths. It is then that the Virginia's Warblers are at the height of their activity. Their colors are the grays and yellows of the new vegetation. The males perch among scrub-oak branches and yellow pines, where they are usually concealed, and do their utmost to outsing their towhee neighbors.

In Nevada, Ridgway (1877) first observed this warbler "among the cedar and piñon groves on the eastern slope of the Ruby Mountains. * * * On the Wahsatch and Uintah Mountains it was more abundant, being particularly plentiful among the scrub-oaks on the foot-hills near Salt Lake City. They lived entirely among the bushes, which there were so dense that the birds were difficult to obtain, even when shot."

In the Charleston Mountains, Nev., according to A. J. van Rossem (1936), "the distribution appeared to be limited to the so-called Upper Sonoran associations of mahogany and Gambel oaks, and therefore the species is considered characteristic of that zone, although the extremes of altitude at which it was found were 6,300 and 9,000 feet. Because of the relative scarcity of oaks, by far the greater number were found in mahogany which here grows as low, dense forest, instead of in the more familiar shrub form in which it is usually known."

In the Great Basin region, Dr. Jean M. Linsdale (1938) found Virginia's warblers in a variety of situations, such as "in sage on rocky, piñon-covered slope 100 yards from a stream; in sage on top of ridge; at tip of mountain mahogany tree; in plum thicket; singing and foraging through upper foliage of tall birches close to creek; in cottonwoods and piñons close to creeks; singing in dead shrub 10 feet high at base of rock slide; in aspen; in thickets of sage, elder, *Ephedra*, and *Symphoricarpos;* in willow; on ground among rocks at crest of ridge." The altitudes ranged from 6,500 to 8,000 feet, with the largest number between 7,000 and 7,500 feet.

In southern Arizona, this warbler, according to Mr. Swarth (1904)—

proved to be very abundant during the spring migration, particularly in the lower parts of the mountains; but the most of them seem to go farther north, and but few, compared with the numbers seen in April and the early part of May, remained through the summer to breed. The earliest arrival noted was on April 10th and soon after they were quite abundant, mostly in the oak region below 5000 feet, remaining so throughout April and up to the first week in May, at which time the migrating birds had about all passed on. All that were seen after that I took to be breeding birds, for they gradually moved to a higher altitude, (6000 to 8000 feet) and were nearly all in pairs. About the middle of April, 1902, I found a few *virginiae*, together with other migrating warblers, in the willows along the San Pedro River, some fifteen miles from the mountains.

*Nesting.*—Ridgway was evidently the first to record the nest of Virginia's warbler, finding it near Salt Lake City on June 9, 1869. "The nest was embedded in the deposits of dead or decaying leaves, on ground covered by dense oak-brush. Its rim was just even with the surface. It was built on the side of a narrow ravine at the bottom of which was a small stream. The nest itself is two inches in depth by three and a half in diameter. It consists of a loose but intricate interweaving of fine strips of the inner bark of the mountain mahogany, fine stems of grasses, roots, and mosses, and is lined with the same with the addition of the fur and hair of the smaller animals" (Baird, Brewer, and Ridgway, 1874).

Shortly afterwards, a nest was found on June 1, 1873, in Colorado, by C. E. Aiken. It was reported by Aiken and Warren (1914) as "the first nest of this species known to science. * * * This was sunk in the ground in a tuft of bunch grass growing in a clump of oak brush, with the dead grass hanging over and completely concealing the nest, which was reached through a small round hole like a mouse hole through the protecting grass."

Dr. Linsdale (1938) reports a nest found in Nevada, at an elevation of 7,700 feet, that "was at the lower edge of a clump of grass 20 inches tall and 2 feet across. The surrounding hillside was of small rocks lying at a maximum angle of rest. A few similar grass clumps were scattered near, about 10 feet apart. The surrounding trees were mountain mahogany and chokecherry. The nest was composed entirely of grass and was in a depression in the loose soil. It was well concealed by dead grass at the base of the tuft."

In the Huachuca Mountains, Ariz., Mr. Swarth (1904) found a nest that "was built on a steep sidehill about ten feet from a much traveled trail, and was very well concealed; being under a thick bunch of overhanging grass, and sunk into the ground besides, so as to be entirely hid from view. This was at an elevation of about 8,000 feet, which seems to be about the upward limit for this species in this region."

We found Virginia's warbler fairly common there in the middle reaches of the canyons, around 7,000 feet, and found a nest being built at the base of a bush of mountain misery; Mr. Willard collected it with a set of three eggs on June 4, 1922; it was made of leaves and strips of bark and was lined with horsehair.

Another nest before me, from the Huachucas, has a foundation of moss and lichens, dry leaves, and strips of cedar mark, over which are finer strips of the bark and shreds of dry weed stalks and grasses, with a lining of still finer fibers; it is a shallow nest, its diameter being 3 by 3½ inches outside and 2 inches inside.

*Eggs.*—While 4 eggs seem to constitute the usual set for Virginia's warbler, as few as 3 and as many as 5 have been reported. These are ovate to short ovate and only slightly lustrous. They are white, finely speckled or spotted with shades of reddish brown, such as "chestnut" and "auburn," intermingled with faint specks of "pale vinaceous-drab." Some eggs are profusely spotted over the entire surface, while others have the markings concentrated at the large end. The measurements of 40 eggs average 15.9 by 12.4 millimeters; the eggs showing the four extremes measure 17.0 by 12.4, 16.0 by 13.0, 14.2 by 12.2, and 16.3 by 11.2 millimeters (Harris).

*Young.*—On the period of incubation and on the development and care of the young we have no information except the following observations of Bailey and Niedrach (1938) : "The hatching time of many species of Colorado birds seems to coincide with an abundance of larvae feeding upon plants among which the birds are nesting. We have noticed time and again, that pests are numerous upon the vegetation when the fledglings are in the nest, but a few weeks later, after the little fellows have taken wing and are able to move to other parts, the caterpillars have gone into the pupa stage." At a nest they were watching, they observed that both parents shared the work of feeding the young, averaging a trip every 6 minutes.

A. J. van Rossem (1936) took young birds that were not fully grown on July 10, and others on July 13 that had nearly completed the post-juvenal molt, from which he inferred that two broods might be raised in a season. H. S. Swarth (1904) noted that the young birds began to appear in the Huachuca Mountains about the middle of July, after which both old and young birds moved down into the foothills.

*Plumages.*—The young Virginia's warbler in juvenal plumage is plain grayish brown above; the throat, chest, and sides are paler brownish gray; the abdomen and center of the breast white; the upper and under tail coverts are dull greenish yellow; there is no chestnut crown patch ; and the greater and median wing coverts are tipped with dull buffy. The sexes are alike.

The postjuvenal molt begins early in July and is often complete before the end of that month. The first winter plumage is similar to that of the adult female at that season. In this plumage the sexes are not very different, and the crown patch is not much in evidence or is altogether lacking in the young female ; both sexes are browner and with less yellow than in the adult plumage, and the female is duller than the male.

A partial prenuptial molt occurs between February and May, mainly about the head, during which the chestnut crown patch is at least partially assumed and the young birds become almost indistinguishable from adults. There is, however, considerable individual variation in the advance toward maturity.

Subsequent molts consist of a complete postnuptial molt in July and August, and a partial prenuptial molt in early spring. The adult male in the fall is browner above and on the flanks, and the yellow on the chest is duller than in the spring, while the chestnut crown patch is concealed by brownish gray tips. The female, also, is browner than in the spring, with little if any yellow on the chest and with the crown patch similarly concealed. In spring birds there is much individual variation, perhaps owing to age, in the amount of yellow on the breast, throat, and chin. Some females are nearly as brightly colored as are the duller males, some have very little yellow on the chest and some lack the chestnut crown patch.

*Food.*—Our information on the food of Virginia's warbler is limited to the observation of Bailey and Niedrach (1938) who saw a pair of these warblers feeding their young on the caterpillars that eat the foliage of the trees and shrubs on their nesting grounds. It is significant that after these caterpillars are no longer available the warbler leaves its breeding haunts and moves down into the foothills, perhaps in search of other food; and it would be interesting to learn what that food is. It has been seen foraging on the ground, as well as in the foliage, and flying up into the air to capture insects on the wing.

*Behavior.*—Virginia's warbler is a shy, retiring species, spending most of its time not far above the ground in the thick underbrush, where it is not easily seen, as its colors match its surroundings. It is also very lively and active, almost constantly in motion, except when it mounts to the top of some dead bush or small tree to sit and sing.

*Voice.*—Dr. Chapman (1907) quotes C. E. Aiken as follows: "The male is very musical during the nesting season, uttering his *swee* ditty continually as he skips through the bushes in search of his morning repast; or having satisfied his appetite, he mounts to the top of some tree in the neighborhood of his nest, and repeats at regular intervals a song of remarkable fulness for a bird of such minute proportions." Henry D. Minot (1880) calls the "ordinary note, a sharp *chip;* song, simple but various (deceptively so); common forms are *ché-we-ché-we-ché-we-ché-we*, *wit-a-wit-wit-wit* (these terminal notes being partially characteristic of *Helminthophagae*) and *che-wé-che-wé-che-wé*, *ché-a-ché-a-ché*". Dr. Linsdale's (1938) comments on singing males follow:

The song varied from 7 to 10 notes, being usually 8, and it occupied about 3 seconds. At the beginning the notes were slow and they came more rapidly at the end. About half a minute elapsed between songs." Another bird "sang

14 times in 3 minutes and 10 seconds. * * * Singing perches on dead limbs that were rather exposed were the rule, but they were not often as high as the tops of tall trees. * * * On June 16, 1930, near Kingston Creek, 7500 feet, a singing male was followed for an hour, beginning at 7:30 a. m. It sang about every 30 seconds. The territory over which it moved was surprisingly large, estimated as extending 400 yards along the cañon slope and vertically about 150 yards, from near the stream to the base of the broken cliffs. * * * The song, compared with that of the Tolmie warbler had a more rapid rhythm and the notes were thinner and weaker. It could be distinguished from that of the Audubon warbler by the lack of rising inflection at the end. The song was represented by the observer (Miller) as *zdl-zdl-zdl-zdl, zt-zt-zt-zt.*

*Field marks.*—Virginia's warbler, with its plain gray upper parts, is an inconspicuous bird, and its shy, retiring habits make it difficult to observe. The chestnut crown patch is not prominent and is often invisible. The yellow on the chest and throat of the male is quite variable and in the female and young much reduced or lacking. The best field marks are the dull yellow rump and upper and under tail covers, which are more or less conspicuous in old and young birds at all seasons.

*Enemies.*—O. W. Howard (1899) says that "the nests of the bird, like those of other ground-nesting birds of this locality, are destroyed by jays and snakes. The jays steal both eggs and young. Often a whole band of these winged wolves will sweep down on a nest and in less time than it takes to tell it they will devour the contents and destroy the nest, the pitiful notes of the helpless parents being drowned by the harsh notes of the marauders."

Frank C. Cross writes to me that Robert J. Niedrach showed him a nest of this warbler that contained a young cowbird and one young warbler.

*Winter.*—By the last of August or early September, Virginia's warblers have retired from their northern breeding haunts, to spend the winter in southern Mexico. Dr. C. William Beebe (1905) writes: "Occasionally in the mornings, numbers of tiny grayish warblers came slowly down the walls of the *barranca,* feeding as they descended, taking short flights, and keeping close to ground among the dense underbrush. These birds lingered at the camp for a time, and then, with soft, low chirps, all passed on to the water, where they alighted on the sand and drank. Then, as if at some silent signal, all flew up and returned quickly, still keeping close to the ground, zig-zagging their way upward in a long line, like tiny gray mice." These were, of course, Virginia's warblers.

## DISTRIBUTION

*Range.*—Western United States to Southern Mexico.

*Breeding range.*—Virginia's warbler breeds **north** to central eastern California (White Mountains); central and northeastern Nevada

(Kingston Creek, Ruby Mountains, and East Humboldt Mountains);
northern Utah (Salt Lake City, Parley's Park, Packs Canyon, and
Ashley); possibly southeastern Idaho (Joe's Gap, Bear Lake County;
one specimen from Bancroft, Bannock County); and northern Colo-
rado (probably Little Snake River, Moffat County, and Estes Park).
East to the eastern slope of the Rocky Mountains in Colorado (Estes
Park, Denver, Manitou, Fountain, and Beulah); in migration has
occurred east to Limon, and Monon in Baca County close to the Kansas
line; and central New Mexico (Tierra Amarilla, Lake Burford, Sandia
Mountain, and Apache, probably). South to southwestern New
Mexico (Apache); and southeastern Arizona (Paradise and the
Huachuca Mountains). West to southeastern and central Arizona
(Huachuca Mountains, Santa Catalina Mountains, and Prescott); and
eastern California (Clark Mountain and White Mountains; casually
in migration to Lemon Grove).

*Winter range.*—In winter Virginia's warbler is found in west central Mexico from northern Jalisco (Bolanas); and Guanajuato (Guanajuato), to Morelos (Yautepec); and Guerrero (Talpa and Chilpancingo).

*Migration.*—A late date of spring departure is: Sonora—Moctezuma, May 10.

Early dates of spring arrival are: Texas—Socorro, April 20. New
Mexico—Cooney, April 10. Colorado—Estes Park, May 2. Arizona—Madera Canyon, Santa Rita Mountains, April 2. Utah—Vernal, May 5. Nevada—South Twin River, April 30.

Late spring migrant in Brewster County, Tex., May 13.

Late dates of fall departure are: Utah—Vernal, September 20.
Arizona—Tombstone, September 11. Colorado—Boulder, September
21. New Mexico—Koehler Junction, September 11. Texas—El
Paso, September 16.

Early dates of fall arrival are: Arizona—Toprock, July 23. Texas—
Toyavale, August 21. Sonora—Guadalupe Canyon, August 31.

*Casual records.*—Two specimens of Virginia's warbler have been
taken in western California: in San Diego County, on September 3,
1931; and at Prisoner's Harbor, Santa Cruz Island, on September 8,
1948. Virginia's warbler has been reported as occurring in Nebraska
and Kansas, but there is no record of a specimen having been taken in
either State.

*Egg dates.*—Arizona: 10 records, May 17 to June 21; 5 records,
May 25 to June 4.

Colorado: 6 records, June 1 to 26.

Nevada: 3 records, June 8 to 15.

VERMIVORA CRISSALIS (Salvin and Godman)

## COLIMA WARBLER

CONTRIBUTED BY JOSSELYN VAN TYNE

HABITS

Described in 1889 from a single specimen collected by W. B. Richardson in the Sierra Nevada de Colima, Mexico, this handsome warbler was, in 1932, still known from only a dozen museum specimens, and not a word had been recorded on its habits. In that year a University of Michigan expedition found the Colima warbler to be common in the higher forests of the Chisos Mountains of southwestern Texas and made the first discovery of its nest and eggs. The basis for the inclusion of this warbler in the A.O.U. Check-List had been a single specimen collected by Frederick M. Gaige in the Chisos in 1928 (Van Tyne, 1929).

The range of the Colima warbler has been recorded only very sketchily, but Bangs (1925) was probably correct in surmising that the specimens from southern Mexico (Colima and Michoacán) were migrant birds. The closely related Virginia's warbler, which nests in the Rocky Mountain States, winters mainly in Michoacán, Guerrero, and Jalisco. Recently R. T. Moore (1942) added a second, more southerly, locality in Michoacán and one in eastern Sinaloa to the known southern range of the Colima warbler. The breeding range is apparently restricted to the highlands of northeastern Mexico and the Chisos Mountains of southwestern Texas. In Texas the Colima warbler occurs at altitudes between 6,000 and 7,500 feet (Van Tyne, 1936) ; in Coahuila, apparently, only above altitudes of approximately 7,500 feet (Burleigh and Lowery, 1942). Records from the southern part of its range, however, show a greater altitudinal spread. The type specimen was taken in Colima at about 8,000 feet, and R. T. Moore (1942) reports two November specimens, one taken at 9,500 feet in northeastern Michoacán, the other at 5,200 feet in Sinaloa. These represent the extremes of the known altitudinal range.

*Courtship.*—Mating behavior has been observed during the first few days of May and sets of eggs noted May 15 (just completed) and May 20 (highly incubated). The only recorded specimen in juvenal plumage was collected July 20. Peet observed pursuit behavior in the Chisos Mountains on May 4 (within a few days of nest building), which may have had some courtship significance, but nothing definite is known of the courtship habits. Sutton noted copulation twice on May 1 in the Chisos, and the gonads of specimens collected that day were much enlarged; there was no indication that the females had begun incubating.

*Nesting.*—Two nests, both in the Chisos Mountains, have been described. The first (discovered in 1932) was lodged between small rocks and deeply imbedded in dead oak leaves on the sloping bank of a dry stream bed. A dense ground cover of vines and other herbaceous plants arched completely over it, leaving an entrance only on the northwest side, toward the stream. The nest had a basic structure of loosely woven fine grasses, the outside reinforced with pieces of green moss and the rim with strips of cedar bark; the cavity (5 centimeters across the rim and 4 centimeters deep) was lined with fine grass, a little fur, and a few hairs (Van Tyne, 1936). The other nest, which was "on the ground, under a little bunch of oak leaves, at the edge of a talus slope, almost at the very base of the cliffs" (Sutton, 1935), was similar, but its basic structure included dry leaves, and the site was concealed by only a partial canopy of leaves (Van Tyne and Sutton, 1937).

Nest building was observed in the Chisos Mountains on May 7, 1932 (Van Tyne, 1936):

As I was crossing the dry stream bed about a hundred yards below Boot Spring, I suddenly saw within twenty-five feet of me a female warbler with nest material in her bill. I stopped instantly and, remaining motionless, was greatly relieved to see the warbler continue undisturbed by my presence. In a moment she dropped to the ground and entered the nest, which was on the sloping right bank of the stream about six feet back from the margin of the rocky stream bed. After working for about twenty seconds the warbler left the nest and flew down the stream bed a hundred and fifty feet. In twelve minutes she was back with more nest material to repeat the performance. Subsequent excursions for building material during the ensuing hour were of three, twelve, six, and twenty-two minutes' duration. Each time she worked at the nest only fifteen to twenty seconds, until the last trip (at 11:43 A. M.) when she worked about two minutes and then departed, probably to feed, for she did not return again while I watched. Each trip to the nest had been made undeviatingly, without any hesitation, from the stream bed or from the forest to the west. Alighting almost directly above the nest, without a pause she dropped through the branches by three or four stages and promptly entered the nest, placed the material, and snuggled down working it into place. After a few moments she seemed to have completed this to her satisfaction, and, leaving the nest, she flew up to the branches ten or twelve feet above, fed for a few moments on the insects among the fresh green leaves of the little oaks and maples, and went away for more material.

When it was evident that the nest building was over for the time I went over to the nest and, examining it more closely, found that it was nearly built. The following day, May 8, it seemed to be finished.

*Eggs.*—Two complete clutches have been found, each containing four eggs. Four eggs collected and measured were 18 by 13.3, 18 by 13.5, 18 by 13.5, and 18.5 by 14 millimeters. They were creamy white, speckled, and blotched in a wreath at the larger end with "vinaceous fawn," "light brownish drab," and "cinnamon drab."

Egg laying, in the one instance observed, was at daily intervals (May 12–15); the first egg was laid four days after completion of the nest. Incubation had begun May 16, the day after the last egg was laid. The length of the incubation period is not known. Females collected on May 12 (Peet), May 17 (Van Tyne), and May 20 (Sutton) had well-marked incubation patches; males collected at the same time had no patch.

*Plumages.*—The Colima warbler differs from its nearest relative, the Virginia's warbler, in being larger; darker, less gray, above; crown paler; rump and upper tail coverts darker and richer in color; yellow of throat and breast absent or, if present, more green and more diffuse; sides and flanks more brownish; crissum darker, more aniline yellow; sexes much more nearly alike. The adult female Colima warbler is slightly darker than the male and is more brown below. It is apparently never yellow on the breast.

The juvenal plumage (known from only one specimen) differs from the adult plumage in lacking the crown spot and in having two buffy wing bars. The rump is also much more yellow (less green) and the crissum is more yellow (less orange). The young Colima warbler differs from the young Virginia's warbler in having a larger bill, darker plumage, and a less ochraceous rump.

The fall plumage differs from that of the spring in being "darker and browner throughout, the gray of head a good deal obscured by deep olive or light brownish olive; crown patch orange rufous; under parts darker with whitish area in middle of belly more distinct and under tailcoverts duller, more nearly aniline yellow" (Bangs, 1925).

George Miksch Sutton's fine color plate (Van Tyne, 1936, frontispiece) of the Colima warbler is apparently the only published figure of the species.

*Behavior.*—In Texas, the Colima warbler was observed feeding on insects (which were not identified), but nothing further has been recorded about its food. All observers seem to agree that it is not a shy bird, although in its preferred cover, the female seems elusive and nests are difficult to find. Sutton has remarked that they are "rather deliberate, even vireo-like in their movements" (Van Tyne and Sutton, 1937). In the Chisos Mountains, they frequented especially the young maples and deciduous oaks along the banks of the dry, boulder-strewn stream bed, and elsewhere on the steep mountain slopes their preference for clumps of small oaks was noted.

*Voice.*—The call note of the Colima warbler is a very sharp, almost explosive *psit*. Its common song is a continuous trill, like that of the chipping sparrow, but shorter (lasting 3 to 4 seconds), more musical, and ending with two separate notes slightly lower in scale. A second, rarer, and more varied song is so clear that it can be heard for three or four hundred feet through the woods although it does not seem loud when heard from nearby. It is perhaps this song that Brandt (1940) describes as resembling the song of the eastern redstart. E. C. Jacot (MS.) reports that the males usually start singing when "a person approaches the territory of a pair, and continues to sing until the intruder has passed." In the Chisos Mountains, Tex., the males were persistent singers. Once several sang even after a dense fog had silenced most other species. They sang usually from bushes and small trees between periods of feeding and moving about but sometimes remained for a while on a higher perch (up to 20 feet), singing at frequent intervals.

## DISTRIBUTION

*Range.*—Chisos Mountains, Tex., and mountains of northeastern Mexico; probably winters in Colima, Michoacán, and Sinaloa.

The Colima warbler has been recorded from: Texas (Chisos Mountains); Coahuila (Sierra Guadalupe and Diamante Pass); Tamaulipas (Miquihuana); Michoacán (Patamba and Sierra Ozumatlan); Sinaloa (5 miles north of Santa Lucia); Colima (Sierra Nevada).

*Egg dates.*—Texas: 2 records, May 15 and 20.

### VERMIVORA LUCIAE (Cooper)

### LUCY'S WARBLER

#### PLATES 18, 19

#### HABITS

Dr. J. G. Cooper discovered this tiny and inconspicuous warbler at Fort Mojave, on the Arizona side of the Colorado River, in the spring of 1861, and named it in honor of Miss Lucy Baird, daughter of Prof. Spencer F. Baird. It might well have been named the mesquite warbler, as its distribution coincides very closely with that of this tree, which seems to furnish its favorite home, most of its nesting sites, and much of its foraging area.

Harry S. Swarth (1905) wrote of conditions then existing:

South of Tucson, Arizona, along the banks of the Santa Cruz River, lies a region offering the greatest inducements to the ornithologist. The river, running underground for most of its course, rises to the surface at this point, and the bottom lands on either side are covered, miles in extent, with a thick growth of giant mesquite trees, literally giants, for a person accustomed to the scrubby bush that grows everywhere in the desert regions of the southwest, can hardly believe that these fine trees, many of them sixty feet high and over, really belong to the same species. This magnificent grove is included in the Papago Indian Reservation, which is the only reason for the trees surviving as long as they have, since elsewhere every mesquite large enough to be used as firewood has been ruthlessly cut down, to grow up again as a scraggly bush.

But this magnificent forest did not long remain in its pristine glory. When I was in Arizona with Frank Willard in 1922, we had looked forward with keen anticipation to visiting the mesquite forest, where he had told me that we should find a thick stand of big trees covering a large area, and some wonderful bird life. We were disappointed in the forest, for the Papago Indians had been cutting down the larger trees unmercifully and had made a network of cart roads all through it for hauling out the firewood. There were only a few large trees left, more or less scattered, and between them many open spaces in which were thickets of small mesquites and thorn or patches of medium-sized mesquites and hackberries. But we were not disappointed in the bird life, for here and in other parts of Pima County, wherever there were mesquites, we found Lucy's warblers really abundant and breeding. The forest fairly teemed with bird life, from the graceful Mexican goshawks soaring overhead to the Gambel's quails whistling on the ground. The constant cooing of the white-winged doves was almost too monotonous, but the rich song of the Arizona cardinal, mingled with the voices of the orioles, towhees, wrens, and vireos made a delightful chorus, among which the sweet song of Lucy's warbler was prominent.

Dr. Joseph Grinnell (1914) writes, referring to the Colorado Valley: "On the California side, both at Riverside Mountain and above Blythe, Lucy warblers were numerous, and very closely confined to the narrow belt of mesquite. The singing males, each representing the forage area and nesting site of a pair, were spaced out very uniformly, so that an estimated strip of about 200 yards in length belonged to each. The birds foraged out to a limited extent from the mesquites towards the river into the arrowweed and willows, and away from the river at the mouths of washes into the ironwoods and palo verdes. But the metropolis was always most emphatically the mesquites."

*Nesting.*—M. French Gilman (1909) had considerable experience with the nesting habits of Lucy's warbler along the Gila River in Arizona, of which he says:

Four general types of nesting sites were noticed, in the following order of frequency: in natural cavities, under loose bark, in woodpecker holes, and in deserted Verdins' nests. Of 23 nests observed, 12 were in natural cavities, 4 under loose bark, 4 in woodpecker holes, and three in Verdins' nests. Natural cavities were of various kinds. Some were where a limb had been broken off; others in the crack made by a large branch splitting from the trunk; and again a decayed spot furnisht a sufficient hollow to conceal the nest. In all cases the site was in a sheltered or protected position; that is, the trunk leaned enough to shade the entrance from above. A mesquite tree was usually selected, tho others were taken. Of the nests observed, 15 were in mesquites, 5 in palo verde, 2 in ironwood, and one in catsclaw. * * *

The nests were small and compact and well hidden in their cavity. Only twice did protruding material betray the location. In one case nesting material protruded from a woodpecker hole, and the other was a bulky nest that showed from each side of a split branch. This last nest I thought must belong to a House Finch, but investigation showed warbler ownership. Nests were made of bark, weeds, and mesquite leaf-stems, and lined with fine bark, horse and cow hair, a few feathers and sometimes a little rabbit fur. The site averaged six and one-half feet from the ground, the lowest being 18 inches and the highest 15 feet. * * *

In nest-building the female seems to do all the work, her mate sometimes accompanying her on trips to and from the tree, but more frequently flitting about the tops of adjacent trees, occasionally uttering his little warble. One pair I watcht had a nest in a Texas Woodpecker hole in a palo verde tree about 15 feet from the ground. The female brought material to the nest three times in two minutes, then a seven minute interval, followed by two trips in three minutes. The male accompanied her on two trips then made himself scarce. He indulged in no singing and both birds were silent, tho in many cases one or both gave the call note at intervals.

Others have mentioned nests of Lucy's warblers in verdins' nests, probably all old winter nests of the male verdin, relined to suit the warbler. O. W. Howard (1899) records such a nest and adds: "Other nests were placed in crevices along river banks where roots of trees were sticking out and one or two were found in natural cavities of the Giant Cactus, or in woodpecker holes therein." We found a nest with young in a cavity in the bleached skeleton of a fallen giant cactus, where I set up my camera and took several photographs of the bird feeding the young. A very pretty nest of this warbler is in the Thayer collection in Cambridge; it was evidently built in the fork of a mesquite limb, supported by a cluster of old and fresh, green twigs; it is made externally of the leaves, petioles, fine green twigs, and flower clusters of the mesquite and is decorated with a few feathers of the white-winged dove; it is lined internally with fine fibers, white cows' hair and black horsehair, and more dove feathers; it measures 4 by 3 inches in outside diameter and 2 by 1⅓ inside; the outside height is nearly 3 inches, and the inside cup is about 1¾ inches deep. A set in my collection was taken from a hole 3 feet above the base of a sandy bank along a wash near the San Pedro River, in Arizona.

*Eggs.*—Lucy's warbler lays from 3 to 7 eggs, but the set usually consists of 4 or 5; the larger sets are rare, but O. W. Howard has found two sets of 7, and several sets of 6 have been recorded. The eggs are ovate to short ovate and have very little lustre. The white or creamy white ground color is finely speckled with shades of "chestnut," "bay," or "auburn." The eggs that have markings in the darker shades of "chestnut" and "bay" frequently have a scattering of minute spots of "brownish drab" that are often lacking on eggs with the lighter markings of "auburn." The spots are usually concentrated at the large end.   The measurements of 50 eggs average 14.6 by 11.4 millimeters; the eggs showing the four extremes measure **16.5** by 11.5, 14.6 by **12.0, 13.2** by 11.2, and 13.7 by **10.7** millimeters. (Harris.)

*Young.*—The period of incubation seems to be unknown, and I can find no information on the development and care of the young.   Evidence points to the conclusion that incubation and brooding are performed entirely by the female, and that at least two broods are reared in a season.   Mr. Swarth (1905) says that "several broods are probably raised, as unfinished nests and incomplete sets were found at the same time that broods of young as large as the adults were seen flying about."

*Plumages.*—Ridgway (1902) says that the young in juvenal plumage are "essentially like adults, but much clearer white beneath; no trace of chestnut on crown; upper tail-coverts ochraceous-buff instead of chestnut; middle and greater wing-coverts tipped with whitish or pale buffy, producing two rather distinct bars."   He might have added that the tertials are edged with cinnamon, and that the primaries and rectrices are edged and tipped with white.

There is apparently a partial postjuvenal molt, some time during the summer, when all the plumage except the flight feathers, remiges, and rectrices, is renewed.   Young birds now become very similar to adults, but can be recognized by the juvenal wings and tail until the edgings wear off.   I can find no evidence of a prenuptial molt in either young or old birds.   I have seen adults in complete postnuptial molt in August.   Fall birds are tinged with brown above and with pale brownish buff below; the chestnut crown patch is concealed by very broad brownish gray tips.   Females are not always distinguishable from males, but usually the chestnut on the crown and upper tail coverts is paler and more restricted.

*Food.*—Nothing definite seems to have been published on the food of Lucy's warbler, but it is evidently largely, if not wholly, insectivorous, as it is often seen foraging in the foliage and flower clusters of the mesquites and in other trees.   Dr. W. P. Taylor tells me that he has seen it feeding on the pendant sprays of ocotillo flowers, probably gleaning insects or other materials from the exterior.   In late spring when the mesquites, palo verdes, the various cacti, and even the **saguaros** burst into full bloom, these gorgeous desert plants are a blaze of color and attract myriads of insects.

*Behavior.*—Mr. Gilman (1909) says that "shyness about the nest seems to be characteristic of these birds."   He was seldom able to flush one from its nest.   "In three cases only, did the parent birds show what might be called proper amount of solicitude when the nest was approacht.   Some of them seemed rather touchy about their nests, leaving them if the nest were toucht even so lightly." Some nests, with incomplete sets, were deserted after they had been inspected; but others were not. "They took good care not to sing in the nest tree, preferring to confine their performances to trees some distance away. The male would frequently meet me several rods from the nest and flit from tree to tree singing at short intervals. Once I made a complete circuit of the nest tree and he accompanied me the entire distance. This was an exceptional case of course. While going from tree to tree and singing, the bird usually tried to keep hidden as much as possible and was rather successful in the effort."

However nest-shy the bird may be when there are eggs in the nest that she does not want discovered, the bird that I watched was not at all shy about her nest, nor was she lacking in parental devotion. For, although my camera stood within a few feet of the nest and I was standing beside it in plain sight, she came repeatedly to feed her young. I should say that these birds are more retiring than shy.

W. L. Dawson (1923) writes: "Albeit an active creature and zealous in song, the Lucy Warbler becomes almost invisible in its habitual setting, and the difficulty of detection is heightened by the bird's instinctive wariness. Again and again I have known a bird which had seemed quite engrossed in song to fall silent at the stir of a footstep a hundred yards away."

*Voice.*—Mr. Dawson (1923) says: "The Lucy Warbler is a loud and industrious singer, but the song has a curious generic quality very difficult to describe. It is *Warbler* song, rather than the song of the Lucy Warbler. It is, perhaps, most like that of the Pileolated Warbler (*Wilsonia pileolata*) in quality. After that, it reminds one of the Yellow Warbler's song, having the same vivacious cadence, but not being so sharply piercing. Again its breathless, haphazard quality suggests one of the Buntings; and I once followed its tantalizing seductions for half an hour under the delusion that I was on the track of the coveted Beautiful Bunting (*Passerina versicolor pulchra*)."

Dr. Grinnell (1914) says that the song "resembles the song of the Sonora yellow warbler in length and frequency of utterance and somewhat in quality, but with a distinct hurried and lisping effect, reminding one of the song of the Lazuli bunting." Several others have noted the resemblance to the song of the yellow warbler. Mrs. Florence Merriam Bailey (1923) puts the song in syllables as follows: "*whee-tee, whee-tee, whee-tee, whee-tee, whee-tee, whee-tee, whee-tee, whee-tee, whee-tee, wheet,* and its call was a faint *chip.*"

*Field marks.*—There are no very striking marks on Lucy's warbler; it is clothed in quiet colors and in general appearance suggests a warbling vireo. The chestnut crown patch of the male can be seen under favorable conditions, but on the female it is seldom in evidence.

The chestnut upper tail coverts can be seen only when the bird is in certain positions. Its activity will mark it as a wood warbler, and it is the only one of this family likely to be found on its breeding grounds among the mesquites in the nesting season.

*Enemies.*—Mr. Howard (1899) says that "many nests are destroyed by wood-rats and snakes." And Mr. Dawson (1923) writes:

Dwarf Cowbirds are prominent in the formidable host of enemies which this tiny bird must face. Sometimes the warblers are able to entrench themselves behind apertures so narrow that the Cowbird cannot get in; and once we saw the Cowbird's foundling resting unharmed, but also harmless, upon the "doorstep," not less than two inches distant from the warbler's eggs. Another nest, more exposed, contained three eggs of the arch enemy, and had been deserted by the troubled owners. The Gila Woodpecker is an especially persistent enemy. Accustomed as he is to poking and prying, he seems to take a fiendish delight in discovering and devouring as many Lucy Warblers' eggs as possible. We caught several of these villains red-handed, and we found reason to believe that more than half of the nests in a certain section had been wrecked by them. Add to these the depredations of lizards, snakes, and, possibly, rats, and the wonder is that these tiny gray waifs are able to reproduce at all.

## DISTRIBUTION

*Range.*—Southwestern United States to central Mexico.

*Breeding range.*—Lucy's warbler breeds **north** to southern Utah (Beaverdam Wash, Zion National Park; Calf Creek, Garfield County; and the San Juan River); and southwestern Colorado (Montezuma County near Four Corners). **East** to Colorado (near Four Corners); western New Mexico (Shiprock, possibly San Antonio, mouth of Mogollon Creek, and Redrock); southeastern Arizona (Bisbee); and northeastern Sonora (Moctezuma). **South** to northern Sonora (Moctezuma and Saric); southern Arizona (Baboquivari Mountains, Menager's Dam, and Gadsden); and southern California (Picacho and Silsbee). **West** to southern California (Silsbee, Mecca possibly, and Chemehuevis Valley); western Arizona (Fort Mojave); and southwestern Utah (Beaverdam Wash).

*Winter range.*—The few available records place the winter home of Lucy's warbler in central western Mexico from Jalisco (Bolaños and Lake Chapala) to eastern Guerrero (Iguala).

*Migration.*—Few migration dates are available for a species with such a limited range. Early dates of arrival are: Arizona—Tucson, March 12. California—Mecca, March 29. Utah—St. George, March 23. A late departure date is: Arizona—Tombstone, October 3.

*Egg dates.*—Arizona: 58 records, April 22 to June 27; 30 records, May 2 to 21, indicating the height of the season.

PARULA AMERICANA PUSILLA (Wilson)

NORTHERN PARULA WARBLER

PLATES 20, 21

HABITS

I have always preferred the old name, blue yellow-backed warbler, as originally used by Wilson and Audubon, to the modern common name; it seems more descriptive of this dainty wood warbler. As to the origin of this newer name, Dr. Spencer Trotter (1909) writes: "The name 'parula' recently in vogue for the warblers of the genus *Compsothlypis* is clearly borrowed from the old Bonaparte genus *Parula* (diminutive of titmouse). The bird (*C. americana*) has appeared under various titles—'the Finch Creeper' of Catesby (I, 64), 'the various coloured little finch creeper' of Bartram (Travels, 292), and the 'Blue Yellow-backed Warbler' of Wilson, Audubon, and later authors." *Parula* was extensively used as the generic name during the last century, and is now reinstated to replace *Compsothlypis*.

The 1931 A. O. U. Check-List of North American Birds recognizes only two races of this species, the subject of this present sketch, *P. a. pusilla*, and the southern race, *P. a. americana*. The two forms together occupy a breeding range covering practically all of the United States east of the Great Plains, as well as parts of southern Canada, the type name being restricted to the birds breeding from the District of Columbia southward to Alabama and Florida.

Ridgway (1902) describes the northern bird as "similar to *C. a. americana*, but slightly larger, with smaller bill and darker, richer coloration; adult male with blue of upper parts deeper, and black of lores more intense; lower throat or upper chest (sometimes both) blackish or dusky (the feathers sometimes tipped with chestnut), forming a more or less distinct, often very conspicuous band; lower chest orange-tawny, tawny, or chestnut (the feathers usually margined with yellow) forming usually a distinct and often abruptly defined patch; sides usually more or less tinged or spotted with chestnut."

In the same work, he describes a third form, *C. a. ramalinae*, as "similar in coloration to" the northern bird, "but smaller even than *C. a. americana*." He gives as its range the Mississippi Valley, from Mississippi, Louisiana, and Texas to Minnesota and Michigan. This western race is not recognized in the 1931 A. O. U. Check-List.

Our experience with the northern parula warbler in Bristol County, Mass., well illustrates the successive changes that nature and man have wrought in the distribution of so many of our birds. Many years ago, perhaps early in the last century or before, some hardy pioneers hewed out a clearing in the forest that clothed the slopes of Rocky Hill in Rehoboth, Mass., planted an apple orchard, and surrounded it with stone walls. All traces of the old farm, if ever there had been one, disappeared before I first visited the locality in 1888, and the forest had begun to encroach on the old clearing. The apple trees even then showed signs of old age and were profusely covered with long festoons of that picturesque tree lichen, often called beard-moss or old-man's-beard (*Usnea barbata, U. longissima,* or *U. trichodea*). This old orchard was a mecca for all local oologists, and many a set of eggs of the blue yellow-backed warbler was taken from it during succeeding years. As time passed, the old trees gradually died, the *Usnea* disappeared, the warblers ceased breeding there, and the forest eventually reclaimed the land until today only the ancient stone walls remain to mark the locally famous haunt of the blue yellow-backs.

I can remember several other old, neglected orchards that were similarly decorated with the long, gray-green lichen and that were inhabited by parula warblers as nesting sites, but they all suffered the same fate; the orchard trees decayed and were replaced by woods and thickets. During the early part of the present century this warbler continued to breed commonly in Bristol County wherever it could find trees infested with *Usnea*—around the edges of swamps and along the shores of ponds, lakes, and sluggish streams; but now this lichen seems for some reason to have entirely disappeared from the County, and the parula warbler has likewise disappeared, although it may still breed in a few similar localities on Cape Cod, Mass., where I have found it a few times in more recent years.

Localities such as those described above seem to be typical of the breeding haunts of the northern parula warbler, at least in New England, southern New York, and New Jersey. Whether the presence of *Usnea* is a sine qua non for the breeding haunts of this wood warbler is an open question; but it may safely be said that where this lichen grows in abundance one is almost sure to find it breeding; and conversely, where this lichen is scarce or lacking, the warbler breeds sparingly or not at all.

Farther westward, northward, and southward, where *Usnea* is scarce or entirely absent, these warblers seem to find congenial haunts in hemlock ravines and in other coniferous woods and swamps; but even there they are more likely to be found where there is at least *some* of one species or another of this lichen, or where the somewhat similar Spanish moss (*Tillandsia usneoides*) grows.

*Spring.*—Parula warblers that have wintered in the West Indies reach southern Florida during the first week in March. Dr. Wetmore (1916) says that it "was the most common of the migrant warblers in

Porto Rico. * * * Migratory movement was apparent among them by February 14, and after this the birds were very restless, especially during early morning, and there was tendency to work from the east to west. In March and April there were distinct waves of migration." But it is well on toward the middle of May before the first migrants reach the northern limits of their breeding range.

Professor Cooke's (1904) records show that the migrants from Mexico and Central America reach the Louisiana coast by the very last of February or early March, while the first arrivals on the lower Rio Grande, in Texas, come two or three weeks later. He observes:

A comparison of the dates shows, first, that the parula warbler arrives in Texas much later than in either of the other States, and hence does not reach the Mississippi Valley by way of Texas; second, that it arrives in northern Florida at least ten days later than it attains the same latitude in Louisiana. From these two facts it would appear that Louisiana is reached by direct flight across the Gulf of Mexico. The average date of arrival at New Orleans coincides closely with the date when the first migrants arrive at the southern end of Florida. It would seem that the birds of Mexico and Cuba are prompted to move northward at the same time, but the flight over the Gulf of Mexico being so much longer than that from Cuba to Florida, the Mexican birds reach a higher latitude by their initial flight.

There are other interesting details in Cooke's account to which the reader is referred.

During migration the parula warbler does not frequent haunts typical of its breeding ground; in fact such are not to be found in much of the country over which it travels; nor does it especially frequent the coniferous woods to which it is partial in summer. It is to be found almost anywhere, in many kinds of trees, though it seems to show a decided preference for deciduous woods. There, it may often be seen drifting through the highest tree-tops in mixed groups of migrating wood warblers, gleaning insects amidst the freshly opening foliage. Referring to the Buckeye Lake region in Ohio, Milton B. Trautman (1940) writes: "The transient Parula Warblers usually displayed a preference for large pin oak and shingle oak trees and a marked preference for one shingle oak in particular. This oak was in the Lakeside Woods, and more Parula Warblers were observed in it than in all of the remaining trees of the woodland. A transient often displays a marked preference for certain types of trees, but it appears unusual for a single tree among many of the same kind to retain yearly so marked an attraction for a particular bird species."

The migrating parula warbler is often seen in roadside trees and in shade trees in parks and gardens. It even visits our orchards, where one of the most charming sights of springtime is to see this gay-colored, tiny warbler flitting about in search of insects among the apple blossoms, a delightful bit of color contrast in a beautiful setting.

*Nesting.*—The nests of the northern parula warbler that we used to find in southern Massachusetts were all located in haunts similar to those described, and mostly in old orchards heavily festooned with beard moss (*Usnea*). We could usually find three to five nests in a well-populated orchard, but they were so well hidden in the hanging moss that we may have overlooked some. A casual observer would never notice one, but with practice we learned to recognize a rounded, cuplike, thick place in a bunch of *Usnea* as indicating a nest. The nests were usually made in bunches of moss that hung from horizontal or sloping branches and were from 5 to 15 feet above the ground, more being below than above 12 feet. Some nests were in red cedars, or savins (*Juniperus virginiana*), scattered among other trees or growing in open stands by themselves; they were located in bunches of *Usnea* close to the center of the tree and often within reach from the ground. Occasionally, isolated trees on the edges of swamps or on the shores of ponds were sufficiently covered with the lichen to contain nests, and these were sometimes as much as 20 feet above the ground. The nearest approach to a colony that I ever found was in a small cedar swamp, not over an acre in extent, that jutted out from the shore of a lake into rather deep water.

The white cedars (*Chamaecyparis thuyoides*) were growing in water that was waist deep or more in places, and the whole place was so obstructed with fallen trees and sunken snags that it was very difficult to explore thoroughly; I managed to find some half a dozen nests, and there may have been others, for many of the trees were well "bearded."

The nests that we have found have all been very simple affairs, apparently merely pockets hollowed out in bunches of hanging *Usnea*, with side entrances slightly above the cups. Some nests were small and suspended only 2 or 3 inches below the supporting branch, practically open baskets accessible from directly above; others were found in long, thick bunches, a foot or more in length, with long streamers hanging below the nest. External measurements were therefore quite variable. Many of the nests were unlined, save with a soft bed of fine shreds of *Usnea;* some were scantily lined with a few pieces of fine grass, two or three pine needles, one or two horsehairs, or a few bits of buff-colored down from the stems of ferns; rarely, a nest was more elaborately lined with the latter material but never as profusely as are the nests of other wood warblers.

Apparently the nests were also difficult to find in Connecticut; "J. M. W." (C. L. Rawson, 1888), who has probably taken more eggs of the blue yellow-backed warbler than any other man, says that the older ornithologists did not realize "that the three Southern New England States were about the centre of its breeding range," until he began sending eggs to Dr. T. M. Brewer. Thomas Nuttall (1833) remarked: "The nest and eggs are yet unknown."

Rawson found the parula warbler nesting in colonies near Norwich, Conn., and says:

I know a swamp where may be found seventy-five pairs of these summer residents. The first time I visited the Preston colony on the 31st of May, I took eight sets of four. The first time I visited another large community in this county on June 5, on a point of land trending into salt water, I took eleven sets of four. * * *

The nests are built on dead or green trees, and on savins or deciduous trees, at varying heights. I took one from the single filament of moss caught on the green twig of a birch, within five inches of the ground, and others close to the trunks of great oaks fifty feet in the air. On the lower swamp, huckleberry brush in the littoral colony is a favorite site.

William Brewster (1906) mentions only one nest taken in the neighborhood of Cambridge, Mass., a region where *Usnea* is scarce:

In shape and general plan of construction the nest closely resembles that of a Baltimore Oriole. It has no hole in the side but instead a wide-mouthed opening at the top through which the bird entered it as the Oriole enters her nest. The upper edges and sides were securely fastened to the fine terminal twigs of a drooping branch where the nest hung suspended among the evergreen foliage of the hemlock, precisely as the Oriole's hammock swings in the dropping spray of an elm. The Warbler's nest has a scanty lining of pine needles and fine grasses but it is otherwise composed entirely of *Usnea*, loosely woven or perhaps merely felted together, evidently by the parent birds. They must have been at some pains to collect this material, for the closest scrutiny on the part of a friend and myself failed to reveal more than a few small and scattered tufts of *Usnea* in the surrounding woods.

Henry Mousley (1924, 1926, and 1928), of Hatley, Quebec, made three attempts to make complete studies of the home life of the northern parula warbler, none of which covered the whole cycle for reasons beyond his control.

The nests were suspended from the branches of coniferous trees, at heights ranging from 26 feet in a spruce to 40 feet in a balsam fir. One of these nests was watched for a total of 24 hours, from May 22 to 31, during the process of construction; during this time the male sang 549 times from a little birch and went with the female to the nest, but brought no material; the female, however, made 206 trips with material, an average of one load every 5.4 minutes. The nest was made entirely of *Usnea*, all brought in, and lined with "some black hair-like rootlets, with two bits of plant down"; it was strengthened with a few fine grass stems. It weighed only 100 grains, or .23 ounce! "Outside diameter 3.25, inside 1.75 inches; outside depth 2.50, inside 1.75 inches. The female after selecting some of the longest threads of the hanging bunch of *Usnea*, attached them to a little twig a few inches off, following this up with that curious process—inherent—of moulding the nest, which in this case, was really an acrobatic performance, there being of course no apparent nest to mould, just a few strands, through which the bird's tail and wings protruded."

Outside New England, where *Usnea* is scarce, the nests are often built in hanging clusters of twigs of hemlocks or spruces, with the use of more or less of this lichen when available. In the lower Mississippi Valley, Spanish moss (*Tillandsia usneoides*) offers a popular substitute and is generally found growing in profusion. But some nests are built of various other materials. George H. Stuart, 3d, writes to me of a nest he found at Pocono Lake, Pa., on June 22, 1916: "This remarkable nest was placed in a horizontal limb of a spruce, 20 feet up and 12 feet from the trunk, near the tip and overhanging a road near the lake." It was "composed mainly of fine dry grasses and the thinnest of bark shreds, with a few bits of down, fashioned together oriole-like, though loosely, with a few coarse grasses projecting suggesting the handiwork of the magnolia warbler. The tiny basket was suspended from the under side of the branch, partially supported by inclining twigs. In form it is an inverted cone or pear, measuring 3 inches deep by 3 inches wide at the rim, the thin walls tapering down to a narrow, pointed bottom. The thinness of the walls in places revealed the eggs from a side view."

Mrs. Nice (1931) reports a curious nest, found by Mr. Kirn near Copan, Okla.; it was fastened to ivy leaves and to a stick which was hanging down, held by the vine. "In this hanging, swaying cluster about two feet long, the nest was built almost entirely of box elder blossoms held together by spider webs on the outside, and sycamore seed down on the inside with a light lining of fine strips of weed stems."

Several nests have been reported as built of various materials in bunches of leaves and other rubbish deposited by freshlets on branches over streams.

Because of the bird's habit of using various materials and sites in its nest building, it may be well to mention some nesting records from the southern Gulf States. Andrew Allison wrote to Dr. Chapman (1907):

The invariable nesting site is a clump of Spanish moss—where this it to be had; I have not observed nests from beyond the range of this plant. The nest is generally placed near the branch from which the long filaments of the 'moss' depend, so that it is well concealed. The height from the ground varies from about eight feet upwards. * * * The nest is nearly hemispherical in shape, opening directly upward. The usual material, in lower Louisiana, is thistle down, which is abundant during the nesting season. Animal hairs are not used, I think. A nest from Bay St. Louis was composed of the very black horse-hair-like inner fiber resulting from the decay of *Tillandsia*.

M. G. Vaiden writes to me that he found a nest near Belzoni, Miss., in a heavy oak swamp where there were clusters of *Usnea* on practically all of the trees. The nest was 16 feet above the ground and 12 feet out on a limb of an oak; it was made like our northern nests and lined with the "moss" and fine rootlets. Another described in his notes was entirely different. It was in a section of Mississippi where there was no *Usnea* growing within 60 miles. The nest was 6 feet from the ground and 4 feet out in the crotch of a limb of a hackberry tree. A pretty nest, it was nicely constructed of leaves and bark from cypress trees, and was lined with small rootlets and very fine twigs.

*Eggs.*—The usual set for the northern parula warbler consists of 4 or 5 eggs; 3 sometimes constitute a full set, and as many as 6 or 7 have been found in a nest; there are 3 sets of 7 in the J. P. Norris collection. The eggs are ovate or short ovate, have only a slight gloss, and are white or creamy white, speckled and spotted with shades of "russet," "chestnut," "bay," and "auburn," with a few underlying spots of "brownish drab." There is much variation; on some eggs the "brownish drab" color is entirely lacking, while on others spots of this color are the most prominent markings; again, the eggs may be almost immaculate, or may have just a few indistinct freckles of "pale wood brown" at the large end. The measurements of 50 eggs average 16.5 by 12.1 millimeters; the eggs showing the four extremes measure 18.3 by 12.7, 16.9 by 12.9, 14.8 by 11.9, and 16.3 by 11.2 millimeters (Harris).

*Young.*—The period of incubation does not seem to have been determined, nor do we know how long the young remain in the nest. Incubation of the eggs and brooding of the young is performed mainly by the female, but the male assists in both to some extent. I have seen a male leave a nest in which there were eggs; and Mr. Mousley (1924) saw a male brood the young for a period of 4 minutes in the absence of the female, but he left as soon as she returned. Both parents feed the young. Mr. Mousley's table shows that during a watching period of 15 hours the male fed the young 45 times and the female fed them only 21 times; the average rate of feeding was once in 13.6 minutes; during this time the male brooded once and the female 34 times, a total of 11 hours and 27 minutes. He "noticed that the food the male brought consisted almost invariably of soft green larvae, whereas, that of the female more often than not consisted of insects, and the portions she brought were usually smaller in proportion than those of her partner."

*Plumages.*—Dr. Dwight (1900) says that the natal down is "smoke-gray." The sexes are alike in the juvenal plumage, which Ridgway (1902) describes as "above plain slate-gray, slightly tinged with olive-green; middle and greater wing-coverts narrowly tipped with white; chin and upper throat pale yellowish; lower throat, chest, sides, and flanks plain light gray (intermediate between mouse gray and gray no. 6); abdomen, anal region, and under tail-coverts white; remiges and rectrices as in adults."

A postjuvenal molt, involving all the contour plumage and the wing coverts but not the rest of the wings or the tail, begins about the middle of July. This produces a first winter plumage in which old and young birds are very much alike and the sexes are recognizable. The young male differs little from the adult male, but the bluish gray of the upper parts is more heavily tinged with olive-green, the yellow of the under parts is duller, and the dark throat band is more or less obscured by yellowish tips on the feathers. The young female differs from the adult female in a similar way and is without any brown throat band.

Dr. Dwight (1900) says that the first nuptial plumage is "acquired by a partial prenuptial moult which involves chiefly the head, chin and throat, but not the rest of the body plumage, the wings nor the tail. The ashy blue crown feathers faintly dusky centrally, the blackish ones of the sides of the head with a white spot above and below the eye and the yellow or chestnut-tinged chin feathers as far as the pectoral band or farther are assumed by moult. Wear brings the back into contrast with the nape and whitens the lower parts. The wings and tail are browner and more worn than in the adult, especially the primary coverts."

A first postnuptial molt in July and early August, which is complete, produces the fully adult plumage. Fall males are similar to spring males, but the blue areas are more or less tipped with greenish and the throat bands with yellowish. Fall females differ in the same way from the spring birds, and there is little, if any, chestnut and no blackish in the throat band.

Subsequent molts and plumages are the same as described above for the young birds.

Charles C. Ayres, Jr., writes to me of a bird he observed near Ottumwa, Iowa: "It was a typical parula warbler with the exception that the blue-gray color extended over the throat and terminated abruptly on the upper breast. Immediately below the termination of the blue-gray color was the well-defined orange-brown breast band, below which the rest of the breast was yellow."

*Food.*—The parula warbler is almost wholly insectivorous. Its food is mainly obtained in the deciduous trees, where it is often seen among the branches and twigs or hanging downward under a cluster of leaves or blossoms like a chickadee searching for small insects, beetles, flies, moths, larvae, and egg clusters. Some flying insects are taken on the wing; and occasionally the bird may be seen feeding on the ground.

Dr. Wetmore (1916) reports on the contents of 61 stomachs from Porto Rico, which contained 97.7 percent animal matter and only 2.3 percent vegetable matter. The latter "consisted of seeds of small berries of the camacey (*Miconia prasina*) and others." In the animal food, beneficial insects and a large number of spiders amounted to about 35 percent, and the remainder were all harmful pests. "Lantern flies (Fulgoridae) (19.09 percent) were identified in 29 stomachs. * * * Other bugs (3.69 percent) comprise small numbers of leaf bugs, species of the chinch bug family, stinkbugs, and a few predaceous assassin bugs. The birds are fond of beetles, and this order supplies 22.53 percent of the food, nearly all being injurious species. Ladybird beetles (1.36 percent) were present in 11 stomachs. Longicorn beetles (1.68 percent) were taken 11 times, and leaf beetles of several species (7.95 percent) were eaten by 30 of these birds." Other beetles taken included darkling beetles, skin beetles, scarred-snout weevils, coffee leaf-weevils, stalk borers, and curculios. Among other items were a few ants and other small Hymenoptera (3.57 percent) and flies (1.19 percent). Caterpillars were found in 18 stomachs and moths in 4. Spiders (29.53 percent) were identified in 29 stomachs. Stuart T. Danforth (1925), from Puerto Rico, adds berries of *Varronia angustifolia* and fleabeetles, and says that large moth eggs were eaten by two birds, forming 25 percent of their food. Forbush (1929) says that "it feeds much on small hairless inch-worms, such as the fall canker-worm and the spring canker-worm, and on the younger and smaller hairy caterpillars, such as the gipsy and the tent caterpillar."

*Behavior.*—The parula warbler is less active in its movements, more sedate and deliberate, than most of the other treetop wood warblers. It creeps along the branches and hops from twig to twig, often clinging to the under side of a cluster like a chickadee, an action that led some of the early writers to refer to it as a small titmouse, and it sometimes clings to the trunk of a tree like a nuthatch in its search for food. The birds are fearless and confiding, and are easily approached. Even when their nest is disturbed they come within a few feet of the intruder, making little, if any, protest or demonstration. George B. Sennett (1878) tells the following story, illustrating the confiding nature of the bird:

Just before we sighted land, imagine our surprise and joy to see a little Blue Yellow-backed Warbler on our mast. It soon flew down to the sail and thence to the deck, where, after a few moments, it felt quite at home. Our sailor caught him, and he was passed around for all to admire and pet. It would nestle in our hands and enjoy the warmth without the least fear. When allowed his freedom, he would hop upon us, fly from one to another, and dart off over the side of the boat as if taking his departure; when lo! back he would come with a fly or moth he had seen over the water and had captured. Several flies were caught in this way. He searched over the whole boat and into the hold for insects. Often he would fly to one or the other of us, as we were lying on the deck, and into our hands and faces, with the utmost familiarity. He received our undivided attention, but could have been no happier than we. Upon reaching shore, amid the confusion of landing we lost sight forever of our pretty friend."

*Voice.*—The parula warbler has a simple, but to my ears a very distinctive, song. In 1900 I recorded the song in my notes as "*pree-e-e-e-e-e, yip*, a somewhat prolonged trill like a pine warbler's, but fainter and more insect-like, ending abruptly in the short *yip* with a decided emphasis." I have always been able to recognize it by the explosive ending, which I never heard from any other wood warbler.

Gerald Thayer wrote to Dr. Chapman (1907) as follows:

The Parula is weak-voiced, and its call notes, as far as I know, are slight and barely peculiar; but it has at least three main songs, with great range of variations.

All may be recognized, or at least distinguished from the weak songs of the *Dendroicae*, like the Blackburnian and Bay-breast, by their beady, buzzy tones. In phrasing, in everything but tone-quality, certain variations of the Parula's and of the Blackburnian's songs very nearly meet and overlap; but the tell-tale tones remain unchanged,—wheezy and beady in the one, smooth as glass in the other. Commonest of the Northern Parula's three main songs is probably the short, unbroken buzz, uttered on an evenly-ascending scale, and ending abruptly, with a slight accentuation of the final note. Next is that which begins with several notes of the same beady character, but clearly separated, and finishes, likewise on an ascending scale, with a brief congested buzz. The third main song is based on an inversion of the second—a buzz followed by a few separate drawled notes, high-pitched like the buzz-ending of the two other songs. All these vary and intervary perplexingly.

Aretas A. Saunders contributes the following notes on the song of this warbler: "The parula warbler has two distinct types of song. One is a simple buzzy trill rising in pitch, and frequently terminated by a short, sharp note of lower pitch. Of 12 records of this song, 7 have the terminal note and 5 do not. The other form has the same buzz-like quality, but begins with three or four short notes on the same pitch, followed by a longer, higher note that is frequently, but not always, slurred upward. Both songs are similar in length and in pitch intervals. They vary from 1⅕ to 1⅗ seconds in length. The rise in pitch varies from one to four and a half tones, and averages about two tones. The actual pitch is exceedingly variable in individuals and varies from A''' to D'''''. Songs vary considerably in loudness, many of them becoming suddenly louder toward the end.

"The species sings throughout migration, and on the breeding grounds till late July. At that season I have seen males still singing while feeding young just out of the nest."

*Enemies.*—Dr. Friedmann (1929) writes; "This bird is practically free from that greatest enemy of most of the warblers, the Cowbird. Occasionally, however, parasitic eggs are found in the dainty pensile nests of the Parula Warbler. Stone found a nest on May 26, 1892, at Cape May Point, New Jersey, containing three eggs of the Warbler and one of the Cowbird. * * * Five other records have come to my notice, from Long Island, New York, Pennsylvania and Connecticut, and the bird is listed as a victim of the Cowbird by several writers, as Bendire, Davie, and Chapman." Mrs. Nice (1931) records two more cases in Oklahoma.

Harold S. Peters (1936) records two lice, *Myrsidea incerta* (Kellogg) and *Ricinius* sp., as external parasites on this species.

*Field marks.*—The parula is one of our smallest warblers. The adult male is well marked, with its blue upper parts, the yellow back being inconspicuous, two conspicuous white wing bands, black lores, yellow breast and chestnut or blackish throat band. The female is duller in all colors, more greenish above and has little or no throat band. Young birds are even less conspicuously marked, as noted in the description of plumages.

*Fall.*—As soon as the young are strong on the wing the family parties desert their breeding grounds, and after the molting season is finished they resort to the deciduous woods and join the migrating hosts of warblers and other small birds drifting southward through the treetops or along the roadside shade trees. The fall migration is apparently a reversal of the springtime routes, as they travel to their winter haunts in Mexico and the West Indies. Professor Cooke (1904) says that this warbler "passes through Florida in countless thousands, being second only to the black-throated blue warbler in the frequency with which it strikes the lighthouses. * * * By the middle of September the great flights begin and continue in full force for a month."

DISTRIBUTION

*Range.*—Southern Canada to Nicaragua and the West Indies.

*Breeding range.*—The Parula warbler breeds **north** to southern Manitoba (Shoal Lake and Caddy Lake); central Ontario (Off Lake, Rossport, and Lake Abitibi); and southern Quebec (Lake Timiskaming, Blue Sea Lake, Gaspé Peninsula, and Anticosti Island). **East** to Anticosti Island (Fox Bay); Prince Edward Island (Tignish); Nova Scotia (Halifax and Yarmouth); and the Atlantic coast south to central Florida (Deer Park, Lake Gentry, and St. Lucie). **South** to central Florida (St. Lucie, Bull Creek Swamp, and Tarpon Springs) and the Gulf coast to south-central Texas (Houston and San Antonio). **West** to central Texas (San Antonio and Kerrville); eastern Oklahoma (Caddo, Red Oak, and Copan); eastern **Kansas**

(Neosha Falls, Topeka, and Leavenworth); central Iowa (Des Moines); north-central Minnesota (Cass Lake and Itasca); and southeastern Manitoba (Shoal Lake).

*Winter range.*—The parula warbler winters **north** to southern Tamaulipas (Tampico); occasionally southern Florida (Tarpon Springs, Sanibel Island, and Miami); the Bahamas Islands (Nassau and Caicos); Hispaniola (Tortue Island and Samaná); Puerto Rico; the Virgin Islands (St. Thomas); and the Lesser Antilles (Saba). **East** to the Lesser Antilles (Saba, St. Christopher, Guadaloupe, and Barbados). **South** to the Lesser Antilles (Barbados); Jamaica (Kingston); and Nicaragua (Río Escondido). **West** to Nicaragua (Río Escondido); El Salvador (Barra de Santiago); western Guatemala (San José and Escuintla); southern Oaxaca (Tehuantepec); Veracruz (Tlacotalpan); and Tamaulipas (Tampico).

The above range is for the species as a whole, of which two geographic races are recognized: the southern parula warbler (*P. a. americana*) breeds in southeastern United States from Maryland southward, east of the mountains; the northern parula warbler (*P. a. pusilla*) breeds in the western and northern portion of the range.

*Migration.*—Late dates of spring departure from the winter home are: El Salvador—Barra de Santiago, April 18. Guatemala—San José, March 7. Yucatán—San Felipe, April 4. Virgin Islands—St. Croix, April 30. Puerto Rico—Mayagüez, May 7. Haiti—Port au Prince, April 4. Cuba—Habana, May 4. Bahamas—Cay Lobos, May 14.

Early dates of spring arrival are: Florida—Daytona Beach, March 3. Alabama—Coosada, March 25. Georgia—Savannah, March 8. South Carolina—Frogmore, March 5. North Carolina—Washington, March 26. West Virginia—Bluefield, April 9. District of Columbia—Washington, April 6. Pennsylvania—Carlisle, April 25. New York—Shelter Island, April 23. Massachusetts—Stoughton, April 25. Vermont—St. Johnsbury, April 21. Maine—Portland, April 29. Nova Scotia—Wolfville, May 8. New Brunswick—St. Stephen, May 9. Quebec—Quebec, May 10. Louisiana—New Orleans, February 15. Mississippi—Bay St. Louis, March 5. Arkansas—Helena, March 24. Tennessee—Athens, April 3. Kentucky—Eubank, April 4. Indiana—Bloomington, April 21. Ohio—Columbus, April 28. Michigan—Ann Arbor, April 29. Ontario—Toronto, May 2. Missouri—Columbia, April 5. Iowa—Grinnell, April 28. Wisconsin—Madison, April 30. Minnesota—Red Wing, May 5. Texas—Hidalgo, March 5. Oklahoma—Caddo, March 25. Kansas—Independence, April 8. Nebraska—Havelock, April 20.

Late dates of fall departure are: Minnesota—St. Paul, October 5. Wisconsin—Milwaukee, October 9. Missouri—St. Louis, October 5.

Ontario—Point Pelee, October 5.   Michigan—Grand Rapids, October 19.   Ohio—Toledo, October 19.   Indiana—Richmond, October 14. Tennessee—Nashville, October 3.   Arkansas—Monticello, October 2. Louisiana—Covington, October 26.   Mississippi—Gulfport, November 2.   Quebec—Hatley, September 30.   New Brunswick—Scotch Lake, September 28.   Maine—Portland, October 24.   New Hampshire—Hanover, October 11.   Massachusetts—Rockport, October 25. New York—Rhinebeck, October 21.   Pennsylvania—Berwyn, October 26.   District of Columbia, Washington, October 17.   West Virginia— French Creek, October 1.   Virginia—Lynchburg, October 17.   North Carolina—Rocky Mount, October 23.   South Carolina—Charleston, October 22.   Georgia—Athens, November 4.   Florida—Gainesville, November 19.

Early dates of fall arrival are: Bahamas—Watling Island, September 28.   Cuba—Habana, August 10.   Dominican Republic—San Juan, October 21.   Puerto Rico—Parguera, September 19.   Nicaragua—Río Escondido, October 20.   Costa Rica—Villa Quesada, October 24.

*Banding.*—Only a single migration record is available from banded birds.   A parula warbler banded as an adult at Flushing, Long Island, New York, on September 16, 1946, was found dead about October 1, 1947, at La Grange, Maine.

*Casual records.*—The parula warbler has been recorded three times in Colorado (in El Paso County, at Kit Carson, and at Denver) ; and three times in Wyoming (once at Cheyenne and twice at Torrington).

*Egg dates.*—Massachusetts: 52 records, May 20 to July 7; 29 records, May 29 to June 10, indicating the height of the season.

Connecticut: 39 records, May 25 to June 25 ; 25 records, June 1 to 10.

South Carolina: 20 records, April 10 to June 24; 10 records, April 30 to May 11.

PARULA AMERICANA AMERICANA (Linnaeus)

SOUTHERN PARULA WARBLER

PLATE 22

HABITS

This southern race of our well-known blue yellow-backed warbler is said to breed from the District of Columbia southward to Florida and Alabama.   William Brewster (1896), in describing and naming the northern race, restricted the Linnaean name *americana* to the southern bird because it was evidently based on Catesby's excellent plate, drawn from a bird taken in South Carolina.   In his comparative diagnoses of the two forms, he describes the southern bird as "averaging slightly smaller but with longer bill.   Adult male with more yellow on the under parts and less black or blackish on the lores and malar region; the dark collar across the jugulum narrow, obscure, often nearly wanting; the chest pale, diffuse russet, without obvious markings." He admits that no one of these characters is quite constant, the best one being the depth and definition of the reddish brown on the chest.   And he suggests that the distribution of the two forms in the breeding season may be roughly correlated with the distribution of *Usnea* in the north and of *Tillandsia* in the south, in which the two forms, respectively, seem to prefer to build their nests.   This, however, is not strictly accurate or universal (for example, see some remarks by M. G. Vaiden, under the preceding form, on the breeding of this species in two different localities in Mississippi).

Arthur T. Wayne (1910) says of the haunts of the southern bird in South Carolina: "As soon as the sweet gum trees begin to bud, the song of this beautiful bird is heard.   It heralds the approach of spring and is one of the first warblers to arrive which does not winter.   The range of this species in the breeding season is entirely governed by the presence or absence of the Spanish moss, and where the moss is growing in profusion the birds are common, but where the moss is absent the birds are absolutely not to be found."

A. H. Howell (1932) calls this southern subspecies "an abundant spring and fall migrant [in Florida]; a common summer resident south at least to Osceola County; and a rare winter resident, chiefly in the central and southern part.   Owing to the presence of a few wintering individuals, it is difficult to determine when spring migration begins.   *   *   *   Positive evidence of migration is furnished by the appearance of large numbers striking the light on Sombrero Key, March 3, 1889, when 250 birds were observed and 30 were killed.   This species is one of the most numerous and regular visitants at the lighthouses on the east coast and on the Keys."   Many of these were, of course, the northern race.   Of the haunts of the southern race, he says: "The dainty little Parula Warbler is found most frequently in cypress swamps or heavily timbered bottomlands, and to a lesser extent in the upland hammocks.   The abundant Spanish moss on the trees furnishes ideal nesting sites for the birds."

*Nesting.*   Except for the fact that the so-called Spanish moss (*Tillandsia*) replaces the beard moss (*Usnea*), the nesting habits of the two races are very much alike.   A. T. Wayne (1910) says that in South Carolina "the nest is always built in the festoons of the Spanish moss, from eight to more than one hundred feet from the ground, and is constructed of the flower of the moss and a few pieces of fine, dry grass."   The nesting habits in Florida are very similar.

In southeastern Virginia, according to Harold H. Bailey (1913) this southern race is:—

a most common breeding bird in its favorite haunts, the cypress or juniper swamps of the southeastern section; Cape Henry southward. These trees seem to furnish particularly fine feeding grounds, and wherever you find one festooned with the long, hanging Spanish moss, here also you are likely to find one or more nests. In this section I should call them a colony bird, for in days past I have seen on the trees in and surrounding one small lake, as many as two hundred pair breeding in company. The Dismal Swamp and its surrounding low territory has been an ideal spot for a feeding and breeding home in years past, but of late, the cutting of the juniper for commercial purposes, and the disappearance of the moss to a great extent, has driven the majority of the birds elsewhere.

*Eggs.*—These are indistinguishable from those of the northern parula warbler. The measurements of 50 eggs average 16.2 by 12.0 millimeters; the eggs showing the four extremes measure 19.5 by 12.7 and 14.0 by 11.0 millimeters (Harris).

*Food.*—Howell (1932) reports: "Examination of the stomachs of four birds taken in Florida in February showed the contents to consist almost wholly of insects and spiders, with a few bud scales. Hymenoptera (ants, bees and wasps) composed the largest item, amounting in two instances to approximately half the total contents. Other insects taken in smaller quantities were lepidopterous larvae, fly larvae, beetles, weevils, scale insects, bugs, and grouse locusts. Spiders were found in three stomachs, and amounted to about 20 per cent of the total food."

### PACULA PITIAYUMI NIGRILORA (Coues)

### SENNETT'S OLIVE-BACKED WARBLER

#### HABITS

This northern race of a wide-ranging species is represented by a number of allied races in Central and South America. From its range in northeastern Mexico it rarely crosses our border into the valley of the lower Rio Grande in southeastern Texas. For its introduction into our fauna and for most of our knowledge of its habits we are indebted to George B. Sennett (1878 and 1879) and to Dr. James C. Merrill (1878). The discovery of the bird in Texas in 1877 is thus described by Mr. Sennett:

On April 20th, soon after reaching Hidalgo, I was directed up the river some four miles by road, and there shot the first three specimens of this new species. On May 3d, another was shot among the mesquite timber of the old resaca, within a mile of town.

On May 8th, another was shot in a dense forest about half a mile from where the first three were obtained. Several more were seen; in fact, they were more abundant than any other Warbler. * * * All of the specimens obtained are males, and I remember of seeing none in pairs.  They were seen usually in little groups of three or four.  They are by no means shy, but frequenting, as they do, the woods, cannot be readily seen.

He visited the locality again the following year and says in his report (1879) :

It is truly a bird of the forest, and delights to be in the upper branches of the tallest trees.  The song of the male is almost continuous as it flies about, and is so clear that it can be heard at a long distance and readily distinguished from all other birds.  By its notes we could locate the bird, and this accounts for our securing so many more males than females.  Were it not for its song, I doubt if we would have taken many, owing to their diminutive size and habit of frequenting the tops of the forest-trees.  As it was, by only taking such as came in our way, we shot over twenty specimens, and could have taken any number more had we set out for them alone.  In feeding habits I could see nothing different from our familiar Blue Yellow-back, *P. americana.*

Dr. Merrill (1878) says of its haunts: "Arrives about the third week in March, and passes the summer among thick woods and near the edges of lagoons where there is Spanish moss."  We found Sennett's warbler fairly common around Brownsville, especially on the edges of the resacas, partially dry old river beds where the trees, mostly small mesquites, are more or less draped with *Usnea* and suggest the places where we would look for parula warblers in the north.

In appearance and behavior they were strikingly reminiscent of our northern friends.  Sutton and Pettingill (1942) found this warbler up to 2,000 feet elevation in southwestern Tamaulipas, in full song on March 14, and a pair copulating on March 20.

*Nesting.*—Dr. Merrill sent to Mr. Sennett (1878) the following description of a nest he found near Brownsville after Mr. Sennett left: "My nest of *Parula* was taken July 5th, about five miles from here.  It was placed in a small thin bunch of hanging moss, about ten feet from the ground, in a thicket; was simply hollowed out of the moss, of which it was entirely composed, with the exception of three or four horsehairs; entrance on side; contained three young about half fledged.  Parents very bold, but thinking they were *americana* I did not shoot them."

The next year, his Mexican guide brought him a nest and a broken egg, which Mr. Sennett (1879) describes as follows:

The nest is exceedingly interesting and beautiful.  It is made in a gray mistletoe-like orchid, an air-plant very common on the Rio Grande, which establishes itself on the small branches of trees, and varies in size up to eight or ten inches in diameter.  This one is six inches long by four and one-half inches wide, quite firm in texture, and was fastened some ten feet from the ground, to the end of a drooping branch of a brazil-tree in open woodland.  The nest is constructed very simply, being formed by parting the gray leaves of the orchid and digging into its centre from the side, a cavity some two inches in diameter being made, with an opening of one and one-quarter inches.  The bottom and sides are lined pretty well up with short cotton wood fibres, forming a fine matting for the eggs to rest upon. A firmer and more secure nest is seldom seen, although so easily made. I imagine a day would complete one, and certainly but little time need be wasted in selecting a site, for thousands of orchids stand out on the partially dead branches on trees with little foliage. That they build also in the hanging trusses of Spanish moss, so abundant everywhere, is true, the young before referred to being found in a nest in one.

There are two nests of Sennett's warbler in the Thayer collection in Cambridge. One of these was taken for F. B. Armstrong in Tamaulipas, Mexico, on July 5, 1911, and held three eggs. It is described as a "nest of hair in bunch of growing moss hanging from limb of cypress tree in river bottom," 8 feet up; it is built right into the *Tillandsia* and is made almost wholly of black and white cattle hair. The other, with a set of four eggs, was taken by James Johnson near Saltillo, Mexico, on May 27, 1906. It is described by the collector as "dug and hollowed in a bunch of pipestem mosses." It is a compact little nest made of very fine rootlets, very fine grasses, shreds of the brown inner bark of the palmetto or palm, and some weed blossoms; it is lined with finer shreds, a little plant down, and a few feathers. Externally it measures 2½ inches in diameter and 2 inches in height; the inside diameter is about 1½ inches; and the depth of the cup about 1¼ inches.

*Eggs.*—Either 3 or 4 eggs seem to constitute the full set, as far as we now know, for Sennett's warbler. The 7 eggs in the Thayer collection vary from ovate to short ovate, and have only a slight lustre. They are white or creamy white and are speckled and spotted with shades of "wood brown," "cinnamon-brown," or "Brussels brown," with underlying spots of "pale brownish drab." On some eggs the markings run to much darker browns, such as "auburn" and "chestnut," and on these the drab spottings are frequently lacking. Usually a loose wreath is formed where the spots are concentrated at the large end, but occasionally they are distributed nearly evenly over the entire surface. The measurements of 36 eggs average 16.3 by 12.2 millimeters; the eggs showing the four extremes measure **19.0** by **13.7** and **15.0** by **11.3** millimeters (Harris).

*Plumages.*—Young Sennett's warblers that I have examined are uniform grayish olive above, inclining to olive-green on the back; the black lores and cheeks are lacking; the median wing coverts are narrowly tipped with whitish, and the greater coverts more broadly so; the chin is pale yellow; the chest and upper breast are shaded with pale gray and centrally tinged yellowish; the abdomen is dull white; and the sides and flanks are shaded with pale olive-grayish. I have not seen enough material to trace subsequent molts and plumages, which doubtless parallel those of the parula warbler.

*Food.*—We have no definite information about the food of Sennett's warbler, but Clarence F. Smith has sent me the following note:

"The only laboratory report available on the food of the species pertains specifically to a South American subspecies of the *pitiayumi* group. The stomach contents were reported to consist of remains of hymenopterous insects and two-winged flies (Zotta, 1932)."

\* \* \*

Nothing further seems to have appeared in print regarding the habits of this warbler. It is much like the well-known parula warbler in appearance and behavior, but can be recognized in the field by the conspicuous black lores and cheeks and by the complete absence of any pectoral band.

### DISTRIBUTION

*Range.*—The species ranges from southern Texas to northern Argentina and Uruguay. The race occurring in the United States is found in southern Texas and northeastern Mexico.

*Breeding range.*—Sennett's olive-backed warbler breeds **north** to northeastern Coahuila (Sabinas); and southern Texas (Hidalgo, Harlingen, and Point Isabel). **East** to southern Texas (Point Isabel and Brownsville); and southeastern Tamaulipas (Altamira and Tampico). **South** to southern Tamaulipas (Tampico); and southern San Luis Potosí (Valles). **West** to eastern San Luis Potosí (Valles); and eastern Coahuila (Cerro de la Silla and Sabinas).

*Winter range.*—While probably not a sedentary form, its winter range very nearly coincides with its breeding range. It has been found in winter from Brownsville, Tex., to northern Hidalgo (Jacala).

*Egg dates.*—Texas: 6 records, April 28 to May 30; 4 records, May 2 to 12, indicating the height of the season.

Mexico: 2 records, May 27 and July 5.

### PARULA GRAYSONI Ridgway

### SOCORRO WARBLER

#### HABITS

The Socorro warbler is closely related to Sennett's warbler and other races of *pitiayumi* but is accepted as a distinct species. It differs from *nigrilora* in having gray, instead of black, lores and cheeks, and in having much less white on the inner webs of the outer rectrices. It was supposed to be confined to Socorro Island, one of the Revillagigedo group, about 250 miles southwest of the southern tip of Baja California. It was added to our fauna by Chester C. Lamb (1925), who states:

On November 3, 1923, I collected one of these birds at Todos Santos, on the Pacific Ocean side of the peninsula of Lower California, some forty miles north of Cape San Lucas. * * * On February 5, 1924, I saw another of these little warblers, within a few feet of me; but my gun was not at hand, so I had to be content with a sight record. The locality was inland, at El Oro, on the east side of the Victoria Mountains, about thirty miles from Todos Santos. The next occurrence, like the first, was at Todos Santos, where, on July 23, 1924, I secured an adult female which is now in my collection at the Los Angeles County Museum, Los Angeles. The taking of these two birds, in the winter and summer of two successive years, would indicate that the species is of more or less regular occurrence in the Cape Region of Lower California. The capture of a specimen in July suggests the possibility of breeding at the point of record.

Nothing more seems to have been heard of the species since. And we know nothing of its habits.

### DISTRIBUTION

*Range.*—Socorro Island and the Cape region of Baja California.

*Breeding range.*—The Socorro warbler is known to breed only on Socorro Island, where it is resident. It has been found in the breeding season near Todos Santos, Baja California.

This warbler has been found in winter in two localities (Todos Santos and El Oro) in Baja California, and appears to be resident in small numbers.

**PEUCEDRAMUS TAENIATUS ARIZONAE Miller and Griscom**

## NORTHERN OLIVE WARBLER

### PLATE 23

### HABITS

The olive warbler was long classed as a species of *Dendroica*, with *Peucedramus* regarded as a subgenus, but it is now properly placed in a genus by itself, for as Dr. Chapman (1907) points out it differs from *Dendroica* chiefly "in its slenderer, more rounded bill, proportionately longer wings (about 1.00 inch longer than the tail) and decidedly forked tail, the central tail feathers being more than .25 inches shorter than the other ones. In general color and pattern of coloration *Peucedramus* is markedly unlike *Dendroica*, from all the species of which the male differs in requiring two years to acquire adult plumage."

For a still longer time it was supposed to be a homogeneous species, until Miller and Griscom (1925) made a study of it and divided the species into five subspecies, mostly Mexican and Central American. In giving this bird the name *P. t. arizonae*, they state that it is entirely different in coloration from the type race; "upperparts plain mouse-gray, in spring plumage almost never tinged with olivaceous, even on the upper tail-coverts, appearing lighter and grayer than typical *olivaceus;* collar on hind neck not so complete, usually invading the occiput; primaries rarely if ever edged with olive-green in spring plumage; head and throat plain ochraceous, duller than in typical *olivaceus;* underparts lighter, the center of the belly purer white, more contrasted with the flanks, which are less olivaceous, more grayish brown; size as in typical *olivaceus.* Throat and side of neck of adult female and immature pale lemon-yellow." They give as its range "mountains of southern and central Arizona south at least to Chihuahua and perhaps east to western Tamaulipas (Miquihuana)."

The species had long been known in Mexico and had been erroneously reported in Texas, but it remained for Henry W. Henshaw (1875) to record it definitely as a North American bird by capturing three specimens on Mount Graham, Ariz., in September, 1874. Since then it has been noted by numerous observers on several other mountain ranges in southern Arizona, where it is now known to be fairly common in summer and where a few remain in winter.

It is a bird of the open pine forests on or near the summits of the mountains. In the Huachucas we found it breeding at about 9,000 feet elevation in the open forests of yellow pine, sugar pine, and fir. As Swarth (1904) says: "I found them only in the pine forests of the highest parts of the mountains, even in cold weather none being seen below 8,500 feet; and more were secured above 9,000 feet than below it."

In the Chiricahuas, Frank Stephens collected a fine series of these warblers for William Brewster (1882a) in March, 1880, in the pine woods at elevations from 10,000 to 12,000 feet. And it was here that W. W. Price (1895) found the first nest in 1894; "the region was a dry open park, thinly set with young pine (*Pinus jeffreyi*), at between nine and ten thousand feet above the sea."

The olive warbler is not always confined to the pines at all seasons, for Dr. Walter P. Taylor tells me that he obtained a single specimen from an oak tree in the Santa Rita Mountains at 5,000 feet on February 4, 1923. It was in the same general locality with bridled titmice and ruby-crowned kinglets, and was alone, perhaps a winter wanderer, foraging nervously through the foliage of the oak.

*Spring.*—According to Swarth (1904), migrating olive warblers reach the Huachuca Mountains, from their winter resorts in northern Mexico, about the first of April. "In 1903 they became fairly abundant, particularly in April, when many small flocks of five or six birds each, were seen. * * * They were seldom in company with other warblers, but when not alone, associated with nuthatches and creepers." Frank C. Willard (1910) says that "the first few days are spent, as it were, in staking out their claims anew. The males at this time are quite pugnacious toward one another, and, tho apparently already mated, they promptly drive any wanderer of the same sex from their selected bit of forest. I believe they return each year to the same locality in which they made their home of the previous year, as I have found them in the same patch of trees year after year while other places near by, with the same apparent advantages, never seem to be chosen." Dr. Taylor (MS.) saw a pair of olive warblers, 20 to 30 feet up in some yellow pines in the Santa Catalina Mountains on May 13, 1928. They kept giving a whistled call with descending inflection. "The two birds were courting apparently, flying about, often facing each other at short range, 6 to 18 inches, calling at very frequent intervals."

*Nesting.*—To William W. Price (1895) belongs the honor of finding the first nest of the Arizona olive warbler. On June 15, 1894, on the Chiricahua Mountains, he—

saw a female, closely followed by a male, fly from a bush of spirea (*Spirea discolor*) to the top of a small pine, and busy itself on a small horizontal limb partially concealed by pine needles. She soon returned to the spirea, followed by the male, which did not enter the bush but perched on a pine branch near by. The female again flew with a dry flower-stem in her bill, from the bush directly to the pine, where a nest was in process of construction. * * * A few days after, a forest fire drove me from my camp, and it was not until July 1 that I was able to visit the nest. The female was sitting, and when frightened from the nest, kept hovering about, but made no sound. The male did not appear at all. The nest was compactly built and placed on a small horizontal branch, about forty feet from the ground, and about six feet from the top of the tree. The eggs, four in number, were in an advanced state of incubation. * * * The body and walls of the nest are composed of rootlets and flower stalks of *Spirea discolor*, and the inner lining consists of fine rootlets and a very small quantity of vegetable down. It is a compactly built structure, measuring about 4 inches in outer diameter by 1¾ inches in depth; the inner cup measures 2 inches in width by 1⅛ inches in depth.

A few years later, O. W. Howard (1899) reported finding four nests in the Huachuca Mountains; one was about 30 feet up in the fork of a large limb of a red fir; another was in a sugar pine near the extremity of a limb and about 30 feet from the ground; a third was near the end of a long slender limb of a yellow pine, about 50 feet up, and well concealed among the long pine needles; the fourth was on a branch of a red fir, not far from the trunk, and over 60 feet from the ground.

F. C. Willard (1910), collecting in the Huachucas, says that "short-leaf pines, long-leaf pines and firs are chosen for the nesting sites." One female that he watched building her nest "was gathering rootlets at the time and seemed very particular about them, picking up and dropping several before selecting one which she thought satisfactory. This she carried into a dense growth at the tip of a branch of a large fir about one hundred yards away. The male was singing and feeding in a tree close by.   After a few trips with material the female would fly into the tree where he was and let him feed her.   This is the only time I have observed nest building going on and the male not following the female in her flights."   In his description of the nest, he says: "It is supported by ten small live twigs from the size of a pencil down, all growing from a branch about five eighths of an inch in diameter. It is composed outwardly of moss and pine bud hulls with plant down scattered thruout.   The proportion of this latter increases until the the lining is reacht where it forms a felt like a hummingbird's nest. This lining is supplemented with a few very fine rootlets."

He gives an interesting account of his attempts to locate another nest in "a short-leaf pine whose branches were weighted down with masses of twigs and cones."   He worked from ten in the morning until three in the afternoon, following the birds about, climbing the suspected tree several times and cutting off many twigs, before he finally found the nest.   "The tree was not a very large one and I had shaken every branch and jarred them with my foot, but until I practically toucht the nest she had stayed on."

While I was in Arizona with Willard he collected for me on May 30 a beautiful nest of the olive warbler, with four fresh eggs.   It was taken at an altitude of 8,500 feet on the Huachuca Mountains and was built in a clump of mistletoe near the tip of a branch of a sugar pine about 20 feet out from the trunk and 55 feet from the ground.   Its construction was similar to those described previously (pl. 23).   The loftiest nest that he ever found was 70 feet from the ground in a pine.

The nest built by the Arizona olive warbler is beautiful, and quite different from that of any other species of its group.   A typical nest (in the Thayer collection in Cambridge) is made mainly of a brown lichen or moss mixed with other lichens and mosses, bud scales, flower scales, and some plant down, reinforced with fine yellowish rootlets. All these are compactly worked into and supported by the living needles of the yellow pine in which the nest was built.   The lining consists of plant down and finer strands of the same yellowish rootlets. It measures 3½ by 3 inches in outside diameter and 2½ in height; the inner cavity is about 2 inches in diameter and 1¼ inches in depth.

*Eggs.*—Three or four distinctive eggs seem to constitute the full set for the northern olive warbler.   These are ovate to short ovate and have a very slight lustre.   They are grayish or bluish white, or even very pale blue, liberally speckled, spotted and blotched with "dark olive-gray," "dark grayish olive," "drab," "olive-brown," or "dark brownish drab."   These are interspersed with undertones of "mouse gray," "deep mouse gray," or "Quaker drab."   On some eggs the spots are sharp and distinct, while on others the olive, brown, and drab markings are clouded into the undertones.   The spottings are usually well scattered over the entire surface, but tend to become heavier at the large end. The measurements of 28 eggs average 17.1 by 12.8 millimeters; the eggs showing the four extremes measure **19.0** by **16.0, 16.0** by 12.2, and 18.1 by **12.0** millimeters (Harris).

*Young.*—Information is lacking on incubation and care of the young.

*Plumages.*—The plumages and molts of the olive warbler are as distinctive as its nest and eggs. The sexes are not quite alike in juvenal plumage. Ridgway (1902) describes the young male as "pileum, hindneck, back, scapulars, rump, and upper tail-coverts plain dull olive or brownish olive; supra-auricular region and sides of neck dull yellowish buffy, the latter tinged with olive; chin, throat, and chest dull yellowish buffy; otherwise like adult female." And of the young female, "similar to the young male but paler and grayer above; supra-auricular and post-auricular regions pale brownish buffy; chin, throat, and chest still paler buffy, the chin and upper throat dull buffy whitish." The white tips of the greater wing coverts are tinged with yellowish.

I have not been able to trace the postjuvenal molt in the series I have examined but it apparently occurs in July and produces very little change, young birds of both sexes in their first winter plumage closely resembling the adult female at that season, though the crown and nape are grayer and the throat and breast are paler. I can find no evidence of a prenuptial molt. Young males evidently breed in this plumage and do not acquire the fully adult plumage until their second fall, or perhaps later. In Brewster's series, collected in March, three males are in this condition, of which he (1882) says that "two of them, although in unworn dress, are absolutely undistinguishable from adults of the opposite sex; the third (No. 77), however, has the throat appreciably tinged with the brownish-saffron of the adult male." This last may be a bird that is one year older, for Ridgway (1902) describes the "second year" male as "identical in coloration with the adult female." Judging from the series that I have examined, including all of Brewster's birds, I am inclined to think that the adult winter plumage is acquired at the first postnuptial molt, or when the bird is a little over one year old.

There can be no doubt, however, that young males breed in this immature plumage, for Price (1895) secured a pair that were feeding a brood of young, and the "male was not in fully adult plumage and was very similar in coloration to the female." Swarth (1904) writes: "The male bird breeds in the immature plumage, for on June 21, 1902, I assisted O. W. Howard in securing a nest, containing four eggs, the parents of which were indistinguishable in color and markings. * * * I was surprised at the large proportion of birds in this immature plumage that were seen.  At a very liberal estimate I should say that the males in adult plumage comprised barely a third of the birds seen in the spring."

Adults have a complete postnuptial molt, mainly in July; all June birds that I have seen are in worn plumage, and August and September birds are in new, fresh feathers.  The fall plumage of the male is similar to that of the spring male, but the colors of the head, neck, and chest are duller, more clay color, the back is more olive and the sides are browner.  In the female at this season the crown is tipped with grayish and the throat and breast with buffy, while the sides are browner than in the spring; the white tips of the greater wing coverts are tinged with yellowish.  The nuptial plumage is acquired mainly, if not entirely, by wear, the edgings wearing away and the colors becoming brighter.

*Food.*—Nothing definite seems to have been recorded on the food of the olive warbler, but its habit of creeping over the branches and twigs of the pines, much after the manner of the pine warbler, would seem to indicate that it was foraging for the many small insects that infest these trees.  It is evidently one of the protectors of the pine forests.  Brewster (1882b) says: "In their actions these Warblers reminded Mr. Stephens of *Dendroeca occidentalis*.  They spent much of their time at the extremities of the pine branches where they searched among the bunches of needles for insects, with which their stomachs were usually well filled.  Occasionally one was seen to pursue a falling insect to the ground, where it would alight for a moment before returning to the tree above."

*Behavior.*—One of the members of Henshaw's (1875) party brought in a specimen of this warbler, on September 20, "which he stated he had shot from among a flock of Audubon's Warblers and Snowbirds, which he had started from the ground while walking the pine woods.  With the rest, it had apparently been feeding upon the ground, and had flown up to a low branch of a pine, where it sat and began to give forth a very beautiful song, which he described as consisting of detached, melodious, whistling notes."

W. E. D. Scott (1885), writing of his field work in the Santa Catalina Mountains in late November, says:

Associated with flocks of the Mexican Bluebird (*Sialia mexicana*), which was, by the way, the only kind of Bluebird observed, was always to be found one and sometimes two representatives of the Olive Warbler (*Peucedramus olivaceus*).  The Bluebirds were generally feeding on some insects in the tall pines, in flocks of from six to ten individuals.  The Olive Warblers were on the best of terms with their blue friends, and as the Bluebirds were shy and restless they made it difficult to obtain or observe very closely their smaller allies.  I did not in these pine woods see the two species apart, and became at length so well aware of the intimacy that existed between them, that I would fire at any small bird passing high overhead in company with Bluebirds. They were chance shots, certainly, but the only two small birds obtained flying in this way with the Bluebirds were Olive Warblers. * * * Generally they preferred the largest branches of the pines when they alighted, though I took one not more than three feet from the ground in a small bush. Their movements while feeding or searching for food are very deliberate, though I noticed now and again certain motions when at the extremity of a bough that reminded me of a Kinglet or a Titmouse.

Swarth (1940) says: "Though frequenting the tree tops to a great extent, they seem singularly tame and unsuspicious, and several times I have had one feeding in some of the lower branches, within arm's reach of me, without its showing the least sign of fear."

*Voice.*—The olive warbler has a rather loud, attractive, and distinctive note, but few observers have referred to it as a song. The "beautiful song" mentioned above consisted of "detached, melodious, whistling notes."

One of its whistling notes sounds very much like the *peto* note of the tufted titmouse and might easily deceive the listener. Scott (1885) observed that these warblers "had a call-note so like that of their associates [the bluebirds] as to be almost identical. It seemed to me only a clearer whistle of more silvery tone." Price (1895) saw a male alight on a twig near his mate, during nest-building, uttering "a liquid *quirt, quirt, quirt,* in a descending scale." Mr. Henshaw (1875) heard "a few strange Vireo-like notes coming" from an olive warbler. A bird that Dr. W. P. Taylor (MS.) watched in apparent courtship gave "a whistled call with descending inflection."

*Field marks.*—In general appearance and behavior the olive warbler suggests the pine warbler, especially as it creeps over the pines. The orange-brown head, neck, and breast of the adult male, with the conspicuous black band through the eye, is distinctive; these colors are much paler and more yellowish in the female, and the band through the eye is grayish. Both adults have two white wing bars, a white area at the base of the primaries and much white in the tail, the white areas being more restricted in the female. Young birds are much like the female (see descriptions of plumages).

*Winter.*—The olive warbler, as a species, is probably permanently resident throughout most of its Mexican and Central American range. But the northern olive warbler is evidently partially migratory, though some individuals, perhaps many, remain in Arizona during part, or all, of the winter. All of the 15 specimens taken by Stephens for William Brewster (1882b) were collected in March, probably too early to be migrants, and he says that Stephens had previously taken one in February 1880, evidently a wintering bird. Mr. Swarth (1904) writes: "I have not found this species very abundant in the Huachucas at any time, but it is probably resident to some extent, for I secured

an adult male on February 21 when the snow was deep on the ground.
During March I saw several more, all adult males and single birds,
usually with a troop of Pygmy Nuthatches; but it was not until the
first of April, when the other warblers were arriving, that they became
at all abundant." Scott (1885) found them on the Catalinas under
winter conditions, with snow on the ground, and says: "I think there
can be little if any doubt that they are residents all the year." And
Dr. W. P. Taylor (MS.) took one in the Santa Ritas on February 4,
1923. Just how far south go the birds that migrate away from Arizona does not seem to be known, but apparently they have not been
detected beyond Chihuahua and Tamaulipas. Perhaps they do not
migrate at all.

### DISTRIBUTION

*Range.*—Southwestern United States to northern Nicaragua.

*Breeding range.*—The northern olive warbler breeds **north** to central Arizona (Baker's Butte and White Mountains) and central western New Mexico (Reserve). **East** to western New Mexico (Reserve
and McKnight's Canyon) ; Chihuahua (Colonia García) ; southeastern
Coahuila (Diamante Pass) ; and southwestern Tamaulipas (Miquihuana). **South** to southwestern Tamaulipas (Miquihuana) and
southern Durango (Durango). **West** to Durango (Durango) ; Sonora
(Sierra Saguaribo) ; and southeastern and central Arizona (Huachuca Mountains, Santa Catalina Mountains, and Baker's Butte).
Other races occur in southern Mexico and Central America.

*Winter range.*—The northern olive warbler is probably migratory
to some extent, individuals withdrawing to the southern part of the
range, but it is found in winter occasionally or in small numbers as
far north as southern Arizona.

*Egg dates.*—Arizona: 14 records, May 23 to July 1; 7 records, June
2 to 18, indicating the height of the season.

### DENDROICA PETECHIA AESTIVA (Gmelin)

### EASTERN YELLOW WARBLER

PLATES 24, 25

### HABITS

The familiar yellow warbler, also commonly called the summer
yellow bird or wild canary, is the best known and the most widely
known of all of our wood warblers. It is one of the few birds that
almost everybody knows by one of the above names. It is universally
beloved as it comes to us in the flush of budding spring, gleaming
in the shrubbery, like a rich yellow flame among the freshly opening
leaves, or bringing to the apple orchards a flash of brilliant sunshine

to mingle with the fragrant blossoms. As Dr. Chapman (1907) says: "In his plumes dwells the gold of the sun, in his voice its brightness and good cheer. We have not to seek him in the depths of the forest, the haunt of nearly all his congeners, he comes to us and makes his home near ours."

The yellow warbler, as a species, is also the most widely distributed member of its family. Its breeding range extends from the Atlantic to the Pacific in both Canada and the United States (110 degrees of longitude), and from the Barren Grounds in northern Canada to Mexico and the Gulf States (40 degrees of latitude). Its winter range covers 54 degrees of longitude and 31 degrees of latitude in Central and South America. Professor Cooke (1904) says: "The extreme points of the yellow warbler's range—northern Alaska and western Peru—are farther separated than the extremes of the range of the black-polled warbler, which is considered the greatest migrant of the family." But it must be remembered that the yellow warbler breeds much farther south than the blackpoll.

*Spring.*—The spring migration of the yellow warbler is long and partially circuitous; eastern yellow warblers that winter as far east as British Guiana probably make a roundabout flight to Central America, as there seem to be no springtime records for this bird in the West Indies and few for it in Florida. These birds may fly across the Gulf from Yucatán to Cuba and Florida, but the main flight is probably directly north from Yucatán to Louisiana and other points on the Gulf coast; they have been repeatedly seen flying northward in the middle of the Gulf. There is also a considerable migration along the coast of Texas, which I have personally observed.

The migration is also prolonged or very irregular, for according to the dates of departure given to me by Alexander F. Skutch (see under *Winter*), the last of these warblers do not leave Central America until the very last of April, or the first of May, after the first arrivals have reached New England; some of these records, however, may apply to one of the western races. After the birds reach the United States, the migration fans out northward and northeastward and seems to be more rapid. Of this Frederick C. Lincoln (1939) says: "Coming north from the Tropics these birds reach New Orleans about April 5, when the average temperature is 65° F. Travelling on northward much faster than does the season, they reach their breeding grounds in Manitoba the latter part of May, when the average temperature is only 47°. Encountering progressively colder weather over their entire route, they cross a strip of country in the 15 days from May 11 to 25 that spring takes 35 days to cross. This 'catching up' with spring is characteristic of species that winter south of the United States and of most of the northern species that winter in the Gulf States."

*Territory.*—Soon after their arrival on their breeding grounds the males begin to select their territories and then to defend them.   Dr. S. Charles Kendeigh (1941) made a study of the territories of birds in a prairie community in northwestern Iowa, and writes:

A special study of the Yellow Warbler indicated that territorial requirements included suitable nest-sites, concealing cover, tall singing posts, feeding areas in trees, and space, and that when certain of these factors were lacking, territorial relations became confused and the behavior of the birds was modified.   *   *   * These warblers possessed territories that averaged about 150 feet in diameter, or approximately two-fifths of an acre.   Even in locations where trees were included, the territories appeared to be of about the same size.   The limits of the territory often did not coincide with the boundaries of the thicket in which the nest was located but extended over the neighboring grassland and often included parts of neighboring thickets.   These territories were defended by the males partly by singing, although in shrubby areas lacking trees they were handicapped by lack of singing posts from which to proclaim their ownership and to advertise themselves.   A few made use of fences from which to sing and also of tall posts and wire from an abandoned electric line that extended through the area.   The role of the female in defense of territory was not determined.

Probably due to this lack of singing posts and to the unusual abundance of birds, chasing was also extensively used as a defense measure, and during the height of the nesting season squabbling birds were a common sight all over the area.   *   *   *   Neighboring males seemed to lack any conception of the limits of each other's territories and moved about indiscriminately until chased out. No actual fighting was observed.   *   *   *   In other parts of the area where trees were available, the males commonly sang at a height of 18 feet, often up to a height of 45 feet, and chasing was not often observed.

For yellow warblers observed by Wendell P. Smith (1943) at Wells River, Vt., "territorial exclusiveness scarcely existed.   In one season a Chestnut-sided Warbler's nest was located within five feet of that of the Yellow Warbler.   The following species were represented by one nesting pair within a radius of thirty feet: House Wren, Catbird, Black and White Warbler, Chestnut-sided Warbler, Northern Yellow-throat and Indigo Bunting.   Unless another individual came very close to the nest, no hostility was shown by either male or female. Too close an approach would bring a swift attack by one or the other, however, but for only a short distance when the pursuer would give up the chase."

A. D. Du Bois mentions in his notes a nest that was about 6 feet from the door of a screened porch in daily use and tells the following story about the territory involved: "Twelve yards south of this nest was a spruce tree.   On several occasions the male met another male at this tree or beyond it.   Both alighted at times in the treetop.   Their boundary arguments had the appearance of pushing-contests in the air; and sometimes the contestants revolved in the air, about an imaginary axis between them.   Once, while one of the warblers was in the tree, the other was seen to poise near the tree on fluttering wings, remaining for two or three seconds as nearly stationary in the air as a hummingbird. Twelve yards beyond the spruce I found a nearly completed nest in tall lilacs; but this nest was not finally occupied." Apparently, a second pair of warblers had tried to build a nest too near the territory of the first pair and had been driven out of the territory.

*Courtship.*—Mr. Smith (1943) says on this subejct:

> Courtship begins soon after arrival of the species. Within a period of from four to six days greatly increased singing is noted which marks its inception. Persistent and lively pursuit of the female by the male was observed, taking place within a restricted area (once within a radius of thirty feet). From one to four days elapsed before courtship was completed. Sexual union may not take place until nest building begins as the following observations in 1938 tend to show. Pursuit of the female began on May 23, continued on the 24th but frequent attempts at intercourse on the part of the male were unsuccessful. On the 26th copulation was seen to take place and on that date the nest was completed. * * * A period of several days intervened between nest completion and egg laying. During two seasons of rather intensive observation, this was two days.

*Nesting.*—Although we have come to regard the yellow warbler as a sociable and friendly little bird that seeks our company and builds its nest in the shrubbery about our homes, often close to our houses or in the bushes under our windows, such were not the original nesting sites and even now are far from being the commonest situations chosen, although they may seem the most evident.

The favorite nesting sites in southern New England are along small streams and brooks, around the borders of swamps and ponds and lakes, or in the more open brushy swamps (where the land is moist but not too wet) among willows, alders, elderberry and blueberry bushes, and other moisture-loving shrubs and small trees. They also nest in drier situations, in shrubbery about open spaces, along brush-grown fences and hedgerows and roadside thickets, or in cut-over lands grown up to sprouts and to thickets of wild raspberry, blueberry, and other bushes.

In such situations the nest is built in an upright fork or crotch of a bush or sapling, seldom over 6 or 8 feet from the ground or less than 3. Nests are sometimes built at higher levels in apple trees in orchards or in small trees about houses but rarely as high as 30 or 40 feet. Near human habitations, clumps of lilac bushes, often close to windows or doors, are decided favorites, while various kinds of ornamental shrubs about our gardens or grounds also provide suitable nesting sites.

Mr. Du Bois has sent me the data for 30 nests of the eastern yellow warbler found in Minnesota, Illinois, and New York. Among these, 4 were in willows, 3 each in lilacs and alders, 2 each in elms and box-elder saplings, and 1 each in a grapevine, an ash sapling, a spirea bush, and a currant bush. One of these latter, in an unspecified bush, was 14 feet from the ground, and another, in a wild grapevine climbing on a tree beside a coalbin, was 8 feet from the ground; those in the elms were 12 and 14 feet, respectively, from the ground. The remainder were mostly 5 feet or less above ground, the lowest being at a height of 2 feet, in a currant bush near a vegetable garden. He tells of a nest that was built in a wild rose bush at the edge of a small run near his vegetable garden; "this nest was so compactly fabricated as to hold water for some time; I saw about one-fourth inch of water standing in the bottom of it after a heavy rain."

On two occasions, he has found the new nest to have been built on top of the old nest of the previous year.

F. G. Schrantz (1943) has published the results of a careful study of 41 nests of the eastern yellow warbler in Iowa, during 1938 and 1939, on the restricted grounds of the Iowa Lakeside Laboratory. Among those at heights from 1½ to 5 feet from the ground were 27 in wolfberry bushes (*Symphoricarpos occidentalis*), 8 in young saplings of boxelder (*Acer negundo*), 2 in wild gooseberry (*Ribes gracile*), 1 in wild currant (*Ribes floridum*), and 1 in an introduced species of honeysuckle. One nest was in a cottonwood at a height of about 10 feet, and another in a boxelder about 15 feet above ground.

Dr. Roberts (1936) says that in the prairie regions of Minnesota, where underbrush is scarce, the yellow warblers build their nests in the cottonwoods in the tree-claims, "against the trunks of the large trees, supporting them on small lateral branches and twigs. * * * These arboreal nests are often fifteen to twenty-five feet from the ground and occasionally still higher." And in the huge cottonwood trees along the river, he has seen nests placed at elevations of 40 to 60 feet. Others have also recorded nests at heights of 40 and 60 feet.

In Dr. Kendeigh's (1941) prairie community, "twenty out of twenty-nine nests were placed in buckbrush, with the rest in boxelder, lilac, willow, or currant. The buckbrush is a low bush usually three or four feet high, growing in rather dense thickets in the open, especially in grassy areas of *Poa* and *Agropyron*. Nests placed here varied between two and three feet above the ground. The nest found closest to the ground (18 inches) was, however, in a small boxelder. In taller shrubs and trees, the nests were found up to about seven feet above the ground."

Mr. Schrantz (1943) watched the building of a nest from the first stages of construction to its completion and the laying of the first egg, covering a period of 4 days.

Construction was first observed at 7:45 a. m., on June 12, 1939, when a female Yellow Warbler was seen carrying a tuft of plant-down into a small boxelder sapling. Upon examination, a mass of plant-down about one and one-half inches in diameter was found at a measured height of two feet three inches from the ground in the fork of the sapling. During an hour of observation the female continued to carry plant-down at intervals of about four minutes although once it did not bring any material for twenty minutes. At noon the plant-down mass had increased to about three inches in diameter and was more compactly pushed into the fork. By 6:45 p. m., there were many strands of plant fibers and grasses woven around and through the plant-down in such a way as to wrap and bind the plant-down around the small twigs of the fork. The nest was just assuming a cup-shaped structure. The female was now bringing large loads of a mixture of grasses and plant fibers and working at a rate of about one trip every four minutes. The first day's building was completed at 7:55 p. m. The nest was now partially surrounded with woven plant fibers and grasses with a slight formation of a rim.

On the second day the work continued and the "rim consisted of plant fibers and grasses woven partly into the original down but mostly into the sides and around the top. At 6:45 p. m., the nest appeared completed with a well-formed cup, plant-fiber and grass rim, and a plant-down floor." The third day was partly rainy and little was accomplished but "by 8 : 00 on the fourth morning, the plant-down inside the nest was smoothed out and contained a few strands of fine grasses. * * * During all the observations on the building of this nest the male at no time was seen to bring any nest material. However, since there were many hours during the day when no observations were made, it is possible that he might have helped at some time. * * * At 6:30 a. m., the following day, one egg was found in the nest. * * * The dates of the beginning of construction and the dates the first eggs were laid were obtained for two other nests, and the time which elapsed in both cases was four days."

Only the female was seen to take part in the building of the nest that Mr. Smith (1943) watched, but my experience was somewhat different. On May 10, 1942, I found a pair of yellow warblers building a nest in the top crotch of a blueberry bush, close to the side of a country road. They were very tame and gave me an unusual opportunity to watch them for over an hour at short range. I parked my car within 5 feet of the nest and took motion and still pictures, with cameras even nearer. The nest was nearly done and they were putting in the lining. Both birds helped in the work, but the female did nine-tenths of it. She came at frequent but rather irregular intervals, bringing a billful of soft plant down that looked like the down from ferns, some of which I found growing nearby, and to which I saw her making frequent trips; the fronds of the cinnamon ferns were just unfolding. This material she deposited in the cup of the nest and settled her body down into it, smoothing the lining into place by turning her body around in different directions, pressing it down with her body and up against the sides of the cup with a sidewise motion of the wings. Occasionally she reached over the rim of the nest, smoothing it with her neck and tucking in the loose ends with her bill. The bottom and outside of the nest seemed to be about finished; one side of it, opposite the most exposed side, was anchored to a nearby twig with strands of plant fiber. The female seemed utterly fearless; the male was more shy, but his streaked breast was occasionally seen at the nest.

Robie W. Tufts tells me that he has seen the male at the nest; he saw a male come to a partly finished nest sit in it for over a minute as though testing the workmanship and sing twice while sitting there. The male is always very attentive during nest-building, following his mate back and forth on her trips for material and keeping close to her most of the time. His interest in the nest is so keen that it would be strange if he did not sometimes help.

The eastern yellow warbler builds a neat, strong nest, the materials being firmly and smoothly interwoven and the lining compactly felted. Five local nests before me show quite a variation in the materials used and in their arrangement. The most obvious material, occurring more or less in all of the nests, consists of the silvery-gray strands from the last-year's stalks of milkweed, Indian hemp, or other similar dead weeds. One nest has a great mass of such material below it on one side, evidently to fill in space in the fork that supported it; mixed with this material are a few strands of grasses, other shredded weed stems, bits of wool, and gray fur. Although this nest is far from neat externally, the cup of the nest is well and firmly made of finer silvery fibers and fine grasses, cinnamon-fern down, with which it is profusely lined, and a few fine white hairs. The rim is strongly reinforced with horsehair and decorated with the cinnamon down. This nest, the largest of the lot, measures nearly 5 inches in height and 3 inches in diameter, externally. The smallest and the neatest of the five is made of finer strands of similar materials, without a trace of cinnamonfern down, the whole being very firmly and smoothly woven into a compact little nest; the rim is neatly made of very fine grasses, and it is smoothly lined with white plant-down; it measures only 2 inches in height and 2¼ inches in diameter, externally. Grasses enter largely into the construction of all the nests. One in particular is lined with both white and buff plant-down and a little very fine grass, and has a solidly built rim of strong grasses very firmly interwoven; the foundation consists of dry brown and gray lichens, or mosses, and a lot of cotton waste, such as is used to clean machinery. A two-story nest, which measures 4 inches in total height, is profusely lined with white cotton in both stories. There is little difference in the internal measurements, which vary from 1¾ to 2 inches in diameter, and from 1¼ to 1½ inches in depth.

None of my nests contain any feathers, but Dr. Roberts (1936) tells of a nest that was made entirely of chicken feathers, with "not a bit of material of any other kind." It was built in a jewelweed

(*Impatiens capensis*), but after a brisk wind and a sharp shower both nest and weed were completely wrecked. He shows a photograph of a nest built almost entirely of sheep wool, and speaks also of the use of fine strips of inner tree bark, which probably occur in many nests, of quantities of fine, white, silky pappus from various plants, and of a few feathers. Du Bois mentions in his notes a nest in which five soft, white chicken feathers were woven into the lining, the largest one when stretched out measuring 3¾ inches; there were also two or three feathers in the body of the nest. In my collection is a beautifully camouflaged nest that was built in the upright crotch of a small poplar and seems to be made very largely of white cotton mixed with fine, light-colored fibers. It is lined with cotton, and with a few green poplar leaves fastened to the exterior, the whole being firmly bound with some of the finest fibers and with spider silk, the light-colored material matches the bark of the tree so closely that it might easily be overlooked.

T. E. McMullen has sent me his data for over 40 nests of the eastern yellow warbler found in New Jersey and Pennsylvania. The lowest nest was only 1 foot from the ground in a small bush, and the highest was 30 feet up in an elm. In addition to the shrubs and trees mentioned above he lists arrowroot, blackberry briers, elder, holly, Osageorange and buttonbushes, birch, wild cherry and oak saplings, and a pear tree.

The well-known habit of building nests one or more stories over cowbirds' eggs will be discussed under the enemies of the yellow warbler.

*Eggs.*—Four or five eggs made up the usual set for the eastern yellow warbler; sometimes as many as six are found, or as few as three. In shape, they vary from ovate to short ovate, or rarely show a tendency to elongate ovate. They are only slightly glossy. These handsome eggs show a great variation, both in ground color and in markings. The most common ground colors are grayish white or greenish white but some eggs have a bluish white or even a soft, pale green ground color. The spots and blotches show an even greater variety of colors. Shades of "fuscous," "olive-brown," "citrine drab," "buffy brown," "buffy olive," "light brownish olive," "raw umber," "metal bronze," or "tawny olive" are intermingled with undertones of "deep gull gray," "neutral gray," "purplish gray," "pale purplish gray," "mouse gray," or "buffy brown." The markings tend to form a wreath around the large end where, on the heavily-marked types, the blotches overlap the undertones and an almost endless number of shades are formed. Sometimes a few spots or scrawls of dark "mummy brown" or "olivaceous black" stand out in sharp contrast to the other markings. Although the eggs are usually well marked, sometimes with blotches a quarter of an inch in diameter, often they are only finely speckled with the gray undertones. The measurements of 50 eggs average 16.6 by 12.6 millimeters; the eggs showing the four extremes measure 17.8 by 13.2, 17.8 by 13.7, 15.2 by 12.7, and 15.8 by 11.7 millimeters (Harris).

*Young.*—The incubation period for the eastern yellow warbler has been recorded as from 8 to 11 days (most observers place it as about 11 days for each individual egg); often, but not always, it begins before the set is complete, making the period appear shorter for the first egg laid. Eggs are generally, though not always, laid on successive days, but at times 1 or 2 days intervene between layings. Incubation is performed wholly by the female. The male stands guard near the nest and feeds the female while she is sitting, but she also leaves occasionally to feed herself. The young remain in the nest from 8 to 15 days, according to several observers, but here again the normal time is probably between 9 and 12 days, if they are undisturbed.

Harry C. Bigglestone (1913) describes the hatching process as follows:

At about 5:30 a. m. on July 3 the writer was attracted by a peculiar rolling motion of the egg in the nest, and noticed upon closer observation, that the shell bulged out in a ring around the middle or a little nearer the smaller end; and soon it began to crack at this place. The egg raised on the small end, leaning against the side of the nest, and the young bird freed himself from the shell by a series of pushes and kicks by the head and feet, respectively. The head escaped from the larger part of the shell and the lower part of the body from the smaller end. The crown of the head and the median line of the back of the nestling were downy. This entire process covered a period of less than four minutes.

The empty shells were broken up and eaten by the parents. He says that brooding was carried on entirely by the female, except that he once saw the male brooding for 7 minutes, and adds:

The female was more careful in brooding the young during the first few days. She would stop for intervals throughout the day, while feeding, and brood the young. Her way of completely covering the brood was to fluff out the under coverts against the rim of the nest and bring the wings down, just inside, so as to effectually close the nest.

* * * The female had different brooding attitudes for the varying circumstances. For protection against the cold of early morning she brooded in the manner described above, completely covering the young. Through the rains she brooded in much the same way as for cold, sheltering the young, so that after an unusually heavy downpour, the nest remained perfectly dry inside. During the heat of midday she usually stood in the nest with wings spread, shielding the young, but without shutting off the circulation of the air. On the contrary, at times she gently flapped her wings, as if fanning the young. During the strong winds she stood in the nest with wings outstretched, and leaned in the direction of the wind, so as to secure a delicate balance and at the same time keep the young in the nest.

Feeding of the nestlings was carried on about equally by both male and female parents for the first 7 days, after which the male was frightened away by a snake and did no more feeding, the female carrying on for the next 4 days. During observations covering nearly all of 10 full days and part of another there were 2373 feedings, 813 by the male and 1560 by the female, there being only 33 feedings during the whole of the last day. "During the first three or four days when the female was brooding, usually the male gave her the food, which she distributed to the nestlings." Some of the food had to be broken up before it was given to the young; and sometimes it had to be thrust down their throats. There were 331 feedings of unrecognized food, and 553 of unidentified insects. The identified food consisted of 659 green worms, 326 fly worms, 162 other worms, 147 May flies, 103 moths, 75 millers, 65 mosquitos, 26 larvae, 25 grasshoppers, 23 spiders, 18 ants, 14 grubs, 8 beetles, 4 damsel flies, 2 tree hoppers, and 1 bee. Feeding began at from 4:29 to 4:50 a. m., and ended at from 7:36 to 8:04 p. m., the average feeding period being 15 hours and 30 minutes per day. The parents were not seen to follow any system of rotation in feeding the young. "At no time while the nest was under observation did the parents feed by regurgitation," though the parents on several irregularly occurring occasions were seen to insert an apparently empty bill into the mouth of a nestling, but it was long after hatching. The excreta were removed by both parents; they were eaten during about the first half of the nest life and carried away after that; the female did most of this. The parents were very watchful of the young, and were seen to drive away such birds as the cowbird, blue jay, wren, chickadee, brown thrasher, kingbird and blackbird, if they came too near the nest; the only bird that was not driven away was a catbird. The presence of a garter snake at the base of the bush caused great excitement; the snake was seen to climb up into the bush and carry off one of the young when it was about six days old; the young bird was dead before it could be rescued.

Schrantz (1943) writes: "The Yellow Warblers are hatched naked except for a scanty amount of down and are an interesting sight with their large bulging eyes and abdomen. It was observed that the eyes were commencing to open on the third day after hatching. By the fifth day the young can completely open their eyes, but in many cases would immediately close them when the nest was approached. At this age they would also duck down in the nest as if trying to hide. A slight tapping on the nests would cause a rapid outstretching of necks with open mouths." Bigglestone (1913) found that almost any slight noise near the nest would produce the same results. Studies of weights by Schrantz showed that—

the young averaged, when hatched, 1.27 gms.; at one day old, 1.87 gms.; at two days old, 2.95 gms.; at three days old, 4.36 gms.; at four days old, 5.57 gms.;

at five days old, 7.26 gms.; at six days old, 8.20 gms.; and at seven days old, 8.78 gms.    *   *   *

Of the 168 eggs in forty-one nests, 119 eggs, representing 70.83%, hatched. Thirty-four eggs, representing 20.24%, disappeared due to wind, abandonment of nest, and unknown causes.    Fifteen eggs, representing 8.93% were addled, two of which were buried with a Cowbird's egg.    Of the 119 nestlings, twenty-eight disappeared.    This represents 16.66% of all eggs laid.    Four of them were seen dead in the nests.    The others disappeared from unknown causes.    Therefore a total of 91 fledglings, representing 54.17% of the original 168 eggs, left the nest.    *   *   *

After all the young left a nest, the parent birds could be found feeding them in the immediate vicinity of the nest for a period of about three days. After this time the birds became more dispersed from the nesting site, but could still be found in the vicinity for a week or ten days.

An unusual casualty is recorded in the following note sent to me by Dr. Harrison F. Lewis: "A nest of this species which I found in a sheep-pasture, was largely built of wool, presumably gathered from the neighboring bushes, where it had been left by the sheep.    One of the young birds in this nest died as a result of having threads of the wool in the nest become entangled about its tongue and bill.    Another member of this brood became entangled in a similar fashion, but I released it."

*Plumages.*—Dr. Dwight (1900) calls the natal down "mouse-gray," and describes the juvenal plumage, in which the sexes are alike, as "above, pale olive-brown.    Wings clove-brown broadly edged with bright olive-yellow paling at tips of the quills, the edge of the outer primary bright lemon-yellow.    Tail pale clove-brown, the inner webs of the rectrices lemon-yellow, the outer edged with olive-yellow.    Below, pale sulphur-yellow, unstreaked."

The first winter plumage is acquired by a partial postjuvenal molt early in July that involves the contour plumage and the wing coverts but not the rest of the wings or the tail.    He describes the young male as "above, pale yellowish olive-green, the edgings of the wing coverts paler.    Below, dull lemon-yellow obscurely, narrowly and sparingly streaked on the throat and sides with pale chestnut."    The female is paler throughout and has no streaking.

The first nuptial plumage is acquired by a partial prenuptial molt in early spring, "which involves most of the body plumage, the wing coverts and the tertiaries, but not the primaries, their coverts, the secondaries, nor the tail.    The whole plumage becomes golden lemon-yellow, greener above and [in the male] brightly streaked on the throat, breast and sides with pale chestnut, somewhat veiled by the feather edgings.    The forehead and crown are yellower than the back and usually chestnut tinged.    The tertiaries and wing coverts are broadly edged with bright lemon yellow."    The female in this plumage is yellower than in the fall and has a few obscure chestnut streaks below. Old and young birds are now very much alike, often practically indistinguishable, except for the worn juvenal wings and tail. Adults have a complete postnuptial molt in July before or while they migrate and a partial prenuptial molt, as in the young bird, before they arrive in the spring. In El Salvador, according to Dickey and van Rossem (1938), "both adults and young of the year were in complete fall (postnuptial) plumage by the time they arrived. * * * An adult male taken April 10 is in the midst of the spring (prenuptial) molt and presents an extremely ragged appearance. Another, collected on April 24, has entirely finished this molt."

In both adult male and female plumages the colors are richer and the streakings below heavier than in the young bird, but the female is always duller in color and the streaking is less prominent or entirely missing.

*Food.*—Edward H. Forbush (1907) writes of the food of the eastern yellow warbler in Massachusetts:

It would be hard to find a summer bird more useful among the shade trees or in the orchard and small-fruit garden than this species. Almost entirely insectivorous, it feeds on many of the greatest pests that attack our fruit trees, vines and berry bushes. Whenever the caterpillars of which it is fond are plentiful, they form about two-thirds of its food. It is destructive to the small caterpillars of the gipsy moth and the brown-tail moth, and is ordinately fond of cankerworms and other measuring worms. Tent caterpillars are commonly eaten. Small bark beetles and boring beetle are eaten, among them the imago of the currant borer. Weevils are greedily taken. A few useful beetles are sacrificed; among them ground beetles, soldier beetles, and small scavenger beetles. The Yellow Warbler has some expertness as a flycatcher among the branches, and seizes small moths, like the coddling moth, with ease, but apparently does not take many parasitic hymenoptera, although some flies are taken. Plant lice sometimes form a considerable portion of its food. No part of the tree where it can find insect food is exempt from its visits, and it even takes grasshoppers, spiders, and myriapods from the ground, grass, or low-growing herbage.

He (1929) says elsewhere: "It attacks none of the products of man's industry, so far as our records go, except the raspberry, of which it has been known to eat a few occasionally."

S. A. Forbes (1883) reports that 5 stomachs from a canker-infested orchard contained 94 percent insects; of which 66 percent were cankerworms, Coleoptera 23 percent, spiders 6 percent, Hymenoptera 2 percent, and Hemiptera 1 percent. A. H. Howell (1907) found a cotton-boll weevil in one stomach from Texas; E. R. Kalmbach (1914) reports that of seven Utah stomachs, two contained alfalfa weevils, forming 25 percent of the food in one; and Prof. Aughey (1878) found an average of 11 locusts in 7 Nebraska birds.

*Behavior.*—The gentle little yellow warbler is not only one of the prettiest but one of the tamest and calmest of our bird neighbors. It comes to us in the most friendly and confiding manner to build its cozy nest and rear its little golden family in the lilac bush under our window or in the climbing rambler over our porch.  Nor does it mind our company in the least as we watch its home life almost within arm's reach.  I have sat for an hour within a few feet of a pair of these lovely birds and watched them building their nest.  The many fine photographs that I have received show that it is an easy subject for close-up pictures; the near presence of the camera does not seem to disturb them in their feeding routine.  Many intimate home-life studies have been very successful, for they are brave and devoted parents.  Robie W. Tufts (1927) has had a male yellow warbler come at least twice to feed a brood of young that he was holding in his hand, and once he even wiped his bill on his thumb.  It is such displays of confidence that endear us to the little golden gem.

*Voice.*—Aretas A. Saunders contributes the following study of the song of this warbler: "The song of the yellow warbler is a bright, sweet and musical refrain of about 8 notes.  My records show that the number varies from 5 to 15 and averages 8½.  The songs are quite variable in form, so much so that it is the quality, rather than the form, that makes the song recognizable.  This quality is difficult to describe, yet that quality, after a little familiarity, is easily recognized; the tones, though musical and pleasing, are not quite clear, but slightly sibilant.

"Two forms of the song are fairly typical, but there are a number of others that vary so much that they are quite unlike either of these.  The most common form begins with four or five notes of even time, and all on the same pitch.  These are followed by two or three more rapid notes on a different pitch, usually lower; and the song is ended by one or two notes back on the original pitch and time.  Such a song, in its simplest form, might be written *see see see see tititi see.*  Of my 87 records, 45 may be classed as this form.

"The second form begins in the same manner, but has all the notes of equal time, and the last three or four successively lower in pitch.  I have records of 24 such songs.  There remain in my records 18 songs so variable that they belong to neither of these forms, and yet no two of them are similar in form.  A number of songs of the different forms begin with slurred notes, the slurs being about equally up or down in pitch.

"Songs vary from 1⅕ to 2 seconds in length, averaging about 1⅗ seconds.  The pitch varies from A ′ ′ ′ ′ to D ′ ′ ′ ′ ′, only three and a half tones altogether.  Single songs vary from one to two and a half tones in range of pitch, averaging about one and a half tones.  Individual birds may sing as many as three different songs, and sometimes sing two different songs in regular alternation.

"Singing continues from the first arrival in migration until the third week of July, ceases for a short time, but is usually revived in August, and is to be heard irregularly until the birds depart for the south."

Francis H. Allen gives me his impressions of the two common songs as follows: "One of these I have been accustomed to render as *wee see wee see wiss wiss'-u*. Occasionally the final *wiss'-u* is doubled. The other of these two songs goes something like *wee wee wee witita weet*, without the drop in the pitch that the first song has at the final note. I have also heard a song of five single notes with no variation in pitch or tempo—*weet weet weet weet weet*. Besides a rather sharp *chip*, which is the ordinary call-note, I have heard a *dzee* from a yellow warbler."

The yellow warbler is an early riser. Mr. Smith (1943) heard one begin singing at 4:56 a. m., "daylight time," and another at 4:05, "but with only one song until 4:08 when seven were given during the space of one minute. During the song period of fifty minutes, 197 songs were given." Dr. Charles W. Townsend told Mr. Allen that he heard one at Ipswich, Mass., on June 13, 1908, that began singing at 3:10 a. m., but this was standard time.

Dr. Winsor M. Tyler (1937) mentions a peculiar note, heard during the migration in August, which had puzzled him for nearly 30 years until he finally traced it to an eastern yellow warbler. "As we walk under the trees, listening, we hear a long, wild, high, sharp bird-note, abrupt, and very slightly vibratory, lasting perhaps half a second. It is a characteristic sound of this time of year, and we hear it best on these quiet, silent days. It comes from a bird moving restlessly up in the trees, and before we can see the bird, it is gone. * * * In pitch, it suggests the call of a migrating Ovenbird, but it is too long-drawn-out; it suggests the *chip* of a Northern Water-Thrush in its sharp abruptness, but again it is too long."

According to Albert R. Brand (1938) there is considerable variation in the pitch of the song of the eastern yellow warbler, from 8,775 vibrations per second in the highest note to 3,475 in the lowest note, and with an approximate mean of 5,900 vibrations per second. This is far below the approximate mean of 8,900 for the black-poll warbler, but well above the average of 4,000 for all passerine birds.

*Field marks.*—One hardly needs field marks to recognize a yellow warbler; it is the yellowest of all our warblers at all seasons, even the wing and tail feathers are edged with yellow, and there is no white in either wings or tail. The youngest birds likewise show some yellow on the under parts and in the flight feathers. See the descriptions of plumages for details.

*Enemies.*—The arch-enemy of the yellow warbler is undoubtedly the cowbird. This warbler is one of the very commonest victims of this parasite, and comparatively few of its nests are not visited at least once by a cowbird in regions where the latter is very common. Dr. Friedmann (1929) has about 500 records of such imposition on the eastern yellow warbler. Everyone who has examined nests of this warbler in any number has found one or more eggs of the cowbird in some of the nests. This parasitic habit has cost this species of warbler many extra hours of unexpected labor and the loss of many eggs and young. But the most interesting fact about it is that the warbler has found a way to combat the evil and, in many cases, to defeat the plans of the cowbird, by either deserting the nest in which the strange egg is deposited or by building a second floor over it and leaving the alien egg to cool off in the "cellar."

The yellow warbler is not the only bird that has learned to do this occasionally, but it is the only one that does it regularly and persistently in spite of repeated contributions from the cowbird. Even if the warbler has one of its own eggs in the nest when the cowbird's egg is deposited it may bury both the eggs by building a story above them, but if there are two or three warbler's eggs in the nest before the alien egg appears, the warbler may feel obliged to incubate and hatch out the stranger, with the usual results of her own young being crowded out and lost. Two or more cowbird's eggs are almost sure to be deserted or buried. But the cowbird is very persistent and keeps on laying, as successive stories are added to the nest by the energetic and persevering warblers. Two-story nests are very common, and as many as three, four, five, and six stories have been recorded. Mr. Forbush (1929) was told by Dr. H. F. Perkins "of one case where a six-storied nest was built, with a cowbird's egg in every one." Mr. Du Bois tells me of a new nest he found in a low bush, with another nest, about half completed and only about a foot below it, containing a fresh, cold cowbird's egg. Out of 43 nests found by Dr. George M. Sutton (1928) in Pymatuning Swamp, Pa., "a Cowbird egg was found in only one nest. This is most unusual, but is due, as elsewhere stated, to the protection against these parasites afforded by the Red-winged Blackbirds which would not tolerate a Cowbird anywhere about the marshes."

Snakes sometimes destroy the young, as related above; squirrels, blue jays, and other predatory mammals and birds rob the nests; and the adults must always be on the alert to escape the many enemies that prey on all small birds.

Harold S. Peters (1936) records only one louse, *Philopterus subflavescens* (Geof.), as an external parasite on the eastern yellow warbler.

*Fall.*—The striking feature of the fall migration of the eastern yellow warbler is its earliness. The birds begin to move away from their nesting haunts as soon as the young are able to take care of themselves, and the southward migration is well under way before midsummer. Smith (1943) says that, in Vermont, "during many seasons, the species is not seen later than July. Departure dates for local summer residents range from July 15 to the 30th. Later records occur between August 18 and September 9th." These later records are probably for birds from farther north. There seems to be a wide spread between the times that the earliest and latest birds leave.

Dr. L. H. Walkinshaw writes to me: "To me it is interesting how soon after nesting has been completed these warblers disappear. After July 10, it is very hard to find one of the species here in Michigan, and after August 10, almost impossible. It does stay some in certain good feeding areas, but the majority have left long before August." According to Milton B. Trautman (1940), the migration in Ohio begins early in July, reaches its height during the first half of August, and only stragglers are seen after September 10.

Arthur T. Wayne (1910) says that, in South Carolina—

the Yellow Warbler is positively uncommon during the spring migrations, but exceedingly abundant in summer and autumn. * * * By July 4, the return migration takes place and a few young birds arrive, but it is not until the 10th or 15th that they are common. * * * The habits of the birds are entirely changed, however, in summer and autumn, for then they frequent the cotton fields, as well as lands which have been planted with peas for forage. It is also not unusual in autumn to see as many as twenty or more of these little birds far out in the salt marshes, where they find food in abundance. The species is so very abundant in late summer and autumn that it is not unusual to encounter hundreds of individuals in a few hours on plantations or in close proximity to salt water.

Prof. W. W. Cooke (1904) writes: "Though in migration the yellow warbler occurs in Florida as far south as Key West and is sometimes fairly common in northern Florida, the numbers that migrate through the southern part of the State must be very small, for not a bird passing north or south has been reported from any of the Florida lighthouses. The migration route of the yellow warblers that breed near the Atlantic coast is evidently southwest to northern Georgia and Alabama, and then across the Gulf of Mexico."

Perhaps the main flight from Florida and the other Gulf States is across the Gulf to Yucatán and then down through Central to South America, for there seem to be no records for Cuba for the eastern yellow warbler. There is a regular migration along the coast of Texas. Dickey and van Rossem (1938) say that "the eastern yellow warbler migrates through El Salvador in fair numbers, but no specimens were taken at any time during the winter. In the fall, particularly, great numbers are in evidence. The first arrivals reached Lake Olomega on August 1, but the main body did not begin to drift through until about the middle of that month."

Frederick C. Lincoln (1939) remarks: "Redstarts and Yellow Warblers, doubtless the more southern breeders in each case, have been seen returning southward on the northern coast of South America just about the time that the earliest of those breeding in the North have reached Florida on their way to winter quarters."

*Winter.*—Dr. Alexander F. Skutch contributes the following winter notes: "This morning as I sat at breakfast a yellow warbler flitted among the shrubbery outside the window. Here in Central America, through 8 or 9 months out of the 12, this well-known bird occupies the same place in dooryard, garden, hedgerow and scrubby pasture as during its briefer sojourn in the more northerly regions where it nests. None of the resident warblers of Central America is quite so abundant and familiar about human dwellings. Everywhere it avoids the heavy forest and prefers the sunlight that floods the clearings made by man.

"It is one of the first of the visitants from the North to arrive in Central America, appearing in Guatemala as early as August 9, reaching Honduras by at least the fourteenth, Costa Rica by the seventeenth, and Panamá by the twenty-second of the month. These early dates are for the Caribbean lowlands, along which it appears to migrate. It arrives later on the Pacific side of the Isthmus, especially in Costa Rica, where it has not been recorded before August 24, at San José, and not until September 11 in the Térraba Valley, still more isolated from the Caribbean flyway by lofty, forested mountains. But by the end of September, it is well distributed as a winter resident over both coasts of Central America, and in the interior up to at least 5,000 feet, becoming rarer at the upper limit of its altitudinal range. Much above 5,000 feet it apparently does not winter; but it is occasionally seen in September in the high mountains as a bird of passage. A heat-loving warbler, it is most common in the lowlands where, in the plantation districts of northern Central America during the winter months, it is among the most abundant birds, whether resident or migratory.

"Although a number of wood warblers which winter in the Central American highlands are gregarious, those that center in the lowlands are typically solitary. In this, the yellow warbler is no exception. Each wintering bird appears to have its own territory, from which it attempts to drive others of its kind. Trespassers are scolded with insistent *chips;* or more rarely, soon after his arrival, a male will sing while defending his claim. Near San Miguel de Desamparados, Costa Rica (4,600 feet), on October 1, 1935, I made the following note: 'This morning, which for a change was bright and calm, I heard a yellow warbler singing in the low fig trees near the house. Upon going out to look, I found that there were two yellow warblers in the trees. One was trying to drive the other away; but the pursued always circled around and returned. I watched them for a long time; but this indecisive action continued without any change in the situation. In the intervals of the pursuit, the warblers (or at least one of them) would sing, but in a low and imperfect fashion, far inferior to the yellow warbler's summer song.' Again, on October 31: 'After the Wilson warbler, the most abundant winter visitor is the yellow warbler. The bird who on October 1 drove its competitor out of the fig trees beside the house still retains these trees and the surrounding *Inga* trees as its domain.'

"The yellow warbler sings far less while in Central America than many other wintering species. Exceptionally, one will be found singing profusely. In early October, 1934, I came upon such a bird among the coffee groves of a great plantation on the lower Pacific slope of Guatemala. His behavior was so far out of the ordinary that I am tempted to copy in full the notes I made upon it at the time: October 5—On the afternoon of my arrival at 'Dolores,' I went out for a walk through the coffee groves. From among the 'chalum' (*Inga*) trees which shaded the coffee bushes, I heard a bird's song which seemed to belong to a warbler; but I did not recognize it as the utterance of any species I knew. After searching for a time among the tree-tops, I spotted the singer, and was surprised to find him a yellow warbler. He was apparently a young bird, for he lacked the chestnut splashes along the sides which distinguish the mature males. He repeated over and over again his little song of four or five notes, which was so unlike the familiar song of the yellow warbler in the eastern United States that I did not at first recognize it; but once I had identified the singer, I realized that I was listening to a shortened and modified form of the typical song.

"As I stood watching and listening to this eccentric warbler, the rain clouds which had been gathering darkly in the west began to surrender their pent-up waters; and the sudden shower approached across the plantation with the roar of a myriad fat drops striking against the large leaves of the Ingas and the far larger ones of the bananas which shaded the plantation. I took refuge from the rain beneath the broad expanse of a banana leaf, which completely shielded me from the beating downpour. Soon the heavy shower exhausted itself; and I emerged from beneath my green roof. The warbler, who had taken shelter from the shower somewhere in the foliage above me, resumed his cheerful singing.

" 'On the next two days, I passed by the spot where I had heard the warbler singing, on the way to and from my botanical collecting ground. Morning and afternoon, I heard the same voice in the same part of the coffee plantation, where the bird seemed to have fixed his residence.'

"Yellow warblers may sing in Central America in the spring as well as the fall. Last year, the male yellow warbler that wintered about my house in Costa Rica sang briefly in the early morning from April 12 to 24. After April 28, I saw no more of his kind in the vicinity.

"From November 1936 until February of the following year, a yellow warbler slept every night in a bush of *Hibiscus mutabilis* beside my cabin in Rivas, Costa Rica. He rested upon one of the long leaf-stalks, where the broad blades of the higher leaves formed a roof above him, but he was exposed on the sides and easily visible from the ground. He always slept alone.

"Early dates of fall arrival in Central America are: Guatemala—passim (Griscom), August 9; Sierra de Tecpán, 8,500 feet, September 4, 1933; Huehuetenango, 6,500 feet, September 11, 1934. Honduras—Tela, August 14, 1930. Costa Rica—Puerto Limón, August 17, 1935; San José (Cherrie), August 24; Cartago, September 6, 1938; Basin of El General, 2,000–3,000 feet, September 13, 1936 and September 11, 1942. Panamá—Canal Zone (Arbib and Loetscher), August 22, 1934.

"Late dates of spring departure are: [British Guiana (Beebe), April 10.] Panamá—Barro Colorado Island, April 23, 1935; Almirante, April 29, 1929. Costa Rica—Basin of El General, April 30, 1936, April 29, 1937, May 7, 1939, May 3, 1940, April 28, 1942; San José (Cherrie), May 11. Honduras—Tela, May 9, 1930. Guatemala—passim (Griscom), May 6; Los Amates, Motagua Valley, May 11, 1932.

Todd and Carriker (1922), reporting for the Santa Marta region of Colombia, say that the eastern yellow warbler is "a common winter resident throughout the whole of the lowlands and lower foothills, but rare above the coastal plain. It frequents shrubbery, open ground with scattering bushes, the low growth along the banks of streams and the sea-beach, etc.—the same kind of covert in general to which it is so partial in the breeding season."

DISTRIBUTION

*Range.*—North America, northern South America and the West Indies.

*Breeding range.*—The yellow warblers of North America breed **north** to north-central Alaska (Kobuk River and Fort Yukon); northern Yukon (Potato Creek, 20 miles above Old Crow River); northwestern Mackenzie (Richard Island, Fort Anderson, Lake St. Croix, and Oot-sing-gree-ay- Island, Great Slave Lake) ; northern Manitoba (Lac Du Brochet, Churchill, York Factory, and Severn House) ; and central Quebec and Labrador (Richmond Gulf, Grand Falls of the Hamilton River, probably Northwest River, and Cartwright). **East** to eastern Labrador (Cartwright) ; Newfoundland (St. Anthony, Twillingate, and St. John's) ; Nova Scotia (Cape Breton Island, Halifax, and Yarmouth) ; and the Atlantic coastal region south to eastern and central North Carolina (Pine Island, Lake Mattamuskeet, Raleigh, and Charlotte) ; central South Carolina (Columbia) ; and central Georgia (Augusta and Macon). **South** to central Georgia (Macon) ; central Alabama, rarely (Autaugaville) ; southern Arkansas (Monticello and Arkadelphia) ; northeastern Texas (Paris, Commerce, and Dallas) ; west-central Oklahoma (Fort Reno and Thomas) ; southern New Mexico (Roswell and Silver City) ; probably southwestern Texas (Fort Hancock and El Paso) ; northern Sonora (Moctezuma, Magdalena, and Colonia Indepencia) ; and northwestern Baja California (El Rosario). **West** to the Pacific coast from northern Baja California (El Rosario) to western Alaska (Frosty Peak, Alaska Peninsula ; Nushagak, Hooper Bay, Saint Michael, and Kobuk River). Wandering birds have been collected at Icy Cape and Wainwright on the northwest coast of Alaska several hundred miles north of the northernmost breeding record.

*Winter range.*—The yellow warbler is found in winter **north** to southern Baja California (La Paz) ; Jalisco (La Barca) ; Morelos (Cuernavaca and Yautepec) ; southern Veracruz (Tlacotalpan) ; Yucatán (Tunkás) ; and Quintana Roo (Akumal) ; occasional or accidental in winter near Brownsville, Tex. **East** to Quintana Roo (Akumal) ; Honduras (Tela and Ceiba) ; Nicaragua (Bluefields) ; Panamá (Almirante and the Canal Zone) ; Venezuela (Trinidad Island) ; British Guiana (Georgetown and the Berbice River) ; Surinam (Paramaribo) ; Cayenne (Cayenne and Approuague) ; and northeastern Brazil (Chaves). **South** to northern Brazil (Chaves, and Bôa Vista on the Rio Branco) and central Perú (La Merced). **West** to central western Perú (La Merced) ; western Ecuador (Guayaquil, Chones, and Esmeraldas) ; western Colombia (Condoto, Medellín, and Turbo) ; western Costa Rica (El General, San José, and Bolson) ; El Salvador (Puerto del Triunfo) ; western Guatemala (San José and Matzantinango) ; Chiapas (Huehuetán) ; Guerrero (Coyuca) ; Colima (Manzanillo) ; and southern Baja California (La Paz).

The range as outlined is divided into several subspecies or geographic races. The Newfoundland warbler (*D. p. amnicola*) breeds from central western Alaska south to central British Columbia, central Alberta, Saskatchewan and Manitoba, central Ontario and Quebec northward and east to Newfoundland; the Alaska yellow warbler

(*D. p. rubiginosa*) breeds in the coastal region of southern Alaska; the Rocky Mountain yellow warbler (*D. p. morcomi*) breeds from southern British Columbia and Washington east through the Rocky Mountains south to northern Nevada, northern Utah and northern New Mexico; the California yellow warbler (*D. p. brewsteri*) breeds west of the Sierras in Oregon and California; the Sonora yellow warbler (*D. p. sonorana*) breeds from southeastern California, southern Nevada, and southern New Mexico to northwestern Mexico and western Texas; the eastern yellow warbler (*D. p. aestiva*) breeds from southern Canada east of the Rocky Mountains southward. The Cuban golden warbler (*D. p. gundlachi*) which is resident in Cuba, the Isle of Pines, and adjacent Cays has been found nesting on Bay Key, Fla. The mangrove, or "golden," yellow warbler (*D. p. castaneiceps*) breeds on both coasts of Baja California from about latitude 27° 14' N. (San Lucas) southward; and on the west coast of Mexico from southern Sonora (Guaymas) south to Nayarit (San Blas). (Apparently it is only slightly migratory, if at all.)

*Migration.*—Early dates of spring departure are: Peru—Iquitos, March 11. British Guiana—Abary River, March 25. Venezuela—Rancho Grande, April 8. Colombia—Santa Marta Region, May 1. Panamá—Canal Zone, May 12. Costa Rica—San José, May 11. El Salvador—Chilata, April 24. Guatemala—Quiriguá, May 11. Honduras—Tela, May 9. Mexico—Tabasco, Balancán, May 11; Nuevo León, Montemorelos, May 21. Florida—Seven Oaks, May 27. Mississippi—Deer Island, May 25. Louisiana—Chenier au Tigre, May 21. Texas—Kerrville, May 31.

Early dates of spring arrival are: Florida—Pensacola, April 6. Georgia, Athens, April 7. South Carolina—Charleston, April 3. North Carolina—Windsor, April 4. Virginia—Lawrenceville, April 13. District of Columbia—Washington, April 2. Pennsylvania—Wayne, April 4. New York—New York, April 19. Massachusetts—Taunton, April 24. Vermont—Burlington, April 28. Maine—Portland, May 2. New Brunswick—Scotch Lake, May 1. Nova Scotia—Wolfville, May 8. Quebec—East Sherbrooke, May 6. Prince Edward Island—North River, May 6. Newfoundland—St. Anthony, June 5. Louisiana—Avery Island, March 23. Mississippi—Shell Mound, April 1. Arkansas—Tillar, April 5. Kentucky—Eubank, April 12. Indiana—Richmond, April 14. Ohio—Oberlin, April 12. Michigan—Ann Arbor, April 19. Ontario—London, April 20. Missouri—St. Louis, April 15. Iowa—Cedar Rapids, April 20. Wisconsin—Reedsburg—April 27. Minnesota—Minneapolis, April 27. Texas—Victoria, March 28. Oklahoma—Stillwater, April 16. Kansas—Topeka, April 16. Nebraska—Red Cloud, April 21. South Dakota—Faulkton, April 22. Manitoba—Aweme, April 30. Saskatchewan—Regina, May 4. Arizona—Fort Lowell, March 19. New Mexico—Albuquerque, April 24. Utah—Provo, April 25. Colorado—Littleton, April 23. Montana—Fortine, May 1. Alberta—Camrose, May 3. Mackenzie—Simpson, May 21. California—Diablo, March 12. Oregon—Portland, April 17. Washington—Camas, April 5. British Columbia—Comox, April 25; Atlin, May 15.

Late dates of fall departure are: Alaska—Ketchikan, September 6. British Columbia—Atlin, August 26; Chilliwack, September 9. Washington—Destruction Island, September 23. Oregon—Newport, September 18. California—Berkeley, October 10. Alberta—Edmonton, September 1. Montana—Great Falls, September 25. Wyoming—Yellowstone National Park, September 21. Colorado Fort Morgan, October 2. Arizona—Organ Pipe Cactus National Monument, October 17. Saskatchewan—East End, September 5. Manitoba—Oak Lake, September 18. North Dakota—Fargo, September 19. South Dakota—Aberdeen, September 20. Kansas—Hays, September 23. Texas—Somerset, October 8. Minnesota—Lanesboro, September 10. Wisconsin—Milwaukee, September 20. Iowa—Marshalltown, September 26. Missouri—Bolivar, October 26. Michigan—Grand Rapids, October 8. Ontario—Ottawa, September 29. Ohio—Cleveland, September 30. Illinois—Chicago, September 29. Kentucky—Hickman, September 23. Mississippi—Gulfport, October 20. Louisiana—New Orleans, October 27. Newfoundland—Tompkins, September 9. Quebec—Montreal, September 3. New Brunswick—St. John, September 2. Nova Scotia—Yarmouth, September 11. Maine—Winthrop, September 23. Vermont—St. Johnsbury, September 21. Massachusetts—Stockbridge, October 1. New York—Rochester, October 30. Pennsylvania—Berwyn, October 7. District of Columbia—Washington, October 12. Virginia—Lexington, October 10. South Carolina—Charleston, October 10. Georgia—Milledgeville, October 27. Florida—Fort Myers, October 25.

Early dates of fall arrival are: Louisiana—New Orleans, July 15. Mississippi—Bay St. Louis, July 7. Florida—St. Marks, July 18. Mexico—Sonora, Sáric, July 31; Oaxaca, Tapanatepec, August 20. Honduras—Lancetilla, August 27. El Salvador—Le Unión, August 1. Nicaragua—Bluefields, August 22. Costa Rica—Puerto Limón, August 17. Panamá—Almirante, August 13. Colombia—Bonda, Santa Marta Region, August 27. Venezuela—Cantaura Anzoatique, September 27. British Guiana—Abary River, September 2. Surinam—Paramaribo, August 28.

*Banding.*—The majority of the banding recoveries indicate the return to the place of banding and give records of longevity. Three birds banded as adults at Wilton, N. Dak., were retrapped at the same station in the following year. One banded at Sioux City, Iowa, on

May 17, 1929, was killed by an auto at the same place June 18, 1932. One banded at Sault Ste. Marie, Mich., on May 30, 1926, was retrapped on May 29, 1929; another banded at the same station, May 20, 1928, was killed by an auto June 28, 1934. A yellow warbler banded at North Eastham, Cape Cod, Mass., on May 28, 1931, was retrapped at the same station May 15, 1932, May 18, 1936, and August 6, 1937.

*Casual records.*—The yellow warbler has twice been collected in Bermuda: November 23, 1875; and October 14, 1903. It has also been observed near Habana, Cuba, on September 3 and 10, 1939. There are three winter records in South Carolina; it was seen at a feeding station at Summerville in the winter of 1939 and on January 21, 1940; and at Charleston on January 18, 1947.

*Egg dates.*—California: 110 records, April 16 to July 15; 56 records, May 21 to June 19, indicating the height of the season.

Massachusetts: 113 records, May 19 to June 30; 82 records, May 27 to June 7.

Minnesota: 26 records, May 29 to June 23; 17 records, May 29 to June 8.

New Jersey: 32 records, May 15 to June 24; 24 records, May 26 to June 7.

Utah: 23 records, May 8 to July 16; 12 records, June 6 to 17.

Washington: 21 records, May 28 to June 24; 11 records, June 2 to 7.

Baja California: 11 records, May 8 to June 12; 6 records, May 15 to June 2, indicating the height of the season.

Mexico: 6 records, June 4 to 20 (Harris).

**DENDROICA PETECHIA AMNICOLA Batchelder**

### NEWFOUNDLAND YELLOW WARBLER

#### HABITS

Based on a series of 14 adult males and 3 adult females from Newfoundland, Charles F. Batchelder (1918) gave the above name to the yellow warblers that breed in that region. After giving a detailed description of the type from Curslet, Newfoundland, he remarks: "When seen in series, the yellow of the under parts is duller, less richly golden, and the chestnut streaks are darker. In comparison with *aestiva*, the female is duskier, less yellowish, throughout the upper parts. * * *

"In general coloring *D. ae. amnicola* shows a certain similarity to *D. ae. rubiginosa*, but it is readily distinguishable from that race by the yellow forehead which, as in *D. ae. aestiva*, contrasts strongly with the green of the back."

Its breeding range extends from Newfoundland to central Alaska, and from Nova Scotia to British Columbia, which includes nearly all of Canada. It migrates through most of the United States, principally through the Mississippi River Basin, and winters in Mexico and possibly South America.

Only a few nesting data are referable to the Newfoundland yellow warbler. Henry Mousley (1926), at Hatley, Quebec, saw a female yellow warbler leaving a large cedar hedge, and says: "Proceeding to the spot from which she came out, I found the nest, which, unlike the usual run of nests of this species, was heavily lined with feathers, instead of plant down * * *. It was nine feet above the ground, in the forks of a small cedar tree."

Roderick MacFarlane (1908) found this warbler abundant in northern Mackenzie, where the nests were "placed on dwarf willows and small scrub pine at a height of a few feet above the ground." Dr. E. W. Nelson (1887) writes:

This is, perhaps, the most abundant warbler throughout Alaska. It is found everywhere in the wooded interior, on the bushy borders of the water-courses, or frequenting the scattered clumps of stunted alders on the shores of Bering Sea, and the coast of the Arctic about Kotzebue Sound. * * * It breeds to the shores of the Arctic Ocean wherever it can find a willow or alder patch wherein to build its nest and shelter its young. * * * In fall, from the last of July to towards the last of August, they come about the houses and native villages to feast on the fare they find provided abundantly in those localities, until, a little later in the season, a few chilling storms send them trooping away with others of their kind to far distant winter quarters.

Dr. Herbert Brandt (1943) writes:

The Newfoundland Yellow Warbler was not observed about Hooper Bay, but as soon as I reached the willows near the mouth of the Yukon River I found it common, and also of like distribution at the other stops that I made on the river as far up as Mountain Village. * * *

The nest of the Newfoundland Yellow Warbler in the Yukon delta is placed usually in a small willow from two to six feet above the ground. The foliage in early July is but partly unfolded, for the alders are yet in their golden curls and the willows in their silver catkins, so the nest is rather conspicuous.

The bird chooses a pronged fork usually with not more than three or four shoots, and in this form constructs its beautiful, trim nest, which is made of plant down and inner bark shreds, all circularly woven and firmly rimmed.

Baird, Brewer, and Ridgway (1874) say: "The notes of Mr. Kennicott and the memoranda of Messrs. McFarlane, Ross, and Lockhart attest the extreme abundance of this species in the farthest Arctic regions. In nearly every instance the nests were placed in willows from two to five feet from the ground, and near water. In one instance Mr. Ross found the eggs of this species in the nest of *Turdus swainsoni*, which had either been deserted or the parent killed, as the eggs were in it, and would probably have been hatched by the Warbler with her own."

As evidence of the late migration of this subspecies, Robie W. Tufts writes to me from Nova Scotia: "The latest date of departure which appears to be normal is October 7, 1936, though they generally leave during the second week of September. On November 25, 1929, a female was collected by me at Wolfville. The bird was searching for food very actively and its general behavior was decidedly abnormal. The bird's body showed slight traces of emaciation." Birds that have been recorded in Massachusetts as late as September 30, long after our local breeding birds have left, were probably of this subspecies.

### DENDROICA PETECHIA RUBIGINOSA (Pallas)

### ALASKA YELLOW WARBLER

#### HABITS

This subspecies was formerly supposed to range throughout most of Alaska, but its breeding range is now understood to be restricted to the coast region of southern Alaska and British Columbia, from Kodiak Island (the type locality) southward to Vancouver Island. It migrates through California to Mexico and Central America, and probably spends the winter in South America. In El Salvador, according to Dickey and van Rossem (1938), "this race was found only as a fairly common spring migrant through the upper levels of the Arid Lower Tropical. As with *D. p. aestiva* the winter range undoubtedly lies farther to the south. It is notable that *rubiginosa* occurs at somewhat higher elevation than the other three forms and was not found at all in the 'tierra caliente.'" This race has been reported in Kansas and in central Texas, but these birds may have been *amnicola*, which somewhat resembles *rubiginosa* and which had not been accepted at that time.

Ridgway (1902) describes the Alaska yellow warbler as "similar to *D. ae. aestiva*, but slightly smaller and much duller in color. Adult male darker and duller olive-green above, the pileum concolor with the back or else becoming slightly more yellowish on forehead (very rarely distinctly yellowish on forehead and fore part of crown); wing-edgings less conspicuous, mostly yellowish olive-green, sometimes inclining to yellow on greater coverts. Adult female darker and duller olive-greenish above, duller yellow below." He might have added that the chestnut streaks on the breast are narrower than in *aestiva*.

Nothing seems to have been published on the nest and eggs of the Alaska yellow warbler, nor on its habits, all of which probably do not differ materially from those of the species elsewhere in similar environment.

DENDROICA PETECHIA MORCOMI Coale

## ROCKY MOUNTAIN YELLOW WARBLER

### HABITS

This is another race that was described many years ago by H. K. Coale (1887) but has only recently been accepted by the A.O.U. Coale gave it its scientific name in honor of J. Frean Morcom and called it the western yellow warbler. The following remarks by Dickey and van Rossem (1938) tell the story very well:

The race of yellow warbler summering in the Great Basin and Rocky Mountain regions of the United States of late years has been generally overlooked and has been synonymized commonly with *aestiva* or, in part, with *brewsteri*. Although not a well differentiated form, its characters are readily apparent in series, and there is no reason why it should not be accorded equal standing with the races currently recognized. The underparts of the males are heavily marked, and in this respect *morcomi* is not distinguishable from *aestiva*. Dorsally, however, *morcomi* is darker and less yellowish green, particularly on the interscapular region. The females are, age for age, more buffy (less yellowish) below and darker and more grayish above than the females of *aestiva*. In comparison with *brewsteri*, *morcomi* (particularly the bill) is larger, and the males are more heavily streaked below. The range of *morcomi* is the Rocky Mountain region of the United States, north to Wyoming and Idaho, west to the eastern slope of the Sierra Nevada, and south (in the western part of its range) to Mammoth, Mono County, California. We have not seen material from the southern Rocky Mountains; so we cannot state the southern limits in that region.

They call it a "common spring and fall migrant and winter visitant in the lowlands," of El Salvador. "Dates of arrival and departure are August 1 and April 9."

Angus M. Woodbury has sent me a copy of the manuscript for "The Birds of Utah," by Woodbury, Cottam, and Sugden, from which I infer that the haunts, nesting, and other habits of the "western yellow warbler," as they call it, do not differ materially from those of the well-known eastern bird. They say of its status in Utah: "This yellow warbler is a common summer resident from early May to late August, the vanguard sometimes reaching here in late April and stragglers sometimes lingering into September, the latest record being September 23. It is primarily a bird of the riparian growths along water edges, either of streams, ponds or lakes or irrigated areas, particularly of the valleys and lower canyons, but occurs higher in the canyons in suitable habitat up to at least 8,000 or 9,000 feet. It does not seem to be attracted to large trees such as cottonwoods, but seems to prefer the more leafy shrubbery and small trees of developmental stages in ecological succession. In migration, it sometimes leaves this niche and may occasionally be found elsewhere. * * *

"In nesting, it is usually found in a bush, chaparral or small tree stratum, seldom going to the ground or to the tops of trees. Its nests

are compactly woven cups generally placed from 3 to 10 feet above
ground, sometimes 15 feet, in rosebushes, willows, choke cherries,
hawk-berries, oaks, young cottonwood or boxelder trees, usually
within a short distance of the water's edge. The nest is usually composed of gray plant fibers, bark shreds or grasses and is usually lined
with some downy substance such as cottonwood or willow cotton or
hair."

DENDROICA PETECHIA BREWSTERI Grinnell

## CALIFORNIA YELLOW WARBLER

### HABITS

The 1931 A.O.U. Check-List gives the breeding range of this subspecies as the "Pacific coast strip from western Washington south
through Oregon and California, west of the Great Basin and southeastern deserts to about lat. 30° in Lower California." It intergrades
with *rubiginosa* on the north and with *morcomi* to the eastward, but
exact boundaries are difficult to define. It seems to range well up into
the mountains, for James B. Dixon tells me that he has found it nesting
in Mono County, Calif., at altitudes of 6,500 to 9,200 feet.

Dr. Joseph Grinnell (1903) in an interesting study of western yellow
warblers, bestowed the above name on the California bird, for which
he gives the following subspecific characters: "Resembling *Dendroica
aestiva aestiva*, from which it differs in smaller size, paler (or less
brightly yellow) coloration, and, in the male, narrower streaking on
under surface; differs from *Dendroica aestiva rubiginosa* in much
smaller size and yellower coloration, and from *Dendroica aestiva
sonorana* in smaller size and much darker coloration."

*Spring.*—Both *rubiginosa* and *brewsteri* occur in California and in
Washington on migrations. As it is difficult to distinguish the two
forms in life, some of the following remarks may refer to either or both
of these two subspecies. Mrs. Amelia S. Allen writes to me that this
species "is the latest of the warblers to arrive in the San Francisco Bay
region for the breeding season. Sometimes they are here by April 8,
but the average date is about April 18. At Lake Tahoe, the first week
of June, breeding pairs were settled in the willows and migrants on
their way farther north were migrating through."

Samuel F. Rathbun says in his Washington notes: "Our experience
with this species, based on many years of observation, is that the birds
in the spring migration progress northward in a series of what may be
called waves. Invariably the first noted will be one or two individuals,
and these are heard for a short time only and evidently move on.
Then there is a break of a day or so before the next are heard, a larger
number. A period of a day, or perhaps two or three, may again elapse
before the main body of birds arrive and they are heard on all sides.

Common in and about the city at this period, it haunts the shade trees lining the streets and the fruit trees in the gardens, but is not at all partial to the outlying sections, except in the more cultivated areas and the orchards. It is essentially a bird of the older settled districts, wherever fruit trees and deciduous trees may abound."

For May 6, 1924, he remarks, "These warblers drifted by all day, in ones and twos or threes, straggling, but, although seemingly widely separated, always within hearing distance of each other. At times there will be a break when apparently none are passing, then in the distance the song will be heard again, soon growing louder, as the bird draws nearer, following in the wake of others that have preceded him, his song in turn growing fainter in the distance after he has passed."

*Nesting.*—The summer haunts and nesting habits of the California yellow warbler are generally similar to those of the eastern bird. Grinnell and Storer (1924) write:

Yellow warblers nest abundantly on the floor of Yosemite Valley. Some of the nests are in growths close to water, whereas others are located in brush tangles or other rank growths back some distance from the streams. A nest found June 7, 1915, may be taken as fairly typical. It was 52 inches above the ground in the crotch of a forking stem of a chokecherry which grew in a clump of the same plant, and was shaded by a black oak. As usual it was higher than wide outside, being 3½ inches in height by 3 to 3¼ inches in diameter. The cup-like cavity was 1¾ inches across at the top and the same in depth at the center. Shreds of bark and flat plant fibers were the principal materials used in construction, the lining being of horsehair and a few feathers.

One nest was "4 feet above the ground in a mountain lilac (*Ceanothus integerrimus*)," and another "was placed about 15 feet above the ground in a small pine tree growing at the margin of a pond. It rested on the next to the topmost whorl of branches and one side was against the slender trunk of the tree."

In the Lassen Peak region, Grinnell, Dixon, and Linsdale (1930) report four nests in willows, one in a wax-berry (*Symphoricarpos*), one in a snowbush, and one fastened between stems of rose and willow at the edge of a clump of rose.

*Eggs.*—Three or four eggs seem to constitute the commonest set for the California yellow warbler. These are hardly distinguishable from those of the eastern bird, though they average, perhaps, more heavily marked. The measurements of 40 eggs average 16.6 by 12.4 millimeters; the eggs showing the four extremes measure **18.3** by 13.5, 17.8 by **15.0**, 14.7 by 12.2, and 16.3 by **11.4** (Harris).

*Food.*—Prof. F. E. L. Beal (1907) analyzed the contents of 98 stomachs of California yellow warblers, and found that the animal matter amounts to 97 percent of the food, consisting wholly of insects and a few spiders.

The largest item is Hymenoptera, which amounts to over 30 percent, almost half of which are ants. The remainder are small bees and wasps, some of which are probably parasitic species, though none were positively identified. * * * Caterpillars, with a few moths, aggregate over 18 percent.

Beetles form nearly 16 percent of the diet, and embrace about a dozen families, of which the only useful one is that of the ladybirds (*Coccinellidae*), which are eaten to a small extent. The great bulk of the beetle food consists of small leaf-beetles (*Chrysomelidae*), with some weevils and several others. One stomach contained the remains of 52 specimens of *Notoxus alamedae*, a small beetle living on trees. Bugs (Hemiptera) constitute over 19 percent of the food, and are eaten regularly every month. Most of them consist of leaf-hoppers (Jassidae) and other active forms, but the black olive scale appeared in a number of stomachs. Plant-lice were not positively identified, but some stomachs contained a pasty mass, which was probably made up of these insects in an advanced stage of digestion.

Flies seem to be acceptable to the summer warbler; they are eaten to the extent of nearly 9 percent. Some of them are of the family of the house fly, others are long-legged tipulids, but the greater number were the smaller species commonly known as gnats. A few small soft-bodied Orthoptera (tree-crickets), a dragon-fly, and a few remains not identified, in all about 5 percent, made up the rest of the animal food.

Only about 2½ percent of the food was vegetable matter, made up mainly of fruit pulp in a single stomach, one or two seeds and rubbish.

Rathbun (MS.) says that this warbler "shows some partiality for feeding on aphids, for we have many times watched it in an orchard carefully scanning the leaves on a tree for this insect."

All other phases of the life histories of this and the following two subspecies do not seem to differ materially from those of the eastern yellow warbler and need not be repeated here.

*Fall.*—According to Rathbun's notes, all the resident, breeding yellow warblers have departed from Washington "by the latter part of August, and in some seasons we have not heard the bird after the twenty-fifth; it is one of the few species that sing more or less during all of its sojourn here, and its song in late summer is almost as good as on its arrival in the spring. A break in the movement south of this species seems to occur about August 20 to 25. Then, early in September, the notes of the yellow warbler begin to be heard again. We have the idea that these may be of the Alaska yellow warbler."

Mrs. Allen writes to me from Berkeley, Calif.: "Breeding birds leave the bay region in late July or early August; migrants from farther north begin to go through in September; the latest date on which I have seen them is October 16, 1920. I usually see them in the shade trees along the streets or in the woods when they come to bathe in my bird pool. But I have two records which show them in very different situations: September 18, 1933, on a hill slope that had been recently burnt over, a group of these warblers with horned larks and Savannah sparrows; and on September 25, 1941, at Point Reyes lighthouse, hunting for food in the low, dry lupines just inside the rocky point. One could not help wondering if they had just come to a landing place after a long flight over the ocean. They were in immature plumage."

According to the 1931 Check-List, the California yellow warbler "migrates through eastern California, Arizona, and Lower California; winters sparsely in the Cape District of Lower California and south to Guatemala, Nicaragua, and Costa Rica."

*Winter.*—Dickey and van Rossem (1938) record this warbler as a "winter visitant and spring migrant in the Arid Lower Tropical Zone," in El Salvador. "The small Pacific coast race, *brewsterii,* is apparently relatively the least common of the four forms found in El Salvador; at any rate, the small number of specimens taken indicates that this is the case. Yellow warblers were common in January at Puerto del Triunfo and in February at Rio San Miguel, but unfortunately only one specimen was taken at each place. Whether all of these winter birds were *brewsteri* and *morcomi* is problematical."

### DENDROICA PETECHIA SONORANA Brewster

### SONORA YELLOW WARBLER

#### HABITS

This is the palest of all the yellow warblers, one of the many pale races of the southwestern desert regions. Its breeding range extends from southeastern California, southern Utah, Arizona, and New Mexico to central western Texas, Sonora, and Chihuahua; and it winters from Mexico southward to Guatemala, Nicaragua, and Costa Rica.

It is best described by Ridgway (1902) as "similar to *D. œ. aestiva,* but much paler; adult male lighter and much more yellowish olive-green above, the back frequently (usually?) streaked with chestnut, pileum usually wholly clear yellow, lower rump and upper tail-coverts yellow, faintly streaked with olive-greenish; wing edgings all yellow; under parts lighter yellow than in *D. œ. aestiva,* and with chest and sides much more narrowly (often faintly) streaked with chestnut; adult female conspicuously paler than in *D. œ. aestiva,* the upper parts often largely pale grayish, the under parts usually very pale buffy yellow."

Woodbury, Cottam, and Sugden (MS.) say of its status in southern Utah: "This race of yellow warbler is a breeder of the streamside fringes of willows, tamarix, and brush of various kinds along the San Juan and lower Colorado Rivers. It undoubtedly extends up the Colorado above the mouth of the San Juan, but how far it extends before yielding to *morcomi* has not been determined. Data available are not sufficient to determine its nesting or migration dates or the length of its stay in Utah."

Swarth (1914) calls it "a common summer visitant in southern and western Arizona, apparently confined almost entirely to the Lower

Sonoran river valleys, the Colorado and the Gila, with their tributaries. * * * I know of no breeding record of a yellow warbler from any point in Arizona north of the Mogollon Divide." Mrs. Bailey (1928) says that "the lower Rio Grande in New Mexico apparently marks the most northern extension of the range of the Sonora Yellow Warbler. It is a common breeder at Mesilla," which is in the southwestern part of the State.

We found the Sonora yellow warbler breeding commonly in the San Pedro Valley, near Fairbank, Ariz., and found several nests in a row of willows along an irrigation ditch. The nests, from 12 to 15 feet above the ground in slender trees, were not very different from those of the eastern bird, being made mainly of willow cotton interwoven with fine strips of inner bark, fine grasses, and plant fibers.

The eggs do not differ greatly from those of the species elsewhere, though what few I have seen are more faintly and finely speckled. The measurements of 40 eggs average 16.9 by 12.8 millimeters; the eggs showing the four extremes measure 18.4 by 13.1, 17.0 by 13.6, 14.9 by 12.5, and 17.8 by 11.4 millimeters (Harris).

### DENDROICA PETECHIA GUNDLACHI Baird

## CUBAN YELLOW WARBLER

#### HABITS

The Cuban yellow warbler was originally described by Baird (1864) as a full species but is now regarded as a subspecies of *Dendroica petechia*. Ridgway (1902) describes it as "similar to *D. p. petechia*, but duller in color; adult male with upper parts much darker olive-green, the pileum usually concolor with the back, sometimes slightly more yellowish, very rarely tinged with orange-ochraceous, and wing-edgings less purely yellow; adult female usually duller in color than in *D. p. petechia*, often grayish olive-green, or even largely gray, above, and dull whitish, merely tinged here and there with yellow, beneath."

Until recently, its range has been supposed to include only Cuba and Isle of Pines. Dr. Barbour (1923) says of its habits: "The Mangrove Canary, as the Cuban Yellow Warbler is called, is abundant wherever there are heavy high mangroves about the coast. I have found it abundant in eastern and western Cuba, and on the Isle of Pines as well. Gundlach reports it nesting in March. I incline to believe that May is more usual; and then the nest of grass, small feathers and woolly down, is placed in a fork on some horizontal mangrove limb. The whole life of the species is passed in the mangrove forests."

Referring to the Isle of Pines, W. E. C. Todd (1916) writes: "This is a bird of the mangroves, to which it is apparently exclusively confined. It is accordingly most numerous along the coast and about the islands of Siguanea Bay, where the mangroves are so constant and pronounced a feature. Mr. Read has observed it along the Pine River also, but it is apparently a rare bird in the northern part of the island, judging from the dearth of records, and, indeed, it cannot be called a common bird in any locality as yet visited. Two nests were found, both in mangroves within a few feet of the water, during the third week in April, but as yet without eggs."

More recently, this warbler has been found breeding on some of the lower Florida Keys. Earle R. Greene (1942) writes:

While exploring one of the Bay Keys in the Great White Heron National Wildlife Refuge off Key West, Florida, on June 15, 1941, with Roger Tory Peterson of the National Audubon Society, a male warbler, in full song, was located. * * * On June 26, the writer located it again on the same key, and on the 28th the male, female and nest were found. The last was in the top part of a red-mangrove tree (*Rhizophora mangle*) and was composed of seaweed and feathers; it contained one egg, white with brownish markings chiefly about the larger end. On July 10, the egg was found broken, apparently jabbed, possibly by a Red-wing nesting nearby. On July 16, the male bird was collected, and on the 30th the female.

Later (1944) he says: "Since then, a male and female were seen on June 16, 1942, on these same keys, and on July 14, 1942, an adult female was noted on the same keys. On August 6, 1942, a male and female, as well as an immature bird, being fed by an adult, were found on Big Mullet Key in the Key West Refuge, which is several miles from the Bay Keys. A letter received from Mrs. Frances Hames states that she found one bird, in song, on one of the Bay Keys on May 30, 1943. I consider it, therefore, a regular nester on certain keys in that area. Additional investigations may determine it as a common breeder."

### DENDROICA PETECHIA CASTANEICEPS Ridgway

### MANGROVE YELLOW WARBLER

#### HABITS

Along both coasts of Baja California southward from about latitude 27° N., and along the Pacific coast of Mexico from Sinaloa to Guatemala, where that curious tree, the red mangrove (*Rhizophora mangle*), bathes its feet in salt water along the shores of bays, estuaries, and tidal creeks, this handsome yellow warbler makes its permanent home. The red mangrove extends its growth on these muddy shores by sending its curving branches outward and downward to take root again in the mud, thus forming an almost impenetrable tangle of roots and branches in an ever-widening band extending outward from the dry land. Its dense, dark foliage forms a low, gloomy forest of branches in which this well-named warbler finds a secure retreat and to which it is almost exclusively confined. It has not always been easy to obtain in these tangles, for Brewster (1902) says that—

during January, February, and a part of March, 1887, Mr. Frazer repeatedly visited all the mangrove thickets that he could find near La Paz, and made every effort to secure a good series of these Warblers, but he took only eight in all and did not shoot more than a pair in any one day. He notes the bird as "rare," but adds that "its numbers increased slightly in March." It cannot be very numerous here at any time, for the total area covered by its favorite mangroves is very limited. Indeed, the place where most of his specimens were obtained "comprises only about two acres, through which winds a small creek, fordable at low tide; but at high water everything is submerged up to the lower branches of the mangroves. I always found the birds working near the surface of the water on the stems of the mangroves or hopping about on the mud, but the males resorted to the tops of the bushes to sing. Their notes are similar in general character to those of the Yellow Warbler."

W. W. Brown was evidently more successful a little later in the season, for, in that same locality in May and June, he collected a large series of these beautiful birds for several American collections, mainly Col. John E. Thayer's. He wrote to Colonel Thayer (1909) :

I found the Mangrove Warbler a rare bird, but my previous experience with this species in Panama, the Pearl Islands, and in Yucatan is what made me successful. I learned its song and alarm note in 1893. The first morning I went into the mangrove swamps of La Paz I whistled the song of the Yucatan species and the birds answered me; this is the secret of my success, for the species is very secretive in its habits. I found it so difficult to get that I offered fifty cents apiece to the duck hunters and others, including the local taxidermist, but they all failed to get it! By covering eight miles of territory I generally managed to get four or five. Sometimes when I shot one it would fall in the mangroves, with a tide running fast. Under such conditions it generally took a long time to find it, and a great deal of cutting with the machete.

Referring to the form found in El Salvador, Dickey and van Rossem (1938) remark: "To add to the difficulties in the path of the collector, the brown and yellow plumage of the males blends perfectly with the dead or dying mangrove leaves which are kept in continual motion by the sea breeze."

*Nesting.*—Brown sent Colonel Thayer (1909) three nests of the mangrove warbler, only one of which contained a set of three eggs. Of this he says: "The nest with eggs is made (and the others resemble it very much) of light green fern down, cobwebs, and light-colored dried grasses, with a few white feathers plastered on the outside. It is beautifully lined with feathers. It is not so perfectly shaped or so well made as the Yellow Warbler's nest."

There are now six beautiful nests of this warbler in the Thayer collection in Cambridge, all collected by Brown near La Paz on dates ranging from May 15 to June 2; all were placed in the red mangroves, either on horizontal branches, mostly near the ends, or in forks; the heights from the ground or water varied from 2 feet to 10 feet. The largest and handsomest nest was 10 feet up on a horizontal branch; it is a very neat, compactly woven cup, made of soft, fine, light buff plant fibers, mixed with plant down, green moss that looks like down (probably the "light green fern down" referred to above or *algae*), a few gray lichens and many whitish flower clusters; it is lined with very fine fibers, apparently from the mangroves, and plenty of feathers; it measures externally 3 inches in diameter and 2½ inches in height; the inner diameter at the top of the in-curved rim is 1¾ inches and the cup is near 2 inches deep. The smallest nest measures only 2¼ inches in outside diameter. The shallowest nest is only 1½ inches high and 1¼ deep inside.

These nests are all works of art and quite distinctive; all the materials are smoothly and compactly felted, being tightly plastered together, as if glued on when wet. The light color and compactness suggest certain hummingbirds' nests. Most of the nests seem small for the size of the birds.

*Eggs.*—Three eggs seems to form the usual set for the mangrove warbler; in the Thayer series there are five sets of three and one set of two. Ed. N. Harrison (MS.) says that "it seems that one egg is a set as often as two." Most of the eggs in this series are ovate, but some are short ovate; they have only a very slight gloss. They are white or creamy white, speckled, spotted or blotched with shades of "mummy brown," "bone brown," "Prout's brown," or "clove brown," with undertones of "light mouse gray," "deep mouse gray," "Quaker drab," or "drab-gray." The browns are frequently so dark as to appear almost black, but some eggs are spotted with lighter shades, such as "cinnamon brown" and "snuff brown." On the more lightly marked types the most prominent markings are the grays, with only a few scattered brown spots. Often a loose wreath is formed around the large end, where the spots are usually concentrated.

The measurements of 32 eggs average 17.9 by 13.4 millimeters; the eggs showing the four extremes measure 19.5 by 13.2, 17.9 by 14.6, 17.0 by 13.2, and 18.3 by 12.9 millimeters (Harris).

*Plumages.*—Although I have examined a large series of mangrove warblers, I have seen no downy young and no summer birds in juvenal plumage. But Dr. Chapman (1907) describes the young female as "above grayish olive-green, rump brighter; tail blackish, externally greenish, webs of all but central narrowly margined with yellow; wings and their coverts blackish, quills margined, coverts tipped with dull greenish; below whitish more or less washed or obscurely streaked with yellow, the under tail-coverts pale yellow."

Young males in the fall are much like adult females, but brighter in color and often with traces of chestnut on the head. Apparently young males wear this femalelike plumage all winter; young males in March show a variable amount of chestnut on the head and throat, and show further progress toward maturity during April, May, and June, indicating a first prenuptial molt. A specimen described by Brewster (1902) is apparently undergoing this molt. "It has the head dull chestnut, very pale and mixed with whitish on the throat, mottled with greenish on the crown; the jugulum, sides of the neck and the middle of the breast *white* with occasional small patches or single feathers of a pale yellow color and numerous fine, chestnut-rufous streaks on the breast; the remainder of the under parts pale primrose yellow mixed with whitish. The back, wings, and tail are nearly as in the adult female. The upper mandible is of the usual dusky horn color, but the basal half of the lower mandible of a pale flesh color. The plumage, generally, has a worn and faded appearance."

This would seem to indicate that the first prenuptial molt is quite extensive, and that young birds become nearly adult after their molt. Adults probably have a complete postnuptial molt sometimes during the summer, but the following descriptions indicate that the prenuptial molt of adults is less extensive. Ridgway (1885) describes the type male, taken December 16, 1882, as follows: "Head rich chestnut, lighter or more rufous on the throat. Upper parts olive-green, the wings dusky, with broad greenish yellow edgings; outer webs of rectrices dusky, edged with yellowish olive-green, the inner webs chiefly primrose-yellow. Lower parts bright gamboge-yellow, the jugulum and breast with a few very indistinct and mostly concealed streaks of chestnut-rufous." And of an adult female, taken December 29, 1882, he says: "Above grayish olive-green; wings grayish dusky, the feathers edged with olive-grayish; rectrices dusky, outer webs edged with olive-green, the inner with primrose yellow. Lower parts dull pale olive-yellowish."

From Dr. Chapman's (1907) descriptions of spring adults it appears that there is very little seasonal change. Male: "Head all around and throat reddish chestnut; back yellow olive-green, the rump brighter; inner webs of all but central tail feathers largely yellow; wings black margined with yellow; underparts, except throat, rich yellow faintly streaked with reddish brown." Female: "Above olive green, much darker and greener than ♂; tail black the two outer feathers with large yellow patches on the inner web near the tip; wings black margined with greenish yellow; below uniform pale, dull yellow."

Laurence M. Huey (1927), referring to the bird life of San Ignacio and Pond Lagoons, on the west coast of Baja California, states that mangrove warblers were found there—

in isolated pairs and gave evidence of early nesting by their singing and by the condition of the sex organs of the specimens collected. This warbler was one of the most interesting species observed. The song of the male was usually delivered from a hidden position amid the dense mangroves, though occasionally the bird was seen perched on a dry twig projecting above the level tops of the thicket. The song was pleasing in tone, and of good volume, suggesting that of the Yellow Warbler, but less shrill. Unlike the song of the Yellow Warbler, it was given with a steady rising inflection. The alarm note is a sharp chirp, audible at some distance even during a brisk wind. This note is uttered at intervals and always in the same tone, much as are the chipping notes of the Orange-crowned Warblers. In searching for food, Mangrove Warblers resemble others of the genus *Dendroica* in their habit of searching each leaf and stem with most careful scrutiny. At times, however, they were seen to launch forth into the air, in true "flycatcher" fashion, after small insects. These aerial sallies were seldom for a distance of over 10 feet, and the bird nearly always returned to the same perch from which it started.

*Enemies.*—The following remarks by Dickey and van Rossem (1938) about the El Salvador race of this species are of interest:

As the entire lives of these birds are spent in an environment which renders them immune from attack by the great majority of the predators which harass species inhabiting the land forest, one is at first inclined to be surprised at their relative scarcity. Raccoons (*Procyon*) are extremely common in the mangroves and were often found prowling through the branches at night. They, as well as carnivorous iguanas, undoubtedly take toll of many nests, but aside from these two it is difficult to conjecture what natural enemy operates to limit the mangrove warbler population. Certainly no "saturation point" has been reached, for pairs may be separated by as much as a mile even in the areas which appear most favorable.

DENDROICA MAGNOLIA (Wilson)

MAGNOLIA WARBLER

PLATES 26–28

HABITS

Wilson secured only two specimens of this pretty warbler, one of which was shot among some magnolia trees near Fort Adams, Miss. He gave it the scientific name *Sylvia magnolia* but called it the black and yellow warbler. This stood for many years as the common name. Nuttall, who had seen it only occasionally in Massachusetts, regarded it as rare. Audubon, on the other hand, found it quite common and even abundant in several places, as we now know it to be. His lively plate of this beautiful bird, one of his best, has always been a favorite of mine; and it seems to me that in the magnolia warbler, more than in any one of the many beautiful species of American wood warblers, are best combined daintiness of attire with pleasing combinations and contrasts of often brilliant colors. Particularly are these qualities apparent when this warbler is seen amongst the dark green firs and spruces of its summer home, where its brilliant array of colors are displayed to advantage as it flits about, sometimes within a few feet of us.

*Spring.*—From their winter quarters in Mexico and Central America, some magnolia warblers migrate straight across the Gulf of Mexico to the Gulf coast between Louisiana and western Florida; they seem to be accidental in Cuba and very rare anywhere in Florida. Another migration, probably of some importance, occurs along the coast of Texas from the mouth of the Rio Grande to Louisiana; I saw a few magnolia warblers in the great migration wave noted on an island in Galveston Bay on May 4, 1923. Professor Cooke (1904) remarks: "The dates of arrival of the magnolia warbler in spring furnish the best evidence yet available in support of the theory that birds migrating across the Gulf of Mexico do not always alight as soon as they reach the shore. The species is a common spring migrant from the Mississippi River to the Atlantic, between latitudes 37° and 39°. South of this district it becomes less and less common, except in the mountains, until in the Gulf States it is rare." It is significant that the earliest date of arrival at Atlanta, Ga., is the same as at the lower Rio Grande in Texas, April 20.

William Brewster (1877) writes:

The Black-and-Yellow Warbler arrives in Massachusetts from the South about the 15th of May. During the next two or three weeks they are abundant everywhere in congenial localities. Willow thickets near streams, ponds, and other damp places, suit them best, but it is also not unusual to find many in the upland woods, especially where young pines or other evergreens grow thickly. Their food at this season is exclusively insects, the larger part consisting of the numerous species of *Diptera*. The males sing freely, especially on warm bright mornings. They associate indifferently with all the migrating warblers, but not unfrequently I have found large flocks composed entirely of members of their own species, and in this way have seen at least fifty individuals collected in one small tract of woodland. By the first of June all excepting a few stragglers have left.

On its migration as well as on its breeding grounds the magnolia warbler seems to avoid the taller treetops and to prefer the lower levels in the forests and in the thickets along the borders of woodlands; it is sometimes seen in garden shrubbery and in orchards, where it adds a brilliant touch of color to the blossoming fruit trees. When it reaches its breeding haunts it prefers low hemlock thickets, or more especially, where these can be found, the dense thickets of small spruces or balsam firs that spring up thickly in old clearings, or grow profusely along the more open woodland paths; the density of the forest depths seems to be avoided in favor of the more open spaces.

In Allegany Park, N. Y., according to Aretas A. Saunders (1938) ; "Magnolia warblers seem to have territory and a definite singing location, but I have seen no animosity toward each other or other species of warblers, such as the black-throated green and blackburnian, birds that have very similar habits and live in the same habitat and sometimes sing regularly in the same tree. * * * Territories are evidently vertical as well as horizontal, that is measured in volume rather than area, so that a clump of big hemlocks furnishes space for several pairs and several species of hemlock-loving warblers."

*Courtship.*—William H. Moore (1904) says: "During the mating season the males are pugnacious little fellows, and many fights do rivals have. They attack each other with much fierceness, seizing hold with their beaks, and hitting with half-opened wings they sprawl about on the ground, until thoroughly overcome. When pressing his suit to the female of his choice, the male displays his colors to great advantage, as they show in fine contrast among the bright green foliage of the trees."

*Nesting.*—All the 14 or more nests that I have seen, in Maine, New Brunswick, Quebec, and Newfoundland, have been in small spruces or balsam firs growing in old clearings, in reclaimed boggy pastures, or along the edges of coniferous woods. These little trees were often less than 6 feet high and generally stood in dense thickets. The lowest nest I find recorded in my notes was only 12 inches above the ground in a tiny fir, and the highest was 8 feet up in a slender balsam in a thick clump of these trees in rather open woods; more nests were below 5 feet than above it. The nests usually rested on horizontal branches or twigs and against the trunk but in a few cases they were placed a few inches or a foot out on a branch.

Similar nesting habits seem to be characteristic of the magnolia warbler in other parts of northern New England, Nova Scotia, and southern Canada according to information received from others; and most of the nests have been placed at similar low levels, though Mr. Brewster (1938) found one near Lake Umbagog that was 25 feet from the ground. In this northeastern region an occasional nest has been found in a cedar, a larch, or a small hemlock, but at a height usually less than 5 feet.

In New York and Pennsylvania hemlock seems to be the favorite tree, and the magnolia warbler more often places its nest at a higher level and well out toward the end of a horizontal branch, where it is usually shaded and sometimes well concealed in dense foliage. Verdi Burtch, of Branchport, N. Y., wrote to Dr. Chapman (1907) that he found nests "in hemlocks usually on a horizontal limb from eight to twenty feet up and over an opening in the woods. Several nests were found in the top of little hemlock saplings from one to five feet

from the ground. One nest was found by Mr. C. F. Stone in a birch
sapling, this being the only instance to my knowledge of its nesting
in a tree other than a hemlock." He has sent me a photograph of a
nest in a wild blackberry bush.

T. E. McMullen has given me the data for 14 nests of the magnolia
warbler found in the Pocono Mountains, Pa.; 10 of these were located
in hemlocks from 30 inches to 30 feet above the ground and from
6 to 12 feet out on the branches; one nest was 30 feet up and one 18,
but the others were all less than 10 from the ground. The other 4
nests were in rhododendrons, in woods, or along the banks of creeks,
and were from 2 to 3 feet up.

Edward A. Preble (Todd, 1940) says that "all but one of more than
fifty nests of this warbler that R. B. Simpson has examined near
Warren [Pa.] were placed in hemlocks. One nest was at the exceptional height of thirty-five feet; another was only a foot from the
ground in some low hemlock brush." Mr. Simpson's other nest was in
a witch-hazel, and Mr. Saunders reported one in a pin cherry, both
under hemlocks.

The magnolia warbler is a poor nest builder; its nests are apparently carelessly built and are very flimsy affairs, much like poorly
built nests of the chipping sparrow; and they are usually insecurely
attached to their supports. Brewster (1877) gives the following good
description of a typical nest: "The framework is wrought somewhat
loosely of fine twigs, those of the hemlock being apparently preferred.
Next comes a layer of coarse grass or dry weed-stalks; while the interior is lined invariably with fine black roots, which closely resemble
horse-hairs. In an examination of more than thirty examples I have
found not one in which these black roots were not used. One specimen has, indeed, a few *real* horse-hairs in the lining, but the roots predominate. This uniform coal-black lining shows in strong contrast
with the lighter aspect of the outer surface of the nest."

Miss Cordelia J. Stanwood, of Ellsworth, Maine, who has sent me
some elaborate notes on the magnolia warbler, gives me this description of one of her best nests: "In this some hay and the fine tips of
cinquefoil served as a foundation, but the greater part of the nest
consisted of a fine black, vegetable fibre, resembling horsehair. So
much of this hairlike material was used that, when the rim was
frescoed with down from the willow pod, a person looking at the
dainty abode in its setting of fir twigs could see nothing but the jet-
black lining and the fluffy, silvery plant-down around the throat of
the nest. The structure was partly pensile, being bound with spiders'
silk to the two branches at right angles to the main stem.

"The front part of the base rested on the branches beneath. It was
placed in a small fir, 2 feet from the ground, surrounded by a growth

of fir and gray birches. * * * The nests were about 2 inches wide at the top on the inside and 1¼ deep. The wall at the top was ¾ inch thick."

A series of eight nests now before me vary considerably in size, compactness, manner of construction, and in the materials used. The largest two measure 4 inches and 3¾ inches, respectively, in outside diameter, and the smallest ones measure from 2¾ to 3 inches. The inner diameter seems to be more constant, varying from 1¾ to 2 inches. All of my nests are shallow, hardly more than an inch deep internally in most cases. Some of them are fairly well made, but most of them are very flimsy and more or less transparent. The neatest nests have the sides and rims well built up with dry grass or weed stems of varying degrees of fineness and density. In some there is no grass, but the sides are well made of the very finest hemlock or larch twigs interwoven with fine, red, fruiting stems of mosses and many fine, black rootlets; they are often slightly decorated or camouflaged with a few weed blossoms or bits of wool or plant down. The lining of black rootlets is present in these and in all other nests of the magnolia warbler that I have seen; it seems to be characteristic of the species and will distinguish the nests from those of other warblers. This jet-black lining forms a fine background against which the handsome eggs are shown in striking contrast.

Miss Stanwood gives in her notes the following account of nest building: "The birds fly with much jolly chattering through the trees and examine any nesting sites that appear desirable. The dainty female, after fitting her little body into many spaces among the twigs, finds one that is entirely adapted to her prospective domicile, and the birds proceed to fashion a basketlike frame of long, fine potentilla or cinquefoil runners, or culms of fine hay. These they fasten to the twigs and needles around the selected space with spiders' web, or tent caterpillar silk, leaving the long ends free. Around the top of the basketlike frame on the interior is laid a culm of hay in the form of an imperfect circle, which is secured to the frame with spiders' silk; many of the long ends are then turned down within, or crumpled into the space for the foundation of the superstructure. In the frame is fashioned the cradle, which is symmetrical and cup-shaped on the inside, but may be formed like the bowl of a spoon on the outside, according to the space which it is designed to fill. The preferred lining materials appear to be a jet-black, hairlike vegetable fibre, and horsehair, but on occasion, the dull orange setae of the birdwheat moss, or the brown fruit stems of maples are used for this purpose.

"Both twittering birds bring the materials while it is damp, if possible, and place it, but being very timid, they work little while an observer is near. At such times the birds come silently, one at a time, deposit the bit of cinquefoil or hairlike fibre hurriedly, the female who is oftentimes less timid than the male, doing most of the modelling, turning around and around in the tiny dwelling and shaping it with her breast. Two birds that I timed carefully spent 4 days building their habitation, and another pair 6 days in doing the same work. The amount of time occupied by the task is determined by the abundance or scarcity of materials and the weather; continuous, heavy, cold and retard the work greatly."

*Eggs.*—Four eggs almost always form a full set for the magnolia warbler, but sometimes there are only three and occasionally five. They vary in shape from ovate to short ovate, or rarely to elongate ovate, and are only slightly glossy. The ground color is white or creamy white and in some instances greenish white. Their markings vary considerably, some being very lightly speckled, while others are boldly spotted, blotched or clouded with "buffy brown," "cinnamon-brown," "Mars brown," "Prout's brown," "mummy brown," "Brussels brown," "chestnut," "auburn," or "tawny-olive," with occasional scrawls of "bay" or black, and with undertones of "vinaceous-drab," "deep brownish drab," or "Quaker drab." There is a tendency for the markings to be concentrated at the large end, where they often form a wreath, or sometimes a solid cap. Many interesting effects are found on the boldly marked eggs, where the large brown blotches are superimposed on the drab undertones. The measurements of 50 eggs average 16.3 by 12.3 millimeters; the eggs showing the four extremes measure 17.9 by 13.2, 15.0 by 12.0, and 15.8 by 11.6 millimeters (Harris).

*Young.*—The period of incubation for the magnolia warbler is said, by different observers, to be 11, 12, or 13 days, and it is evidently performed by the female only. Miss Stanwood tells me that incubation sometimes begins after the second egg is laid. One egg is laid each day until the set is complete. The young remain in the nest from 8 to 10 days, usually the latter. The eyes of the young are opening on the third or fourth day. On the sixth day, the feathers are breaking the sheaths, and by the eighth or ninth day the young are well feathered. The female does all the brooding of the young, of which Miss Stanwood writes in her notes:

"At first the mother bird covered the young much of the time, as the infant birds were fragile and the weather was cold and damp. Every few minutes the brooding bird moved back on the nest far enough to feed the nestlings regurgitated or digested food, and to cleanse the nest of biting pests such as ants, which might endanger the lives of the baby birds. The father bird sang gaily, far away and near at hand, throughout the long summer day. When he came to the nest with food, he flirted his tail, fluttered his wings, quivered all over and twittered very prettily to his mate, who responded in like manner.

"He presented his first tender moths and juicy caterpillars to the mother bird, who ate part of them, but the remainder she crushed and mixed with digestive juices in her mouth and placed well down the throats of the baby birds.

"The little ones were not many hours old before the male insisted on presenting to them a few tidbits himself; and in a few days the parents fed the young almost exclusively on fresh insect food, which grew larger and tougher as the days went by."

She mentions two attempts of the parent birds to draw her away from their young: "Once I accidentally flushed a brooding magnolia. The bird disappeared into the underbrush, but soon attracted my attention to herself by calling from the top of a second-growth fir, a few yards from where her precious secret was concealed. Then she fell from branch to branch, striking the boughs with a thud, like a dead weight, and dragged an apparently helpless leg or wing over the ground, but always away from where her treasures were hidden. On another occasion, when I visited a family of magnolias that were quite ready to fly, the little ones spilled over the side of the cradle into the surrounding grasses and ferns. Both parent birds, with spread wings and tail, tumbled from all the seedlings in the vicinity and trailed around in widening circles, calling piteously. At last the male bird poised himself in air on fluttering wings between me and a callow youngster, but the moment I lessened the distance between us he vanished."

Henry Mousley (1924) recorded his observations on two nests of magnolia warblers, and found that during a period of 15 hours, at one nest containing very young birds, the male fed the young 34 times and the female 58 times; the average rate of feeding was once in 9.8 minutes; the female did all the brooding for a total of 6 hours and 19 minutes; the faeces were eaten 9 times and carried away 17 times, about equally by each sex.

Margaret Morse Nice (1926) made a very elaborate study of the happenings at another nest; her account, containing many interesting observations, to which the reader is referred, is too detailed to be quoted here. Her table shows that she watched the nest for a total of 26½ hours, spread over a period of 9 days; during this time, the young were fed by the male 118 times and by the female 91 times; the average rate of feeding was once in 7.8 minutes; the female brooded 33 times for a total of 352 minutes; the faeces were eaten 8 times and carried away 38 times.

Aretas A. Saunders (1938) writes: "After the young have left the nest, they are much in evidence in the forests. As soon as this happens, whatever territory there was is abandoned. The young wander away, keeping together, and the parents care for them, feeding them frequently for the first few days.  Both sexes feed the young, but after a day or two only the male is likely to be in attendance. Young in this stage are easily located by the incessant hunger calls. These calls consist of three or four high-pitched notes, *tsee tsee tu—tsee tsee tsee tu—tsee tsee*, etc.  I cannot distinguish the call made by young of this species from those made under similar circumstances by the young of the black-throated green and blackburnian warblers."

I have also received from Mrs. Doris Huestis Speirs and from Mrs. Louise de Kiriline Lawrence very full reports on their observations at two nests of magnolia warblers in Ontario.  Many of their observations were similar to those mentioned; however, the following should be noted here: Mrs. Lawrence found the incubation period to be about 11 days, incubation and brooding being by the female only. The young were fed by both parents by regurgitation for the first 3 days, and after that on solid food, mostly caterpillars; in 49 minutes, the male fed them 7 times and the female 5 times.  During 5½ hours, the male ate or carried away the fecal sacks 15 times.  The young left the nest on the ninth day after hatching, and were fed by their parents up to the twenty-fifth day after leaving the nest; after that they were seen feeding themselves.  Mrs. Speirs kept an accurate record of the brooding periods, which were from 8 to 45 minutes in length, but seldom less than 20 minutes, the female leaving the nest for periods of from 3 to 15 minutes.  At times she closed her eyes and seemed to doze; occasionally she rose and turned the eggs with her feet or bill.  The presence of birds of other species approaching or flying over did not seem to disturb her but the movements of a red squirrel in the vicinity kept her alert.  The story of this nest ended in tragedy; some predator destroyed all but one of the young, the female finally disappeared and eventually there was nothing in the nest but an unhatched egg.  A sharp-shinned hawk had been seen flying over.

*Plumages.*—Dr. Dwight (1900) calls the natal down "sepia-brown," and describes the juvenal plumage as "above, dark sepia-brown, soon fading, usually paler on the crown and obscurely streaked with clove-brown.  Wings and tail dull black, chiefly edged with ashy or plumbeous gray, the secondaries, tertiaries and wing coverts with drab, two wing bands pale buff; the rectrices white on inner web of basal half. Below, pale sulphur-yellow, dusky or grayish on the throat, and streaked or mottled except on the abdomen and crissum with deep olive-brown.  Lores and orbital region ashy brown."

The amount of yellow on the under parts is quite variable, the youngest nestlings showing very little or none at all.  The sexes are practically alike in the juvenal plumage, but become recognizable during the first fall.

The postjuvenal molt begins early in July and involves all the contour plumage and the wing coverts, but not the rest of the wings or the tail.

This produces the first winter plumages, in which the young of each sex closely resemble their respective adult counterparts at that season but the colors are all duller, the crown and back are browner, there is a dusky band on the upper breast, and the black streaking is paler or obscure.

Dr. Dwight (1900) says: "First nuptial plumage acquired by a partial prenuptial moult which involves most of the body plumage, the wing coverts and sometimes a few tertiaries, but not the rest of the wings nor the tail. Young and old become practically indistinguishable except by the wings and tail, especially the primary coverts, all of which are usually browner and more worn than in adults." According to Dickey and van Rossem (1938) this takes place in El Salvador early in April and is completed very rapidly.

Subsequent molts of adults consist of a complete postnuptial molt in July and August and an extensive prenuptial molt in April, as described above. Dr. Chapman (1907) says that the adult male in the fall is quite unlike the spring male; "crown and nape brownish gray; eye-ring whitish [instead of white spot below and a white line behind the eye]; * * * rump yellow; tail as in Spring; wing-coverts *tipped* [instead of broadly marked and forming a conspicuous white patch] with white forming two white bars; below yellow, sides with partly concealed black streaks, upper breast with a faint dusky band." The fall female differs in a similar way from the spring female, having a browner crown and the dusky band on the upper breast well developed, much as in the young male in the fall. The female is always much duller than the male in all plumages.

*Food.*—Ora W. Knight (1908) writes: "The food consists largely of beetles, grubs, flies, worms and similar insects. I have seen the birds prying frequently into the deformities on spruce and fir produced by a species of licelike insects (*Adelges*), and feel very sure that they do good work in destroying these pests, which are becoming very numerous in some sections of the State [Maine] and injuring the spruce and fir trees."

W. L. McAtee (1926) praises its good looks as well as its usefulness by saying: "The beautiful Black and Yellow Warbler is a common summer resident of the higher parts of the Catskill and Adirondack regions, and breeds sparingly in local cool spots elsewhere in the State [New York]. * * * So far as known its food in our region consists entirely of insects and associated creatures, as spiders and daddy-long-legs. Almost all of its known items of insect food are sorts injurious to woodlands. It takes weevils, leaf bettles,

and click beetles, leaf hoppers, plant lice, and scale insects, sawfly
larvae and ants, and caterpillars and moths. Surely a record of good
deeds to match the excellence of appearance of this feathered gem."

F. H. King (1883) reports from Wisconsin: "Of seventeen specimens examined, three had eaten four hymenoptera, among which were
two ants; one, one moth; six, seventeen caterpillars; six, fifteen diptera; six, twelve beetles; and one, two larvae. Two tipulids were
represented among the diptera." Professor Aughey (1878) counted
as many as 23 locusts, probably in nymphal stages, in the stomach of a
magnolia warbler collected in Nebraska. And F. L. Burns (1915a)
included this species with the Cape May warbler as feeding on cultivated grapes.

*Behavior.*—The magnolia warbler is not only one of the most beautiful—to my mind, the most beautiful—of wood warblers, it is one of the
most attractive to watch. It frequents, especially on its breeding
grounds, the lower levels in its forest haunts, where it can easily be seen.
It is most active and sprightly in its movements as it flits about in the
small trees or bushes, with its wings drooping and its tail spread almost
constantly, showing the conspicuous black and white markings in
pleasing contrast with the brilliant yellow breast, the gray crown, and
the black back; it seems to be conscious of its beauty and anxious to
display it. Its rich and vivacious song, almost incessantly uttered
during the early part of the nesting season, attracts attention and
shows the nervous energy of the active little bird. It is not particularly shy and is quite apt to show itself at frequent intervals, as if from
curiosity. The female sits closely on her nest until almost touched,
and then slips quickly off to the ground and disappears. But both of
the parents are devoted to their young and quite bold in their defense,
as mentioned above by Miss Stanwood. At the nest that Mrs. Nice
(1926) was watching the warblers paid no attention to a red squirrel
that several times came within 15 feet of the nest. "In general the
relations of these warblers with other birds was not unfriendly; no
attention was paid to passing Chickadees nor to Chewinks and Maryland Yellow-throats that nested near. The only birds towards whom
the male showed animosity were a male Myrtle Warbler that he drove
away both during incubation and while the young were in the nest, and
the male of his own species who came to call July 2. On July 8 the
female warbler gave short shrift to an inquisitive female Black-
throated Green Warbler that seemed to wish to inspect the household."

The intimate studies made by Mrs. Nice and Henry Mousley indicate
that these warblers will tolerate a reasonable amount of human
intimacy without showing too much timidity.

*Voice.*—My earliest impression of the song of the magnolia warbler
was written in 1891 as *wee-chew, wee-chew* in full, rich notes. Later I

attempted to syllabilize it quite differently; once I wrote it *switter*, *switter*, *swirr*, or *swicher*, *swich*, *a-swirr*. On another occasion it sounded like *wheet*, *tit*, *chéw*, or *wheet*, *wheet*, *tit*, *chéw*.

Mrs. Nice (1926) noted only two songs, "the day song and perch song *weechy weech* and the feeding and vesper song *sing sweet* with its variation *sing sing sweet*. He used three different notes: *tit* the alarm note, *kree* the love note, and *eep*, the significance of which I never fathomed."

Gerald Thayer wrote to Dr. Chapman (1907):

> The Magnolia belongs among the full-voiced Warblers, and is a versatile singer, having at least two main songs, both subject to much and notable variation. The typical form of the commoner song is peculiar and easily remembered: *Weeto wecto weétee-eet*,—or *Witchi*, *witchi*, *witchi tit*,—the first four notes deliberate and even and comparatively low in tone, the last three hurried and higher pitched, with decided emphasis on the antepenult *weet* or *witch*. The other song has the same general character, and begins with nearly the same notes, but instead of ending with the sprightly, high-pitched *wéetee-eet'*, it falls off in a single perfunctory-sounding though emphatic note, of *lower* tone than the rest. In syllables it is like *Witti witti wét,'*—*weetee weetee wúr*.

He proceeds to mention some variations:

> One such variant I have fixed in my own recollection by the syllables *Ter-whiz wee-it*; and another, almost unrecognizable, by the syllables *Weé-yer weé-yer wee-yer*. Still another beginning like *Weechi wéech*, ended with a hurried confusion of small notes, some low, some high. But throughout these and all the many other surprising variations I have heard about Monadnock, the characteristic tone-quality was preserved unchanged, and so were certain minor tricks, scarcely describable, of emphasis and phrasing. The tone is much like the Yellow Warbler's and also the Chestnut-side's, though distinctly different from either. In loudness it averages lower than the Yellow's and about equal to the Chestnut-side's.

Then he mentions a peculiar call note, *tlep*, *tlep*, a lisping note with a slight metallic ring, that reminded him of the siskin or of Henslow's sparrow.

The following remarkable list of seven distinct songs recognized by Stewart Edward White (1893) is included because it represents either some very unusual variations or very keen observation:

> 1. Three notes followed by one lower: *che-weech che-weech che-ó*. 2. Three sharp clear whistles with a strong *r* sound, then a warble of three notes, the middle the highest, the latter clear and decisive: *pra pra pra r-é-oo*. 3. Two quick sharp notes followed by a warble of three notes, the middle the highest: the warble is soft and slurred: *prút pút purreao*. 4. A soft falsetto warble, different in tone from any other bird song: *purra-ĕ-whuy-a*. 5. Of the same falsetto tone uttered rapidly: *prut-ut-ut-ut-ut*. 5. A harsh note like, in miniature, the cry of a Jay: *d kay kay kay*. 7. A harsh *k-e-e-e-dl*, the last syllable higher by a shade, quick, and subordinated to the first part. The alarm note is a sharp *zeek*.

Mr. Brewster (1877) has written his impression of the song in words as, "*she knew she was right; yes, she knew she was right*."

Elsewhere, he writes it: *"Pretty, pretty Rachel."* The latter version seems to suggest the rhythmic swing of the song very well.

Francis H. Allen (MS.) gives me several somewhat similar renderings, and mentions a migrating bird that sang for a long time early one morning in the spruces and hemlock near his house: "It was such steady and unintermittent singing as I have seldom if ever heard from any other warbler, and the bird alternated very regularly between the first and second songs—*weetle weetle weetle weet*, then *will' you wée sip*, or *will' you will' you wée sip*, the latter song not so emphatic as usual and weaker than the other." This alternation is not uncommon with some species of warblers, as the redstart, but I have no records of it for the magnolia. He also mentions a common call note, "a dry 2-syllabled note, *tizic*, a little suggestive, perhaps, of the song of the yellow-bellied flycatcher", which he thinks has no counterpart among our warbler notes.

Aretas A. Saunders has lately sent me a full account of the song of this warbler, saying, in part: "The song of the magnolia warbler is a short one, commonly of six or seven notes, of a weak, rather colorless, but musical quality. My 49 records of this song show that the number of notes varies from 4 to 9, all but 8 of them being of either 6 or 7 notes. The 6-note songs usually consist of three, 2-note phrases. The first two are just alike, the 2 notes of each phrase on different pitches. The third phrase is either higher or lower in pitch, and frequently with the order of pitch from low to high or from high to low reversed.

"The majority of the songs have a range, in pitch, of two or two and a half tones, nearly always between A ′ ′ ′ and D ′ ′ ′ ′. A few songs range as much as three and a half tones, and may be as low as F ′ ′ ′ or up to E flat ′ ′ ′ ′, but the range for the species is only five tones.

"The songs are quite short, ranging from ⅗ second to 1⅖ seconds. Individual birds often sing two or three different songs, or vary songs by dropping or adding notes.

"The song period extends from the arrival of the bird in migration to late July or early August. The average date of the last song in 14 years in Allegany Park is August 1. The earliest is July 26, 1933, and the latest August 15, 1937."

*Enemies.*—Dr. Friedmann (1929) mentions only a few cases in which the magnolia warbler has been imposed upon by the cowbird, but E. H. Eaton (1914), says that the cowbird "seems to make a specialty of presenting this Warbler with one or more of its eggs, generally puncturing the eggs of the Magnolia before leaving the nest." However, it is probable that this warbler is a rather uncommon victim, perhaps because the cowbird is not particularly common in the places where the warbler breeds.

Harold S. Peters (1936) lists two lice, *Degeeriella eustigma* (Kellogg) and *Myrsidea incerta* (Kellogg), as external parasites on this warbler.

*Field marks.*—The adult magnolia warbler of both sexes is so conspicuously marked that it should be easily recognized. The gray crown, black back and cheeks, yellow breast and rump, the two broad white wing bars and the large amount of white in the tail, midway between the base and the tip, are all good field marks. The female is only a little less brilliant than the male. The young bird in juvenal plumage is quite different, but the position of the white in the tail is distinctive.

*Fall.*—When the young birds are well able to take care of themselves, they and their parents join the gathering throngs of warblers and other small birds in preparation for the southward migration. Brewster (1877) writes:

In Eastern Massachusetts this species occurs as a fall migrant from September 21 to October 30, but it is never seen at this season in anything like the numbers which pass through the same section in spring, and the bulk of the migration must follow a more westerly route. Its haunts while with us in the autumn are somewhat different from those which it affects during its northward journey. We now find it most commonly on hillsides, among scrub-oaks and scattered birches, and in company with such birds as the Yellow-Rump (*Dendroeca coronata*) and the Black-Poll (*D. striata*). A dull, listless troop they are, comparatively sombre of plumage, totally devoid of song, and apparently intent only upon the gratification of their appetites.

Brewster was probably correct in assuming that the main trend of the fall migration is more westerly. Milton B. Trautman (1940) says of the fall migration of the magnolia warbler at Buckeye Lake, Ohio: "A persistent search in mid-August always resulted in recording a few early transients, and by the last of the month several were seen each day. The numbers increased gradually through early September. From September 10 to 25 the greatest daily numbers were attained, and 50 to 125 birds a day were noted. The numbers were slightly higher than they were in spring. The fall transients frequented the same types of habitat as did the spring birds, except that more were found in brushy fields or pastures, especially those dotted or thicketed with hawthorn and wild plum."

Prof. W. W. Cooke (1904) writes:

Over much of the southern part of the United States the magnolia warbler, though rare in spring, is common in fall. * * * The general path of migration of the species seems to cross the middle of the Gulf of Mexico. It is bounded approximately on the east by a line drawn from the north central part of Georgia to eastern Yucatan, while few individuals seem to proceed farther west than the coast line from eastern Texas to southern Vera Cruz. In common with some twenty other species of birds the magnolia warbler seems to make its flight between the United States and Yucatan without taking advantage of the peninsula of Florida or using Cuba as a stopping place. At the southern end of the Allegheny Mountains it is a common migrant, while it has been noted only three times in Florida and only once in Cuba.

*Winter.*—Dr. Alexander F. Skutch contributes the following from Costa Rica: "The magnolia warbler is one of the abundant winter visitants of northern Central America. Although its known winter range extends to Panamá, it only rarely migrates so far south. I have never seen the bird either in Panamá or Costa Rica; nor did Carriker have any record of it when he prepared his list of the birds of the latter country. But in the Caribbean lowlands of Honduras and Guatemala, it is common and widespread from October to April, sharing with the yellow warbler the distinction of being the member of the family most often seen during this period. While it appears to be present in somewhat smaller numbers than in the Caribbean region, it is still far from rare on the Pacific side of Guatemala. Here I found it fairly abundant, during the winter months, on the great coffee plantations between 2,000 and 4,000 feet above sea-level. It was not uncommon in the bushy growth about the shores of Lake Atitlán (4,900 feet), at the end of October; and I even found a few among the pines and oaks at Huehuetenango, at an altitude of 6,600 feet in the western highlands, on November 12, 1934; but I am not at all certain whether they remained so high during the cooler months that followed. In its winter home, this sprightly bird lives singly rather than in flocks. It frequents open groves, light second-growth woodland, thickets, and the riverside vegetation, rather than the heavy forest.

"The magnolia warblers arrive in Guatemala and Honduras in their dull winter dress, at the end of September or in October. By early April, the males are in full nuptial attire, so bright and gay that their approaching departure will deprive the region of one of its most beautiful birds. They linger until the end of April; and I have seen males as late as females.

"Early dates of fall arrival in Central America are: Guatemala— passim (Griscom), October 12; Colomba, September 30, 1934; Finca Helvetia, October 6, 1934. Honduras—Tela, October 6, 1930.

"Late dates of spring departure from Central America are: Honduras—Tela, April 24, 1930. Guatemala—passim (Griscom), April 15; Motagua Valley, near Los Amates, April 30, 1932."

Dickey and van Rossem (1938) record it for El Salvador as a—

rare fall migrant, but common winter visitant and spring migrant in the Arid Lower Tropical Zone. Although found from sea level to 3,500 feet, the species is much more numerous below 2,000 feet than above that altitude. Dates of arrival and departure are October 12 and April 24. * * *

In December perhaps a dozen all told were seen on Mt. Cacaguatique, always as single birds with small flocks of Tennessee and other warblers. By January they had become very common, and at Puerto del Triunfo during the whole of that month and in February at Rio San Miguel almost every flock of blue honey creepers was accompanied by one or more magnolia warblers. There was no noticeable decrease in numbers until after the middle of April, and even on the 24th (the last date on which the species was noted) they were recorded as common.

## DISTRIBUTION

*Range.*—Central Canada to Panamá.

*Breeding range.*—The magnolia warbler breeds **north** to southwestern Mackenzie (Wrigley, Providence, and Resolution) ; northeastern Alberta (Chipewyan) ; central Saskatchewan (Flotten Lake, Emma Lake, and Hudson Bay Junction) ; central Manitoba (Cedar Lake, Norway House, and Oxford House) ; northern Ontario (Red Lake, Lac Seul, and Moose Factory) ; southern Quebec (Lake Mistassini, Mingan, and Natashquan) ; and northern Newfoundland (Northeast Brook, Canada Bay). **East** to eastern Newfoundland (Northeast Brook, Badger, and Princeton) and Nova Scotia (Baddeck, Cape Breton Island). **South** to Nova Scotia (Baddeck, Halifax, and Barrington) ; southern Maine (Ellsworth, Bath, Portland, and Saco) ; southern New Hampshire (Concord and Monadnock) ; northwestern Massachusetts (Winchendon and Pelham) ; northeastern Pennsylvania (Lords Valley, Delaware Water Gap, and Pottsville) ; western Maryland (Cumberland) ; central western Virginia (Sounding Knob) ; central eastern West Virginia (Watoga and Pickens) ; occasionally western North Carolina (Asheville) ; northeastern Ohio (Pymatuning Bog and Conneaut) ; possibly northwestern Ohio (Toledo) ; northern Michigan (Grayling, Wequetansing, and the Beaver Islands) ; northern Wisconsin (Kelley Brook, Ashland, and Superior) ; northern Minnesota (McGregor, Leech Lake, and White Earth) ; southern Manitoba (Winnepeg and Brandon) ; southern Saskatchewan (Indian Head, Wood Mountain, and Maple Creek) ; central Alberta (Stony Plain, Lesser Slave Lake, and Winagami) ; and central British Columbia (Field, Quesnel, Mukko Lake, and Hazelton). **West** to western and northern British Columbia (Hazelton and Liard Crossing) ; and southwestern Mackenzie (Nahanni Mountains and Wrigley). Accidental or casual north to Fort Franklin.

*Winter range.*—The magnolia warbler is found in winter **north** to northern Puebla (Metlatoyuca) ; Veracruz (Tlacotalpan) ; and Quintana Roo (Puerto Morelos and Cozumel Island). **East** to Cozumel Island; British Honduras (Orange Walk and Belize) ; Honduras (Tela and Ceiba) ; Nicaragua (Río Escondido) ; and Panamá (Canal Zone). **South** to Panamá (Canal Zone and Almirante). **West** to western Panamá (Almirante) ; Costa Rica (Guayabo) ; El Salvador (Puerto del Triunfo) ; Guatemala (San Lucas) ; Oaxaca (Tehuantepec); western Veracruz (Motzorongo); and northern Puebla (Metlatoyuca). Occasional or accidental in winter (possibly from delayed migration), in southern Sonora (Alamos); Texas (Brownsville, Dallas, and Huntsville); Mississippi (Edwards and Gulfport); Alabama (Tupelo); and Florida (New Smyrna). It has also occurred rarely in migration in the West Indies; Cuba (Habana); Dominican Republic (Puerto Plata); and Puerto Rico (Mayagüez).

*Migration.*—Late dates of spring departure from the winter home are: Nicaragua—Edén, March 29. El Salvador—Chilata, April 24. Guatemala—Chuntuqui, April 25. Honduras—Tela, April 24. Veracruz—Minatitlán, April 27. Puerto Rico—San Germán, April 20. Cuba—Santiago de las Vegas, May 4.

Early dates of spring arrival are: Florida—Palm Beach, March 3. Alabama—Long Island, April 10. Georgia—Savannah, April 13. South Carolina—Summerton, April 17. North Carolina—Waynesville, April 14. Virginia—Lynchburg, April 18. West Virginia—White Sulphur Springs, April 25. District of Columbia—Washington, April 22. Pennsylvania—Pittsburgh, April 22. New York—Canandaigua, April 23. Massachusetts—Amherst, April 29. Vermont—St. Johnsbury, April 29. Maine—Dover-Foxcroft, May 5. New Brunswick—Scotch Lake, May 2. Nova Scotia—Wolfville, May 6. Quebec—Quebec, May 4. Prince Edward Island—Mount Herbert, May 4. Louisiana—Avery Island, April 6. Mississippi—Edwards, April 17. Arkansas—Helena, A p r i l 20. Tennessee—Knoxville, April 17. Kentucky—Bowling Green, April 23. Illinois—Le Roy, April 19. Ohio—Oberlin, April 19. Michigan—Grand Rapids, April 26. Ontario—London, April 30. Missouri—Marionville, April 20. Iowa—Iowa City, April 27. Wisconsin—Milwaukee, April 26. Minnesota—Crystal Bay, April 29. Texas—Brownsville, April 3. Nebraska—Lincoln, April 29. South Dakota—Yankton, May 2. North Dakota—Argusville, May 11. Manitoba—Aweme, May 11. Saskatchewan—Wiseton, May 5. Colorado—Derby, May 3. Alberta—Glenevis, May 22. Mackenzie—Simpson, May 23.

Late dates of spring departure of transients are: Florida—Dry Tortugas Island, May 22. Alabama—Leighton, May 10. Georgia—Margret, May 25. South Carolina—Spartanburg, May 18. North Carolina—Raleigh, May 18. Virginia—Naruna, May 25. District of Columbia—Washington, June 4. Louisiana—Cameron Farm, May 15. Mississippi—Deer Island, May 21. Arkansas—Winslow, May 22. Tennessee—Nashville, May 22. Kentucky—Danville, May 27. Illinois—Chicago, June 8. Ohio—Youngstown, June 3. Missouri—St. Louis, June 3. Iowa—Mount Vernon, June 2. Texas—Waco, May 23. Oklahoma—Arnett, May 28. Kansas—Stockton, May 21. Nebraska—Stapleton, May 23. South Dakota—Yankton, June 6. North Dakota—Argusville, June 12.

Late dates of fall departure are: Alberta—Glenevis, September 18. Saskatchewan—Wiseton, September 27. Manitoba—Shoal Lake, September 28. North Dakota—Fargo, October 9 (bird banded). South Dakota—Lennox, October 5. Texas—Cove, November 13. Minnesota—St. Paul, October 2. Wisconsin—Appleton, October 18. Iowa—Sigourney, October 20. Ontario—Toronto, October 16. Ohio—Cleveland, November 2. Indiana—Elkhart, October 16. Kentucky—Bowling Green, November 10. Tennessee—Nashville, November 11. Mississippi—Gulfport, November 8. Louisiana—New Orleans, November 4. Newfoundland—Tompkins, September 25. Prince Edward Island—North River, September 8. Quebec—Quebec. September 19. New Brunswick—Saint John, October 12. Maine—Portland, September 28. New Hampshire—Hanover, October 16. Massachusetts—Lynn, October 28. New York—Long Beach, October 27. Pennsylvania—Jeffersonville, October 15. District of Columbia—Washington, October 28. Virginia—Lawrenceville, October 25. North Carolina—Raleigh, October 20. South Carolina—Cherokee Plantation, November 12. Georgia—Atlanta, November 4. Florida—Pensacola, October 31.

Early dates of fall arrival: North Dakota—Fargo, September 3. South Dakota—Aberdeen, August 26. Nebraska—Monroe Canyon, Sioux County, September 12. Texas—Brownsville, September 3. Wisconsin—New London, August 12. Iowa—Grinnell, August 20. Illinois—Chicago, August 12. Indiana—Indianapolis, August 25. Kentucky—Wurtland, August 8. Tennessee—Nashville, August 27. Mississippi—Edwards, September 7. Louisiana—September 11. District of Columbia—Washington, August 15. Virginia—Charlottesville, September 3. North Carolina—Asheville, August 28. Georgia—Athens, September 7. Alabama—Birmingham, September 13. Florida—St. Augustine, September 3. Cuba—Habana, November 3. Yucatán—Chichén-Itzá, October 7. Honduras—Truxillo. September 27. Guatemala—Colomba, September 30. El Salvador—Divisadero, October 12. Nicaragua—Río Escondido, October 27. Panamá—Cocoplum, October 24.

*Casual records.*—A specimen was secured in Bermuda on May 7, 1878; a specimen was collected at Godthaab, Greenland, in 1875; a bird was picked up, recently dead, at Salem, Oreg., in January 1907; and on October 1, 1913, a specimen was picked up dead on the sea ice a mile off shore from Humphrey Point, Alaska. Eight specimens have been taken in California: Farallon Islands, May 29 and June 2, 1911; at sea about 10 miles west of Halfmoon Bay, June 8, 1943; Yosemite Valley, October 6, 1919; Santa Cruz Island, May 23, 1908; Santa Barbara Island, May 15, 1897; and Los Angeles, October 21, 1897, and October 5, 1901.

*Egg dates.*—Maine: 95 records, June 4 to 30; 74 records, June 7 to 15, indicating the height of the season.

New Brunswick: 59 records, June 7 to 28; 37 records, June 13 to 19.

New York: 23 records, June 3 to July 1; 13 records, June 5 to 12.

Pennsylvania: 41 records, May 28 to June 13; 32 records, May 30 to June 8 (Harris).

DENDROICA TIGRINA (Gmelin)

CAPE MAY WARBLER

PLATE 29

HABITS

This is the bird that made Cape May famous. Dr. Stone (1937) suggests that it has "served to advertise the name of Cape May probably more widely than has been done in any other way." The inappropriate name Cape May warbler was given to it by Alexander Wilson (1831), who described and figured it from a specimen of an adult male taken by his friend, George Ord, in a maple swamp in Cape May County, N. J., in May, 1811. He never saw it in life and never obtained another specimen. Audubon never saw it in life, the specimens figured by him having been obtained by Edward Harris near Philadelphia. Nuttall apparently never saw it.

Dr. Stone (1937) writes: "Curiously enough it seems never to have been recorded again at Cape May until September 4, 1920, when I recognized one in a shade tree on Perry Street in company with some Chestnut-sided Warblers. Since then we have seen a few nearly every year in spring and fall both at Cape May and at the Point." It is perhaps not to be wondered at that the early ornithologists knew so little about it before 1860, for bird observers were few and widely scattered in those days, and the Cape May warbler is only a hurried migrant through the United States over a very wide immigration range, nowhere very abundant, and its numbers seem to fluctuate from year to year.

Some years before Wilson named the Cape May warbler, a specimen of the same bird flew aboard a vessel off the coast of Jamaica and was painted and described by George Edwards. This was the basis of Gmelin's name *tigrina*, little tiger. Although not striped exactly like a tiger, it has carried this name ever since.

*Spring.*—Cape May warblers leave their winter home in the West Indies in March and pass through the Bahamas and Florida in March and April, northward along the Atlantic coast, and branch out westward to southern Missouri and up through the Mississippi Valley to Minnesota and Canada. Very few stop to settle much short of the Canadian border. Dr. Chapman (1907) writes of the spring migration: "In early May in Florida, I have seen this species actually common, feeding in weedy patches among a rank growth of poke-berries. It seemed like wanton extravagance on the part of nature to bring so many of these generally rare creatures within one's experience in a single morning. Both on the east and west coasts of the State the bird is at times a common migrant, possibly bound for its summer home by way of the Mississippi Valley, where it is more numerous than in the north Atlantic States."

Amos W. Butler (1898) says:

The Cape May Warbler is generally considered a rare bird everywhere. While this is true, and some years it is altogether absent, there are years when it is common and even abundant. In Indiana it appears as a migrant, perhaps more numerous in fall than spring. * * * Some years with us they are found upon the drier uplands, among the oak woods, where they usually keep among the lower branches or upon the high bushes and smaller trees. They are not very active, but keep persistenly hunting insects. At other times, we find them among our orchards, even coming into towns, where they occupy themselves catching insects among the foliage and about the blossoms of all kinds of shade and fruit trees.

In Ohio, according to Milton B. Trautman (1940), "the bird was uncommon in every spring except 1, and seldom more than 10 individuals were noted in a day. Between May 14 and 20, 1926, the species was very numerous throughout central Ohio. On May 16 I noted at least 40 individuals in Lakeside Woods, and it was evident that hundreds were present in the area on that day." Referring also to Ohio, W. F. Henninger (1918) writes: "This year, on May 25, 1917, we entered a large patch of woods about half a mile from the Grand Reservoir early in the morning, just when the fog had barely raised above the treetops, and the warblers were fairly swarming there, among them numbers of Cape May's. I counted more than fifty, but got tired counting and then gave it up, after taking a fine pair." Rev. J. J. Murray (MS.) refers to this warbler as common in the vicinity of Lexington, Va., in the spring from April 29 to May 18, where it seems to prefer conifers at that season.

I have seen the Cape May warbler fairly common in Florida at times and I have collected it there, but I have never seen it in my corner of Massachusetts. Mr. Forbush (1929) tells the story very well for this State:

For nearly one hundred years at least this species had been considered very rare in New England, but about 1909 it seemed to become more common. In May, 1912, at Amesbury, Massachusetts, one chilly morning I found bright males scattered through the village. A cold wave, catching them in night migration, had brought them down, and they could be seen here and there on or near the ground, and in low bushes by the roadside. In the dooryards and along the streets these lovely birds hopped and fluttered fearlessly in their search for food, paying little attention to passers-by. By 1915 they had appeared more generally, and in May, 1917, they were well distributed over a large part of New England.

Since that time Cape May Warblers have been not uncommon transients in certain years, and they have never been as rare as they formerly were. In migration they may be found in trees and shrubbery about dwellings and along village streets almost as commonly as in woods or in swampy thickets, where at this season they find many insects. Occasionally a few may be seen in blossoming orchards.

*Courtship.*—Information on the courtship behavior of the wood warblers is so scanty that it seems worthwhile to include two small items on this subject for the Cape May warbler. While watching a pair at their nest-building, Dr. Merriam (1917) observed that "on June 11 the male was seen to chase the female. The next day nest building was apparently complete. An hour's watching on the 13th also failed to show any further nest construction, although the female was frequently heard in the low growth. Once she flew ten feet up in a spruce and gave a peculiar note at the same time lifting her tail. Immediately the male flew down and copulation took place. The whole proceeding resembled very much that of the Chipping Sparrow." James Bond (1937) noted at times that, "when the female was working on the nest, the male would fly with rigid wings just above her. This was a characteristic courting display, noted with other individuals."

*Nesting.*—The Cape May warbler seeks for its summer home the country of the pointed firs and spruces that tower like tapering church spires in the Canadian Life Zone of our northern border and in Canada. It seems to prefer an open, parklike stand of these noble trees rather than the denser coniferous forests, though it often finds a congenial home along the borders of the forests or in the more open spaces within them, especially where there is a mixture of tall white or yellow birches, or a few hemlocks. Its breeding range follows the Canadian Zone rather closely, as along the cool coastline of eastern Maine. James Bond writes to me of its interesting distribution in that state: "In the eastern half of the state it is found mainly along the coast, as far south as Hog Island, Knox County. It ranges across Maine through Washington, Aroostook and northern Penobscot Counties, but is a rare species in the interior, and is unknown in summer from the Bangor and Lincoln sections of Penobscot County. I found it most abundant in southern Mount Desert Island in the vicinity of Ship Harbor. Here several pairs nest every year in the cool, often fog-drenched woods, although I have found but one nest."

The first published report of the nesting of the Cape May warbler was perhaps based on an error in identification. Montague Chamberlain (1885) reported that his friend James W. Banks found a nest apparently "just outside the city limits" of Saint John, New Brunswick; he states that it "was hid among a cluster of low cedars growing in an exposed position, on a rather open hill-side, near a gentleman's residence, and within a stone's throw of a much frequented lane. The nest was placed less than three feet from the ground and within six inches of the tips of the branches." The location of this nest, as will be seen from the accounts that follow, was entirely different from that of the many nests found since; both nest and eggs were said to resemble somewhat those of the magnolia warbler; no male Cape May warbler was seen or heard, and the bird Banks reports having shot from the nest may have been wrongly identified, since the females of the two species are somewhat alike. Referring to this account, James Bond (1937) remarks: "It would be wise to regard the 'classical' nest taken near Saint John, New Brunswick, by Banks as that of a Magnolia Warbler, as is indicated not only by its situation but by its construction, for the nest of the Cape May Warbler is a decidedly more bulky affair. I mention this since recent books still perpetuate this undoubted error, ignoring the information that has been gleaned during the past twenty years."

Probably the first undoubted nest of the Cape May warbler was found on an island in Lake Edward, Quebec, on June 7, 1916, by Dr. H. F. Merriam, who published an interesting account of it (1917). He watched the building of the nest for some days before the nest was taken on the eighteenth. The female was seen carrying nesting material into the thick top of a spruce about 40 feet from the ground in a rather open part of the woods, consisting for the most part of spruce and balsam of moderate size interspersed with large white and yellow birches.

The female was not at all timid and apparently gathered most of her nesting material at two places, both within sixty feet of the nest tree. * * * While searching in the low growth she was absorbed in manner, giving only occasionally a sharp chip. In going to the nest her actions were more rapid and she chipped more frequently, generally alighting ten to twenty feet below the nest and working her way up from limb to limb on the outside of the tree. * * * The male was not seen to carry any nest material but seemed to be generally in the immediate neighborhood. At times he accompanied the female part way to or from the nest and sometimes remained near her in the low spruces. * * *

The nest was placed about six feet from the top of the tree on a short branch nine inches from the trunk and an equal distance from the tip. From the ground it could not be seen even with field glasses. From a few feet below the nest was apparently a green ball of moss. Closer examination, however, showed it to be a neatly cupped nest resting on the branch and short twigs. To these it was not securely tied and was lifted intact from its position without difficulty.

The exterior of the nest was of green Sphagnum moss, interwoven with vine stems, and a very few twigs, bound lightly with plant down, small wads of which appeared here and there over the moss. The body of the nest consisted of fine grass stems. Within this was a lining of white hairs apparently from the rabbit, one small partridge feather and a few fine black rootlets. The nest was bulky but very neatly and fairly compactly put together. At the rim one side was very smoothly finished. This was probably the entrance side toward the tree trunk. It was an unusual and beautiful nest.

Its dimensions were: outside, 4 inches wide by 2¼ deep; inside, 1¾ inches wide by 1 inch deep.

Two years later, Philipp and Bowdish (1919) found four nests in northern New Brunswick. "They were in rather high spruce trees, within two or three feet of the extreme top, usually as near the top as suitable site and cover could be secured. All were built in very thick foliage, against the main stem of the tree, resting lightly on twigs and foliage, but fairly secured thereto by webs, and were entirely invisible from the ground, in every case." The nests were from 35 to 40 feet above the ground, and were not substantially different in size and construction from that described by Dr. Merriam. They add that the thick lining of hair, feathers, and a little fur, all smoothly felted, serves to distinguish the nests from those of the black-poll and myrtle warblers, and note that the nest tree is usually "fairly openly situated, at least as to one side, although this is not always the case, since other pairs watched were very evidently nesting in trees where it was much more difficult to detect them."

Richard C. Harlow has sent me the data for seven nests of the Cape May warbler that he collected in Tabusintac, New Brunswick, in 1919. Two of these were 55 feet from the ground in a fir, and the others were 35, 45, 50, 55, and 60 feet up, respectively, in black spruces. All were in the very topmost shelters of the trees, and three of them were in heavy forests, the others being on the edges. In other respects they were similar to those described above. The females sat very closely until almost touched, and then dropped down to the ground.

The nest found by James Bond (MS.) on Mount Desert Island, Maine, was against the trunk of a red spruce 38 feet above ground and about 4 feet from the extreme top of the tree. In construction it was similar to those described above. In his published (1937) paper the tree was said to be a black spruce, but he now writes to me that it was a red spruce and that there were no black spruces in the immediate vicinity; these two spruces are difficult to distinguish.

Dr. Paul Harrington, of Toronto, writes to me that he found a nest of the Cape May warbler in an open spruce forest near Dorcas Bay, Bruce Peninsula, on June 12, 1934. "The tree was about 35 feet high, a typical 'church spire.' Near the top was a heavy clump, but I could see nothing that indicated a nest; when I put my hand in the heavy needles near the trunk a bird popped out and straight down. * * * I carefully groped about and eventually found the nest, built near the trunk in the uppermost clump of needles."

*Eggs.*—Mr. Harlow tells me that the Cape May warbler lays from 4 to 9 eggs to a set. The larger numbers must be very rare, but 6 or 7 seem to be the commonest numbers among my records, and sets of 4 seem to be uncommon. The eggs vary in shape from ovate to short

ovate and are almost lusterless. They are creamy white, richly
spotted and blotched with shades of reddish brown, such as "auburn,"
"chestnut," "sayal brown," "bay," or "snuff brown," with an occasional
scrawl of black. The undermarkings are of "fawn," "light brownish
drab," "brownish drab," or "light mouse gray." The markings are
more concentrated at the large end. The measurements of 50 eggs
average 16.8 by 12.5 millimeters; the eggs showing the four extremes
measure 18.4 by 12.3, 18.0 by 14.0, 15.0 by 12.0, and 16.0 by 11.5 millimeters (Harris).

*Plumages.*—Dr. Dwight (1900) describes the juvenal plumage, in
which the sexes are alike, as "above, dark hair-brown, olive tinged on
the back. Wings and tail black, edged chiefly with dull brownish
olive-green, the coverts with drab and tipped with buffy white. The
two outer rectrices with subterminal white spots. Below, including
sides of head, mouse-gray with dusky mottling or streaking on the
breast and sides; the abdomen and crissum dingy white faintly tinged
with primrose-yellow."

The partial postjuvenal molt, beginning early in July, involves the
contour plumage and the wing coverts, but not the rest of the wings
or the tail. This produces the first winter plumage, in which the
sexes begin to differentiate. Dr. Dwight describes the first winter
male as "above, dull olive-green, each feather centrally clove-brown
veiled with olive-gray edgings; the rump canary-yellow, the feathers
basally black. Below, including sides of neck, superciliary lines and
spot under eye, canary-yellow, palest on abdomen and crissum, narrowly streaked on sides of chin, on the throat, breast and sides with
black which is veiled by grayish edgings; auriculars mouse-gray."
The young female, he says, is "duller and browner above, and generally without yellow below, being dull white with gray streaking."

The first nuptial plumage is acquired by a partial prenuptial molt
beginning in late winter, "which involves much of the body plumage
but not the wings nor the tail. The black crown, the streaks on the
back, the chestnut ear-patches and the streaked yellow of the throat
and breast are acquired," in the male. The female in first nuptial
plumage "shows a little yellow assumed by a limited prenuptial
moult." Both sexes are now in nearly fully adult plumage, except
for the worn juvenal wings and tail.

Adults have a complete postnuptial molt in July and probably a
partial prenuptial molt, as in the young bird, though there is not
enough pertinent material available to prove the latter. Dr. Dwight
(1900) says that the adult winter plumage of the male is "similar to
first winter plumage but the head black, the back streaked and everywhere veiled with smoke-gray edgings. Below, whitish edgings
obscure the black streaks, the chestnut ear-coverts and the bright

lemon-yellow areas. The wings and tail are blacker than in first winter, the back is black, either streaked or spotted, and the yellow below is deeper." Of the female, he says: "The adult winter plumage is similar to the male in first winter dress, the yellow below rather paler and with less heavy streakings."

*Food.*—Throughout most of the year the Cape May warbler is insectivorous, and mainly beneficial, but for a short time on its fall migration it undoubtedly causes damage to ripe grapes by puncturing them to obtain the juice, often ruining a large percentage of the crop. Many complaints have been made and several have been published. Frank L. Burns (1915a) claimed that about 50 percent of his crop was destroyed at Berwyn, Pa., and says: "I believe that grape juice was the principal food of the Cape May Warbler during its lengthy visit in this neighborhood. It was present in countless numbers at Berwyn and vicinity as far as a mile south of the village, apparently by far the most abundant species for a period; the complaints of the the 'little striped yellow bird' were many, and so far as I am able to learn, all unbagged grapes were ruined; the loss must have been many tons worth several hundred dollars." He sent ten stomachs to the Biological Survey for analysis and received the following reply:

Hymenoptera constituted on an average 57.5 percent of the contents of the stomachs. A third perhaps of this material was parasitic Hymenoptera and their destruction counts against the bird. The others were ants and small bees and are of neutral importance except perhaps the ants which may be injurious. Diptera made up 16.7 percent of the stomach contents and again a large proportion of them were parasitic species. Lepidoptera (small moths) constitute 16.7 per cent, beetles 7.8 percent and the remainder was made up of Hemiptera, spiders and miscellaneous insects. Except for the spiders the food was entirely composed of insects, and a large proportion of useful species were taken and no decidedly injurious ones. I should say that these Cape May Warblers did very little to pay for the destruction of grapes.

McAtee (1904), after investigating the damage done on grapes by this and the Tennessee warbler in Indiana, published the following report on the contents of a single stomach of a Cape May warbler:

8 *Typlocyba comes,* an especial pest of the grape, "an exceedingly abundant and destructive" jassid; 3 *Aphodius inquinatus* and one Carabid, kinds which may be considered neutral economically, but, in case of a departure from their ordinary diet, would on account of vegetarian tendencies become injurious; 1 *Drasterias sp.* (click-beetle), 1 tortoise-beetle, 1 flea-beetle (*Haltica chalybea*), all injurious beetles, the last of which is a particular enemy of the grape, which "appears on the vine in early spring and bores into and scoops out the unopened buds, sometimes so completely as to kill the vine to the roots," and later in the season in both larval and adult stages feeds upon the foliage, and if abundant "leaves little but the larger veins"; 1 *Notoxus* sp., a weevil, with all the undesirability characteristic of the creatures bearing that name; 2 ants, harmful, if for no other reason than harboring plant lice; and a vespoidean hymenopteron (wasp) of neutral significance. * * *

The feeding habits of the birds may, from the present knowledge, be declared practically entirely beneficial. In return it seems not too much to expect that we should without complaint furnish, for a few days in the year, the drink to wash the great numbers of our insect enemies down to their destruction; and to consider these two little fellows as among the worthiest as they are among the prettiest of our warbler friends.

Prof. Maurice Brooks (1933), speaking of this warbler in West Virginia, says:

We had at that time [1909] a small commercial vineyard, and during the first week in September, when the crop was just ripening, we were surprised to find in the vineyard swarms of Cape May Warblers. We were not long in doubt as to their purpose there, for within a week they had destroyed practically every grape we had. * * * Their method was to puncture the skin of the berry at one point, extract a little juice, and move on to the next. They would systematically work over every berry in the cluster, if undisturbed, and they soon became exceedingly tame. It is no exaggeration to say that there were hundreds of the birds in the locality.

After the birds had made one puncture, swarms of bees and wasps soon finished the work of destruction. There was no way of frightening so many birds away, and we were driven to sacking our grapes in the future. The next year, 1910, they returned in numbers again, destroying practically all unsacked clusters, and completely cleaning out the vines of our neighbors, who raised just a few grapes for their home use.

These and other warblers have been seen drinking sap from the holes dug in trees by sapsuckers, but they also obtain some insects from such borings and perhaps also from the punctured grapes, which make fine insect traps. However, the damage does not seem to be universal, and occurs only where the birds are abundant, and then for only a short time. In view of his record as an insect destroyer, the laborer may be worthy of his hire.

To the insects mentioned as food for this warbler, A. H. Howell (1932) adds small crickets, flies, leaf hoppers, termites, larvae of moths, dragonflies, and daddy-long-legs.

*Behavior.*—Brewster (1938) writes:

It keeps invariably near the tops of the highest trees whence it occasionally darts out after passing insects. It has a habit of singing on the extreme pinnacle of some enormous fir or spruce, where it will often remain perfectly motionless for ten or fifteen minutes at a time; on such occasions the bird is extremely hard to find, and if shot is almost certain to lodge on some of the numerous spreading branches beneath. * * * In rainy or dark weather they came in numbers from the woods to feed among the thickets of low firs and spruces in the pastures. Here they spent much of their time hanging head downward at the extremity of the branches, often continuing in this position for nearly a minute at a time. They seemed to be picking minute insects from the under surface of the fir needles. They also resorted to a thicket of blossoming plum trees directly under our window, where we were always sure of finding several of them. There were numerous Hummingbirds here also, and these, the Cape Mays were continually chasing.

While watching a pair at their nest building, Dr. Merriam (1917) saw a female on the ground gathering material; she "was attacked by a Junco and after a chase the Junco actually caught and held her. At this commotion the male Cape May flew down and lit close by but took no active part in the argument. The Junco was apparently victor for after one more flight to her nest the female Cape May was not again seen to trespass on the Junco's territory or do any more nest building that morning." However, in his notes from West Virginia, Dr. J. J. Murray says that "this warbler is more active and restless in its feeding than any of our warblers, except possibly the myrtle; and it is also noisier and more aggressive in its attitude toward other warblers which seek to share its feeding places." Harlow also says that "the male Cape May is the tiger of the north woods in defending his territory. He attacks all birds that come close to the nest, up to the size of the olive-backed thrush, and is absolutely fearless."

*Voice.*—Aretas A. Saunders sends me the following note on the song of this warbler: "I have had few opportunities to study the song of the Cape May warbler, and have only five records. These show that the song is weak, high-pitched and somewhat sibillant. The notes are mainly all on one pitch, in even rhythmic time and from eight to eleven in number. They are pitched on E'''' and F''''. Two of the songs have one or two notes, near the end, a half-tone higher in pitch than the others. The songs are from 1⅗ to 2 seconds in length."

Francis H. Allen (MS.) heard one singing and feeding in some Norway spruce in West Roxbury, Mass., on May 10. "He had *chip* notes very much like a familiar note of the chipping sparrow. (I have also recorded a *prssp* like that of the blackpoll warbler but fainter and sometimes doubled.) This bird had a variety of songs. The simplest one resembled the black and white warbler's song and a short simple song of the redstart, but was thinner and harder in quality than the latter. Then there were other, more elaborate songs, some divided into two parts and some into three. Two or three times he sang several times with no pauses between, making what was practically a long continuous song. The chief characteristic of the songs, I should say, was short and staccato double notes, the latter part of which were very high-pitched. These repeated several times formed the simplest of the songs. The song in three parts reminded me of that of the Tennessee warbler, but was higher pitched and not so full and loud. The bird had long periods of silence, but sang freely when he did sing."

Brewster (1938) says that "the song of this Warbler is harder—or at least sharper and more penetrating—than that of either the Bay-breast or Blackburnian. In these respects it resembles the song of *Protonotaria* but the tone or quality is more wiry and, indeed, very close to that of *Mniotilta*."

*Field marks.*—The adult male Cape May warbler should be unmistakable in his brilliant spring plumage, with his black cap, chestnut cheeks, white lesser wing coverts, and bright yellow breast conspicuously streaked with black.

The female lacks the black cap and chestnut cheeks; her breast is pale yellow streaked with pale dusky; and all her colors are duller. Young birds are much like the female, but are still duller in coloration. See descriptions of other plumages. The tail-tilting habit is quite pronounced.

*Fall.*—The fall migration starts in August and is prolonged through September, or even into October or a little later. The birds are numerically more abundant in the fall because of the large families of young, but they are less conspicuous while the foliage is still on the trees and while they are clad in dull autumn and immature plumages. Deciduous woods seem to be their favorite haunts at this season. The migration route is a reversal of the spring route, the main flight being between the Mississippi and the Alleghenies.

In this area, the birds are often excessively abundant, as shown by the accounts in the preceding paragraphs under food. They are common in Florida on migration on their way to the Bahamas and West Indies. C. J. Maynard (1896) writes:

"They were very abundant at Key West in November, frequenting the gardens near the houses where they were searching among the tropical trees and shrubs for inescts. The birds were very unsuspicious, often clinging to branches which overhung the sidewalks within a few feet of the passengers. They appeared to prefer the inhabited portion of the Key, for I rarely found them in wooded districts. The majority left the island before the first of December, but a few remained all winter."

*Winter.*—Maynard (1896) says: "These birds are also common on all of the northern Bahamas which I have visited, occurring in the thickets about gardens as well as in the dense scrub. I found them abundant on Inagua in February, 1888. Here they were feeding upon the juices of a large tubular flower of a peculiar species of vine, in company with the Bahama Honey Creeper and the Lyre-tailed Hummingbird."

In Cuba, according to Dr. Barbour (1923), "a few arrive from time to time during the autumn, but in February they become really common; they stay until May. They are great flower feeders and haunt aloes and the majagua tree when it is in bloom. Many may be seen about the sisal plantations near Matanzas and in gardens where agaves blossom."

Wetmore and Swales (1931) write: "Though the Cape May warbler is found through the Greater Antilles Hispaniola appears to be the winter metropolis of the species as the birds are found throughout the island often in considerable numbers. In fact their abundance in some localities is almost bewildering to one acustomed to their rarity as migrants in the eastern United States."

### DISTRIBUTION

*Range.*—Eastern North America and the West Indies.

*Breeding range.*—The Cape May warbler breeds **north** to northeastern Alberta (Chipewyan); possibly southwestern Mackenzie (Simpson); northern Saskatchewan (north shore of Lake Athabaska near Fair Point); central Ontario (Moose Factory); and southern Quebec (Lake Abitibi, Lake Edward, and Anticosti Island). **East** to eastern Quebec (Anticosti Island and Grand Grève); New Brunswick (Tabusintac and Saint John); and Nova Scotia (Wolfville and Stewiacke). **South** to Nova Scotio (Stewiacke); southern Maine (Ship Harbor, Mount Desert Island; Hog Island, Muscongus Bay; Pemaquid Point; and Auburn); northern New Hampshire (Lake Umbagog); south-central Vermont (Mount Killington); northern New York (North Elba); southern Ontario (Dorcas Bay and Biscotasing); northern Michigan (Newberry and Camp Cusino); northern Wisconsin (Kelley Brook and Harbster); rarely northeastern Minnesota (Gabro Lake); southwestern Ontario (Lac Seul); and central Alberta (Lesser Slave Lake and Sturgeon Lake). **West** to west-central and northeastern Alberta (Sturgeon Lake and Chipewyan). The Cape May warbler probably breeds in northern Manitoba since it is a regular, though not abundant, migrant in the southern part of the province.

*Winter range.*—The winter home of the Cape May warbler is in the West Indies **north** to the Bahamas (Nassau and Watling Island), **east** and **south** to St. Lucia, and **west** to Jamaica and western Cuba (Isle of Pines and Habana). It has also been found on the island of Roatán, Honduras. It was found in Quintana Roo not far from Xcopén on March 13 which is the second record for Mexico; the other is simply "Yucatán."

*Migration.*—Late dates of spring departure from the winter home are: Virgin Islands—St. Croix, April 25. Puerto Rico—Mayagüez, April 8. Haiti—Île à Vache, April 30. Cuba—Habana, May 4. Bahamas—Nassau, May 15.

Early dates of spring arrival are: Florida—Key West, March 6. Georgia—Macon, April 7. South Carolina—Chester, April 15. North Carolina—Greensboro, April 13. District of Columbia—Washington,

April 19. Pennsylvania—Carlisle, April 30. New York—Geneva, April 30. Massachusetts—Amherst, May 4. Vermont—Clarendon, May 7. Maine—Auburn, May 4. New Brunswick—Scotch Lake, May 8. Nova Scotia—Pictou, May 11. Quebec—Montreal, May 14. Tennessee—Nashville, April 16. Kentucky—Russellville, April 27. Indiana—Bloomington, April 22. Ohio—Oberlin, April 27. Michigan—Ann Arbor, April 27. Ontario—London, May 1; Moose Factory, May 28. Iowa—Davenport, May 2. Wisconsin—Racine, May 2. Minnesota—St. Paul, May 2. South Dakota—Sioux Falls, May 12. North Dakota—Argusville, May 11. Manitoba—Aweme, May 10. Saskatchewan—Indian Head, May 16. Alberta—Medicine Hat, May 17.

Some late dates of spring departure of transients are: Florida—Warrington, May 18. Alabama—Anniston, May 7. Georgia—Round Oak, May 15. South Carolina—Clemson (College), May 17. North Carolina—Arden, May 19. Virginia—Naruna, May 29. District of Columbia, Washington, May 30. Pennsylvania—Doylestown, May 26. New York—Watertown, June 1. Massachusetts—Northampton, June 6. Tennessee—Nashville, May 15. Kentucky—Bowling Green, May 10. Illinois—Chicago, June 3. Indiana—Lafayette, May 31. Ohio—Austinburg—June 2. Michigan—Sault Ste. Marie, June 7. Ontario—Ottawa, June 7. Minnesota—Minneapolis, June 1. South Dakota—Sisseton, June 3. North Dakota—Grafton, June 5. Manitoba—Aweme, June 1.

Late dates of fall departure are: Alberta—Camrose, August 26. Saskatchewan—Eastend, August 29. Manitoba—Winnipeg, October 7. North Dakota—Fargo, October 3 (bird banded). Wisconsin—Racine, October 16. Iowa—Iowa City, November 27. Michigan—Detroit, October 16. Ontario—Point Pelee, October 5. Ohio—Cleveland, November 2. Indiana—Waterloo, October 15. Illinois—Rantoul, October 23. Kentucky—Bowling Green, October 15. New Brunswick—Scotch Lake, September 28. Massachusetts—Belmont, November 25. New York—Hewlett, November 15. Pennsylvania—West Chester, October 31. District of Columbia—Washington, November 26. Virginia—Sweet Briar, November 29. North Carolina, Raleigh, November 1. South Carolina—Mount Pleasant, November 3. Georgia—St. Marys, October 31. Florida—Lemon City, November 25.

The Cape May warbler sometimes lingers very late in fall migration. It has been found on Long Island at Hewlett as late as December 4; at Harrisburg, Pa., one was trapped and banded on December 5; it has twice been collected at Washington, D. C., on December 16; one was found at Bethany, W. Va., on December 7; one seen at Brownsville, Tex., on December 22; and reported in December at Key West, Fla.

Early dates of fall arrival are: Manitoba—Winnipeg, August 20. North Dakota—Fargo, September 18. Minnesota—Minneapolis, August 25. Wisconsin—Green Bay, August 1. Illinois—Chicago, August 19. Ontario—Cobalt, August 12. Michigan—Whitefish Point, August 5. Ohio—Toledo, August 14. New Hampshire—Pequaket, August 24. Vermont—Wells River, August 4. Massachusetts—Harvard, August 30. New York—Rhinebeck, August 3. Pennsylvania—Pittsburgh, August 28. District of Columbia—Washington—August 4. Virginia—Charlottesville, September 4. North Carolina—Weaverville, September 15. South Carolina—Charleston, September 13. Georgia—Savannah, September 23. Florida—Sombrero Key, September 17. Bahamas—Cay Lobos, October 20. Cuba—Santiago de las Vegas, September 20. Dominican Republic—Sánchez, October 23. Puerto Rico—Faro de Cabo Rojo, September 17.

*Banding.*—The one banding recovery available is especially interesting as it indicates a peculiar migration. A Cape May warbler banded at Elmhurst, Long Island, N. Y., on September 12, 1937, was caught by a cat October 15, 1937 at Cleveland, Tenn.

*Casual records.*—In British Columbia one was collected June 17, 1938, at Charlie Lake. In California one was collected at Potholes on the Colorado River, September 23, 1924. A specimen labeled "Arizona" taken before 1876 is in the museum in Paris. The Cape May warbler has been once observed in Bermuda, April 3, 1909.

*Egg dates.*—Maine: 2 records, June 6 to 15.

New Brunswick: 68 records, June 10 to 29; 43 records, June 12 to 20; indicating the height of the season.

## DENDROICA CAERULESCENS CAERULESCENS (Gmelin)

### NORTHERN BLACK-THROATED BLUE WARBLER

PLATES 29, 30

#### HABITS

This neatly dressed warbler is one of our commonest migrants throughout the eastern half of the United States, but as a breeding bird it is confined mainly to the northernmost States and to extreme southern Canada, almost wholly within the Canadian Zone. Its rather long common name describes this dainty bird.

*Spring.*—From its principal winter resort in the West Indies, the black-throated blue warbler migrates through the Bahamas and Florida to the Atlantic States and northward, along the Alleghenies and to the eastward of them, to its northeastern breedings grounds. According to Prof. W. W. Cooke (1904) the earliest arrivals usually strike the Sombrero Key lighthouse in Florida around the middle of April, although there are two or three exceptionally early records in March. As the average dates of arrival in New England and New Brunswick are only about a month later, it would seem that the migration is fairly rapid. But the dates of earliest arrival do not tell the whole story, for Frederick C. Lincoln (1939) observed this species in the mountains of Haiti in the middle of May, showing that there are always many late migrants.

Professor Cooke's records show that this species arrives at Asheville, N. C., a few days earlier than at Raleigh, N. C., suggesting that this is one of the few species that appear in the mountains earlier than on the plains.

There is a northward migration west of the Alleghenies corresponding almost exactly in time with that along the Atlantic slope. Cooke says that "in southern Louisiana and southern Mississippi the black-throated blue warbler is almost unknown." He gives only very few records for any point south of Indiana, and some of these may have come across the Gulf of Mexico. The inference is that the bulk of the birds that migrate northward through the central States may have crossed the lower Alleghenies into these valleys. According to his records, it takes the birds only about 10 days to migrate from Brookville, Ind., to points in Ontario.

On its migration the black-throated blue warbler shows a preference for the lower shrubbery in various kinds of woodlands, but it may also be seen almost anywhere in such suitable cover in our parks and gardens or about human dwellings. Milton B. Trautman (1940) says that, in Ohio, these and the Canada warblers "were close associates in migration and frequented the same habitat niches."

In its summer home this warbler is even more of a woodland bird, frequenting heavy deciduous woods where there is more or less thick undergrowth of mountain-laurel, rhododendron, creeping yew, deciduous bushes, small saplings, or tiny conifers. My most intimate acquaintance with the black-throated blue warbler was made while visiting at Asquam Lake, N. H., with Mr. and Mrs. Richard B. Harding. From their camp the land slopes downward to the shore of the lake and is heavily wooded with tall white oaks, swamp white oaks, red oaks, beeches, maples, paper birches, and other deciduous trees; there are also some white pines and hemlocks scattered through the forest, and a heavy undergrowth of mountain-laurel, striped maple, witch-hazel, and other shrubbery. The black-throated blue warblers and the veeries were the commonest breeding birds in this area.

Gerald Thayer wrote to Dr. Chapman (1907) that about Monadnock, N. H., this is "a bird of the ampler deciduous undergrowth in deep, moist woods—mixed virgin timber or very old second growth.

It is peculiarly partial to these woodland conditions, and is common wherever they occur, especially between the altitudes of 1,000 and 2,500 feet.   Creeping yew is almost always common in woods where these Warblers breed, and they sometimes, perhaps often, nest in a clump of it." And William Brewster (1938) says that around Umbagog Lake, Maine, "the local population was chiefly concentrated wherever there were extensive patches of yew (*Taxus canadensis*)." I can find no evidence that this warbler is ever common in clear stands of coniferous trees, but is often found in mixed woods where there is a scattering of the evergreens, especially if there are small seedlings of spruce, fir, or hemlock, in which they sometimes build their nests.

*Territory.*—In favored regions, where the population is fairly dense, as it often is, the males arrive ahead of the females and establish their breeding and feeding territories, which they often have to defend against intruding males of the same species.   John Burroughs (1895) describes such an encounter as follows: "Their battle-cry is a low, peculiar chirp, not very fierce, but bantering and confident.  They quickly come to blows, but it is a very fantastic battle, and, as it would seem, indulged in more to satisfy their sense of honor than to hurt each other, for neither party gets the better of the other, and they separate a few paces and sing, and squeak, and challenge each other in a very happy frame of mind.   The gauntlet is no sooner thrown down than it is again taken up by one or the other, and in the course of fifteen or twenty minues they have three or four encounters, separating a little, then provoked to return again like two cocks, till finally they withdrawn beyond hearing of each other,—both, no doubt, claimin the victory."

*Nesting.*—I believe that John Burroughs (1895) was the first naturalist to discover the nest of the "black-throated blue-backed warbler," as he called it, and he wrote an interesting account of his hunt for it in "Locusts and Wild Honey."   It was found in July, 1871, in Delaware County, N. Y., and contained four young and one addled egg.   "The nest was built in the fork of a little hemlock, about fifteen inches from the ground, and was a thick, firm structure, composed of the finer material of the woods, with a lining of very delicate roots or rootlets."   The young birds were nearly fledged and were frightened from the nest.   "This brought the parent birds on the scene in an agony of alarm.   Their distress was pitiful.   They threw themselves on the ground at our very feet, and fluttered, and cried, and trailed themselves before us, to draw us away from the place, or distract our attention from the helpless young."

Mrs. Harding showed me some half dozen nests of this warbler in the locality near her camp at Asquam Lake, N. H.   All were in low bushes of mountain-laurel (*Kalmia latifolia*) from 12 to 18 inches above the ground and were not very well concealed. They were well made of strips of inner bark, canoe birch bark, straws, fern fronds, and dry leaves, and were lined with black horsehair and fine black rootlets. Altogether, Mrs. Harding (1931) found 15 nests similarly placed in low mountain-laurels, from 9 to 15 inches up, and all made of similar materials, but she says that "skunk fur is used freely as a substitute and sometimes pine needles or bits of moss," in the lining. So far as I know, she has not found pieces of rotten wood in the nests, as commonly reported by others.

Miss Cordelia J. Stanwood, of Ellsworth, Maine, tells me that the nests she finds near her home are placed in small firs or spruces. Frederic H. Kennard mentions in his notes a Maine nest wonderfully well hidden in a clump of little spruces about one foot from the ground. He also reports two Vermont nests, one about 2 feet from the ground in a tangle of raspberry vines beside a logging road, the other about 8 or 10 inches up in a little thicket of low-growing mountain maple. Robie W. Tufts tells me that the few nests he has examined in Nova Scotia were all built in "small spruce or fir seedlings two or three feet from the ground in heavy woods of mixed or coniferous growth."

Francis H. Allen writes to me of a nest he found in an unusual situation in Waterville, N. H.: "It was placed about a foot from the ground in the small twigs of a fallen beech, on which were the dead leaves of last season. * * * I collected the nest July 3 after the young had left it. The measurements were: Diameter, outside, 3½ inches; inside, 2 inches; depth, outside, 2¼ inches; inside, 1⅛ inches. It was composed mainly of fragments and shreds of dead wood, apparently stuck together by some glutinous substance, and in one place it had what seemed to be a web of some kind binding it. A few beech buds and bud scales were worked in, and a bleached leaf fragment, a shred of yellow birchbark, and a small dangling strip of canoe-birch paper—the last perhaps for ornament—completed the body of the nest. The lining was of fine black rootlets. The general effect of the outside was a light yellow or bright straw-color. It was an interesting and a beautiful nest."

Dr. Chapman (1907) says that "nests found by Burtch (MS.) at Branchport, New York, were built in birch saplings eighteen and twenty inches from the ground, and in a blackberry bush fourteen inches from the ground." He quotes from the manuscript of Egbert Bagg, of Utica, N. Y., who found nests very similar to the one described above by F. H. Allen. But he says that "one nest had some of the finer quills of our common porcupine (even large enough for their barbs to be visible to the naked eye). This sort of lining might be satisfactory to the old bird, protected by her coat of feathers, but would seem to be somewhat dangerous to her naked fledglings." One of his nests, evidently built in an upright fork, measured "diameter, outside, 3½ inches, inside, 2¼ inches; height, outside, 5 inches; depth, inside, 1½ inches."

T. E. McMullen has sent me the data for 22 nests, found in the Pocono Mountains, Pa. All of these were built in rhododendrons in woods, two on hillsides, one on the edge of a road, one on the edge of the woods, one near a creek, and three along a creek bank. Most of Mr. Brewster's (1938) Lake Umbagog nests were placed low down in yews (*Taxus canadensis*). Apparently, the favorite nesting sites of the black-throated blue warbler are in the broadleaf evergreens, mountain-laurels and rhododendrons, where these are available; next in popularity come the other evergreens (spruces, firs, and hemlocks) of small size; but nests have been found in many places in deciduous seedlings, saplings and sprouts, mainly maple and beech, or in various other bushes or tangles.

Mrs. Harding gave me an account of the building of a nest, which she watched during a period of four days. Most of the work was done by the female, but the male helped shape the nest occasionally. The beginning of the nest and much of the main part of it was made of thin strips of the paperlike bark of the white, or canoe, birch firmly bound in place with great quantities of cobwebs; during the early stages of building the rim was anchored with several strands of cobweb to the surrounding leaves and twigs to secure it while the nest was being shaped; this the bird did by sitting in the nest and turning around in all directions, molding it inside with her feet and breast and pressing her tail down over the edge to smooth the exterior. The male sang in the vicinity and brought some of the material, and once he drove away another male. The nest was finished on the fourth day. This process is described in more detail in Mrs. Harding's (1931) paper, where she notes "there is usually an interim of at least twenty-four hours before the first egg is laid. The female lays the eggs at intervals of twenty-four hours—frequently early in the morning. * * * On the morning of the fourth day when the clutch is complete the female commences incubating."

*Eggs.*—The black-throated blue warbler lays normally four eggs, three are not a rare complement, but five are seldom found. Richard C. Harlow tells me that in over 200 nests that he has examined he has found only 4 sets of five.

The eggs vary in shape from ovate to short ovate, rarely tending to elongate ovate, and are only slightly lustrous. They are white or creamy white, speckled, blotched, or clouded with tones of "pecan brown," "russet," "Mars brown," "cinnamon-brown," "chestnut-brown," "bay," or "auburn," with undertones of "benzo brown," "light brownish drab," "light violet-gray," or "pale Quaker drab." There is quite a little variation in the markings, ranging from spots and undertones that are distinct and clearly defined to spots clouded together and undertones only faintly discernible. The markings are usually concentrated at the large end, often forming a loose wreath, or sometimes a solid cap of brown. Occasionally, markings are well scattered over the entire egg. There seem to be two distinct types, one having spots of two or three shades of brown, with gray undertones, the other with tones of only one shade of brown, with drab undertones. The measurements of 50 eggs average 16.9 by 12.8 millimeters; the eggs showing the four extremes measure 18.9 by 13.0, 16.7 by 13.5, 15.2 by 12.2, and 17.0 by 11.8 millimeters (Harris).

*Young.*—The period of incubation for the black-throated blue warbler, according to Miss Stanwood's notes, is about 12 days; and the young remain in the nest for about 10 days. Incubation of the eggs and brooding of the young is done by the female only, but feeding the young and cleaning the nest is shared about equally with the male. She saw the young fed with daddy-longlegs, white moths, caterpillars, crane-flies, mosquitoes, and many other insects.

Quoting from the notes of J. A. Farley, Mr. Forbush (1929) gives the following picture of a brooding female: "She had spread the white feathers of her lower parts out so completely over her young that there was not a vestige now visible of the four young that I had found a short time previously filling the nest so full. She 'fluffed' herself out so as to hide all traces of the young. * * * She made a beautiful picture. The whole effect was wonderful. The bird seemed to be sitting in a billowy mass of eider down, or cotton wool, that swelled, or rather bulged, up all around her, a regular bed of down."

Mrs. Nice (1930b) watched a brood of young black-throated blue warblers, in Pelham, Mass., for 7 consecutive days, June 24 to 30, and for a total of 36½ hours. During this time the female fed the young 193 times and the male, 201 times; the average feeding time was once in 5.6 minutes; the female brooded 22 times, a total of 200 minutes, mainly in the earlier half of the period; the feces were eaten by the female 6 times and by the male 13 times; they were carried away by the female 47 times and by the male 67 times.

As to the food of the young, Mrs. Harding (1931) writes:

As soon as the young hatch the female begins feeding them. I have seen no evidence of regurgitation. She thoroughly crushes caterpillars, etc., between her mandibles before giving them to the young. Their food for the first day consists of small insects, soft white grubs and a large number of half inch, smooth, green caterpillars, which are found on hemlock trees. From the second to the eighth day their diet consists chiefly of small green caterpillars, insects, white grubs and an occasional may-fly or gray and cream colored caterpillar without spines. On the ninth and tenth day their diet still includes white grubs and green caterpillars, but dragon flies and may-flies are the chief staples. Slugs, winged ants, white cabbage butterflies and moths are also on the menu.

From the time the young hatch until they are five days old the parents swallow the faecal sacs. After that they carry them away from the nest and place them on the branches of neighboring trees—frequently using dead branches.

She gives a detailed account of the development of the young and their manner of leaving the nest naturally on the tenth day. During the 6 days when she thought it safe to handle them without driving them out of the nest too soon, one increased in weight from 22 grains to 141, and another from 24 to 147 grains.

*Plumages.*—The sexes differ slightly in the juvenal plumage. The young male is olive-brown above; the wings are blackish, the primaries edged with bluish-leaden-gray; the wing coverts, secondaries, and tertials are margined with olive-green, and there is a white patch near the base of the primaries, as in the adult; the tail is much like that of the adult; the under parts are brownish, tinged with yellowish on the throat and abdomen; the lores and two submalar streaks are dusky, and the superciliary stripe is yellowish white. The young female is similar, but has dull brown wings and tail with greenish instead of bluish edgings, and the white area in the primaries is smaller, more dingy and sometimes obscure.

A partial postjuvenal molt occurs in late July and August involving the contour plumage and the wing coverts but not the rest of the wings or the tail, producing a first winter plumage in which the sexes become decidedly differentiated and not very different from the adults at that season. This is one of the few wood warblers in which the fall plumage is very much like the spring dress. In the young male the blue of the upper parts is not as clearly blue as in the adult; the feathers of the back are faintly edged with olive-green, those of the black throat veiled with dull whitish, and the abdomen is tinged with yellowish. The young female differs from the fall adult in being greener above, without bluish tinge, and more buffy or yellowish below.

There is a limited prenuptial molt about the head, and wear has removed most of the edgings and fading has made the under parts clearer. At this age, young birds can be distinguished from adults by the worn and dull brown wings and tail. Subsequent molts and plumages, in which young and old are alike, consist of a complete postnuptial molt in July and August and a limited prenuptial molt about the head. The adult male in the fall is only slightly tipped with greenish above and with whitish on the black throat, which may be somewhat less in extent.

*Food.*—No thorough study of the food of the black-throated blue warbler seems to have been made, but probably all of the items mentioned as food for the young are also eaten by the adults.  Forbush (1929) adds the hairy tent caterpillar, flies, beetles, and plant lice. Aughey (1878) found 23 locusts and 15 other insects in one stomach collected in Nebraska.  Dr. Wetmore (1916) reports on the contents of eight stomachs collected in Puerto Rico, in which animal matter formed 75.5 percent and vegetable matter 24.5 percent of the food. "The vegetable food was found in the three stomachs taken in December and January and consisted of seeds of the camacey (*Miconia prasina*)." The principal items in the animal food were lantern flies (Fulgoridae), 19.46 percent, various weevils, 14.25 percent, flies, 10.09 percent, and spiders, 12.62 percent.  A few beetles and one ant were eaten.  Most of the food consisted of harmful insects.

*Behavoir.*—The black-throated blue warbler is one of the tamest and most confiding of all our wood warblers.  I was able to photograph (pl. 30) the female incubating and both sexes feeding the young at very short range without any special concealment; they are very devoted parents and show great concern when the safety of their young is threatened, trailing along the ground with the broken-wing act in great distress.

Gerald Thayer wrote to Dr. Chapman (1907) : "In its movements the Black-throated Blue is more deliberate than many of its relatives, but it has at the same time a somewhat Redstart-like way of 'spiriting' itself from one perch to another, and, while perched, of partly opening its white-mooned wings;—a habit and a marking shared by the boldly blue-and-black-and-white males and the dimly green and yellowish females and young."

Henry D. Minot (1877) writes:

They are very dexterous in obtaining their insect prey; sometimes seizing it in the air, with the skill of a true Flycatcher, and at other times finding it among the branches of the various trees which they frequent.  Now they twist their heads into seemingly painful postures, the better to search the crannies in the bark or blossoms, now spring from a twig to snap up an insect in the foilage above their heads, instantly returning, and now flutter before a cluster of opening leaves, with the grace of a Hummingbird.  Occasionally they descend to the ground, and are so very tame that once, when I was standing motionless, observing some Warblers near me, one hopped between my feet to pick up a morsel of food.

*Voice.*—Aretas A. Saunders has sent me the following study of the song: "The song of the black-throated blue warbler, in its more typical forms, is one of only three or four slowly drawled notes in a peculiarly husky voice, the last note commonly slurred upward.  While the number of notes in the songs varies in my 41 records from two to seven, more than half of them are of only three notes, and most of the others are of four or five.  In all, 22 songs end with the upward slur of the last note, 14 in an unslurred note and 5 in a downward slur.

The general trend of the pitch is upward in 29 records, downward in 10, and ending in the same pitch as the first note in 2.

"The pitch of songs varies from G''' to E'''', a range of four and a half tones. Single songs range from half a tone to three tones, the majority covering one and a half or two tones. The length of the songs is from 1⅕ to 2 seconds. This indicates the slowness of the three or four notes, for other warbler songs with twice as many notes are about the same length. In the few songs of this bird that have more notes the notes are shorter and faster, so that the songs are not longer.

"This species shows a greater tendency to sing unusual songs than most warblers. On three occasions I have heard a warbler song that I could not recognize, and when I located the bird, found it to be a black-throated blue.

"Two of these songs were of rapid notes, in a clear, ringing quality, not at all like the ordinary song of this bird. The third was two rather long notes in a clear, sweet whistle, the second higher in pitch than the first, so that it resembled the *phoebe* whistle of the chickadee reversed.

"The average date of the last song in 14 summers in Allegany State Park is July 21. The earliest is July 14, 1927 an 1940, and the latest July 29, 1931. The song is rarely revived in August, after the molt."

Francis H. Allen (MS.) writes the two common songs as "*quee quee quee-e-e'* " and "*que-que-que-que quee-ee'*," and says further, "in June 1907, I heard a bird in Shelburne, Vt., that sang persistently a short song like *kū quee-e-e'* besides singing occasionally one of the ordinary songs. In May, 1910, at Jaffrey, N. H., I heard a bird sing over and over *qui-qui-qui-qui-qui-qui-qui-qui-quee'*, but most of the birds of the region seemed to sing *zee zee zee-ee*, with a falling inflection, while some sang the ordinary *quee quee quee-e-e'*, with rising inflection. The *quee* songs have a nasal tone. The call note is a dry *chut* or *chet*, resembling the *chip* of the black-throated green but not so thick."

Mrs. Nice (1930b) describes four different songs; and Gerald Thayer, in Chapman (1907), gives four main songs, with variations, but the versatility of this singer seems to be well enough shown in the previous descriptions.

*Field marks.*—The male black-throated blue warbler could hardly be mistaken for anything else; there is no other American warbler that is at all like it. The blue back, the extensive black throat, the white patch near the bases of the primaries, the white under parts, and the white spots on the inner webs of the three outer tail feathers are all diagnostic. Fortunately, the fall plumage is essentially the same. But the female is one of the most difficult of the warblers to recognize, olive-green above and buffy below; the only distinctive marks are the white patches in the wings and tail, similar to those of the male, but smaller, duller, and sometimes obscure.

*Fall.*—As soon as the molting season is over, late in August, old and young birds begin to drift away from their summer haunts; most of them depart from New England during September or even late August.  Birds from New England and farther north pass through the Atlantic Coast States to Florida and the West Indies, while those from the interior migrate slightly southeastward and across the lower Alleghenies to join them.  Professor Cooke (1904) writes:

"Black-throated blue warblers strike the lighthouse at Sombrero Key in greater numbers than any other kind of bird, particularly during the fall migration. * * * In five years' time they struck the light on seventy-seven nights, and as a result 450 dead birds were picked up on the platform under the lantern. Probably a still larger number fell into the sea.  Adding to these those that were merely stunned and that remained on the balcony under the light until able to resume their journey, the keeper counted 2,000 birds that struck.  There were two nights, however, when the numbers of this species were so great that no attempt was made to count them.  The Fowey Rocks lighthouse was struck on thirty different nights.  It is certain, therefore, that the black-throated blue warbler passes in enormous numbers along both coasts of southern Florida.

*Winter.*—Professor Cooke (1904) observes that "the winter home of the black-throated blue warbler is better defined than that of any other common warbler, and allows a very exact determination of the square miles of territory occupied by it at this season.  Cuba, Haiti, and Jamaica, with a combined area of 74,000 square miles, are doubtless occupied during the winter by the great majority of the individuals of the species.  The remaining birds do not probably cover enough territory to bring the total to 80,000 square miles.  This is a small area compared with that occupied during the breeding season."  In his Birds of Cuba, Dr. Thomas Barbour (1923) writes:

The Black-throated Blue Warbler is excessively common, early to arrive and late to leave.  It is one of the tamest and most confiding species, and one to be found in all sorts of situations.  Early pleasant days in Cuba spent at Edwin Atkins' plantation, Soledad, near Cienfuegos, brought a great surprise, for I found it not uncommon to have these little Warblers enter my room through the great ever open windows and flit from couch to chair.  This happened often, notably at Guabairo, not far from Soledad.  So inquisitive and confiding are they, that one can hardly recognize the rather retiring dweller in woodland solitude which we know in the North.

### DISTRIBUTION

*Range.*—Eastern North America, from southern Canada to northern South America.

*Breeding range.*—The black-throated blue warbler breeds **north** to southwestern and central Ontario (Lac Seul, Kapuskasing, and Lake

Timiskaming) ; and southern Quebec (Blue Sea Lake, Quebec, God-bout, and Mingan). **East** to southern Quebec (Mingan, Grand Grève, and the Magdalen Islands) ; eastern Nova Scotia (Cape Breton Island and Halifax) ; southern Maine (Ellsworth and Auburn) ; southeastern Massachusetts (Taunton) ; Connecticut (Hadlyme) ; northeastern Pennsylvania (Lords Valley and Pocono Mountain) ; and southward through the Alleghanies to Northwestern South Carolina (Mountain Rest) ; northeastern Georgia (Rabun Bald, Brasstown Bald, and Young Harris). **South** to northern Georgia (Young Harris) ; southeastern Tennessee (Beersheba Springs) ; southeastern Kentucky (Log Mountain and Black Mountain) ; northeastern Ohio (Wayne Township and Pymatuning Bog) ; northern Michigan (Douglas Lake and Wequetonsing) ; northern Wisconsin (Fish Creek, Mamie Lake, and Perkinstown) ; and northern Minnesota (Kingsdale, Cass Lake, and White Earth; possibly sometimes near Minneapolis). **West** to northern Minnesota (White Earth) and western Ontario (Lac Seul). The species very probably breeds rarely in Manitoba or Saskatchewan where there are as yet only a few records and it is a recent arrival. At Emma Lake, Saskatchewan, 40 miles north of Prince Albert, 5 were observed June 27 to July 2, 1939. The first record for the Province was a specimen collected on October 21, 1936, at Percival, 100 miles east of Regina. It is a rare but tolerably regular migrant through eastern North and South Dakota, suggesting that there is some as yet unknown breeding area. The species has been recorded in migration, more often in fall, in Wyoming, Colorado, Nebraska, Kansas, Oklahoma, and Texas.

Observers at Aweme, Manitoba, in 38 years recorded it only twice. Another observer at Eastend, southwestern Saskatchewan, recorded it for the first time on September 21, 1937, after at least twenty years of continuous observation.

On the basis of such information it seems probable that the species is slowly spreading its breeding range westward.

*Winter range.*—The principal winter home of the black-throated blue warbler is in the West Indies where it is found **north** to the Bahamas (Andros, Nassau, and Watling Islands). **East** to Puerto Rico (Río Piedras) and the Virgin Islands (St. Croix). **South** to Puerto Rico (Maricas) ; Hispaniola (Paraíso, Dominican Republic; and Jérémie, Haiti) ; Jamaica (Spanishtown) ; and the Swan Islands. **West** to the Swan Islands; Cozumel Island; Cuba (Habana) ; and the Bahamas (Andros). It is also casual north to southern Florida (Sanibel Island, Key West, and Sombrero Key) ; accidental in Guatemala (Cobán) ; and in northern South America; Venezuela (Ocumare and Rancho Grande) ; and Colombia (Las Nubes, Santa Marta region, and Pueblo Viejo).

The species as outlined is divided into two subspecies or geographic races. The black-throated blue warbler (*D. c. caerulescens*) is found in Canada and in the United States south to Pennsylvania; Cairns' warbler (*D. c. cairnsi*) breeds in the Appalachian Mountains from southwestern Pennsylvania southward.

*Migration.*—Late dates of departure from the winter home are: Puerto Rico—Consumo, April 3. Haiti—Morne à Cabrits, May 6. Cuba—Habana, May 11. Bahamas—Cay Lobos, May 14.

Early dates of spring arrival are: Florida—Fort Myers, March 4. Georgia—Fitzgerald, April 11. South Carolina—Spartanburg, April 5. North Carolina—Weaverville, April 19. Virginia—Lynchburg, April 21. District of Columbia—Washington, April 19. Pennsylvania—Swarthmore, April 25. New York—New York, April 28. Massachusetts—Amherst, May 2. New Hampshire—East Westmoreland, April 29. Maine—Auburn, May 3. Novia Scotia—Scotch Lake, May 7. Quebec—Quebec, May 7. Louisiana—New Orleans, March 22. Tennessee—Chattanooga, April 14. Kentucky—Lexington, April 24. Illinois—Urbana, April 26. Ohio—Canton, April 22. Michigan—Battle Creek, April 28. Ontario—Reaboro, May 3. Missouri—St. Louis, April 18. Iowa—Sigourney, April 21. Wisconsin—Ripon, April 28. Minnesota—Hibbing, May 8.

Late dates of the departure of transients in spring are: Florida—Daytona Beach, May 21. Georgia—Darien, May 20. South Carolina—Clemson (College), May 15. North Carolina—Raleigh, May 19. Virginia—Charlottesville, May 22. District of Columbia—Washington, May 30. Pennsylvania—Berwyn, June 3. Ohio—Ashtabula, May 29. Indiana—Fort Wayne, June 2. Michigan—Detroit, June 2. Illinois—Lake Forest, June 8. Wisconsin—Racine, June 4. Iowa—National, May 27.

Late dates of fall departure are: North Dakota—Fargo, October 21 (bird banded). Minnesota—Minneapolis, October 3. Wisconsin—Milwaukee, October 16. Iowa—Sigourney, October 20. Illinois—Chicago, October 25. Michigan—Grand Rapids, November 1. Indiana—Indianapolis, October 14. Ontario—Port Dover, October 27. Ohio—Medina, October 30. Kentucky—Eubank, October 22. Tennessee—Athens, October 18. Mississippi—Gulfport, October 12. Quebec—Montreal, October 15. New Brunswick—Saint John, October 11. Maine—Portland, October 17. New Hampshire—Water Village, October 8. Massachusetts—Cambridge, November 7. New York—Fire Island, October 24. Pennsylvania—Harrisburg, October 24. District of Columbia—Washington, October 29. Virginia—Lexington, October 15. North Carolina—Highlands, November 14. South Carolina—Clemson (College), October 17. Georgia—Athens, November 2. Florida—Fernandina, November 15.

Early dates of fall arrival are: Wisconsin—New London, August 23. Michigan—Grand Rapids, August 26. Ohio—Toledo, August 24. Illinois—La Grange, August 24. District of Columbia—Washington, August 21. Virginia—Charlottesville, September 12. North Carolina—Mount Mitchell, September 1. South Carolina—Mount Pleasant, August 30. Georgia—Savannah, August 28. Florida—Coconut Grove, August 29. Cuba—Cienfuegos, September 2. Dominican Republic—El Río, October 5. Puerto Rico—Las Marías, October 12.

*Casual records.*—On the Farallon Islands, Calif., a specimen was found dead on November 17, 1886; it had been previously observed for three weeks. In New Mexico a specimen was taken at Gallinas Mountain on October 8, 1904, and on October 9, 1938 another was collected in Milk Ranch Canyon near Fort Wingate. In Bermuda a specimen was collected October 2, 1902; and it is considered a rare winter visitor. An individual spending the winter at a feeding stand in the suburbs of Washington, D. C., was observed closely from December 22, 1930, to January 16, 1931.

At sea the black-throated blue warbler has been observed on October 27, 1921, 12 hours run out from Port-au-Prince, Haiti, toward New York; and on March 29, 1918, in the Gulf of Mexico, 125 miles from Sabine Pass, La.

*Destruction at lighthouses.*—Lighthouses with fixed white lights have caused considerable destruction of bird life during migration and the black-throated blue warbler seems to have been especially lured to those in southern Florida. Records were received from several of these lighthouses over a period of 5 or 6 years. Those from Sombrero Key are most detailed and give an interesting picture of migration at that point, since they include date, weather conditions, number of birds that struck, number killed, and hours during which the birds struck the light.

Comparatively fewer birds struck the light in spring than in fall. The spring dates are from March 9 to May 29; but in 4 years birds are reported to have struck the light only on 24 nights and 4 individuals is the greatest number reported.

In the fall, the records extend from September 3 to December 5, the heaviest nights being from the middle of September to late October. In two different years birds struck the light on 19 nights in two months. The greatest number in one night was 400 with 56 killed. In one of those years 1146 birds struck the light; of these 193 were killed. It was not only on stormy nights that the birds were attracted, as 130 struck and 15 were killed on a night described as calm and dark. Sometimes they kept striking all night, but on others the flight seems to have been concentrated, as when 300 birds struck in 3½ hours. On a few occasions the mortality was as high as one-third of the birds that struck.

On the night of January 26, 1886, two birds struck the light. These were either wintering birds or extremely early migrants.

*Egg dates.*—Massachusetts: 6 records, May 28 to July 5; 3 records, June 2 to 8.

New Hampshire: 17 records, June 3 to 22; 9 records, June 10 to 15.

New York: 51 records, May 29 to June 20; 37 records, June 3 to 12, indicating the height of the season.

Pennsylvania: 57 records, May 25 to June 26; 32 records, May 30 to June 6.

North Carolina: 10 records, May 5 to June 22; 6 records, June 4 to 11.

Virginia: 19 records, May 26 to June 18; 14 records, May 27 to June 4 (Harris).

## DENDROICA CAERULESCENS CAIRNSI Coues

### CAIRNS' WARBLER

#### PLATE 31

##### HABITS

This local race of the black-throated blue warbler, breeding in the southern Alleghenies, was named by Dr. Elliott Coues (1897) in honor of its discoverer and original describer, John S. Cairns of Weaverville, N. C. Dr. Coues, at that time, mentioned only the characters of the male, but those of the female are fully as well, perhaps more satisfactorily, marked than those of the male. Ridgway (1902) describes both very well and concisely as follows:

"Similar to *D. c. caerulescens*, but adult male darker above, especially the pileum, which is not lighter blue than the back, the latter usually more or less spotted or clouded with black, sometimes chiefly black, the pileum sometimes streaked with black; adult female darker and duller olive above and less yellowish beneath, with the olive of flanks darker and more strongly contrasted with the pale olive-yellowish of abdomen." In discussing its distribution, he was unable to define its breeding range with any degree of accuracy; and adds in a footnote: "On the whole, the form is not a very satisfactory one, one of the two characters on which it was based (smaller size) failing altogether (*D. c. cairnsi* averaging slightly larger, in fact, than *D. c. caerulescens*), and the other only partially so, since many specimens of *D. c. cairnsi* have little if any black on the back, while many of *D. c. caerulescens* have quite as much as the average amount shown in *D. c. cairnsi*."

The 1931 A. O. U. Check-List gives the breeding range of *cairnsi* as from Maryland to Georgia, but no definite line can be drawn; birds from southern Pennsylvania and Maryland, and perhaps the Virginias, are variably intermediate in their characters, and specimens can be found that are referable to either one or the other form.

Before this race had been separated from the northern form, Cairns (1896) wrote of its haunts:

High up on the heavily timbered mountain ranges of western North Carolina is the summer home of the Black-throated Blue Warbler.

Here in precipitous ravines, amid tangled vines and moss-covered logs, where the sun's rays never penetrate the rank vegetation and the air is always cool, dwells the happy little creature, filling the woods from dawn to twilight with its song. * * *

These birds are a local race; breeding from one generation to another. They arrive from the south nearly ten days earlier than those that pass through the valleys on their northward migration. It is common to observe migrants through the valleys while breeders on the higher mountains are already nest-building and rearing their young.

This statement agrees with Professor Cooke's (1904) later data, and with his statement: "The species is one of the few that appear in the mountains earlier than on the plains, and the case seems to sustain the theory that the individuals of a species that breed farthest south are the first to migrate in the spring."

*Nesting.*—Cairns (1896) writes on this subject:

Nesting begins in May and continues until the end of June. The nests are placed in various shrubs, such as laurel, wild gooseberry, and chestnut, but the blue cohosh or papoose-root (*Caulophyllum thalictroides*) seems to be the favorite. These thick weeds grow rapidly to a height of from three to five feet, entirely hiding the ground, and thus afford the birds considerable protection. * * * The nests are never placed over three feet from the ground; usually about eighteen inches; one I examined was only six inches. * * *

The nests show little variation in their construction, though some are more substantially built than others. Exteriorly they are composed of rhododendron or grape-vine bark, interwoven with birch-bark, moss, spider-webs, and occasionally bits of rotten wood. The interior is neatly lined with hair-like moss, resembling fine black roots, mixed with a few sprays of bright red moss, forming a strikingly beautiful contrast to the pearly eggs. The female gathers all the materials, and builds rapidly, usually completing a nest in from four to six days if the weather is favorable. She is usually accompanied by the male, which, however, does not assist her in any way.

Bruce P. Tyler of Johnson City, Tenn., has sent me some fine photographs (pl. 31) of the nests of this warbler, and says in his notes: "The Cairns warbler is found breeding in May, and later, on the southerly slope of Beech Mountain, just across the Tennessee line in North Carolina, at an elevation of 4,800 to 5,200 feet above sea level. The nest is built in small upright saplings or sprouts, 3 to 4 feet above the ground, and is constructed of shredded bark from the dying chestnut trees, rotten wood, etc., bound together with spiders' webs, and lined with fern rootlets and fine grass."

Thomas D. Burleigh (1927a) records four nests found, during May and June, on the slopes of Brasstown Bald in the northeastern part of Georgia: Two of these were in laurel bushes, 2 and 2½ feet from the ground; another was 2 feet up in the fork of a small viburnum; and the fourth was 5 feet from the ground, "saddled near the end of a drooping limb of a rhododendron at the base of a large yellow birch well up the mountainside." A nest in my collection was taken by H. H. Bailey in Giles County, Va., at an elevation of 4,000 feet, on May 22, 1914; it was placed in a horsechestnut sprout alongside of a road, 1 foot above the ground. This and another nest before me are very similar to those described above.

*Eggs.*—The 3 or 4 eggs laid by Cairn's warbler are practically indistinguishable from those of the black-throated blue warbler. The measurements of 30 eggs average 17.3 by 12.7 millimeters; the eggs showing the four extremes measure 19.0 by 13.0, 17.9 by 13.4, and 16.0 by 12.0 millimeters (Harris).

## DENDROICA CORONATA CORONATA (Linnaeus)

### EASTERN MYRTLE WARBLER

#### PLATES 31–33

#### HABITS

We used to call this the yellow-rumped warbler, a none too distinctive name, as other warblers have yellow rumps. Another early and slightly better name, "yellow-crowned wood warbler," reflected the scientific name *coronata* and was based on the old Edwards name "golden-crowned fly-catcher." The present name, Eastern myrtle warbler, comes from its fondness for the berries of the waxmyrtle (*Myrica cerifera*); and in the south, where it is common in winter, it is often called the myrtlebird.

Next to the yellow warbler, this is probably the best known of the wood warblers and is about the second one of the group that the novice learns to recognize. All through the eastern United States this is by far the most abundant warbler on both migrations, being about the first to arrive in the spring and the last to leave in the fall, often remaining all winter nearly up to the southern limits of its breeding range. It is a large, conspicuous warbler, not at all shy, and is to be found almost anywhere, often in enormous numbers. The breeding range of the species is one of the most extensive, extending from the tree limit in Alaska and northern Canada down through the coniferous forests into the northern tier of States, and even farther south in the mountains. Its winter range is still more extensive. It spends the winter farther north than any other wood warbler, although more or less sparingly and irregularly in the northern States, and its range extends through the Bahamas, the northern West Indies, Mexico, and Central America to Panamá. There is no wonder that it is well known. But neither Wilson, Audubon, nor Nuttall ever found its nest.

*Spring.*—Professor Cooke (1904) writes:

The myrtle warbler is one of the first migrants to move northward. A large flight struck the Alligator Reef lighthouse February 23, 1892, and some 60 birds struck the Sombrero Key lighthouse March 3, 1889. By the middle of March migration is well under way over all the winter range, and the foremost birds keep close behind the disappearance of frost. * * * By the last of March all the myrtle warblers have departed from Jamaica, Haiti, Cuba, and the Bahamas. The latest recorded date of striking of this species at any of the Florida lighthouses is April 3, 1889. By the middle of the month the latest northbound birds have left southern Florida. * * * Most of the migrants cross the Rio Grande into Texas about the middle of March, and it is the middle of April before the last have passed north.

Charles L. Whittle (1922) witnessed a heavy migration of myrtle warblers along the coastal islands of South Carolina on March 4, 1920, that seemed to have been influenced largely by the presence of the waxmyrtle (*Myrica cerifera*). He says:

Perhaps half a mile from the northeast end of Sullivan Island the belt of waxmyrtle trees narrows to a width, measured northwest and southeast, of about three hundred feet. Here, near a seashore resort, a road had been recently cut across the belt of waxmyrtle trees at right angles to the sand bar. Streams of warblers flying along the shore northeasterly from Folly and Morris Islands, just south of the entrance to Charleston harbor, dropped to the land and converged at the southwest end of the mantle of myrtle trees and passed across the open swath cut for the new road. Posting ourselves here we counted the birds moving northeast, minute by minute as they passed the opening, for half an hour. The flight was continuous, many of the birds lighting on the ground and trees from time to time, and the number crossing per minute varied from twenty to two hundred, and accordingly averaged about one hundred per minute. As far as we could judge the number was no greater than it had been all the time since our arrival at the shore. Taking, therefore, the average at one hundred per minute, 24,000 Myrtle Warblers passed northward between nine in the morning and one in the afternoon. Not only so, but additional warblers passed close by both to the east and to the west of the stream of birds under observation. No doubt also the migration began prior to nine in the morning and did not cease at one in the afternoon.

He points out that the northern species of myrtle, or bayberry (*Myrica pensylvanica*), extends all along the coast from New Brunswick and Nova Scotia to Florida; and he suggests that if these warblers prefer to migrate along a coastal route where these myrtles reach their maximum development and where the climate may be milder than at higher elevations inland, it may explain why they generally arrive in New Brunswick a week earlier than in Pennsylvania.

Milton P. Skinner (1928) says that, in the North Carolina sand-hills, "early in March the movement becomes conspicuous, and great numbers of these warblers are then seen constantly moving through the forests and across the fields in steady streams, flitting about a few minutes, and then passing on to the northeast. These movements are near the ground, or among the tree trunks, but at other times the birds are above the tallest trees. The general direction is from the south-west to the northeast, with fifty to a hundred warblers passing over a field each hour of every day for at least two weeks."

At Buckeye Lake, Ohio, according to Milton B. Trautman (1940)—

No warbler species migrated through the area in such consistently large num-bers as did the Myrtle Warbler, and none had a more prolonged spring or fall migration. The first spring transients, mostly brilliant colored males, were gen-erally seen between April 12 and 20. Thereafter the number of individuals in-creased rapidly, and from May 1 to May 5 between 100 and 200 birds, mostly males, could generally be daily noted. A marked decrease usually followed this migration wave. Between May 10 and 18, during the period of maximum num-bers for most warbler species, there was a second large wave and then 150 to 500, mostly females and young males, were observed daily. A drastic decline in numbers took place shortly after May 18, and by May 23 few or none remained.

The migration is about the same in Massachusetts. The birds come in waves, the adult males preceding the females. We usually see the first arrivals about the middle of April, drifting through the leafless treetops in the tall deciduous woods where we look for hawks' nests; in their brilliant new plumage with gleaming yellow patches they are easily recognized as myrtle warblers, even in the tops of the 60-foot trees. Mr. Forbush (1929) gives this picture of the later waves:

In the latter days of April or very early in May when the south wind blows, when houstonias and violets begin to bloom on sunny southern slopes, when the wild cherry and apples trees and some of the birches, sumacs and the shrubbery in sheltered sunny nooks begin to put out a misty greenery of tiny leaflets, then we may look for the Myrtle Warblers, the males lovely in their nuptial dress of blue-gray, black, white and lemon-yellow. Then they may be found fluttering about in sheltered bushy bogs, catching the early insects that dance in the sun-shine along the water-side. All through early May they move northward, or westward toward the mountains, migrating by day or night indifferently as the case may be.

Soon most of them have passed beyond our borders and reached their summer homes in the coniferous forests of the Canadian Zone, the first of the family to come, close on the heels of retreating winter and while frost and snow still linger in the northern woods.

*Courtship.*—The courtship of the myrtle warbler must be a very pretty performance. Two brief accounts of it have been published: "As summer approaches the males begin their courtship of the females, following them about and displaying their beauties by fluffing out the feathers of their sides, raising their wings and erecting the feathers

of the crown, so as to exhibit to the full their beautiful black and
yellow markings.   After much time spent in courting they mate, and
at once look about for a nesting place" (Forbush, 1929).   Males seeking mates "made advances to the female contingency, hopping from
twig to twig with outspread wings, chipping and fluttering, now re-
pulsed by the fair one, and now accepted by another one to whom
advances were made, to finally spend a few days in a favorable spot
and begin nest building" (Knight, 1908).

*Nesting.*—On August 1, 1907, at Clarkes Harbor, Nova Scotia, I
found the first and only nest of the myrtle warbler that I have ever
seen; it was about 15 feet from the ground on a horizontal branch of a
large spruce tree, about 5 feet out from the trunk, and contained three
young birds that were nearly fully feathered.   Robie W. Tufts says in
his Nova Scotia notes: "I have seen these nests built at varying heights
from 5 to 50 feet high.   One found on June 6, 1919, contained four
slightly incubated eggs.   It was placed close to the stem of a pine tree,
near the top, about 50 feet up.   My field experiences tend to support
the theory that these birds normally raise two broods a year."   He
found one nest built in an apple tree in an orchard, of which he says:
"Of the large number of nests of this species I have examined, this is
the only one not built in a conifer."

There are two Nova Scotia nests of the myrtle warbler in the Thayer
collection in Cambridge, both taken by H. F. Tufts.   They are slightly
different in composition and structure, but are probably fairly typical
of the species.   One, found saddled on a spruce limb 10 feet from the
ground, is rather bulky and loosely built; the foundation and sides are
made of fine coniferous twigs mixed on the bottom with grasses and
rootlets and around the rim firmly interwoven with black horsehair,
or perhaps moose hair, and finer rootlets; the cup is smoothly lined
with finer hair and feathers.   Externally it measures, roughly, 4 by
5 inches in diameter and about 2 inches in height; the cup is about 2
inches in diameter and 1¾ inches deep.   The other, a very pretty nest
found 8 feet up in a small spruce, close to the trunk, is more firmly and
compactly built; the base and sides are made up mainly of green
mosses and a few gray lichens mixed with fine twigs and a few fine
grasses, all firmly interwoven; internally the cup is smoothly lined
with fine black and white hairs on top of a few feathers.   Externally
it measures 2¼ inches in height and 3 by 3½ inches in diameter; the
cup is 2 inches in diameter and about 1½ inches deep.

Of nestings in Maine, Knight (1908) says: "As soon as nest building
begins, the favorite locality selected is a thicket of evergreen trees near
the highway, some open pasture containing a few clumps of scattered
evergreens, small thickets of evergreens along the banks of some stream
or river or about the shore of a pond or lake, or a row of trees about

some country dwelling or in an orchard. In the vast majority of cases an evergreen tree is selected as a nesting site, though occasionally some hardwood tree, such as maple, apple or birch, may be taken. A majority of nests seem to be placed in cedar trees, with fir and spruce following as close second choices."

Forbush (1929) mentions two Massachusetts nests in tall white pines. A nest studied by Mrs. Nice (1930a), at Pelham, Mass., was "six feet up in a small red cedar on a branch next to the trunk. It was a rather shallow affair, composed of cedar twigs and bark, plant fibers, a piece of string and pine needles, and was lined with a few horse hairs and many Ruffed Grouse feathers."

Dr. Paul Harrington has sent me his notes based on the study of 44 nests of the myrtle warbler in Simcoe County, Ontario. He says that the white pine is generally chosen as a nesting tree, the nests being placed from 6 to 40 feet up, averaging 15 feet; "28 nests were built on horizontal limbs about two-thirds out from the trunk, but none at the outermost end. They were conspicuous from below but not from above, as clumps of needles overhung them in such a way as to afford good protection." Of the remainder, 2 were built in the top clump of needles in young trees; 5 were in small spruces, the lowest 3 feet, the highest 15, and all on horizontal limbs, 3 near the trunk and 2 half-way out on the limb; 5 were about 15 feet up in crotches of small cedars; 3 were found in red pines, in the outermost clumps of needles 10 to 15 feet from the ground; and 1 nest was 6 feet up in a small balsam. He says that the nest is lined thickly with feathers and a few hairs. "The feathers are so placed that, as well as lining the nest, they form a screen over the inside when the bird is not sitting. This is done by the shafts of the feathers being woven or imbedded into the inside of the nest and the vane lying free." At Petawa he found these birds nesting in small jack pines.

Dr. F. A. E. Starr, in his notes from northern Ontario, also says that any conifers are suitable nesting sites: "I have found only one exception to the use of a conifer. This nest was built in a hawthorn, and when I collected the nest, the birds moved to a cedar." A. D. Henderson writes to me: "The myrtle warbler is a fairly numerous summer resident at Belvedere, Alberta, and in the Fort Assiniboine District. It nests mainly in the muskegs in tamarack and spruce trees, but occasionally in deciduous trees close to a muskeg." The nests are mostly from 10 to 15 feet up. One nest was in a jack pine, "in a bunchy growth at the end of a limb." Baird, Brewer, and Ridgway (1874) state that MacFarlane found nests on the ground in the Anderson River region.

*Eggs.*—Most observers agree that four or five eggs form the usual set for the myrtle warbler. Tufts (MS.) says that "five eggs are more commonly found than four." Dr. Starr says in his notes that "four eggs are rarely laid, two and three being the usual numbers, while sometimes only one is laid, along with those of the cowbird." This is probably an abnormal situation in which the cowbird fills the nest with its own eggs, leaving little room for those of the warbler.

The eggs are ovate to short ovate and slightly glossy. The ground color is creamy white and is speckled, spotted, or blotched with "auburn," "argus brown," "Brussels brown," "chestnut brown," or "cinnamon-brown," with undermarks of "light brownish drab," "vinaceous gray," or "purplish gray." Generally the spots are concentrated at the large end, forming a wreath, but some are marked all over and may also have a few scrawls of blackish brown. I think the handsomest are those having the rich creamy white ground almost immaculate except for a solid wreath, around the large end, of spots and blotches of the browns overlapping and intermingled with the undertones of gray, so that they resemble somewhat the eggs of the wood pewee. On lightly marked eggs the drab or gray spots are the most prominent. The measurements of 50 eggs average 17.5 by 13.3 millimeters; the eggs showing the four extremes measure 20.3 by 13.2, 17.9 by 14.8, 14.8 by 12.9, and 16.0 by 12.4 millimeters (Harris).

*Young.*—The incubation period for the myrtle warbler is from 12 to 13 days and the young remain in the nest normally from 12 to 14 days. Incubating the eggs and brooding the young is apparently done entirely by the female, but both parents are active in feeding the young and in cleaning the nest. Mrs. Nice (1930a), with the help of Miss Lucille Baker, watched a nest containing young for a total of 19 hours, over a period of 6 days. On the first day the female brooded 25 percent of the time, but less later on; the brooding periods averaged 9 minutes.

A great deal of her energy was expended in delousing the nest—thirty-six minutes on July 28 and seventy-four minutes during the forenoon of the next day, but after that there was little trouble. Once, during thirteen minutes she made over 250 captures, all of which she ate. * * *

The male brought food sixty times, the female forty-eight times, so that the young were fed once in 10.9 minutes. About one-third of the time the male brought two insects, while the female did so on about one-sixth of her trips. During the fourteen hours of observation, the male brought food once in every nineteen minutes, the female once in every twenty-eight minutes. During the last five and one-half hours, the male brought food once in twenty-two minutes, the female once in eighteen minutes. * * *

Excreta were eaten by the female through July 29, but she carried one away at 7:05 P. M., July 28. She ate twelve sacs and carried eleven; her mate carried twenty-five and ate one. * * * He picked lice off his legs and gave them to the babies.

Mr. Knight (1908) says: "The female does most of the work of incubation, but on very rare and exceptional occasions I have found the male bird incubating and even engaged in song while on the nest. * * * The natal down rapidly dries and fluffs out on the young birds and is sepia-brown in color. At the end of six to seven days pin feathers begin to appear, and by the twelfth to fourteenth day the young are well advanced in their juvenal plumage and able to scramble out of the nest. Two to three days after leaving the nest they are able to essay short flights."

*Plumages.*—Mr. Knight (1908) refers to the natal down as sepia-brown. Dr. Dwight (1900) describes the juvenal plumage, in which the sexes are alike, as "above, the feathers centrally dull black, edged with drab and buffy brown, producing a streaked effect. Below, much whiter but similarly streaked, a tinge of pale primrose-yellow on the abdomen. Wings and tail dull black, edged with drab, palest on primaries and outer rectrices. Two very indistinct buffy white wing bands. Upper and lower eyelids with dull white spots."

The first winter plumage is acquired by a partial postjuvenal molt in August, which involves the contour plumage and the wing coverts, but not the rest of the wings or the tail. This plumage is entirely different from the juvenal and the sexes are only slightly differentiated. Dr. Dwight (1900) describes the young male as "above, sepia-brown, grayer on the back and obscurely streaked with black, the rump and a concealed crown spot lemon-yellow, the upper tail coverts black, broadly edged with plumbeous gray. Wing coverts black, plumbeous edged and tipped with white tinged with wood-brown forming two wing bands. Below, dull white, washed with pale buff on the throat and sides and obscurely streaked on the breast and sides with black, veiled by whitish edgings. Sides of breast with dull yellow patches. Incomplete orbital ring and faintly indicated superciliary stripe white or buffy." He says of the young female: "The black streaking of this dress is less obvious both above and below than in the male, the plumage everywhere is browner, and the crown patch very obscure."

The extensive prenuptial molt begins early, usually in March, before the birds have left their winter quarters; a few new feathers may be assumed even in late February but most of the molt occurs in April while the birds are migrating; it is, however, generally completed by the time the birds have reached their breeding grounds. Dr. Dwight (1900) says this molt "involves most of the body plumage and wing coverts, occasionally a tertiary but not the rest of the wings nor the tail. The black and gray of the upper surface, the white wing bars and the yellow crown and rump are new, some of the old upper tail coverts and a part of the feathers of the abdomen and crissum being retained in many cases, those of the back and elsewhere less often. Young and old become practically indistinguishable although the young usually have browner and more worn wings and tails, obvious in the primary coverts, but the differences are not absolute." In the female, "the first nuptial plumage is assumed by a restricted moult, leaving behind many brown feathers. The brown feathers of the lores and auriculars are assumed by moult."

The adult winter plumage is acquired by a complete postnuptial molt, beginning late in July. In the male, this "differs little from the first winter dress, but the wings and tail are blacker with brighter gray edgings, noticeable especially in the primary coverts. The back is usually grayer and the lower parts whiter, with broader streakings above and below." In the female there are similar differences, the adult winter female resembling the young male at that season. Adults have a complete postnuptial molt in July and a prenuptial molt as in the young birds.

*Food.*—Forbush (1929) sums up the food of this warbler very well as follows:

The Myrtle Warbler is one of the few warblers that can subsist for long periods upon berries and seeds, although undoubtedly it prefers insects when it can get them. Along the coast during the milder winters there are many flies rising from the seaweed in sheltered spots on mild days even in January, and there are eggs of plant-lice and some hibernating insects to be found on the trees, but the principal food of the Myrtle Warbler in New England during the inclement season is the bayberry. They can exist, however, on the berries of the Virginia juniper or red cedar and these seem to form their principal food when wintering in the interior; berries of the Virginia creeper or woodbine, those of viburnums, honeysuckle, mountain ash, poison ivy, spikenard and dogwoods also serve to eke out the birds' bill of fare. In the maple sugar orchards in early spring they occasionally drink sweet sap from the trees. In the southern Atlantic states they take palmetto berries. North and south they also eat some seeds, particularly those of sunflower and goldenrod. During spring and summer they destroy thousands of caterpillars, small grubs and the larvae of saw-flies and various insects, leaf-beetles, dark-beetles, weevils, wood-borers, ants, scale insects, plant-lice and their eggs, including the woolly apple-tree aphis and the the common apple-leaf plant-louse, also grasshoppers and locusts, bugs, house-flies and other flies including caddice-flies, crane-flies, calcid-flies, ichneumon-flies and gnats, also spiders.

To the above comprehensive list there is little to be added, although wild cranberries and the berries of the poison sumac might have been included. Myrtle warblers are doubtless instrumental in spreading the seeds of poisonous species of *Rhus*, which is not to their credit; they also help to disseminate the red cedar, as they digest only the outer covering of these three and the bayberries. These warblers are often seen on the beaches and sand dunes eating the seeds of the beachgrass, or in open fields feeding on grass seed and doubtless various weed seeds. They frequent the fresh holes bored by sapsuckers to drink the flowing sap and eat the insects that are attracted to it. In Florida, in winter, they drink the juice of fallen oranges in the groves and even the broken oranges on the trees.

They are somewhat expert as flycatchers, taking mosquitos and gnats in the air. Knight (1908) writes: "During the fall months they enter the city gardens and orchards, climb over the roofs and along the gutters of houses, peering into every nook and cranny. They hover on beating wings about such crannies of the clapboards and finish where they may have spied some delicious, big fat spider, chrysalis or other delectable morsel, and such finds are speedily devoured. Now peering, now hovering, and now springing into the air after some winged insect, they stop about a building for a few hours or days, slowly but surely retreating southward."

*Behavior.*—Much of the behavior of this friendly little bird has been referred to in connection with its activities about our homes and gardens and its nesting habits. Tilford Moore tells me that "these birds seem to have a tendency toward 'creeperism,' in that they are often seen hanging to the bark of a vertical trunk or branch, and are usually on the larger branches rather than among the smaller twigs. They often flutter a lot when hanging to the bark." And Wendell Taber sends me this note: "On May 5, 1940, Richard Stackpole and I watched a flock in West Newbury, Mass. The birds were running about on the grass near a stream. Again, they would alight at the base of a tree and run up it several feet. I think all the birds that performed this feat were females. They were most deceptive, and we kept thinking we were seeing brown creepers until we put field glasses on them."

William Brewster (1938) writes of the behavior of a female about her nest, 35 feet from the ground in a hemlock: "The female Yellow-rump was sitting and for some time she absolutely refused to leave her eggs. Watrous first shook the branch and then with a long stick poked and shook smartly the twigs within an inch or two of her head. At length she hopped out of the nest and stood for a moment or more on its rim looking about her. Then she fluttered down towards the ground with quivering wings and wide spread tail, moving slowly and alighting several times on a branch or cluster of twigs where she would lie prostrate for a moment beating her wings feebly and simulating the movements of a wounded or otherwise disabled bird."

Dr. Stone (1937) describes the flight of the myrtle warbler very well:

We soon learn to identify their rather jerky flight as they rise from the bushes, and with a series of short wing flips turn now to the right, now to the left, in their zigzag progress, rising somewhat with the beats, and falling in the intervals. Sometimes a bird will go but a short distance, flitting from bush to bush, while others will climb higher and higher in the air, drifting in their jerky way across the sky like wind-blown leaves. * * *

As soon as a Myrtlebird alights on a bush there is a short, sharp flip of the tail, not a seesaw action, but one involving the body as well, and as it comes to rest the head is drawn in and the plumage ruffled up making the outline more nearly globular, while the wings are dropped slightly so that their tips are a little below the base of the tail.

Francis H. Allen has sent me the following notes on the behavior of this species: "Aug. 27, 1915, Mt. Sunapee, N. H.  On the summit of the mountain an immature myrtle warbler, very tame, flitted and hopped about on the ground, over moss and rocks, and in bushes and trees, feeding industriously on small insects.  It seemed to pay no attention to my companion and me, and at one time hopped between us when we stood about 6 feet apart, and came within 2 feet of my outstretched hand as I held a crumb out towards it.  I followed it about a little and found it quite fearless, except when I made a sudden movement.  The bird could fly well and seemed perfectly well able to take care of itself.

"July 5, 1931, Mt. Whiteface, N. H.  One or more were seen flying up fifty or a hundred feet above the tops of the low spruces and darting about up there after insects—doubtless the black flies which were abundant on the summit.

"Oct. 25, 1941, Plymouth, Mass.  A sizable flock were feeding actively, flying back and forth across the narrow Eel River, feeding among foliage, catching flies and eating bayberries.  One came within 6 feet of me and calmly ate bayberry after bayberry."

*Voice.*—Aretas A. Saunders contributes the following account of the songs: "The songs of the myrtle warbler show some differences from those heard from birds on migration or on the breeding grounds. The song in general is a series of short, rapid notes in a rather colorless simple, but musical quality.  The number of notes, in my 41 records, varies from 7 to 21 and averages about 12.  The songs heard on migration, however, average 11 while those on the breeding grounds average 14.

"The songs heard on migration are quite indefinite in form; the pitch rises and falls irregularly, and no two songs are much alike. An individual bird may sing many variations, each song it sings often being a little different from the others.  The notes, however, are all about the same length and loudness, accented notes that stand out from the others being rare.  This song shows indications of a somewhat primitive character.

"The song on the breeding grounds is somewhat more definite; the notes are often joined in 2-note phrases, the first note of each phrase higher in pitch than the second and each phrase successively higher, so that the song trends upward in pitch.  This is true of 10 of my 13 records of the song on the breeding grounds in the Adirondacks. The other 3 have a slight downward trend.  In addition to the more regular form, these songs have a somewhat brighter, livelier, and more musical sound than those heard on migration.

"Songs of this species vary from 1 to 2⅘ seconds in length. There are usually about seven notes per second. Only 3 of my records show any irregularity in the time of the notes, that is having some notes that are shorter or longer than the others. Pitch of the songs varies from F'''' to E'''', a half tone less than an octave. Single songs vary from one to four and a half tones, averaging about two and a half tones; only 5 records are greater in range, and only 16 are less, nearly half of the records having the average range.

"Since the myrtle warbler winters in Connecticut, I am able to get the first dates of singing. In 30 years of records the average date is April 13; the earliest April 2, 1923, and the latest April 25, 1920. In the Adirondacks the last date of singing noted was July 31, 1926.

"The call note, *tchick*, is louder than in most warblers. I found it pitched on D''. Another note is a fainter *tseet tseet*, usually doubled and pitched on F-sharp'''."

Francis H. Allen (MS.) describes the song in a different way as follows:

"The only syllabifications I find in my notes are of a bird heard at West Bridgewater, Vt., June 19, 1907, which sang *whee whee whee whee whee whee whee whee hew hew*, sometimes with three or even four *hews* at the end and sometimes with only one; and one of a bird at South Tamworth, N. H., July 23, 1942, whose song consisted of two trills, *ching ching ching ching ching weedle weedle weet*.

"The ordinary call-note is a hoarse *chep*, easily distinguished from the call of any other New England warbler. I have also heard occasionally a slight *tsip* or *tsit*, suggesting a chickadee. The feeding call of the young out of the nest is a rapid succession of several explosive *chips* or *pits* with a rolling quality—a sort of chatter or chippering."

On June 7, 1900, in Washington County, Maine, I recorded the song of the myrtle warbler as *wheedle wheedle wheedle wheedle wheedle*, repeated five to seven times so rapidly as to be hard to count and all on one key, usually ending abruptly but occasionally in a little trill.

Few writers have accorded the song of the myrtle warbler much praise, but Bradford Torrey (1885) pays it this tribute: "For music to be heard constantly, right under one's window, it could scarcely be improved: sweet, brief, and remarkably unobstrusive, without sharpness or emphasis; a trill not altogether unlike the pine-creeping warbler's, but less matter-of-fact and business-like. I used to listen to it before I rose in the morning, and it was to be heard at intervals all day long."

*Field marks.*—The male myrtle warbler in spring plumage is easily recognized at a considerable distance in its blue-gray, black, and white plumage, offset by conspicuous patches of bright yellow on rump, sides, and crown, and by the black sides and cheeks. The female is much duller and browner, the yellow being less conspicuous and the black cheeks lacking. Young birds and fall adults are much like the female, but the yellow rump, showing plainly as the bird flies away from the observer, will distinguish the species at any season or age.

*Enemies.*—So much of the breeding range of the myrtle warbler is beyond the normal breeding range of the cowbirds that, until recently, it was supposed to be largely free from the imposition of this parasite. When Dr. Friedmann (1929) published his book on the cowbirds he had only three records of such molestation, but more have turned up since, particularly in the Middle West where the ranges of the two species overlap considerably. Dr. Paul Harrington writes to me from Toronto: "Sixty-five percent of the nests examined contained eggs or young of the cowbird; it would not be exaggerating to say that two-thirds of the initial nests are parasitized. The egg or eggs of the cowbird are often deposited before the nest is completed, leading to many a deserted nest. Twice I have found a cowbird's egg imbedded, as so often happens in the yellow warbler's nest, but in both cases yet another was in the nest with the owner's. Twelve percent of the nests with eggs of the cowbird were deserted, but none in which the owner's eggs were also present. Generally but one of the parasite's eggs was found, occasionally two and rarely three."

Dr. F. A. E. Starr says in his notes from Ontario: "Occasionally, when a cowbird usurps a nest, the birds continue building till the cowbird's egg is imbedded. This is all in vain, however, as out of 30 nests, I have yet to find one which did not contain from one to three eggs of the cowbird." And A. D. Henderson mentions in his notes from Belvedere, Alberta, a nest that held five eggs of the myrtle warbler and one egg of the Nevada cowbird, and another nestful consisting of four eggs of the warbler and two of the cowbird. Probably very few young of the warbler are likely to survive in nests with young cowbirds, which means that this parasite must seriously interfere with the normal increase in the warbler population.

Harold S. Peters (1936) lists two lice, two flies, and two mites as external parasites on the myrtle warbler.

*Fall.*—The myrtle warbler is one of the latest of its family to move southward and is also one of the most leisurely in migration; the migration covers practically the whole of September and October and much of November, the earliest arrivals sometimes reaching the Gulf States before the last ones have left Canada. Abundant in the spring, it is much more so in the fall, when it can often be seen in enormous numbers. As the birds drift along southward, many stop along the way where food is abundant and some spend the winter at no great distance from the southern limits of the breeding range. In Massachusetts, we usually look for them during the latter half of September or during those golden October days when woods are ablaze with the gorgeous autumn colors. As we stroll along the sunny side of the woods on some bright morning after a frosty night, the air is full of pleasing bird music. The robins, now wild woodland birds, are twittering or uttering their wild autumn calls as they drift through the trees; the white-throated and the song sparrows, from the brushy thickets below, give forth their faint, sweet notes like soft echoes of their springtime songs; and the myrtle warblers mingle their distinctive call-notes with these other voices as they glean for aphids on the birches. In the open grassy fields and weed patches, too, we find many myrtle warblers associated with the scattered flocks of juncos and field and chipping sparrows, feeding on the ground. And later in the fall, we find them in the bayberry patches near the seacoast, or even on the salt marshes or among the sand dunes with the Ipswich and savanna sparrows.

Southward along the Atlantic coast the flight is heavy; Dr. Stone (1937) says that, at Cape May, N. J., "on October 13, 1913, Julian Potter encountered a great flight of Myrtle Warblers which he estimated at 3,000. * * * October 31, 1920, was a characteristic Myrtle Warbler day. All day long they were present in abundance. The air seemed full of them wherever one went. Thousands were flittering here and there in the dense growth of rusty Indian grass (*Andropogon*), in the bayberry thickets, in pine woods and in dune thickets."

From their breeding grounds in the northern interior these warblers continue to drift southward during October, not in compact flocks but straggling in a continuous stream, some alighting while others are moving on. In Ohio, according to Trautman (1940), "the numbers continued to increase rapidly until approximately October 5. Between October 5 and 20 the species was more numerous over the entire land area than it was at any other season, and thousands were daily present. It was particularly abundant on Cranberry Island, where it fed upon insects, cranberries, poison sumac, and other berries. On several occasions an estimated number between 1000 and 1200 individuals was seen within an hour on this island. After October 20 there was a rather gradual decline in numbers. By November 1, comparatively few remained, and in some years the birds had disappeared."

*Winter.*—The myrtle warbler winters abundantly throughout the southern half of the United States east of the Great Plains, commonly as far north as southeastern Kansas, southern Illinois, southern Indiana and northern New Jersey, and less commonly or rarely and irregularly farther north. It is the only one of the wood warblers that is hardy enough to brave the rigors of our northern winters amid ice and snow and sometimes zero temperatures.

Robert Ridgway (1889) writing of its winter habits in southern Illinois, says:

It may often be seen in midwinter, when the ground is covered with snow, in the door-yards along with Snowbirds (*Junco hyemalis*), Tree Sparrows, and other familiar species, gleaning bread crumbs from the door-steps, or hunting for spiders or other insect tidbits in the nooks of the garden fence or the crevices in the bark of trees; and at evening, flying in considerable companies, to the sheltering branches of the thickest tree tops (preferably evergreens), where they pass the night. Not infrequently, however, they roost in odd nooks and crannies about the buildings, or even in holes in the straw- or hay-stacks, in the barn-yard. A favorite food of this species are the berries of the Poison-vine (*Rhus toxicodendron*), and during the early part of winter large numbers of them may be seen wherever vines of this species are abundant.

What few myrtle warblers remain in southern Massachusetts are usually to be found in situations similar to those frequented in late fall, especially near the coast where there is a good supply of bay-berries and other berries. When this supply is exhausted they move elsewhere, though they can subsist to some extent on the seeds of the pitch pine, on grass seed, and on various weed seeds. In New Jersey, they are found in similar situations. Farther south they are abundant inland as well as on the coast, living in all kinds of environments— old fields, cultivated lands, thickets, brushy borders of the woodlands, and in woods of scrub oaks and pine. They are common to abundant on both coasts of Florida and in the interior and often come into the orange groves, to feed on the fallen oranges. A. H. Howell (1932) says: "Not infrequently they may be found in numbers on the Gulf beaches, or in reeds in the salt marshes of the coast or in the Everglades. They are partial to the borders of streams or sloughs, and sometimes venture out on the floating vegetation in rivers or lakes."

The following is contributed by Dr. Alexander F. Skutch: "In December, 1932, it was vividly brought home to me how widely the myrtle warblers are spread over the earth during the winter months, and in what varied climates they dwell. On the ninth, a clear, cold, winter day, I met a small party of these yellow-rumped birds in a barren field at the edge of a woods in Maryland. On the twenty-fourth, I watched them fly above the tatters of melting snow in New Jersey, within view of the skyscrapers of New York. That afternoon I embarked upon a ship, and a week later arrived upon a banana plantation in Guatemala, where the air was balmy and the landscape vividly green, where snow and bleak winds seemed to belong to another world. Yet here, too, were myrtle warblers, hundreds of them, feeding in the open pastures and along the roadways, wherever the vegetation was not too dense, then rising up in compact flocks, wheeling and dropping together, moving always as though actuated by a true group spirit. During three days on that plantation, I met 23 kinds of winter visitants from the North; yet the myrtle warbler appeared to be the most abundant of them all: certainly, I saw far more of them than of any other migratory bird; yet this was in part because they foraged in more exposed places. Of all the warblers I found here, this was the only species that moved in flocks; for most of the wood warblers that winter in the Central American lowlands are strict individualists. It is also significant that of all the 23 species of wintering birds, this, the most abundant in December, was the only one then common that I had not recorded from February to June of the same year, when I passed 4 months studying the birds on that same plantation.

"Although it has been recorded from Central American localities as early as October and as late as April, the myrtle warbler is certainly most abundant as a winter visitant from November to March. All my own records from points in Guatemala, Honduras, and Costa Rica fall within these 5 months. It arrives later and departs earlier than warblers less tolerant of cold.

"The myrtle warbler winters in a variety of situations. At Puerto Castilla, on the northern coast of Honduras, I found these warblers abundant at the end of January, 1931. Here they foraged upon the lawns between the cottages, hopping rather than walking like waterthrushes, and when alarmed flew up to rest upon the broad fronds of the coconut palms that lined the sandy beach. At the other extreme, I have found them in mountain pastures, rarely as high as 8,500 feet above sea level. In the highlands, this bird is likely to be confused with the Audubon warbler, from the mountains of western United States, in similar dull winter attire. But the Audubon warbler, even at this season, wears five patches of yellow—on the crown, throat, both sides and rump—while the myrtle warbler shows only four, lacking that on the throat. The presence or absence of yellow on the throat is a distinguishing feature.

"At the end of December, 1937, I found myrtle warblers abundant in the vicinity of Buenos Aires de Osa, a hamlet in the lower Térraba Valley of Costa Rica, of interest to the bird-watcher because, although lying in a region covered by the heaviest lowland forest, it is surrounded by extensive open savannas which support a rather different bird-life. Here fork-tailed flycatchers were also abundant, roosting by night in some orange trees behind the padre's house, by day spreading in small flocks over the savannas, where they perched in the low bushes, only a few feet above the ground, and darted down to snatch up the insects they descried. It was surprising to find the myrtle warblers associating intimately with the flycatchers; just as, in the

Guatemalan highlands, I had found Audubon's warblers flocking with bluebirds. The myrtle warblers not only foraged about the bushes which served the flycatchers as watch-towers; but the two kinds of birds, so dissimilar in size and habits, changed their feeding grounds together. While I sometimes found the warblers alone, I saw them in company with the fork-tailed flycatchers too often for the association to be looked upon as accidental. I could not discover that either warbler or flycatcher derived any material advantage from the presence of the other. It seemed to be a case of pure sociability.

"Central American dates are: Guatemala—Motagua Valley, near Los Amates, December 31, 1932; Sierra de Tecpán, March 16, 1933; Finca Mocá, January 20–26, 1935; Nebaj (Griscom), April 27; La Primavera (Griscom), April 8. Honduras—Puerto Castilla, January 27, 1931; Tela (Peters), March 17. Costa Rica—Vara Blanca, December 13, 1937, to February 28, 1938; Guayabo (Ridgway and Zeledón), March 18; Carrillo (Underwood), October 2; Guacimo (Carriker), December 4; Las Cañas, Guanacaste, November 21, 1936; El General, January 12, 1936; Buenos Aires de Osa, December 24–30, 1937."

DISTRIBUTION

*Range.*—North America.

*Breeding range.*—The myrtle warbler breeds **north** to northern Alaska (Kobuk River and timberline on the south slope of the Brooks Range); northern Yukon (La Pierre House); northern Mackenzie (Aklavik; Fort Anderson; MacTavish Bay, Bear Lake; Lake Hardisty, and Artillery Lake); northern Manitoba (Lac du Brochet, Cochrane River, and Churchill); northern Ontario (Moose Factory); southern Labrador (Grand Falls and Rigolet, possibly Nain and Okkak). **East** to eastern Labrador (Rigolet and Cartwright); Newfoundland (St. Anthony, Canada Bay, and St. John's); and Nova Scotia (Cape Breton Island, Sable Island, Halifax, and Yarmouth). **South** to southern Nova Scotia (Yarmouth); New Brunswick (Grand Manan); southern Maine (Gouldsboro, Deer Isle, Bath, and Auburn); New Hampshire (Concord); central and southern Massachusetts (Marlboro, Webster, and Pelham); southwestern Vermont (Bennington); northern New York (Falls Pond and Buffalo); rarely northeastern Pennsylvania (Pocono Lake); accidentally in northern Maryland (Havre de Grace); southern Ontario (London and Sarnia); northern Michigan (Crawford County and Douglas Lake); northern Wisconsin (Antigo, probably, Trout Lake, Namekagon Lake, and Superior); central Minnesota (St. Cloud, Brainerd, and Bemidji); southern Manitoba (Winnipeg and Aweme); central Saskatchewan (Flotten Lake and Prince Albert); central Alberta (Flagstaff, Camrose, Lobstick River, and Wipiti River); northern British Columbia

(Fort St. John, Ingenika River, and Buckley Lake); and southern Alaska (Admiralty Island, Sitka, Seldovia, and Nushagak). West to western Alaska (Nushagak, Russian Mission, St. Michael, and the Kobuk River).

*Winter range.*—The myrtle warbler winters in two discontinuous areas. The principal winter home is **north** to central Oklahoma (Oklahoma City); northern Arkansas (Winslow, Little Rock, and Helena); western Tennessee (Memphis); southern Illinois (Anna and Mount Carmel); southern Kentucky (Bowling Green); central Virginia (Lexington); District of Columbia (Washington); southeastern Pennsylvania (Philadelphia); northern New Jersey (Morristown and Elizabeth); southern Connecticut (New Haven); Rhode Island (Providence); and northeastern Massachusetts (Cape Ann). It also occurs in winter irregularly **north** to Holly, Colo.; Hays and Manhattan, Kan.; Madison, Wis.; Chicago, Ill.; Battle Creek and Rochester (one banded in January), Mich.; Rochester, N. Y.; and Portland, Maine. **East** to Massachusetts (Cape Ann) and along the Atlantic coast to Florida (Miami and Key West); the Bahama Islands (Little Abaco and Caicos); Dominican Republic (Puerto Plato and Sánchez); Puerto Rico (San Juan); St. Croix Island; and rarely, Antigua. **South** to Antigua, northern Colombia, rare or accidental (Santa Marta region); and Panamá (Pearl Islands). **West** to Panamá (Pearl Islands, Canal Zone, and Almirante); Costa Rica (El General and Guayabo); eastern Nicaragua (Greytown and the Río Escondido); northern Honduras (Puerto Castilla and Lancetilla); western Guatemala (Dueñas and Tecpán); eastern Oaxaca (Tehuantepec); Veracruz (Orizaba); Tamaulipas (Victoria); Nuevo León (Monterrey); southwestern Texas (mouth of the Pecos River, Camp Barkeley, Taylor County, and Fort Worth); and central Oklahoma (Oklahoma City).

The western winter range is **north** to central Western Oregon (Newport and Albany). **East** to western Oregon (Albany); central California (Marysville, Stockton, Mariposa County, Redlands, and Potholes); southern Arizona (Tucson and Tombstone); and southwestern Sonora (Guaymas). **South** to southern Sonora. **West** to western Sonora (Guaymas and the Colorado River delta); western California (San Clementi Island, Santa Barbara, San Francisco Bay region, and Eureka); and western Oregon (Coss Bay and Newport).

The species as outlined is divided into two subspecies or geographic races. The Alaska myrtle warbler (*D. c. hooveri*) breeds from western Alaska and northwestern Mackenzie to central Alberta and central British Columbia; the eastern myrtle warbler (*D. c. coronata*) from western Saskatchewan eastward.

*Migration.*—Late dates of spring departure from the winter home are: Costa Rica—Guayabo, March 18. El Salvador—Volcán de San

Miguel, March 22. Guatemala—Nebaj, April 27. Honduras—Lancetilla, March 17. Mexico—Valles, San Luis Potosí, May 2. Puerto Rico—Mayagüez, April 8. Haiti—Port-au-Prince, April 27. Cuba—Habana, April 28. Bahamas—New Providence, April 2. Florida—Pensacola—May 13. Alabama—Birmingham, May 8. Georgia—Atlanta, May 20. South Carolina—Greenwood, May 12. Louisiana—Mansfield, May 2. Mississippi—Oxford, May 8. Tennessee—Nashville, May 17. Arkansas—Helena, May 18. Texas—Bonham, May 6. Oklahoma—Norman, May 3.

Early dates of spring arrival are: New York—New York, April 1. Massachusetts—Lynn, April 11. Vermont—St. Johnsbury, April 12. Maine—Portland, April 6. New Brunswick—Scotch Lake, April 11. Nova Scotia—Yarmouth, April 11. Quebec—Hatley, April 22. Newfoundland—St. Anthony, April 25. Labrador—Cartwright, May 24. Illinois—Chicago, March 24. Indiana—Bloomington, March 26. Ohio—Youngstown, April 1. Ontario—Harrow, April 3. Michigan—Sault Ste. Marie, April 9. Missouri—Columbia, March 27. Iowa—Sigourney, April 3. Wisconsin—New London, April 1. Minnesota—Minneapolis, April 4. Kansas—Independence, April 7. Nebraska—Red Cloud, April 1. South Dakota—Brookings, April 7. North Dakota—Fargo, April 13. Manitoba—Aweme, April 12. Saskatchewan—Eastend, April 22. Mackenzie—Simpson, May 7. New Mexico—San Antonio, April 18. Colorado—Colorado Springs, April 17. Wyoming—Laramie, April 15. Montana—Kirby, April 29. Alberta—Glenevis, April 14. Washington—Seattle, March 14. British Columbia—Courtenay, March 31; Atlin, April 21. Yukon—Sheldon Lake, April 26. Alaska—Wrangell, April 29; Fairbanks, May 7.

Late dates of spring departure of transients are: District of Columbia—Washington, June 1. Pennsylvania—Warren, June 6. Illinois—Chicago, June 3. Indiana—Waterloo, June 3. Ohio—Oberlin, May 31. Missouri—Concordia, May 25. Iowa—Grinnell, June 1. Nebraska—Nenzel, May 27. North Dakota—Argusville, May 30. California—Red Bluff, May 3. Nevada—Quinn River Crossing, May 21. Washington—Tacoma, May 3.

Late dates of fall departure are: British Columbia—Atlin, September 19; Courtenay, October 14. Mackenzie—Nahami River, October 25. Wyoming—Laramie, November 25. Saskatchewan—Yorkton, October 14. Manitoba—Brandon, October 31. North Dakota—Argusville, November 15. South Dakota—Faulkton, November 15. Kansas—Lawrence, November 12. Minnesota—St. Paul, November 5. Wisconsin—Racine, November 16. Iowa—Wall Lake, November 15. Missouri—Kansas City, November 16. Illinois—Murphysboro, November 21. Michigan—Detroit, November 19. Indiana—Indianapolis, November 20. Ontario—Point Pelee, November 23. Ohio—

Toledo, November 17. Newfoundland—Tompkins, October 4. Prince Edward Island—North River, October 15. Quebec—Kamouraska, November 9. New Brunswick—Saint John, November 4. Maine—Portland, November 9. New Hampshire—Durham, November 4. Massachusetts—Boston, November 27. New York—Brooklyn, November 22. Pennsylvania—Doylestown, November 29.

Early dates of fall arrival are: Washington—Bellingham, September 28. Oregon—Thurston, October 5. California—Eureka, October 12. Wyoming—Yellowstone Park, August 25. North Dakota—Fargo, September 8. South Dakota—September 15. Nebraska—Fairbury, September 30. Kansas—Lawrence, September 26. Oklahoma—Oklahoma City, October 12. Texas—Somerset, October 10. Iowa—Grinnell, September 6. Missouri—St. Louis, September 17. Illinois—Chicago, August 31. Indiana—Hobart, September 2. Ohio—Austinburg, August 25. Kentucky—Bowling Green, September 14. Tennessee—Athens, October 3. Arkansas—Rogers, October 4. Louisiana—Monroe, September 26. Mississippi—Edwards, September 22. New York—Rhinebeck, August 31. Pennsylvania—Pittsburgh, September 8. District of Columbia—Washington, September 9. West Virginia—Bluefield, September 12. Virginia—Naruna, September 22. North Carolina—Mount Mitchell, September 30. South Carolina—Spartanburg, September 21. Georgia—Round Oak, October 10. Alabama—Anniston, October 8. Florida—New Smyrna, October 4. Bahamas—Cay Lobos, November 22. Cuba—Habana, November 17. Dominican Republic—San Juan, October 1. Puerto Rico—Mayagüez, December 14. Costa Rica—Carrillo, October 2.

*Banding.*—The myrtle warbler comes rather more readily than other warblers to banding traps, especially in winter, and so has yielded several records of migration and of longevity for return to the place of banding. A myrtle warbler banded at Elmhurst, Long Island, on October 19, 1936, was recovered on December 9, 1936, at Awensdaw, S. C. One banded on October 2, 1932, at Fargo, N. D., was found dead December 5, 1932, at Clarence, La. Another banded at Wilton, N. D., on September 25, 1939, was found in January 1940 at Leola, Ark. One banded on February 2, 1930, at Gastonia, N. C., was shot on December 25, 1930, at Kings Creek, Cherokee County, S. C.

A banding station at Thomasville, Ga., obtained several records indicative of the birds' tendency to return to the same wintering place. Three birds banded in March 1920, were retrapped in February and March of 1921. One banded February 24, 1921, was retrapped February 5, 12, and 13, 1924, and found dead, apparently of starvation, on the fifteenth. A myrtle warbler banded on February 28, 1917, was retrapped in March 1920 and several times between March 1 and 17,

1921. It was then at least 5 years old and had made four round trips to the breeding grounds.

Another myrtle warbler banded at Huntington, Long Island, on October 23, 1933, was killed February 1, 1940, at Dunbar, S. C.; it was then at least 6½ years old.

*Casual records.*—At least six specimens of the myrtle warbler have been collected in Greenland: Fiskenaes, May 21, 1841; Julianehaab, about 1847; Godhavn, July 31, 1878; Nanortalik, May 23, 1880; Agpamiut, in Sukkertoppen District, October 15, 1931; and Kangea, near Godthaab, October 28, 1937. A specimen was taken from the stomach of a white gyrfalcon October 7, 1929, killed near the Post on Southampton Island. Two specimens have been collected on the Arctic Coast of Alaska: one on June 3, 1898, at Point Tangent; and one June 4, 1930, near Point Barrow. A myrtle warbler was collected May 25, 1879, on the northeast coast of Siberia at latitude 67° N. At sea about 100 miles from Cape Hatteras, several myrtle warblers were noted on October 16 and 31, 1930.

*Egg dates.*—Maine: 16 records, May 26 to June 23; 10 records, June 11 to 20, indicating the height of the season.

New Brunswick: 10 records, June 5 to 28; 6 records, June 13 to 21.

Nova Scotia: 14 records, May 23 to June 21; 7 records, June 3 to 17 (Harris).

**DENDROICA CORONATA HOOVERI McGregor**

**ALASKA MYRTLE WARBLER**

**HABITS**

The Alaska myrtle warbler is another subspecies that was described many years ago but only recently admitted to the A. O. U. Check-List. Richard C. McGregor (1899) described this warbler, from specimens collected in California, as a western race and named it for his friend Theodore J. Hoover, who collected the type and placed his material at his disposal. He called it *Dendroica coronata hooveri*, Hoover's warbler. In his description of it he says that it is "in colors and markings like *Dendroica coronata*, but with wing and tail much longer." His table of measurements shows that the wings of California males average .15 inch longer than those of eastern birds, and the tails .14 inch longer, less than ⅙ inch! Among the wing measurements of eastern males the individual variation is as great as the difference in his averages, the shortest measuring 2.80 and the longest 2.95 inches! It appears to be a quite finely drawn subspecies.

Dr. Oberholser (1938) says of it: "The Myrtle Warblers breeding in Alaska are recognizable as a western race of this species. They differ from the eastern bird in larger size and more solidly black breast in the male. The upper parts in winter plumage and in the young are also less rufescent than in the eastern bird."

The breeding range of this race, so far as known, extends from northwestern Mackenzie to western Alaska, and southward to central British Columbia and central Alberta. It has been found in winter from California to southeastern Louisiana, in the southeastern United States, and in northern Baja California and in southern Veracruz, in Mexico. It may be commoner than is supposed, as it is recognizable only with specimens in hand.

Dr. Joseph Grinnell (1900) writes of its habits in northern Alaska:

Hoover's Warblers were numerous summer residents of the timber tracts throughout the Kowak Valley from the delta eastward. In the latter part of August scattering companies were frequenting the spruce, birch and cottonwoods, among the foliage of which they were constantly searching, with oft-repeated 'chits,' just as are their habits in winter in California. The last observed, a straggling flock of six or eight, were seen in a patch of tall willows about sunset of August 30th. The following spring the arrival of Hoover's Warblers was on May 22nd. They were already in pairs and the males were in full song. At this season they were confined exclusively to the heavier spruce woods. In the Kowak delta, on the 23rd of June, a set of five considerably-incubated eggs was secured. The nest was in a small spruce in a tract of larger growth, and only four feet above the ground. It is a rather loose structure of fine dry grass-blades, lined with ptarmigan feathers.

In the Atlin region of northern British Columbia, according to Mr. Swarth (1926), it is a common species, breeding mostly in the lowlands:

A nest with five fresh eggs (Mus. Vert. Zool. no. 1992) was taken by Brooks on June 15. It was in a slender spruce, one of a small thicket in a locality that is largely poplar grown, about forty feet from the ground and near the top of the tree. It rested on the twigs forming the terminal forks of a branch, about three feet from the trunk. The outer walls of the nest were built mostly of the shredded bark of the fire-weed stalks, with a little fire-weed 'cotton,' some coarse grass and small twigs, and several wing and tail feathers of a small bird. In the lining there was some horse hair, mountain sheep hair and a few soft feathers.

Another nest, containing newly hatched young on June 28, was in a small jack pine in open woods on the shore of Lake Atlin.

During the last week in August and the first week in September the southward exodus was at its height. Flocks of warblers, mostly this species, flitted rapidly through the poplar woods, and there was a constant stream of myrtle warblers making long flights overhead. The last one, a single bird, was seen September 19.

As the breeding ranges of Hoover's warbler and Audubon's warbler approach each other in British Columbia and may even overlap it would not be strange if hybrids between these two closely related species should occasionally turn up. Joseph Mailliard (1937) calls attention to a number of such hybrids between both forms of *coronata* and *auduboni*. And more recently, Fred M. Packard writes to me: "I have inspected skins in most of the major museums in America to detect these hybrids, and have been surprised at the number I have found. All but two were taken in the Rockies or farther west, so that presumably the subspecies concerned is *D. c. hooveri*."

### DENDROICA AUDUBONI AUDUBONI (Townsend)

## PACIFIC AUDUBON'S WARBLER

PLATE 34

HABITS

The Pacific Audubon's warbler is a handsome western species closely related to our familiar myrtle warbler, which to a large extent it replaces, and is much like it in behavior and appearance; but it has one more touch of color in its brilliant yellow throat, five spots of yellow instead of four, and it has more white in the wings and tail. Although its breeding range does not extend nearly as far north as that of the myrtle warbler, it extends farther south, and to considerably higher altitudes, breeding largely in the Canadian Zone among the pines, firs, and spruces. Including the range of the Rocky Mountain form (*memorabilis*), which has not yet been admitted to the A. O. U. Check-List, the type race breeds from central British Columbia, central Alberta, and west-central Saskatchewan southward to southern California, northern Arizona, New Mexico, and western Texas. Throughout most of this range it is widely distributed in the lowlands only during the winter, retiring to the mountains for the breeding season.

In the mountains of New Mexico it has been found breeding at altitudes of form 7,500 feet to over 11,000 feet. In Colorado it breeds at similar elevations and perhaps up to nearly 12,000 feet. In southern California, Dr. Joseph Grinnell (1908) found it breeding in the San Bernardino Mountains from 9,000 feet "almost to timber limit, 10,500 feet elevation, at least. * * * This was one of the most abundant birds of the San Bernardino mountains, and was widely distributed from the lower edge of the Transition zone up through the Boreal." Grinnell and Storer (1924) write:

The Audubon Warbler is the most widely distributed and the most abundant of all the species of wood warblers found in the Yosemite region. It occurs in numbers throughout the main forested districts of the mountains during the summer season, and it frequents the deciduous trees and brush of the foothill and valley country in the winter time.

Altitudinally its summer range extends from the beginning of the Transition Zone yellow pines on the west slope, at 3300 to 3500 feet, up through the lodgepole pines and other conifers of the Canadian and Hudsonian zones to the upper limit of unstunted trees at 10,000 feet or a little higher. * * *

During the summer season the Audubon Warbler keeps mainly to coniferous trees, foraging from 10 to 50 feet or more above the ground. In the Transition Zone and part of the Canadian Zone it shares this habitat with the Hermit Warbler, but at the higher altitudes it is the only warbler present in the evergreen forest.

Farther north, in Mono County, Calif., James B. Dixon tells me that he found it nesting between 7,600 and 9,500 feet elevation. Referring to the Toyabe region in Nevada, Dr. Jean M. Linsdale (1938) found the Rocky Mountain form in a somewhat different environment: "In the mountains the area occupied by this warbler agreed fairly well with the area covered with trees. Individuals were seen most often in aspens, limber pines, birches, willows, and mountain mahoganies." Angus M. Woodbury (MS.) says of the breeding range of the Rocky Mountain form in Utah: "It summers in altitudes ranging from about 7,000 to 10,000 feet and nests in almost any of the components of the forests in those altitudes; pine, fir, spruce, aspen, or oak."

In Washington, Audubon's warbler is common and well distributed from near sea level in the vicinity of Seattle and Tacoma up to about 8,000 feet in the mountains. Near Tacoma, D. E. Brown showed us some typical lowland haunts of this warbler in the so-called "prairie region." On this smooth, flat land, a fine growth of firs and cedars was scattered about in the open; the two or three local species of firs were most abundant and were growing to perfection, being well branched down to the ground.

*Spring.*—There is a northward as well as an altitudinal migration in the spring. Samuel F. Rathbun says in his notes from Seattle: "Although the Audubon's is of frequent if not regular occurrence during the winter, a migration of the bird through the region is to be noted each spring and fall." Near Seattle the first birds are seen and their song is heard about March 10 to 15, and numbers are seen passing through up to the latter part of April. "By way of comparison, in the Lake Crescent section the first are seen about April 2, at the earliest, and after three weeks the last appear to have passed by, as the species performs its spring migration in a leisurely manner." A later wave of migrants passes through Seattle between April 10 and 25, probably birds that nest farther north.

Migration is evident in Utah, for Woodbury (MS.) says: "In addition to its summer residence, it is a common migrant through the state, and a sparse winter resident, mainly at low altitudes. It migrates through the streamside and cultivated trees of the valleys, including shade trees and orchards. The migrations cover a period of about 6 weeks each in spring and fall, usually from about mid-April to the end of May and from mid-September to the end of October, but in different years the waves may be a little earlier or later."

In California, there is a gradual exodus of Audubon's warblers from the lowlands to the mountains during April and May. Mrs. Amelia S. Allen tells me that "by the end of April they have disappeared from the San Francisco Bay region." And Swarth (1926b) says that in May, following the spring molt, "there is a gradual withdrawal of the birds to the higher mountains and to more northern latitudes."

Audubon's warbler occurs abundantly on the Huachuca Mountains, Ariz., but as a migrant only, during March, April, and May. Swarth (1904) writes:

Though distributed over all parts of the mountains, they were at all times more abundant in the higher pine region, than elsewhere; and on April 24, 1903, I found them particularly numerous along the divide of the mountains, evidently migrating. They could hardly be said to be in flocks on this occasion, for along the ridge, which runs almost due north and south, there was for several miles a continuous stream of Audubon Warblers travelling rapidly from tree to tree, always moving in a northerly direction; sometimes a dozen or more in one pine, and sometimes only two or three, but never stopping long and all moving in the same direction. Almost all that were seen on this occasion were high plumaged males, hardly half a dozen females being observed for the day.

This was about two weeks before the local breeding race (*D. a. nigrifrons*) might be expected to arrive.

Dr. Merrill (1888), at Fort Klamath, Oreg., found Audubon's warblers "extremely abundant during the migrations. A few males were seen at Modoc Point on the 8th and 9th of April, and at the Fort on the 15th; by the 20th they were quite plentiful. A second 'wave' composed of both males and females, which latter had not previously been seen, arrived about the 4th of May, when they suddenly became more abundant than ever, bringing *D. aestiva morcomi* and *H. lutescens* with them."

*Nesting.*—The only two nests of Audubon's warbler that I have seen were shown to me in Washington, near the State University at Seattle. The University is located on high land at the north end of Lake Washington, where the steep banks, sloping down to the lake, are heavily wooded with a mixed growth of large and small firs of at least two species, as well as cedars, alder trees, and maples. In the more open part of the woods I was shown, on April 29, 1911, a nest of this warbler placed about 30 feet from the ground on two small branches and against the trunk of a tall Douglas fir beside a woodland path. The other nest I saw in the previously described "prairie region" near Tacoma on May 14, 1911; it was placed only 9 feet from the ground but 10 feet out from the trunk of a dense Douglas fir growing in the open, and was well concealed in the thick foliage.

These nests were evidently typical for the region, according to Rathbun. He mentions in his notes two other nests. One, found

May 2, 1909, on the east side of Lake Washington and along a road, was 30 feet from the ground in a small hemlock, near the extremity of one of the limbs and 7 feet out from the trunk. The other, found May 11, 1913, was in a small fir about 30 feet up and about 4 feet from the trunk on one of the lower limbs. "The nest is a very beautiful structure, constructed outwardly of very small twigs from the fir or hemlock, inside of which are placed smaller ones of the same character, with black rootlets, and lined with feathers, of which a quantity are used, and a few horsehairs. It is a compactly built affair." Dawson and Bowles (1909) say that the nests are placed from 40 to 50 feet up, and usually measure 4 inches in width outside by 2¾ in depth; and inside 2 by 1½ inches. They are made externally of such materials as fir twigs, weed tops, flower pedicels, rootlets, and catkins, and are heavily lined with feathers of various birds—including grouse, ptarmigan or domestic fowls—these feathers often curving upward and inward so as partially to conceal the eggs.

Dr. J. C. Merrill (1898) found a very different type of nesting near Fort Sherman, Idaho: "Here a majority of the nests I found were in deciduous trees and bushes, generally but a few feet from the ground. One was in a small rose bush growing at the edge of a cut bank overhanging a road where wagons daily passed close to it. * * * Occasionally one was seen in deep woods by the roadside near where hay had been brushed off a load on a passing wagon; this was utilized for the entire nest except lining, making a conspicuous yellow object in the dark green fir or pine in which it was placed."

P. M. Silloway (1901) found a nest of Audubon's warbler near Flathead Lake, Mont., that was 18 feet from the ground in a fork of a willow. "The fork containing the nest was in a main stem, upright, a number of feet below the leaf-bearing part of the tree, so that the nest was exposed quite fairly to view." H. D. Minot (1880) found one at Seven Lakes, Colo., in an odd situation: "The nest, composed of shreds and feathers, with a few twigs without and hairs within, was built in a dead, bare spruce, about twenty feet from the ground, compressed between the trunk and a piece of bark that was attached beneath and upheld above, where a bough ran through a knot-hole, so compressed that the hollow measures 2¼ x 1¾, and 1½ inches deep." Dr. Chapman (1907) describes a nest from Estes Park, Colo., as "loosely constructed of weed-stems and tops, and strips of bark, lined with fine weeds and horse-hair."

Mr. Woodbury (MS.) describes Utah nests as "compactly woven, cup-shaped structures, usually of fine grasses, plant fibers or shredded bark, lined with feathers or some substitute, and camouflaged with some fine stringy material holding bracts or other small particles in place." He reports nests in such conifers as spruce, balsam, and ponderosa pine, and in aspen and oak.

J. Stuart Rowley writes to me: "In California, I have found several nests of this species in the San Bernardino Mountains and in the Mono County area in the northern part of the State. The nests I have found have all been beautifully made structures, securely fastened to small, low hanging branches of lodgpole pine, and placed about 10 to 12 feet from the ground."

Dr. Grinnell (1908) records three nests, found in the San Bernardinos; one "was twenty feet above the ground in the thick foliage of a short drooping fir bough. It was compactly composed of weathered grasses, frayed-out plant fibres, and tail and wing feathers of juncos and other small birds. Internally it was thickly lined with mountain quail feathers, some of the chestnut-colored ones sticking above the rim conspicuously. This feather feature seems to be characteristic of Audubon warblers' nests, as it was noticeably present in all that we saw." Another nest was 25 feet from the ground in one of the lowest branches of a yellow pine. The third "was snugly tucked away in a small clump of mistletoe on an alder branch twelve feet above the ground."

J. K. Jensen (1923) says of New Mexico nests: "The nests are usually placed on a horizontal limb of a pine or spruce, but also among dead twigs on the trunks of cottonwoods, and even in a cavity of some tree. All nests found were lined with a few feathers of Bluebirds and Long-crested Jay."

Nests in tamarack, cedar, and birch have been reported by other collectors.

*Eggs.*—Audubon's warbler lays from 3 to 5 eggs, almost always 4. They are ovate, tending toward short ovate, and are slightly glossy. They are grayish or creamy white, spotted and blotched with "raw umber," "Brussels brown," "argus brown," and sometimes "auburn," with underlying spots of "pale brownish drab," "light brownish drab," or "light mouse gray." The markings are often confined to the large end, and frequently the drab undertones are in the majority, sometimes running together to form a cap, and this is relieved with a few superimposed spots or blotches of dark "argus brown," or scattered small scrawls so dark as to appear almost black. The eggs generally are sparsely but rather boldly marked. The measurements of 50 eggs average 17.6 by 13.5 millimeters; the eggs showing the four extremes measure 19.4 by 14.0, 19.1 by 14.5, and 15.4 by 12.3 millimeters (Harris).

*Young.*—The period of incubation is probably between 12 and 13 days, as with the Myrtle warbler. Mrs. Wheelock (1904) writes:

In the brood whose incubation was closely watched, I found that twelve days elapsed between the laying of the last egg and the advent of the young. The female did most of the brooding; the male was found on the nest only once, but was usually perched on a neighboring tree warbling his enthusiastic little song, "cheree-cheree-cheree-cheree." After the young were feathered enough to leave the nest, which occurred when they were two weeks old, the male forgot to sing and became a veritable family drudge with the brood ever at his heels clamoring for food. * * * The pair whose young had hatched so early were very friendly, feeding them without much fear while I sat within three or four feet of the nest and on a level with it. They usually came with nothing to be seen in their beaks, but the insect food they had gleaned and carried in their own throats was regurgitated into the throats of the young. When the latter were five days old the mother bird, for the first time, brought an insect large enough to be seen, and crammed it into the open bill of one of the nestlings, and from that time on most of the food brought was eaten by the young while fresh.

The general opinion seems to be that two broods are often, perhaps usually, raised in a season. The young birds are the first to leave their mountain resorts, probably driven out by their parents, and are the first to appear in the lowlands.

*Plumages.*—The plumages and molts of Audubon's warbler are similar in sequence to those of the myrtle warbler; in juvenal and first fall plumages the two species are almost indistinguishable, though there is always more white in the tail feathers of the western bird, in which the white spot usually reaches the fourth feather even in young birds. In any plumage the white areas in the tail of Audubon's warbler occupy two more feathers on each side of the tail than in the myrtle warbler.

The juvenal Audubon's warbler is brown above, streaked with black and white, and white below, streaked with black; the sexes are alike. This plumage is worn but a short time; Dr. Grinnell (1908) says that it "is of very short duration, not more than fifteen days, I should say"; and Swarth (1926) says that is "worn but a few weeks. Tail and wing have scarcely attained full length when the first winter plumage begins to appear, and by the time the birds are drifting back into the lowlands in September the last vestige of the juvenal plumage is gone." This postjuvenal molt involves all the contour plumage and the wing coverts, but not the rest of the wings or the tail.

In the first winter plumage there is but slight difference between the sexes, the female being somewhat duller than the male and often with little or no yellow on the throat. In both sexes the plumage is browner throughout, the yellow areas are paler and less pronounced, the black streaks are less prominent, and the white areas in the tail are more restricted than in fall adults. Swarth continues: "All winter long these drab-colored birds pervade the lowlands, conspicuous only through force of numbers. Then, the latter part of March, comes the prenuptial molt that brings such marked changes to the male. This molt is extensive, far more so than with most of our birds in the spring, since it includes all of the plumage except flight-feathers and tail-feathers. At the close of the spring molt, about the middle of April as a rule, the male emerges, gorgeous in black breast and yellow trimmings, and with a showy white patch on either wing. The female, with similarly extensive molt, has changed but little in appearance." He probably intended this as a description of the adult prenuptial molt, but that of the young bird is practically the same. However, the young bird in first nuptial plumage can always be recognized by the faded and worn primaries and tail feathers; otherwise, young and old are essentially alike. Adults have a complete postnuptial molt in August and a partial prenuptial molt, as outlined, in early spring. Mr. Swarth (1926) says: "In winter plumage, old and young, male and female, are all very similar, but there are minor differences by which the old male, at least, may be told from the others. The dark streaks on the sides of the breast are a little more pronounced, the yellow markings a little brighter, and the body color a little clearer gray, as compared with the browner young birds."

Hybrids, or intergrades, occur occasionally between the different races of *auduboni* and *coronata* where their ranges approach or overlap.

*Food.*—Professor Beal (1907) examined the stomachs of 383 Audubon's warblers taken in California from July to May, inclusive. The food consisted of 85 percent of animal matter (insects and spiders) and a little more than 15 percent of vegetable matter. The largest item was Hymenoptera, 26 percent, consisting mostly of ants, with some wasps, and a few parasitic species. Diptera accounted for 16 percent, including house flies, crane-flies, and gnats, many of which must have been caught on the wing, as this warbler is a good fly-catcher. Bugs, Hemiptera, amounted to nearly 20 percent of the food, including the black olive scale, other scales, plant-lice, stink bugs, leaf-hoppers and tree-hoppers. "Plant lice (Aphididae) were contained in 39 stomachs, and from the number eaten appear to be favorite food. Several stomachs were entirely filled with them, and the stomachs in which they were found contained an average of 71 percent in each." Caterpillars amounted to nearly 14 percent and beetles more than 6 percent of the food; most of the beetles were injurious species. Other insects and spiders made up about 2 percent.

The vegetable food consisted of fruits, mostly wild and of no value, less than 5 percent, and seeds, over 9 percent, mostly weed seeds and seeds of the poison oak. These warblers have been known to puncture grapes and they probably eat some late fruit, but they do very little damage to cultivated fruits and berries. C. S. Sharp (1903) observed a flock of 200 birds, mostly Audubon's warblers, greedily eating the raisins in the tray shed of his packing house; they had to be constantly driven away. Mrs. Amelia S. Allen says in her notes that they collect in great flocks in the live oaks to feed on the oak worms in the spring, and that they eat myrica berries in the fall. John G. Tyler (1913) says: "Audubon warblers share with Say Phoebes the habit of catching flies from a window, sometimes becoming so engrossed in this occupation as to cling for several seconds to the screen where a south-facing window offers a bountiful supply of this kind of food."

*Behavior.*—Audubon's warbler is a lively and active bird that seems to be always in a hurry, constantly moving in pursuit of its prey. Mrs. Bailey (1902) writes:

Its flight and all its movements seem to be regulated by gnats, its days one continuous hunt for dinner. When insects are scarce it will fly hesitatingly through the air looking this way and that, its yellow rump spot always in evidence, but when it comes to an invisible gauzy-winged throng it zigzags through, snapping them up as it goes; then, perhaps, closing its wings it tumbles down to a bush, catches itself, and races pellmell after another insect that has caught its eye. In the parks it is especially fond of the palm tops frequented by the golden-crowned sparrows, and dashes around them in its mad helter-skelter fashion. The most straight-laced, conventional thing it ever does is to make flycatcher sallies from a post of observation when it has caught its insect. If it actually sits still a moment with wings hanging at its sides, its head is turning alertly, its bright eyes keen for action, and while you look it dashes away with a nervous *quip* into midair, in hot pursuit of its prey.

It is not especially timid, being easy to approach when at its nest, and it shows its confidence in human nature by building its nest in trees in parks, over highways, in gardens, and even close to houses. Its behavior in the defense of its young shows a solicitude for their welfare. Jensen (1923) says: "If a nest with young is discovered, both parent birds try every means possible to draw the attention of the intruder away from the nest. Often I have seen them drop with folded wings from the top of a tree and flutter among the leaves as if each had a broken wing." And Grinnell, Dixon, and Linsdale (1930) write:

June 15, 1925, a female Audubon warbler was seen which showed concern whenever the observer went near a certain thicket of very small pines and willows. The bird came to within three meters of the intruder and distracted his attention by going through an elaborate display. The bird spread its tail fan-wise, showing the white spots to greatest effect, and quivered the partly spread wings, toppling over backwards at the same time, as if unable to hold to the perch. For an instant the observer thought the bird's foot was caught in the forking twigs. The inference finally made was that partly fledged young were in the low vegetation somewhere very near.

*Voice.*—Samuel F. Rathbun sends me the following note on the song of Audubon's warbler: "The first note or two is given rather slowly, then its utterance is more rapid and with a somewhat rising inflection, the song closing a little hurriedly. It is quite a strong and sprightly song, but its charm lies mostly in the fact that it is one of the first, if not the very first, of the warbler songs heard in the spring. The call note given by both sexes is the same, a quick and slightly lisping one that is also used in the autumn and at times in flight."

Dr. Walter P. Taylor (MS.) says of a song heard at Fort Valley, Ariz., on June 12, 1925: "The song seems much less full and seems lacking in quality, as compared with that of the Audubon in Washington State. It was so lacking in strength and quality that I took it for a Grace warbler." He wrote it as *wheetlea, wheetlea,* repeated 7 or 8 times, or *wheetoo,* 7 times repeated, or again *wheetleoo wheet,* the final syllable a little different from the others.

Mrs. Bailey (1902) says: "His song is of a strong warbler type, opening toward the end, *chwee, chwee-chwee-ah, chwee,* between the song of the yellow warbler and that of the junco." At Lake Burford, N. Mex., in May and June, according to Dr. Wetmore (1920), "males were found singing from the tops of the tallest pines and were slow and leisurely in their movements in great contrast to their habit at other seasons. Frequently while singing they remained on one perch for some time so that often it was difficult to find them. The song resembled the syllables *tsil tsil tsil tsi tsi tsi tsi.* In a way it was similar to that of the Myrtle Warbler but was louder and more decided in its character."

Dr. Merrill (1888) says: "On two or three occasions I have heard a very sweet and peculiar song by the female, and only after shooting them in the act of singing could I convince myself of their identity."

*Field marks.*—The male in his gay spring plumage is not likely to be confused with any other warbler except the myrtle warbler, from which it differs in having a brilliant yellow throat instead of a white one; in other words, *auduboni* has five patches of yellow against four for *coronata*. In immature and fall plumages the two species are much alike, but *auduboni* has four or five large white patches on each side of the tail, while *coronata* has only two or three, in the different plumages; these white markings are diagnostic in any plumage. The yellow rump is always conspicuous at any season, even when the other yellow markings are more obscured.

*Fall.*—The fall migration is a reversal of the spring migration, from the north southward and from the mountains down to the valleys and lowlands. Rathbun tells me that the southward migrants pass through Washington during October and November, but that a few remain there and even farther north, in winter. In California, Audubon's warblers that have bred in the mountains begin to drift downward to lower levels in August, the young birds coming first, so that by September they are well spread out over the lowlands almost down to sea-level. Soon after the first of October, the first of the migrants cross the border into Mexico on their way to winter quarters. Dr. Taylor tells me that in New Mexico during October these warblers are abundant in the aspens, being "by far the most numerous species of bird."

*Winter.*—Audubon's warbler is a hardy bird. At least some individuals remain in winter almost up to the northern limit of its breeding range; and while it retires entirely from its summer haunts in the mountains, most of its breeding range elsewhere is not wholly deserted. It probably remains as far north as it can make a living; its adaptability in finding a food supply helps in this and makes it one of the most successful of western birds as well as one of the most abundant in all parts of its range. A few remain, perhaps regularly, in coastal British Columbia, for Theed Pearse has given me five December dates and four February dates, spread out over a period of 10 years, on which he has recorded one or more Audubon's warblers on Vancouver Island; on one of these dates, February 10, 1943, the temperature dropped to −6° F.

Rathbun tells me it is "of frequent, if not regular, occurrence during the winter" in Washington. And in Oregon Gabrielson and Jewett (1940) record it as a "permanent resident that has been noted in every county during summer and throughout western Oregon in winter. * * * Its little song is heard on every side during May and June, and its peculiarly distinct call or alarm note is a familiar sound throughout the balance of the year. This is true not only of the wooded slopes and bottoms but equally so of the weedy fence rows of the Willamette Valley, where during the short days of fall and winter these warblers may be found associating with the Golden-crowned Sparrows and Willow Goldfinches or sitting on the telephone wires with the Western Bluebirds." Swarth (1926) writes:

In much of the West, especially in the Southwest, the Audubon's warbler is one of the dominant species during the winter months. In southern California it vies with the Intermediate Sparrow and House Finch in point of numbers. Wherever there are birds at all, this bird is sure to be there. From the seacoast to the mountains, in city parks and gardens, in orchards and in chaparral, the Audubon's warbler is equally at home. On any country walk scores are sure to be seen, starting up from the ground or out of the trees with wavering and erratic flight, showing in departure a flash of white-marked tail-feathers and a gleaming yellow rump spot, and uttering the incessant *chip* that, better than any marking, serves to identify the fleeting bird.

In colder sections there are some fatalities; in the Fresno district, according to Tyler (1913), "a period of two or three unusually cold nights frequently results disastrously for these little warblers, and my observations show that there is a greater mortality among this species than in all other birds combined. After a hard freeze it is not an uncommon occurrence to see certain individuals that appear so benumbed as to be almost unable to fly, and not a few dead birds have been been found under trees along the streets."

From much farther south, in Central America, Dr. Alexander F. Skutch (MS.) writes:

"Audubon's warbler is a moderately abundant winter resident in the higher mountains of Guatemala, yet like the closely related myrtle warbler, appears to be less regular in its time of arrival and departure and less uniformly distributed, than the majority of the more common winter visitants. These attractive warblers were abundant on the Sierra de Tecpán from January until April, 1933; but strangely enough they did not return in August or September with all the other warblers that winter there; and none had appeared by the end of the year, although I kept close watch for them. Yet in the middle of the following September, I found them numerous among the pine and alder trees on the Sierra Cuchumatanes, nearly 11,000 feet above sea-level. The males were then resplendent in their full nuptial dress of yellow, black, white and gray, and sang enchantingly. I believe it not impossible that they breed in this remote, little-known region—for here also I found a breeding representative of the savannah sparrow, hitherto known only as a migrant in the country—and it is to be hoped that some day an ornithologist will study the bird-life of this lofty plateau during the breeding season, from April to August.

"During the winter months, the Audubon warblers are truly social, and are nearly always met in flocks, sometimes containing 25 or more individuals. They are versatile in their modes of finding food. Sometimes, from the tops of the tall cypress trees near the summit of the Sierra de Tecpán, they would launch themselves on long and skillfully executed sallies to snatch up insects on the wing. As they twisted about in the air, they would spread their tails to reveal the prettily contrasting areas of black and white. At other times they foraged on the ground, like the myrtle warblers; and this habit brought them into contact with the bluebirds (*Sialia sialis guatemalae*), which are likewise arboreal birds that frequently descend to hunt on the ground. At altitudes of 8,000 to 9,000 feet I almost always found the Audubon warblers and the bluebirds together in the bare, close-cropped pastures where there were scattered, low, oak trees; and this association was so constant that it could not have been accidental. Both kinds of birds were exceedingly wary as they hunted over the ground, and would fly up into the trees if they espied a man approaching them, even from a long way off. The Audubon warblers, probably because they more frequently enter open, exposed places, where they are conspicuous and far from shelter and must exercise great caution not to be surprised, were by far the shiest and most difficult to approach of all the warblers of the Sierra, whether resident or migratory. This was true whether they happened to be in the trees or on the ground.

"In the evening, foraging over the ground as they went, the Audubon warblers and bluebirds would go together to bathe in one of the rivulets that flowed through the pastures. After splashing vigorously in the shallow water they would fly up together into the raijón bushes, shake the drops from their feathers, sometimes wipe their wet faces against the branches, and put their plumage in order again. The last Audubon warbler that I saw in the spring was a lone female, who foraged in company with a pair of the resident bluebirds in the open pasture. She must have appreciated the companionship of the bluebirds more than ever, after all of her own kind had departed for more northerly regions.

"Guatemalan dates are: Sierra de Tecpán, January 16 to April 23, 1933; Sierra Cuchumatanes, September 13, 1934; Chichicastenango (Griscom), November 16."

## DISTRIBUTION

*Range.*—Western North America from central British Columbia to Guatemala.

*Breeding range.*—Audubon's warbler breeds **north** to central British Columbia (Hazelton, Fort St. James, and Nukko Lake) and central western Alberta (Smoky River). **East** to southwestern Alberta (Smoky River, Jasper Park, Banff National Park, and Crowsnest Lake); casually to southwestern Saskatchewan (Cypress Hills); western Montana (Fortine, Teton County, Bozeman, and Fort Custer); western South Dakota (Harding County and the Black Hills); northwestern Nebraska (Warbonnet Canyon, Sioux County); central Colorado (Estes Park, Gold Hill, Colorado Springs, Wet Mountains, and Fort Garland); central New Mexico (Taos, Ruidoso, and Cloudcroft); western Texas (Guadalupe Mountains); and western Chihuahua (Pinos Altos); in migration much farther east. **South** to central western Chihuahua (Pinos Altos); southeastern to north-central Arizona (Huachuca Mountains, Santa Catalina Mountains, Flagstaff, and Grand Canyon); southwestern Utah (Zion National Park); southern Nevada (Charleston Mountains); central southern California (San Bernardino Mountains and the Santa Rosa Mountains); and northern Baja California (Sierra San Pedro Mártir). **West** to northern Baja California (Sierra San Pedro Mártir); southwestern California (San Jacinto Mountains and Mount Wilson); central eastern California (Yosemite Valley and Big Trees); western California (Diablo, Mount Tamalpais, Fort Ross, and Trinity Mountains); western Oregon (Coos Bay, Eugene, Corvallis, and Netarts); western Washington (Cape Disappointment, Shelton, and the San Juan Islands); and western British Columbia (Cowichan Lake and Port Hardy, Vancouver Island; and Hazelton).

*Winter range.*—The Audubon warbler is found in winter **north** to southwestern British Columbia (Comox and Chilliwack). **East** to southwestern British Columbia (Chilliwack); central Washington (Yakima); occasionally eastern Washington (Cheney); northeastern Oregon, casually (Pendleton and Legrande); central California (Marysville and Fresno); casually to southwestern Utah (St. George and Zion National Park); central Arizona (Fort Mojave, Fort Verde, Salt River National Wildlife Refuge, and Tombstone); southern Texas (El Paso, rarely Knickerbocker, and Brownsville); Tamaulipas (Matamoros and Victoria); western Veracruz (Orizaba); and central Guatemala (San Jerónimo). **South** to Guatemala (San Jerónimo, Tecpán, and San Lucas); casual or accidental south to central Costa Rica (Juan Viñas). **West** to western Guatemala (San Lucas and Totonicapán); Oaxaca (Parada); Guerrero (Chilpancingo and Coyuca); western Jalisco (Tonila); Nayarit (Tepic); southern Sinaloa (Mazatlán); western Baja California (Santa Margarita and Natividad Islands); and the west coast of the United States to southwestern British Columbia (Comox).

The preceding range is for the species as a whole of which two subspecies or geographic races are recognized. The Pacific Audubon's warbler (*D. a. auduboni*) breeds south to southern California, central Arizona, and New Mexico; the black-fronted Audubon's warbler (*D. a. nigrifrons*) breeds from the Huachuca Moutains, Ariz., through the mountains to southwestern Chihuahua.

*Migration.*—Late dates of spring departure from the winter range are: Guatemala—Tecpán, April 23. Sonora—Moctezuma, May 23. Texas—Marathon, May 18. Kansas—Fort Wallace, May 27. Arizona—Prescott, May 19. California—Fresno, May 3.

Early dates of spring arrival are: Kansas—Garden City, April 22. Nebraska—Hastings, April 14. New Mexico—Apache, March 7. Colorado—Colorado Springs, April 12. Wyoming—Laramie, April 21. Montana—Fortine, April 14. Alberta—Banff, April 23. Utah— St. George, March 8. Nevada—Carson City, April 10. Idaho—Sandpoint, April 16. California—Grass Valley, April 10. Oregon—Prospect, March 6. Washington—Shelton, March 4. British Columbia— Summerland, March 30.

Late dates of fall departure are: British Columbia—Okanagan Landing, October 24. Washington—Pullman, November 13. Oregon—Prospect, November 18. Idaho—Bayview, October 26. Utah— St. George, December 7. Alberta—Edmonton, September 11. Montana—Fortine, October 24. Wyoming—Laramie, November 9. Colorado—Fort Morgan, October 30. New Mexico—Silver City, November 10.

Early dates of fall arrival are: California—San Diego, September 2. Texas—Fort Davis, September 9. Sonora—Las Cuevas, September 3. Guatemala—Chichicastenango, November 16.

*Banding.*—An Audubon's warbler that was banded at Santa Cruz, Calif., on February 17, 1931, was found dead November 5, 1931, at Glenwood, Calif. Another, banded at Altadena, Calif., on December 1, 1935, was retrapped at the same station on February 13, 1940, being then nearly 5 years old, at the least.

*Casual records.*—A specimen of Audubon's warbler was collected at Cambridge, Mass., on November 15, 1876. Another was collected at West Chester, Pa., November 8, 1889. In Ohio one was closely watched at Cleveland April 30 and May 3, 1931; and a second one at Richmond on October 5, 1941. On April 28, 1928, one was closely watched at Minneapolis, Minn.

*Egg dates.*—California: 53 records, May 11 to July 30; 28 records, June 13 to 25, indicating the height of the season.

Colorado: 10 records, June 18 to July 6; 5 records, June 19 to 29.

Washington: 11 records, April 19 to June 29; 5 records, May 14 to June 13.

## DENDROICA AUDUBONI NIGRIFRONS (Brewster)

## BLACK-FRONTED AUDUBON'S WARBLER

### HABITS

The black-fronted Audubon's warbler was originally described by William Brewster (1889) as a distinct species, based on a series of five specimens collected by M. A. Frazar in the Sierra Madre Mountains of Chihuahua, Mexico, in June and July, 1888. He gave as its characters: "Male similar to *D. auduboni* but with the forehead and sides of the crown and head nearly uniform black, the interscapulars so closely spotted that the black of their centres exceeds in extent the bluish ashy on their edges and tips, the black of the breast patch wholly unmixed with lighter color. Female with the general coloring, especially on the head, darker than in female *auduboni;* the dark markings of the breast and back coarser and more numerous; the entire pileum, including the yellow crown patch, spotted finely but thickly with slaty black." He admits that it is closely related to *D. auduboni*, "so closely in fact that the two may prove to intergrade," but he found no indications of such intergradation. Later, however, Leverett M. Loomis (1901) called attention to the fact that several birds, collected in the Huachuca and Chiricahua Mountains, in Arizona, showed signs of intergradation with breeding birds from central California. These were taken by W. W. Price, establishing this bird as an addition to our fauna, and resulting in its reduction to sub-specific rank. It is known to breed in the Huachuca Mountains and in the high Sierras of northwestern Mexico, ranging south to Guatemala. Swarth (1904) says of the status of the black-fronted warbler in Arizona:

This, the only form of *auduboni* that breeds in the Huachucas, occurs during the summer months, though in rather limited numbers, in the higher pine regions from 8500 feet upwards. On one occasion, April 5, 1903, I secured a male *nigrifrons* from a flock of *auduboni* feeding in some live-oaks near the mouth of one of the canyons at an altitude of about 4500 feet, but this is the only time that I have seen it below the altitude given above; and it is also exceptional in the early date of its arrival. No more were seen until the second week in May, which seems nearer the usual time of arrival, for in 1902, the first was seen on May 9th. * * * Several specimens were taken intermediate in their characteristics between *auduboni* and *nigrifrons;* some, of the size of the latter, though in color but little darker than *auduboni*, while some show every gradation of color between the two extremes.

The black-fronted warbler averages somewhat larger than the Audubon's.

*Nesting.*—Before this warbler was known to be the breeding form in Arizona, O. W. Howard (1899) reported on two nests found in the Huachuca Mountains in 1898, and said that he had found "several nests" of Audubon's warblers in 1897 and 1898, all in these mountains. These were all, doubtless, nests of the black-fronted warbler. One of these was in a red fir tree about 15 feet up, and the other "was placed in the lower branches of a sugar-pine about fifty feet from the ground, and twelve feet out from the trunk of the tree. * * * The nests are very loosely constructed, being composed almost entirely of loose straws with a few feathers and hair for a lining." One of Howard's nests of this warbler, with four eggs, is in the Thayer collection in Cambridge. It was found in the same mountains, at an elevation of about 9,000 feet, saddled on the limb of a red spruce tree 35 feet above ground and well concealed in the foliage. It is rather a bulky nest made of shredded weed stems, fine strips of inner bark, fine rootlets and various other plant fibers, mixed with feathers of the Arizona jay, three long wing feathers of small birds and two small owl feathers; it is lined with fine fibers, horse and cattle hair, and jay feathers. Externally it measures about 3½ inches in diameter and 2½ in height; the inside diameter is about 2 inches and the cup is about 1¾ inches deep.

James Rooney has sent me the data for a set of four eggs of the black-fronted warbler, taken by Clyde L. Field in the Santa Catalina Mountains in Arizona, June 2, 1938. The nest, placed 15 feet above ground at the end of a pine limb, was made of twigs and was lined with deer hair and a few feathers. A nest with four eggs, in the collection of Charles E. Doe, in Florida, was taken by the same collector in the same mountains on June 8, 1937; it was in a crotch of an aspen, 30 feet up.

*Eggs.*—The measurements of 16 eggs average 18.5 by 13.6 millimeters; the eggs showing the four extremes measure 19.8 by 14.0, 19.5 by 14.4, 17.3 by 13.9, and 17.6 by 12.4 millimeters (Harris).

DENDROICA NIGRESCENS (Townsend)

BLACK-THROATED GRAY WARBLER

PLATE 35

HABITS

The black-throated gray warbler is neatly dressed in gray-black and white, with only a tiny spot of bright yellow in front of the eye. Its breeding range extends from southern British Columbia, Nevada, northern Utah, and northwestern Colorado southward to northern Lower California, southern Arizona, and southern New Mexico. It spends the winter in Mexico.

As a summer resident it is common and sometimes abundant in western Washington, even at lower elevations where, Samuel F. Rathbun tells me, it "prefers a locality somewhat open, with a second growth of young conifers; this may occur in the rather heavy forest, if such condition exists there, or along the edge of the timber; the species is partial to this character of growth."

In southern Oregon, according to C. W. Bowles (1902), it seems to combine the habitat requirements of the eastern black-throated green and the prairie warbler. Like the former, it seeks tall trees, preferably conifers, well scattered and interspersed with bushes, since it nests in both. Like the prairie warbler, it chooses high dry places with dry ground underneath for its nest.

Farther south, the black-throated gray warbler seems to prefer growths of hardwood and underbrush for its summer haunts—oaks, scrub oak, pinyon, juniper, manzanita, and the like. Dr. Walter K. Fisher wrote to Dr. Chapman (1907) that, in California, "it lives in chaparral such as deer brush, wild lilac of various species, scrub oak, and sometimes, particularly in the humid coast districts, among evergreens. It is fond of the neighborhood of clearings where it works constantly and carefully among low growth." Dr. Grinnell (1908) says that in the San Bernardino Mountains, "this warbler appeared to be be confined exclusively to the golden oak belt during the breeding season." Referring to the Great Basin region, Dr. Linsdale (1938) writes: "The black-throated gray warbler was one of the few species adapted to occupy the piñon belt on the Toyabe Mountains. Not only did this bird tolerate conditions on dry slopes, but it was practically limited to them. The pairs were scattered far apart, but because this type of habitat takes up so much of the total area, this warbler must rank high among all the summer resident birds on the basis of numbers."

This warbler is a common breeding bird in the mountains of southern Arizona. In the brushy foothills and canyons of the Huachucas, we found it between 4,000 and 7,000 feet in altitude, in the oak belt about halfway up the canyons, principally among the scrub oaks and manzanita bushes. In New Mexico, according to Mrs. Bailey (1928), it is found in summer at slightly higher levels, 5,500 to 8,000 feet, in the oak and pinyon pine country.

*Nesting.*—In Washington, the black-throated gray warbler seems to nest in fir trees exclusively, at heights ranging from 7 or 8 feet up to 50 feet above the ground. Rathbun has sent me the data for seven nests, all in firs, at heights ranging from 7½ to 35 feet; they were all on horizontal branches and from 4 to 10 feet out from the trunk. He describes in his notes a typical nesting site as follows: "From a distance I saw a fir tree the character of which, from my experience, was favored by this warbler as a nesting place. It was of considerable size, one of a number scattered along the edge of the forest, and had considerable undergrowth beneath. After a very careful examination I located the nest near the extremity of one of the large lower limbs, at a distance from the trunk of 9 feet and at a height above the ground of 23 feet. The nest was placed at the side of the limb and was securely attached at a point where grew several small twig-like branches." He says that this bird is very regular in its nesting date, the average date for fresh eggs is between June 3 and 8, and that the nest is always a neat one. He describes a typical nest as follows: "Plant fibers, dry grasses and a few very small weed-stalks were all neatly woven together to form the walls of the nest. The lining was a few feathers—two being those of the ruffed grouse, with others from sparrows, the quill of each being worked into the walls of the nest; next to this lining were soft and very fine plant fibers, with a few horsehairs."

C. W. Bowles (1902) mentions a nest in southern Oregon that "was six feet up in a manzanita bush in a patch of bushes of the same variety about three acres in extent." But he adds that—

the nests were from three feet and three inches to twenty-five feet from the ground, oaks seeming the favorite in southern Oregon and fir near Tacoma. The usual situation is in a small clump of leaves that is just large enough to almost completely conceal the nest, and yet so very small that a crow or jay would never think of anything being concealed in them. * * * The nests externally are about 3 x 2¾ inches and internaly 1¾ x 1¾ inches in diameter and depth. They are composed externally of grass and weed-stalks, that must be several seasons old, (being bleached and very soft) moss and feathers; and lined with feathers (one had evidently been lined from a dead Stellar jay), horse, cow and rabbit hair or fur, and sometimes the very fine stems of the flowers of some kind of moss. The male has never been seen to assist either at nest-building or incubation.

In the Yosemite region, where Grinnell and Storer (1924) found the black-throated gray warbler in fair numbers among the golden oaks on the north walls of the Valley, they found a nest "placed 5 feet 6 inches above ground in a mountain lilac (*Ceanothus integerrimus*) bush against a main stem."

From southern California, James B. Dixon writes to me: "This bird breeds sparingly from 2,500 feet to the tops of our mountain ranges in San Diego, Riverside and San Bernardino Counties. During my observations since 1898, I have seen but five nests. One was in a live oak tree, two in manzanita bushes and two in golden oak saplings." A nest in Riverside County, at 5,500 feet elevation, was in "a scrub growth area which was well wooded with sapling golden oak and manzanita, buck thorn, and other sparsely growing bushes." The nest was "located 12 feet from the ground in a deep, vertical crotch of a golden oak sapling, and could be seen from only one angle, much like the nest of a gnatcatcher or wood pewee." Another nest was found "in the dense growth of a young manzanita bush. * * * The locations of the two nests were extremely different, one was carefully concealed in a comparatively bare oak sapling, and the other in the dense foliage of a rank-growing young manzanita bush."

In the Huachuca Mountains of Arizona, I found but one nest of the blackthroated gray warbler. It was 5 feet up in the main crotch of a small oak growing on a steep slope on the side of a branch of Ramsey Canyon; the slope was sparsely covered with scrub oaks and other bushes, with a scattering of tall pines; the nest was so well concealed that I could not get a clear photograph of it. Howard (1899) found three nests in these mountains in upright forks of oak saplings, and says: "I found other nests, some placed in large white oaks and some in sycamores and have known the birds to build high up in pines." One of his nests from these mountains, in the Thayer collection, was found only 18 inches up in a young fir tree in a thicket; lying against the main stem, it was supported, surrounded, and well concealed by live twigs. Four other nests in this collection, were all taken in the Huachuca and Chiricahua mountains from oaks at heights ranging from 6 to 16 feet above ground. All much alike, their decidedly gray appearance makes them less visible among the gray branches. They are made of light gray, old, shredded stems of dead weeds and grasses, very fine gray plant fibers and a few dead leaves, bits of string, and thread, all firmly bound with spider's web and

decorated with numerous bits of spider cocoons. They are lined with
fine brown and white hairs and small, soft feathers.

In New Mexico, Jensen (1923) reports two nests in piñon pines;
one was 3 feet and the other 5 feet above ground.

*Eggs.*—From 3 to 5 eggs, usually 4, constitute a full set for the
black-throated gray warbler. These are ovate to short ovate and are
only slightly glossy. The ground color is white or creamy white
and is speckled, spotted, and sometimes blotched with "chestnut,"
"auburn," "bay," or "russet," occasionally with "mummy brown,"
with underlying spots of "light brownish drab," or "light vinaceous
drab." The spots are usually concentrated at the large end, forming
a loose wreath, with the drab markings frequently in the majority.
Some eggs are only lightly speckled, while others are boldly marked.
The measurements of 50 eggs average 16.5 by 12.5 millimeters; the
eggs showing the four extremes measure 18.2 by 12.3, 18.1 by 13.1,
14.6 by 12.9, and 16.2 by 11.6 millimeters (Harris).

*Young.*—The period of incubation does not seem to have been
recorded for this warbler. It is probably performed by the female
entirely, but both parents share in the feeding of the young. Information on this subject is scanty.

*Plumages.*—The young black-throated gray warbler in juvenal
plumage shows the characters of the species more than do the young
of other wood warblers; the black and white areas about the head
and throat are strongly indicated in a duller pattern and there are
two broad white bars tipping the median and greater wing coverts
(see pl. 35); these markings are more subdued in the female than
in the male, thus making a slight sexual difference. The back is
brownish gray and the underparts grayish white, faintly streaked
with black.

I have not been able to trace the postjuvenal molt, but it is perhaps
less extensive than in most other warblers. In first winter plumage
the young male is much like the adult male at that season, but it is
more strongly washed with brown above and with yellowish beneath,
the chin is white, the black throat is mottled with white, and the
streaking above and below is duller and more obscured. The young
female differs from the adult female in about the same way.

Apparently, the nuptial plumage is produced mainly by wear, or
by a limited prenuptial molt. The postnuptial molt is evidently complete in late summer.

The adult winter plumages of both sexes differ but little from the
spring plumages; in the male, the feathers of the upper parts and
cheeks are margined with brownish gray and the throat with white,
the sides are washed with brown and the black streaks are obscured;
in the female, the plumage is tinged with brownish in the same way
and the black streaks are obscured.

*Food.*—No extensive study of the food of the black-throated gray warbler seems to have been made. It is evidently mainly, if not wholly, insectivorous, for several observers have mentioned its zeal in foraging among the foliage of trees and bushes for insects, with a special fondness shown for oak worms and other green caterpillars. Bowles (1902) says that "it seems to prefer oak trees in the spring because of the small green caterpillars that are very numerous on them and which are devoured on all occasions. One female must have eaten nearly half its weight of them (from three-fourths to one and one-half inches long) while its nest was being taken." Mrs. Wheelock (1904) writes in the same vein: "In the spring these oaks are particularly infested with the green caterpillars, and the Warblers never seem to tire of devouring the pests. They lean way over to peer under every leaf, or reach up to the twigs overhead, never missing one. Twenty of these worms is an average meal for a Black-throated Gray Warbler, and the total for a day must reach into the hundreds."

*Behavior.*—The black-throated gray warbler is not one of the most active wood warblers except when it is busy feeding; even then it goes about it in a quiet, businesslike manner, without much concern over the presence of humans. At other times, it is rather shy and retiring, difficult to follow, as it slips away silently in the thick underbrush, where it spends so much of its time. Its nest is difficult to find, for it is not only well concealed, but the bird is careful not to betray it; our usual method of following a bird to its nest was not very successful, as it was soon lost to sight while we were watching it.

Mr. Bowles (1902) writes of its behavior that an incubating female "passed the time eating caterpillars while the nest was being examined. She did not go over five feet from it this time, till I left when she followed for about twenty feet, and kept almost within reach, watching me very closely. * * * Black-throated gray warblers do not object to human association at all; one nest was fifteen feet up on an oak branch, directly over a trail that was used at least six times a day by people going for mail, and generally much oftener."

William L. Finley (1904a) describes quite different behavior at a nest containing young: "The moment the mother returned and found me at the nest she was scared almost out of her senses. She fell from the top of the tree in a fluttering fit. She caught quivering on the limb a foot from my hand. But unable to hold on, she slipped through the branches and clutched my shoe. I never saw such an exaggerated case of the chills. I stooped to see what ailed her. She wavered like an autumn leaf to the ground. I leaped down, but she had limped under a bush and suddenly got well. Of course I knew she was tricking me! But I never saw higher skill in a feathered artist."

*Voice.*—The simple, but pleasing song of the black-throated gray warbler is described in Rathbun's notes as follows: "The song as ordinarily sung consists of three rather quickly given notes, of a somewhat lisping quality, that rise and fall but are alike in construction and a closing fourth note that may slur upward with a decided accent, or may fall. The real construction of this song is lost unless the singer is close by, for then it will be found that each of the first three notes is a double one. It is a clear and pleasing song, of good carrying quality, and somewhat smooth when heard at a distance. During the nesting season the males will be heard in song much of the time during the day. The habit of the bird is to perch on or near the top of a young evergreen tree and sing repeatedly without shifting its perch, then to fly to another tree of similar character and repeat its actions."

As I heard it in Washington, I wrote it *swee, swee, ker-swee, sick,* or *swee, swee, swee, per-swee-ee, sic.* Dr. Walter P. Taylor writes it in his notes *zee zeegle, zeegle, zeegle, zort, tseeee.* Grinnell and Storer (1924) describe it as "a rather lazy, drawling utterance, deep-toned rather than shrill. *Wēē-zy, wēē-zy, wēē-zy, wēē-zy-weet; tsewey, tsewey, tsewey, tsewey-tsew; zuēē, zuēē, zuēē, soop; sĭ-sĭ-wēēzy, wēēzy we-tsú; owēzē-wēzē-wēzē-wēzē-chŭr,* are syllabifications written by us at different times when individual birds were singing close at hand. There are modifications in the song; sometimes the terminal syllable is omitted and again only three of the two-syllabled notes are given. The ordinary call is a rather low, one-syllabled *chit.*"

Mrs. Bailey (1902) says that "its song is a simple warbler lay, *zee-ee-zee-ee, ze, ze, ze,* with the quiet woodsy quality of *virens* and *caerulescens,* so soothing to the ear." Bowles (1902) heard an unusual song that "was on the principle of a yellow-throated vireo or a scarlet tanager; but the quality of a blue-headed vireo in addition, making a very strong and rich song."

*Field marks.*—The gray back, white breast with a few black streaks, two white wing bars, and, particularly, the conspicuous black and white pattern of the head and throat will make this warbler almost unmistakable. The tiny yellow spot in front of the eye is visible only at close quarters. Young birds and adults in the fall show the same characters more or less obscured by brownish edgings. The female has a white throat instead of a black one.

*Enemies.*—Jays of different species and crows evidently take heavy toll of the eggs and young, as they are persistent nest hunters and often have their own broods to feed near by. Bowles (1902) says that "one pair of California jays seemed to have located every nest that was built in a gulch where they were building their own nest." One of the Grinnell and Storer (1924) party "interrupted an attack by a California Striped Racer upon a brood of Black-throated Gray Warblers. The female parent was much excited, flying from twig to twig, calling, and fluttering her wings. Near by, on the ground, was one of the young warblers. There was good evidence that the snake had already swallowed another member of the brood." This warbler seems to have escaped any interference by cowbirds.

*Fall.*—The southward migration begins in September and is mainly accomplished during that month; Washington is generally vacated during September, but migration continues through California during the first half of October; after the middle of October even southern California is deserted, and the black-throated gray warblers have gone to their winter haunts in Mexico.

## DISTRIBUTION

*Range.*—Western North America from central British Columbia to southern Mexico.

*Breeding range.*—The black-throated gray warbler breeds **north** to southwestern British Columia (Hagensborg and Lillooet). **East** to southwestern British Columbia (Lillooet and Chilliwack); western Washington (Bellingham and Leavenworth); central northern Oregon (The Dalles); possibly southwestern Idaho (Riddle); southwestern Wyoming, possibly (Mountain); western and southern Colorado (probably Escalante Hills, Coventry, and the Culebra Range); central New Mexico (Santa Fe); and northeastern Sonora (San Luis Mountains). **South** to northeastern Sonora (San Luis Mountains); southeastern to north-central Arizona (Huachuca Mountains, Santa Rita Mountains, Santa Catalina Mountains, and Bill Williams Mountain); and northeastern Baja California (Sierra San Pedro Mártir). **West** to northern Baja California (Sierra San Pedro Mártir); western California (San Jacinto Mountains, Glendora, Santa Lucia Peak, and Lakeport); western Oregon (Kirby, Coos Bay, Corvallis, and Portland); western Washington (Spirit Lake and Shelton); and southwestern British Columbia (Victoria, Stuart Island, and Hagensborg).

*Winter range.*—The principal winter home of the black-throated gray warbler is in western Mexico. It is found in winter **north** to extreme southern Arizona (Yuma, occasionally in the Baboquivari Mountains, and Tucson). **East** to southeastern Arizona (Tucson); eastern Sonora (Tesia and Alamos); southwestern Durango (Chacala); northern Michoacán (Patambán); Mexico (city of Mexico); and central Oaxaca (Oaxaca). **South** to central Oaxaca. **West** to western Oaxaca (La Parada); Guerrero (Chilpancingo); western Michoacán (Los Reyes); southern Sinaloa (Escuinapa and Mazatlán); southern Baja California (Victoria Mountains and San José del

Rancho) ; and southwestern Arizona (Yuma). It has also been found at this season casually, south to Duenas, Guatemala, and north to Pasadena and Eureka, Calif., and Cameron County, Tex.

*Migration.*—Early dates of spring arrival are: New Mexico—Cooney, April 6. Arizona—Santa Rita Mountains, March 21. California—Grass Valley, March 24. Oregon—Portland, April 14. Washington—Tacoma, April 10. British Columbia—Chilliwack, April 16.

Late dates of fall departure are: British Columbia—Courtenay, September 7. Washington—Yakima, October 27. Oregon—Eugene, October 11. California—Diablo, November 11. Arizona—Phoenix, November 8.

*Casual records.*—A black-throated gray warbler was picked up dead at Lenox, Mass., on December 8, 1923. A specimen was collected at Ithaca, N. Y., on November 15, 1936. On December 8, 1941, an individual was observed on Bull's Island, S. C.; and from December 26, 1942, to January 5, 1943, one was under observation at Miami, Fla.

*Egg dates.*—Arizona: 12 records, May 4 to June 19; 7 records, May 17 to 26.

California: 32 records, May 1 to July 3; 18 records, May 20 to June 10, indicating the height of the season.

Washington: 8 records, May 29 to June 28; 5 records, June 5 to 23 (Harris).

### DENDROICA TOWNSENDI (Townsend)

### TOWNSEND'S WARBLER

#### HABITS

This warbler always reminds me of our familiar black-throated green warbler, which it resembles slightly in color pattern but more particularly in its habits and its drowsy song. Its voice is as much associated with the northwestern forests of tall firs as is that of our eastern bird with the pine woods of New England. Its breeding range is confined to the coniferous forests from Prince William Sound and the upper Yukon in Alaska south to Washington and east to southwestern Alberta and western Montana, but it is better known as a migrant through the Rocky Mountain region in general and as a winter visitant in California.

Samuel F. Rathbun writes to me from Seattle, Wash., that Townsend's warbler is widely distributed throughout that region. "It is found in the lowlands to some extent as a summer resident, but by far the greater number of the birds will be found summering in the more mountainous and unsettled parts of the region. In some parts it is abundant. During the migrations I have noted it following the deciduous growth and nearby conifers along water courses, but when settled in its summer home, it is almost entirely restricted to the high conifers, a habit that seems to be followed even during rainy and stormy days. I am of the opinion that it must nest at a considerable height, for on several occasions I have seen the birds carrying material into trees at a height of over one hundred feet."

Taylor and Shaw (1927) write: "On entering the great forest of the Pacific Northwest, with its solitude, the deep-shaded grandeur of its brown-barked pillars and its stillness, one can almost imagine himself in a different world. Incessantly repeated, apparently from the very crowns of the trees, comes the song of the Townsend warbler, denizen of upper foliage strata. Found in early summer from Alaska south to the State of Washington, the Townsend warbler finds on Mount Rainier approximately the southern limit of its breeding range." Similar haunts seem to have been chosen wherever the species has been found breeding.

*Spring.*—The spring migration, apparently directly northward from Mexico, seems to be quite prolonged. Dr. Alexander F. Skutch tells me that the last of the winter visitors do not leave Guatemala until about the first of May. Professor Cooke (1904) says that "an early migrating Townsend warbler was seen on April 9 in the Huachuca Mountains of Arizona. Migrants from Mexico begin to enter southern California April 14 to 20. * * * First arrivals have been reported from Loveland, Colo., May 11, 1889." And "the average date of the first seen during five years at Columbia Falls, Mont., is May 7." Mrs. Amelia S. Allen writes to me from Berkeley, Calif., that Towsend's warbler is an abundant fall and spring migrant in California, where it is also a common winter visitant. "In the spring they begin to increase about the middle of March, when singing flocks go through the live oak trees, feeding on the small oak worms. They become less conspicuous after the middle of April, but if there are rains in the first half of May to delay migrations, occasional flocks are seen. My latest date is May 17, 1915."

Rathbun, in his Washington notes, writes: "In the spring of 1916, in the Lake Crescent region, a great majority of the individuals came in two distinct waves. The first occurred on April 28 and this lasted for two days, on the second of which the birds were less numerous. After an interval of a day on which we failed to see any of these warblers, there followed a second wave, on May 1, much larger than the one preceding. It consisted of hundreds of these warblers, together with individuals of other species, the main body of which followed the belt of deciduous trees along the shore of the lake. This fact we verified by ascending the adjacent mountain side to a considerable elevation during the movement, where we found but few birds. Descending to the lake level to note the migration, we found the birds close to the ground, the trees being of small size. As most of the Townsend's warblers were males in high plumage, the sight was most attractive. All were in constant song and flitting about with rapid movements. In their company were many chestnut-backed chickadees, a few Sitka kinglets, many Hammond's flycatchers, and now and then an Audubon's warbler and a red-breasted nuthatch. This movement began about half past eight in the morning and lasted until ten o'clock, when the number of birds began to diminish rapidly, and during the remainder of the day was inconsequential."

On April 25, 1917, he saw a similar flight at the same place. "The day was rather warm and somewhat overcast, and the wave continued intermittently throughout the greater part of the day, the song of Townsend's warbler being much in evidence most of the time. In this movement the birds passed by in small detached companies at intervals, but the aggregate number was large."

*Nesting.*—Not too much is known about the nesting habits of Townsend's warbler, but enough is known to indicate that nests reported in willows during the last century were evidently wrongly identified. The species is now known to nest only in firs, though possibly it may sometimes be found to select other conifers as nesting sites. Nests and eggs are still very scarce in collections.

The first authentic nests were found by J. H. Bowles (1908) near Lake Chelan, Wash., on June 20, 1908. The two nests, each containing four newly hatched young—

were both placed about twelve feet up in small firs, one some five feet out on a limb, the other close against the main trunk. Both were saddled upon the limb, and not placed in a fork nor in a crotch.

The construction of both nests was identical, and entirely different from any of the descriptions that I have read. They were firmly built, rather bulky, and decidedly shallow for the nest of a warbler. The material used appeared to be mostly cedar bark, with a few slender fir twigs interwoven. Externally they were patched with a silvery flax-like plant fiber, while the lining seemed to be entirely of the stems of moss flowers. To an eastern collector it resembled an unusually bulky and considerably flattened nest of the Black-throated Green Warbler, lacking any sign of feathers, however, in its construction.

A nest with five eggs is in the Thayer collection in Cambridge, taken by C. deB. Green on Graham Island, British Columbia, June 24, 1912. It is described as placed "on top of the big limb of spruce tree," and is large, compact, and well-built, being made largely of fine plant fibers, mixed with strips of grasses, mosses, lichens, fine strips of inner bark, plant down, and a few spider coccoons—all firmly woven together and neatly and smoothly lined with long, fine, white hairs and one feather. It measures externally 2¼ inches in height and 3 by 3½ in diameter; the cup is 1½ inches deep and about 2 inches in diameter.

A set in my collection now in the U. S. National Museum was taken by F. R. Decker in Chelan County, Wash., on June 23, 1923; the nest was about 15 feet up and 8 feet out on a limb of a fir tree and contained five fresh eggs. Both birds remained close while the nest was being taken. Two nests in the Doe Museum, at Gainesville, Fla., were taken by J. H. Bowles in Washington, 9 and 10 feet up in small, slender firs, June 2 and 4.

*Eggs.*—Either 3, 4, or 5 eggs are the numbers in the few recorded sets. The 5 eggs in the Thayer collection are ovate and have only a slight gloss. The white ground color is speckled and spotted with tones of "bay," "auburn," "chestnut brown," "Mars brown," or "russet," with undertones of "pale brownish drab," or "vinaceous drab." Some of the eggs have markings of two or three shades of the darker browns, such as "bay," or "auburn," while others have tones of a single lighter brown, such as "russet," interspersed with the drab spots. There is not a well defined wreath on any of these eggs, although the spots are denser at the large end. The measurements of 40 eggs average 17.4 by 12.9 millimeters; the eggs showing the four extremes measure **19.0** by 12.7, 17.3 by **13.6**, **15.2** by 12.7, and 17.4 by **12.3** millimeters (Harris).

*Plumages.*—Maj. Allan Brooks (1934) gives the following good description of the juvenal plumage of Townsend's warbler: "Upper surface brownish olive, greener on dorsum and grayer on crown; lores and auriculars dusky brown, a broad supercilium and malar stripe whitish, faintly tinged with yellow; chin and throat dusky olive gray passing into white on the ventral region and crissum, the flanks and breast streaked with dusky; wings with two white bars formed by the tips of the greater and lesser coverts, tertials edged with ash gray, the black central shafts of the white bars seen in the second (first winter) plumage are barely indicated; tail as in second plumage."

Evidently the juvenal plumage is worn for only a very short time, for in the bird thus described, collected on July 7, "a few yellow feathers of the second plumage are appearing." Apparently, the postjuvenal molt is completed in July and August, and involves the contour plumage and the wing coverts only.

The young male in first winter plumage is similar to the old male at that season, but with less black on the head and throat, cheeks more olive, black streaks on back and sides obsolete, and yellow of the throat paler. The young female differs from the adult female in a similar way. There is evidently a partial prenuptial molt in late winter or early spring, but I have not been able to trace it. Apparently the black throat is acquired by the young male at this molt, and perhaps enough of the head and body plumage to make the young bird appear nearly adult, though the worn and faded juvenal wings and tail will distinguish it.

Adults have a complete postnuptial molt in July and August. Ridgway (1902) describes the fall and winter male plumage as "similar to the spring and summer plumage, but all the black areas much broken or obscured; that of the pileum and hindneck by broad olive-green margins to the feathers, the black forming mesial or central streaks, that of the auricular patch overlaid by olive-green tips to the feathers, and that of the throat replaced by nearly uniform lemon yellow, with black appearing as spots or blotches on sides of chest; black streaks on back, etc., more or less concealed." The adult female fall plumage is "similar to the spring and summer plumage, but upper parts slightly browner olive-green, with the streaks obsolete, or nearly so; sides and flanks tinged with brownish."

Although considerable wearing away of the concealing tips of the feathers occurs during the winter, thus brightening the nuptial plumage, there is evidently at least a partial prenuptial molt, especially about the head and throat, at which the clear black throat of the male is assumed and perhaps more of the body plumage renewed.

Stanley G. Jewett (1944) describes four specimens of adult males that are clearly hybrids between this species and the hermit warbler.

*Food.*—Professor Beal (1907) examined the contents of 31 stomachs of Townsend's warblers taken in California from October through January, of which he says: "The animal food consists of insects and a few spiders, and amounts to over 95 percent of the food during the time specified. Of this, bugs make up 42 percent, mostly stink-bugs (Pentatomidae) and a few leaf-hoppers and scales." Several stomachs were entirely filled with stink-bugs.

Hymenoptera, consisting of both wasps and ants, are eaten to the extent of 25 percent of the food. Most of them are winged species. Perhaps the most striking point in the food of this bird is the great number of weevils or snout-beetles represented. They amount to over 20 percent of the food, while all other beetles form less than 1 percent. The greater number of these insects were of the species *Diodyrhynchus byturoides*, a weevil which destroys the staminate blossoms of coniferous trees. Five stomachs contained, respectively, 68, 65, 53, 50, and 35 of these beetles, or 271 in all. * * * Representatives also of another family of snout-beetles very destructive to timber were present in a few stomachs. These were the engravers (Scolytidae), which lay their eggs beneath the bark of trees, where they hatch, and the larvae bore in every direction. Caterpillars and a few miscellaneous insects and some spiders make up the remainder of the animal food.

The less than 5 percent of vegetable food "consists of a few seeds and leaf galls."

Gordon W. Gullion tells me that in Eugene, Oreg., from early January until the first of April 1948, Townsend's warblers were observed at a feeding station almost daily, eating cheese, marshmallows, and peanut butter.

*Behavior.*—A marked characteristic of Townsend's warblers is their
fondness for the tree tops, especially on their breeding grounds and to
some extent at other seasons. In the coniferous forests which they
frequent in summer, they confine their activities almost entirely to
the tops of the tallest fir trees, where they travel rapidly, stopping
only long enough to glean their food and then hastening onward, returning, perhaps, over the same trees in their active restless foraging.

Later in the summer and as migration time draws near, they are
frequently seen at lower levels, among deciduous trees and in second
growth woods, often in association with kniglets, chickadees, other
warblers, and juncos.

*Voice.*—Mrs. Allen (MS.) renders the song as a *"weazy weazy
weazy weazy tweea,* rising in spirals, and the call-note a soft *chip,* not
so metallic as the lutescent's, and less emphatic than the Audubon's."
According to Rathbun (MS.), "its song is heard during May and
June quite persistently under all climatic conditions." Dr. Merrill
(1898) says that the song, as he heard it in Idaho, "usually consists
of five notes, *deé deé deé—dĕ dĕ,* all, especially the first three, uttered
in the peculiar harsh drawl of *D. virens.* Later in the season this
song changes somewhat." This second song was heard in low second
growth. Mr. Rathbun also refers in his notes to a different song,
heard in some young second growth; the bird was "singing softly
as if to itself, this being a much more finished performance than the
ordinary song, although identical in construction, the distinction being an elaboration of the song in full in softer tones." Ralph Hoffmann (1927) found the song of Townsend's warbler difficult to distinguish from that of the black-throated gray warbler. "The Townsend Warbler's song has less of the drawling inflection in the opening notes than the Black-throated Gray's and often ends with a prolonged *ee-zee.* A song noted by the writer in the Olympics in western
Washington was transcribed as a hoarse *swee swee swee zee.*"

*Field marks.*—The adult male Townsend's warbler is distinctively
marked, having the crown, cheeks, and throat black, with bright yellow spaces between these areas, and an olive-green back and bright
yellow breast, both streaked with black; it has two prominent white
wing bars and considerable white on the outer tail feathers. The
female has a similar pattern, but the colors are much duller and she
has no black throat. Young and adults in the fall are much like the
adult female in spring, but are more or less clouded with brownish.
There is no other western warbler that is much like it.

*Fall.*—Theed Pearse tells me that he has seen Townsend's warblers
on migration through Vancouver Island, British Columbia, as early
as August 13 and as late as October 9, but gives no winter records.
Rathburn gives me two winter records for the vicinity of Seattle,

Wash.; D. E. Brown took two males on January 9, 1921, and saw "a number of others"; and a week later he collected a female. These were doubtless, winter casuals, as the summer residents and transients pass through Oregon in October or earlier.

Mrs. Allen writes to me from Berkeley, Calif.: "The Townsend Warbler is an abundant fall and spring migrant and a common winter visitor. In Berkeley the average date of arrival in the fall is September 28 (18 records), the earliest August 27, 1931. They are most abundant during October, after which they are reduced to winter numbers."

Henshaw (1875) writes:

At Mount Graham, Ariz., in September, this warbler was found in considerable numbers, though the few taken were procured with no little difficulty, for they almost invariably were seen in the tops of the tallest trees, where a glimpse might now and then be had of them as they dashed out after flying insects, or flew from tree to tree in their always onward migratory course. The tracts of pine woods they shunned entirely, but affected the firs and spruces, and their flights from point to point were regulated and made longer and shorter by the presence or absence of these trees. Their movements were exceedingly rapid; a moment spent in passing in and out the interlacing branches, a few hurried sweeps at their extremities, and they were off to the next adjoining tree to repeat the process again and again till lost sight of in the dense woods.

*Winter.*—A few straggling Townsend's warblers spend the winter occasionally as far north as Oregon and Washington; the species is fairly common from central California southward; but the main body of the species retires to Mexico and Central America. Mrs. Allen tells me that they are quite abundant in the redwood trees of California in winter; and in midwinter, she has "many records of their coming under the eaves of the house, where they seem to be taking spiders."

Dr. Skutch has contributed the following account: "Townsend's warblers winter in vast numbers in the highlands of Guatemala. From their arrival in September until shortly before the departure of the last in May, I considered these the most abundant of all birds, whether resident or migratory, between 7,000 and 10,000 feet above sea-level on the Sierra de Tecpán in west-central Guatemala. Here they were almost equally numerous in the forest of pine, oak, alder and arbutus and in the nearly pure stands of lofty cypress trees (*Cupressus benthamii*) on the mountain-top. But they are widespread over the Guatemalan altos, from 5,000 to 10,000 feet above sea-level, and even pass the winter at considerably lower altitudes, where pine woods locally replace the broad-leafed forest prevalent in these less elevated regions. Thus on the Finca Mocá, a huge coffee plantation lying on the southern side of the Volcán Atitlán, a local stand of pine reaches to about 3,000 feet above sea-level. Among these pines I found Townsend's warblers wintering down to at least 3,400 feet, in company with such birds as hermit warblers and Coues' flycatchers—all of them highland species which I failed to find at so low an altitude in the neighboring dicotyledonous woods more typical of the region.

"By the time the Townsend's warblers began to arrive from the North, the great majority of the resident birds of the Sierra de Tecpán had finished breeding for the year, and those of sociable habits had begun to flock. The pretty Hartlaub's warblers (*Vermivora super-ciliosa*) formed the nuclei of the mixed companies of small birds which roamed through the rain-drenched woods at the beginning of September. The newly arrived Townsend's warblers at once joined these flocks, falling in with the resident birds as though they had never been absent in far northern lands. Soon they outnumbered all other birds in these motley parties. They were monotonously abundant; and despite their beauty, I was more than once exasperated, when I had striven until my neck ached to obtain an adequate glimpse of some small, elusive bird flitting through the high treetops, to find at last that it was just one more Townsend's warbler. There was always another of the same kind much lower among the branches, which I might have admired with less flexure of the neck! At 5,000 feet and below, the plainly attired Tennessee warbler replaces the elegant Townsend's warbler as the most abundant member of the mixed flocks.

"By the middle of April, the Townsend's warblers on the Sierra de Tecpán began to sing—a dreamy, lazy sort of song, which reminded me much of that of the black-throated green warbler. Through the remainder of the month, I repeatedly heard this simple song, sounding always as though it came from far away. Soon the ranks of the Townsend's warblers began to thin; and after May 2 I saw them no more. Males were present as late as April 28; but the last that I saw, on May 2, was a female. The withdrawal of the countless black-and-yellow warblers, together with that of the other migratory species that flocked with them, left a void among the treetops, which was not filled until their return just 4 months later.

"Early dates of fall arrival in Guatemala are: Guatemala City (Anthony), September 7; Sierra de Tecpán, September 2, 1933; Hue-huetenango, September 11, 1934. Late dates of spring departure from Guatemala are: Guatemala City (Anthony), May 1; Sierra de Tecpán, May 2, 1933."

Dickey and van Rossem (1938) say that "Townsend's warbler is a decidedly uncommon species in El Salvador, which probably marks about the southern limit of the winter range. The winter distribution, locally, is practically confined to the oaks and pines of the interior mountains where conditions most closely parallel those prevailing in the breeding range."

DISTRIBUTION

*Range.*—Western North America.

*Breeding range.*—Townsend's warbler breeds **north** to southern Alaska (Seldovia, Port Nell Juan, and Cordova) ; and southern Yukon (Lapie River and Sheldon Lake). **East** to eastern Yukon (Sheldon Lake and Lake Marsh) ; central to southeastern British Columbia (Atlin, Bear Lake, Tacla Lake, and Revelstoke) ; southwestern Alberta (Banff National Park) ; and western Montana (Fortine, Columbia Falls, Great Falls, and Red Lodge). **South** to central southern Montana (Red Lodge) ; northwestern Wyoming (Mammoth Hot Springs) ; northern Idaho (Falcon and Moscow) ; and southern Washington (Blue Mountains, Preston, and Mount Adams). **West** to western Washington (Mount Adams, Mount Rainier, Seattle, and Bellingham) ; western British Columbia (Comox, Vancouver Island, and the Queen Charlotte Islands) ; and southern Alaska (Craig, Baranof Island, Glacier, Cordova, and Seldovia).

*Winter range.*—The Townsend's warbler is found in winter in two widely separated areas. It is found in varying numbers in the coastal region of California from Mount St. Helena, Sonoma County, south to San Diego, and on the Santa Barbara Islands. A specimen collected at Patagonia, southeastern Arizona on December 3, may have been wintering. It also winters in the mountains of western Mexico and Central America from Guerrero (Tlalixtaquilla) ; and the Federal District (Tlalpan) ; through Oaxaca (La Parada and Totontepec) ; Guatemala (Huehuetenango, Tecpán, Dueñas, and Guatemala) ; El Salvador (Los Esesmiles and Mount Cacaguatique) ; to central northern Nicaragua (Matagalpa).

*Migration.*—Late dates of spring departure are: El Salvador—San José del Sacore, March 16. Guatemala—Tecpán, May 2. Nayarit—Tres Marías Islands, May 11. Sonora—Oposura, May 31. Texas—Boot Spring, Chisos Mountains, May 16. New Mexico—Rinconada, May 6. Arizona—Rock Canyon, Santa Catalina Mountains, May 25. California—Buena Vista, May 10.

Early dates of spring arrival are: Hidalgo—Jacala, March 28. New Mexico—Apache, April 23. Arizona—Tombstone, April 3. Colorado—Loveland, May 11. Wyoming—Cheyenne, May 11. Montana—Columbia Falls, May 4. Idaho—Coeur d'Alene, April 29. Oregon—Sutherlin, April 21. Washington—Bellingham, April 25. British Columbia—Courtenay, March 28; Atlin, May 18. Alaska—Craig, April 27.

Late dates of fall departure are: Alaska—Ketchikan, September 5. British Columbia—Atlin, September 1; Okanagan Landing, September 15. Washington—Tacoma, October 3. Alberta—Jasper Park, September 8. Idaho—Priest River, September 10. Montana—Missoula, August 31. Wyoming—Laramie, October 18. Colorado—Fort Morgan, October 12. Utah—Bryce Canyon, October 7. Arizona— Mineral Creek, Pinal County, November 2. New Mexico—near Corona, October 18. Oklahoma—Kenton, September 27. Texas— Glenn Springs, Brewster County, October 19. Chihuahua—Durazno, November 7.

Early dates of fall arrival are: Oregon—Fremont National Forest, August 20. California—August 26. Utah—Beaver Creek Canyon, August 10. Arizona—San Francisco Mountain, August 21. Wyoming—Laramie, August 11. Colorado—Estes Park, August 14. New Mexico—Apache, August 2. Texas—Pulliam Canyon, Chisos Mountains, August 26. Chihuahua—Saltillo, August 28. Guatemala— Tecpán, September 2. El Salvador—Divisadero, September 27.

*Casual records.*—On May 12, 1868, a Townsend's warbler was collected near Coatesville, Pa. A female sepcimen was collected September 17, 1939, at Gulfport, Miss. On August 18, 1934 one was reported seen at East Hampton, Long Island; another was closely observed by several competent observers in Prospect Park, Brooklyn, N. Y., May 8 to 10, 1947.

*Egg dates.*—British Columbia: 2 records, June 7 and 24.

Oregon: 3 records, June 7 to 21.

Washington: 18 records, May 24 to June 24; 9 records, June 8 to 19, indicating the height of the season (Harris).

DENDROICA VIRENS VIRENS (Gmelin)

### NORTHERN BLACK-THROATED GREEN WARBLER

PLATES 36–38

#### HABITS

The northern black-throated green warbler I have always associated with the white pine woods, the delightful fragrance of fallen pine needles carpeting the forest floor, and the murmuring of the warm summer breeze. The song has been written as "trees, trees, murmuring trees," appropriate words that seem to call vividly to mind the pretty little bird in its sylvan haunts and its delicious and soothing voice.

In southeastern Massachusetts, from late April until after midsummer one can seldom wander far in the thick groves of white pine (*Pinus strobus*), either in the open stands or in mixed woods where these pines predominate, without hearing the delightful drawling notes of this warbler, though the tiny singer in the treetops is not so easily seen. It is not, however, exclusively confined even in the breeding season to such woods, for sometimes we find it in open stands of pitch pines (*Pinus rigida*) or in old neglected pastures and hillsides where there is a scattered growth of red cedars (*Juniperus virginiana*).

Gerald Thayer wrote to Dr. Chapman (1907) that, in the Monadnock region of New Hampshire, the black-throated green warbler is "a very common or abundant summer bird through all the region, high and low; ranging from the pine woods of the lowest valleys to the half open copses of spruce and mountain ash along Monadnock's rocky ridge—2,500 to 3,160 feet. * * * Though decidedly a forest Warbler, it favors second growth, and pasture-bordering copses, rather than the very heavy timber, and is particularly partial to dry white pine woods."

Farther north, in the Canadian Zone, these warblers are at home in the forests of spruce and fir, but even here they seem to prefer pines, if they can find them, for Ora W. Knight (1908) says that in Maine "in the breeding season they resort to the pine woods by preference, and as a result are rather common in the pine barrens of the coastal plain. Inland the species is common, and while preferring the pines still, also occurs in rather open mixed woods where cedars, hemlocks and spruces predominate, and in northern Maine is found in spruce woods, seemingly because no other kinds are available."

Farther west, in northern Michigan, this warbler breeds on the open jack pine plains and in mixed growths containing a fair percentage of other conifers. Frank A. Pitelka (1940b) writes: "During the breeding season the Black-throated Green Warbler is one of the more frequent Compsothlypids in the conifer regions of northern lower Michigan, though it is by no means to be included among the common birds. Locally it occurs in spruces of mature bog communities and in upland developmental forests of mixed pine and deciduous growth."

In western Pennsylvania, "its local breeding range is correlated rather closely with the distribution of the white pine and the hemlock. Where these conifers prevail, the Black-throated Green appears, although in the mountains it is by no means averse to hardwood timber, if high and dense" (Todd, 1940). And, in the Pymatuning Swamp region, "wherever tall black birches and equally tall, slender hemlocks grew side by side, the Black-throated Green Warblers were almost sure to be found, and no less than twenty pairs were located" (Sutton, 1928). Referring to the central Allegheny Mountain region, Prof. Maurice Brooks (1940) says that "this species, in its distribution within our area, presents one of the most puzzling problems with which we have to deal. It occurs everywhere at high elevations, in spruce, hemlock, northern hardwoods, white pine, oak-pine scrub, and oak-hickory."

Still farther south, on Mount Mitchell, in western North Carolina, Thomas D. Burleigh (1941) found it to be "a plentiful breeding bird in the thick fir and spruce woods at the top of the mountain, appearing in April when the ground is frequently still covered with snow and lingering in the fall until early October."

*Spring.*—From its winter home in Mexico and Central America, the black-throated green warbler, starting early in March, migrates northward through eastern Texas and up the Mississippi Valley, mainly in the forested areas. I noted it in the great wave of warblers migrating along the Texas coastal islands early in May. The fact that it is so rare in southern Florida, and still rarer in Cuba, suggests that many individuals must make the perilous flight from Yucatan across the Gulf of Mexico to the Gulf States. From Louisiana it takes a more northeasterly route, mainly along the Alleghenies, to New England and beyond. It is one of the earlier warblers to arrive in Massachusetts, often during the last week in April. The birds come along in waves, the first wave consisting mainly of males and later waves containing the females in larger numbers. The passage of individuals seems to be fairly rapid, but the species may be present for nearly a month at any point along its migration route. While migrating it may be seen, like other warblers, almost anywhere—in the tops of woodland trees, in roadside trees and shrubbery, in gardens and in parks, before it settles down in its favorite breeding haunts. There must be a very heavy migration through Ohio, for Milton B. Trautman (1940) says that in the "larger flight 50 to 125 were daily recorded, and it was evident that there were several thousands present."

*Nesting.*—Although the black-throated green warbler is one of our commonest breeding warblers, I have never found its nest in my home territory, though I have spent many hours hunting for it in its favorite pine woods. While hunting through a somewhat open tract of pitch pines on Martha's Vineyard, Mass., on June 8, 1919, with Frank C. Willard, we found a nest with four fresh eggs 8 feet from the ground in a small pine; it was saddled on an upward-slanting limb and partially supported by a whorl of three small branches. It was a pretty nest, made of grasses, seaweed, and strips of inner bark, and was lined with fine grasses, cowhair, horsehair, and a few white feathers. The male was incubating and was very tame, coming within a few feet of us; he also returned and sat on the empty nest after Mr. Willard had removed the eggs.

On June 4, 1910, Herbert K. Job showed me a nest near New Haven, Conn., in mixed deciduous woods; it was about 11 feet from the ground, built against the trunk of a large chestnut sprout and supported by a small dead branch and two live twigs; the leaves on this twig screened the nest from above, one leaf forming a complete canopy over the nest, the tip of it being tucked into the rim. It was made largely of materials similar to those in the one previously described, there being three large feathers on the rim and many small feathers in the lining.

The only other nest I have ever seen was found on the island of Grand Manan, New Brunswick, on June 11, 1891; it was placed only 3 feet from the ground between two horizontal branches and against the trunk of a small spruce beside a cowpath in coniferous woods. It was a compact, deeply hollowed, structure made of fine twigs, mosses, birch bark, strips of inner bark, and weed stems, and it was lined with white cowhair and a few feathers.

There is a set in my collection, given to me by Fred H. Carpenter, said to have been taken from a nest only 8 inches from the ground in a small red cedar in an old neglected pasture in Rehoboth, Mass. The nest, now before me, seems to be typical of the species.

The nests mentioned in some notes sent to me by Miss Cordelia J. Stanwood, of Ellsworth, Maine, were in spruces or hemlocks at low or moderate heights, but Knight (1908) says that "near Bangor the species builds fifty to seventy feet up in the larger, taller pine trees." Robie W. Tufts tells me that, of some 20 or 30 nests that he has seen in Nova Scotia, "all have been built in conifers, including hemlock, spruce, and pine." In New York and Pennsylvania, hemlocks seem to be the favorite nesting trees, but nests are sometimes placed in beeches or yellow birches; the nests in hemlocks are usually placed on horizontal branches at a considerable height from the ground and generally well hidden in the foliage. A nest examined by Dr. George M. Sutton (1928) at Pymatuning Swamp "was saddled on a horizontal bough only about twenty-five feet from the ground, in a comparatively small hemlock. The nest was very deep and beautifully constructed, its lining including bits of hair, fur, and soft feathers, and its foundational material consisting chiefly of slender and uniform twigs of dead hemlock."

The two nests studied by F. A. Pitelka (1940), in northern lower Michigan, were on horizontal branches of Norway pines (*Pinus resinosa*), 23 and 12 feet from the ground, respectively. The materials used in the nests were largely similar to those mentioned above, with the addition of woollike plant fibers and short pine twigs in the lining, and with "a considerable quantity of hypnaceous mosses and bits of birch bark" used as trimmings.

Dr. Paul Harrington writes to me: "I have found this bird nesting in pure deciduous forests on two occasions." One nest was 40 feet up in the crotch of an ironwood, and the other was 20 feet from the ground in a small elm, both in Ontario. Edward R. Ford has sent me the following note: "On Gull Island, about ten acres in extent, which lies in northwestern Lake Michigan, we found the black-throated green warbler in an unusual nesting niche. About half of the island's area is northern hardwood forest, whose floor cover is largely of American yew (*Taxus canadensis*). At a height of but two or three feet, among the sprays of this ground-hemlock, we discovered two nests of the species named. Each of these, July 12, 1918, held four eggs. There was a third nest, empty but evidently used that season."

Nests have also been found in maples, in white, gray, and black birches, in alders and probably in other deciduous trees and bushes. And the following unusual nesting sites are of interest: William Brewster (1906) mentions a nest that he found "in a barberry bush growing in an open pasture at Arlington Heights, one hundred yards or more from the nearest woods." He also has a nest, taken by C. H. Watrous in Connecticut, that was on the ground "among a large clump of ferns in a very low and damp place under a heavy growth of hemlocks" (Brewster, 1895). John C. Brown (1889), of Portland, Maine, mentions a nest that was built in a grapevine growing luxuriantly about a pagoda at some distance from any woods; it was well hidden from the outside by the foliage, but in plain sight from inside the pagoda. And B. S. Bowdish (1906) records a New Jersey nest that "was built between the stems of a 'skunk cabbage' plant, and fastened to a catbriar and the twigs of a dead bush, and was about fourteen inches from the ground, in a very wet part of the swamp."

Miss Stanwood (1910) watched a pair of black-throated green warblers building a nest in a fir tree, of which she writes:

First they laid knots of spider's silk and little curls of white birch bark in the shape of the nest, on the horizontal fork about midway of a branch six feet long. Next bits of fine grass, a little usnea moss, and cedar bark fibre. Both the male and female worked on the nest, until observed, the female shaping it with the breast each time they added a bit of material. Around the top were carefully laid the finest gray spruce twigs. These were bound together with masses of white spider's silk. The white curls of birch bark, the much weathered twigs, the fluffy shining bands and knots of spider's silk, made a very dainty looking structure. After the first morning, I did not see the male about the nest. As a general thing, I find that, if birds are observed building, the male usually leaves his part of the work to the female. The lady bird continued to shape the nest with her breast, turning around and around, as if swinging on a central pivot, just her beak and tail showing above the rim. If I came too near, she stood up in the nest as if to fly. If I withdrew to a respectful distance, say three yards, she went on with her work of shaping the nest. On the second day the rim of the nest seemed about completed. It was narrower than the rest of the cup and beautifully turned. Nothing to speak of had been done to the bottom. On the fourth day, by touching the inside of the nest with the tips of my fingers, I judged that the lining was about finished. It consisted of rabbit-hair and horse-hair, felted or woven together so as to be very thick and firm. Between the foundation of twigs and bark and the hair lining was a layer of fine hay of which the mouth of the nest was chiefly shaped. I never saw a more substantial looking little nest. It was also one of the most beautiful I have ever found, a perfect harmony in grays.

A very pretty nest in my collection is largely made, externally, of usnea and is profusely decorated with masses of the curly outer bark of the yellow birch. The larger of two nests before me measures about 4 by 3½ inches in outer diameter, the smaller about 3 inches; both are about 2 inches high, nearly 2 inches wide and 1½ deep inside.

*Eggs.*—The black-throated green warbler usually lays 4 eggs to a set, but quite often 5. These are ovate to short ovate and slightly glossy. The ground color is grayish white or creamy white. The markings consist of specks, spots, blotches, or small scrawls of reddish browns, such as "auburn," "chestnut," "bay," "Mars brown," or "russet," with underlying spots of "light brownish drab," "deep brownish drab," or "light purplish drab." Generally the markings are concentrated at the larger end, where they usually form a wreath, but occasionally the spots are well scattered over the entire egg. There is considerable variation. Some eggs have a faint wreath of the pale drab coloring which is relieved with a few bold spots or scrawls of dark "bay" or "Mars brown." Others are richly spotted and blotched equally with browns and drabs, or they may have a solid ring of "russet" blotches which completely covers and conceals the drab undertones. The measurements of 50 eggs average 17.0 by 12.7 millimeters; the eggs showing the four extremes measure 18.8 by 12.8, 17.2, by 13.4, 15.5 by 12.2, and 18.0 by 12.0 millimeters (Harris).

*Young.*—It is generally conceded that the period of incubation is about 12 days and that the young remain in the nest from 8 to 10 days, depending on the amount of disturbance. Probably the female does most, or all, of the incubating and brooding, but both sexes assist in feeding the young and in swallowing or removing the fecal sacs. Miss Stanwood (1910b) refers to the development of the young as follows: "On the third day the young birds grow rapidly, burnt-orange in color, covered with an abundant supply of burnt-umber down. The quills and pin feathers showed blue-gray through the skin, and the eyes were just beginning to open." At another nest, "on the eighth day, the nest was simply stuffed full of little green-gray birds, strikingly like the color of the nest.

   *   *   *   On the eleventh day, quite early in the morning, as I neared the nesting place, I heard the fledglings calling from the tree-tops. Soon I caught a glimpse of the Black-throated Green Warblers marshalling their little band away."

Margaret M. and L. B. Nice (1932) made detailed studies of two nests of this warbler, to which the reader is referred. I quote from their summary:

1. The young in the first nest were raised with no assistance from the male until the last two days, when he brought 11 meals in contrast to his mate's total of more than 245. The young in the second nest were raised entirely by the female. 2. The first female incubated for periods ranging from 34 to 50 minutes, absenting herself for periods ranging from 9 to 26 minutes. The second female once incubated for 99 minutes at a stretch; her absences varied from 13 to 20 minutes. 3. Both females brooded for longer periods than the majority of arboreal Warblers that have been studied, averaging 15.1 and 18.3 minutes respectively. 4. Both females fed at slow rates, the average for the first being once in 19.7 minutes, for the second once in 16.3 minutes. * * * (6). Both females made definite efforts to get their last young out of the nest and to lead them to a distance.

Pitelka (1940b) gives many interesting details on the home life of the black-throated green warbler, illustrated with charts and tables that are not suitable for inclusion here, but his paper is well worth careful study.

Reading and Hayes (1933) made some intimate studies of these warblers at their nest; referring to the food of the young, they say: "Observations at less than two feet revealed the tremendous value of these birds as insect destroyers. Spiders, mayflies, green caterpillars (Anisota), ants, small noctuid moths, ichneumon flies, crane flies, and many smaller diptera made up the whole of their menu. While the few spiders and ichneumon flies were harmless or possibly beneficial, many of the other insects were injurious."

*Plumages.*—Dr. Dwight (1900) calls the natal down sepia-brown and describes the juvenal plumage, in which the sexes are alike, as "above, sepia-brown or drab. Wings and tail dull black, edged with ashy or olive-gray; two wing bands white; the outer three rectrices largely white. Below, dull white, dusky on the throat, spotted on the breast and sides with dull olive-brown. Indistinct grayish white superciliary line. Dusky transocular streak."

A partial postjuvenal molt, beginning in July and involving the contour plumage and the wing coverts but not the rest of the wings or the tail, produces the first winter plumage, in which the sexes are distinguishable. He describes the young male as—

above, greenish olive-yellow, the upper tail coverts ashy or plumbeous gray edged with olive yellow. The feathers of the crown and back especially have concealed black shaft streaks. The wing coverts are black, edged with olive green; two broad white wing bands tipped faintly with yellow. Below, faint primrose-yellow, white on the crissum; the breast and a spot on the flanks canary, the chin, sides of head and neck and superciliary line bright lemon-yellow; a variable area on the throat seldom including the chin, black, veiled by long narrow edgings, the sides and flanks broadly streaked and similarly veiled. Transocular and rictal streaks dusky; lores grayish. * * * In first winter plumage the female is browner than the male, without the black throat and the side streaks obscure; some specimens with much black may, however, easily be mistaken for dull first winter males.

The first nuptial plumage is acquired by a partial prenuptial molt, "which involves chiefly the head, chin and throat and not the rest of the plumage. The black chin is assumed by the male and the forehead becomes yellower by moult, wear removing the edgings everywhere so that the streakings below and the throat become jet-black. Young and old become practically indistinguishable, except that the wings and tail of the young bird will average browner and more worn with the edgings duller." In the female, "the first nuptial plumage differs very little from the first winter, wear bringing out the streaking, while a few feathers are assumed by moult on the chin."

A complete postnuptial molt occurs in July, producing the adult winter plumage, in which the male "differs somewhat from the first winter, the black of the throat extending uninterruptedly to the apex of the chin, further down on the throat, and in broader stripes on the sides; the wings and tail are blacker and the edgings grayer, especially on the tertiaries; the concealed black of the back more extensive. The veiling is conspicuous on the throat." The adult winter female is much like the first winter male, "and may have considerable black on the throat, and even the chin."

The adult nuptial plumage is acquired mainly by wear, with only slight indications of molt, as in the young bird. Dr. Dwight says of the female: "The adult nuptial plumage is, in extreme examples, hardly distinguishable from the male, but usually the black is much restricted and the chin yellow, merely spotted with black."

*Food.*—We have only scattering reports on the food of the black-throated green warbler. S. A. Forbes (1883) examined the stomach of one taken in an orchard infested with canker-worms in Illinois, and found it to contain 70 percent of these destructive caterpillars, 15 percent beetles, 5 percent Hemiptera, and the remaining 10 percent Hymenoptera, gnats, coleopterous larvae and mites. Five stomachs of Nebraska birds, collected by Professor Aughey (1878), contained an average of 23 locusts and 21 other insects. Of twelve specimens examined by F. H. King (1883) in Wisconsin, "one had eaten a moth; three, seven caterpillars; one, two diptera; one, six larvae—probably caterpillars; three, eleven beetles; and one, a heteroptera."

Knight (1908) from Maine writes: "The food consists almost entirely of insects, including beetles, flies, moths, spiders, grubs, larvae and in general the sorts of insects found on the limbs and foliage of the various evergreen trees and especially on the pines. Only rarely do they take their prey in the air, preferring to diligently seek it out among the branches and foliage."

Probably all the items mentioned in the food of the young are also eaten by the adults. Forbush (1929) adds to the list leaf rollers, leaf-eating caterpillars of various kinds, and plant-lice. Evidently these warblers are among the best protectors of our forest trees. W. B. Barrows (1912) says that they are "particularly fond of the berries of the poison-ivy, and to a less extent of those of the junipers." J. K. Terres (1940) saw them tearing open the nests of tent caterpillars, devouring large quantities of the larvae, which were about three-quarters of an inch long.

*Behavior.*—Although the black-throated green warbler is one of our tamest and most confiding wood warblers, as shown by the intimate studies of its home life made by several observers, it is much more often heard than seen, for it is a tiny mite and spends most of its time in the tree-tops, gleaning in the foliage of both coniferous and deciduous trees. As Miss Stanwood (1910b) says: "The bird is quick in its movements, but often spends periods of some length on one tree, frequently coming down low to peep inquisitively at an observer, once in a while flying toward a person as if to alight on his hand or head." Forbush (1929) draws a picture of its confidence: "Like all the wood warblers it is fond of bathing, its bath tub often some pool in a mountain trout brook. One day as I stood beside such a brook, a very lovely male, disregarding my presence, alighted on a stone at my feet, and at once hopped into the clear spring water and performed his ablutions, dipping into the stream and throwing off the sparkling drops in little showers. As he stood there in the sunlight which streamed through an opening in the tree-tops, he left an enduring picture in my memory."

Those who have studied the home life of the black-throated green warbler have noted its intolerance of some avian intruders in the vicinity of its nest, and its tolerance of others. Pitelka (1940b) writes:

On the eighth day after the hatching, a red squirrel (*Sciurus hudsonicus*) was observed to approach the blind, coming to within seven feet of the nest. At this time, the female simply left the vicinity of the nest at once and gave no alarm notes. Later the same day, when a young Black and White Warbler approached the nest to a distance of five feet, the female pounced upon it and struck with considerable force. When the intruder returned a second time the female flew at it and drove it away. The indifference to red squirrels and at the same time the offensive reaction toward small passerine intruders (*Vireo olivaceus* and *Penthestes atricapillus*) has also been noted by the Nices (1932: 160).

Reading and Hayes (1933) write: "While at the nest, we noticed an inquisitive Chestnut-sided Warbler in a maple a short distance away. He hung around for several minutes, peering at us, until suddenly the male, ably seconded by his mate, attacked him and drove him off. A male Blackburnian met the same fate a little while later, while peacefully hunting insects in the big spruce and, about an hour after that a Red-eyed Vireo changed his intended route at the first warning note and promptly withdrew. Curiously enough, a small family of Black-capped Chickadees travelling slowly through the spruce was totally disregarded."

The black-throated green warbler is seldom bothered by the cowbird, although mentioned by several writers as imposed upon.

*Voice.*—Aretas A. Saunders has sent me the following full account of the two songs of the black-throated green warbler: "The quality of the songs is sweet and musical and exceedingly pleasing. With the possible exception of the yellow warbler, this species has the most attractive of the *Dendroica* songs. The quality has something indescribable that is all its own and enables those familiar with it to recognize the song, however variable the form.

"The black-throated green warbler has two distinct forms of song. Both may be sung by the same individual, and both are equally common in the migration and through the nesting season, so that they cannot be considered as territory and nesting songs. I distinguish them as first and second, but my choice is purely arbitrary. Both are delivered in the same quality. The first is a little longer than the second, for it contains more notes; but it is not proportionately longer, for the notes are shorter.

"The first song has notes on three different pitches. The first notes, three to nine but commonly four or five, are all on the same pitch, usually the highest; the next note, usually a major third lower, is the lowest; the next, and last, is between them. Such a song might be written *sree sree sree sree sree tro tray*, all the notes being of equal length. I have 34 records of this song, 23 of which follow this form. A few are arranged with the last note highest, or lowest, or on the same pitch as the first. The first notes are sometimes varied by alternating short and long notes or sometimes are united in a long trill.

"The second song consists of four or five notes only, with a definite time arrangement—3 2 1 1 or 3 2 1 1 1; that is, the first note is three times as long as the last and the second note twice as long. The third and fourth notes are on the same pitch, but the others are on different pitches, so that the song might be written *treee tray to to*, or a 5-note song *treee tray tray to-to tay*. The notes, as in the first song, are on three different pitches, but they vary in every possible way as to which note is highest and which lowest, so that there are six possible arrangements of these different pitches in a 4-note song where the last two notes are always on the same pitch. In my collection of 52 records of this song I have samples of all six, and of these 33 are of four notes, while only 19 have the fifth note added.

"Songs of this species vary from 1⅕ to 2 seconds in length, the first song from 1⅖ to 2 seconds, and the second 1⅕ to 1⅘ seconds. The pitch varies from F''' to E'''', a half tone less than an octave. One peculiar song of the first type, however, was prefixed by a wrenlike chatter that was pitched on B″, but the remaining song was normal in pitch. Single songs average about one and a half tones in range, but the majority of the songs of the first type range two tones, and those of the second type two and a half tones.

"The song is to be heard from the first arrival of the species in migration until shortly after the first of August. In 14 seasons the average date of late song in Allegany State Park is August 2, the earliest is July 25, 1927, and the latest August 11, 1935 and 1937. While there is no regular revival of full song after the molt, there is occasional singing of a primitive character."

C. Russell Mason tells me of a song in which the high, musical note was given six times instead of the usual once. Francis H. Allen has heard some variations in the songs and has sent me these notes: "One bird added at the end of the familiar *zee zee zee zoo zee* a coda of an intricate and wrenlike quality, and sang this beautiful song constantly. Another introduced a trill after the second note of the 'trees, trees' song and ended it with a low note. Another bird sang a variant of the 'trees, trees' song, in which it substituted for the final high note a lower-pitched *su-eet su-eet* without the familiar *z* quality." He and Dr. W. M. Tyler heard one that "sang in addition to one of the characteristic songs of the species an entirely unrecognizable one that went something like *ti-ti-ti-ti-ti-zp*. The first five notes were very thin and slight with a very short pause before the last one, and the final note was a short emphatic buzz. Once this song ran into a characteristic song without a pause between." He refers to the ordinary call-note as a distinctive *chet*, suggesting that of the myrtle warbler, but thinner. "On the occasion in early June, I heard from a male bird a succession of chippering notes which I had formerly attributed to the young alone. He alternated these notes with singing."

Many other somewhat similar renderings have appeared in print, both in syllables and in human words, most of which seem to recall the song to mind. Some of the best of the wordings are *trees, trees, murmuring trees* and *sleep, sleep, pretty one, sleep* (Torrey, 1885); *good Saint Theresa* (Maynard, 1896); and *take it, take it, leisure-ly* (Stanwood, 1910b). Miss Stanwood pays this tribute to the charm of the song: "His voice is suggestive of the drowsy summer days, the languor of the breeze dreamily swaying the pines, spruces, firs, and hemlocks. It recalls the incense of evergreens, the fragrance of the wild strawberry, the delicate perfume of the linnea. No other bird voice is so potent to evoke that particular spell of the northern woods."

The black-throated green warbler is a most persistent singer. The Nices (1932) say that the first warbler "gave 466 songs in a single hour and more than 14,000 in the 94 hours of observation." According to Albert R. Brand (1938), the approximate mean number of vibrations per second in the song is 6,025, in the highest note 6,750 and in the lowest note 5,125. This compares with a mean of 8,900 for the black-polled warbler, which is the shrillest passerine bird song.

*Field marks.*—The conspicuous, bright yellow cheeks, the olive-green back, the prominent black throat, the two white wing bands, and the white outer webs of the lateral tail feathers will distinguish the male in breeding plumage. The female is duller and has less black, or none at all, on the throat. Young birds in the fall are much like the female. See the descriptions under Plumages.

*Fall.*—The fall migration of the black-throated green warbler begins during the latter part of August, continuing through September and often through much of October. It seems to be a reversal of the route followed in the spring. Similar haunts are frequented in the fall in the company of vast congregations of other species. A remarkable flight of various species of warblers was seen by Rev. W. F. Henninger in Scioto County, Ohio, an account of which is quoted by W. L. Dawson (1903) as follows:

On September 28, 1899, I ran into a company of warblers which I would place conservatively at two thousand individuals. It was like a regular army as it moved up a long sloping hillside, and with wonderful rapidity. The wind was blowing almost a gale from the north, and the birds allowed themselves to be urged before it in the direction of their ultimate retreat, like half-stubborn autumn leaves. Lisping, chipping, whirling, driving, they hurried on and I after at full speed, panting, and wishing devoutly for a better chance to identify the fleeing forms. Arrived at the top of the hill the army suddenly halted and when I arrived breathless I had time to note the arrangement by species, not rigid indeed, but sufficiently striking to command attention. In the center were seen Hooded Warblers and a sprinkling of Chestnut-sides. On either side of these in turn were Black-throated Greens and Sycamores, about two hundred of each; while the wings proper were held by Bay-breasts and Black-polls in enormous numbers. * * * As the birds deployed to feed the specific lines were not quite obliterated.

*Winter.*—The following notes are contributed by Dr. Alexander F. Skutch: "The black-throated green warbler is an abundant winter resident in the Central American mountains, where it is well distributed on both the Caribbean and Pacific slopes. In Guatemala, it winters from 1,000 to about 8,500 feet above sea-level, but is not abundant at either of these extremes of altitude. Farther south, in Costa Rica, it prefers slightly higher elevations. Here I have not recorded it between 2,000 and 2,900 feet, although the greater part of my bird-watching in the country has been done in this altitudinal belt. From 2,900 feet, where it is rare as a winter resident, it ranges up to nearly 10,000 feet. At this elevation, I found it abundant on the Volcán Irazú in late November. Less sociable than the Townsend warbler, it does not form flocks, and except during the actual period of migration, is more often seen alone than in the company of others of its kind.

"As a rule the black-throated green warbler arrives late, and has rarely been recorded before mid-October. But on August 9, 1933, I found a lone male in full nuptial plumage with a mixed flock of small resident birds in an open oak wood on the Sierra de Tecpán in the Guatemalan highlands. He sang his dreamy, unsubstantial song as he foraged along with his newly found companions. I saw only one other of his kind—or possibly it was the same individual again—before early October, when the species began to arrive on the Sierra de Tecpán in numbers.

"Another early arrival appeared on September 28, 1938, in the yard of the cottage I occupied at Vara Blanca, at an altitude of 5,500 feet on the northern slope of the Cordillera Central of Costa Rica. During the following days, it came every afternoon to forage in the low cypress hedges that surrounded the dwelling. Possibly it was attracted to these because of associations with its native land, for these trimmed cypresses were the only coniferous trees in the vicinity—indeed, in Costa Rica, the warblers find no native conifers save two species of *Podocarpus*, a genus whose center of distribution is in the Southern Hemisphere rather than in the North. At times the newly arrived warbler descended to the bare ground in the flower garden, where it appeared to find something edible. On October 2 it was for the first time accompanied by a second of its kind. Throughout the winter months a black-throated green warbler continued to visit these cypress hedges.

"This is another migrant warbler that plucks the dainty white protein corpuscles from the velvety cushions at the bases of the long petioles of the Cecropia tree. In excessively humid highland regions, as at Vara Blanca, the wide, hollow internodes of these trees are much of the time flooded with water, and therefore uninhabitable by the Azteca ants which at lower elevations usually colonize them. In the absence of the ants, whose food these tiny morsels are, the birds find an abundance of them on the Cecropia trees. A number of small native birds, including finches, tanagers, warblers, honeycreepers and ovenbirds (Furnariidae), share them with the migratory warblers.

"By mid-March the males are in resplendent nuptial plumage. On April 27, 1933, I heard a male black-throated green warbler singing among the alder trees beside a rivulet on the Sierra de Tecpán. On April 4 and 5, 1938, a male sang repeatedly at the edge of the forest at Vara Blanca; and from this date until the disappearance of the species from the region on April 14 I often heard their song.

"There is a certain amount of evidence that with the increasing aridity of the dry season the black-throated green warblers withdraw early in the year from districts on the Pacific slope where they were present during the wetter closing months of the preceding year. Thus, on the Sierra de Tecpán I met none between December 7 and April 20, when the northward movement was in progress, and the birds seen were doubtless transients rather than winter residents. And in the higher parts of the Basin of El General in southern Costa Rica I have recorded the species only in October, November, and December, after which the nearly rainless season begins. But in the wetter climate of Vara Blanca, they were seen throughout February and March until their northward departure in April.

"The black-throated green warbler withdraws from Costa Rica about the middle of April, and by the end of the first week of May has vanished from Guatemala.

"Early dates of fall arrival in Central America are: Guatemala—passim (Griscom), October 15; Sierra de Tecpán, August 9, 1933; Finca Mocá, October 29, 1934. Honduras—Tela, October 26, 1930. Costa Rica—Vara Blanca, September 28, 1937; San José (Underwood), October 16; Basin of El General, October 22, 1936.

"Late dates of spring departure from Central America are: Costa Rica—Juan Viñas (Carriker), April 17; Vara Blanca, April 14, 1938. Guatemala—passim (Griscom), May 4; Sierra de Tecpán, May 6, 1933.

The following account of its winter haunts in El Salvador by Dickey and van Rossem (1938) is also interesting:

All through the mountainous districts, both in the interior and coastwise, the black-throated green warbler is an extremely common winter visitant; in fact, it constitutes, at levels between 3,500 and 5,000 feet, fully 90 per cent of the nonresident warbler population. The numerous flocks of from a dozen to half a hundred individuals invariably formed the nuclei about which gathered smaller numbers of other insectivorous species resident and nonresident. The black-throated green warbler showed decided preference for the oak and pine association at the altitudes mentioned, although it was by no means confined to such environments.

Many were seen in the coffee cover down to 3,000 feet on Mt. Cacaguatique and 2,300 feet at San Salvador. A few birds reach as high as 8,000 feet, at which level they were found in both pines and cloud forest on Los Esesmiles. * * * The average winter range of *virens* lies approximately 3,000 feet below that of *townsendi*, although strays and vagrants make the extremes of altitude nearly the same in both cases.

## DISTRIBUTION

*Range.*—Eastern North America from southern Canada to Panamá.

*Breeding range.*—The black-throated green warbler breeds **north** to central western and northeastern Alberta (Grande Prairie, Peace River and Chipewyan); central Saskatchewan (Big River and Emma Lake); southern Manitoba (Brandon and Hillside Beach); southern

Ontario (Lac Seul, Rossport, Chapleau, and Lake Abitibi; casual or accidental at Moose Factory); central Quebec (Mistassini Post, Upper St. Maurice River, Godbout, Mingan, and Natashquan); and casually in southeastern Labrador (Battle Harbor). **East** to southeastern Quebec (Natashquan); southwestern Newfoundland (Spruce Brook and Tompkins); Nova Scotia (Sydney, Halifax, and Barrington); the coast of New England; Long Island (Miller's Place); northern New Jersey (Demarest and Dover); central Pennsylvania (Pottsville and Carlisle); central Maryland (Thurmont); central and southeastern Virginia (Charlottesville and Dismal Swamp); North Carolina (Lake Mattamuskeet); and central South Carolina (Charleston). **South** to South Carolina (Charleston); northern Georgia (Pinelog Mountains and Lookout Mountain); northeastern Alabama (Sand Mountain); southeastern Kentucky (Big Black Mountain and Jackson); central Michigan (Bay City and Mason County); northern Wisconsin (New London and Ladysmith); central Minnesota (Lake Minnetonka, Mille Lacs, and Cass Lake); southwestern Manitoba (Aweme); and southern Alberta (Brooks). **West** to western Alberta (Brooks, Glenevis, Sturgeon Lake, and Grande Prairie).

*Winter range.*—The black-throated green warbler is found in winter **north** to southern Texas (Arroya Colorado, Willacy County); and Yucatán (Tunkas and Chichén-Itzá). **East** to Yucatán (Chichén-Itzá); the coast of Quintana Roo; northeastern El Salvador (Mount Cacaguatique); eastern Costa Rica (Volcán Irazú); and central Panamá (Veragua); casual or accidental to northern Colombia (one record; Cincinnati, Santa Marta region). **South** to Panamá (Veragua and Volcán de Chiriquí). **West** to western Panamá (Volcán de Chiriquí); western Costa Rica (El General); western El Salvador (San Salvador); western Guatemala (Volcán de Agua and Dueñas); Oaxaca (Tehuantepec); western Morelos (Curnavaca); Puebla (Metlatoyuca); southern Tamaulipas (Altamira); probably eastern Nuevo León (Linares); and southern Texas (Santa Maria and Arroya Colorado).

The black-throated green warbler has apparently extended its winter range northward in recent years. Except for a single specimen taken at Brownsville in January 1911, it was not known to winter in Texas until 1933–34, when about 30 birds were seen. Since then it has increased and spread over most of Cameron County and to the southern border of Willacy County. One was recorded on Bull's Island, S. C., on January 8 and 9, 1940.

The species is also rare or casual in winter or migration in the West Indies: Cuba (Habana and Isle of Pines); Jamaica; Haiti (Île à Vache); Puerto Rico (Adjuntas); and the islands of St. Croix, Guadeloupe, and Dominica; also Watling Island, Bahamas.

The ranges as outlined apply to the entire species of which two geographic races are recognized. The northern black-throated green warbler (*D. v. virens*) is found in all the breeding range except the coastal region, from southeastern Virginia to South Carolina, which is occupied by Wayne's black-throated green warbler (*D. v. waynei*).

*Migration.*—Late dates of spring departure from the winter home are: Costa Rica—Juan Viñas, April 17. Guatemala—Tecpán, May 6. Tamaulipas—Xicoténcatl, May 11. Cuba—Habana, May 1.

Early dates of spring arrival are: Florida—Key West, March 3. Alabama—Eutaw, April 1. Georgia—Atlanta, March 26. South Carolina—Mount Pleasant, March 22. North Carolina—Raleigh, March 22. Virginia—Lawrenceville, April 3. West Virginia—French Creek, April 10. District of Columbia—Washington, April 18. Pennsylvania—Erie, April 19. New York—Rhinebeck, April 20. Massachusetts—Cambridge, April 19. New Hampshire—Tilton, April 26. Maine—Portland, April 26. New Brunswick—Scotch Lake, May 1. Nova Scotia—Wolfville, May 3. Quebec—Montreal, May 4. Louisiana—Avery Island, March 23. Mississippi—Oxford, March 10. Tennessee, Chattanooga, March 19. Kentucky—Eubanks, March 23. Arkansas—Delight, March 26. Missouri—Forsyth, April 8. Illinois—Murphysboro, April 11. Indiana—Bicknell, April 16. Ohio—Oberlin, April 13. Michigan—Vicksburg, April 13. Ontario—Guelph, April 20. Wisconsin—Milwaukee, April 19. Minnesota—Brainerd, April 25. Texas—Rockport, February 5. Kansas—Independence, April 1. North Dakota—Fargo, May 5. Manitoba—Aweme, April 30. Alberta—Edmonton, May 5.

Late dates of the spring departure of transients are: Florida—Pensacola, May 7. Alabama—Long Island, May 16. Georgia—Athens, May 14. South Carolina—Greenwood, May 17. North Carolina—Chapel Hill, May 24. Virginia—Norfolk, May 26. West Virginia—Fairmont, May 23. District of Columbia—Washington, June 10. Pennsylvania—Beaver, May 27. Louisiana—Lobdell, May 9. Mississippi—Horn Island, May 12. Tennessee—Knoxville, May 31. Arkansas—Delight, May 30. Missouri—St. Louis, May 22. Illinois—Chicago, June 3. Indiana—Notre Dame, June 2. Ohio—Toledo, June 5. Texas—Brownsville, May 15. Oklahoma—Tulsa, May 18. Kansas—Lawrence, May 16. Nebraska—Syracuse, May 27.

Early dates of fall departure are: Alberta—Glenevis, August 30. Manitoba—Brandon, September 24. North Dakota—Fargo, September 19 (bird banded). Nebraska—Stapleton, October 17. Oklahoma—Oklahoma City, November 2. Minnesota—Minneapolis, November 2. Wisconsin—Madison, November 1. Michigan—Detroit, November 1. Ontario—Ottawa, October 25. Ohio—Columbus, October 31. Illinois—Rantoul, October 31. Kentucky—Madison-

ville, October 24. Tennessee—Memphis, October 28. Mississippi—
Gulfport, November 18. Louisiana—New Orleans, November 4.
Newfoundland—Tompkins, October 4. Nova Scotia—Sable Island,
October 7. New Brunswick—Saint John, October 12. Quebec—
Quebec, October 3. Maine—Ellsworth, October 19. Vermont—
Woodstock, October 19. Massachusetts—Harvard, November 2.
New York—Scarsdale, October 26. Pennsylvania—McKeesport, Oc-
tober 25. District of Columbia—Washington, October 21. North
Carolina—Weaverville, October 31. Georgia—Athens, November 1.
Alabama—Fairhope, November 19. Florida—Sombrero Key, No-
vember 10 (two struck lighthouse, one killed).

Early dates of fall arrival are: North Dakota—Wilton, September 4.
Kansas—Lake Quivira, September 6. Oklahoma—Tulsa, August 13.
Texas—Cove, July 26. Ohio—Toledo, August 20. Indiana—Waterloo, August 14. Illinois—Chicago, August 15. Kentucky—Versailles, August 13. Missouri—Montier, August 25. Arkansas—
Winslow, August 13. Tennessee—Memphis, August 7. Mississippi—
Hernando, July 30. Louisiana—Breaux Bridge, August 12. Pennsylvania—Pittsburgh, August 20. District of Columbia—Washington, August 22. West Virginia—Bluefield, August 29.—Virginia—
Charlottesville, September 3. North Carolina—Montezuma, August
27. Georgia—Atlanta, September 6. Florida—Pensacola, September 9. Cuba—Habana, September 30. Mexico—Cuernavaca, Morelos, September 14. Guatemala—Tecpán, August 9. Costa Rica—Vara
Blanca, September 28.

*Banding.*—A few interesting records of banded birds are available.
One banded at Hanover, N. H., on September 16, 1930, was found dead
at Milledgeville, Ga., on February 25, 1935. Since the bird was an
adult when banded it had lived at least five years and eight months.
Another banded at Groton, Mass., on May 24, 1933, was "caught" at
West Memphis, Ark., on October 22, 1933. A third bird, banded at
Overbrook, Philadelphia, Pa., was killed by an Indian near Tetela,
Oaxaca, Mexico, about April 1, 1936.

*Casual records.*—A specimen of the black-throated green warbler
was collected on one of the Farallon Islands on May 29, 1911, and
another seen on June 1. There are three records for Arizona: one
collected in Ramsay Canyon, Huachuca Mountains, on May 9, 1895;
one recorded seen in the same mountains in August 1932; and one
collected May 30, 1933, in Toroweap Valley, Mohave County, on the
brink of Grand Canyon. One was noted on the Teton River below
Collins, Mont., on June 4, 1916. A specimen was collected at Barr
Lake, Colo., May 20, 1909. In Monroe Canyon, Sioux County, Nebr.
one was noted October 8, 1920. At Julianehaab, Greenland, a specimen was taken in 1853; and another at Sukkertoppen in the fall of

1933. There are three records for Bermuda: May 7, 1878; February 1927; and May 1, 1928. A specimen was secured on the island of Heligoland, Germany, on November 19, 1858.

*Egg dates.*—Massachusetts: 26 records, May 21 to July 11; 15 records, May 30 to June 10, indicating the height of the season.

New Brunswick: 13 records, June 13 to 28; 9 records, June 5 to 19.

New York: 19 records, May 30 to July 16; 10 records, June 2 to 11.

Nova Scotia: 13 records, June 7 to 28; 9 records, June 13 to 20 (Harris).

## DENDROICA VIRENS WAYNEI (Bangs)

### WAYNE'S BLACK-THROATED GREEN WARBLER

CONTRIBUTED BY ALEXANDER SPRUNT, JR.

#### HABITS

It was a silent world, this great cypress swamp where I sought the nest of the Wayne's black-throated green warbler in the company of the man whose name it bears and who first made it known to science. A vast flooded expanse of trees and water—colorful, eerie, and mysterious—it was a realm of gray-green gloom. Huge trunks towered on all sides; long aisles of wine-dark mirror-smooth water stretched illimitably away among the buttressed columns. The grayness that predominated, from the furrowed knees and smoother trunks of the great trees to the shrouds of moss festooned from their branches, was relieved here and there by contrasting splotches of bright green overhead where occasional shafts of brilliant sunlight penetrated the canopy of feathery foliage.

Our dugout made no sound as it slid along. Only the slight splash of the paddle entering and leaving the water gave evidence of any means of propulsion. Now and again the silence was broken by the calls echoing down the flooded aisles—the clear whistle of the prothonotary warbler ringing sweetly, the full-voiced carol of the yellow-throated warbler, the strident call of the pileated woodpecker answered by the distant cry of a hunting red-shouldered hawk. Occasionally the deep, resonant "whoo-aw" of a barred owl reverberated solemnly among the cypresses, and once a sombre anhinga flapped ahead of the dugout to plunge cleanly into the still water in full career.

But above these evidences of swamp life, above the swish of breaking bass, the crashing splash of a disturbed alligator, the clamor of a startled heron or ibis, sounded one persistent call from the high branches—a song of seven notes, five on the same tone, one ascending, the last descending. It was this call that drew us on, the song of the bird whose nest we sought that morning, Wayne's warbler, the southern race of the black-throated green warbler.

To find the black-throated green warbler in a cypress swamp might seem strange indeed to one who knows the species in its spruce and balsam highlands, in the rhododendron and laurel thickets of the Blue Ridge, in the evergreens of the Adirondacks and Maine! Yet here it is, one of the characteristic avian dwellers of the warm swamplands of the South Carolina Low Country, arriving in the spring to nest amid the green cypress twigs, the drooping limbs of the magnolias, and the majestic spread of the live oak.

When Arthur T. Wayne of Mount Pleasant, S. C., discovered the first nesting of this race he was sure it was not a typical *Dendroica virens virens*, and on April 25, 1918 he sent a male to Outram Bangs of the Museum of Comparative Zoology in Cambridge, Mass. Later he sent him six other specimens. Upon comparing them with specimens of *D. v. virens*, Bangs (1918) described it as a different race, giving it the name of the discoverer, *waynei*. Extracts from his published material are illuminating. He states, for instance, that "this series proves to represent a form easily distinguishable from true *Dendroica virens* (Gmelin). I take great pleasure in naming it after the keen ornithologist and excellent observer and collector who discovered it, and who noticed its peculiarities even without sufficient material with which to compare it."

The subspecific differences are mainly a duller coloration, less yellowish, and of a paler shade, and the throat patch more restricted. Its principal variation from *virens* is its much smaller and more delicate bill. As Bangs points out, "measurements of a bill so small do not convey the same impression that an actual comparison of specimens does. The bill of the new form when compared to that of *D. v. virens*, appears not more than two-thirds as large." Certainly this is true. So marked is the difference that a specimen of *waynei* placed amid a score or more of *virens* can easily be picked out even at some distance.

The southern limit of the breeding range of *virens* appears to be the high mountains of Carolina and Georgia and northern Alabama, usually at elevations of more than 4,000 feet; *waynei* is confined to a coastal strip (in some cases less than 5 miles from the ocean) so that the intervening area between it and *virens* averages about 300 miles. In all that distance, no northern black-throated green warbler appears except in scattered and isolated instances. The migratory route of *waynei* is as yet imperfectly known, but since *virens* is so scarce along the lower Atlantic coast as to be virtually absent, and since it has never yet been secured or reported along the Carolina and Georgia or northern Florida coasts, it would seem that any specimen seen in those localities would be *waynei*.

*Spring.*—Wayne (1910) said of this bird in South Carolina: "This species arrives with great regularity [Charleston County] as the following dates will show, viz., March 26, 1890; March 27, 1900; March 27, 1912; March 23, 1916. It is not common until the middle of April and its passage through the coast region requires so long a time that one not acquainted with the migrations of birds might readily believe that it bred here . . . that this species should remain on the coast until June, and not breed is very surprising."

At that time he was, of course, unaware that the species contained two races, but, as Outram Bangs has pointed out (1918), these March arrival dates in coastal South Carolina occur when "true *D. virens* is still in winter quarters in Mexico and Central America." Thus, it will be seen that the migration times must vary considerably, and the arrival of the coastal race is in advance of the true species, indicating a different and less distant winter home, another phase to consider when comparing the two.

There is almost a complete dearth of additional information on arrival dates in other southern states. My records of South Carolina arrival dates in recent years do not vary much from Wayne's, and he has no earlier ones. I have but once encountered *waynei* in spring elsewhere than in South Carolina, this being a specimen observed in full song in Rhetta Lagoon, Cumberland Island, Ga., on April 15, 1932. However, that it was, in fact, a migrant is beyond all question for it is not present in its United States range in late fall and winter.

In his description of the race in 1918, Bangs stated that "it would seem not unlikely that the South Carolina form is resident and nonmigratory, and I hope Mr. Wayne will be able to prove whether or not this is so." This belief of Bangs' was carried into the A. O. U. Check-List (1931) which gives the range of this form as "resident in the coastal district of South Carolina." This is not the case; *waynei* does not remain in winter, and is therefore not resident but migratory, as I have previously pointed out (1932).

The migration of this race is as yet imperfectly known. While any coastal migrant black-throated green warbler would probably be referable to it, as *virens* appears to keep to the interior when travelling north, as a matter of fact there are almost no records of migratory occurrences. S. A. Grimes (MS.) tells me that he has never observed any black-throated green warbler in the area about Jacksonville, Fla., where he lives and where he is much afield, having had years of experience. Earle R. Greene (MS.) similarly states that his experience of over two years in the Okefenokee Swamp in southern Georgia failed to produce "a single individual." Strictly in line with his observations are those of Francis Harper (MS.) whose experience in the Okefenokee is even more extensive than

Greene's. He writes in response to my request, "I have never found the slightest trace of the bird there." This is strange, as the Okefenokee would seem to be typical habitat for the Wayne's Warbler, but it evidently does not occur there.

*Courtship.*—Nothing is known of the courtship behavior of this bird, owing to the difficulty of observation, the very restricted range of the bird, and the dearth of local observers.

*Nesting.*—Wayne was under the impression that he was the discoverer of the first known nest of this race, but search of the literature reveals that he was in error, though the first nests found were not recognized as those of *waynei*. Wayne secured the first eggs, and these still appear to be the only ones in existence, as all other breeding records deal with young birds. Authentic breeding information is exceedingly scanty, and since this is the case, all of the instances are mentioned herewith.

The first recorded breeding was in coastal North Carolina, and is mentioned by Pearson and the Brimleys (1919). They included it under the black-throated green warbler, as the species at that time had not been divided into two races. One nest was found at La Grange, Lenoir County, in June 1905 (Smithwick), and the other at Lake Ellis, Craven County, June 1910. Adults were seen feeding very young birds.

Continually impressed with the birds' presence in coastal South Carolina so late in spring, Wayne sought evidences of nesting and, on April 11, 1917, saw a female carrying nesting material in a large cypress swamp in Charleston County, but could not locate the nest. On the twenty-eighth of the same month he detected both a male and female in the same procedure but again failed to find the nest. His (1918) comment on this follows: "The brief account of this bird written in 'Birds of South Carolina' is, in the main, correct. Although I had never found it breeding when the book went to the press I was absolutely certain that it really bred on the coast." A year later, on April 28, 1918, he saw another female engaged in nest building, and again was unable to find the nest. Those who knew Wayne's untiring energy in such work can readily understand the extreme difficulty experienced in locating this elusive bird's home. It was on this last date that he secured the type specimen from which Bangs described the race. The following year finally brought success. Wayne (1919) states:

"On March 20, 1919, I visited the place where the type specimen was taken. * * * A few males were heard singing from the topmost branches of tall, gigantic, deciduous trees, and were also seen to fly into very tall pines." He again visited this spot on April eighteenth with Henry Moessner and the latter located a nest. It "was built in a live oak tree and on the end of a horizontal branch among twigs * * * absolutely concealed * * * about 38 feet above the ground." Wayne climbed a nearby tree and with Moessner's help from below, attempted to pull the oak limb toward him in order to reach the nest, when "sad to relate, without a moment's warning, the limb snapped off and the four fresh eggs that the nest contained were dashed in fragments on the ground."

The nest itself was preserved, and Wayne describes it as "small and compact, measuring 1¾ inches in height and 1½ inches in depth. It is constructed of strips of fine bark and weed stems, over which is wound externally the black substance that is invariably present in the lining of the nests of Bachman's Warbler (*Vermivora bachmanii*). The interior * * * is chiefly composed of a beautiful ochraceous buff substance, doubtless from the unfolding leaves of some fern, and a few feathers."

On the twenty-eighth, ten days after this nest was found, Wayne returned to the swamp with the Misses Louise Ford and Marion Pellew and found "a very young bird just from the nest and unable to fly more than a few feet, being fed by the male parent, which shows that the birds breed irregularly."

The party proceeded to another part of the swamp where a female was seen to enter a large magnolia. "Miss Ford * * * saw the female go to her nest * * * built near the extremity of a long drooping magnolia limb, but on the horizontal portion of it and about 25 feet above the ground." This nest held four heavily incubated eggs, these being the first ones actually taken. This nest had a quantity of caterpillar silk binding the fibres of Spanish and hypnum moss outside, and was "lavishly lined with the beautiful ochraceous buff substance from young fern leaves, as in the first nest."

Edward S. Dingle (MS.) writes that "on the morning of April 25, 1923, a Wayne's warbler was observed building in a cypress tree; the bird collected material from the ground and also from the trunk of a large cypress nearby. The male was not seen." On the third of May following, I accompanied Wayne and Dingle to the site; there Dingle located the nest, climbed the tree, and secured it, with four eggs. This nest was 62 feet from the ground and 5 feet out from the trunk. This is the third, and last nest from South Carolina with eggs, on which data are extant. All, with the exception of the first, were in Wayne's collection at his death, and are now in the Charleston (S. C.) Museum. The sites in each case, were found by Wayne, but the nests were actually located by Moessner, Dingle, and Miss Ford.

Commenting on these discoveries, Wayne (1919) states: "I have known this bird ever since May 4, 1885 when I took a male in Caw-caw Swamp, Colleton County, S. C., while on a collecting trip with my friend, the late William Brewster. I gave the bird to him in the flesh, and in his collection it still remains. The nest and eggs have remained unknown until brought to light by this season's research."

Russell Richardson (1926) reported black-throated green warblers in the Dismal Swamp, on the North Carolina side, in June. No evidence of nesting was found by him, and he did not, apparently, realize that the birds he saw were *waynei*. In 1932 Drs. W. R. McIlwaine and J. J. Murray visited Dismal Swamp on May 23–26, and "found Wayne's warblers rather common." From Murray (1932) we find that they "heard two singing males on May 23rd as we came down the Washington Ditch to the Lake; two males singing on the 24th near the entrance to the Feeder Ditch * * * and six males on the 26th." They also found two family parties of adults feeding small birds on the 24th. One of these parties was near the mouth of the Feeder Ditch; the other a half mile up the Jericho Ditch from the Lake (Drummond). * * * The young birds were out of the nest and could fly well. They looked like big bumble-bees buzzing across from one tree to another; staying rather high up. The adults ranged low in gathering food, both male and female feeding the young birds."

*Eggs.*—The eggs of *waynei* are similar to those of *virens*. Wayne has described them (1919) as "of a white or whitish color speckled and spotted in the form of a wreath around the larger end with brownish red and lilac." The sets previously described are the only ones of which the writer is aware, and may be the only ones in collections. Whether any have ever been secured outside of South Carolina is doubtful. Measurements of Wayne's two sets average 16.79 by 12.25 and 15.12 by 12.03 mm., a trifle under the average for eggs of *virens*. The breeding records for the Dismal Swamp (Virginia) and two localities in North Carolina, concern young birds only.

*Plumages.*—Data available are not sufficient for a detailed description of the plumages but they are probably the same as those of *virens*.

*Food.*—No positive information on the food of *waynei* exists, as far as I can ascertain, except that in July 1939, G. H. Jensen examined the stomach contents of a single specimen secured by Howell and Burleigh at Murrells Inlet, S. C., June 6, 1932. It was full and contained 100 percent animal matter, consisting of 3 Lepidoptera larvae, 98 percent; 1 *Formica* sp., 2 percent. That the race is insectivorous goes without saying, but more than that remains to be worked out. Howell (1932) cites Barrows as saying that *virens* consumes plant lice, span-worms, and leaf-rollers together with berries of poison ivy. Probably *waynei* indulges similar tastes.

*Behavior.*—Wayne's warbler is essentially a high-ranging bird. It spends much of its time amid the topmost branches of cypress, magnolia, gum, and other swamp trees, rarely descending to even mid-sections of this characteristic growth while feeding. Highly restless and exceedingly active in movements, it is constantly on the go and, as a consequence, is rather difficult to see and study satisfactorily, the oft-repeated song being the best indication of its whereabouts. As might be supposed, the female is even more elusive, and flits about like some swamp wraith, silent and mysterious. The failure of as keen an observer as Wayne to locate the nests of building females gives an idea of its secretiveness.

In these respects it differs materially from *virens*, at least in my experience with that race, which is frequency found at rather low elevations. Doubtless the type of growth is responsible, for *virens* is a spruce-balsam-hemlock dweller, and these evergreens are dense trees with branches often beginning only a few feet from the ground, so that it can be seen and watched rather easily.

While several authors have referred to *virens* as a tame bird, the same cannot be said for *waynei*. In years of experience with the latter, I have always found it shy and retiring. Singing freely enough if unaware of observation, it often ceases when it detects an intruder, and since the song is one of the surest means of locating it, great care has to be taken in moving about, particularly near the nest.

The nest is impossible to find without watching the female, for it is more often than not completely invisible from the ground. *D. v. waynei* is found in the same habitat with yellow-throated and parula warblers, but, unlike them, never utilizes the hanging clumps of Spanish moss (*Tillandsia*) in which they invariably nest. I have climbed a tall cypress and collected a nest and eggs of *D. d. dominica* while *waynei* was singing in the near vicinity. The preference of *waynei* for heavy, old-growth swamp forests is so marked that if this timber is cut out, the bird disappears from the area completely, even though other growth is left standing. In the South Carolina Low Country, this characteristic is shared by both Bachman's and Swainson's warblers, both of which nest in heavy-swamps.

*Voice.*—Though it was the cuckoo which Bryant characterized as "a wandering voice," he might well have written the words with respect to this tiny warbler for the bird is heard far more readily than it is seen. As a songster it is all but indefatigable. Perhaps this is because the depths of the cypress swamps and the old "backwaters" are cooler than the surrounding highlands, but no matter how warm the day, or close the atmosphere, the constantly reiterated, seven-note song resounds through the air most of the day. The ornithologists I have guided to the haunts of *waynei* all agree that the song is very close to that of *virens*. Perhaps it is a shade more deliberate and studied, as might be expected of a southerner! However, to all intents and purposes, it is the same song.  I am inclined to describe it as slower and more pronounced, but after all the difference is minor.

Arthur H. Howell (1932) describes the song of *virens* as "a drowsy, drawled ditty of four or five notes, *wee-wee-wee-su-see*, the next to last note on a lower pitch and the final one distinctly higher." This portrays quite well the song of *waynei*, except for the number of notes, which are much oftener seven than less, the first five being exactly alike, the sixth descending, and the seventh ascending.

Frank M. Chapman (1907), quoting Gerald Thayer, says of *virens* that "most of the individuals in a region sing nearly alike . . . but about one in forty does queer tricks with its voice.  Among the commonest of these tricks is the introduction into all parts of the song of a pronounced quaver or tremulo. . . . The song is sometimes disguised almost past recognition." He states further that the "deliberate song of five (sometimes six or eight) notes, is the one usually described in books."

I have never noted any "quaver or tremulo" in the song.  It may occur, but in the scores of times I have heard the song it has not taken place.  Nor can I recall any song of eight notes.  Occasionally, *waynei* will utter only five notes, but this is the marked exception and not the rule.  Certainly, individuals in a given region sing exactly alike, and indeed, all the specimens I ever heard sounded alike, except for the occasional slight variation in number of notes.

*Fall.*—The length of stay of *waynei* in its summer range has not yet been determined with certainty.  Few departure dates have been recorded, but in all probability the bird is a rather early migrant.  Occurrence of the song decreases markedly after the nesting season, making the birds' movements much more difficult to trace.  It will be recalled that young were noted flying on May twenty-fourth, in the Dismal Swamp of Virginia.  South Carolina birds were seen to fly "a few feet" on April twenty-eighth, almost a month earlier.  The North Carolina records show that young were noted "in June", probably early in the month.  That multiple broods are raised is also something of an open question, though it seems that in South Carolina two are raised  Henry H. Kopman (1904) states that on July 30, 1897, he took one at Beauvoir, Miss., on the Gulf coast, and later comments (1905) that "Professor Cooke [W. W.] is inclined to think" that the Beauvoir bird was a stray.  Probably it was a stray, and in view of what we know today, the chances are that the bird was a specimen of *waynei*.  Many of the birds of course linger much later than that; on September 29, 1935, Earle R. Greene [MS.] noted one at Lake Mattamuskeet, N. C.  This is doubtless a rather late date and may be taken as about the limit of its stay along the Atlantic coast.

Enough remains to be learned about this most interesting race to keep students busy. The highly attractive type of habitat, the marked isolation of nesting pairs even in a restricted range, the active character and handsome appearance of the bird itself, all these combine to render Wayne's warbler distinctive and appealing.

## DENDROICA CHRYSOPARIA Sclater and Salvin

### GOLDEN-CHEEKED WARBLER

#### HABITS

This elegant warbler is confined in the breeding season to a very narrow range in south-central Texas, the timbered parts of the "Edwards Plateau" region. It has been reported as breeding in Bandera, Bexar, Comal, Concho, Kendall, Kerr, and Tom Green Counties, and rarely north to Bosque and McLennan Counties. It winters in the highlands of southern Mexico and Guatemala.

The golden-cheeked warbler was entirely unknown to early American ornithologists. William Brewster (1879) gives the following brief account of its early history: "The original specimens were procured by Mr. Salvin in Vera Paz, Guatemala. Since that time, with the exception of a male obtained by Mr. Dresser, near San Antonio, Texas, about 1864, no additional ones have apparently been taken. The specimen mentioned by Mr. Purdie was taken by George H. Ragsdale in Bosque County, Texas, April, 1878." The bird is now well known in the limited region outlined above, and many specimens of the birds, their nests, and their eggs have found their way into collections.

The first comprehensive account of its habits was given to Dr. Chapman (1907) by H. P. Attwater, of San Antonio, Tex. He says of its summer haunts in the counties named above:

The Goldencheek is not a bird of the forest, being seldom met with in the tall timbered areas in the wilder valleys along the rivers, or in the tall trees which fringe the streams in the cañons; but its favorite haunts are among the smaller growth of trees, on the rough wooded hillsides, and which covers the slopes and "points" leading up from the cañons, and the boulder strewn ridges or "divides" which separate the heads of the creeks. The trees which compose this growth consist chiefly of mountain cedar (juniper), Spanish or mountain oak, black oak, and live oak on the higher ground, and live oak and Spanish oak clumps or thickets on the lower flats among the foothills, interspersed in some localities with dwarf walnut, pecan and hackberry. All these trees grow on an average from 10 to 20 feet high, the cedar often forming almost impenetrable "brakes". Whatever space remains among the oaks and cedars is generally covered with shin oak brush, which is a characteristic feature of the region. The cedar or juniper appears to possess some peculiar attraction for this bird for they are seldom found at any great distance from cedar localities, and they seem to divide the greater part of their time between the cedars and Spanish oaks, searching for insects, with occasional visits to other oaks, walnuts, etc., but seldom descending as low as the shin oak brush, which averages four to five feet. It is quite probable that future observations will show, that some favorite insect food which comprises a portion of their "bill of fare," is found among the cedar foliage.

*Spring.*—The golden-cheeked warblers arrive in central Texas about the middle of March, sometimes a little earlier or later. The adult males precede the young males and females by about 5 days. Mr. Attwater (Chapman, 1907) says: "The song of the male is the first unmistakable notification of its arrival and within a few days it is quite common and the females are also observed. In the localities described the Golden-cheeked Warbler is by no means a rare bird, and it is by far the most abundant of the few Warblers, which breed in the same region."

*Nesting.*—W. H. Werner was apparently the first to find the nest of the golden-cheeked warbler, in Comal County, Tex., in 1878, about which he wrote to Mr. Brewster (1879): "The four nests that I have found were similar in construction, and were built in forks of perpendicular limbs of the *Juniperus virginiana*, from ten to eighteen feet from the ground. The outside is composed of the inner bark of the above-mentioned tree, interspersed with spider-webs, well fastened to the limb, and in color resembling the bark of the tree on which it is built, so that from a little distance it is difficult to detect the nest." Two of these nests were examined by Mr. Brewster both so much alike that the following description of one will suffice:

It is placed in a nearly upright fork of a red cedar, between two stout branches to which it is firmly attached. Although a large, deep structure, it by no means belongs to either the bulky, or loosely woven class of bird domiciles, but is, on the contrary, very closely and compactly felted. In general character and appearance it closely resembles the average nest of the Black-throated Green Warbler (*Dendroica virens*). It is, however, of nearly double the size, in fact, larger than any Wood Warbler's nest (excepting perhaps that of *D. coronata*) with which I am acquainted. It measures as follows: external diameter, 3.50; external depth, 3.45; internal diameter, 1.60; internal depth, 2.00. The exterior is mainly composed of strips of cedar bark, with a slight admixture of fine grass-stems, rootlets, and hemp-like fibres, the whole being kept in place by an occasional wrapping of spider-webs. The interior is beautifully lined with the hair of different quadrupeds and numerous feathers; among the latter, several conspicuous scarlet ones from the Cardinal Grosbeak. The outer surface of the whole presents a grayish, inconspicuous appearance, and from the nature of the component materials is well calculated to escape observation. Indeed, it must depend for concealment upon this protective coloring, as it is in no way sheltered by any surrounding foliage.

Attwater (Chapman, 1907) says:

Of over fifty nests of this bird which I have examined, most of them were securely placed in perpendicular forks of the main limbs of cedar trees, about two-thirds up in the tree; average fifteen feet from the ground. My highest record is twenty-one feet, and lowest six feet. I have also found them in similar

positions in small black oak, mountain oak, walnut and pecan trees.  *  *  *
The favorite nesting haunts are isolated patches or clumps of scrubby cedars,
with scant foliage, on the summits of the scarped cañon slopes, and in the
thick cedar "brakes." In cedar the older growth of trees is always selected, and
no attempt at concealment is made. I have never found a nest in a young
thrifty cedar with *thick* foliage.

The male is always to be heard singing in the vicinity of the nest, and the
old nesting localities, and occasionally the same tree is selected apparently and
returned to one year after another.

Nearly all the nests reported by others were in cedars and were
similar in construction to those described. There are five nests of
the golden-cheeked warbler in the Thayer collection in Cambridge,
of which only one was in a cedar; two were in Spanish or mountain
oaks and two in live oaks; four of these had more or less admixture
of lichens, mosses, bits of dry leaves, and plant down in the bases,
and feathers of quail, cardinal and other birds in the linings. The
smallest nest in the series measures externally 2½ inches in diameter
and 2 inches in height; it is very neatly and firmly woven.

*Plumages.*—Ridgway (1902) describes the juvenal plumage of the
golden-cheeked warbler as follows: "Pileum, hindneck, back, scapulars, rump, and upper tail-coverts plain grayish brown or brownish
gray; sides of head, chin, throat, chest, and sides pale brownish gray;
rest of under part white, the breast very indistinctly streaked with
pale gray; wings and tail essentially as in adults, but middle coverts
with a mesial wedge-shaped mark of dusky."

Apparently there is a partial postjuvenal molt early in the summer, which is similar to that of other wood warblers. This produces
the first winter plumages, in which the sexes are recognizable and
much like the respective adults at that season. In the young male the
upper parts are streaked with olive-green and black, the upper tail
coverts are margined with olive-green and gray, and the white tips
of the median wing coverts have narrow, black shaft streaks instead of
the dusky wedges seen in the juvenal coverts. Ridgway (1902) says
of the young female: "Similar to the adult female but pileum, hindneck, back, scapulars, rump, and upper tail-coverts plain olive-green,
or with very indistinct narrow streaks of dusky on pileum and back;
throat and chest pale grayish (the feathers dusky beneath surface),
the former tinged with yellow anteriorly; sides and flanks indistinctly
streaked with dusky."

I have seen no specimens showing a prenuptial molt, which is probably finished before the birds arrive in Texas. The first and subsequent nuptial plumages may be largely produced by wear, as the fall
and winter plumages are much like those of spring birds, but are
concealed by the tips and margins of the feathers. However, it would
be strange if there were no prenuptial molt, especially in young birds.

Young birds in first nuptial plumage can be recognized by the worn and faded wings and tail.

*Eggs.*—Four eggs make up the regular set for the golden-cheeked warbler, although sometimes only three and very rarely five are found. They are ovate to short ovate and have only a very slight lustre. They are white or creamy white, finely speckled and spotted with "bay," "auburn," or "chestnut," and occasionally "argus brown," intermingled with spots of "vinaceous drab," "brownish drab," or "light mouse gray." They are generally finely marked, but sometimes eggs will have spots which are large enough to be called blotches, or even a few small scrawls of very dark brown. The markings are concentrated at the large end, where frequently a fine wreath is formed, or the speckles may be so dense as to almost obscure the ground; occasionally the markings are scattered over the entire egg. The measurements of 50 eggs average 17.7 by 13.1 millimeters; the eggs showing the four extremes measure 18.9 by 13.0, 17.8 by 13.7, and 15.6 by 12.4 millimeters (Harris).

*Young.*—We have no information on incubation or on the care and feeding of the nestlings. Attwater (Chapman, 1907) has this to say:

The young birds out of the nest, which are being fed by the parents late in April and in May, are from early nests which have escaped destruction by "northers" on account of their sheltered positions and situations, and it is possible that then another nest is built and a second brood reared. * * * During June the family groups wander about together, chiefly in the cañons and along the lower hillsides, keeping together till the young are old enough to take care of themselves. While being fed by the parents the "twittering" of the young birds is continually heard, with the cautions "tick, tick" alarm notes of the female when enemies approach. Early in July they begin to scatter, as most of the young birds are then able to shift for themselves.

*Food.*—Very little has been mentioned regarding the food of this wood warbler beyond the fact that it seems to be mainly, if not wholly, insectivorous. Mr. Attwater (1892) says: "Upon examining the stomachs of a number of young birds which were being fed, I found they all contained (with other insects) a number of small black lice (*Aphis* sp.) which I watched the old birds collecting from the green cedar limbs."

*Behavior.*—Mr. Attwater wrote to Dr. Chapman (1907):

Like most of the same sex of other Warblers, the female of this species is very shy, and seldom noticed except when an intruder disturbs the nest or when feeding the young after leaving it, but the male Golden-cheeked Warbler is by no means a shy bird. He keeps continually flying from tree to tree in search of insects, and on fine days uttering his song at short intervals from early dawn until after sundown, and before nest building begins shows little alarm upon being approached. I have stood under a tree a number of times within five or six feet of a wandering male Golden-cheek, which appeared as pleased and

interested in watching *me* as I was in observing him.   Seemingly he was desirous
of assisting me to describe his song in my note-book, by very obligingly repeating
it frequently for my special benefit.

Mr. Werner told Mr. Brewster (1879) that "their habits were
similar to those of *D. virens;* they were very active, always on the
alert for insects, examining almost every limb, and now and then
darting after them while on the wing."

*Voice.*—The song evidently bears a resemblance to that of the black-
throated green warbler in quality.   Mr. Werner wrote it *tsrr weasy-
weasy tweah*, and referred to the notes as soft.   Mr. Attwater wrote
to Dr. Chapman (1907) : "It would be difficult to describe the Golden-
cheek's song with any real satisfaction.   It varies somewhat, being
uttered much more rapidly by some individuals than by others.   At
a distance only the louder parts are heard, so that it sounds quite
different than when heard at close quarters.   The hurried song might
be given as *tweah, tweak, twee-sy*, with some individuals introducing
an extra note or two, and the slower or more deliberate style *twee-ah,
eseah, eachy*.   After the young leave the nests the males gradually
stop singing, and at this period sometimes only use a part of the
regular song."

George Finlay Simmons (1925) describes the song as "ventrilo-
quistic, elusive, seeming to come from here, there, everywhere; *ter-
wih-zeee-e-e-e, chy*, the first, second, and fourth notes short and soft,
the third longest, most distinct, and with the shrill buzzing *z-z-z-z*
quality of the Black-throated Green Warbler's song.   * * *   Sung
by male from conspicuous perch atop a small tree near nest and hidden
female; heard commonly in spring in the Golden-cheek habitat; males
gradually stop singing when young have left nest.   Call, chirping in
migration; female, a soft, scolding *check, check, check* or *tick, tick*,
uttered slowly, a note at a time."

*Enemies.*—According to Dr. Friedmann (1929), the golden-cheeked
warbler is "apparently a rather rare victim of the Dwarf Cowbird."
He mentions only three authentic cases.

*Field marks.*—The golden-cheeked warbler might at first glance be
mistaken for a black-throated green warbler, but the upper parts in
the adult male are deep black from crown to tail, instead of olive-
green, and the under parts, except for the black throat, are white and
not tinged with yellow.   The female differs from the eastern bird in
the same way.

*Fall.*—Golden-cheeked warblers do not remain on their breeding
grounds very long and leave for their winter resorts in Mexico and
Central America before the end of summer.   Mr. Attwater told Dr.
Chapman (1907) that "early in July they begin to scatter, as most of
the young birds are then able to shift for themselves.   By the middle

of July most of the old males have stopped singing, and by the end of July old and young have disappeared from their usual haunts. I have noticed a few stragglers during the first two weeks in August, and all probably leave before September first."

*Range.*—Texas to Nicaragua.

*Breeding range.*—During the breeding season the golden-cheeked warbler is confined to a few counties in south central Texas: **North** to Kerr (Ingram and Kerrville) and Travis (Austin) Counties; **south** to Bexar (San Antonio) and Medina (Castroville) Counties; and **west** to Real County (West Frio Canyon). It is probably not so narrowly confined as the definite records indicate. It has been recorded in summer, but with no indication of breeding, at Waco, Hunt, and Commerce.

*Winter range.*—Little is known of the golden-cheeked warbler in winter. At that season it has been found at Teziutlán, western Veracruz; Tactic, central Guatemala; and Matagalpa, central northern Nicaragua. On November 23, 1939, and January 8, 1940, a male was observed on the island of St. Croix, Virgin Islands. It has been observed in Tamaulipas and Nuevo León in March, probably on migration.

*Migration.*—The golden-cheeked warbler is an early migrant both in spring and fall. It has arrived at Kerrville, Tex., as early as March 5, and the majority of the birds have left by the middle of July; latest, Ingram, August 18.

*Egg dates.*—Texas: 29 records, April 1 to June 27; 10 records, April 11 to 24; 10 records, May 18 to 28 (Harris).

**DENDROICA OCCIDENTALIS (Townsend)**

**HERMIT WARBLER**

PLATE 39

HABITS

This well-marked wood warbler lives in summer in the high coniferous forests of the west, from British Columbia southward to the southern Sierra Nevadas in California, and spends the winter in Mexico and Central America. This is another of those species discovered by J. K. Townsend along the Columbia River, of which he wrote to Audubon (1841): "I shot this pair of birds near Fort Vancouver, on the 28th of May, 1835. I found them flitting among the pine trees in the depth of a forest. They were actively engaged in searching for insects, and were frequently seen hanging from the twigs like Titmice. Their note was uttered at distant intervals, and resembled very much that of the Black-throated Blue Warbler, *Sylvia canadensis*."

In northwestern Washington the hermit warbler is not common and is decidedly local in its summer haunts, being regularly found in certain favored regions and entirely absent in other somewhat similar localities. It is partial to a certain type of coniferous forest, and when one learns to recognize the proper environment he is quite likely to find it. D. E. Drown and S. F. Rathbun showed me some typical haunts of this warbler near Tacoma, where J. H. Bowles has found it nesting. This is level land covered with a more or less open growth of firs and cedars, the largest trees, giant Douglas firs, are somewhat scattered and tower above the rest of the forest, some reaching a height of 200 feet or more. As the warblers spend most of their time in the tops of these great trees and are very active, it is difficult to identify them even with a good glass, and still more difficult to follow them to their nests.

Chester Barlow (1901) says that in the central Sierra Nevada, in California, "the hermit warbler is pre-eminently a frequenter of the conifers, although it feeds in the bushes and black oaks in common with other species." In the Yosemite region, according to Grinnell and Storer (1924), "the Hermit Warbler is a bird of the coniferous forests at middle altitudes. Pines and firs afford it suitable forage range and safe nesting sites. The birds keep fairly well up in the trees, most often at 20 to 50 feet from the ground. The Hermit may thus be found in close association with the Audubon Warbler, although the latter ranges to a much greater altitude in the mountains."

*Spring.*—Dr. Chapman (1907), outlining the migration of the hermit warbler, says that it "enters the United States in April being reported from Oracle, Arizona, April 12, 1899, and the Huachuca Mountains, Arizona, April 9, 1902. Records of the earliest birds seen in California are Campo, April 27, 1877, and Julian, April 25, 1884. A Hermit Warbler was noted at Burrard Inlet, British Columbia, April 20, 1885." Swarth (1904) says that the first arrivals in the Huachucas "appeared in the very highest parts of the mountains, but a little later they could be found in all parts of the range, and on April 17, 1902, I saw a few in some willows near the San Pedro River." Mrs. Amelia S. Allen's notes from the San Francisco Bay region, give dates of arrival from April 24 to May 10. In northwestern Washington, according to Bowles (1906), "the hermits make their first appearance early in May and the fact is only to be known thru their notes; for they frequent the tops of the giant firs which cover large sections of our flat prairie country."

*Nesting.*—The first undoubted nests of the hermit warbler were found by C. A. Allen in Blue Cañon, California, two in 1886 and one about eight years previously, about which he wrote to William Brewster (1887) : "All three nests were similarly placed;—in 'pitch pines,' from twenty-five to forty feet above the ground, on thick, scraggy limbs, where they were so well concealed that it would have been impossible to find them except by watching the birds, as was done in each instance." One of these nests held two eggs on June 4, but they were destroyed before they could be collected; the other two nests contained three young each. One of the nests with three young was sent to Brewster, who writes:

The nest with young, taken June 7, 1886, is now before me. It is composed of the fibrous stalks of herbaceous plants, fine dead twigs, lichens (*Evernia vulpina*), and a little cotton twine, and is lined with soft inner bark of some coniferous tree and fine long hairs, apparently from the tail of a squirrel. The bright, yellow *Evernia*, sprinkled rather plentifully about the rim, gives a touch of color to the otherwise cold, gray tone of the exterior and contrasts agreeably with the warm, reddish-brown lining. Although the materials are coarse and wadded, rather than woven, together, the general effect of this nest is neat and tasteful. It does not resemble any other Warbler's nest that I have seen, but rather recalls the nest of some Fringilline bird, being perhaps most like that of the Lark Finch. It measures externally 4.50 inches in width by 2 inches in depth. The cavity is 1.25 inches deep by 2.50 inches wide at the top. The walls at the rim average nearly an inch in thickness.

Chester Barlow (1901), who has had considerable experience with the nesting of the hermit warbler in the central Sierra Nevada, refers to the records up to that time as follows:

On June 10, 1896, Mr. R. H. Beck collected a nest and four eggs from a limb of a yellow pine 40 feet up, near the American River at 3,500 feet altitude. The nest was reached by means of a ladder carried a long distance up the mountain. (See *Nidologist*, IV, p. 79). On June 14, 1898, I had the good fortune to discover a nest opposite the station at Fyffe, it being built at the end of a small limb of a yellow pine 45 feet up. The nest was located by searching at random and contained four eggs about one-fourth incubated. This nest was described at length in *The Auk* (XVI, pp. 156–161.) * * * While walking through the timber at Fyffe on June 8, 1899, Mr. H. W. Carriger came upon a nest of this species but 2½ feet up in a cedar sapling. It contained four eggs, advanced in incubation (See CONDOR I, pp. 59 60). A nest containing young about four days old found by Mr. Price's assistant at Fyffe on June 11, 1897, was placed twelve feet up near the top of a small cedar, next to the trunk and well concealed. Thus it is probable that Fyffe has afforded more nesting records of this species than has any other part of the state.

Of the nest described in *The Auk*, Barlow (1899) says:

The nest was 45 feet from the ground in a yellow pine, built four feet from the trunk of the tree on an upcurved limb 18 inches from the end. * * * The nest is not fastened to the limb, resting merely upon the limb and pine needles and is wider at the bottom than at the top, its base measuring four inches one way and three inches the other. It is very prettily constructed, the bottom layer being of light grayish weed stems, bleached pine needles and other light materials held securely together by cobwebs and wooly substances. The nest cavity is lined with strips of red cedar bark (*Libocedrus*) and the ends, instead of being woven smoothly, project out of the nest. The inner lining is of a fine brownish fiber resembling shreds of soap-root. The composition of the nest gives it a very pretty effect.

J. H. Bowles (1906) found a nest in northwestern Washington on June 11, 1905, "in a grove of young hundred-foot firs near a small swamp." The female sat so close that he was obliged to lift her from the nest with his hand—

and she then flew only a few feet where she remained chipping and spreading her wings and tail. * * * The nest was placed twenty feet from the ground in a young fir, and was securely saddled on a good sized limb at a distance of six feet from the trunk of the tree. It is a compact structure composed externally of small dead fir twigs, various kinds of dry moss, and down from the cotton-wood flowers, showing a strong outward resemblance to nests of *D. auduboni*. But here the likeness between the two is at an end; for the lining consists of fine dried grasses, and horsehair, with only a single feather from the wing of a western bluebird. The measurements are, externally, four inches in diameter and two and three-quarters inches deep; internally, two inches in diameter by one and a quarter inches deep."

A nest in the Thayer collection in Cambridge was collected by O. W. Howard "70 feet above ground, near the end of a limb of a yellow pine, in a bunch of needles," in Tulare County, Calif. Gordon W. Gullion tells me of an Oregon nest that was "about 125 feet above the ground."

*Eggs.*—The hermit warbler lays 3, 4, or 5 eggs to a set; 5 are apparently not rare. Bowles (1906) says of his 5 eggs: "They have a rather dull white ground with the slightest suggestion of flesh color, heavily blotched and spotted with varying shades of red, brown and lavender. * * * I think they may be considered the handsomest of all the warblers' eggs." The 4 eggs in the Thayer collection in Cambridge are ovate, with a very slight lustre. They are creamy white, finely speckled and spotted with "chestnut" and "auburn," with intermingling spots of "light brownish drab." The markings are concentrated at the large end, forming a broad, loose wreath. The measurements of 50 eggs average 17.0 by 13.1 millimeters; the eggs showing the four extremes measure **18.0** by 13.4, 17.0 by **13.7,** 15.2 by 12.7, and 16.3 by **11.8** millimeters (Harris).

*Young.*—We have no information on the incubation of the eggs, nor on the care and development of the young.

*Plumages.*—I have examined the nestlings sent to Brewster by C. A. Allen; they are about two-thirds fledged on the body and wings; the heads still show the long natal down, "hair brown" in color; the feathers of the back are "olive brown"; the wings are "clove brown," with two narrow, white wing bars, faintly tinged with pale yellow; the breasts and sides are pale "hair brown" to "light grayish olive"; and the rest of the under parts are yellowish white. A young bird in fresh plumage, collected July 1, is probably in full juvenal plumage; its body plumage is similar to that of the nestlings, but there is some yellow on the forehead and throat, and the sides of the head and neck are decidedly yellow; however, this may be a bird that has assumed its first winter plumage at an unusually early date.

In first winter plumage, young birds of both sexes are much like the adult female at that season, mainly grayish olive-green above, with black streaks concealed or absent; forehead, sides of the head, and chin pale yellow; and the rest of the under parts buffy white, the sides browner. The broad, white tips of the lesser wing coverts have a black shaft streak or wedge, apparently characteristic of this plumage. There is probably a prenuptial molt involving much of the head and body plumage and the wing coverts, but the dull juvenal wings are retained until the next molt.

The complete postnuptial molt occurs in July and August. The fall plumages of both sexes are like the spring plumages, but the clear blacks and yellows are largely concealed by olive above and by buffy below.

*Food.*—The only item I can find on the food of the hermit warbler is the following short statement by Bowles (1906) : "Their food consists of small spiders, caterpillars, tiny beetles, and flying insects which they dart out and capture in a manner worthy of that peer of flycatchers the Audubon warbler."

*Behavior.*—The most marked trait of the hermit warbler is its fondness for the tree tops, spending much of its time in the tops of the tallest firs, often 200 feet or more above the ground, where it is very active and not easy to follow. But it builds its nest at lower levels, and often comes down to forage in the lower branches, in smaller trees and even in the underbrush, where it is not particularly shy and can be easily approached. It is a close sitter while incubating; Bowles had to lift one off its nest.

A hermit warbler watched by Miss Margaret W. Wythe, in Yosemite Valley, "was foraging in the upper parts of the trees and never came to the lower branches. Starting from near the trunk of a pine it would work out to the tip of one branch before going to another. Its demeanor while foraging was much more deliberate than that of any of the other warblers" (Grinnell and Storer, 1924).

*Voice.*—Rathbun (MS.) writes: "The song is quite strong, can be heard a considerable distance, and when given in full consists of five or six notes. The first note, rather faint, rises and then falls, with a slight accent at its close; if one is quite close to the singer, the note has a light lisping sound. This note is followed by another, similar but stronger and more prolonged. Then come three or four short, clear notes quickly given, the song ending with a prolonged rising one that closes sharply. Our interpretation of the song would be *zweeo-zweeo-zwee-zwee-zwee-zweeck*. Whenever an additional note is given, it is of the intermediate kind. One or two of these notes are, to us, suggestive of some heard in the song of Townsend's warbler. The song is quite rapidly sung in an energetic way, being very distinctive and is pleasing. It resembles the song of no other warbler in the region."

Bowles (1906) says that the song of the hermit warbler "consists of four distinct notes, as a rule, and is described as *zeegle-zeegle, zeegle-zeek*, uttered somewhat slowly at first but ending rather sharply." Barlow (1899) states that "though not loud it would penetrate through the woods quite a distance and very much resembled *tsit, tsit, tsit, tsit, chee chee chee*, the first four syllables being uttered with a gradual and uniform speed, ending quickly with the *chee chee chee*." Grinnell and Storer (1924) write:

> The song of the male Hermit Warbler, while varying somewhat with different individuals, is suficiently distinct from that of the other warblers of the region to make possible identification by voice alone. The song is most nearly like that of the Audubon Warbler but usually not so clear or mellow. A male bird observed at Chinquapin seemed to say *seezle, seezle, seezle, seezle, zeek, zeek;* just that number of syllables, over and over again. The quality was slightly droning, but not so much so as that of the Black-throated Gray Warbler. Another song, clearer in quality, heard in Yosemite Valley, was written *ter'-ley, ter'-ley, ter'-ley, sic', sic'*, thus much more nearly like the song of the Audubon Warbler. Other transscriptions ranged between these two as to timbre. A rendering set down at Glacier Point June 16, 1915, was as follows: *ser-weez', ser-weez', ser-weez', ser', ser'*. The marked rhythm throughout, and the stressed terminal syllables, are distinctive features of the Hermit's song. The call note is a moderate *chip*."

Writing of warbler songs of early dawn, Dawson (Dawson and Bowles, 1909) indulges in the following flowery praise of the hermit's sing: "There is Audubon with his hastening melody of gladness. There is Black-throated Gray with his still drowsy sonnet of sweet content. Then there is Hermit hidden aloft in the shapeless greenery of the under-dawn—his note is sweetest, gladdest, most seraphic of them all, *lilly, lilly, lilly, leê-oleet.* It is almost sacrilege to give it form—besides it is so hopeless. The preparatory notes are like the tinkle of crystal bells, and when our attention is focused, lo! the wonder happens, the exquisite lilt of the closing phrase, *leê-oleet.*"

*Field marks.*—The yellow head, the black throat, the dark back, and the white, unmarked under parts will distinguish the male in spring. The head of the female, of young birds, and of fall birds is also more or less yellowish and the back is more olivaceous.  The two white wing bars are also common to several other species.  Its song is said to be distinctive.

*Fall.*—The fall migration of the hermit warbler begins early. Bowles (1906) says that, in Washington, "about the middle of July both young and old assemble in good-sized flocks and frequent the water holes in the smaller growths of timber.  At such times I have never seen them associating with any other kinds of birds."  W. W. Price wrote to Mr. Barlow (1901) of the migration in the Sierra Nevada:

The adults are very rare during June and July in the neighborhood of my camp at Silver Creek, but late in July and early in August a migration of the young birds of the year takes place and the species is very abundant everywhere in the tamaracks from about 6000 to 8000 feet.  A hundred or more may be counted in an hour's walk at my camp, 7000 feet, on Silver Creek.  They are very silent, uttering now and then a 'cheep,' and always busy searching among the leaves and cones for insects.  Among some fifty collected in the first week in August, 1896, there were only two or three adults.  The young males have the most coloring, but they in no way approach adult plumage.  These great flights of the hermit warbler are intermingled with other species, Hammond flycatcher, Calaveras and lutescent warblers, Cassin vireo, and sometimes Louisiana tanagers and red-brested nuthatches.  Each year the flight has been noted, it comes without warning of storm or wind, and after a few days disappears to be seen no more.

In the Huachuca Mountains of Arizona, according to Swarth (1904), "they reappeared in August, but at this time were seen only in the pines above 8500 feet.  It is rather singular, and in contradiction to the idea that in the migrations the old birds go first in order to show the way, that the first secured in the fall was a young female, taken August 7th.  The young birds then became very abundant, and on August 14th the first adult female was taken; and not until August 19th was an adult male seen.  The adults then became nearly as abundant as the juveniles, and both together were more numerous than I have ever seen them in the spring, on several occasions as many as fifteen to twenty being seen in one flock."

*Winter.*—Dr. Skutch writes to me: "The hermit warbler is a moderately abundant winter resident in the Guatemalan highlands, found chiefly between 5,000 and 10,000 feet above sea level, but ranging downward to about 3,500 feet on the Pacific slope and possibly somewhat lower on the Caribbean slope, where pine forests push down into the upper levels of the Tropical Zone.  These treetop birds are usually found in the mixed flocks of small birds, of which Townsend's warblers form the predominant element.  During the early part of their sojourn in Guatemala, I sometimes saw two, three, or more hermits in the same flock; but in February and March, there was as a rule only one. In 1933, I saw the last of these warblers on the Sierra de Tecpán on March 29, and recorded the first fall arrival on September 13, when four individuals were seen."

DISTRIBUTION

*Range.*—Western North America from Puget Sound to Nicaragua.
*Breeding range.*—The hermit warbler breeds **north** to northwestern Washington (Lake Crescent and Tacoma). **East** to the Cascades of Washington (Tacoma); Oregon (Prospect); and the Sierra Nevada in California (Meadow Valley, Pinecrest, Yosemite Valley, Taylor Meadow, and the San Bernardino Mountains). **South** to the San Bernardino Mountains and La Honda. **West** to the Pacific coast from central western California northward (La Honda, Cahto, and Garberville); western Oregon (Kerby and Tillamook); and northwestern Washington (Lake Crescent).
*Winter range.*—The hermit warbler has been found in winter **north** to central Mexico (Taxco, Cuernavaca, and Mexico City). **East** to Mexico City and central Guatemala (San Gerónimo and Alotepeque). **South** to southern Guatemala (Alotepeque); probably farther south since specimens have been taken at Los Esesmiles, El Salvador, and Metagalpa, Nicaragua. **West** to western Guatemala (Altopeque, Tecpán, and Momostenango); western Oaxaca (La Parada); and northern Guerrero (Taxco).

The hermit warbler has been taken three times in January in central western California (San Geronimo and Point Reyes, Marin County; and Pacific Grove, Monterey County).
*Migration.*—Late dates of spring departure from the winter home are: Guatemala—Tecpán, March 29. Sonora—Rancho la Arizona, May 8. Arizona—Huachuca Mountains—May 28.

Early dates of spring arrival are: Tampico—Galindo, March 19. Coahuila—Sierra de Guadeloupe, April 20. Arizona—Oracle, April 12. California—Witch Creek, April 10. Washington—Tacoma, April 25.

Late dates of fall departure are: Washington—Edwards, October 19. California—Monterey, October 20. Arizona—Santa Catalina Mountains, September 29. Tamaulipas—Guiaves, October 7.

Early dates of fall arrival are: California—Berkeley, July 9. Arizona—Graham Mountains, July 30. New Mexico—Animas Peak, August 3. Michoacán—Tancitaro, August 16. Guatemala—Tecpán, September 13.

*Casual records.*—Specimens of the hermit warbler have been collected in the Huachuca Mountains in Arizona on June 16, 1894; at Basin in the Chisos Mountains in Texas on May 3, 1935; and near Cambridge, Minn., on May 3, 1931.

*Egg dates.*—California: 10 records, May 14 to June 25; 6 records, June 3 to 14, indicating the height of the season.
Washington: 3 records, June 5 to 11 (Harris).

DENDROICA CERULEA (Wilson)

CERULEAN WARBLER

PLATE 39

HABITS

This heavenly-blue wood warbler was first introduced to science, figured, and named by Wilson in the first volume of his American Ornithology.  Only the male was figured and described from a specimen received from Charles Willson Peale and taken in eastern Pennsylvania.  The female was not known until Charles Lucien Bonaparte described it in his continuation of Wilson's American Ornithology.  Strangely enough the discovery of this specimen was also made by a member of the famous Peale family, Titian Peale, the bird having been taken in the same general region, on the banks of the Schuylkill, August 1, 1825.  Audubon met with it later, but was almost wholly wrong in what he wrote about it, though his plate is good.

The species is now known to occupy a rather extensive breeding range located mainly west of the Alleghenies and east of the Great Plains from southern Ontario and central New York southward to the northern parts of some of the Gulf States and Texas.  It is, however, decidedly local in its distribution over much of this range.

This warbler, a bird of the treetops in heavy deciduous woods, where its colors make it difficult to distinguish among the lights and shadows of the lofty foliage and against the blue sky, is well named cerulean!  In his notes from central New York, Samuel F. Rathbun writes: "The type of growth to which the cerulean warbler is partial appears to be the rather open forests in the lowlands and often along some stream.  During the nesting season, it will not be found to any extent in the better class of hardwood trees of the uplands; in fact, this warbler shows a strong liking for areas where large elms and soft maples and black ash are the dominant trees."  Verdi Burtch wrote to Dr. Chapman (1907) that near Branchport, N. Y., this warbler is "locally abundant in mixed growths of oak and maple with a few birch and hickory."  In other portions of its range, it is found in mixed woods of maples, beech, basswood or linden, elm, sycamore, or oaks.  Frank C. Kirkwood (1901) found that, in Maryland, "the species has a decided preference for high open woods clear of underbrush. * * * The trees are principally chestnuts, with oaks, hickorys, tulip trees, etc."

*Spring.*—The main migration route of the cerulean warbler is through the Mississippi Valley, from the Alleghenies westward; it is rare in the Atlantic States, especially the more southern ones, and hardly more than casual in Florida and the West Indies. It enters the United States, in Texas and Louisiana, in April, and reaches its breeding grounds in the interior early in May.

Rathbun (MS.) says of the spring migration in central New York: "The cerulean warbler arrives in this region about the middle of May, its coming being announced by its song. With rare exceptions, it is not found in the spring migration with other warblers and it appears to move in very small groups or singly; even in the large spring-time movements of warblers known as 'waves,' some of the birds of which remain while others pass through the region, I have observed very few cerulean warblers. Not much time elapses after its arrival before mating takes place and nest building begins."

*Nesting.*—The earlier ornithologists knew nothing about the nesting habits of the cerulean warbler; Audubon's description of its nest was entirely erroneous, and it was about 50 years after the bird was discovered that its nest was reported. This is not strange, as the nest is not easy to find and still more difficult to secure. Rathbun (MS.) writes in his notes: "During our stay in New York State, we found only three of its nests, because they were rather difficult to locate. We found the first at a height of 55 feet in a little cluster of small, twig-like branches growing on the side of a feathered elm; these clusters were close enough together to be of great use in climbing the tree, which was at least 3 feet in diameter. The nest was discovered by seeing the bird fly into the cluster. Within the next week a second nest was found by watching the female bird; it was at a height of 45 feet in a very small, flat crotch of a soft maple. The third nest was at a height of about 30 feet.

"The nests were identical in all respects except as to shape, which varied because of its situation. Each was nicely made but not unusual in appearance. The material used was almost wholly the fine strips of the grayish bark of small weed stalks, neatly interwoven. Each was smoothly and beautifully lined with the fresh stems of ground mosses of a brownish red color, which contrasted nicely with the gray outer material. Of great interest was the smoothness with which the material was woven in."

Burtch wrote to Dr. Chapman (1907) that near Branchport, N. Y., where the bird is locally common, "the nest is usually placed on a horizontal branch or drooping branch of an elm, ranging from twenty-five to sixty feet from the ground, and from four, to fifteen, or eighteen feet from the body of the tree *over an opening.*"

W. E. Saunders (1900) reports eight nests found in southern Ontario; two of these were in oaks, 20 and 23 feet up, two in maples,

30 and 35 feet from the ground, and four in basswoods (lindens), from 17 to 50 feet above ground. He gives the measurements of three nests; they measured externally from 1¾ to 2 inches in height and 2¾ inches in diameter; internally they varied from ⅞ to 1 inch in depth and from 1⅞ to 1¾ inches in diameter. He remarks: "A feature that interested me very much was the extreme shallowness of the nests; all the other warblers with which I am acquainted building a comparatively deep nest, and the query arises, Does the bird build a shallow nest because it places it on a substantial limb, or does it place it on a substantial limb because its nests are shallow? The attachment of the nest, also, is exceedingly frail, and I am inclined to think that few of these nests would remain in position long after the young had left."

A nest found by Kirkwood (1901) in Baltimore County, Md., is described as follows: "The nest is made of brown bark fibre, with some fine grass stems among it, and is finished inside with a few black horse-hairs. Outside it is finished with gray shreds of bark, spider web, and a few small fragments of newspaper that had been water-soaked. * * * As the branch sloped, one part of the rim is within ¾ of an inch of it, while the opposite part is 1¾ inches above it, the material comes down on one side of branch to 2¼ inches below the rim. On this side a tiny twig arches out from branch and extending to the rim is embedded in the nest, and the leaves which grew from its top shaded the nest." The nest was 48 feet and 6 inches up from the ground and 15 feet out from the trunk of a tulip tree, with no other limb between it and the ground.

A neat little nest before me is made of materials similar to those mentioned. It is lined with the reddish brown flowering stems of mosses smoothly woven with other very fine brownish fibres into a compact rim, and it is decorated externally with various brown and gray lichens and mosses. Other nests have been reported in sycamores, beeches, rock maples, sugar maples, and white oaks.

*Eggs.*—The cerulean warbler lays from 3 to 5 eggs, usually 4. They are ovate to short ovate and have a slight luster. The ground color is grayish white, creamy white, or even very pale greenish white, and they are speckled, spotted or blotched with "bay," "chestnut," or "auburn," intermingled with spots of "light brownish drab," or "brownish drab." Some eggs have spots scattered all over the surface, but usually they are concentrated at the large end, where a loose wreath is formed. Generally the eggs are finely marked, but occasionally are quite heavily blotched. The measurements of 50 eggs average 17.0 by 13.0 millimeters; the eggs showing the four extremes measure 17.9 by 13.0, 17.0 by 13.7, 16.0 by 12.4, and 17.2 by 12.0 millimeters (Harris).

*Young.*—The period of incubation seems to be unknown, and we have no information on the care and development of the young. Incubation is said to be performed by the female alone, but both parents assist in feeding the young. After the young are out of the nest, they may be seen travelling through the woods in family parties with their parents. There seems to be no evidence that more than one brood is raised in a season.

*Plumages.*—Ridgway (1902) describes the young cerulean warbler in nestling (juvenal) plumage as "above uniform brownish gray (deep drab gray), the pileum divided longitudinally by a broad median stripe of grayish white; sides of head (including a broad superciliary stripe) and entire under parts white; a narrow postocular stripe of deep drab gray; wings as in adults, but edgings greenish rather than bluish."

The first winter plumage is assumed by a partial postjuvenal molt, involving the contour plumage and the wing coverts, but not the rest of the wings nor the tail. Dr. Dwight (1900) describes the young male in this plumage as "above, deep bice-green, partly concealing cinereous gray which is conspicuous on the rump and upper tail coverts, the latter and the feathers of the back often black centrally. The wing coverts with bluish cinereous gray edgings; two wing bands white, faintly tinged with canary-yellow. Below, white, strongly washed except on the chin, abdomen and crissum with primrose-yellow, the sides and flanks streaked obscurely with dull black. Superciliary line primrose-yellow; lores and orbital regions whitish; a dusky transocular streak."

The first nuptial plumage is acquired by a partial prenuptial molt "which involves much of the body plumage and wing coverts, but not the rest of the wings nor the tail. The grayish cerulean blue, the black streaks on the back and the white wing bands are acquired; below, the plumage is white with a narrow bluish black band on the throat and the sides distinctly streaked. Young and old become practically indistinguishable, except by the duller wings and tail of the juvenal dress."

The adult winter plumage is acquired by a complete postnuptial molt in July, which he says "differs from first winter in being much bluer and whiter, the wings and tail blacker and the edgings a bluer gray. Resembles the adult nuptial, but rather grayer on the back and the throat band incomplete." The adult nuptial plumage is acquired by a partial-prenuptial molt as in the young bird.

He says of the plumages of the female: "The plumages and moults correspond to those of the male. In juvenal plumage the edgings of the wings and tail are greener tinged than those of the male. In first winter plumage the green above is duller and the black of the back and tail coverts is lacking; below there is more yellow and the side streaks are obscure. The first nuptial plumage is acquired by a moult limited chiefly to the head and throat which become bluer and whiter respectively. Later plumages are brighter, but green always replaces the blue of the male."

*Food.*—No thorough study of the food of the cerulean warbler seems to have been made, but it is known to be insectivorous, foraging among the foliage, twigs, branches, and even on the trunks of trees. It is an expert fly catcher, darting out into the air for flying insects. A. H. Howell (1924) says that "examination of 4 stomachs of this species taken in Alabama showed the food to consist of Hymenoptera, beetles, weevils, and caterpillars." Professor Aughey (1878) observed this warbler catching locusts in Nebraska.

*Behavior.*—S. Harmsted Chubb (1919) describes the behavior of the cerulean warbler as follows:

A bird more difficult to observe I have rarely if ever met with. His life seemed to be confined almost entirely to the tops of the tallest deciduous trees, where he would generally feed, with apparent design, on the side most remote from the would-be observer, exhibiting a wariness not expected on the part of a warbler, and finally leaving the tree, the first intimation of his departure being a more distant song. He never remained in the same tree top more than eight or ten minutes at a time and yet rarely ventured out of hearing distance from the center of his range. Fortunately, he would sometimes take a perch on a bare twig and sing for several minutes, but the perch was always high and generally with the sky as a poor background for observation. Had it not been for the almost incessant singing, being heard almost constantly from daybreak until nearly dark, the task of identification would have seemed hopeless.

*Voice.*—Aretas A. Saunders writes to me: "I have but six records of the song of this bird. There is probably more variation in the song than these records show, for all six are much alike. The song consists of four to eight notes, of even time and all mainly on one pitch, followed by a trill about a tone higher, the latter, in all of my records, pitched on C''''. The first notes, in one of my records, are upward slurs, and in two others the first note of the group slurs upward, but in all of the others all of the notes are of even pitch and not slurred. The pitch varies from G''' to C''''. The songs are undoubtedly between one and two seconds in length, but I had no stop watch at the time, so did not time them. The song is rather loud and not particularly musical. In form the song is much like that of the Blackburnian warbler, but the loudness, different quality, and lower pitch distinguish it."

Francis H. Allen (MS.) writes the song as "*wee wee wee wee bzzz,* heard many times without any apparent variation." This was somewhat different from the song of a cerulean I heard, which had a "chippy" beginning that suggested the song of a yellow palm warbler, and also that of the parula warbler.  Rev. J. J. Murray writes to me from Virginia: "The songs of the parula and cerulean in this section are very similar, but not difficult to distinguish.  The pattern is reversed in the two; the parula's song is 'bzz, bzz, bzz, trill', while that of the cerulean is a 'trill, trill, trill, bzz'.  The cerulean's song can be expressed by the phrase *'Just a little sneeze.'*"  A. D. DuBois tells me that "the beginning of the song is similar to that of the redstart, but it ends with a fine, 'wiry,' grasshopper-like trill, ascending in pitch and drawn out to nothing at the end."  Mr. Chubb (1919) describes two songs of the cerulean warbler as follows:

> The musical exercises of the bird consisted of an alternation of two distinctly different songs, so different indeed that until the bird was caught in the act we never for a moment suspected a single authorship.  One song suggested slightly that of the Magnolia Warbler but rather softer, four syllables, though not quite so well defined as in the Magnolia.  The other, for want of something better, might be compared with the song of the Parula Warbler, a short buzzing trill rising in the scale, much louder and less lispy than the song of the Parula. The songs were each of about one second duration, rendered approximately eight or ten times per minute.  Altogether the performance was quite musical, in sweetness far above the average warbler song.  These two songs were generally alternated with clock-like regularity, though occasionally the bird preferred to dwell upon one or other of his selections for the greater part of the day.

Kirkwood (1901) says: "It also gives its song in a low tone as if it whispered it, and unless the bird is carefully watched the observer might be led to believe that he heard a second bird singing in the distance.  I have watched a bird sing thus between each regular song, at other times it would not give it at all, or only occasionally, while on two or three occasions I heard it given for quite a while to the exclusion of the regular song, and quite often have heard it given two or three or even more times in succession between regular songs." He has heard the cerulean warbler singing through July and until the middle of August; on August 19, he heard them singing "immature or imperfect (?) songs."

*Enemies.*—The cerulean warbler is a rather uncommon victim of the eastern cowbird; not more than 10 cases seem to have been recorded.

*Field marks.*—No other American wood warbler has a similar shade of heavenly blue on its back as the male cerulean; its under parts are pure white, relieved by a narrow black necklace, and it has two white wing bars.  Females, young birds, and even fall males are similar, and are tinged with blue above and with pale yellow below, with a whitish or yellowish line over the eye.  In this plumage they resemble the young parula warbler, but the latter is much deeper yellow on the breast and has no line over the eye.

*Fall.*—Rathbun says in his notes from central New York: "When July comes the warblers will be found quite widely dispersed in any sort of forest, because they are now moving through the country in little family groups. Now and then will be heard snatches of the spring song. This is but preparatory for their departure from the region, which takes place in the latter part of August; we have never seen this warbler after the first week in September.

Professor Cooke (1904) writes:

The cerulean warbler is a rare migrant in the States along the Atlantic coast, though it has been noted in the Carolinas, Georgia, and Florida. In northeastern Texas and Louisiana it is not uncommon. Its main route of migration seems to cross the Gulf of Mexico chiefly from Louisiana and Mississippi. The species is one of the first to start on the southward migration. By the middle of summer it has reached the Gulf coast and is well on its way to its winter home. At Beauvoir and Bay St. Louis, on the coast of Mississippi, it has appeared in different years on dates ranging from July 12 to 29. For a few days it is common, attaining the height of its abundance about the first week in August. It then passes southward so rapidly that Cherrie was able to record its presence on August 24, 1890, at San José, Costa Rica. By November it reaches central Ecuador. Though the bulk of the birds perform their migration at this early date, some laggards remain behind until late in the season.

Dr. A. F. Skutch tells me it is "exceedingly rare in Guatemala. * * * I have never seen the cerulean warbler in Central America. In Ecuador, I found a male in the Pastaza Valley, at an altitude of about 4,000 feet, on October 15, 1939. Two days later this warbler had become fairly common in this locality, and I saw several individuals.

*Winter.*—Says Professor Cooke (1904) : "The cerulean warbler is chiefly found in winter in South America from Panamá south to Perú, in which country it seems to have its center of abundance. In western Perú Jelski (Taczanowski, Proc. Zool. Soc. London, p. 508, 1847) found it common at Monterico and other places in the mountains east of Lima at 10,000 to 13,000 feet elevation, always in wandering flocks, which were sometimes quite large and contained both old and young birds."

### DISTRIBUTION

*Range.*—North and South America from southern Canada to Perú and Bolivia.

*Breeding range.*—The cerulean warbler breeds **north** to southern Minnesota (Minneapolis); southern Wisconsin (Barahoo Bluffs, Madison, and Racine, possibly as far north as New London); central Michigan (Saginaw, Locke, and Detroit) ; southern Ontario (Thedford, Plover Mills, Warren, and Delta ; perhaps Manotick) ; and southern New York (Lockport, Rochester, Ithaca, Santa Cruz Park, and Wappingers Creek, Dutchess County). **East** to southeastern New York (Dutchess County) ; rarely northeastern Maryland (Towson) ; southwestern Delaware (Seaford) ; western Virginia (Charlottesville and Natural Bridge) ; western North Carolina (Morganton and Pink Beds) ; and northern Georgia (Lumpkin County and Atlanta). South to north-central Georgia (Atlanta) ; south-central Alabama (Autaugaville and Greensboro) ; northern Louisiana (Monroe and Caddo Lake) ; and northern Texas (Texarkana and Dallas). West to northeastern Texas (Dallas) ; northeastern Oklahoma (Copan) ; southeastern Kansas (Independence) ; eastern Nebraska (Omaha and Pilgrim Hill, Dakota County) ; western Iowa (Sioux City) ; and southern Minnesota (Minneapolis).

*Winter range.*—The winter home of the cerulean warbler is northwestern South America, in the valleys of the Andes from central Colombia (Antioquia, Medellín, and Bogotá) through Ecuador (Río Napo, Sara-yacu, and the Pataza Valley) ; to southern Perú (Huachipa and Lima). It has also been found occasionally or accidentally in central northern Venezuela (Rancho Grande) ; and in western Bolivia (Nairapi and Tilotilo near La Paz). Casual in winter or migration in the Cayman Islands and western Cuba.

*Migration.*—Late dates of spring departure are: Perú—Huambo, March 15. Ecuador—near San José, March 31. Colombia—Buena Vista, March 4. Florida—Pensacola, April 26. Texas—Austin, April 30.

Early dates of spring arrival are: Florida—Dry Tortugas Island, March 23. Alabama—Greensboro, March 26. Georgia—Atlanta, April 13. South Carolina—Clemson (College), April 21. North Carolina—Asheville, April 23. Virginia—Charlottesville, April 13. West Virginia—Wheeling, April 23. Pennsylvania—McKeesport, April 23. New York—Corning, April 25. Louisiana—Grand Isle, March 27. Arkansas—Tillar, April 6. Tennessee—Athens, April 4. Kentucky—Eubank, April 5. Illinois—Olney, April 18. Indiana—Bloomington, April 11. Michigan—Bay City, April 26. Ohio—Toledo, April 20. Ontario—Hamilton, April 25. Missouri—St. Louis, April 12. Iowa—Hillsboro, April 18. Minnesota—Faribault, April 29. Texas—Victoria, March 17. Oklahoma—Copan, March 27. Kansas—Independence, April 24.

Late dates of fall departure are: Ontario—Point Pelee, September 5. Michigan—Detroit, September 5. Ohio—Ashtabula, September 27. Indiana—Whiting, October 4. Illinois—Chicago, September 28. Kentucky—Versailles, September 4. Tennessee—Athens, September 27. Mississippi—Gulfport, September 17. Oklahoma—Copan, October 1. Texas—Austin, September 27. New York—New York, September 18. Pennsylvania—Berwyn, September 29. North Carolina—Raleigh, September 16. Georgia—Augusta, September 16. Alabama—Birmingham, September 21. Florida—Pensacola, September 18. Costa Rica—San José, October 24.

Early dates of fall arrival are: Texas—Austin, July 20. Mississippi—Beauvoir, July 12. Virginia—Sweet Briar, July 20. Georgia—Athens, July 28. Florida—Pensacola, July 23. Costa Rica—Villa Quesada, August 23. Ecuador—Río Oyacachi, August 10. Perú—Huachipa, October 3.

*Casual records.*—The majority of the cerulean warblers found east of the Allegheny Mountains might be considered as casual. All records for New England should as yet be so considered, though the species has increased in eastern New York in recent years. About 10 individuals have been recorded in Massachusetts; two in Rhode Island, and one in New Hampshire. On June 2, 1924, one was collected at Whitewater Lake, in southwestern Manitoba, the farthest north that the species has been found. There are two records for North Dakota; one near Jamestown on May 28, 1931, and another near Minot on May 24, 1937. A cerulean warbler was recorded near Denver, Colorado, on May 17, 1883, and a specimen collected on September 2, 1936, on Cherry Creek in Douglas County. A bird "observed at the Mimbres during the latter part of April" is the only record for New Mexico. On October 1, 1947, a specimen was collected at the southeastern edge of the Salton Sea in California; and on October 2, 1925, a specimen was collected near La Grulla in the Sierra San Pedro Mártir, Baja California.

*Egg dates.*—Ontario: 3 records, June 2 to 13.

New York: 22 records, May 29 to July 9; 15 records, June 1 to 4.

Pennsylvania: 5 records, May 16 to 26.

**DENDROICA FUSCA (Muller)**

**BLACKBURNIAN WARBLER**

PLATES 40, 41

HABITS

Bagg and Eliot (1937) give the following account of the history of the naming of the Blackburnian Warbler:

Some time in the later eighteenth century, a specimen (apparently female) was sent from New York to England, and there described and named for a Mrs. Blackburn who collected stuffed birds and was a patron to ornithology. *Blackburniae*—Gmelin's latinization, in 1788, of this English name—was its scientific designation until quite recently, when in an obscure German publication, dated 1776, were discovered a description of a specimen from French Guiana (which is well east of the species' normal winter range), and the name *fusca*, blackish. Wilson recognized the male as a rare transient near Philadelphia, but when he shot a female (apparently, though he called it a male) in the Great Pine Swamp, Pa., he named it *Sylvia parus*, the Hemlock Warbler. Audubon, too, considered the Blackburnian and Hemlock Warblers distinct."

Blackburnian seems to be a doubly appropriate name, for its upper parts are largely black and its throat burns like a brilliant orange flame amid the dark foliage of the hemlocks and spruces. A glimpse of such a brilliant gem, flashing out from its sombre surroundings, is fairly startling.

Throughout most of the eastern half of the United States the Blackburnian warbler is known only as a migrant, mainly from the Mississippi Valley eastward. Its summer range extends from Manitoba eastward to Nova Scotia, from Minnesota to New England, and southward in the Allegheny Mountains to South Carolina and Georgia, in the Lower Canadian and Upper Transition Zones. For its breeding haunts it prefers the deep evergreen woods where spruces, firs, and hemlocks predominate, or often swampy woods where the black spruces are thickly draped with *Usnea*, offering concealment for birds and nests.

In Massachusetts, which is about the southern limit of its breeding range in New England, William Brewster (1888) describes its haunts at Winchendon as follows: "On both high and low ground, wherever there were spruces in any numbers, whether by themselves or mixed with other trees, and also to some extent where the growth was entirely of hemlocks, the Blackburnian Warbler was one of the most abundant and characteristic summer birds, in places even outnumbering the Black-throated Green Warbler, although it shunned strictly the extensive tracts of white pines which *D. virens* seemed to find quite as congenial as any of the other evergreens."

Gerald Thayer wrote to Dr. Chapman (1907) that at Monadnock, New Hampshire, it is "a very common summer resident. It is one of the four deep-wood Warblers of this region, the other three being the Black-throated Blue, the Northern Parula and the Canada. While all the other summer Warblers of Monadnock seem better pleased with various sorts of lighter timber, these four are commonest in the small remaining tracts of primeval woodland, and in the heaviest and oldest second growth. But despite this general community of habit, each of the four has marked minor idiosyncrasies. The Blackburnian favors very big trees, particularly hemlocks, and spends most of its life high above the ground."

Professor Maurice Brooks (1936) says that Blackburnian warblers "are thoroughly at home in the deciduous second-growth timber that in so many places has replaced the coniferous forest. They range down to elevations of 2,500 feet in northern West Virginia. Here they associate with Golden-winged and Chestnut-sided warblers. A favorite perch is on some chestnut tree that has been killed by the blight." Rev. J. J. Murray tells me that, in Virginia, it is "common above 1,500 feet, wherever there are conifers." And Thomas D. Burleigh (1941) says of its status on Mount Mitchell in western North Carolina: "Although not known to breed above an altitude of approximately 5,000 feet, this species is fairly plentiful during the late summer in the fir and spruce woods at the top of the mountain, appearing regularly in July and lingering through September."

*Spring.*—The Blackburnian warbler is apparently rare in spring in the Atlantic States south of North Carolina; its migration range extends westward to the plains of eastern Texas, eastern Kansas, and eastern Nebraska, but it is rare west of the forested regions of the Mississippi Valley. Professor Cooke (1904) says that the average rate of migration "from the mouth of the Mississippi to its source, where it breeds, appears to be scarcely 25 miles per day." Forbush (1929) writes:

It is generally regarded as rare in migration in Massachusetts, though probably untold numbers pass over the state every year, but only a few stop here. It is not when the birds are migrating that we see them, but when they *stop* to rest. * * * I can recall but two instances in my lifetime when myriads of Blackburnian Warblers stopped here, though other similar flights probably have come when I was not there to see. At sunrise one morning in early May, many years ago, when the tiny green leaves were just breaking forth on the tall trees of the woods near Worcester, Blackburnians were everywhere in the tree-tops. They swarmed in the woods for miles. Years later, in Amesbury, on another May morning, the night flight, having met a cold wave from the north with a light frost, had come down to earth and the birds were busily looking for food; many Blackburnians and many other warblers were in the low shrubbery, in the grass, and even on plowed fields in every direction all through the village and about the farms. The sudden cold had stopped them. A few hours later as the day grew warmer they disappeared and were not seen again.

Brewster (1906) says: "We see the beautiful Blackburnian oftenest during the later part of May, in extensive tracts of upland woods, where it spends much of its time in the tops of the larger trees, showing a decided preference for hemlocks and white pines. In Cambridge I have repeatedly observed it in our garden and the immediate neighborhood, usually in tall elms or in blossoming apple trees."

*Nesting.*—So far as I can learn, the nest of the Blackburnian warbler is almost always placed in a coniferous tree at heights ranging from 5 feet to over 80 feet above the ground; nests have been reported many times in hemlocks, which seems to be a favorite tree, but also in spruces, firs, tamaracks, pines and even a cedar. Ora W. Knight (1908) says: "I have found them breeding in colonies as a rule, that is to say, in a rather dense, mossy carpeted tract of evergreen woods near the pond at Pittsfield [Maine], covering perhaps a square mile, there were about ten pairs of these birds to be found, and in a tract of similar woods about half this size at Bangor there are often six or eight pair nesting. In other words, in suitable localities they tend to congregate in loosely scattered assemblies, while in less suitable spots, generally none, or at most a single pair will be found." Of a nest found near Winchendon, Mass., Brewster (1888) writes:

The nest, which was found by watching the female, was built at a height of about thirty feet above the ground, on the horizontal branch of a black spruce, some six feet out from the main stem. Its bottom rested securely near the base of a short, stout twig. Above and on every side masses of dark spruce foliage, rendered still denser by a draping of *Usnea* (which covered the entire tree profusely), hid the nest so perfectly that not a vestige of it could be seen from any direction. This nest is composed outwardly of fine twigs, among which some of the surrounding *Usnea* is entangled and interwoven. The lining is of horse hair, fine, dry grasses, and a few of the black rootlets used by *D. maculosa*. The whole structure is light and airy in appearance, and resembles rather closely the nest of the Chipping Sparrow.

The highest nest of which I can find any record is one reported by Dr. C. Hart Merriam (1885), found by A. J. Dayan in a grove of large white pines (*Pinus strobus*), in Lewis County, N. Y. It was saddled on a horizontal limb of one of the pines, about 84 feet from the ground and about 10 feet out from the trunk. "The nest is large, substantial, and very compact. It consists almost entirely of a thick and densely woven mat of the soft down of the cattail (*Typha latifolia*), with seeds attached, and is lined with fine lichens, horse hair, and a piece of white thread. On the outside is an irregular covering of small twigs and rootlets, with here and there a stem of moss or a bit of lichen."

The lowest nests that I have heard of are recorded in Frederic H. Kennard's notes from Maine; one was only 5½ feet up and the other 9 feet from the ground in small spruces. Mrs. Nice (1932) found a nest near her mother's home in Pelham, Mass., that was "18 feet from the ground near the top of a cedar among comparatively open, young growth, 40 yards south of the house and 150 yards to the east of the great pines and hemlocks where the male habitually sang." The only nest of this warbler that I have ever seen was found by watching the female building it, on June 16, 1913, on an island in Lake Winnipegosis, Manitoba; it was only about 10 feet from the ground, near the end of a drooping branch of a large black spruce that stood on the edge of some coniferous woods next to an open swale. The nest, shaded from above, was partly concealed from below by dense foliage and was, apparently, well made of soft fibers, deeply cupped, and lined with some dark material and a little willow cotton. I was not able to visit the island again.

In New York State and in Pennsylvania, the nests of the Blackburnian warbler are almost invariably placed in hemlocks. All of the four nests recorded by T. E. McMullen (MS.) from the Pocono Mountains, Pa., were in hemlocks. And Todd (1940) states that with one exception all the nests found by R. B. Simpson, of Warren,

Pa., were in hemlocks, "at elevations varying from twenty to fifty feet. The exceptional nest was in a large chestnut, sixty feet from the ground."

Dr. Roberts (1936) mentions a Minnesota nest "situated in an arbor vitae tree, directly over the entrance to a cabin," and one "placed in a small spruce, close to the trunk, about 2 feet from the top of the tree and about 20 feet from the ground. Another was found in "a jack-pine tree, 20 feet from the ground, 6 feet from the trunk, resting in a tangle of small branches, and concealed by a closely overhanging branch."

*Eggs.*—The Blackburnian warbler lays normally 4 or 5 eggs, usually 4; in a series of 14 sets there are only 3 sets of 5. They are ovate to short ovate and slightly glossy. The ground color is snowy white or very pale greenish white, and is handsomely spotted and blotched with "auburn," "bay," "argus brown," "Mars brown," or "mummy brown," with undertones of "brownish drab," or "light vinaceous-drab." On some eggs the drab marks are the most prevalent, with fewer but more prominent spots or blotches of dark brown shades, such as "Mars brown" and "mummy brown." Others have spots of "auburn" and "bay" so concentrated that they form a solid band around the large end. In addition a few small scrawls of brownish black are often found. Generally speaking the markings tend to form a wreath, but some eggs are spotted more or less evenly all over the surface. The measurements of 50 eggs average 17.2 by 12.8 millimeters; the eggs showing the four extremes measure 18.0 by 13.6, 17.0 by 13.7, 15.6 by 12.5, and 17.1 by 12.0 millimeters (Harris).

*Young.*—We have no information on incubation and very little on the care of the young. The male has been seen to go onto the nest, and evidently shares occasionally in the duty of incubation. Both parents help in feeding the young, as noted by Mrs. Nice (1932) at the nest she was watching. When Mrs. Nice's daughter climbed a tree near the nest, the female "assumed a peculiar attitude, her tail outspread and dropped at right angles to her body, her wings flipping rapidly and occasionally held stiffly up or down. The excitement caused the young to jump out on the ground where they could not be found."

*Plumages.*—Dr. Dwight (1900) calls the natal down sepia-brown, and in speaking of the males, describes the juvenal plumage as "above, dark sepia-brown obscurely streaked on the back with clove-brown. Wings and tail clove-brown edged with olive-buff, the tertiaries and coverts with white forming two wing bands at tips of greater and median coverts; the outer three rectrices largely white. Below, white, washed with wood brown or buff on breast and sides, spotted, except on chin, abdomen and crissum, with dull sepia. Superciliary stripe cream-buff, spot on upper and under eyelid white; lores and auriculars dusky."

A partial postjuvenal molt begins early in August, involving the contour plumage and the wing coverts but not the rest of the wings or the tail. This produces the first winter plumage, which he describes as "above, deep yellowish olive-gray, flecked on the crown and streaked on the back with black; obscure median crown stripe straw-yellow; rump and upper tail coverts black, edged with olive-gray. Wing coverts clove-brown edged with olive-gray and tipped with white forming two broad wing bands. Below, straw-yellow brightening to orange-tinged lemon on the throat, fading to buffy white on the crissum and narrowly streaked on the sides with black veiled by yellow edgings. Superciliary stripe and postauricular region lemon-yellow orange-tinged. Auriculars, rictal streak and transocular stripe olive-gray mixed with black. Suborbital spot yellowish white."

He says that the first nuptial plumage is "acquired by a partial prenuptial moult which involves most of the body plumage (except posteriorly), the wing coverts and sometimes the tertiaries but not the rest of the wings nor the tail. The full orange and black plumage is assumed, young and old becoming practically indistinguishable, the orange throat equally intense in both, the wings and tail usually browner in the young bird and the primary coverts a key to age."

The adult winter plumage is acquired by a complete postnuptial molt in July, and "differs little from the first winter dress, but the yellow more distinctly orange, the transocular and rictal streaks, the crown and auriculars distinctly black, veiled with orange tips, the streaking below heavier and broader, the wings and tail blacker and the edgings grayer." The adult nuptial plumage is acquired as in the young bird; this molt evidently begins in February, while the birds are in their winter quarters, and is usually finished before they reach their summer homes.

Of the females, Dr. Dwight says:

The plumages and moults correspond to those of the male. In juvenal plumage the wing edgings are usually duller, the first winter plumage being similar to that of the male but browner, the yellow tints nearly lost and the streakings obscure and grayish. The first nuptial plumage, assumed by a more or less limited prenuptial moult, is grayer above and paler below, except on the chin and throat where new pale orange feathers contrast with the worn and faded ones of the breast. The adult winter plumage is practically the same as the male first winter, the auriculars and transocular stripe usually duller. The adult nuptial plumage is brighter below than the first nuptial and with more spotting on the crown, but the black head and bright orange throat of the male are never acquired.

*Food.*—The Blackburnian warbler is mainly insectivorous like other wood warblers, feeding almost entirely on the forest pests that are so injurious to the trees. F. H. King (1883), writing of its food in Wisconsin, says: "Of nine specimens examined, four had eaten nine small beetles; five, nineteen caterpillars; one, ants; and one, small winged insect. In the stomachs of three examined collectively, were found four caterpillars, four ants, one dipterous insect .09 of an inch long, one medium sized heteropterous insect, four large crane-flies, and one ichneumon-fly (?). Another bird had in its stomach one heteropterous insect (*Tingis*), nine small caterpillars, two leaf-beetles, and two large crane-flies."

Ora W. Knight (1908) writes: "In general I have found large quantities of the wing cases and harder body portions of beetles in the stomachs of such Blackburnian Warblers as I have dissected, also unidentifiable grubs, worms, larvae of various lepidopterous insects and similar material. As a rule they feed by passing from limb to limb and examining the foliage and limbs of trees, more seldom catching anything in the air."

R. W. Sheppard (1939), of Niagara Falls, Ontario, observed a male Blackburnian warbler in his garden for several days, November 5 to 11, 1938, that appeared to be traveling with two chickadees, among some willow trees. "An examination of the row of low willow trees which appeared to be so attractive to this particular warbler, revealed the presence of numbers of active aphids and innumerable newly laid aphis eggs, and it is probable that these insects and their eggs provided the major incentive for the repeated and prolonged visits of this very late migrant."

Henry D. Minot (1877) observed "a pair feeding upon ivy berries" on April 21, when insects were not yet common in Massachusetts.

*Behavior.*—William Brewster (1938) describes what he thought was the unique behavior of a female Blackburnian warbler at its nest, although a similar habit has been observed in other wood warblers. Even though the eggs "were perfectly fresh the female sat so closely that thumping and shaking the tree (a slender one) failed to start her, and when Watrous climbed it he nearly touched her before she slipped off. She then dropped like a stone to the ground over which she crawled and tumbled and fluttered with widespread tail and quivering wings much like a Water Thrush or Oven Bird and evidently with the hope of leading us away from the nest."

The Blackburnian is preeminently a forest warbler and a treetop bird. On migrations it frequents the tops of the trees in the deciduous forests, often in company with other wood warblers; and on its breeding grounds in the coniferous forests the male loves to perch on the topmost tip of some tall spruce and sing for long periods, his fiery breast gleaming in the sunlight. As his mate is probably sitting on her nest not far away, his serenity may be disturbed by the appearance of a rival; but the intruder in his territory is promptly driven away and he resumes his singing.

*Voice.*—Aretas A. Saunders has sent me the following study: "The song of the Blackburnian warbler is one that is usually of two distinct parts, the first a series of notes or 2-note phrases all on one pitch, and the second a faster series, or a trill, on a different pitch. It is very high in pitch, with a thin, wiry quality, rather unmusical, and not loud but penetrating.

"Of my 34 records, 25 have the second part higher in pitch than the first, while in the other 9 it is lower. I do not think, however, that this means that the higher ending is commoner, for there is reason to think that the difference is geographical. Of 11 records of migrating birds in Connecticut, 10 end in the higher pitch. Of 15 records from breeding birds in the Adirondacks, 13 end in the higher pitch; but of 8 records of breeding birds in Allegany State Park in western New York, only 2 end in the higher pitch, and 6 in the lower.

"In 20 of the records the first part of the song is of 2-note phrases, but the remainder is of single repeated notes. In 6 records, ending in a higher pitch, the final trill slurs upward in pitch, suggesting the ending of a typical parula song in form. In 10 of the records the second part is much shorter than the first.

"Songs vary from 1⅖ to 2⅖ seconds, averaging a little longer than those of other species of this genus. The number of notes in songs, excepting those with trills, varies from 7 to 25, and averages 14. Pitch varies from D'''' to F'''', one and a half tones more than an octave. It ranks with the blackpolled and bay-breasted warblers in the very high pitch of its upper notes but shows more variation in pitch than either.

"The song of this bird ceases earlier in summer than most others. In 14 summers in Allegany Park, the average date of the last song was July 12, the earliest July 4, 1929, and the latest July 22, 1935. I have never heard singing in late summer after the molt."

Francis H. Allen sends me his impressions as follows: "Like so many of our warblers, the Blackburnian has two song-forms, but both are subject to great individual variation. An extremely high note is almost an invariable characteristic. In one form it is the closing note, and in the other it ends each repeated phrase of a succession that constitutes the main part of the song. The first song resembles that of the parula, but ends with this high note, while the main part is less buzzy and more what I might call pebbly in character. The second I have been accustomed to call the chickawee song because of the repeated phrase which suggests those syllables. At Sherburne, Vt., in June, 1907, I found the Blackburnians singing a song that I rendered as *chĭ-ee chĭ-ee chĭ-ee chĭ-ee chip*. Another rendering of the same or a similar song, recorded at Jaffrey, N. H., May 30, 1910, was *serwée serwée serwée serwée serwíp*, with the emphasis on the *wip*. At New London, N. H., in June, 1931, where this was perhaps the commonest of the warblers, I was particularly impressed by the variability of both the songs. In some, the very high and attenuated notes were so short that for some time I failed to recognize their source. One bird sang *chiddle chiddle chiddle chick-a chick-a cheet*. At Hog Island in Muscongus Bay, Maine, in June, 1936, I heard a song of which only a sweet *weet weet weet weet* carried to a distance, but of which, heard near at hand, the end was found to be a short, confused succession of high-pitched, dry notes concluding with a very high, short note. This was, I think, the most pleasing performance I have ever heard from this species."

Mrs. Nice (1932) mentions three different songs; the commonest and shortest, like the parula's in form, lasts for one second and is given at intervals of 7½ to 10 seconds; the rarest and longest lasts for two seconds and is given at intervals of 10 or 14 seconds.

A. D. DuBois tells me that the Blackburnian warbler "has a song not unlike that of the dickcissel in its general form, although much subdued in volume." Gerald Thayer wrote to Dr. Chapman (1907) of two or more different songs of this warbler, and says:

Its voice is thin, but, unlike the Parula's, exquisitely smooth, in all the many variations of its two (or more) main songs. * * * Even the tone quality is not quite constant, for though it never, in my experience, varies toward huskiness, it does occasionally range toward full-voiced richness. Thus I have heard a Blackburnian that began his otherwise normal song with two or three clear notes much like those of the most full and smooth-voiced performance of the American Redstart's, and another that began so much like a Nashville that I had to hear him several times, near by, to be convinced that there was not a Nashville chiming in. Sometimes, again, tone and delivery are varied toward excessive languidness; and sometimes, contrariwise, toward sharp, wiry "thinness."

*Enemies.*—Dr. Friedmann (1929) calls the Blackburnian warbler "a very uncommon victim of the Cowbird." Dr. Merriam (1885) records a nest of this warbler that was 84 feet from the ground, containing four warbler's eggs and one of the cowbird, of which Friedmann remarks: "This is probably the altitude record for a Cowbird's egg, bettering by some twenty feet my highest record at Ithaca, a Cowbird's egg in a nest of a Pine Warbler about sixty feet up."

Harold S. Peters (1936) records two species of lice, *Menacanthus chrysophaeum* (Kellogg) and *Ricinus* pallens (Kellogg), and one mite, *Proctophyllodes* sp., as external parasites of this warbler.

*Field marks.*—The adult male Blackburnian warbler in spring plumage is unmistakable, with its black upper parts, large white patch in the wings, orange stripe in center of the crown and another over the eye, and, especially, the flaming orange throat and breast. The female in the spring and the male in the fall are similarly marked, but the colors are much duller.  The colors of young birds in the fall are even duller, and the back is brownish, but the white outer web of the basal half of the outer tail feather should indicate the species.

*Fall.*—Early in August, young and old birds begin to gather into flocks preparing to migrate, and before the end of that month most of them have left their breeding grounds.  All through August and most of September, we may see them drifting through our deciduous woods in mixed flocks with other species of warblers.  These migrating flocks are generally so high up in the tree tops and are so active in their movements that it is not easy to identify them in their dull winter plumages.

By early October, most of the Blackburnian warblers have passed beyond the United States, en route to their winter home in South America.  Professor Cooke (1904) says: "By the middle of October the earliest migrants have reached Venezuela and Ecuador.  The main army of the Blackburnians pass the south end of the Alleghenies between September 25 and October 5, and during the first two weeks of October are moving through San José, Costa Rica, and by early in November are settled for the winter in Perú."

Dickey and van Rossem (1838) refer to it as a "fairly common fall migrant and very rare winter visitant in the Arid Lower Tropical Zone" in El Salvador, but "not seen in spring."

*Winter.*—Dr. Alexander F. Skutch contributes the following notes: "Rarely recorded, and apparently only as a bird of passage, in Guatemala, the Blackburnian warbler is a moderately abundant winter resident in Costa Rica.  Here it passes the winter months on both slopes of the Cordillera, from about 1,500 to 6,000 feet above sea-level, but is far more abundant above than below 3,000 feet.  It is found in mid-winter both in heavy forest and among scattered tall trees. Although the birds appear to arrive in flocks in late August or September, they soon disperse through the woodland and show slight sociability.  Yet one or two may at times join a mixed flock of Tennessee warblers and other small birds.  Restlessly active, the Blackburnian warbler forages well above the ground, where it is difficult to see.  I have never heard its song in Central America.

"Early dates of fall arrival are: Guatemala—Chimoxan (Griscom), October 1; Panajachel (Griscom), October 4.  Costa Rica—San José (Cherrie), September 8; San José (Underwood), Septem 10; La Hondura (Carriker), September 19; San Isidro de Coronado, September 8, 1935; Vara Blanca, August 19, 1937; Cartago, September 13, 1938; Murcia, September 14, 1941; Basin of El General, September

16, 1936; Ujarrás (Carriker), September 12. Ecuador—Volcán Tungurahua, 7,400 feet, October 12, 1939.

"Late dates of spring departure from Central America are: Costa Rica—Basin of El General, March 25, 1936, March 13, 1937 and April 18, 1943; Vara Blanca, May 7, 1938; Pejivalle, April 23, 1941; Bonilla (Basulto), April 10. Guatemala—Finca Sepacuite (Griscom), May 10."

## DISTRIBUTION

*Range.*—Southern Canada east of the Great Plains to Central Perú.

*Breeding range.*—The Blackburnian warbler breeds **north** to southern Manitoba (Lake St. Martin and Berens Island, Lake Winnipeg); central Ontario (Lac Seul, Lake Abitibi, and North Bay; has occurred at Trout Lake); and central Quebec (Blue Sea Lake, Lake Albanel, rarely; Lake St. John and Gaspé; possibly Pointe de Monts and Natashquan). **East** to eastern Quebec (Gaspé); eastern New Brunswick (Bathurst and Tabusintac); and eastern Nova Scotia (Antigonish and Halifax). **South** to Nova Scotia (Halifax); southern Maine (Calais, Lewiston, and Portland); Massachusetts (Cambridge, Springfield, and Sheffield); northern New Jersey (Kittatinny Mountains); central Pennsylvania (Mauch Chunk and Carlisle); and south through the mountains of Maryland, Virginia, West Virginia, North and South Carolina and Tennessee to northern Georgia (Brasstown Bald and Burnt Mountain); western Pennsylvania (Leasureville and Meadville); northeastern Ohio (Pymatuning Swamp and possibly Geneva); northern Michigan (Bay City and Wequetonsing); northern Wisconsin (New London, Unity and Ladysmith); and northern Minnesota (Elk River, Onamia, and Itasca Park). **West** to northwestern Minnesota (Itasca Park) and southeastern Manitoba (Winnipeg and Lake St. Martin).

A possible future extension of range westward is seen in records from Saskatchewan: it was recorded four times near Indian Head 1888–1901; one at Last Mountain Lake in 1920, at Lake Johnston in 1922; and at Emma Lake in the summer of 1939, possibly breeding.

*Winter range.*—The Blackburnian warbler is reported to winter commonly in Costa Rica, but as yet has been found in Panamá only as a migrant. In South America it is found **north** to northern Colombia (Santa Marta region); and central northern Venezuela (Rancho Grande). **East** to northwestern Venezuela (Rancho Grande, Mérida, and Páramo de Tamá); the eastern slope of the Andes in Colombia (Pamplona, Bogotá, and San Antonio); Ecuador (Mount Sumaca, Machay, and Zamora); and Perú (Chinchao and Huambo). **South** to central Perú (Huambo and Anquimarca). **West** to western Perú (Anquimarca and Tambillo); Ecuador (Ambato, Quito, and Parambo); and Colombia (Concordia, Medellín, and the Santa Marta region). It is casual in migration in the Bahamas and Cuba.

*Migration.*—Late dates of spring departure from the winter home are: Perú—Chelpes, April 22. Ecuador—Quito, May 10. Venezuela—Rancho Grande, April 22. Colombia—La Porquera, April 24. Costa Rica—Vera Blanca, May 7.

Early dates of spring arrival are: Panamá—Garachiné, March 5. Florida—Pensacola, April 5. Alabama—Hollins, April 4. Georgia—Athens, March 29. South Carolina—Aiken, April 17. North Carolina—Weaverville, April 16. Virginia—Lynchburg, April 25. West Virginia—White Sulphur Springs, April 17. District of Columbia—Washington, April 23. Pennsylvania—Renovo, April 27. New York—Rochester, April 26. Massachusetts—Melrose, April 29. Vermont—Wells River, April 30. Maine—Portland, May 4. New Brunswick—Scotch Lake, May 5. Quebec—Montreal, May 10. Louisiana—Lake Borgne, March 27. Mississippi—Gulfport, March 27. Tennessee—Chattanooga, March 31. Kentucky—Lexington, April 12. Indiana—Brookville, April 15. Ohio—Oberlin, April 19. Michigan—Hillsdale, April 22. Ontario—London, April 27. Arkansas—Huttig, April 15. Missouri—Bolivar, April 20. Iowa—Davenport, April 28. Wisconsin—Unity, April 27. Minnesota—Waseca, April 30. Texas—Boerne, March 31. Nebraska—Stapleton, May 1. South DakotaVermilion, May 3. Monitoba—Aweme, May 14.

Late dates of spring departure of transients are: Florida—Pensacola, May 9. Alabama—Autaugaville, May 12. Georgia—Athens, May 7. South Carolina—Spartanburg, May 12. North Carolina—Greensboro, May 17. Virginia—Charlottesville, May 28. District of Columbia—Washington, June 3. Pennsylvania—Norristown, May 30. New York—New York, June 7. Louisiana—New Orleans, April 23. Mississippi—Corinth, May 12. Kentucky—Lexington, May 16. Illinois—Lake Forest, June 9. Ohio—Toledo, June 12. Arkansas—Rogers, May 12. Missouri—Kansas City, May 30. Iowa—Sigourney, June 1. Texas—Commerce, May 18. Nebraska—Fairbury, May 26. South Dakota—Yankton, June 2.

Late dates of fall departure are: Saskatchewan—Last Mountain Lake, September 1. Nebraska—Fairbury, October 14. Texas—Brownsville, October 2. Minnesota—Saint Paul, September 25. Wisconsin—Madison, September 27. Ontario—Hamilton, October 3. Michigan—Ann Arbor, October 8. Indiana—Waterloo, October 17. Kentucky—Danville, October 16. Missouri—St. Louis, October 6. Tennessee—Memphis, October 28. Arkansas—Chicat, October 4. Mississippi—Eudora, October 24. Louisiana—New Orleans, October 9. Quebec—Hatley, September 30. New Brunswick—Scotch Lake, September 28. Maine—Phillips, September 17. New Hampshire—

Hanover, September 24. Massachusetts—Wellesley, October 23. New York—Canandaigua, October 12. Pennsylvania—Berwyn, October 19. District of Columbia—Washington, October 10. West Virginia—Bluefield, October 8. Virginia—Sweet Briar, November 1. Georgia—Tifton, November 2. Alabama—Birmingham, October 25. Florida—Arcadia, October 30. Cuba—Bosque de la Habana, October 30.

Early dates of fall arrival are: North Dakota—Argusville, August 23. Texas—Commerce, August 28. Illinois—Glen Ellyn, August 19. Ohio—Little Cedar Point, July 31. Kentucky—Versailles, August 31. Tennessee—Nashville, August 29. Mississippi—Bay St. Louis, August 11. New York—New York, August 11. Pennsylvania—Berwyn, August 19. District of Columbia—Washington, August 2. Virginia—Charlottesville, August 10. North Carolina—Mount Mitchell, July 30. Georgia—Savannah, August 10. Florida—Key West, July 29. Cuba—Santiago de las Vegas, September 20. Costa Rica—San José, August 17. Colombia—Santa Isabel, September 22. Venezuela—Escorial, October 14. Ecuador—Tumbaco, October 12. Perú—Tambillo, November 19.

*Casual records.*—A specimen of Blackburnian warbler was collected at Frederickshaab, Greenland, on October 16, 1845. One was taken at Ogden, Utah, in September 1871, and another near Fort Bayard, N. M., in May 1876. On August 21, 1924, a male was watched closely for sometime near Libby, Mont.

*Egg dates.*—Maine: 5 records, June 2 to 17.

New York: 23 records, May 29 to July 6; 16 records, June 7 to 17, indicating the height of the season.

New Hampshire: 6 records, May 23 to June 18.

Pennsylvania: 5 records, May 28 to June 9.

Quebec: 2 records, June 15 and 20.

### DENDROICA DOMINICA DOMINICA (Linnaeus)

### EASTERN YELLOW-THROATED WARBLER

CONTRIBUTED BY ALEXANDER SPRUNT, JR.

PLATES 42, 43

### HABITS

One of the botanical attractions of the South is the Spanish moss (*Tillandsia usneoides*) that drapes with its graceful, swaying strands the cypresses in the lagoons and backwaters, the live oaks that stand in spectacular avenues on the approaches of so many plantations of the Carolina Low Country and in magnificent groves throughout the Coastal Plain, and even the pines that forest wide reaches of Georgia and northern Florida. To many ornithologists the thought of this

Spanish moss brings to mind the birds partial to it, particularly the eastern yellow-throated warbler.  Indeed, in the coastal part of the range of this bird the two are all but synonymous, so that where the moss is scarce, so, too, is the eastern yellow-throated warbler.  Since childhood I have thought of this little gray and yellow sprite, one of the handsomest of a handsome tribe, as the animated spirit of the Spanish-moss country.

*Spring.*—The eastern yellow-throated warbler is much less migratory than many species of its genus.  In the southern portion of its range it is a permanent resident, though of course, quiet at that season and therefore difficult to find; but it occurs throughout the year and can be seen on almost any day in winter from the Charleston, S. C., area southward to Lake Okeechobee, Fla.

In Florida, though it is resident in much of the state, a marked increase of migrants from the south occurs in late February and early March.  Arthur H. Howell (1932) states that "the beginning of spring migration is indicated by the appearance of the birds at Sombrero Key Light March 11th."  He also states that F. M. Chapman noted arrivals at Gainesville on March 2.  (Some birds are mated by March 11 in the vicinity of Charleston.)  Thus, the spring migration seems a rather erratic and long-drawn-out movement.

In the Pensacola region of Florida, F. M. Weston (MS.) writes: "Birds that have wintered commence singing, and thus become conspicuous, early in March.  Incoming migrants gradually add to the number until, by the first of April, the species is common and widely distributed in all areas where Spanish moss is present.  Howell considers this species as one of the typical birds of the pine forests, but in this region, where the moss is never found in pure stands of pine, the bird is absent from the pine woods.  In the Dead Lakes area, south of Marianna, Fla., a drowned cypress swamp, the cypresses are covered with dense masses of moss and the yellow-throated warbler is one of the characteristic birds."

Arrival dates in Georgia are similar to those in South Carolina.  Around Charleston, there are comparatively few birds in evidence from November until late February, though individuals may be seen throughout this period.  The barrier islands, typified by Bull's Island, seem to be favorite wintering localities.  In late February the song period begins, coinciding with a distinct influx from the south, and soon the birds seem almost everywhere.  Arthur T. Wayne (1910) puts the twenty-seventh of the month as the advent of the spring migration in Charleston.  This coincides with all my observations, though some variation may occur when the spring is early or late.

In North Carolina the bird is much more common in the coast region than the interior, but does occur scatteringly in the middle portion of the state and sometimes considerably to the westward. It is absent in the mountains but a few may be noted in the valleys of the foothills. According to the findings of Pearson and the Brimleys (1942) it appears about Raleigh on March 9. Probably the coastal areas are visted earlier, perhaps by March 1. Uncertainty prevails regarding the arrival of birds in the western parts of the state. These authors quote T. D. Burleigh as stating that the earliest date near Asheville is March 28, 1935, and that "at no time were any seen on the mountainsides."

In Virginia one finds this warbler appearing in the Tidewater area "as early as March 20th," according to H. H. Bailey (1913). May T. Cooke (1929) states that it usually comes to the Washington region around April 15, the earliest record being March 30. Its summer status there is characterized as "local"; moist woodlands along the Potomac River are its favorite spots. Further inland, Ruskin H. Freer (MS.) says that he has seen it but twice at Lynchburg, on April 11, 1933, and September 30, 1930. Lynchburg, in the foothills of the Blue Ridge, is probably a western limit.

Professor E. A. Smyth never saw it in Montgomery County and J. J. Murray (MS.) has not recorded it about Lexington in Rockbridge County (MS.), localities in the Shenandoah Valley of Virginia. According to Dr. Murray "the bird is unknown west of the Blue Ridge in Virginia. It is a migrant in the foothills and upper Piedmont on the eastern side of the Blue Ridge. From Washington south through central Virginia it is an uncommon summer resident in the eastern third of the State, becoming more common as the coast is approached, but even in the tidewater region and on the Eastern Shore it is abundant only locally."

My experience with this warbler in Virginia is limited to the southern portion of the Eastern Shore. There, in the area about Eastville, Cheriton, and Cape Charles during June and half of July 1940, I found it fairly numerous in the woodlands but discovered no nests. This locality appears to be the extreme northern limit of the Spanish moss for only a few bedraggled clumps were noted in the woods near Eastville on the Chesapeake Bay side of the peninsula. This moss ceases to be prevalent as one comes to the bay on the Norfolk side and the dejected evidences of the growth across that body of water suggest that it may have had its origin in windblown shreds that gained and maintain a precarious foothold.

*Nesting*—It is in its domestic habits that *dominica* exhibits its unalterable affinity for *Tillandsia usneoides* where the ranges coincide. The nest is rarely placed anywhere except in a clump of it, and the tree concerned is usually an oak, as this species offers more foothold for the Spanish moss than others and, as a consequence, is more heavily draped. Although I have found nests both in pines and cypresses, there is little question but that the live oak holds them more often than any other tree. The long plantation avenues are splendid sites, and Arthur T. Wayne once told me that he had climbed every tree in the long approach to Oakland Plantation in Christ Church Parish near Charleston, for nests of this bird!

The height at which the nest is placed varies from 10 or 12 feet to 50 or 75, and in some cases to nearly 100. The lowest nest I ever found was in my yard (in 1943) ; it was built in a clump of moss in a cassina bush (*Ilex vomitoria*) barely 3½ feet from the ground. However, the average height might be put at about 35 feet.

Nest building materials are not of wide choice, usually consisting of fine grasses, caterpillar silk, weed stems, and plant down, with a lining of plant down or sometimes feathers. The moss among which the nest is suspended is woven into the structure to some extent. Horsehair and skeletonized leaves are sometimes employed. The nest is fairly deeply cupped and averages about 3 inches in outside diameter, 2½ in inside diameter, and the same in depth. The writer has never seen a nest not built in moss, but Wayne (1910) gives two other locations in coastal South Carolina, his only such in 50 years of field work. Both were in short-leaf pines, one 45 and the other 50 feet up, and both were hidden in masses of needles and burs, invisible from below. One of these nests is in the Brewster collection and the other in J. E. Thayer's.

Dr. E. E. Murphey, writing of the bird in the Savannah River Valley of Georgia (1937), states that it prefers moss "whenever it is present" but adds, "contrary to the experience of Arthur T. Wayne in the coastal area, it breeds also in pine woods which at places come very close to the margins of the swamps * * * Here the Yellow-throated Warbler nests not uncommonly, building far out on the end of the horizontal limbs, well concealed by the needles." He states that "two broods are usually reared." W. H. LaPrade, Jr. (1922) describes the nesting in the Atlanta area as similar to that noted by Dr. Murphey about Augusta. In the coastal strip and the offshore islands conditions identical with those in South Carolina prevail.

In the latter State birds are usually mated by March 11. Nest building is begun by the middle of the month unless the season is delayed or adverse weather hinders operations, in which case nests are not found at times until early April. Georgia and Florida nestings correspond closely. In areas where Spanish moss is not found, *dominica* reverts to saddling its nest on the horizontal branches of trees. Pearson and the Brimleys (1942) state that in the Raleigh, N. C., area the nest is frequently constructed in pines "at a height of from 20 to 40 feet." They also say that in the coastal region where the cypress occurs the bird "frequently nests in the long, gray moss hanging from the trees." North Carolina nesting commences in late April.

The nest is constructed mostly by the female, sometimes completely so, but D. J. Nicholson (1929) has seen the male assisting in Florida. In the spring of 1942 a nest was built in a banner of moss no more than 20 feet from the porch of my home, at the extremity of a drooping live-oak limb. The female brought material as often as twice a minute, disappearing completely within the moss clump which could be seen bulging now and then with her movements. She was utterly unconcerned by observers on the porch, even the noise made by children not disturbing her in the least. The male sang constantly nearby.

Two broods are raised in coastal South Carolina. The young of the first are fully fledged by April 22, according to Wayne. The second nest is begun soon after the first brood is away. The yellow-throated warbler will, of course, lay again if accident befalls the nest and eggs. Little time is lost in the interim and illustrative of this tenacity of purpose are some interesting notes of C. S. Brimley (1943) dealing with experiments made by him and his brother, H. H. Brimley of Raleigh, N. C. On April 25, 1890 they collected a set of four eggs from the nest in a pine tree, 42 feet up. Four days later (April 29) another nest was being built in a smaller pine nearby, at an elevation of 47 feet. On May 12 a set of eggs was taken from it and three days later (May 15) the birds again began to build, this time in a very slender pine which had to be stayed with ropes when eggs were removed from the nest on May 26. Two days later the fourth nest was started in a large pine, 44 feet up. On June 7 additional eggs were secured. All sets consisted of four eggs. No further attempts were made on this persevering pair but "they may have built a fifth nest * * * for all we know to the contrary."

Although it seems remarkable that Audubon apparently failed to remark particularly on the moss-nesting habits of this warbler, it will be recalled that his observations seem to have been made largely in Louisiana, for he stresses this State in his account of the species; but he could hardly have failed to observe it elsewhere in the South, particularly on his visits to Rev. John Bachman in Charleston. Of the nest Audubon (1841) says that it is "placed on a horizontal branch of a cypress, twenty, thirty, or even fifty feet above the ground, and is with difficulty discerned from below, as it resembles a knot or a tuft of moss." Certainly, moss is abundant in Louisiana and it would seem that the birds there share this preference despite the fact that the form of this warbler found there is *albilora*.

*Eggs.*—[AUTHOR'S NOTE: Dr. Chapman (1907) says that the yellow-throated warbler lays 4 or 5 eggs, but very rarely 5, and adds:

"Ground color a dull greenish gray-white, in a large series the peculiar color of the markings seem to tinge the ground color; the markings are very mixed, numerous under shell marks, in the form of blotches and specks, of pale lavender and purplish gray overlaid with heavier surface markings of wine-red, umber and deeper shades of purplish gray and blackish. The heaviest markings are at the larger end, which is sometimes well wreathed, with many spots and specks over rest of egg." The measurements of 50 eggs average 17.1 by 13.0 millimeters; the eggs showing the four extremes measure **19.0** by 13.6, 17.6 by **14.0**, 15.4 by 12.7, and 16.0 by **11.9** millimeters.]

*Plumages.*—[AUTHOR'S NOTE: Dr. Dwight (1900) describes the juvenal plumage, in which the sexes are apparently alike, as "above olive-brown with dull black streaking. Below, dull white, streaked with clove-brown chiefly anteriorly." A postjuvenal molt, beginning early in June in Florida, and involving the contour plumage and the wing coverts but not the rest of the wings or the tail, produces the first winter plumages. These are much like those of the adults, but are generally more brownish, the female being browner than the male. The yellow throat is assumed at this molt.

The first nuptial plumage is acquired by wear, the brownish wash wearing away and the back becoming grayer and the black markings clearer. Young birds are now indistinguishable from adults, except by the browner and more worn wings.

Adults have one complete postnuptial molt in midsummer, after which the fully adult plumage is assumed, the colors of the female being similar to those of the male but duller.]

*Food*—The food of the yellow-throated warbler has apparently not been well investigated. Little appears in the literature, an illustration of the need to learn more of the diet of small, woodland birds. Records of the examination of seven stomachs reveal that insects compose most of its diet, for according to Howell (1932) "beetles, moths and their larvae, flies, bugs, grasshoppers, grouse locusts, crickets, scale insects, and spiders" are included in the food. Witmer Stone (1937) in writing of the first observance of this warbler at Cape May Point, N. J., on July 13, 1920, states that he saw it take "a green caterpillar about an inch in length." D. J. Nicholson has noted (1929) that while watching one of these birds in Volusia County, Fla., he saw it eat at least ten "worms" in a few minutes as it searched the trees near where he sat.

I have often watched these warblers feeding in my yard and have seen them take small, active caterpillars on numerous occasions. There seems little doubt that scale insects are often taken, as the yellow-throated warbler, creeping about the limbs of trees as it does, undoubtedly finds many of these tiny, but destructive pests. There can be little question as to its benefit to agriculture.

*Behavior*—There is much that is reminiscent of the brown creeper in the habits of the yellow-throated warbler. Its actions are deliberate and methodical, with none, or very little, of the nervous energy so characteristic of many species of *Dendroica*. As a result it is easier to watch than many other warblers, and its technique of hunting frequently brings it close to the observer. Pearson and the Brimleys (1942) state that it confines its creeping search to the limbs of trees, omitting the trunks altogether. However I have seen this warbler in my yard, feeding on the trunks of both pines and oaks. In this posture, it acts almost exactly like the black-and-white warbler (*Mniotilta varia*) and the brown creeper (*Certhia familiaris*). D. J. Nicholson of Orlando, Fla. (1929), mentions that he has seen them feeding on the "mossy trunks" of trees.

Milton P. Skinner (1928) writes:

> Yellow-throated warblers are gentle and friendly, but are not really socially inclined, either toward other members of their own kind or toward other species. * * * In the trees, their movements are quick, nervous and active, and they are very neat and trim in appearance for they spend much time in preening * * * As usual with warblers, these little birds are skillful insect catchers, and eat house flies, mosquitoes, ants, crickets, beetles and many other varieties of the smaller insects. Once I saw one on an artificial feeding station eating bread crumbs.

> These warblers seem even fonder of bathing than most other warblers. They go regularly and often to their baths, and after bathing they spend several minutes carefully preening their feathers.

*Voice*—The song of the yellow-throated warbler is one of its distinctive characteristics. Completely unlike the thready, insectlike notes of many of its family, it is difficult to describe verbally, and interpretations of it must necessarily vary according to impressions made on human ears. That it is loud, with a definitely ringing character, is agreed upon by all, and in this respect resembles the beautiful song of the prothonotary warbler (*Protonotaria citrea*) another dweller of the cypress lagoons.

R. T. Peterson (1939) says that the song is "slightly suggestive" of those of the indigo bunting (*Passerina cyanea*) and the Louisiana water-thrush (*Seiurus motacilla*), although I had not noticed this resemblance, and describes the notes as "starting with several clear, slurred notes and dropping slightly down the scale." This is true; the preliminary or "clear" notes vary in number from five to eight, and are run together at the end. F. M. Weston (MS.) says that there are "several distinct repetitions of a single note, ending weakly in an anticlimax trill," also a satisfactory description. Rendered into words (always inaccurate and often misleading) it has been written as *ching-ching-ching-chicker-churwee*. F. M. Chapman (1907) remarks that he was familiar with the song for some years before being impressed

with its resemblance to that of *S. motacilla*, and follows with the
statement that it is not so much the form of the notes themselves "as
their wild, ringing, carrying quality which recalls the song of the
water-thrush," in which quality a resemblance is readily under-
standable, and further says that the song has been compared to that of
the indigo bunting "not without reason." Howell (1932) simply
characterizes it as "loud and attractive," and also compares it with that
of the indigo bunting and the water-thrush.

Aretas A. Saunders (MS.) writes: "The song is bright, musical and
lively, beginning with high-pitched two-note phrases, sounding something like *cheeka-cheeka-cincha-cincha*, and then dropping down in
pitch in a series of rapid notes. It is fairly loud, with a clear ringing
quality." This is much the best description I have seen of this highly
individual song.

This warbler is an indefatigable songster. From early March
through May (about Charleston) it sings almost incessantly, practically from dawn to dusk. Often only seconds intervene between the
renditions. As June approaches, the frequency of its singing drops
sharply, and by the middle of that month only a very occasional song
is heard.

*Enemies.*—The yellow-throated warbler is open to the various dan-
gers which beset any of the smaller passerine species, but I know of
no single enemy that operates against it particularly. However, it
occasionally falls into a somewhat novel trap, becoming entangled in
tough spider-webs. In much of the cypress country of the southeast
the large Carolina silk spider makes its home and spins a magnificent
golden web high up amid the straight-trunked columns of the trees.
Some of these webs may stretch for many yards and on two occasions
I have seen this warbler caught therein. In one instance it was the
convulsive fluttering of the bird, apparently stationary in midair,
which attracted attention and after some moments of violent activity,
it succeeded in breaking the strands which held it. In the other, a
dead specimen was found inextricably entangled. Although two experiences such as this are by no means conclusive of any marked
mortality, it at least indicates that this may occur more often than
one would realize.

*Field marks.*—The brilliant yellow throat is always diagnostic and
is usually readily seen because of the bird's tameness and deliberate
actions. The grayness of the plumage is also apparent. A brief
glimpse is enough to establish its identity, even if the characteristic
song is unfamiliar.

*Fall.*—The yellow-throated warbler leaves the northern portions of
its range rather early. A very late specimen in the northern perim-

eter of the range was found dead by J. K. Potter (MS.) at Collingwood, N. J., on November 2, 1943. According to H. H. Bailey (1913)
departure dates for southeastern Virginia are in the "latter part of
July." May T. Cooke (1929) gives the latest occurrence about Washington as September 11, 1927. Near Lynchburg, R. H. Freer (MS.)
has seen it once on September 30. These are all considerably later
than Bailey's late July, and though very late, dates indicate that the
species may remain in Virigina well into August. C. W. Richmond
and J. D. Figgins secured specimens on July 28, 1889, at Four Mile
Run (near Washington), these being noted by William Rives (1890)
in his catalog of Virginia birds.

Late September sees the last migrants leaving central and western
North Carolina; the twenty-fifth of that month in the Raleigh area
and the twenty-eighth in the Asheville region (Pearson and the Brimleys, 1942). In the coastal area the average is probably a little later.

From South Carolina southward, as already noted, the species is a
permanent resident though the scattered wintering individuals are
quite probably birds that nested in the northern portion of the range.
About Charleston birds can be seen through July and August, but
being quiet are not nearly so noticeable, and their numbers fall off
in September and October. The young appear to leave much earlier,
indeed, shortly after the cessation of the song period in mid-June,
though doubtless early July sees some of them still here.

In Florida I have not seen this warbler south of the Lake Okeecho-
bee-Kissimmee Prairie region in winter but occasional individuals
are seen there throughout January and February in the "hammocks"
and they begin to sing in early March. In the western part of the
state F. M. Weston writes from Pensacola that the "fall migration is
hardly noticeable in this region, for the birds have been silent and
inconspicuous since June, and the migratory movement consists merely
of a quiet withdrawal from the area." Of its winter status in that
area he follows with the statement that the "yellow-throated warbler
winters regularly in small numbers, at which season it is confined to
the live oak groves. In order to find it, an observer must scan
carefully every chickadee-titmouse group found in situable situations.
The composition of such a group would be half-a-dozen each of the
tufted titmouse, Florida chickadee, myrtle warbler and ruby-crowned
kinglet, a blue-gray gnatcatcher, a blue-headed vireo, an orange-
crowned warbler and one or two yellow-throated warblers."

Alexander Wilson (1832) in speaking of the first specimen of this
warbler he ever saw (in Georgia) stated that it was late in February
and was the first spring appearance of the species in that area, following this at once with the explanation that "they leave the U. S.

about three months during winter and, consequently, go to no great distance." He was in one of his few errors here for the warbler is, as we have abundantly seen, present in southeastern United States through the whole of the winter.

## DISTRIBUTION

*Range.*—Southeastern United States to Panamá and the West Indies.

*Breeding range.*—The yellow-throated warbler breeds **north** to northern Illinois (Knoxville, Hennepin, Saint Charles, and possibly Waukegan); northern Indiana (Elkhart and Waterloo); northern and eastern Ohio (Wauseon, Sandusky, Cleveland, and Cadiz); northern West Virginia (Doddridge County); northern Maryland (Baltimore); and southern Delaware (Seaford and Frankford). Its occurrence, without indication of breeding has been reported north to Sigourney, Iowa; Lake Koshonong and Racine, Wis.; Kalamazoo, Battle Creek, and Detroit, Mich.; Frankfort Springs and Narberth, Pa.; Mamaroneck, N. Y.; Hartford, Conn.; and Dedham, Mass. **East** to southeastern Delaware (Frankford); and the Atlantic coast to central eastern Florida (Titusville). **South** to south-central and western Florida (Titusville, Bassinger, Punta Rossa, Tarpon Springs, St. Marks, and Pensacola); the Gulf coast of Mississippi and Louisiana to eastern and central Texas (Port Arthur, Houston, Brazoria County, San Antonio, and Ingram). **West** to eastern Texas (Ingram, Austin, Waco, Rhome, and Gainesville); central Oklahoma (Dougherty, Oklahoma City, and Ponca City); southeastern Kansas (Neosha Falls), central Missouri (Columbia); and western Illinois (Knoxville).

The territory as outlined is occupied by two geographic races: the eastern yellow-throated warbler (*D. d. dominica*) breeds from Maryland southward and east of the mountains; the sycamore yellow-throated warbler (*D. d. albilora*) breeds from the mountains westward.

*Winter range.*—The two races appear not to mingle in winter. The yellow-throated warbler winters **north** to northwestern Florida (Pensacola and St. Marks); and casually to southern Georgia (Thomasville and Brunswick). **East** to southeastern Georgia (Brunswick); the Bahamas (Watling and Great Inagua Islands); Dominican Republic (Samaná); Puerto Rico; and St. Thomas; casually to Montserrat. **South** to Montserrat, casually; Haiti (Port au Prince); and Jamaica. **West** to Jamaica; Grand Cayman; western Cuba (Isle of Pines and Habana); and western Florida (Pensacola).

The sycamore warbler winters regularly **north** to southern Sinaloa (Mazatlán); Nayarit (Tepic); southern Veracruz (Tlacotalpan); Yucatán (Progreso); and Quintana Roo (Cozumel Island). **East** to Quintana Roo (Cozumel Island and Xcopén); British Honduras

(Belize) ; central northern Honduras (Ruatán Island and Puerto Castilla) ; southeastern Nicaragua (Greytown) ; and central Costa Rica (San José and Cartago). **South** to Costa Rica. **West** to western Costa Rica (Cartago) ; western Guatemala (Dueñas and Totonicopán) ; western Guerrero (Acapulco) ; western Michoacán (Coahuayana) ; Colima (Colima) ; and southwestern Sinaloa (Mazatlán). It also winters in small numbers in Cameron County, Tex.

*Migration.*—Late dates of departure from the winter home are: Puerto Rico—Ponce, February 26. Haiti—Île à Vache, April 29. Cuba—Cienfuegos, April 15. Bahamas—New Providence, April 15. Veracruz—Tres Zapotes, March 25.

Early dates of spring arrival are: Alabama—Greensboro, March 10. Georgia—Augusta, March 2. South Carolina—Columbia, March 23. North Carolina—Raleigh, March 13. Virginia—Lawrenceville, March 19. District of Columbia—Washington, March 24.

Late dates of fall departure are: Ohio—Toledo, September 28. Indiana—Bloomington, October 9. Missouri—St. Louis, October 11. Kentucky—Bowling Green, October 5. Tennessee—Nashville, October 3. Arkansas—Helena, October 10. Mississippi—Biloxi, October 12. Louisiana—Monroe, October 16. Texas—Brownsville, October 8. District of Columbia—Washington, September 27. Virginia—Lynchburg, October 6. North Carolina—Chapel Hill, October 6. Georgia—Athens, October 11.

Early dates of fall arrival are: Bahamas—Nassau, July 26. Cuba—Guantánamo, July 11. Jamaica, August 16. Dominican Republic—Monte Viejo, August 26. Puerto Rico—Fortuna, August 28. Mexico—Chiapas, Ocote, August 13. Guatemala—San Lucas, August 7. Honduras—Truxillo, September 26. Costa Rica—San José, September 17.

*Casual records.*—A number of specimens of the sycamore warbler have been taken on the Atlantic seaboard.

*Egg dates.*—Florida : 11 records, April 17 to June 9 ; 7 records, April 20 to 29.

South Carolina : 31 records, April 2 to May 22 ; 21 records, April 14 to 26, indicating the hight of the season (Harris).

**DENDROICA DOMINICA ALBILORA Ridgway**

**SYCAMORE YELLOW-THROATED WARBLER**

PLATE 44

HABITS

This western form of the yellow-throated warbler makes its summer home in the Mississippi Valley, from southern Wisconsin and southern Michigan southward, and it winters in Mexico and Central America.

Although its winter range is so widely separated from that of the eastern form and its summer range, mainly west of the Alleghenies, is quite distinct, the two forms are very much alike in characters and habits. Ridgway (1902) describes it as similar to the yellow-throated warbler, "but with much smaller bill, the superciliary stripe more rarely yellow anteriorly, and with white areas on inner webs of lateral rectrices averaging decidedly larger."

Allison wrote to Dr. Chapman (1907) that in southern Louisiana, "it has a strong liking for woods shrouded in heavy festoons of Spanish moss, and, therefore, keeps much to the cypress swamps; but it is common in the less damp woods in the same regions; on the northern shores of Lake Pontchartrain it spreads slightly from the cypress swamp into the pines. It is essentially a bird of the larger trees, and swampy forest may be considered its typical habitat." M. G. Vaiden, of Rosedale, Miss., tells me that he always looks for the sycamore warbler in the cypresses, and that it is seldom found elsewhere, except on migrations.

Ridgway (1889) says of its haunts in Illinois: "The Sycamore Warbler is a common summer resident in the bottom-lands, where, according to the writer's experience, it lives chiefly in the large sycamore trees along or near water courses." In Indiana, according to A. W. Butler (1898), "the Sycamore Warbler does not depart from the vicinity of streams, even following small creeks, along which sycamores grow, for quite a distance towards their source. They seem to prefer these trees, spending much time among their highest branches, but they may also be found among all the trees fringing waterways, sometimes quite near the ground, and often are seen among our orchards, lawns, and even the shade trees along the streets of towns in the valleys."

It seems to be partial to the large, picturesque, stream-loving sycamores in other parts of its range, as far north and east as Michigan and Ohio, thus deserving its well-chosen name. In many places these fine trees have disappeared, and the warblers have become scare or have gone entirely.

*Spring.*—The sycamore yellow-throated warbler is one of the earliest wood warblers to enter the United States from its winter home, arriving in Louisiana around the first week in March, reaching Indiana about the middle of April, and appearing in Michigan as early as April 20. In Ohio, according to Dr. Wheaton (1882), "this is the first of the family to arrive in spring. It is always to be seen before the Yellow-rumped and Yellow Warblers make their appearance, sometimes before the last snow and ice. I have seen them in considerable numbers on the 13th of April, and have known of its occurrence as early as April 9th. When on their migrations they confine themselves almost exclusively to the trees which skirt the streams, and move northward by day with considerable rapidity."

The main migration route seems to be almost directly northeastward, from western México and Central America to western North Carolina and Ohio, and more directly northward through the broad Mississippi Valley to Michigan and Wisconsin. This is markedly different from the migration route of the eastern race, which migrates nearly northward along the Atlantic coast.

*Nesting.*—Whether the nest of the sycamore warbler is in a cypress or in a sycamore, it is always placed at a considerable height from the ground, for this is a treetop bird. Nests have been recorded at heights ranging from 10 to 120 feet above the ground, but probably most of them are between 30 and 60 feet up. Mr. Butler (1928) describes two Indiana nests of similar construction. One was—

built about 35 or 40 feet above the ground in a flat crotch, on an approximately horizontal limb of a large sycamore tree. * * * The nest measures as follows: Outside diameter 2.50 inches; inside diameter 1.65; outside height 2 inches; inside depth 1.75 inches. The heavier frame was composed of shreds of grapevine bark, bits of the covering and coarser fibre of weeds, mingled with which were many small pieces of cotton cord or ravelings. The nest was lined and its entire bottom was composed of the soft down obtained from dry sycamore balls. In fact the nest really had no foundation for the bottom, the lining material reaching through to the limb. [The other] was about 75 feet above the ground in a crotch of small branches toward the end of a sycamore limb which was not strong enough to bear one's weight. It was so hidden by the foliage that it could not be seen until some of the leaves fell this autumn.

A set of four eggs is in the Richard C. Harlow collection, taken by W. C. Avery, Greensboro, Ala., April 24, 1893. The nest was in a liquidambar tree, 26 feet up and 9 feet out from the body of the tree, on a horizontal branch and nearly concealed in the *Tillandsia* in which it was built. George Finlay Simmons (1925) says that in Texas the nests are sometimes built in an elm or a pecan tree, from 12 to 35 feet from the ground.

*Eggs.*—The sycamore warbler lays from 3 to 5 eggs; in most cases 4 eggs seem to complete the set. Mr. Simmons (1925) describes them as "dull greenish gray-white; marked with distinct and clouded blotches, specks, and under-shell markings of lavender, purplish-gray, umber, and brownish-red; and sometimes even blackish spots; usually wreathed about the larger end." The measurements of 10 eggs average 16.9 by 12.7 millimeters; the eggs showing the four extremes measure **17.6** by **12.1, 16.2** by 12.8, and 16.6 by **13.0** millimeters.

*Plumages.*—The sequence of plumages and molts is probably the same as for the yellow-throated warbler.

*Food.*—Very little seems to have been published on the food of this warbler, but it probably does not differ materially from that of the other wood warblers. Professor Aughey (1878) found remains of 15 locusts and 24 other insects in the stomach of one collected in Nebraska. A. H. Howell (1924) says: "Examination of 9 stomachs of this bird from Alabama showed its food to be mainly flies, beetles, ants and other Hymenoptera, and spiders."

*Behavior.*—Ridgway (1889) says that "in its motions, this warbler partakes much of the character of a creeper, often ascending or descending trunks of trees or following their branches, much in the manner of a *Mniotilta.*" Butler (1898) says that "its longer flights much resemble those of the Chipping Sparrow. Its shorter ones, as with quivering wings it beats rapid strokes when moving from limb to limb, remind one of the movements of the Kingbird." Referring to its general habits in Texas, Simmons (1925) says it is—

observed singly or in pairs, moving very slowly about in the tops of the trees, particularly the sycamores along streams, carefully keeping limbs and branches between itself and any chance observer. Movements very deliberate, sometimes stopping for several minues, *creeping* along by small hops, among upper branches, never on trunks or larger limbs; thus, in actions, strikingly different from most members of the warbler family. Usually keeps to the tops of the tallest trees; hops from one perch to another very slowly; occasionally comes down among the lower branches. Usually quiet, the song being uttered at wide intervals; however, at times in spring it may be heard almost constantly singing.

*Voice.*—Butler (1898) writes: "The song of the Sycamore Warbler, as I catch it, is as follows: *Twit, che-e, che-e, che-e, che-e, che-e, che-á.* This is about its usual length. The first syllable is abrupt, with rising inflection, then, after a slight pause, the remainder is uttered at the same pitch until the last syllable, which ends sharply with a slight rise in tone. The whole song is very unique. Its notes are clear and distinct, and it is pitched in such a key that it may be heard under favorable circumstances over a quarter of a mile."

Mr. Allison wrote to Dr. Chapman (1907) as follows: "The call-note is a rather lively chipping, like that of an agitated Parula Warbler, or perhaps somewhat more like that of Pine Warbler. The song is like the Indigo Bunting's, much softened, and with a falling cadence all the way through; thus: *See-wee, see-wee, see-wee, swee, swee, swee, swee*—the last four notes uttered more rapidly, but becoming fainter, until the last one is very indistinct."

Mrs. Nice (1931) writes: "The songs of this lovely warbler made one think of evergreen forests; they gave a wistful, haunting touch to the somber, leafless woods, where most of the bird notes were loud and ringing. The bird in the Oliver's woods in 1927 had two songs. 'A' was in a continuously descending scale except for the last note which was slightly higher than that preceding—*see see see see see see chérwer;* the ending was abrupt. 'B' was more musical; it consisted of four notes on the same pitch, then three descending, ending with one on a somewhat higher pitch. Both songs were given five and six times a minute."

*Winter.*—Dr. Skutch contributes the following note: "The sycamore warbler is a rare winter resident in Central America, infrequently recorded in both the highlands and the Caribbean lowlands. Although Griscom states that in Guatemala it is a common winter visitant, the statement scarcely seems supported by the paucity of published records. Carriker knew of but one specimen taken in Costa Rica. I have myself seen this bird only thrice during 12 years in Central America. On January 22, 1935, I found one in a flock of Townsend's and black-throated green warblers in the pine woods on the Finca Mocá, on the Pacific slope of Guatemala at 3,500 feet. My one Honduran record is of a bird seen among the coconut trees by the shore at Puerto Castilla, on January 27, 1931. Peters secured a single specimen from a coconut palm near Tela, in the same general region, on January 18, 1928. In Costa Rica, I found one of these rare warblers in the garden of the hacienda Las Cóncavas, near Cartago, at 4,600 feet above sea-level, on November 3, 1935.

"Griscom's record of the sycamore warbler at San Lucas, Guatemala, on August 7, indicates early arrival. The single published Costa Rican date is of a bird collected by Underwood at San José on September 17. The date of the spring departure appears to be quite unknown."

## DENDROICA GRACIAE GRACIAE Baird

### NORTHERN GRACE'S WARBLER

#### HABITS

This pretty little warbler was discovered by Dr. Elliott Coues (1878) and named by him in honor of his sister and for whom, as he expresses it, "my affection and respect keep pace with my appreciation of true loveliness of character." Of its discovery, he states: "While journeying through New Mexico, *en route* to Fort Whipple, Arizona, in July, 1864, I found Grace's Warbler on the summit of Whipple's Pass of the Rocky Mountains, not far from the old site of Fort Wingate, and secured the first specimen on the second of the month just named." He afterwards found it to be "the most abundant bird of its kind, excepting Audubon's Warbler," in the pine forests on the mountains of Arizona, and says that Henshaw found it to be "one of the commonest of the summer Warblers in the White Mountains. * * * His observations confirm my own in regard to the pine-loving character of the birds; he found them almost invariably in coniferous forests, passing swiftly along the smaller branches of these tall trees, or darting into the air to capture passing insects; and even in August, when various families had united into small flocks, and were lingering in company with other insectivorous birds, before their departure for the South, their preference for their native pines was still evident."

I found it fairly common in the upper reaches of Ramsey Canyon in the Huachuca Mountains of Arizona, among the tall, scattered yellow pines, at elevations between 6,000 and 7,000 feet, where a nest with young was found on June 4, 1922. Swarth (1904) found it more common there as a migrant than as a breeding bird and rather irregular in its abundance.

Grace's warbler, now well-known as a summer resident in the mountains of southern Colorado, New Mexico, Arizona, Sonora, and Chihuahua, is apparently closely related to the yellow-throated warbler of the southern States and to Adelaide's warbler of Puerto Rico; it has a slightly differentiated subspecies in Central America.

*Nesting.*—What is probably the first authentic nest of Grace's warbler to be reported was taken in Yavapai County, Ariz., on June 23, 1890, by H. Keays for H. P. Attwater. This nest is described by Samuel B. Ladd (1891) as "placed on limb of pine sixty feet from the ground. Nest very compact; outside diameter 3 in. by 1½ in. high; inside diameter 1¾ in. by 1¼ in. deep. The body of this nest is composed of horse-hair, strings and vegetable fibres. The most abundant vegetable material interwoven consists of the staminate catkins and bud scales of *Quercus emoryi*. There is also some wool, vegetable down, and insect webbing, in which are entangled the exuviae of some caterpiller. Attached on the outside was a small staminate cone of a species of *Pinus*. Nest well lined with feathers and horse-hair."

O. W. Howard (1899) found two nests in Arizona; one nest was "placed deep down in the middle in a large bunch of pine needles and was entirely hidden from view." The other he found "in a red fir tree. It was placed in a thick bunch of leaves at the extremity of a limb about fifty feet from the ground." A nest with four eggs, in the Doe Museum in Gainesville, Fla., taken by O. C. Poling on May 25, 1891, at 8,000 feet in the Huachuca Mountains, was built in a bunch of pine needles and cones at the end of a long branch of a red pine, 20 feet from the ground.

*Eggs.*—From 3 to 4 eggs, apparently more often 3, make up the set for Grace's warbler. They are ovate with a tendency toward elongate ovate, and are only slightly glossy. They are white or creamy white, finely speckled and spotted with "auburn," "bay," or "chestnut brown," intermingled with "light brownish drab," "deep brownish drab," or "pale vinaceous drab." The markings are concentrated at the large end, where they frequently form a distinct wreath, leaving the lower half of the egg immaculate. Occasionally eggs are speckled all over; and some are marked with blotches. Generally the drab spots are in the majority, when the fewer brown spots, which are often as dark as to appear almost black, are more prominent. The measurements of 38 eggs average 16.9 by 12.7 millimeters; the eggs showing the four extremes measure 18.2 by 13.1, 18.0 by 13.3, 14.8 by 12.7, and 15.4 by 11.7 millimeters (Harris).

*Young.*—Nothing seems to have been published on incubation or on the development and care of the young.

*Plumages.*—Ridgway (1902) describes the young male in first plumage as "above plain grayish hair brown or drab-gray, the feathers ash gray beneath the surface; sides of head similar but rather paler; malar region, chin, and throat pale brownish gray, minutely and sparsely flecked with darker, the chest similar, but with rather large roundish spots of dusky; rest of under parts dull white streaked or spotted with dusky gray medially, dull grayish laterally."

Swarth (1904) writes of the postjuvenal molt:

A young male taken July 13th is in the brown streaked plumage, but yellow feathers are beginning to appear along the median line of the throat and upper breast, and the yellow superciliary stripe is also beginning to show. Another, a little older, has the streaks of the lower parts restricted to the sides and flanks, and the yellow markings nearly perfect. A male taken on July 30th, which has just discarded the juvenile for the winter plumage, differs from the autumnal adults in having the white of the under parts more strongly tinged with buff; and whereas the adult has the back decidedly streaked, though the markings are overcast by the brownish edgings to the feathers, in the juvenile these markings are but imperfectly indicated.

Apparently, the nuptial plumage is assumed by wear alone, for no available specimens show any signs of prenuptial molt and both young birds and adults in the fall are much like the spring birds, but browner and with the markings obscured by brownish tips that probably wear away before spring.

Young birds and females have duller colors than the adult males and are browner in the fall than in the spring. Adults doubtless have a complete postnuptial molt in late summer.

*Behavior.*—Grace's warbler is a bird of the pines, spending most of its time in the towering tops of the tallest trees. It is sometimes seen in other conifers such as hemlocks and spruces, but very seldom on or even near the ground. Dr. Wetmore (1920) says: "Usually they were found in the tops of the Yellow Pines where they worked about rather leisurely, exploring the smaller limbs and at short intervals pausing to sing. * * * Occasionally one was found working about through the oak undergrowth at times coming down almost to the ground. The flight was undulating and rather quick and jerky."

Dr. Coues (1878) writes: "They are seen coursing among the branchlets, skipping at apparent random through the endless intracacies of the foliage, hovering momentarily about the terminal bunches of needles, and then dashing far out into clear space, to capture the passing insect with a dexterous twist and turn.   So the season passes, till the young are on wing, when the different families, still with bonds unbroken, ramble at leisure through the woods, the young birds timid and feeble at first, venturing shorter flights than their parents, who seem absorbed in solicitude for their welfare, and attend them most sedulously, till they are quite able to shift for themselves."

We found Grace's warbler to be an active, restless species.   We could often locate one by its song coming from lofty top of some tall pine, but before we could see its diminutive form, we would hear its song coming from some distant tree farther up the mountain side; and so we would follow the little songster from tree to tree, seldom getting more than a fleeting glimpse of it.   At times, however, when it was more interested in feeding than in singing, we could see it quietly gleaning its insect food along the smaller branches and twigs after the manner of the pine warbler.   We never saw it on or near the ground.

*Voice.*—Dr. Wetmore (1920) says that the song of Grace's warbler, as heard by him at Lake Burford, N. Mex., "was a rapid repetition of notes somewhat reminiscent of the efforts of the Chipping Sparrow, but with the notes evenly spaced, not blurred at the end, and closing abruptly, so that the last syllable was as strongly accented as any of the others.   It resembled the syllables *chip chip chip chip chip* given in a loud tone."

Dr. Walter P. Taylor has sent me some notes on the song, which he calls "rather a modest utterance conspicuously lacking in strength. Song, *tseet tseet tseet tseet zeekle zeet.*   A better rendering is *tsew tsew tsew tsew tsew tsee tsee tsee tsee tseeeip!*   The song has something of a yellow warbler quality.   I find it extremely hard to put down on paper anything that remotely resembles it."   Again he writes it "*tchew tchew tchew*, more slowly uttered, followed by *tsip tsip tsip tsip tsip*, rapidly repeated."

*Field marks.*—Grace's is one of the smallest of our wood warblers, a tiny bird.   It shows a striking resemblance to the yellow-throated warbler, but it is much smaller, has no black in the cheeks, and it has a yellow rather than a white mark below the eye.   The adult male in spring is light bluish gray above, marked on the head and back with black spots, with a bright yellow throat, two white wing bars, and much white in the tail.   Females, young birds, and males in the fall are similar but browner.

### DISTRIBUTION

*Range.*—Southwestern United States to central Mexico.

*Breeding range.*—Grace's warbler breeds **north** to southern Utah (Zion National Park); southwestern Colorado (Fort Lewis and Pagosa Springs); and central northern New Mexico (Tres Piedras; possibly Sierra Grande). **East** to central New Mexico (Tres Piedras and Mesa Yegua); western Texas (Guadalupe Mountains); and northwestern Chihuahua (Colonia García). **South** to northwestern Chihuahua (Colonia García) and southeastern Sonora (Rancho Santa Bárbara). **West** to western Sonora (Rancho Santa Bárbara, Moctezuma, and Nogales); eastern central and western Arizona (Huachuca Mountains, Tucson, Fort Whipple, Hualpai Mountains, and Mount Trumble); and southwestern Utah (Zion National Park).

*Winter range.*—In winter Grace's warbler seems to be confined to a small area in central western Mexico, from central Jalisco (Bolaños) southeast to east central Michoacán (Patambán and Patzcuaro); and west to south central Jalisco (Zapotitlán); occasional north to northern Nayarit (Santa Teresa).

*Migration.*—Very little information is available regarding the migratory movements of Grace's warbler. Dates of spring arrival are: Sonora—Mina Abundancia, April 11. New Mexico—Silver City, April 20. Arizona—Santa Rita Mountains, March 15. The latest date of one recorded at Albuquerque, New Mexico, is September 7. A resident race occurs in Central America.

*Egg dates.*—Arizona: 9 records, May 3 to June 27; 5 records, May 30 to June 8, indicating the height of the season.

New Mexico: 2 records, May 22 and June 13 (Harris).

*PLATES*

PLATE 1

Morristown, N. J.

R. T. Peterson

BLACK-AND-WHITE WARBLER

PLATE 2

Eliot Porter

BLACK-AND-WHITE WARBLER, MALE

Maine, June 29, 1940

PLATE 3

Dennis, Mass., June 17, 1921 A. C. Bent

Johnson City, Tenn., May 10, 1942 B. P. Tyler

NESTS OF BLACK-AND-WHITE WARBLER

PLATE 4

Reelfoot Lake, Tenn., July 9, 1940                    L. H. Walkinshaw

PROTHONOTARY WARBLER

PLATE 5

Duval County, Fla., May 8, 1935          S. A. Grimes

PAIR OF PROTHONOTARY WARBLERS

PLATE 6

Duval County, Fla., May 22, 1931        S. A. Grimes

Duval County, Fla., June 14, 1935        S. A. Grimes

NESTS OF PROTHONOTARY WARBLER

PLATE 7

Duval County, Fla., May 13, 1936

NEST OF SWAINSON'S WARBLER

PLATE 8

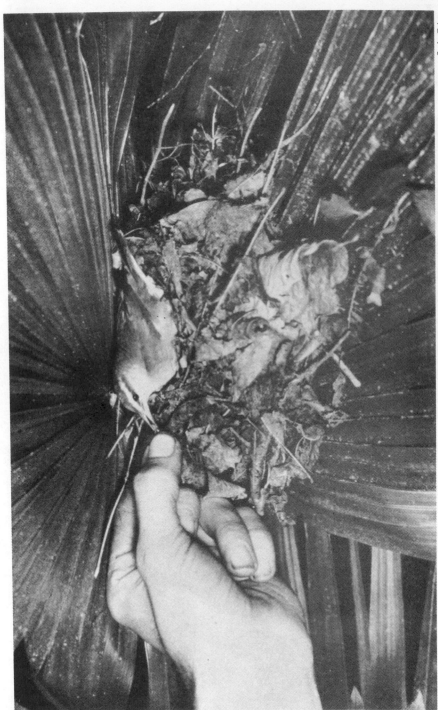

SWAINSON'S WARBLER

Duval County, Fla., May 1936

PLATE 9

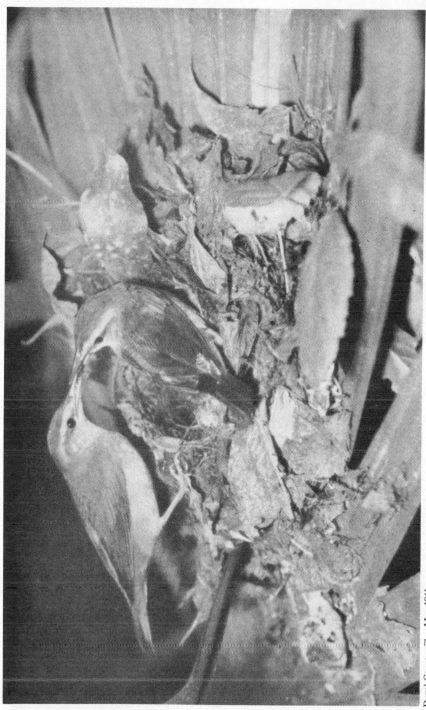

Duval County, Fla., May 1941

PAIR OF SWAINSON'S WARBLERS

PLATE 10

Allen Frost        Calhoun County, Mich., June 9, 1937        L. H. Walkinshaw

WORM-EATING WARBLER (LEFT) AND GOLDEN-WINGED WARBLER (RIGHT)

PLATE 11

Near Branchport, N. Y.

GOLDEN-WINGED WARBLER AND NEST

C. F. Stone

PLATE 12

A. C. Bent

F. H. Shoemaker

Hadlyme, Conn., June 1, 1934

Near Omaha, Nebr., June 8, 1901

NESTS OF BLUE-WINGED WARBLER

PLATE 13

New Britain, Conn., June 5, 1932

New Britain, Conn., May 27, 1932      E. W. Schmidt and D. D. MacDavid

BLUE-WINGED WARBLER AND NEST

PLATE 14

Tabusintac, New Brunswick

B. S. Bowdish

TENNESSEE WARBLER AND NEST

PLATE 15

J. S. Rowley

Santa Catalina Island, Calif., April 16, 1939

NESTS OF DUSKY ORANGE-CROWNED WARBLER

PLATE 16

Yates County, N. Y.                                    C. F. Stone

Tabusintac, New Brunswick                             B. S. Bowdish

NESTS OF EASTERN NASHVILLE WARBLER

PLATE 17

W. J. Brown

Tabusintac, New Brunswick

B. S. Bowdish

Saint Dorothee, Quebec, June 4, 1943

NESTS OF EASTERN NASHVILLE WARBLER
(Note two cowbird eggs in nest on left)

PLATE 18

Huachuca Mountains, Ariz.                                          F. C. Willard

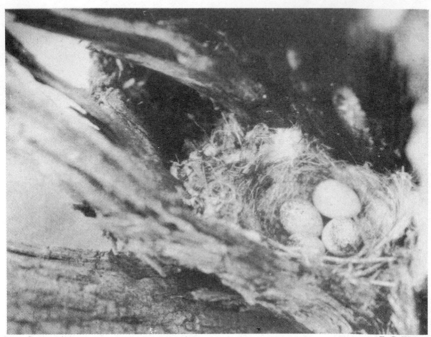

Pima County, Ariz.                                                 F. C. Willard

NESTS OF VIRGINIA'S WARBLER (UPPER) AND LUCY'S WARBLER (LOWER)

PLATE 19

Eliot Porter

LUCY'S WARBLER

Arizona, April 29, 1941

PLATE 20

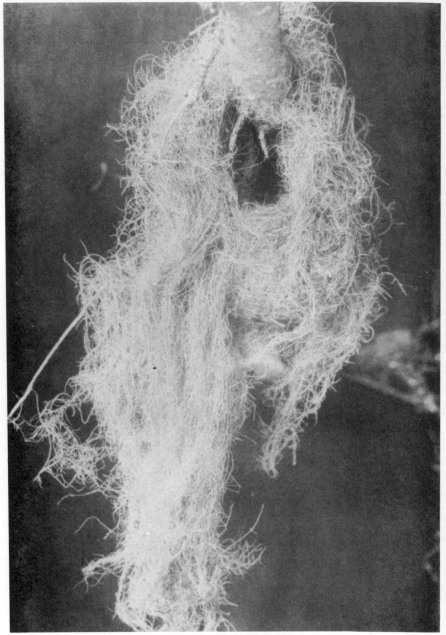

Maine C. J. Stanwood

NEST OF NORTHERN PARULA WARBLER

PLATE 21

Maine, July 9, 1939

Eliot Porter

NORTHERN PARULA WARBLER, MALE

PLATE 22

Duval County, Fla., May 4, 1936                                          S. A. Grimes

SOUTHERN PARULA WARBLER, MALE

PLATE 23

Huachuca Mountains, Ariz., May 30, 1922

A. C. Bent

NESTING SITE AND NEST OF NORTHERN OLIVE WARBLER

PLATE 24

S. A. Grimes

NEST OF EASTERN YELLOW WARBLER

PLATE 25

Grice and Grice

EASTERN YELLOW WARBLERS

Taunton, Mass.  May 31, 1941

PLATE 26

NEST OF MAGNOLIA WARBLER IN A HEMLOCK

Pocono Lake, Pa.

PLATE 27

S. A. Grimes

Wyoming County, N. Y., June 5, 1928

NEST OF MAGNOLIA WARBLER

PLATE 28

Maine, July 6, 1940

Eliot Porter

MALE MAGNOLIA WARBLER WITH YOUNG

PLATE 29

Tabusintac, New Brunswick                                                        B. S. Bowdish

Maine                                                                                    C. J. Stanwood

NESTS OF CAPE MAY WARBLER (UPPER) AND NORTHERN BLACK-THROATED BLUE
WARBLER (LOWER)

PLATE 30

Asquam Lake, N. H., June 25, 1927                                      A. C. Bent

NORTHERN BLACK-THROATED BLUE WARBLER, FEMALES

PLATE 31

Beech Mountain, N. C., June 4, 1942                          B. P. Tyler

East Wallingford, Vt., June 2, 1907                          Owen Durfee

**NESTS OF CAIRNS' WARBLER (UPPER) AND EASTERN MYRTLE WARBLE (LOWER)**

PLATE 32

EASTERN MYRTLE WARBLER

Maine, 1945

PLATE 33

Eliot Porter

Maine, June 18, 1940

EASTERN MYRTLE WARBLER, FEMALE

PLATE 34

San Bernardino County, Calif., May 19, 1940 — J. S. Rowley

Phoenix, Ariz., Jan. 3, 1942 — H. L. and Ruth Crockett

NEST OF PACIFIC AUDUBON'S WARBLER AND BIRD IN WINTER PLUMAGE

PLATE 35

Oregon                                                                    W. L. Finley

BLACK-THROATED GRAY WARBLERS AND NEST

PLATE 36

Kensington, Conn., June 8, 1924        E. W. Schmidt and D. D. MacDavid

NORTHERN BLACK-THROATED GREEN WARBLER AND NEST

PLATE 37

Eliot Porter

NORTHERN BLACK-THROATED GREEN WARBLER, MALE

Maine, June 29, 1939

PLATE 38

Eliot Porter

Maine, July 24, 1940

NORTHERN BLACK-THROATED GREEN WARBLER, FEMALE

PLATE 39

Eldorado County, Calif., May 14, 1913      O. F. Heinman (Courtesy *The Condor* and M. S. Ray)

Yates County, N. Y., June 1915      C. F. Stone

HERMIT WARBLER'S NEST (UPPER) AND CERULEAN WARBLER (LOWER)

PLATE 40

Cass County, Minn., June 22, 1929                                    S. A. Grimes

BLACKBURNIAN WARBLER'S NEST
(Note two cowbird eggs in nest)

PLATE 41

Cass County, Minn., June 1929

S. A. Grimes

BLACKBURNIAN WARBLER, MALE
(One cowbird egg in nest)

PLATE 42

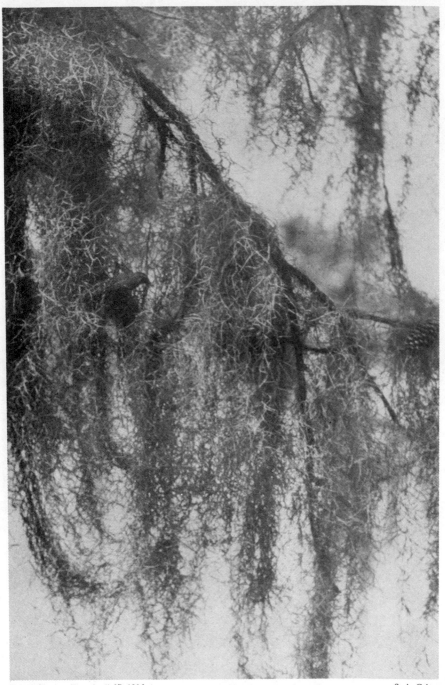

Duval County, Fla., April 27, 1936                                    S. A. Grimes

EASTERN YELLOW-THROATED WARBLER

PLATE 43

Duval County, Fla., May 1934 S. A. Grimes

Duval County, Fla., May 2, 1931 S. A. Grimes

EASTERN YELLOW-THROATED WARBLER AND NEST

PLATE 44

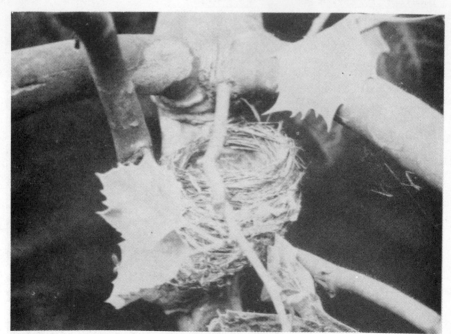

Tennessee                                    H. S. Vaughn

NESTS OF SYCAMORE YELLOW-THROATED WARBLER

# A CATALOGUE OF SELECTED DOVER BOOKS
# IN ALL FIELDS OF INTEREST

AMERICA'S OLD MASTERS, James T. Flexner. Four men emerged unexpectedly from provincial 18th century America to leadership in European art: Benjamin West, J. S. Copley, C. R. Peale, Gilbert Stuart. Brilliant coverage of lives and contributions. Revised, 1967 edition. 69 plates. 365pp. of text.

21806-6 Paperbound $3.00

FIRST FLOWERS OF OUR WILDERNESS: AMERICAN PAINTING, THE COLONIAL PERIOD, James T. Flexner. Painters, and regional painting traditions from earliest Colonial times up to the emergence of Copley, West and Peale Sr., Foster, Gustavus Hesselius, Feke, John Smibert and many anonymous painters in the primitive manner. Engaging presentation, with 162 illustrations. xxii + 368pp.

22180-6 Paperbound $3.50

THE LIGHT OF DISTANT SKIES: AMERICAN PAINTING, 1760-1835, James T. Flexner. The great generation of early American painters goes to Europe to learn and to teach: West, Copley, Gilbert Stuart and others. Allston, Trumbull, Morse; also contemporary American painters—primitives, derivatives, academics—who remained in America. 102 illustrations. xiii + 306pp.

22179-2 Paperbound $3.00

A HISTORY OF THE RISE AND PROGRESS OF THE ARTS OF DESIGN IN THE UNITED STATES, William Dunlap. Much the richest mine of information on early American painters, sculptors, architects, engravers, miniaturists, etc. The only source of information for scores of artists, the major primary source for many others. Unabridged reprint of rare original 1834 edition, with new introduction by James T. Flexner, and 394 new illustrations. Edited by Rita Weiss. 6⅝ x 9⅝.

21695-0, 21696-9, 21697-7 Three volumes, Paperbound $13.50

EPOCHS OF CHINESE AND JAPANESE ART, Ernest F. Fenollosa. From primitive Chinese art to the 20th century, thorough history, explanation of every important art period and form, including Japanese woodcuts; main stress on China and Japan, but Tibet, Korea also included. Still unexcelled for its detailed, rich coverage of cultural background, aesthetic elements, diffusion studies, particularly of the historical period. 2nd, 1913 edition. 242 illustrations. lii + 439pp. of text.

20364-6, 20365-4 Two volumes, Paperbound $6.00

THE GENTLE ART OF MAKING ENEMIES, James A. M. Whistler. Greatest wit of his day deflates Oscar Wilde, Ruskin, Swinburne; strikes back at inane critics, exhibitions, art journalism; aesthetics of impressionist revolution in most striking form. Highly readable classic by great painter. Reproduction of edition designed by Whistler. Introduction by Alfred Werner. xxxvi + 334pp.

21875-9 Paperbound $2.50

THE ARCHITECTURE OF COUNTRY HOUSES, Andrew J. Downing. Together with Vaux's *Villas and Cottages* this is the basic book for Hudson River Gothic architecture of the middle Victorian period. Full, sound discussions of general aspects of housing, architecture, style, decoration, furnishing, together with scores of detailed house plans, illustrations of specific buildings, accompanied by full text. Perhaps the most influential single American architectural book. 1850 edition. Introduction by J. Stewart Johnson. 321 figures, 34 architectural designs. xvi + 560pp.
22003-6 Paperbound $4.00

LOST EXAMPLES OF COLONIAL ARCHITECTURE, John Mead Howells. Full-page photographs of buildings that have disappeared or been so altered as to be denatured, including many designed by major early American architects. 245 plates. xvii + 248pp. 7⅞ x 10¾.
21143-6 Paperbound $3.50

DOMESTIC ARCHITECTURE OF THE AMERICAN COLONIES AND OF THE EARLY REPUBLIC, Fiske Kimball. Foremost architect and restorer of Williamsburg and Monticello covers nearly 200 homes between 1620-1825. Architectural details, construction, style features, special fixtures, floor plans, etc. Generally considered finest work in its area. 219 illustrations of houses, doorways, windows, capital mantels. xx + 314pp. 7⅞ x 10¾.
21743-4 Paperbound $4.00

EARLY AMERICAN ROOMS: 1650-1858, edited by Russell Hawes Kettell. Tour of 12 rooms, each representative of a different era in American history and each furnished, decorated, designed and occupied in the style of the era. 72 plans and elevations, 8-page color section, etc., show fabrics, wall papers, arrangements, etc. Full descriptive text. xvii + 200pp. of text. 8⅜ x 11¼.
21633-0 Paperbound $5.00

THE FITZWILLIAM VIRGINAL BOOK, edited by J. Fuller Maitland and W. B. Squire. Full modern printing of famous early 17th-century ms. volume of 300 works by Morley, Byrd, Bull, Gibbons, etc. For piano or other modern keyboard instrument; easy to read format. xxxvi + 938pp. 8⅜ x 11.
21068-5, 21069-3 Two volumes, Paperbound $10.00

KEYBOARD MUSIC, Johann Sebastian Bach. Bach Gesellschaft edition. A rich selection of Bach's masterpieces for the harpsichord: the six English Suites, six French Suites, the six Partitas (Clavierübung part I), the Goldberg Variations (Clavierübung part IV), the fifteen Two-Part Inventions and the fifteen Three-Part Sinfonias. Clearly reproduced on large sheets with ample margins; eminently playable. vi + 312pp. 8⅛ x 11.
22360-4 Paperbound $5.00

THE MUSIC OF BACH: AN INTRODUCTION, Charles Sanford Terry. A fine, non-technical introduction to Bach's music, both instrumental and vocal. Covers organ music, chamber music, passion music, other types. Analyzes themes, developments, innovations. x + 114pp.
21075-8 Paperbound $1.25

BEETHOVEN AND HIS NINE SYMPHONIES, Sir George Grove. Noted British musicologist provides best history, analysis, commentary on symphonies. Very thorough, rigorously accurate; necessary to both advanced student and amateur music lover. 436 musical passages. vii + 407 pp.
20334-4 Paperbound $2.75

ALPHABETS AND ORNAMENTS, Ernst Lehner. Well-known pictorial source for decorative alphabets, script examples, cartouches, frames, decorative title pages, calligraphic initials, borders, similar material. 14th to 19th century, mostly European. Useful in almost any graphic arts designing, varied styles. 750 illustrations. 256pp. 7 x 10. 21905-4 Paperbound $4.00

PAINTING: A CREATIVE APPROACH, Norman Colquhoun. For the beginner simple guide provides an instructive approach to painting: major stumbling blocks for beginner; overcoming them, technical points; paints and pigments; oil painting; watercolor and other media and color. New section on "plastic" paints. Glossary. Formerly *Paint Your Own Pictures.* 221pp. 22000-1 Paperbound $1.75

THE ENJOYMENT AND USE OF COLOR, Walter Sargent. Explanation of the relations between colors themselves and between colors in nature and art, including hundreds of little-known facts about color values, intensities, effects of high and low illumination, complementary colors. Many practical hints for painters, references to great masters. 7 color plates, 29 illustrations. x + 274pp.
20944-X Paperbound $2.75

THE NOTEBOOKS OF LEONARDO DA VINCI, compiled and edited by Jean Paul Richter. 1566 extracts from original manuscripts reveal the full range of Leonardo's versatile genius: all his writings on painting, sculpture, architecture, anatomy, astronomy, geography, topography, physiology, mining, music, etc., in both Italian and English, with 186 plates of manuscript pages and more than 500 additional drawings. Includes studies for the Last Supper, the lost Sforza monument, and other works. Total of xlvii + 866pp. 7⅞ x 10¾.
22572-0, 22573-9 Two volumes, Paperbound $10.00

MONTGOMERY WARD CATALOGUE OF 1895. Tea gowns, yards of flannel and pillow-case lace, stereoscopes, books of gospel hymns, the New Improved Singer Sewing Machine, side saddles, milk skimmers, straight-edged razors, high-button shoes, spittoons, and on and on . . . listing some 25,000 items, practically all illustrated. Essential to the shoppers of the 1890's, it is our truest record of the spirit of the period. Unaltered reprint of Issue No. 57, Spring and Summer 1895. Introduction by Boris Emmet. Innumerable illustrations. xiii + 624pp. 8½ x 11⅝.
22377-9 Paperbound $6.95

THE CRYSTAL PALACE EXHIBITION ILLUSTRATED CATALOGUE (LONDON, 1851). One of the wonders of the modern world—the Crystal Palace Exhibition in which all the nations of the civilized world exhibited their achievements in the arts and sciences—presented in an equally important illustrated catalogue. More than 1700 items pictured with accompanying text—ceramics, textiles, cast-iron work, carpets, pianos, sleds, razors, wall-papers, billiard tables, beehives, silverware and hundreds of other artifacts—represent the focal point of Victorian culture in the Western World. Probably the largest collection of Victorian decorative art ever assembled— indispensable for antiquarians and designers. Unabridged republication of the Art-Journal Catalogue of the Great Exhibition of 1851, with all terminal essays. New introduction by John Gloag, F.S.A. xxxiv + 426pp. 9 x 12.
22503-8 Paperbound $4.50

How to Know the Wild Flowers, Mrs. William Starr Dana. This is the classical book of American wildflowers (of the Eastern and Central United States), used by hundreds of thousands. Covers over 500 species, arranged in extremely easy to use color and season groups. Full descriptions, much plant lore. This Dover edition is the fullest ever compiled, with tables of nomenclature changes. 174 full-page plates by M. Satterlee. xii + 418pp. 20332-8 Paperbound $2.75

Our Plant Friends and Foes, William Atherton DuPuy. History, economic importance, essential botanical information and peculiarities of 25 common forms of plant life are provided in this book in an entertaining and charming style. Covers food plants (potatoes, apples, beans, wheat, almonds, bananas, etc.), flowers (lily, tulip, etc.), trees (pine, oak, elm, etc.), weeds, poisonous mushrooms and vines, gourds, citrus fruits, cotton, the cactus family, and much more. 108 illustrations. xiv + 290pp. 22272-1 Paperbound $2.50

How to Know the Ferns, Frances T. Parsons. Classic survey of Eastern and Central ferns, arranged according to clear, simple identification key. Excellent introduction to greatly neglected nature area. 57 illustrations and 42 plates. xvi + 215pp. 20740-4 Paperbound $2.00

Manual of the Trees of North America, Charles S. Sargent. America's foremost dendrologist provides the definitive coverage of North American trees and tree-like shrubs. 717 species fully described and illustrated: exact distribution, down to township; full botanical description; economic importance; description of subspecies and races; habitat, growth data; similar material. Necessary to every serious student of tree-life. Nomenclature revised to present. Over 100 locating keys. 783 illustrations. lii + 934pp. 20277-1, 20278-X Two volumes, Paperbound $6.00

Our Northern Shrubs, Harriet L. Keeler. Fine non-technical reference work identifying more than 225 important shrubs of Eastern and Central United States and Canada. Full text covering botanical description, habitat, plant lore, is paralleled with 205 full-page photographs of flowering or fruiting plants. Nomenclature revised by Edward G. Voss. One of few works concerned with shrubs. 205 plates, 35 drawings. xxviii + 521pp. 21989-5 Paperbound $3.75

The Mushroom Handbook, Louis C. C. Krieger. Still the best popular handbook: full descriptions of 259 species, cross references to another 200. Extremely thorough text enables you to identify, know all about any mushroom you are likely to meet in eastern and central U. S. A.: habitat, luminescence, poisonous qualities, use, folklore, etc. 32 color plates show over 50 mushrooms, also 126 other illustrations. Finding keys. vii + 560pp. 21861-9 Paperbound $3.95

Handbook of Birds of Eastern North America, Frank M. Chapman. Still much the best single-volume guide to the birds of Eastern and Central United States. Very full coverage of 675 species, with descriptions, life habits, distribution, similar data. All descriptions keyed to two-page color chart. With this single volume the average birdwatcher needs no other books. 1931 revised edition. 195 illustrations. xxxvi + 581pp. 21489-3 Paperbound $4.50

JOHANN SEBASTIAN BACH, Philipp Spitta. One of the great classics of musicology, this definitive analysis of Bach's music (and life) has never been surpassed. Lucid, nontechnical analyses of hundreds of pieces (30 pages devoted to St. Matthew Passion, 26 to B Minor Mass). Also includes major analysis of 18th-century music. 450 musical examples. 40-page musical supplement. Total of xx + 1799pp.
(EUK) 22278-0, 22279-9 Two volumes, Clothbound $15.00

MOZART AND HIS PIANO CONCERTOS, Cuthbert Girdlestone. The only full-length study of an important area of Mozart's creativity. Provides detailed analyses of all 23 concertos, traces inspirational sources. 417 musical examples. Second edition. 509pp. (USO) 21271-8 Paperbound $3.50

THE PERFECT WAGNERITE: A COMMENTARY ON THE NIBLUNG'S RING, George Bernard Shaw. Brilliant and still relevant criticism in remarkable essays on Wagner's Ring cycle, Shaw's ideas on political and social ideology behind the plots, role of Leitmotifs, vocal requisites, etc. Prefaces. xxi + 136pp.
21707-8 Paperbound $1.50

DON GIOVANNI, W. A. Mozart. Complete libretto, modern English translation; biographies of composer and librettist; accounts of early performances and critical reaction. Lavishly illustrated. All the material you need to understand and appreciate this great work. Dover Opera Guide and Libretto Series; translated and introduced by Ellen Bleiler. 92 illustrations. 209pp.
21134-7 Paperbound $1.50

HIGH FIDELITY SYSTEMS: A LAYMAN'S GUIDE, Roy F. Allison. All the basic information you need for setting up your own audio system: high fidelity and stereo record players, tape records, F.M. Connections, adjusting tone arm, cartridge, checking needle alignment, positioning speakers, phasing speakers, adjusting hums, trouble-shooting, maintenance, and similar topics. Enlarged 1965 edition. More than 50 charts, diagrams, photos. iv + 91pp. 21514-8 Paperbound $1.25

REPRODUCTION OF SOUND, Edgar Villchur. Thorough coverage for laymen of high fidelity systems, reproducing systems in general, needles, amplifiers, preamps, loudspeakers, feedback, explaining physical background. "A rare talent for making technicalities vividly comprehensible," R. Darrell, *High Fidelity*. 69 figures. iv + 92pp. 21515-6 Paperbound $1.00

HEAR ME TALKIN' TO YA: THE STORY OF JAZZ AS TOLD BY THE MEN WHO MADE IT, Nat Shapiro and Nat Hentoff. Louis Armstrong, Fats Waller, Jo Jones, Clarence Williams, Billy Holiday, Duke Ellington, Jelly Roll Morton and dozens of other jazz greats tell how it was in Chicago's South Side, New Orleans, depression Harlem and the modern West Coast as jazz was born and grew. xvi + 429pp.
21726-4 Paperbound $2.50

FABLES OF AESOP, translated by Sir Roger L'Estrange. A reproduction of the very rare 1931 Paris edition; a selection of the most interesting fables, together with 50 imaginative drawings by Alexander Calder. v + 128pp. 6½x9¼.
21780-9 Paperbound $1.25

AMERICAN FOOD AND GAME FISHES, David S. Jordan and Barton W. Evermann. Definitive source of information, detailed and accurate enough to enable the sportsman and nature lover to identify conclusively some 1,000 species and sub-species of North American fish, sought for food or sport. Coverage of range, physiology, habits, life history, food value. Best methods of capture, interest to the angler, advice on bait, fly-fishing, etc. 338 drawings and photographs. 1 + 574pp. 6⅝ x 9⅜.
22383-1 Paperbound $4.50

THE FROG BOOK, Mary C. Dickerson. Complete with extensive finding keys, over 300 photographs, and an introduction to the general biology of frogs and toads, this is the classic non-technical study of Northeastern and Central species. 58 species; 290 photographs and 16 color plates. xvii + 253pp.
21973-9 Paperbound $4.00

THE MOTH BOOK: A GUIDE TO THE MOTHS OF NORTH AMERICA, William J. Holland. Classical study, eagerly sought after and used for the past 60 years. Clear identification manual to more than 2,000 different moths, largest manual in existence. General information about moths, capturing, mounting, classifying, etc., followed by species by species descriptions. 263 illustrations plus 48 color plates show almost every species, full size. 1968 edition, preface, nomenclature changes by A. E. Brower. xxiv + 479pp. of text. 6½ x 9¼.
21948-8 Paperbound $5.00

THE SEA-BEACH AT EBB-TIDE, Augusta Foote Arnold. Interested amateur can identify hundreds of marine plants and animals on coasts of North America; marine algae; seaweeds; squids; hermit crabs; horse shoe crabs; shrimps; corals; sea anemones; etc. Species descriptions cover: structure; food; reproductive cycle; size; shape; color; habitat; etc. Over 600 drawings. 85 plates. xii + 490pp.
21949-6 Paperbound $3.50

COMMON BIRD SONGS, Donald J. Borror. 33⅓ 12-inch record presents songs of 60 important birds of the eastern United States. A thorough, serious record which provides several examples for each bird, showing different types of song, individual variations, etc. Inestimable identification aid for birdwatcher. 32-page booklet gives text about birds and songs, with illustration for each bird.
21829-5 Record, book, album. Monaural. $2.75

FADS AND FALLACIES IN THE NAME OF SCIENCE, Martin Gardner. Fair, witty appraisal of cranks and quacks of science: Atlantis, Lemuria, hollow earth, flat earth, Velikovsky, orgone energy, Dianetics, flying saucers, Bridey Murphy, food fads, medical fads, perpetual motion, etc. Formerly "In the Name of Science." x + 363pp.
20394-8 Paperbound $2.00

HOAXES, Curtis D. MacDougall. Exhaustive, unbelievably rich account of great hoaxes: Locke's moon hoax, Shakespearean forgeries, sea serpents, Loch Ness monster, Cardiff giant, John Wilkes Booth's mummy, Disumbrationist school of art, dozens more; also journalism, psychology of hoaxing. 54 illustrations. xi + 338pp.
20465-0 Paperbound $2.75

ADVENTURES OF AN AFRICAN SLAVER, Theodore Canot. Edited by Brantz Mayer. A detailed portrayal of slavery and the slave trade, 1820-1840. Canot, an established trader along the African coast, describes the slave economy of the African kingdoms, the treatment of captured negroes, the extensive journeys in the interior to gather slaves, slave revolts and their suppression, harems, bribes, and much more. Full and unabridged republication of 1854 edition. Introduction by Malcom Cowley. 16 illustrations. xvii + 448pp. 22456-2 Paperbound $3.50

MY BONDAGE AND MY FREEDOM, Frederick Douglass. Born and brought up in slavery, Douglass witnessed its horrors and experienced its cruelties, but went on to become one of the most outspoken forces in the American anti-slavery movement. Considered the best of his autobiographies, this book graphically describes the inhuman treatment of slaves, its effects on slave owners and slave families, and how Douglass's determination led him to a new life. Unaltered reprint of 1st (1855) edition. xxxii + 464pp. 22457-0 Paperbound $2.50

THE INDIANS' BOOK, recorded and edited by Natalie Curtis. Lore, music, narratives, dozens of drawings by Indians themselves from an authoritative and important survey of native culture among Plains, Southwestern, Lake and Pueblo Indians. Standard work in popular ethnomusicology. 149 songs in full notation. 23 drawings, 23 photos. xxxi + 584pp. 6⅝ x 9⅜. 21939-9 Paperbound $4.50

DICTIONARY OF AMERICAN PORTRAITS, edited by Hayward and Blanche Cirker. 4024 portraits of 4000 most important Americans, colonial days to 1905 (with a few important categories, like Presidents, to present). Pioneers, explorers, colonial figures, U. S. officials, politicians, writers, military and naval men, scientists, inventors, manufacturers, jurists, actors, historians, educators, notorious figures, Indian chiefs, etc. All authentic contemporary likenesses. The only work of its kind in existence; supplements all biographical sources for libraries. Indispensable to anyone working with American history. 8,000-item classified index, finding lists, other aids. xiv + 756pp. 9¼ x 12¾. 21823-6 Clothbound $30.00

TRITTON'S GUIDE TO BETTER WINE AND BEER MAKING FOR BEGINNERS, S. M. Tritton. All you need to know to make family-sized quantities of over 100 types of grape, fruit, herb and vegetable wines; as well as beers, mead, cider, etc. Complete recipes, advice as to equipment, procedures such as fermenting, bottling, and storing wines. Recipes given in British, U. S., and metric measures. Accompanying booklet lists sources in U. S. A. where ingredients may be bought, and additional information. 11 illustrations. 157pp. 5⅝ x 8⅛. (USO) 22090-7 Clothbound $3.50

GARDENING WITH HERBS FOR FLAVOR AND FRAGRANCE, Helen M. Fox. How to grow herbs in your own garden, how to use them in your cooking (over 55 recipes included), legends and myths associated with each species, uses in medicine, perfumes, etc.—these are elements of one of the few books written especially for American herb fanciers. Guides you step-by-step from soil preparation to harvesting and storage for each type of herb. 12 drawings by Louise Mansfield. xiv + 334pp. 22540-2 Paperbound $2.50

THE RED FAIRY BOOK, Andrew Lang. Lang's color fairy books have long been children's favorites. This volume includes Rapunzel, Jack and the Bean-stalk and 35 other stories, familiar and unfamiliar. 4 plates, 93 illustrations x + 367pp.
21673-X Paperbound $2.50

THE BLUE FAIRY BOOK, Andrew Lang. Lang's tales come from all countries and all times. Here are 37 tales from Grimm, the Arabian Nights, Greek Mythology, and other fascinating sources. 8 plates, 130 illustrations. xi + 390pp.
21437-0 Paperbound $2.50

HOUSEHOLD STORIES BY THE BROTHERS GRIMM. Classic English-language edition of the well-known tales — Rumpelstiltskin, Snow White, Hansel and Gretel, The Twelve Brothers, Faithful John, Rapunzel, Tom Thumb (52 stories in all). Translated into simple, straightforward English by Lucy Crane. Ornamented with headpieces, vignettes, elaborate decorative initials and a dozen full-page illustrations by Walter Crane. x + 269pp.
21080-4 Paperbound $2.50

THE MERRY ADVENTURES OF ROBIN HOOD, Howard Pyle. The finest modern versions of the traditional ballads and tales about the great English outlaw. Howard Pyle's complete prose version, with every word, every illustration of the first edition. Do not confuse this facsimile of the original (1883) with modern editions that change text or illustrations. 23 plates plus many page decorations. xxii + 296pp.
22043-5 Paperbound $2.50

THE STORY OF KING ARTHUR AND HIS KNIGHTS, Howard Pyle. The finest children's version of the life of King Arthur; brilliantly retold by Pyle, with 48 of his most imaginative illustrations. xviii + 313pp. 6⅛ x 9¼.
21445-1 Paperbound $2.50

THE WONDERFUL WIZARD OF OZ, L. Frank Baum. America's finest children's book in facsimile of first edition with all Denslow illustrations in full color. The edition a child should have. Introduction by Martin Gardner. 23 color plates, scores of drawings. iv + 267pp.
20691-2 Paperbound $2.50

THE MARVELOUS LAND OF OZ, L. Frank Baum. The second Oz book, every bit as imaginative as the Wizard. The hero is a boy named Tip, but the Scarecrow and the Tin Woodman are back, as is the Oz magic. 16 color plates, 120 drawings by John R. Neill. 287pp.
20692-0 Paperbound $2.50

THE MAGICAL MONARCH OF MO, L. Frank Baum. Remarkable adventures in a land even stranger than Oz. The best of Baum's books not in the Oz series. 15 color plates and dozens of drawings by Frank Verbeck. xviii + 237pp.
21892-9 Paperbound $2.25

THE BAD CHILD'S BOOK OF BEASTS, MORE BEASTS FOR WORSE CHILDREN, A MORAL ALPHABET, Hilaire Belloc. Three complete humor classics in one volume. Be kind to the frog, and do not call him names . . . and 28 other whimsical animals. Familiar favorites and some not so well known. Illustrated by Basil Blackwell. 156pp.
(USO) 20749-8 Paperbound $1.50

TWO LITTLE SAVAGES; BEING THE ADVENTURES OF TWO BOYS WHO LIVED AS INDIANS AND WHAT THEY LEARNED, Ernest Thompson Seton. Great classic of nature and boyhood provides a vast range of woodlore in most palatable form, a genuinely entertaining story. Two farm boys build a teepee in woods and live in it for a month, working out Indian solutions to living problems, star lore, birds and animals, plants, etc. 293 illustrations. vii + 286pp.

20985-7 Paperbound $2.50

PETER PIPER'S PRACTICAL PRINCIPLES OF PLAIN & PERFECT PRONUNCIATION. Alliterative jingles and tongue-twisters of surprising charm, that made their first appearance in America about 1830. Republished in full with the spirited woodcut illustrations from this earliest American edition. 32pp. 4½ x 6⅜.

22560-7 Paperbound $1.00

SCIENCE EXPERIMENTS AND AMUSEMENTS FOR CHILDREN, Charles Vivian. 73 easy experiments, requiring only materials found at home or easily available, such as candles, coins, steel wool, etc.; illustrate basic phenomena like vacuum, simple chemical reaction, etc. All safe. Modern, well-planned. Formerly *Science Games for Children*. 102 photos, numerous drawings. 96pp. 6⅛ x 9¼.

21856-2 Paperbound $1.25

AN INTRODUCTION TO CHESS MOVES AND TACTICS SIMPLY EXPLAINED, Leonard Barden. Informal intermediate introduction, quite strong in explaining reasons for moves. Covers basic material, tactics, important openings, traps, positional play in middle game, end game. Attempts to isolate patterns and recurrent configurations. Formerly *Chess*. 58 figures. 102pp.     (USO) 21210-6 Paperbound $1.25

LASKER'S MANUAL OF CHESS, Dr. Emanuel Lasker. Lasker was not only one of the five great World Champions, he was also one of the ablest expositors, theorists, and analysts. In many ways, his Manual, permeated with his philosophy of battle, filled with keen insights, is one of the greatest works ever written on chess. Filled with analyzed games by the great players. A single-volume library that will profit almost any chess player, beginner or master. 308 diagrams. xli x 349pp.

20640-8 Paperbound $2.75

THE MASTER BOOK OF MATHEMATICAL RECREATIONS, Fred Schuh. In opinion of many the finest work ever prepared on mathematical puzzles, stunts, recreations; exhaustively thorough explanations of mathematics involved, analysis of effects, citation of puzzles and games. Mathematics involved is elementary. Translated by F. Göbel. 194 figures. xxiv + 430pp.     22134-2 Paperbound $3.00

MATHEMATICS, MAGIC AND MYSTERY, Martin Gardner. Puzzle editor for Scientific American explains mathematics behind various mystifying tricks: card tricks, stage "mind reading," coin and match tricks, counting out games, geometric dissections, etc. Probability sets, theory of numbers clearly explained. Also provides more than 400 tricks, guaranteed to work, that you can do. 135 illustrations. xii + 176pp.

20338-2 Paperbound $1.50

JIM WHITEWOLF: THE LIFE OF A KIOWA APACHE INDIAN, Charles S. Brant, editor. Spans transition between native life and acculturation period, 1880 on. Kiowa culture, personal life pattern, religion and the supernatural, the Ghost Dance, breakdown in the White Man's world, similar material. 1 map. xii + 144pp.
22015-X Paperbound $1.75

THE NATIVE TRIBES OF CENTRAL AUSTRALIA, Baldwin Spencer and F. J. Gillen. Basic book in anthropology, devoted to full coverage of the Arunta and Warramunga tribes; the source for knowledge about kinship systems, material and social culture, religion, etc. Still unsurpassed. 121 photographs, 89 drawings. xviii + 669pp.
21775-2 Paperbound $5.00

MALAY MAGIC, Walter W. Skeat. Classic (1900); still the definitive work on the folklore and popular religion of the Malay peninsula. Describes marriage rites, birth spirits and ceremonies, medicine, dances, games, war and weapons, etc. Extensive quotes from original sources, many magic charms translated into English. 35 illustrations. Preface by Charles Otto Blagden. xxiv + 685pp.
21760-4 Paperbound $4.00

HEAVENS ON EARTH: UTOPIAN COMMUNITIES IN AMERICA, 1680-1880, Mark Holloway. The finest nontechnical account of American utopias, from the early Woman in the Wilderness, Ephrata, Rappites to the enormous mid 19th-century efflorescence; Shakers, New Harmony, Equity Stores, Fourier's Phalanxes, Oneida, Amana, Fruitlands, etc. "Entertaining and very instructive." *Times Literary Supplement.* 15 illustrations. 246pp.
21593-8 Paperbound $2.00

LONDON LABOUR AND THE LONDON POOR, Henry Mayhew. Earliest (c. 1850) sociological study in English, describing myriad subcultures of London poor. Particularly remarkable for the thousands of pages of direct testimony taken from the lips of London prostitutes, thieves, beggars, street sellers, chimney-sweepers, street-musicians, "mudlarks," "pure-finders," rag-gatherers, "running-patterers," dock laborers, cab-men, and hundreds of others, quoted directly in this massive work. An extraordinarily vital picture of London emerges. 110 illustrations. Total of lxxvi + 1951pp. 6⅝ x 10.
21934-8, 21935-6, 21936-4, 21937-2 Four volumes, Paperbound $14.00

HISTORY OF THE LATER ROMAN EMPIRE, J. B. Bury. Eloquent, detailed reconstruction of Western and Byzantine Roman Empire by a major historian, from the death of Theodosius I (395 A.D.) to the death of Justinian (565). Extensive quotations from contemporary sources; full coverage of important Roman and foreign figures of the time. xxxiv + 965pp. 21829-5 Record, book, album. Monaural. $3.50

AN INTELLECTUAL AND CULTURAL HISTORY OF THE WESTERN WORLD, Harry Elmer Barnes. Monumental study, tracing the development of the accomplishments that make up human culture. Every aspect of man's achievement surveyed from its origins in the Paleolithic to the present day (1964); social structures, ideas, economic systems, art, literature, technology, mathematics, the sciences, medicine, religion, jurisprudence, etc. Evaluations of the contributions of scores of great men. 1964 edition, revised and edited by scholars in the many fields represented. Total of xxix + 1381pp. 21275-0, 21276-9, 21277-7 Three volumes, Paperbound $7.75

INCIDENTS OF TRAVEL IN YUCATAN, John L. Stephens. Classic (1843) exploration of jungles of Yucatan, looking for evidences of Maya civilization. Stephens found many ruins; comments on travel adventures, Mexican and Indian culture. 127 striking illustrations by F. Catherwood. Total of 669 pp.
20926-1, 20927-X Two volumes, Paperbound $5.00

INCIDENTS OF TRAVEL IN CENTRAL AMERICA, CHIAPAS, AND YUCATAN, John L. Stephens. An exciting travel journal and an important classic of archeology. Narrative relates his almost single-handed discovery of the Mayan culture, and exploration of the ruined cities of Copan, Palenque, Utatlan and others; the monuments they dug from the earth, the temples buried in the jungle, the customs of poverty-stricken Indians living a stone's throw from the ruined palaces. 115 drawings by F. Catherwood. Portrait of Stephens. xii + 812pp.
22404-X, 22405-8 Two volumes, Paperbound $6.00

A NEW VOYAGE ROUND THE WORLD, William Dampier. Late 17-century naturalist joined the pirates of the Spanish Main to gather information; remarkably vivid account of buccaneers, pirates; detailed, accurate account of botany, zoology, ethnography of lands visited. Probably the most important early English voyage, enormous implications for British exploration, trade, colonial policy. Also most interesting reading. Argonaut edition, introduction by Sir Albert Gray. New introduction by Percy Adams. 6 plates, 7 illustrations. xlvii + 376pp. 6½ x 9¼.
21900-3 Paperbound $3.00

INTERNATIONAL AIRLINE PHRASE BOOK IN SIX LANGUAGES, Joseph W. Bátor. Important phrases and sentences in English paralleled with French, German, Portuguese, Italian, Spanish equivalents, covering all possible airport-travel situations; created for airline personnel as well as tourist by Language Chief, Pan American Airlines. xiv + 204pp.
22017-6 Paperbound $2.00

STAGE COACH AND TAVERN DAYS, Alice Morse Earle. Detailed, lively account of the early days of taverns; their uses and importance in the social, political and military life; furnishings and decorations; locations; food and drink; tavern signs, etc. Second half covers every aspect of early travel; the roads, coaches, drivers, etc. Nostalgic, charming, packed with fascinating material. 157 illustrations, mostly photographs. xiv + 449pp.
22518-6 Paperbound $4.00

NORSE DISCOVERIES AND EXPLORATIONS IN NORTH AMERICA, Hjalmar R. Holand. The perplexing Kensington Stone, found in Minnesota at the end of the 19th century. Is it a record of a Scandinavian expedition to North America in the 14th century? Or is it one of the most successful hoaxes in history. A scientific detective investigation. Formerly *Westward from Vinland*. 31 photographs, 17 figures. x + 354pp.
22014-1 Paperbound $2.75

A BOOK OF OLD MAPS, compiled and edited by Emerson D. Fite and Archibald Freeman. 74 old maps offer an unusual survey of the discovery, settlement and growth of America down to the close of the Revolutionary war: maps showing Norse settlements in Greenland, the explorations of Columbus, Verrazano, Cabot, Champlain, Joliet, Drake, Hudson, etc., campaigns of Revolutionary war battles, and much more. Each map is accompanied by a brief historical essay. xvi + 299pp. 11 x 13¾.
22084-2 Paperbound $6.00

PLANETS, STARS AND GALAXIES: DESCRIPTIVE ASTRONOMY FOR BEGINNERS, A. E. Fanning. Comprehensive introductory survey of astronomy: the sun, solar system, stars, galaxies, universe, cosmology; up-to-date, including quasars, radio stars, etc. Preface by Prof. Donald Menzel. 24pp. of photographs. 189pp. 5¼ x 8¼.
21680-2 Paperbound $1.50

TEACH YOURSELF CALCULUS, P. Abbott. With a good background in algebra and trig, you can teach yourself calculus with this book. Simple, straightforward introduction to functions of all kinds, integration, differentiation, series, etc. "Students who are beginning to study calculus method will derive great help from this book." Faraday House Journal. 308pp. 20683-1 Clothbound $2.00

TEACH YOURSELF TRIGONOMETRY, P. Abbott. Geometrical foundations, indices and logarithms, ratios, angles, circular measure, etc. are presented in this sound, easy-to-use text. Excellent for the beginner or as a brush up, this text carries the student through the solution of triangles. 204pp. 20682-3 Clothbound $2.00

TEACH YOURSELF ANATOMY, David LeVay. Accurate, inclusive, profusely illustrated account of structure, skeleton, abdomen, muscles, nervous system, glands, brain, reproductive organs, evolution. "Quite the best and most readable account,' *Medical Officer.* 12 color plates. 164 figures. 311pp. 4¾ x 7.
21651-9 Clothbound $2.50

TEACH YOURSELF PHYSIOLOGY, David LeVay. Anatomical, biochemical bases; digestive, nervous, endocrine systems; metabolism; respiration; muscle; excretion; temperature control; reproduction. "Good elementary exposition," *The Lancet.* 6 color plates. 44 illustrations. 208pp. 4¼ x 7. 21658-6 Clothbound $2.50

THE FRIENDLY STARS, Martha Evans Martin. Classic has taught naked-eye observation of stars, planets to hundreds of thousands, still not surpassed for charm, lucidity, adequacy. Completely updated by Professor Donald H. Menzel, Harvard Observatory. 25 illustrations. 16 x 30 chart. x + 147pp. 21099-5 Paperbound $1.25

MUSIC OF THE SPHERES: THE MATERIAL UNIVERSE FROM ATOM TO QUASAR, SIMPLY EXPLAINED, Guy Murchie. Extremely broad, brilliantly written popular account begins with the solar system and reaches to dividing line between matter and nonmatter; latest understandings presented with exceptional clarity. Volume One: Planets, stars, galaxies, cosmology, geology, celestial mechanics, latest astronomical discoveries; Volume Two: Matter, atoms, waves, radiation, relativity, chemical action, heat, nuclear energy, quantum theory, music, light, color, probability, antimatter, antigravity, and similar topics. 319 figures. 1967 (second) edition. Total of xx + 644pp. 21809-0, 21810-4 Two volumes, Paperbound $5.00

OLD-TIME SCHOOLS AND SCHOOL BOOKS, Clifton Johnson. Illustrations and rhymes from early primers, abundant quotations from early textbooks, many anecdotes of school life enliven this study of elementary schools from Puritans to middle 19th century. Introduction by Carl Withers. 234 illustrations. xxxiii + 381pp.
21031-6 Paperbound $2.50

# CATALOGUE OF DOVER BOOKS

VISUAL ILLUSIONS: THEIR CAUSES, CHARACTERISTICS, AND APPLICATIONS, Matthew Luckiesh. Thorough description and discussion of optical illusion, geometric and perspective, particularly; size and shape distortions, illusions of color, of motion; natural illusions; use of illusion in art and magic, industry, etc. Most useful today with op art, also for classical art. Scores of effects illustrated. Introduction by William H. Ittleson. 100 illustrations. xxi + 252pp.

21530-X Paperbound $2.00

A HANDBOOK OF ANATOMY FOR ART STUDENTS, Arthur Thomson. Thorough, virtually exhaustive coverage of skeletal structure, musculature, etc. Full text, supplemented by anatomical diagrams and drawings and by photographs of undraped figures. Unique in its comparison of male and female forms, pointing out differences of contour, texture, form. 211 figures, 40 drawings, 86 photographs. xx + 459pp. 5⅜ x 8⅜.

21163-0 Paperbound $3.50

150 MASTERPIECES OF DRAWING, Selected by Anthony Toney. Full page reproductions of drawings from the early 16th to the end of the 18th century, all beautifully reproduced: Rembrandt, Michelangelo, Dürer, Fragonard, Urs, Graf, Wouwerman, many others. First-rate browsing book, model book for artists. xviii + 150pp. 8⅜ x 11¼.

21032-4 Paperbound $2.50

THE LATER WORK OF AUBREY BEARDSLEY, Aubrey Beardsley. Exotic, erotic, ironic masterpieces in full maturity: Comedy Ballet, Venus and Tannhauser, Pierrot, Lysistrata, Rape of the Lock, Savoy material, Ali Baba, Volpone, etc. This material revolutionized the art world, and is still powerful, fresh, brilliant. With The Early Work, all Beardsley's finest work. 174 plates, 2 in color. xiv + 176pp. 8⅛ x 11.

21817-1 Paperbound $3.00

DRAWINGS OF REMBRANDT, Rembrandt van Rijn. Complete reproduction of fabulously rare edition by Lippmann and Hofstede de Groot, completely reedited, updated, improved by Prof. Seymour Slive, Fogg Museum. Portraits, Biblical sketches, landscapes, Oriental types, nudes, episodes from classical mythology—All Rembrandt's fertile genius. Also selection of drawings by his pupils and followers. "Stunning volumes," Saturday Review. 550 illustrations. lxxviii + 552pp. 9⅛ x 12¼.

21485-0, 21486-9 Two volumes, Paperbound $10.00

THE DISASTERS OF WAR, Francisco Goya. One of the masterpieces of Western civilization—83 etchings that record Goya's shattering, bitter reaction to the Napoleonic war that swept through Spain after the insurrection of 1808 and to war in general. Reprint of the first edition, with three additional plates from Boston's Museum of Fine Arts. All plates facsimile size. Introduction by Philip Hofer, Fogg Museum. v + 97pp. 9⅜ x 8¼.

21872-4 Paperbound $2.00

GRAPHIC WORKS OF ODILON REDON. Largest collection of Redon's graphic works ever assembled: 172 lithographs, 28 etchings and engravings, 9 drawings. These include some of his most famous works. All the plates from Odilon Redon: oeuvre graphique complet, plus additional plates. New introduction and caption translations by Alfred Werner. 209 illustrations. xxvii + 209pp. 9⅛ x 12¼.

21966-8 Paperbound $4.00

THE PRINCIPLES OF PSYCHOLOGY, William James. The famous long course, complete and unabridged. Stream of thought, time perception, memory, experimental methods—these are only some of the concerns of a work that was years ahead of its time and still valid, interesting, useful. 94 figures. Total of xviii + 1391pp.
20381-6, 20382-4 Two volumes, Paperbound $8.00

THE STRANGE STORY OF THE QUANTUM, Banesh Hoffmann. Non-mathematical but thorough explanation of work of Planck, Einstein, Bohr, Pauli, de Broglie, Schrödinger, Heisenberg, Dirac, Feynman, etc. No technical background needed. "Of books attempting such an account, this is the best," Henry Margenau, Yale. 40-page "Postscript 1959." xii + 285pp.
20518-5 Paperbound $2.00

THE RISE OF THE NEW PHYSICS, A. d'Abro. Most thorough explanation in print of central core of mathematical physics, both classical and modern; from Newton to Dirac and Heisenberg. Both history and exposition; philosophy of science, causality, explanations of higher mathematics, analytical mechanics, electromagnetism, thermodynamics, phase rule, special and general relativity, matrices. No higher mathematics needed to follow exposition, though treatment is elementary to intermediate in level. Recommended to serious student who wishes verbal understanding. 97 illustrations. xvii + 982pp.
20003-5, 20004-3 Two volumes, Paperbound $6.00

GREAT IDEAS OF OPERATIONS RESEARCH, Jagjit Singh. Easily followed non-technical explanation of mathematical tools, aims, results: statistics, linear programming, game theory, queueing theory, Monte Carlo simulation, etc. Uses only elementary mathematics. Many case studies, several analyzed in detail. Clarity, breadth make this excellent for specialist in another field who wishes background. 41 figures. x + 228pp.
21886-4 Paperbound $2.50

GREAT IDEAS OF MODERN MATHEMATICS: THEIR NATURE AND USE, Jagjit Singh. Internationally famous expositor, winner of Unesco's Kalinga Award for science popularization explains verbally such topics as differential equations, matrices, groups, sets, transformations, mathematical logic and other important modern mathematics, as well as use in physics, astrophysics, and similar fields. Superb exposition for layman, scientist in other areas. viii + 312pp.
20587-8 Paperbound $2.50

GREAT IDEAS IN INFORMATION THEORY, LANGUAGE AND CYBERNETICS, Jagjit Singh. The analog and digital computers, how they work, how they are like and unlike the human brain, the men who developed them, their future applications, computer terminology. An essential book for today, even for readers with little math. Some mathematical demonstrations included for more advanced readers. 118 figures. Tables. ix + 338pp.
21694-2 Paperbound $2.50

CHANCE, LUCK AND STATISTICS, Horace C. Levinson. Non-mathematical presentation of fundamentals of probability theory and science of statistics and their applications. Games of chance, betting odds, misuse of statistics, normal and skew distributions, birth rates, stock speculation, insurance. Enlarged edition. Formerly "The Science of Chance." xiii + 357pp.
21007-3 Paperbound $2.50

MATHEMATICAL PUZZLES FOR BEGINNERS AND ENTHUSIASTS, Geoffrey Mott-Smith. 189 puzzles from easy to difficult—involving arithmetic, logic, algebra, properties of digits, probability, etc.—for enjoyment and mental stimulus. Explanation of mathematical principles behind the puzzles. 135 illustrations. viii + 248pp.
20198-8 Paperbound $1.75

PAPER FOLDING FOR BEGINNERS, William D. Murray and Francis J. Rigney. Easiest book on the market, clearest instructions on making interesting, beautiful origami. Sail boats, cups, roosters, frogs that move legs, bonbon boxes, standing birds, etc. 40 projects; more than 275 diagrams and photographs. 94pp.
20713-7 Paperbound $1.00

TRICKS AND GAMES ON THE POOL TABLE, Fred Herrmann. 79 tricks and games—some solitaires, some for two or more players, some competitive games—to entertain you between formal games. Mystifying shots and throws, unusual caroms, tricks involving such props as cork, coins, a hat, etc. Formerly *Fun on the Pool Table*. 77 figures. 95pp.
21814-7 Paperbound $1.00

HAND SHADOWS TO BE THROWN UPON THE WALL: A SERIES OF NOVEL AND AMUSING FIGURES FORMED BY THE HAND, Henry Bursill. Delightful picturebook from great-grandfather's day shows how to make 18 different hand shadows: a bird that flies, duck that quacks, dog that wags his tail, camel, goose, deer, boy, turtle, etc. Only book of its sort. vi + 33pp. 6½ x 9¼. 21779-5 Paperbound $1.00

WHITTLING AND WOODCARVING, E. J. Tangerman. 18th printing of best book on market. "If you can cut a potato you can carve" toys and puzzles, chains, chessmen, caricatures, masks, frames, woodcut blocks, surface patterns, much more. Information on tools, woods, techniques. Also goes into serious wood sculpture from Middle Ages to present, East and West. 464 photos, figures. x + 293pp.
20965-2 Paperbound $2.00

HISTORY OF PHILOSOPHY, Julián Marías. Possibly the clearest, most easily followed, best planned, most useful one-volume history of philosophy on the market; neither skimpy nor overfull. Full details on system of every major philosopher and dozens of less important thinkers from pre-Socratics up to Existentialism and later. Strong on many European figures usually omitted. Has gone through dozens of editions in Europe. 1966 edition, translated by Stanley Appelbaum and Clarence Strowbridge. xviii + 505pp. 21739-6 Paperbound $3.00

YOGA: A SCIENTIFIC EVALUATION, Kovoor T. Behanan. Scientific but non-technical study of physiological results of yoga exercises; done under auspices of Yale U. Relations to Indian thought, to psychoanalysis, etc. 16 photos. xxiii + 270pp.
20505-3 Paperbound $2.50